THE GLOSSARY OF
USER-INTERFACE PATTERNS

Compiled & Edited By:
Manasi Pathak
Dr. Padmaja Saha

Rhythm

Independent
Publication

THE GLOSSARY OF USER-INTERFACE PATTERNS

Compiled & Edited By:
Manasi Pathak
Dr. Padmaja Saha

Copyright ©2023, All rights reserved.

ISBN:9798861761161

9798861761161

Published by:

Rhythm Independent Publication,

Jinkethimmanahalli, Varanasi, Bengaluru, Karnataka, India - 560036

For all types of correspondence, send your mails to the provided address above.

The information presented herein has been collated from a diverse range of sources, comprehensive perspective on the subject matter.

360-Degree Product View

A 360-Degree Product View is a UI pattern commonly used in design systems to enhance the user experience of exploring and understanding a product. It allows users to interactively view and examine a product from all angles, simulating a real-life experience of holding and inspecting the product physically. In this UI pattern, a series of images or a video is stitched together to create a seamless rotation effect, representing a full rotation of the product. Users can either control the rotation manually or set it to auto-rotate at a predefined speed. They can also pause the rotation to focus on a specific angle or zoom in to see fine details. The 360-degree product view is typically implemented using JavaScript or HTML5/CSS3 animations to control the rotation and zoom effects. It may also incorporate other interactive features like hotspots to highlight specific product details or annotations to provide additional information. This UI pattern is especially useful in e-commerce or product showcase websites where users need to make informed decisions about a product before making a purchase. By providing a 360-degree view, users can have a better understanding of the product's design, features, and overall quality. It helps to bridge the gap between online shopping and the traditional in-store experience, where customers can physically handle and examine the products. The 360-degree product view is also advantageous for businesses, as it can boost conversion rates and reduce potential returns. By giving customers a more accurate representation of the product, it minimizes the possibility of dissatisfaction due to inaccurate expectations. It can also help reduce the number of customer inquiries by providing a comprehensive visual representation of the product's key features. Overall, the 360-degree product view is an effective UI pattern in design systems that provides a dynamic and engaging way for users to explore and understand products online. It enhances the user experience by simulating the physical experience of handling and inspecting products, ultimately leading to better-informed purchasing decisions. The End>

360-Degree Video Playback

360-Degree Video Playback is a UI pattern and design system that allows users to view video content from all angles in a fully immersive experience. This feature provides an interactive and engaging way for users to explore videos and feel like they are a part of the scene. In the context of UI patterns and design systems, 360-Degree Video Playback offers a way to display videos that capture a full 360-degree view of the surroundings. It employs panoramic video technology to capture a complete scene, allowing users to pan around and see every possible angle. The 360-Degree Video Playback UI pattern is typically implemented by displaying the video content within a specialized player. This player allows users to navigate through the video by dragging or swiping their fingers across the screen, moving the view in any direction. Users can also interact with the video playback by zooming in or out to focus on specific details. Designing a user-friendly 360-Degree Video Playback UI involves providing intuitive controls and indicators that enable users to easily navigate through the video and understand their position within the 360-degree field of view. This may include visual cues such as a compass or orientation indicator, as well as on-screen controls for play/pause, volume adjustment, and timeline scrubbing. Implementing a 360-Degree Video Playback UI within a larger design system requires careful integration with existing components and guidelines. It is important to ensure consistency in terms of color, typography, and overall visual language. Additionally, accessibility considerations should be taken into account to ensure that users with disabilities can still have a meaningful experience with the 360-degree video content. In conclusion, 360-Degree Video Playback is a UI pattern and design system that enables users to interactively view video content from all angles. By providing a fully immersive experience, this feature enhances engagement and allows users to explore videos in a unique and captivating way.>

3D Animations

1

3D animations in the context of UI patterns and design systems refer to the use of three-dimensional visual effects to enhance the user experience and engagement with the user interface. These animations are created using computer graphics techniques to bring objects and elements to life, providing a sense of depth, realism, and interactivity.

3D animations can be applied to various UI patterns and design system elements, such as buttons, menus, transitions, and illustrations. They can be used to guide user attention, communicate status changes or feedback, and create immersive and interactive interfaces.

3D Elements

3D Elements in the context of UI patterns and design systems refers to graphical elements that have perceived depth and appear three-dimensional. These elements are designed in a way that they mimic real-life objects or spaces, creating an immersive user experience.

These 3D elements can be implemented in various ways, such as using gradients, shadows, and lighting effects to create the illusion of depth. They can be applied to buttons, icons, illustrations, backgrounds, or any other element within a user interface.

404 Error Page

A 404 Error Page is a standardized user interface pattern and design element that is displayed when a user tries to access a web page that does not exist. It is an integral part of a design system, which is a collection of reusable components and guidelines for creating a consistent and cohesive user experience across a website or application. A 404 Error Page serves as a helpful mechanism to inform users that the requested content is unavailable. It is designed to provide clarity and guide users in navigating back to the main website or finding alternative content. The purpose of the page is to minimize frustration and improve the overall user experience by effectively communicating the error and providing relevant options for the user to continue their journey. When designing a 404 Error Page, there are several key elements that should be considered: 1. Error Message: The page should clearly indicate the error with a user-friendly message. It should use simple language and avoid technical jargon so that users can easily understand the issue. 2. Branding: The page should maintain the same visual identity and branding as the rest of the website or application. This helps users recognize that they are still within the same context and instills trust and familiarity. 3. Navigation: The page should include clear navigation options to direct users back to the main website or provide alternative content. This can be achieved through a prominent homepage link, search functionality, or related content suggestions. 4. Visual Hierarchy: The page should prioritize the most important information and actions. This can be done by using headings, typography, and color to guide users' attention and emphasize the main call to action. 5. Error Code: In addition to the error message, the page can include the relevant error code to provide more technical information for advanced users or support purposes. By following these design principles, a 404 Error Page can effectively communicate the error, guide users to relevant content, and maintain a consistent user experience within the overall design system.

HTML:

A 404 Error Page is a standardized user interface pattern and design element that is displayed when a user tries to access a web page that does not exist. It is an integral part of a design system, which is a collection of reusable components and guidelines for creating a consistent and cohesive user experience across a website or application.

AI-Generated Content

AI-generated content refers to text, images, or other forms of content that are created or generated by artificial intelligence algorithms. In the context of UI patterns and design systems, AI-generated content can be used to automate and streamline the process of creating user interfaces, improving efficiency and consistency.

UI patterns are recurring solutions to common design problems in user interfaces. They provide designers with a set of guidelines and best practices to follow when creating user interfaces. AI-generated content can be used to generate variations of UI patterns or to automatically generate

2

UI patterns based on specific design requirements.

AI-Personalized Content

AI-Personalized Content refers to content that is dynamically generated and tailored to the individual user based on their preferences, behavior, and other relevant data. It is a UI pattern commonly used in designing systems and interfaces that aim to provide personalized experiences for users.

In the context of UI patterns and design systems, AI-Personalized Content involves the use of artificial intelligence algorithms to analyze user data and generate content that is relevant and meaningful to each individual. This can include personalized recommendations, customized product suggestions, targeted advertising, and personalized messaging.

AI-Generated Artwork

AI-generated artwork refers to visual designs and graphics that are created using artificial intelligence algorithms and techniques. It involves the use of machine learning and deep learning models to generate novel and unique artwork.

In the context of UI patterns and design systems, AI-generated artwork can be utilized to enhance the visual appeal and creativity of user interfaces. It can be used to create customized illustrations, icons, backgrounds, and other graphical elements that align with the overall design theme and branding of the product.

AI-Generated Music

AI-generated music refers to musical compositions that are created or composed using artificial intelligence algorithms and techniques. It involves using machine learning algorithms to analyze and understand patterns, styles, and structures in existing music and then generate new musical pieces based on that analysis.

UI patterns and design systems play a crucial role in the presentation and implementation of AI-generated music. UI patterns are reusable solutions to common design problems, while design systems are comprehensive collections of design guidelines, components, and standards that ensure consistency and cohesiveness in the user interface.

The integration of AI-generated music into UI patterns and design systems requires careful consideration of various factors. Firstly, the user interface should provide a seamless and intuitive way for users to interact with the AI-generated music. This may involve creating dedicated modules or components that allow users to select or customize the desired style or genre of the music. Additionally, the UI should offer controls that enable users to modify parameters such as tempo, mood, or complexity to personalize the music according to their preferences.

Furthermore, design systems can help establish a visual language and hierarchy for presenting AI-generated music. This involves defining consistent color schemes, typography, and iconography that convey the nature and characteristics of the music. The design system should also consider the ability to visually represent the underlying AI algorithms and processes, providing users with transparency and control over the generation and customization of the music.

Overall, the integration of AI-generated music within UI patterns and design systems aims to provide users with a compelling and engaging musical experience. By leveraging AI techniques, users can explore and discover new musical compositions while benefiting from the convenience and personalization offered by the user interface. The seamless integration of AI-generated music into UI patterns and design systems contributes to a cohesive and immersive user experience, enhancing the overall usability and enjoyment of the music application.

AR Navigation

AR navigation refers to the user interface (UI) pattern and design system that enables users to navigate and interact with augmented reality (AR) content. AR navigation serves as a tool for users to explore and engage with digital 3D objects and virtual environments overlaid onto the real world. Using AR technology, AR navigation provides users with a spatial understanding of their surroundings by placing virtual elements within the physical environment. It allows users to move around, interact with objects, and access information in a more intuitive and immersive way. AR navigation leverages the capabilities of a device's camera and sensors to analyze the surroundings and accurately superimpose digital content onto the real-world view. The primary objective of AR navigation is to enhance the user experience by providing intuitive and easily understandable interactions. It enables users to explore and understand the virtual content by using gestures, voice commands, or touch inputs. AR navigation typically includes features such as object manipulation, spatial mapping, scene understanding, and menu navigation. Object manipulation allows users to interact with virtual objects within the AR environment. This can involve actions such as rotating, scaling, or moving objects. Spatial mapping uses the device's sensors to create a digital representation of the physical environment, enabling virtual objects to interact with real-world surfaces and physical objects. Scene understanding helps the AR system identify and interpret the context and layout of the surroundings, ensuring accurate placement of virtual content. Menu navigation provides users with access to additional features and settings, allowing them to customize their AR experience. Designing a consistent and user-friendly AR navigation system involves adhering to established UI patterns and design principles. It is essential to consider factors such as the placement and visibility of AR elements, the use of intuitive gestures and interactions, and the legibility of text and icons within the AR interface. A well-designed AR navigation system should seamlessly integrate digital content with the real world, providing users with a smooth and immersive experience. In conclusion, AR navigation is a UI pattern and design system that enables users to navigate and interact with augmented reality content. It utilizes AR technology to superimpose virtual objects onto the real world, allowing for intuitive and immersive interactions. By designing a user-friendly and consistent AR navigation system, users can seamlessly explore and engage with AR content.

AR Shopping Experience

Augmented Reality (AR) Shopping Experience is a user interface (UI) pattern and design system that combines virtual reality and real-world environments to create an immersive shopping experience. It allows users to visualize and interact with virtual products in their physical environment, providing a more engaging and personalized shopping experience. In an AR Shopping Experience, users can use their smartphones or other devices with AR capabilities to scan their surroundings and place virtual products within their physical space. This enables them to see how the products would look in real life, helping them make more informed purchase decisions. The UI pattern of an AR Shopping Experience typically involves a user-friendly interface that guides users through the process of scanning their environment and selecting virtual products to be placed. It may include features such as a virtual catalog, search functionality, product descriptions, and user reviews. The design system of an AR Shopping Experience focuses on creating realistic and immersive virtual representations of products. This involves using high-quality 3D models, realistic textures, and accurate sizing and proportions. The design system also considers factors such as lighting and shadows to ensure that the virtual products blend seamlessly with the real-world environment. The goal of an AR Shopping Experience is to bridge the gap between online and in-person shopping by providing a digital platform that offers the advantages of both. It allows users to explore a wider range of products without the limitations of physical stores while still being able to see and interact with the products in a realistic way. Overall, an AR Shopping Experience offers an innovative and interactive way for users to shop for products. By bringing virtual products into the physical world, it enhances the shopping experience and helps users make more confident purchasing decisions.

AR Shopping Experience is a UI pattern and design system that combines virtual reality and real-world environments to create an immersive shopping experience. It allows users to visualize and interact with virtual products in their physical environment, providing a more engaging and personalized shopping experience.

AR Shopping Experience includes a user-friendly interface that guides users through the process of scanning their environment and selecting virtual products. The design system focuses on creating realistic and immersive virtual representations of products to ensure a seamless integration with the real world. The goal is to enhance the shopping experience by offering a digital platform that offers the advantages of both online and in-person shopping.

AR-Enhanced Shopping

AR-Enhanced Shopping is a user interface (UI) pattern and design system that integrates augmented reality (AR) technology to enhance the shopping experience for users. It leverages AR capabilities to provide virtual product visualization, try-on experiences, and interactive product information in real-world environments.

The UI pattern of AR-Enhanced Shopping involves the seamless integration of AR technology into the shopping process. Users can access AR features through a dedicated application or a web-based platform. The design system adheres to a consistent visual language and user experience to provide a coherent and intuitive interaction model.

AR-Enhanced Art Exhibitions

AR-enhanced Art Exhibitions refer to the use of augmented reality technology to enhance traditional art exhibitions. This entails the integration of virtual elements into the physical exhibition space, providing visitors with an immersive and interactive experience. In terms of UI patterns and design systems, AR-enhanced Art Exhibitions require careful consideration of the user interface to ensure intuitive navigation and seamless integration of virtual content. This involves the use of consistent visual cues and clear instructions to guide visitors in interacting with the augmented reality features. The design system for AR-enhanced Art Exhibitions should prioritize simplicity and ease of use, allowing visitors to focus on the art while effortlessly engaging with the augmented reality components. This includes the use of visual hierarchy to highlight important information and minimize distractions, as well as the implementation of intuitive gestures or controls to interact with virtual elements. Furthermore, the UI patterns for AR-enhanced Art Exhibitions should facilitate a smooth transition between the physical and virtual realms. This may involve the use of markers or triggers to activate augmented reality content when visitors approach specific artworks, as well as the integration of spatial mapping technology to ensure accurate placement of virtual objects within the exhibition space. In summary, AR-enhanced Art Exhibitions utilize augmented reality technology to enhance the visitor experience by seamlessly integrating virtual elements into the physical exhibition space. The UI patterns and design system for such exhibitions should prioritize simplicity, intuitive navigation, and a seamless transition between the physical and virtual realms.

AR-enhanced Art Exhibitions refer to the use of augmented reality technology to enhance traditional art exhibitions. This entails the integration of virtual elements into the physical exhibition space, providing visitors with an immersive and interactive experience.

In terms of UI patterns and design systems, AR-enhanced Art Exhibitions require careful consideration of the user interface to ensure intuitive navigation and seamless integration of virtual content. This involves the use of consistent visual cues and clear instructions to guide visitors in interacting with the augmented reality features.

AR-Enhanced Historical Tours

AR-enhanced Historical Tours refer to user interfaces and design systems that incorporate augmented reality (AR) technology to enhance the experience of historical tours.

AR-enhanced Historical Tours utilize AR technology to overlay virtual content onto the real-world environment, providing users with immersive and interactive experiences. These tours often include a mobile application or a web-based platform that allows users to explore historical sites and landmarks with the help of their devices.

The user interface (UI) patterns and design system associated with AR-enhanced Historical Tours aim to provide users with intuitive and seamless interactions. The UI patterns focus on guiding users through the tour, presenting relevant historical information, and displaying AR content in a visually appealing way.

One common UI pattern is the use of markers or points of interest (POIs) to indicate historical sites. These markers can be displayed on a map or through the device's camera view, allowing users to easily navigate and discover nearby points of interest. The design system for these markers can include visual cues such as icons or colors to differentiate between different types of historical sites.

Another UI pattern involves the use of AR overlays to provide users with contextual information about the historical sites they are visiting. These overlays may include historical photos, videos, or 3D models that are superimposed onto the real-world environment. The design system for these overlays focuses on ensuring that the virtual content seamlessly blends with the real-world surroundings, creating a cohesive and immersive experience.

In addition to UI patterns, AR-enhanced Historical Tours often incorporate a design system that ensures a consistent and coherent visual language throughout the application or platform. This design system may include guidelines for typography, color palettes, and iconography that align with the historical theme of the tour.

AR-Enhanced Learning

AR-enhanced Learning refers to the use of Augmented Reality (AR) technology to enhance the learning experience. It involves the integration of virtual elements into the real-world environment, creating an interactive and immersive learning environment. AR-enhanced Learning utilizes UI patterns and design systems to create a seamless and intuitive user interface. UI patterns refer to commonly used design solutions for specific interface problems, while design systems provide a set of guidelines and standards for designing consistent and coherent user interfaces. In the context of AR-enhanced Learning, UI patterns are used to design the interactions between the user and the virtual elements. These patterns help to guide the user in navigating and interacting with the augmented content, ensuring a smooth and intuitive learning experience. For example, common UI patterns such as swipe gestures, tap interactions, and buttons can be used to enable users to interact with the virtual objects and access additional information. Design systems play a crucial role in ensuring a consistent and cohesive user interface throughout the AR-enhanced Learning experience. They provide a set of standardized design elements, such as colors, typography, and iconography, that maintain visual consistency across different AR learning applications. Design systems also define layout guidelines and spatial considerations, ensuring that the AR content is properly integrated into the real-world environment. By leveraging UI patterns and design systems, AR-enhanced Learning aims to provide an effective and engaging learning experience. The use of familiar UI patterns helps users quickly understand how to interact with the augmented content, reducing the learning curve and allowing users to focus on the educational material. Consistent design systems ensure a visually pleasing and immersive experience, enabling learners to fully engage with the AR-enhanced content. In conclusion, AR-enhanced Learning is the integration of virtual elements into the real-world environment to enhance the learning experience. By utilizing UI patterns and design systems, it aims to create intuitive interactions and visually consistent interfaces. Ultimately, AR-enhanced Learning seeks to provide an effective and engaging learning experience by leveraging the capabilities of augmented reality technology.

AR-Enhanced Museums

AR-enhanced Museums refer to museums that incorporate Augmented Reality (AR) technology to enhance the visitor's experience by overlaying digital content onto the real-world exhibits and environments. These museums use UI patterns and design systems to create a seamless and immersive interaction between the physical and virtual elements.

AR-enhanced Museums utilize various UI patterns, such as gesture-based interactions, marker-based AR, and location-based AR, to facilitate user engagement and exploration. Gesture-based interactions allow visitors to interact with the digital content using gestures, such as tapping, swiping, or pinching. This enables a more intuitive and natural way of exploring the AR-enhanced exhibits. Marker-based AR involves using physical markers, such as QR codes or image targets, to trigger and anchor the digital content in the real-world environment. Visitors can scan these markers with their mobile devices, which then display the corresponding AR content associated with the exhibit. Location-based AR uses GPS or beacons to determine the visitor's location within the museum and deliver context-specific AR content accordingly.

AR-Enhanced Training Simulations

AR-enhanced training simulations are a user interface (UI) pattern that combines augmented reality (AR) technology with interactive training simulations to provide an immersive and realistic learning experience. This pattern is a part of a comprehensive design system that focuses on optimizing the user interface and user experience of AR training simulations.

AR-enhanced training simulations typically involve the use of AR headsets or devices that overlay virtual elements onto the real-world environment. These virtual elements can include 3D objects, animations, instructions, and information relevant to the training scenario. By blending the real and virtual worlds, AR enhances the trainee's perception and understanding of the training content.

Access Request Form

Access Request Form refers to a user interface (UI) pattern within a design system that allows users to request access to a particular resource or feature. It serves as a formal means for users to express their need for access to something that is restricted or controlled by an organization or system. The Access Request Form typically consists of a set of fields and options that users need to fill out in order to submit their request. These fields may include personal information such as name, email address, and job title, as well as the reason for requesting access and any additional details or documents required to support the request. The purpose of the Access Request Form is to streamline the process of granting or denying access to authorized users. By providing a standardized form, organizations can ensure that all necessary information is collected and evaluated in a consistent manner. This helps to maintain security and control over sensitive resources, while also promoting transparency and accountability. The design of the Access Request Form should be intuitive and user-friendly, guiding users through the process step by step. Clear instructions and descriptive labels should be included for each field, helping users to understand what information is required. Validation checks can also be implemented to ensure that all necessary fields are completed correctly before submission. From a design system perspective, the Access Request Form should adhere to the overall visual and interaction design principles of the system. This ensures consistency and coherence across different UI components and patterns. The form should use the same color scheme, typography, and visual hierarchy as other elements within the design system. In summary, an Access Request Form is a UI pattern within a design system that provides a formal way for users to request access to restricted resources or features. It is designed to streamline the access granting process while maintaining security and control. By adhering to the principles of the design system, the form ensures consistency and a unified user experience.>

Accessibility Feedback Form

Accessibility refers to the design and development of products, services, and environments that can be accessed and used by individuals with disabilities. In the context of UI patterns and design systems, accessibility focuses on ensuring that digital interfaces are inclusive and usable by a wide range of users, including those with visual, auditory, motor, and cognitive impairments.

Accessibility in UI patterns and design systems involves incorporating principles and techniques that enable people with disabilities to perceive, understand, navigate, and interact with digital content effectively. This includes considerations such as providing alternative text for images, using color contrast to ensure legibility, avoiding the use of solely color-coded information, and using semantic HTML markup to enhance screen reader support.

Accordion Menu

The accordion menu is a UI pattern commonly used in web design to organize and display hierarchical information in a compact and intuitive manner. It consists of a vertical stack of collapsible panels, where only one panel can be expanded at a time, while the rest remain collapsed. When a panel is clicked or tapped, it expands to reveal its content, typically revealing subcategories or additional details. This behavior allows users to easily navigate through a complex hierarchy without overwhelming them with too much information at once. By hiding content until it is needed, the accordion menu helps conserve screen space and provide a clear and manageable interface. Each panel in the accordion menu typically consists of a header or title that provides a brief description of its content. This header is usually clickable and serves as a trigger to expand or collapse the panel. When expanded, the header may change its appearance to indicate its active state and provide visual feedback to users. The accordion menu is a versatile and widely-used design pattern that can be applied to various contexts, such as navigation menus, FAQ sections, product filters, or any situation where there is a need to present information in a hierarchical structure. Its simplicity and efficient use of space make it a popular choice for responsive and mobile-friendly designs. Overall, the accordion menu offers an accessible and organized way to present hierarchical information, allowing users to navigate and explore content at their own pace. Its collapsible panels help manage limited screen space while providing a visually appealing and interactive experience.

The accordion menu is a UI pattern commonly used in web design to organize and display hierarchical information in a compact and intuitive manner. It consists of a vertical stack of collapsible panels, where only one panel can be expanded at a time, while the rest remain collapsed.

When a panel is clicked or tapped, it expands to reveal its content, typically revealing subcategories or additional details. This behavior allows users to easily navigate through a complex hierarchy without overwhelming them with too much information at once. By hiding content until it is needed, the accordion menu helps conserve screen space and provide a clear and manageable interface.

Accordion Menus

An accordion menu is a user interface (UI) design pattern that allows users to toggle between different sections of a webpage or application, displaying or hiding the content within each section as desired. It typically consists of a vertical list of clickable headers, with each header representing a section or category of content. When a header is clicked, the corresponding section expands or collapses, revealing or hiding its content. Accordion menus are commonly used in the context of a design system, which is a collection of reusable components and guidelines that ensures consistency and efficiency in UI design. By including accordion menus as part of the design system, designers and developers can easily implement this UI pattern across various projects, promoting a unified and intuitive user experience. When designing an accordion menu, it is essential to consider the following principles: 1. Clear and intuitive navigation: The accordion menu should have clearly labeled headers that accurately represent the content within each section. Users should easily understand how the menu functions and navigate through the different sections effortlessly. 2. Responsive design: With the increasing use of mobile devices, it is crucial for accordion menus to be responsive and adapt to different screen sizes. The menu should collapse or expand accordingly, ensuring optimal usability on both desktop and mobile interfaces. 3. Animation and transition effects: Adding smooth animation and transition effects when expanding or collapsing the sections can enhance the user experience. These visual cues provide feedback to the user and create a more engaging interaction. Implementing an accordion menu in pure HTML can be achieved using a combination of HTML, CSS, and JavaScript. To create the basic structure, we can use nested HTML elements, such as and

, along with CSS classes for styling. JavaScript is then used to add interactivity by toggling the visibility of the sections.

Section 1

Content of section 1

Section 2

Content of section 2

Account Closure Form

An account closure form is a UI pattern and design system element that allows users to terminate or close their account with a particular service or platform.

The purpose of an account closure form is to provide a structured and streamlined process for users who wish to permanently close their accounts. It typically includes a series of fields and options that users must complete in order to initiate the closure process. These fields may include personal information such as name, email address, and account username, as well as additional information that may be required to ensure the security and validity of the closure request.

By providing an account closure form, the service or platform aims to gather all necessary information from the user in a systematic manner, thereby reducing the risk of errors or incomplete submissions. This not only ensures a more efficient and effective closure process, but also helps protect the user's data and privacy by verifying their identity and intentions.

An account closure form typically includes clear instructions and guidance on how to complete the form and what to expect after the account has been closed. This may include information regarding any outstanding payments, data deletion processes, and the permanent removal of the user's personal information from the service or platform's databases.

Overall, an account closure form is a crucial element in a UI pattern and design system, as it allows users to exercise their rights and choices by providing a formal and structured process to close their accounts. By implementing this design pattern, services and platforms can enhance user trust and confidence, while also ensuring compliance with data privacy and protection regulations.

Account Deactivation Form

An account deactivation form is a user interface pattern and design system element that allows users to deactivate their account on a website or app.

This form typically consists of a series of input fields and options that the user must complete in order to successfully deactivate their account. The purpose of this form is to provide a clear and structured process for account deactivation, ensuring that users fully understand the consequences and implications of their action.

Account Management

Account Management refers to a set of user interfaces (UI) patterns and design systems that facilitate the management and control of user accounts within a digital application or platform. It encompasses the various features, functions, and actions that enable users to modify, update, and access their account settings, personal information, and privacy preferences. In the context of UI patterns, Account Management typically includes common design elements such as user profiles, login and registration forms, password resets, and account settings pages. These elements enable users to create new accounts, log into existing accounts, update their personal information (such as name, email, and profile picture), and manage their privacy and security settings (such as password changes and two-factor authentication). A well-designed Account Management system ensures that users have a seamless and intuitive experience when interacting with their accounts. It focuses on providing clear and easy-to-understand navigation, intuitive user flows, and informative feedback to guide users throughout the account management process. In addition to the basic functionalities mentioned above, Account Management systems often include more advanced features such as account linking (e.g., connecting social media accounts), email preferences management, and data export options. These additional features contribute to enhancing the overall user experience and providing users with more control over their accounts. Moreover, a design system plays a crucial role in Account Management by providing a set of consistent visual components, user interface elements, and design guidelines. This helps maintain a cohesive look and feel across different account-related pages and ensures a unified user experience throughout the entire application or platform. Overall, Account Management is an essential part of any digital application or platform that deals with user accounts. A well-designed and user-friendly Account Management system not only enables users to effectively manage their accounts but also enhances their overall satisfaction and trust in the application or platform.

Adaptive Icons

Adaptive Icons are a type of user interface (UI) pattern and design system element that provide a consistent visual representation of an app icon across different devices and platforms. They are specifically designed to adapt to various shape and size requirements imposed by different operating systems and launcher interfaces. In the realm of UI design, consistency and coherency are crucial for users to easily recognize and interact with app icons. However, different platforms have different guidelines and specifications for icon shape and size. For instance, Android devices may require square icons, while iOS devices may require rounded icons. This disparity can create a fragmented and inconsistent visual experience for users. To address this challenge, Adaptive Icons were introduced as part of the Android Oreo update in 2017. They establish a level of standardization by allowing app developers to create a single icon design that can dynamically adapt to various shapes and sizes. This is achieved through the use of two distinct layers within the icon: a mask layer and a background layer. The mask layer acts as a silhouette or shape template that defines the overall form of the icon. It is designed to fit various geometric shapes, such as circles, squares, rounded squares, and squircles. The app developer creates the mask layer based on the desired boundaries and shape guidelines of each platform. The background layer, on the other hand, fills the space within the mask layer and provides the visual representation of the app icon. It can include designs, colors, gradients, or textures that reflect the branding or identity of the app. When implemented correctly, Adaptive Icons ensure consistency across different devices and launcher interfaces. As users switch between devices or customize their launcher settings, the app icons seamlessly adapt to the required shape and size, maintaining visual harmony within the user's environment. In conclusion, Adaptive Icons are a UI pattern and design system element that allow app icons to adapt to different shapes and sizes dictated by various operating systems and launcher interfaces. They consist of a mask layer that establishes the overall shape and a background layer that represents the visual content. This adaptive nature ensures a consistent and cohesive user experience across multiple platforms.>

Advanced Search Form

An advanced search form is a user interface (UI) pattern and design system component that allows users to perform complex search queries and retrieve specific information from a large database or website. It provides an enhanced search experience by offering more advanced search options and filters, enabling users to narrow down their search criteria and find desired results more accurately and efficiently. The advanced search form typically consists of multiple fields and controls that users can interact with to define their search parameters. These fields may include options such as keywords, categories, dates, locations, price ranges, or any other relevant attributes depending on the context of the search. By providing a range of filters and options, the advanced search form empowers users to customize their search queries according to their specific requirements. To ensure a seamless user experience, the advanced search form should follow established design system guidelines. This means incorporating consistent visual elements, such as color, typography, and layout, that align with the overall design language of the application or website. The form should also be intuitive and easy to navigate, with clear labels and instructions to guide users through the search process. One key aspect of an effective advanced search form is the ability to handle complex queries and provide real-time feedback to users. As users interact with the form and input their search criteria, the system should validate and update the search parameters accordingly. This could involve dynamically adjusting the available options, displaying relevant suggestions, or providing error messages when invalid inputs are entered. Ultimately, the goal of an advanced search form is to empower users to find specific information quickly and accurately. By offering more advanced search options and filters, it enables users to refine their queries and retrieve the most relevant results. An effective advanced search form not only improves the user experience but also enhances the overall usability and discoverability of the underlying system or website.

In summary, an advanced search form is a UI pattern and design system component that provides enhanced search options and filters, enabling users to perform complex search queries and retrieve specific information more accurately and efficiently. It should follow established design system guidelines, handle complex queries, and provide real-time feedback to users.

Affiliate Links

Affiliate links are a type of URL used in UI patterns and design systems to track referrals and earn commissions for recommending products or services. These links contain a unique identifier that identifies the source of the referral, allowing the affiliate to receive credit for any resulting sales or conversions.

When a user clicks on an affiliate link, they are directed to the merchant's website or product page. The unique identifier in the URL is typically associated with the affiliate's account, so that when a purchase or conversion occurs, the affiliate can be credited with the referral and earn a commission.

Agent Escalation

Agent Escalation refers to the process in which a user interface (UI) pattern or design system enables the transfer of a support request from a self-service system to a human agent or higher level of support. It is a crucial element in providing a seamless user experience and ensuring that users can easily access additional help when required.

In the context of UI patterns and design systems, Agent Escalation typically involves a transition from self-service options, such as an automated chatbot or a knowledge base, to a live chat or phone conversation with a human agent. This escalation can be triggered by various factors, including the complexity of the user's request, the inability of the self-service system to provide a satisfactory solution, or the user's explicit request for human assistance.

When implementing Agent Escalation, a well-designed UI pattern or design system should ensure a smooth and intuitive transition for the user. This may involve clear and prominent placement of a "Contact Support" button or link within the self-service interface, which allows users to initiate the escalation process easily. The UI should also provide clear instructions or hints to guide users through the process, ensuring they understand how to request assistance and what to expect next.

Furthermore, the UI pattern or design system should facilitate the transfer of relevant information from the self-service system to the human agent. This could involve capturing contextual information about the user's previous interactions or providing a summary of the user's current issue. Such information enables the human agent to understand the user's context and provide more personalized and effective support.

In summary, Agent Escalation is a UI pattern or design system component that facilitates the transfer of support requests from a self-service system to a human agent. It ensures a seamless user experience by providing a clear transition mechanism and transferring relevant information to the agent. By incorporating this component into a UI pattern or design system, organizations can enhance their support capabilities and deliver a more satisfying user experience.>

App Walkthrough

A walkthrough in the context of UI patterns and design systems refers to a step-by-step guide or tutorial that helps users navigate and understand the functionality of an app. It provides a structured approach to familiarize users with the app's features and user interface, ensuring a smooth and intuitive user experience. An app walkthrough serves as an instructional tool, guiding users through the various screens, controls, and interactions within the app. It often includes explanatory text, visual cues, and interactive elements to enhance the understanding and engagement of users. The primary goal of an app walkthrough is to onboard and educate users, particularly those who are new to the app or may not be familiar with its specific features. By presenting relevant information and instructions in a clear and concise manner, the walkthrough aims to eliminate confusion, reduce friction, and enable users to quickly grasp the app's purpose and functionality. A well-designed app walkthrough takes into consideration the target audience and their level of knowledge or experience with similar apps. It leverages UI patterns and design principles to ensure consistency, reduce cognitive load, and improve usability. Consistent visual elements, such as colors, typography, and icons, are often employed to create a cohesive and visually appealing walkthrough. Furthermore, an effective app walkthrough adapts to the user's progress and allows for customization or skipping of certain steps. This flexibility caters to individual preferences and helps prevent users from feeling overwhelmed or frustrated by a rigid tutorial. In a design system, the app walkthrough

11

component plays a vital role in maintaining a consistent user experience across different products or platforms. By following established UI patterns and design guidelines, designers can create walkthroughs that align with the overall visual and interactive language of the system. This ensures a cohesive and familiar experience for users who interact with multiple apps or services within the same design system. Overall, an app walkthrough is an essential component of UI patterns and design systems. It serves as a guiding tool to help users understand and navigate through an app, ensuring a smooth and intuitive user experience. By leveraging consistent design principles and considering the needs of the target audience, designers can create effective walkthroughs that onboard and educate users effectively.

An app walkthrough in the context of UI patterns and design systems is a step-by-step guide or tutorial that helps users navigate and understand the functionality of an app.

A well-designed app walkthrough utilizes UI patterns and design principles to ensure consistency, reduce cognitive load, and improve usability for a smooth and intuitive user experience.

App Widget

An App Widget is a small and interactive user interface component that can be added to the home screen or displayed as a floating element within an application. It is designed to provide users with quick access to important information or functionality from a specific app without requiring them to open the full app. App Widgets are typically used to display timely and relevant information to users, such as weather updates, news headlines, or calendar events. They can also be used to perform common tasks directly from the home screen, such as playing music, toggling settings, or writing a note. In terms of UI patterns, App Widgets are considered as a part of the "glanceable" or "microinteraction" design patterns. Glanceable design patterns aim to provide users with easily digestible information at a quick glance, while microinteraction patterns focus on simple, single-purpose interactions that require minimal effort from the user. From a design system perspective, App Widgets should follow the visual and interaction guidelines of the platform they are built for. This ensures consistency across different apps and provides users with a familiar experience. Design systems often provide a set of pre-defined styles, layouts, and components that developers can use to create App Widgets that seamlessly integrate with the overall system and other apps. To create an App Widget in HTML, you can use the available frameworks and libraries that provide support for building widgets, such as React, Angular, or Vue.js. These frameworks allow you to define the structure and behavior of the widget using HTML markup, combined with JavaScript for interactivity and data fetching. Using pure HTML, you can create a basic App Widget by defining a container element and adding the necessary content and styling. Here is an example:

Weather Widget

Today's temperature: 25°C

In this example, we have a simple App Widget that displays the current weather temperature. The container element has a class of "widget-container" for styling purposes. Inside the container, we have a title element with a class of "widget-title" and a content element with a class of "widget-content". The title and content can be dynamically updated with data from an external source. Overall, App Widgets are an essential component of modern UI design, providing users with quick access to important information and functionality right from the home screen or within an app.>

Application Form

An application form is a structured interface that allows users to input and submit information for a specific purpose or action. It is an essential component of user interface (UI) patterns and design systems in various digital platforms. Application forms typically include a set of fields, labels, and input elements that gather relevant data from users. These fields can vary depending on the purpose of the form, such as user registration, feedback submission, or online purchases. The design of an application form aims to provide a seamless and intuitive experience for users, enabling them to efficiently complete the required actions. The form begins with clear and concise instructions, guiding users on how to fill out the necessary information. Labels are commonly used to indicate the purpose and requirement of each input field. Text inputs allow users to type in alphanumeric characters, while other input elements like checkboxes, radio buttons, and dropdown menus provide options for users to select from. Validation is a crucial aspect of application forms. It ensures that the information submitted by users is accurate and complete. Typically, validation can be done in real-time or upon form submission. Real-time validation instantly alerts users about any errors or missing fields as they fill out the form, while submission validation provides a comprehensive error message after the form is submitted. To enhance the usability of application forms, design systems incorporate visual cues to highlight active and selected fields. These visual cues can include changes in color, border, or text style. Furthermore, grouping related fields and structuring the form layout in a logical manner assist users in understanding the required information and completing the form with ease. Overall, an application form is a vital tool that enables users to interact with digital platforms by providing their information, preferences, or feedback. It forms an integral part of UI patterns and design systems, as it guides users through the process of inputting and submitting data efficiently. The design of application forms should prioritize usability, clarity, and validation to ensure a seamless user experience.

Appointment Booking Form

An Appointment Booking Form is a User Interface (UI) pattern and design system that allows users to schedule, modify, or cancel appointments or reservations. It serves as a digital gateway that streamlines the appointment booking process, saving time and enhancing user experience. The Appointment Booking Form typically consists of different sections and fields, which enable users to provide the necessary information for their appointment. These sections may include personal details, such as name, contact information, and any additional notes or comments. Users may also be prompted to specify the type or purpose of the appointment, along with the desired date and time. The design system of an Appointment Booking Form adheres to principles of usability, accessibility, and visual consistency. To ensure usability, the form should have clear labels and instructions, guiding users through the process step by step. Field validation is also essential, ensuring that users provide accurate and relevant information. Accessibility is crucial in the design of an Appointment Booking Form to ensure that all users, including those with disabilities, can seamlessly make appointments. The form should comply with accessibility standards, such as providing alternative text for images, using appropriate color contrasts, and maintaining a logical tab order for keyboard navigation. Visual consistency is significant in the design system of an Appointment Booking Form to create a cohesive and professional interface. Consistent typography, color schemes, and layout elements help users navigate the form easily and understand the information they need to provide. The Appointment Booking Form can be enhanced with additional features to improve user experience. For example, implementing a live calendar view can allow users to see available appointment slots, reducing the need for back-and-forth communication. Integrating notifications, reminders, or confirmation emails can also help users stay informed about their appointments. Overall, an Appointment Booking Form is a vital UI pattern and design system that simplifies the appointment booking process for users. It provides a structured and intuitive interface, ensuring that users can easily schedule, modify, or cancel appointments, ultimately enhancing their overall experience.

Answer: An Appointment Booking Form is a User Interface (UI) pattern and design system that allows users to schedule, modify, or cancel appointments or reservations. It serves as a digital gateway that streamlines the appointment booking process, saving time and enhancing user experience.

The design system of an Appointment Booking Form adheres to principles of usability, accessibility, and visual consistency. To ensure usability, the form should have clear labels and instructions, guiding users through the process step by step. Field validation is also essential, ensuring that users provide accurate and relevant information.

Appointment Booking Widgets

An appointment booking widget is a UI pattern and design system component that allows users to schedule and manage appointments or reservations through a user-friendly interface. It is typically used in applications or websites that offer services requiring pre-planned time slots, such as booking appointments with healthcare professionals, reserving tables at restaurants, or scheduling meetings with colleagues.

The appointment booking widget provides a seamless and intuitive experience for users to select the date, time, and duration of their desired appointment. It displays an interactive calendar or dropdown menus for users to choose the desired date and time, along with additional options such as selecting the service or provider, adding personal notes or requirements, and viewing availability in real-time.

Article Reader

An article reader is a UI pattern and design system component that is specifically designed to display and present lengthy textual content, such as articles, blog posts, or news stories, in an easily readable and visually appealing manner.

This component typically includes features such as a clean and well-structured layout, typography optimization for readability, interactive navigation options (e.g., scrolling, pagination, or table of contents), and options for user customization (e.g., font size or theme selection).

Attendance Tracking Form

An Attendance Tracking Form is a user interface pattern used in design systems to collect and record attendance data. This form allows users to input attendance information for individuals or groups, typically for events, classes, meetings, or other scheduled activities. The purpose of an Attendance Tracking Form is to provide a structured and organized way for users to track attendance and gather necessary information. It simplifies the process of recording attendance by providing a standardized format that can be easily understood and used by both the people responsible for taking attendance and the individuals whose attendance is being recorded. An Attendance Tracking Form typically consists of various fields and elements that enable the user to input data accurately. These may include: 1. Date: The field where the user can specify the date of the attendance record. 2. Event/Activity: A field to describe the specific event or activity for which attendance is being recorded. 3. Participants: A field for listing the names or identities of the individuals who attended. 4. Attendance Status: A dropdown or radio button group that allows the user to indicate if someone is present, absent, or has a different status. 5. Notes/comments: An optional field for additional information or comments related to the attendance record. In addition to these basic elements, an Attendance Tracking Form may also include additional features to enhance usability and efficiency. This may include options for bulk entry of attendance data, the ability to import or export attendance records, or the integration of automated attendance systems. The design of an Attendance Tracking Form should prioritize clarity, consistency, and ease of use. It should follow the overall visual and interaction design guidelines of the design system to ensure a cohesive look and feel across all UI components. Clear labeling, logical ordering of fields, and proper spacing are important to enhance user comprehension and facilitate efficient data entry. By utilizing an Attendance Tracking Form as part of a design system, organizations can improve the accuracy and consistency of their attendance records. It simplifies the task of tracking attendance and provides a standardized interface that can be easily understood and used by both administrators and participants.>

Audiobook Player

An Audiobook Player is a user interface (UI) pattern specifically designed to provide a seamless and user-friendly experience for playing audiobooks. It is part of a larger design system that encompasses various UI elements and patterns.

The Audiobook Player typically consists of different components and controls that facilitate the navigation, playback, and management of audiobooks. These components may include:

The Play/Pause Button: This button allows users to start or pause the playback of the audiobook. When pressed, it toggles between a play and pause icon to reflect the current state of the playback.

The Progress Bar: This visual representation displays the progress of the audiobook playback. It indicates the elapsed time and total duration of the audiobook, allowing users to easily track their listening progress and navigate to specific sections of the audiobook.

The Skip Backward/Forward Buttons: These buttons enable users to skip backward or forward in the audiobook playback. By clicking these buttons, users can move to the previous or next chapter, section, or a specific time point in the audiobook.

The Volume Control: This control allows users to adjust the volume of the audiobook playback. It typically includes a slider or buttons to increase or decrease the volume level. Users can customize the volume according to their preferences and environment.

The Bookmarking Feature: This feature enables users to bookmark sections or specific moments in the audiobook that they find interesting or want to revisit later. It allows users to easily return to these bookmarks and continue listening from where they left off.

Overall, the Audiobook Player strives to provide a visually appealing and intuitive interface that enhances the user's listening experience. It ensures that users can easily control and navigate through their audiobooks, adjusting settings, and accessing important features with ease. By adhering to consistent design patterns and principles, the Audiobook Player creates a cohesive and enjoyable user experience for audiobook enthusiasts.

Augmented Reality (AR) Gaming

Augmented Reality (AR) gaming refers to the integration of virtual elements into the real-world environment through the use of technology. It combines the physical world with computer-generated sensory inputs, such as sound, video, graphics, or GPS data, to provide an immersive experience for the users. AR gaming utilizes various UI patterns and a design system to create interactive and engaging gameplay.

In the context of UI patterns, AR gaming incorporates user-centered design principles to enhance the user experience. It involves the use of intuitive visual cues, such as markers or triggers, to enable users to interact with the virtual elements seamlessly. These cues serve as entry points for the AR experience, allowing users to trigger actions or access additional information about the game. By using clear and recognizable visual indicators, AR gaming ensures that users can easily understand and navigate the augmented environment.

Furthermore, AR gaming also utilizes UI patterns like overlays and pop-ups to provide contextual information and instructions to the users. Overlays are used to display informative text or graphics on top of the real-world view, guiding users through the gameplay or providing them with relevant information. Pop-ups, on the other hand, offer additional interactive features, such as menus or options, that allow users to control and customize their gaming experience.

AR gaming heavily relies on a well-defined design system to maintain consistency and coherence throughout the gameplay. A design system in AR gaming encompasses a set of visual and interaction guidelines that dictate the overall look and feel of the augmented environment. It includes the use of consistent color palettes, typography, and iconography to provide visual cues that align with the game's theme and style. The design system also ensures that the interactive elements, such as buttons or input fields, adhere to the same visual language and behavior, promoting familiarity and ease of use for the users.

In conclusion, Augmented Reality (AR) gaming utilizes various UI patterns and a well-defined design system to create immersive and interactive gameplay. By incorporating user-centered design principles, AR gaming enhances the user experience through intuitive visual cues, overlays, and pop-ups. The design system ensures consistency and coherence in the augmented environment, providing a seamless and engaging gaming experience for the users.

Augmented Reality (AR) Integration

Augmented Reality (AR) Integration refers to the incorporation of virtual elements or information into the real-world environment through digital technologies. In the context of UI patterns and design systems, AR integration involves the seamless integration of augmented reality features and functionalities into the user interface to enhance the user experience and interaction. AR integration often entails the use of various sensors, cameras, and computer vision algorithms to overlay digital content onto the physical world. This allows users to perceive and interact with virtual objects or information as if they were part of the real environment. By integrating AR into UI patterns and design systems, designers and developers can create more immersive and interactive experiences for users. The integration of AR into UI patterns and design systems requires careful consideration of various factors. This includes the design and placement of AR elements, the use of appropriate visual cues and feedback, and the optimization of performance and usability. Designers need to ensure that the AR elements harmoniously blend with the overall design and do not disrupt or overwhelm the user experience. In terms of UI patterns, AR integration can be implemented using various techniques such as marker-based tracking, markerless tracking, surface detection, and object recognition. Marker-based tracking involves the use of predefined markers or images that act as triggers for AR content. Markerless tracking, on the other hand, relies on computer vision algorithms to detect and track real-world objects or surfaces. Surface detection focuses on recognizing and identifying flat surfaces in the physical environment, while object recognition involves detecting and tracking specific objects or images. Design systems play a crucial role in ensuring consistency and coherence in the integration of AR into UI patterns. By providing guidelines, standards, and reusable components, design systems help designers and developers maintain a unified and cohesive AR experience across different screens and devices. Design systems can also facilitate collaboration and streamline the development process by offering a library of pre-designed AR elements and interactions. Overall, AR integration in UI patterns and design systems opens up new possibilities for interactive and immersive user experiences. Through careful design and development, AR can seamlessly enhance the real world with virtual elements, transforming how users engage with digital content and information. By leveraging the capabilities of AR, designers and developers can create truly dynamic and engaging interfaces that bridge the gap between the physical and digital realms. >

Augmented Reality (AR) Overlays

Augmented Reality (AR) overlays refer to visual elements and information that are superimposed onto the real-world environment through the use of a digital device, such as a smartphone or smart glasses. These overlays are designed to enhance and augment the user's perception of reality by adding digital content to their physical surroundings. In the context of UI patterns and design systems, AR overlays play a crucial role in providing a seamless and intuitive user experience. They enable users to interact with their environment in new and innovative ways, by providing relevant and contextually rich information overlaid on top of real-world objects. AR overlays can be used in a variety of applications, ranging from navigation and wayfinding to gaming and education. For example, in a navigation app, AR overlays can display real-time directions and points of interest directly on the user's field of view, eliminating the need to constantly switch between the app and the physical environment. In terms of UI patterns, AR overlays often follow the principles of minimalism and user-centered design. The overlays should be visually lightweight, unobtrusive, and easy to understand. They should also adapt to the user's context and provide information that is relevant to their current task or situation. To achieve these goals, AR overlays should be designed with careful attention to typography, color, and layout. Clear and legible text, along with visually distinct icons and symbols, should be used to communicate information effectively. The layout of the overlays should be optimized for different screen sizes and orientations, ensuring that the content is displayed in a visually pleasing and easily accessible manner. In conclusion, AR overlays are a powerful tool in enhancing the user experience and enabling new forms of interaction with the real world. By carefully designing and implementing these overlays, designers can create intuitive and immersive experiences that seamlessly blend digital and physical elements.

Augmented Reality (AR) Product Try-On

Augmented Reality (AR) Product Try-On is a UI pattern that allows users to virtually try on products, such as clothing, accessories, or makeup, using their own device screen. This interactive and immersive experience leverages computer-generated imagery to overlay the virtual representation of the product onto the user's real-world environment in real-time. AR product try-on leverages the camera capabilities of the user's device, such as a smartphone or tablet, to capture and analyze their physical surroundings. The AR technology then superimposes the virtual product onto the live video feed, ensuring accurate placement, alignment, and scale. This enables users to visualize how the product would look and fit in their real-world context without physically having to try it on. The UI design system for AR product try-on should provide a seamless and intuitive user experience. It should include clear instructions and guidance on how to use the AR feature, as well as an easily accessible toggle to activate and deactivate the AR overlay. The UI should also include options to switch between different product variations or styles for a comprehensive try-on experience. To ensure accuracy and realism, the design system should consider factors such as lighting conditions, shadows, and reflections in the virtual representation of the product. This will enhance the user's perception of how the product would look in their actual environment. Additionally, the UI pattern should provide interactive elements, such as the ability to rotate, zoom, or move the virtual product within the user's camera view. This allows users to examine the product from different angles and perspectives, enhancing the overall try-on experience. AR product try-on can significantly benefit both users and businesses. Users can make more informed purchase decisions by virtually experiencing the product before making a purchase. This reduces the risk of disappointment and returns, while also providing an engaging and enjoyable shopping experience. For businesses, AR product try-on can increase customer satisfaction, boost sales, and differentiate their brand from competitors. In summary, the AR product try-on UI pattern enables users to virtually try on products using their device's camera and AR technology. The design system should prioritize user experience, realism, and interactivity to provide an immersive and accurate visualization of the product within the user's real-world context.

Author Bio On Blog Posts

An author bio on blog posts is a brief description of the author that appears at the end of their written content. It provides readers with relevant information about the author, such as their name, background, and expertise. This bio section helps to establish credibility and build trust with the audience, as it gives them a sense of who is behind the content they are consuming.

From a UI patterns and design system perspective, the author bio serves as an essential component of the overall blog post layout. It is usually presented in a visually distinct section, separate from the main content, often with a different background color or border to highlight its importance. The use of typography, spacing, and layout techniques are employed to create a clear visual hierarchy that draws attention to the author's information.

Back To Top Button

A back to top button is a UI pattern and design system element commonly used in websites or applications to provide easy navigation to the top of the page. It is typically represented by a small arrow or icon placed at the bottom right corner of the screen that appears as the user scrolls down the page. When a user scrolls down a lengthy page, it becomes cumbersome to manually scroll all the way back to the top. The back to top button serves as a convenient shortcut to quickly return to the beginning of the content without repetitive scrolling. It enhances the user experience by saving time and effort, providing a seamless navigation experience. The back to top button is designed to be unobtrusive yet easily noticeable when needed. It usually remains hidden until the user starts scrolling downwards. Once the user scrolls a certain distance, the button becomes visible, allowing them to click on it to instantly jump back to the top. In terms of implementation, the back to top button can be achieved using HTML and CSS. It is often placed within a container element, such as a ``, and styled using CSS to position it at the bottom right corner of the screen. Additionally, JavaScript or jQuery can be utilized to add functionality to the button, making it smoothly scroll back to the top when clicked. Including a back to top button is particularly beneficial for long-scrolling pages, blog posts, news articles, or any content-heavy pages where users are likely to scroll extensively. It enhances usability, allowing users to navigate the content more efficiently and providing a positive user experience. In conclusion, the back to top button is a UI pattern that facilitates easy navigation to the top of a page. It saves time and effort for users who have scrolled through lengthy content, allowing them to quickly return to the starting point. By implementing the back to top button, websites and applications can enhance their overall usability and improve the user experience.

Billing Address Form

A Billing Address Form is a user interface pattern used in web design to collect necessary information from users for billing purposes. It is a specific form that enables users to provide their billing address, typically associated with financial transactions or online purchases, in a structured and standardized format.

The Billing Address Form is an essential element of a design system, which is a collection of reusable components and guidelines that ensures consistency and coherence across different interfaces. It serves as a standard design pattern that allows designers and developers to create a user-friendly and efficient form that meets the needs of both the business and the user.

Billing And Payment History

The Billing and Payment History is a UI pattern that provides users with a visual representation of their financial transactions, including bills and payments made over a specific period of time. It is an essential component of a design system as it allows users to easily track and manage their billing information.

In this UI pattern, the Billing and Payment History typically consists of a chronological list or table of transactions, organized by date and time. Each transaction entry includes details such as the transaction type (e.g. bill or payment), the amount, the date of the transaction, and any additional notes or reference numbers. The most recent transactions are usually displayed at the top of the list, allowing users to quickly view their most recent activity.

Biometric Authentication

Biometric Authentication in the context of UI patterns and design system refers to the use of unique physiological or behavioral characteristics of individuals to verify their identity. It involves the use of biometric technologies, such as fingerprint recognition, iris scanning, face recognition, and voice recognition, to authenticate users. Biometric authentication offers a more secure and user-friendly way to verify one's identity compared to traditional methods like passwords or PINs. By leveraging the distinct features that are unique to each individual, it provides a high level of accuracy in verifying user identity. In terms of UI patterns and design system, biometric authentication typically involves integrating the biometric technology within the user interface in a seamless and intuitive manner. This ensures that the user experience remains consistent and familiar across different applications and devices. The design of biometric authentication UI patterns focuses on providing clear instructions to users on how to interact with the biometric sensors or devices. This includes guiding users to properly position their finger on a fingerprint scanner, aligning their face within a frame for facial recognition, or providing voice prompts for voice authentication. Furthermore, it is essential to provide visual feedback to users during the authentication process. This can be accomplished through the use of progress indicators, animations, or color changes to indicate successful or unsuccessful authentication attempts. In terms of accessibility, it is important to ensure that biometric authentication UI patterns cater to users with different abilities. This includes providing alternative authentication methods for individuals with disabilities who may have difficulty using certain biometric technologies. Additionally, considering privacy concerns, it is crucial to provide clear information and obtain user consent for the collection and storage of biometric data. Overall, biometric authentication in the context of UI patterns and design system provides a secure and user-friendly method for verifying user identity. By integrating biometric technologies seamlessly into the user interface, it offers a consistent and intuitive authentication experience across different applications and devices.

Biometric Authentication in the context of UI patterns and design system refers to the use of unique physiological or behavioral characteristics of individuals to verify their identity. It involves the use of biometric technologies, such as fingerprint recognition, iris scanning, face recognition, and voice recognition, to authenticate users.

Biometric authentication offers a more secure and user-friendly way to verify one's identity compared to traditional methods like passwords or PINs. By leveraging the distinct features that are unique to each individual, it provides a high level of accuracy in verifying user identity.

Bot Mentions

A bot mention is a user interface pattern and design system element commonly used to highlight and display messages or interactions involving a bot. In a user interface, a bot mention acts as a visual cue to draw attention to the presence of a bot and emphasize its participation in the conversation or task.

In the context of UI patterns and design systems, a bot mention typically consists of distinct visual styling or formatting that sets it apart from other user messages or system notifications. This can include a different color scheme, font style, or iconography. The purpose of these visual cues is to ensure clarity and help users easily recognize and differentiate bot-generated content from human-generated content.

Brand Logo

A brand logo is a visual representation of a brand or company. It is a unique symbol or design that is used consistently across various touchpoints to identify and differentiate the brand. In the context of UI patterns and design systems, brand logos play a crucial role in creating a cohesive and memorable user experience.

Brand logos are typically created through a thoughtful and strategic design process. They are often a combination of typography, colors, shapes, and symbols that visually communicate the personality, values, and message of the brand. The logo should be simple, scalable, and instantly recognizable, ensuring it can be effectively used across different mediums and sizes.

Breadcrumb Navigation

Breadcrumb Navigation is a UI pattern commonly used in website and application design systems. It provides a clear and concise way for users to understand their current location within a website's hierarchy and navigate back to previously visited pages. In a breadcrumb navigation, a series of links are displayed horizontally, typically at the top of a webpage or application interface. Each link represents a specific level within the hierarchy of pages or sections, with the leftmost link representing the top-level or home page. The purpose of breadcrumb navigation is to enhance the user experience by providing a visual trail that allows users to easily understand where they are in relation to the overall structure of the website or application. This helps users orient themselves, navigate between pages, and explore related content more efficiently. One key benefit of breadcrumb navigation is that it reduces the cognitive load on users by providing them with a clear and predictable way to navigate. Instead of relying solely on the browser's back button or complex navigation menus, users can simply click on the desired breadcrumb link to return to a higher-level page. Additionally, breadcrumb navigation can be particularly useful for websites or applications with deep hierarchies or complex structures. By visually representing the hierarchy, users can quickly understand the relationships between different pages and sections, making it easier for them to find the information they are looking for. The implementation of breadcrumb navigation in HTML can be straightforward. Each link in the breadcrumb is wrapped in an anchor tag, and the links are separated by a separator character, such as a forward slash ("/") or a greater-than sign (">"). By applying appropriate CSS styling, the breadcrumb can be visually enhanced to provide a clear and intuitive navigation experience. Overall, breadcrumb navigation is an effective UI pattern that contributes to the overall usability and user experience of websites and applications. By providing users with a clear visual representation of their location within a hierarchy, it simplifies navigation and helps users efficiently explore and interact with content.>

Breadcrumbs

A breadcrumb is a navigation component commonly used in user interfaces to provide users with a way to understand their current location within a website or application and easily navigate back to higher-level pages. It is typically displayed as a horizontal trail of clickable links, starting from the home page and ending with the current page.

Each link in the breadcrumb represents a higher-level page in the hierarchy, allowing users to quickly jump to any previous pages they have visited. The links are often displayed in a chronological order, with the current page usually being the last link in the trail. The links are also usually separated by a delimiter, such as a forward slash ("/"), to visually distinguish them.

Bug Report Form

A bug report form is a user interface (UI) pattern used in design systems to collect information about bugs or issues that users encounter while using a software application. It provides a structured format for users to report and describe the problem they are facing, allowing developers to understand and resolve the issue more effectively. The bug report form typically consists of various input fields and components that prompt the user to provide specific details about the bug. These fields may include: 1. Title: A brief but descriptive title that summarizes the issue. 2. Description: A text area where the user can provide a detailed explanation of the problem they encountered. This section may also include instructions on what kind of information should be included, such as steps to reproduce the bug, expected behavior, and actual behavior. 3. Severity/Priority: A dropdown or radio buttons that allow the user to indicate the urgency or impact of the bug. This helps prioritize the resolution process. 4. Attachments: An option to upload any files or screenshots that may help illustrate or provide more context to the issue. 5. Browser/Device information: Fields to capture details about the browser, operating system, and device the user was using when the bug occurred. This information can be valuable in replicating and troubleshooting the issue. 6. Contact information: Fields for the user to enter their name and email address, allowing developers to follow up with any clarifications or updates. By using a bug report form, developers can gather consistent and structured information about bugs, eliminating the need for back-and-forth communication with users to gather necessary details. This saves time and improves the efficiency of the bug-fixing process. Example of a bug report form:

Title:

Description:

Note: This is a simplified example for demonstration purposes. In a real-world scenario, the form would likely include additional fields and components, validation, and styling to enhance usability and capture all necessary bug-related information.>

Calendar View

A calendar view is a user interface (UI) design pattern commonly used in the context of design systems. It presents a visual representation of dates and events in a structured and organized manner. The primary purpose of a calendar view is to help users easily navigate through dates, manage events, and get an overview of their schedule.

A calendar view typically consists of a grid-like structure, with each cell representing a specific date. The cells are organized into rows and columns, forming a monthly or weekly layout. Days of the week are usually displayed as headers, providing a contextual reference for the dates displayed below.

Call To Action (CTA) Buttons

Call to Action (CTA) Buttons are commonly used UI elements in web design that prompt users to take a specific action. They are typically designed as clickable buttons or links with text, often in a contrasting color, that stands out from the rest of the interface. CTA buttons serve as visual cues that guide users towards completing a desired action or goal, such as making a purchase, signing up for a newsletter, or downloading a file. They play a crucial role in user experience by providing clear directions and reducing cognitive load. When designing CTA buttons, several factors should be considered to ensure their effectiveness. Firstly, the language used in the button text should be concise, action-oriented, and compelling. It should clearly convey the purpose of the action, such as "Buy Now," "Subscribe," or "Download." Additionally, the text should create a sense of urgency or offer a value proposition to entice users to click. The visual design of CTA buttons is equally important. They should be visually distinct from other elements on the page to attract users' attention. The use of color, typography, and spacing can help emphasize the button and make it stand out. It is common to use contrasting colors, such as a vibrant color for the button background and a lighter color for the text, to create visual contrast. Size and placement are also key considerations in CTA button design. Buttons should be large enough to be easily clickable on both desktop and mobile devices. They should be strategically

20

placed in a prominent position within the layout, such as above the fold or near important content. Proper spacing around the button can also help draw attention to it and ensure it is easily distinguishable from surrounding elements. CTA buttons play a vital role in guiding users through a desired user flow and achieving conversion goals. By following best practices in their design and placement, designers can effectively prompt users to take action and enhance overall user experience.

Call to Action (CTA) Buttons are commonly used UI elements in web design that prompt users to take a specific action. They are typically designed as clickable buttons or links with text, often in a contrasting color, that stands out from the rest of the interface.

CTA buttons serve as visual cues that guide users towards completing a desired action or goal, such as making a purchase, signing up for a newsletter, or downloading a file. They play a crucial role in user experience by providing clear directions and reducing cognitive load.

Camera Interface

A camera interface is a user interface pattern or design system that allows users to interact with a camera device or application. It provides a set of controls and options to enable users to capture and manipulate images or videos. The camera interface typically consists of various elements, such as viewfinder, controls, settings, and feedback. The viewfinder displays the live preview of what the camera sees and helps users frame their shots. The controls allow users to capture images or videos, switch between different camera modes, adjust settings, and access additional features. The settings provide options to modify image quality, resolution, exposure, focus, flash, and other parameters. In terms of design, the camera interface aims to provide a user-friendly and intuitive experience. It should be visually appealing, with clear and easily understandable icons or labels for each control or setting. The interface should also provide clear feedback, such as visual indicators or sounds, to inform users about the camera's status, focus, or exposure. A well-designed camera interface follows established UX principles, such as simplicity, consistency, and discoverability. It should present the most commonly used controls prominently, while keeping less frequently used options accessible but not overwhelming. The interface should also allow for easy navigation between different screens or modes, using gestures or clear navigation elements. In terms of implementation, the camera interface can be developed using HTML, CSS, and JavaScript. HTML provides the structure and layout for the interface, CSS is used for styling and visual design, and JavaScript is used for interactivity and capturing user input. Overall, a camera interface is a crucial component of camera applications or devices, providing users with an intuitive and enjoyable way to capture and manipulate images or videos. Its design and implementation should prioritize user needs and expectations, while adhering to established UX principles and best practices.

The camera interface is a user interface pattern or design system

that allows users to interact with a camera device or application. It provides a set of controls and options to enable users to capture and manipulate images or videos.

Canvas Menu

The Canvas Menu is a user interface pattern and a design system component used in web applications to present a group of options and actions in a visually appealing and organized manner. It is commonly utilized to provide navigation menus, dropdown menus, or expandable menus in modern websites. At its core, the Canvas Menu consists of a container element that houses the menu items or links. The container typically takes the shape of a rectangular box, which can be customized with various styles, such as background color, border, or shadow effects. The menu items within the Canvas Menu are displayed in a vertical or horizontal layout, depending on the design and user preferences. Each menu item is usually represented by a text label, which can be accompanied by an icon or image to enhance the visual representation and aid in quick recognition. These items often serve as shortcuts to different sections or pages of the web application. To interact with the Canvas Menu, users can employ various input devices, such as a mouse, touchpad, or touchscreen. When the user hovers over or clicks on a menu item, it may trigger a specific action, such as navigating to a different page, displaying additional submenus, or executing a particular function within the web application. One of the key advantages of the Canvas Menu is its flexibility and adaptability. It can be seamlessly integrated into different design systems and user interfaces without compromising the overall aesthetic or user experience. Designers can customize the appearance of the Canvas Menu to match the look and feel of their website or application, ensuring consistent branding and visual coherence. Moreover, the Canvas Menu can accommodate a varying number of menu items, allowing designers and developers to scale it based on the application's complexity and navigation requirements. This scalability also extends to mobile devices, as the Canvas Menu can be responsive and adapt to different screen sizes. In conclusion, the Canvas Menu is a versatile user interface pattern and design system component that provides an intuitive and visually appealing way to present menu options and actions in web applications. It offers flexibility in customization, scalability, and responsiveness, making it a valuable tool for enhancing the overall navigation experience for website visitors.

Car Rental

A car rental UI pattern refers to a standardized design and layout that is used to provide a seamless and user-friendly experience for customers who want to rent a car. It includes a set of predefined elements, components, and interactions that are used consistently throughout the entire car rental system. These UI patterns are part of a larger design system that aims to ensure a cohesive and consistent user experience across different platforms and devices. The main goal of a car rental UI pattern is to simplify the process of renting a car and make it as intuitive as possible for users. It should allow users to easily search for available cars, view their details, select dates and locations for pickup and drop-off, and complete the reservation process. The design should be clean, uncluttered, and visually appealing, with clear and concise labels, instructions, and error messages. The UI pattern should also take into account the needs and preferences of different user groups. For example, it should be accessible and have a responsive design that adapts well to different screen sizes, making it easy for users to rent a car on their smartphones or tablets. It should also provide multiple language options, allowing users to choose their preferred language for a more personalized experience. In terms of navigation, the UI pattern should provide a clear hierarchy and logical flow that guides users through each step of the car rental process. It should have a consistent layout and placement of elements, such as search filters, sorting options, and reservation summaries. The pattern should also include clear and intuitive navigation elements, such as breadcrumbs or a progress bar, to help users understand where they are in the process and how to proceed. Furthermore, a car rental UI pattern should prioritize user trust and security. It should clearly display important information, such as rental terms and conditions, insurance options, and payment details. It should also use secure and encrypted connections for handling sensitive information, such as credit card details, to ensure the privacy and security of users' data. Overall, a car rental UI pattern is an essential component of a design system, providing a consistent and user-friendly interface for customers to rent cars easily, efficiently, and securely.>

Card Sorting

Card sorting is a user research method used in the context of UI patterns and design systems to gather insights and organize information through user input. It involves presenting users with a set of items or pieces of content (represented as cards) and asking them to group and sort them into categories based on their own understanding and organization. The process of card sorting is typically conducted in a controlled environment, such as a usability lab or remote online platform. Participants are given a set of cards, either physical or virtual, each containing a single item or concept. They are then asked to group the cards together in a way that makes sense to them and label each group with a category name. The participants have the freedom to create as many or as few groups as they see fit and can rename or modify groups later on. By observing users as they perform card sorting, designers and researchers can gain insights into how users perceive and organize information. This method helps uncover patterns, similarities, and differences in users' mental models and provides valuable input for the design and organization of user interfaces, navigational structures, and content categorization. Card sorting can be conducted in two main forms: open card sorting and closed card sorting. In open card sorting, participants have the freedom to create their own categories and group the cards as they see fit. This helps reveal the natural organization and mental models of users. Closed card sorting, on the other hand, provides pre-defined categories or groups that participants must sort the cards into. This method is useful for testing existing navigational structures or evaluating the effectiveness of a design system. The outcome of a card sorting session is often represented as a card sort diagram or matrix, illustrating the relationships and hierarchy between groups and items. The data gathered from card sorting sessions can be analyzed quantitatively and qualitatively, allowing designers to refine and optimize the information architecture, content organization, and interaction design of their UI patterns and design systems. In conclusion, card sorting is a user-centered research method that provides valuable insights into how users organize and categorize information. It helps inform the design of UI patterns and design systems, ultimately leading to more user-friendly and intuitive interfaces.

Carousel Sliders

Carousel sliders are a UI pattern commonly found in website design systems. They are used to showcase multiple pieces of content or images in a visually appealing and interactive manner. A carousel slider typically consists of a horizontal strip or container that holds a series of content or image cards. These cards are displayed one at a time, with the ability to navigate to the next or previous card using navigation buttons or gestures. The main purpose of a carousel slider is to allow users to easily browse through a set of content or images, without overwhelming them with too much information at once. It provides a way to present a collection of related items in a compact and engaging format. Carousel sliders are often used in situations where there is limited screen space or when there is a need to highlight multiple pieces of content within a specific area. They are commonly used on homepages, landing pages, and product pages to showcase featured products, recent articles, testimonials, or any other type of content that needs to be highlighted. The design of a carousel slider can vary depending on the specific requirements and goals of the website or application. It can be simple and minimalistic, with just the content or image cards and navigation buttons. Alternatively, it can be more elaborate with additional elements such as captions, overlays, autoplay functionality, or thumbnail navigation. When designing a carousel slider, it is important to consider factors such as the number of items to be displayed, the size and aspect ratio of the content or images, and the user's interaction patterns. It is also crucial to ensure that the carousel slider is accessible and responsive across different devices and screen sizes. In conclusion, carousel sliders are a popular UI pattern used in web design systems to showcase multiple pieces of content or images in an engaging and easily navigable way. They provide a compact and visually appealing format for presenting collections of related items, and can be customized to suit different design needs and goals.

Cart Checkout Form

A cart checkout form is a user interface component that allows customers to securely complete the purchasing process for their selected items in an online shopping website or application. It serves as the final step before finalizing the transaction and making the payment.

The cart checkout form typically consists of a series of input fields and sections where users can enter their personal and payment information to complete the purchase. These input fields include details such as the customer's name, shipping address, billing address, email address, contact number, and payment method. Some forms may also include additional fields to capture any special instructions or discount codes.

Cascading Style Sheets (CSS) Grid

p { font-family: Arial, sans-serif; font-size: 16px; line-height: 1.6; text-align: justify; }

Cascading Style Sheets (CSS) Grid is a flexible layout system that allows web developers to create complex and responsive user interface (UI) patterns and design systems. It is a two-dimensional grid-based layout system, providing a powerful and intuitive way to design and arrange elements on a webpage.

With CSS Grid, developers can define rows and columns of the grid using simple CSS properties. Elements within the grid can be placed and sized precisely, allowing for fine-grained control over the layout. This makes it ideal for creating consistently aligned grids, multi-column layouts, and overlapping content.

The grid can be divided into areas, which can be assigned names for easier reference. By using grid-template-areas, developers can visually define the layout of the grid by assigning names to

23

each area and placing elements within those areas. This approach simplifies the code and enhances readability, making it easier to understand and maintain complex layouts.

CSS Grid also offers powerful features for responsive design. Developers can define different layouts for different screen sizes by using media queries. This allows for adapting the grid layout based on the screen dimensions, ensuring a consistent and user-friendly experience across a wide range of devices.

In addition, CSS Grid provides the ability to control the space between rows and columns, specify grid gaps, alignment, and feature dynamic sizing. It offers a range of properties like grid-template-columns, grid-template-rows, grid-gap, justify-content, align-items, and more, which give developers precise control over the layout of elements within the grid.

Overall, CSS Grid is a versatile layout system that empowers developers to create complex and flexible UI patterns and design systems. By using the grid structure, developers can easily control the placement and sizing of elements, achieve responsive designs, and enhance the overall user experience on the web.

Case Resolution Form

Case Resolution Form is a UI pattern and design system component that is used to capture and organize information related to resolving a specific case or issue. It provides a structured way for users to input and track relevant details, such as the nature of the problem, the steps taken to resolve it, and any additional notes or comments.

The form typically consists of various input fields, checkboxes, dropdown menus, and text areas, allowing users to enter and select the required information. These fields may include options to specify the type of case, priority level, and the individuals or teams involved. Additional fields might be included to track the status of the case, such as "Open," "In Progress," or "Resolved."

The Case Resolution Form follows a user-centered design approach, ensuring that the interface is intuitive, straightforward, and easy to navigate. It is important to provide clear instructions and labels for each field, enabling users to quickly understand what information is expected. The form should also include validation rules to prevent any errors or missing data entries.

The design system for a Case Resolution Form should adhere to the overall visual consistency and branding guidelines of the application or website. This ensures that the form aligns with the established design language, such as color palette, typography, and layout, reinforcing a cohesive user experience throughout. Consistency in design also aids in user familiarity and recognition, reducing cognitive load and potential confusion.

In conclusion, the Case Resolution Form is a crucial tool in documenting and managing the resolution process for specific cases or issues. It provides a structured and organized approach for capturing relevant information and allows all involved parties to track the progress and status of a resolution. By following user-centered design principles and aligning with the overall design system, the form can effectively facilitate the resolution process and enhance user experience.

Case Submission Form

Case Submission Form is a UI pattern and design system element used to collect and gather information from users in a structured manner. It serves as a standardized template that allows users to provide specific details or submit requests, feedback, or any other form of communication. The Case Submission Form typically consists of various input fields, such as text fields, checkboxes, radio buttons, dropdown menus, and text areas, accompanied by clear and concise labels. Each input field is designed to capture specific information, ensuring that users provide all the necessary details while minimizing errors or omissions. The main purpose of a Case Submission Form is to streamline the process of data collection and facilitate efficient communication between users and the system. By offering a well-organized and intuitive interface, it enables users to articulate their needs or concerns effectively. By standardizing the structure and format, it ensures consistency and accuracy in the data collected, making it easier for the system to process and analyze the information. In terms of design system, Case Submission Forms are typically created using HTML and CSS, following the design guidelines and principles set forth by the organization or brand. The form's layout and styling should align with the overall visual language and branding, ensuring a cohesive user experience. By providing a Case Submission Form, businesses and organizations can gather valuable insights, feedback, and requests from their users. This information can be utilized to improve products or services, address user concerns or inquiries more efficiently, and make informed decisions based on the data collected. Overall, the Case Submission Form is a fundamental component of UI patterns and design systems, as it plays a crucial role in facilitating communication and data collection between users and the system. Its standardized structure and intuitive design enhance the user experience and enable efficient processing and analysis of user-generated content.

Case Submission Form is a UI pattern and design system element that collects user information in a structured manner. It streamlines the process of data collection and facilitates efficient communication between users and the system. By offering a well-organized interface with various input fields, it allows users to provide specific details and minimizes errors or omissions.

Created using HTML and CSS, Case Submission Forms align with the organization's design guidelines and branding. They provide valuable insights, feedback, and requests for businesses or organizations. This information can be utilized to improve products or services, address user concerns, and make informed decisions.

Challenge Response Form

A UI pattern is a recurring, reusable solution that solves common design problems in user interface (UI) design. It is a best practice or a proven approach to addressing specific design challenges in a consistent and systematic way. UI patterns help designers and developers create intuitive and familiar user experiences by providing a set of guidelines and conventions. They promote consistency and efficiency in design by ensuring that similar problems are solved in a similar manner throughout the application or website. UI patterns can be classified into different categories based on their purpose and functionality. For example, there are navigation patterns that define how users can move through the interface, such as drop-down menus or tabs. There are also input patterns that provide guidelines for data entry and validation, such as forms or input fields. Design systems, on the other hand, are a comprehensive collection of reusable components, guidelines, and assets that define the visual and interactive elements of a product or brand. They serve as a single source of truth for design and development teams to ensure consistency and efficiency in creating user interfaces. A design system encompasses not only UI patterns but also other design elements such as typography, color palette, iconography, and spacing. It provides a holistic approach to design by considering the entire user experience and the brand identity. Design systems are built on the principles of modularity and scalability. They allow designers and developers to easily create new interfaces by assembling pre-defined components and patterns. This not only speeds up the design process but also ensures consistency across different parts of the application or website. In conclusion, UI patterns and design systems play a crucial role in guiding designers and developers to create user-friendly and visually consistent interfaces. They provide a systematic and reusable approach to solving design challenges and ensure a cohesive user experience.>

Chat Head Interface

A chat head interface is a UI pattern commonly used in messaging applications that allows users to view and interact with ongoing conversations in a compact and convenient manner. It typically appears as a circular or rounded profile picture (head) of the person or entity engaged in the conversation, overlaid on top of the application's main interface. When clicked or tapped on, the chat head expands to display the full conversation thread, allowing users to read, send, or interact with messages without leaving their current context. One key advantage of the chat head interface is its multitasking capability. As the chat heads float on top of the main UI, users can continue using the application or performing other tasks while still having easy access to ongoing conversations. This enables a seamless and uninterrupted user experience, as users no longer need to switch between different screens or applications to engage in conversations. Furthermore, the chat head interface typically supports multiple simultaneous chat heads, allowing users to view and manage multiple conversations at once. In terms of design system, chat heads introduce a distinct visual element that needs to be consistent with the overall

25

aesthetic of the application. The design should prioritize clarity and instant recognition of the conversation partners, often accomplished by displaying their profile pictures or avatars at a relatively large size within the circular or rounded boundary. The chat head should also display an indication of unread messages, such as a badge or a highlighted border, to provide users with a quick visual cue that new messages are awaiting their attention. When designing the expanded chat head view, it is important to maintain consistency with the main conversation or messaging interface. This ensures that users can easily navigate between the two views without confusion or loss of context. The expanded view should display the conversation thread in a readable and interactive manner, allowing users to easily scroll through messages, view media, and send replies. In conclusion, the chat head interface is a UI pattern that enhances multitasking and convenience in messaging applications. It provides users with quick access to ongoing conversations while allowing them to continue their primary tasks. By carefully considering the design system and maintaining consistency with the main messaging interface, the chat head interface can offer a seamless and efficient user experience.

Chat Interface

A chat interface in the context of UI patterns and design systems is a user interface element that is designed to facilitate communication between users in a digital environment. It typically consists of a series of messages exchanged between users, displayed in a conversational format.

The chat interface is commonly used in various applications and platforms, such as messaging apps, social media platforms, customer support systems, and collaborative workspaces. It allows users to engage in real-time or asynchronous conversations, enabling efficient and effective communication.

Chatbots

A chatbot is a user interface (UI) pattern and a component of a design system that enables interaction between humans and computer systems through conversation. It is programmed to provide automated responses based on natural language processing (NLP) algorithms. The primary purpose of a chatbot is to simulate human conversation and deliver information or perform tasks in a conversational manner. It serves as a virtual assistant, capable of understanding and responding to user queries, initiating predefined actions, and providing relevant suggestions or recommendations. Chatbots are typically integrated within messaging platforms, websites, or applications. They can be implemented as standalone interfaces or embedded within existing user interfaces. When a user interacts with a chatbot, they can ask questions, make requests, or provide commands using text or voice inputs. The chatbot then processes the input and generates an appropriate response based on its programming. Designing a chatbot involves considering the overall user experience (UX) and ensuring that the conversation flow feels natural and intuitive. The design system for chatbots encompasses various elements, such as dialogue design, message categorization, and system feedback. Dialogues should be designed to anticipate and understand user intents, enabling the bot to respond accurately. Message categorization involves organizing responses into relevant groups to ensure coherence and clarity in communication. System feedback ensures that users receive appropriate confirmation or clarification during the conversation. In terms of UI patterns, chatbots may employ speech bubbles or text bubbles to visually represent conversation threads. These bubbles may be color-coded to differentiate between user messages and bot responses. Additionally, elements like typing indicators, message timestamps, user avatars, or system avatars can be used to enhance the chatbot's visual presentation and improve the overall user experience. Overall, chatbots play a vital role in streamlining interactions between users and computer systems, providing seamless customer support, information retrieval, or task automation. Their design and integration within UI patterns and design systems are focused on delivering conversational interfaces that are intuitive, efficient, and helpful to users.

Checkout Screen

A checkout screen refers to a user interface pattern and design system that is commonly used in e-commerce websites and applications. It is a crucial part of the online shopping experience, allowing users to review and finalize their purchases. The checkout screen typically consists of several sections and elements that guide users through the payment process. It is designed to be intuitive, user-friendly, and efficient, ensuring a smooth transaction flow. One of the primary components of a checkout screen is the order summary. This section displays a summary of the items selected for purchase, including their quantities, prices, and any applicable discounts. It allows users to review their choices before proceeding further. The next significant element is the billing and shipping information form. Users are required to fill in their personal details and shipping address in this section. Depending on the website or application, the form may be divided into multiple subsections for better organization and ease of completion. Following the personal information, the checkout screen includes a payment section. Here, users can select their preferred payment method, such as credit card, PayPal, or other available options. The necessary fields for each payment method are provided, ensuring users can securely provide their payment details. Additionally, the checkout screen may include a section for applying coupon codes or promotional offers. This feature allows users to enter any valid codes they may have, providing them with the corresponding discounts or benefits. The screen should display the applied discounts and any changes to the order total dynamically. Another essential aspect of the checkout screen is the order review and confirmation step. This gives users a final chance to review all the information they have provided before completing the purchase. It is crucial for users to have a clear and concise summary of their order, including the total cost, shipping details, and estimated delivery time. In terms of design system, a checkout screen should align with the overall branding and visual identity of the website or application. Consistency in typography, colors, and spacing promotes a seamless experience for users. It is also important to consider mobile responsiveness to provide an optimal checkout experience on various devices. Overall, a checkout screen is a vital element of any e-commerce platform, enabling users to finalize their purchases securely and efficiently. By employing a well-designed and intuitive interface, businesses can enhance customer satisfaction and reduce cart abandonment rates.

A checkout screen is a crucial part of the online shopping experience, allowing users to review and finalize their purchases. It typically includes an order summary, billing and shipping information form, payment section, coupon code application, and order review and confirmation step. The design system should align with the overall branding and visual identity of the platform, offering consistency in typography, colors, and spacing. A well-designed checkout screen enhances customer satisfaction and reduces cart abandonment rates.

Coding And Programming

Coding and programming, within the context of UI patterns and design systems, refer to the technical processes involved in creating and implementing user interfaces. UI patterns, also known as user interface patterns, are standardized solutions to common design problems in the field of user interface design. They provide a set of guidelines and best practices for designing user interfaces that are intuitive, user-friendly, and visually appealing. UI patterns help designers and developers save time and effort by offering pre-defined solutions for common problems, allowing them to focus on customizing the interface to meet specific project requirements. Design systems, on the other hand, are comprehensive collections of design guidelines, rules, and assets that help ensure consistency and coherence across different interfaces and platforms. A design system provides a centralized source of truth for design and development teams, ensuring that all UI elements and components in a project are designed and implemented consistently. It includes guidelines for typography, color schemes, iconography, spacing, and more. Coding, within the context of UI patterns and design systems, involves writing the necessary code to transform the design concepts into functional user interfaces. This includes using programming languages such as HTML, CSS, and JavaScript to structure and style the interface elements. HTML (Hypertext Markup Language) is used to define the structure and content of web pages, while CSS (Cascading Style Sheets) is used to control the visual presentation and layout. JavaScript is often used to add interactivity and dynamic elements to the interface. Programming, in the context of UI patterns and design systems, refers to the broader process of writing code to create and implement user interfaces. This includes not only coding the individual UI elements, but also developing the necessary logic and functionality to make them work together seamlessly. In summary, coding and programming are essential technical processes in the field of UI patterns and design systems. They involve writing code to transform design concepts into functional and visually appealing user interfaces, following standardized UI patterns and design system guidelines. HTML, CSS, and JavaScript are often used in combination to achieve this.>

Collapsible Panels

Collapsible panels are a UI pattern commonly used in designing user interfaces and creating responsive web experiences. They are elements that can expand or collapse when triggered by the user, allowing for the display of additional content or options without cluttering the interface. Collapsible panels typically consist of a header or toggle element and a content section. The header serves as a control to expand or collapse the content, often in the form of an arrow or icon. When clicked, the content section slides open or closed, revealing or hiding its contents. This behavior provides a way to present additional information or functionality when needed, while keeping the interface clean and organized by hiding non-essential elements by default. The use of collapsible panels can enhance user experience by reducing visual clutter and allowing users to focus on the content that is relevant to them. They also help save screen real estate, especially in mobile or responsive designs where space is limited. Additionally, collapsible panels can be used to create a modular and flexible design system, where panels can be easily added, removed, or rearranged to accommodate different use cases or content variations. To implement collapsible panels in HTML, the use of JavaScript or CSS is typically required for the interactive behavior. However, the following HTML code demonstrates a basic structure for a collapsible panel:

Panel 1

content of panel 1

Panel 2

content of panel 2

In this example, each panel consists of a header (the first

element) and a content section (the second

element). Through JavaScript or CSS, clicking on the header would trigger the expansion or collapse of the respective content section. Overall, collapsible panels are a versatile UI pattern that can greatly enhance the usability and organization of a user interface. By allowing users to control the visibility of content, they provide a more interactive and user-centric experience.>

Color Contrast Checker

A Color Contrast Checker is a tool designed for the evaluation of color combinations used in user interface (UI) patterns and design systems. It assesses the contrast between foreground and background colors to ensure readability and accessibility for users with varying visual abilities. The tool displays the contrast ratio between two selected colors and provides guidance on whether the combination meets the accepted accessibility standards, such as those outlined in the Web Content Accessibility Guidelines (WCAG). These guidelines emphasize the importance of sufficient contrast to enable users to perceive and distinguish content properly. To use the Color Contrast Checker, designers and developers input the hexadecimal or RGB values of the foreground and background colors they intend to use. The tool then calculates the contrast ratio between these two colors and indicates whether the combination passes or fails the accessibility criteria. Typically, a contrast ratio of 4.5:1 or higher for normal text is recommended, while a contrast ratio of 3:1 or higher is suggested for larger text and graphical objects. For UI patterns and design systems, where consistency is key, the Color Contrast Checker plays a crucial role. It helps maintain a unified visual identity while ensuring that the color combinations used meet accessibility requirements. By implementing accessible color schemes, designers increase the usability of their interfaces and enhance the overall user experience. Integrating a Color Contrast Checker into the design and development workflow ensures that accessibility considerations are not overlooked or delegated to a later stage. It empowers designers to make informed color choices from the outset, reducing the need for subsequent revisions or costly accessibility fixes. By offering a simple yet effective evaluation of color combinations, the Color Contrast Checker enables designers to create inclusive and user-friendly interfaces. It promotes a design mindset that prioritizes accessibility, reinforces the principles of inclusive design, and fosters equal access to digital content for all users. In conclusion, the Color Contrast Checker is a vital tool for designers and developers working on UI patterns and design systems. Its purpose is to assess the contrast between foreground and background colors, providing guidance on accessibility and ensuring optimal reading experiences for users with diverse visual abilities.

Color Picker

A color picker is a user interface (UI) pattern and design system component that allows users to select and apply colors within an application or design tool. A color picker typically consists of a visual representation of a color spectrum or a grid of color swatches. This representation helps users visualize and choose the desired color for their UI elements, such as backgrounds, text, or icons. The main purpose of a color picker is to provide users with an intuitive and efficient way to select colors that harmonize with their overall design. By offering a range of colors, gradients, and shades, a color picker enables users to explore various color options and find the ones that best fit their design aesthetic. In addition to the visual representation, a color picker often includes control elements that allow users to fine-tune their color selection. These controls may include sliders or input fields for adjusting the hue, saturation, brightness, and opacity of a color. Implementing a color picker in a design system is crucial for maintaining consistency across an application or a suite of products. By defining a set of colors and providing a standardized color picker component, designers and developers can ensure that the selected colors adhere to the established design guidelines. Furthermore, a color picker in a design system can offer advanced features such as color palettes, color history, or color accessibility tools. These additional functionalities assist designers in creating cohesive designs and meeting accessibility standards. In conclusion, a color picker is a UI pattern and design system component that empowers users to select and apply colors to their designs. It provides an interface for visually exploring and adjusting colors, fostering consistency and enhancing the overall visual appeal of a digital product or application.

A color picker is a UI pattern and design system component that allows users to select and apply colors within an application or design tool. It consists of a visual representation of a color spectrum or swatch grid, enabling users to choose colors for various UI elements. A color picker is crucial in maintaining consistency and adherence to design guidelines within a design system.

Comment Form

UI patterns refer to recurring design solutions that solve common user interface problems. They are reusable, proven solutions that provide a consistent and familiar experience to users, promoting usability and efficiency. UI patterns are commonly used in the development of design systems, which are a collection of reusable components and guidelines that ensure a consistent and cohesive look and feel across an entire product or application. Design systems are a framework or set of tools that help design and development teams create and maintain a unified visual style and user experience. They provide a comprehensive set of guidelines, principles, and components that enable teams to efficiently build and maintain a consistent UI. Design systems promote efficiency, reduce inconsistencies, and improve collaboration between designers and developers. In terms of UI patterns, they can be categorized into various types based on their purpose and functionality. Some common UI patterns include: 1. Navigation patterns: These patterns deal with how users navigate through an application or website. Examples include menus, tabs, and breadcrumbs. 2. Input patterns: These patterns focus on the input methods and elements used by users to interact with an application. Examples include forms, input fields, and dropdowns. 3. Feedback patterns: These patterns provide users with feedback on their actions and help them understand the system's state. Examples include notifications, tooltips, and progress indicators. 4. Layout patterns: These patterns define the overall structure and organization of content within an application. Examples include grids, cards, and sidebars. 5. Visual patterns: These patterns deal with the visual aspects of an application, such as colors, typography, and iconography. Examples include style guides, color palettes, and icon sets. By utilizing UI patterns within a design system, designers and developers can maintain consistency, efficiency, and usability throughout the entire product or application. Whether it's through navigation, input, feedback, layout, or visual patterns, UI patterns provide solutions to common problems and ensure a seamless and intuitive user

29

experience. Design systems, on the other hand, provide the framework and guidelines necessary for maintaining a consistent and cohesive design across the entire product or application. In conclusion, UI patterns and design systems play a crucial role in creating intuitive and efficient user interfaces. By applying UI patterns within a design system, teams can ensure consistency, reusability, and a seamless user experience.

Comment Section

UI patterns are reusable solutions to common design problems that arise during the development of user interfaces. They provide a set of guidelines for creating consistent and intuitive user interfaces, ensuring that users can easily navigate, understand, and interact with digital products. A design system, on the other hand, is a comprehensive set of rules, components, and guidelines that dictate the visual and functional aspects of a user interface. It defines the overall look and feel of a product, ensuring that all UI elements are visually cohesive and work together seamlessly. UI patterns and design systems work hand in hand to create user-friendly and visually appealing interfaces. By following established patterns and using predefined components provided by the design system, designers and developers can save time and effort in creating consistent and high-quality user interfaces. UI patterns can include various elements such as navigation menus, search bars, forms, buttons, and more. These patterns are based on common user behaviors and expectations, making it easier for users to understand and interact with the interface. By using familiar patterns, users can quickly and intuitively navigate through the application, reducing cognitive load and improving overall user experience. Design systems, on the other hand, provide a structured framework for implementing these patterns. They include a library of reusable components, such as buttons, typography styles, color schemes, and iconography. By using these predefined components, designers and developers can ensure that the user interface remains consistent and visually pleasing, regardless of the size or complexity of the application. In summary, UI patterns and design systems are crucial tools in the field of user interface design. UI patterns provide guidelines and solutions for common design problems, while design systems offer a comprehensive set of rules and components to create visually cohesive and user-friendly interfaces. By following these principles, designers and developers can create interfaces that are both aesthetically pleasing and intuitive to use.>

Comments Section

A comments section is a user interface (UI) design pattern commonly used in websites, mobile applications, and other digital platforms to allow users to engage in conversations, share opinions, and provide feedback on specific content or topics. It is typically implemented as a section or area where users can post comments, reply to existing comments, and interact with other users.

The primary purpose of a comments section is to create a sense of community and enable user-generated content. It provides a platform for users to express their thoughts, ask questions, offer suggestions, and engage in discussions related to the content being viewed. This fosters user engagement and encourages users to spend more time on the platform, ultimately enhancing the overall user experience.

Community Guidelines Violation Report Form

A community guidelines violation report form is a user interface (UI) pattern and design system component that allows users to report instances of content or behavior that are in violation of the community guidelines established by a platform or online community.

The purpose of the community guidelines violation report form is to provide users with a straightforward and accessible method to report any content or behavior that goes against the established rules and standards of the community. This could include things like spam, hate speech, harassment, or any other form of behavior that violates the community guidelines.

The form typically consists of a series of fields or inputs that users can fill out to provide information about the violation. Common fields include the user's name or username, a description of the violation, and any additional details or evidence that can support the report. In some cases, the form might also include optional fields for the user's contact information or any other relevant information that can assist in the investigation of the report.

The design of the form follows the principles of usability and accessibility to ensure that it can be easily understood and used by all users. It often includes clear labels and instructions for each field, error handling mechanisms, and a submit button to finalize the report.

By providing a clear and accessible means for users to report violations of community guidelines, the community guidelines violation report form plays a critical role in maintaining a safe and respectful online environment. It allows the platform or community administrators to effectively enforce the guidelines and take appropriate actions against users who repeatedly violate the rules, ultimately fostering a more positive and inclusive community for all users.

Community Safety

Community Safety refers to the measures and strategies implemented to ensure the well-being, security, and protection of individuals within a community.

In the context of UI patterns and design systems, Community Safety involves the application of user interface elements and design principles to create digital products that prioritize the safety and security of users.

Comparison Tables

Comparison Tables are UI patterns used in design systems to present and compare multiple items or pieces of information in a structured and organized manner. These tables allow users to easily analyze and understand the similarities and differences between the items being compared. In a design system, comparison tables are typically designed using a grid-like layout. Each row of the table represents an item or element being compared, while each column represents a specific characteristic or attribute of the items. The table cells contain the relevant information for each item and attribute. The use of consistent typography, colors, and alignment helps to provide a clear and visually appealing presentation. The main purpose of a comparison table is to facilitate comparison and decision-making for users. By presenting information in a tabular format, users can quickly scan and compare different attributes across multiple items. This enables users to make informed choices based on their specific needs or preferences. The information in a comparison table is typically presented in a concise and structured manner. Headers are used to label the columns and provide a clear indication of the attribute being compared. The table cells contain the specific data for each item and attribute, arranged in a logical order. The use of clear and concise language helps to ensure that the information is easily understandable and accessible to users. To enhance usability, comparison tables often include interactive features. For example, users may be able to sort the table based on specific attributes, allowing them to prioritize and focus on the most important information. Filters or search functionality can also be incorporated to further refine the view, enabling users to find specific items or attributes of interest. In summary, comparison tables are UI patterns used in design systems to present and compare multiple items or pieces of information. By presenting data in a structured and organized format, these tables facilitate comparison and decision-making for users. The clear and concise presentation of information, along with interactive features, enhances usability and user experience.

Complaint Form

A complaint form is a user interface (UI) pattern and design system that allows users to express their dissatisfaction or grievances regarding a product, service, or experience. It provides users with a formal structure to articulate their complaints, ensuring that the necessary information is captured accurately and efficiently. To create a complaint form in HTML, you can use the

tag to structure the content. Here is an example:

Name:

Email:

In this example, the complaint form begins with a paragraph (

) tag that includes a label and an input field for the user to provide their name. The "for" attribute in the label is used to associate it with the corresponding input field using the "id" attribute. The "name" attribute is used for form submission. Another paragraph tag (

) is used for the email input field, following the same structure as the name input field. The "type" attribute of the input field specifies that it should accept email addresses, and the "required" attribute ensures that the field must be filled out before submission. This basic structure can be expanded to include additional fields relevant to the complaint, such as a subject line, a description box, or even file upload options for supporting evidence. These fields can be added within their respective

tags, following the same pattern. By using this complaint form UI pattern and design system, users can provide detailed and structured feedback to address their concerns. It allows for efficient handling of complaints by capturing the necessary information in a standardized format, helping businesses and organizations to address grievances more effectively.>

Compose Email

Subject: Definition of UI Patterns and Design System Dear [Recipient's name], I hope this email finds you well. The purpose of this email is to provide a formal definition of UI (User Interface) patterns and design systems in the context of web development. UI patterns refer to recurring design solutions that address common usability issues. These patterns provide a tried and tested approach to solve problems that users often encounter when interacting with a website or application. UI patterns can be thought of as best practices in design that have been refined over time to enhance user experience. On the other hand, a design system is a comprehensive set of guidelines, components, and tools that ensure consistency and efficiency in visual design and development processes. It encompasses the UI patterns mentioned earlier and provides a framework for creating consistent and coherent user interfaces across different platforms. Design systems help designers and developers maintain a unified look and feel throughout a project by establishing a set of rules and standards. These rules cover various aspects of design, such as typography, color schemes, button styles, icons, spacing, and interaction patterns. By adhering to a design system, teams can reduce design and development challenges, streamline the process, and ultimately deliver a more polished product. In summary, UI patterns are specific design solutions that address usability issues, while design systems are comprehensive frameworks that provide guidelines and components for consistent and efficient design and development. I hope this definition helps you to gain a better understanding of UI patterns and design systems in the context of web development. If you have any further questions or need additional clarification, please feel free to reach out. Thank you for your attention. Best regards, [Your Name]>

Confirmation Form

A confirmation form is a user interface pattern and component of a design system that is used to gather explicit user consent or confirmation before performing a specific action or completing a process.

It typically consists of a form that presents the user with a message or prompt asking them to confirm their intent or decision. The message should clearly explain what action or process the user is confirming and provide any necessary context or details. The confirmation form often includes buttons or options for the user to either confirm or cancel their action.

Consent Form

A consent form is a formal document in the context of UI patterns and design systems that obtains permission or agreement from a user or participant before they engage in certain activities or disclose personal information. In the design of user interfaces, consent forms play a crucial role in adhering to ethical standards and regulations, such as data protection laws and privacy policies. These forms are used to inform users about the purpose and scope of their interaction with a system, as well as the potential risks and benefits associated with it. The goal is to ensure that users understand and voluntarily agree to the terms and conditions before proceeding. Consent forms in UI design typically contain the following elements: 1. Purpose: The form clearly states the purpose of obtaining consent, such as collecting personal data for account creation or tracking user behavior for analytics. 2. Scope: It outlines the specific activities for which consent is being sought, such as sharing data with third-party services or conducting user research. 3. Terms and Conditions: The form includes a summary or link to the terms and conditions that govern the overall use of the system, including rights and responsibilities of both parties. 4. Data Collection and Usage: It provides information on what data will be collected and how it will be used, stored, and potentially shared with other parties. 5. Duration and Revocability: The form specifies the duration of consent, such as whether it is a one-time agreement or ongoing until revoked by the user. It also explains how users can withdraw their consent if they choose to do so. 6. Acknowledgment: The form includes a statement or checkbox where users explicitly indicate their consent by acknowledging that they have read and understood the provided information. By incorporating consent forms into UI patterns and design systems, designers can ensure that users are well-informed and empowered to make decisions about their personal data and online interactions. This not only promotes transparency and trust but also helps organizations to meet legal requirements and address user privacy concerns.>

Contact Form

A contact form is a user interface (UI) pattern commonly used in design systems to provide a structured way for users to communicate with a website or application. It serves as a means for users to submit their inquiries, feedback, or any other types of messages to the website or application owner. The contact form typically consists of various input fields where users can enter their name, email address, subject, and message. These input fields are designed to capture the necessary information from the user in a structured format, making it easier for the recipient of the form submission to understand and respond to the user's message. In addition to the input fields, contact forms often include a submit button that users can click to send their message. This button triggers a server-side process that collects the form data and sends it to the designated recipient. Design systems play a significant role in defining the appearance and functionality of contact forms. They provide a set of standardized design elements, layout guidelines, and user interaction patterns that ensure consistency and enhance the overall user experience. The design of a contact form should align with the overall visual style of the website or application. This includes consistent typography, color scheme, and button styles. By following the design system's guidelines, contact forms can maintain visual harmony with other UI components on the website or application. In terms of functionality, contact forms should adhere to usability principles to ensure they are user-friendly and accessible. This means using clear and concise labels for the input fields, providing helpful error messages for incorrect form submissions, and offering additional features like CAPTCHA to prevent spam. In conclusion, contact forms are a vital component of UI patterns and design systems. They provide a structured way for users to communicate with website or application owners, while following the guidelines and visual style defined by the design system. By implementing contact forms that align with these principles, websites and applications can enhance the user experience and capture valuable information from their users.>

Contact Information Form

A contact information form is a user interface (UI) pattern and component of a design system that allows users to enter or update their contact details in a structured and organized manner. It is commonly used in web applications, mobile apps, and websites to collect and store user information for communication purposes. The contact information form typically consists of several input fields that prompt users to enter their personal details such as name, email address, phone number, and physical address. These input fields are accompanied by labels that describe the purpose of each field, helping users understand what information is required. The form may also include additional fields for optional details, such as a website URL or social media handles. In the UI design system, the contact information form adheres to certain design principles and guidelines to ensure consistency and usability across different platforms and devices. It follows a clean and minimalist design approach, with clear labels and input fields that are easy to read and interact with. The form may include validation mechanisms to ensure that the entered information is accurate and in the correct format. This can include verifying the email address format, restricting the phone number field to numerical input only, and offering suggestions or auto-filling options for the address field. A well-designed contact information form not only provides a seamless user experience but also aligns with accessibility standards. It should be accessible to users with disabilities, such as providing proper color contrast for visually impaired users and ensuring form elements are compatible with assistive technologies like screen readers. Overall, the contact information form is an essential component of the UI design system and plays a crucial role in enabling effective communication between users and the platform. It helps collect accurate user information and provides a convenient way for users to update their contact details. By adhering to design principles and accessibility guidelines, the contact information form ensures a user-friendly experience and contributes to the overall usability of the application or website.

A contact information form is a UI pattern that allows users to enter or update their contact details in a structured manner.

It includes input fields for name, email address, phone number, and other relevant information, along with labels and validation mechanisms for accuracy and usability.

Contact Information

Contact Information refers to the details that allow users or customers to get in touch with a business, organization, or individual. In the context of UI patterns and design systems, Contact Information is an essential element that provides users with a means to communicate, inquire, or seek support. It typically includes information such as phone numbers, email addresses, physical addresses, and sometimes social media profiles or website URLs. Including Contact Information in a UI pattern or design system is crucial as it enables users to easily find and interact with the relevant contact details. Whether it is a customer trying to inquire about a product or service or a user seeking technical support, having accessible contact information improves user experience and helps build trust. To ensure a seamless user experience, Contact Information should be displayed in a prominent and consistent manner across all screens and pages. It is common for UI patterns and design systems to have a dedicated section or component that showcases contact details, often located in a header or footer. When designing Contact Information for a UI pattern or design system, it is important to consider usability and accessibility. Ensure that the contact details are prominently displayed and legible, using clear typography and appropriate spacing. Providing alternative contact methods, such as a contact form or live chat, can also enhance the user experience. In terms of design, Contact Information should align with the overall aesthetic and branding of the UI pattern or design system. This includes using consistent colors, fonts, and visual elements to ensure a cohesive look and feel. Consider using icons or labels to distinguish between different types of contact details, such as a phone icon for phone numbers and a mail icon for email addresses. Overall, Contact Information is a crucial component of UI patterns and design systems. By providing users with easily accessible and visually consistent contact details, businesses and organizations can enhance user experience, promote effective communication, and build trust with their users.

Contacts Screen

A Contacts screen is a user interface element commonly found in mobile applications and websites. It is part of the UI pattern and design system for managing and displaying a collection of contacts. This screen provides a user-friendly way to organize and access contact information. The Contacts screen typically consists of a list or grid that displays the names or images of contacts. Each contact is represented as a separate entry in the list, allowing users to easily scroll and browse through their contacts. Tapping or clicking on a contact entry opens a detailed view with more information about the selected contact. In addition to displaying contact names or images, the Contacts screen may also include other relevant details such as phone numbers, email addresses, or social media profiles. It is common for the screen to provide search functionality that allows users to quickly find specific contacts by typing in a search query. The Contacts screen is designed to be intuitive and user-friendly. It often follows a consistent visual style and layout to ensure a seamless experience for users. Design systems and UI patterns help to establish and maintain this consistency across different screens and applications. To create a Contacts screen in HTML, you can use the tag to represent the contact entries. Each contact can be wrapped in its own

tag, allowing for consistent spacing and formatting. Within each

tag, you can include the contact name or image, along with any other relevant information. For example:

Contact Name 1

Contact Name 2

Contact Name 3

... By using the

tags, you can easily add or remove contacts from the screen by simply adding or deleting the corresponding

tag. This makes it convenient to update and manage the contact list dynamically. In conclusion, the Contacts screen is a crucial component of UI patterns and design systems that allow users to manage and access their contacts efficiently. By following consistent design principles and using the appropriate HTML tags, developers can create an intuitive and visually appealing Contacts screen in their applications.>

Content Cards

A content card is a UI element that is used to showcase information or content in a concise and visually appealing manner. It is a part of the design system that helps in creating consistent and cohesive user interfaces.

Content cards are typically rectangular in shape and are organized in a grid or a list. They can contain a variety of content types such as text, images, icons, or even multimedia elements like videos or audio. The content within a card is usually self-contained and is designed to be easily scannable, allowing users to quickly grasp the main information without having to read lengthy passages.

Content Download Request Form

A content download request form is a user interface (UI) pattern that allows users to request or download content from a website or application. It is a form used to capture user information and preferences for the content they wish to download, such as ebooks, whitepapers, or case studies. The purpose of the content download request form is to gather information from the user that is necessary for providing them with the desired content. This includes basic contact information like name, email address, and sometimes phone number. The form may also ask for additional details, such as job title, company name, or industry, in order to personalize the content or for marketing purposes. The design of the content download request form should be simple and intuitive, with clear labels and prompts for each field. It is important to strike a balance between collecting enough information to qualify leads or personalize content and not overwhelming the user with too many fields or asking for overly personal information. Some best practices for designing a content download request form include: - Minimizing the number of required fields to reduce friction and increase completion rates. - Using clear and concise language for the form instructions and labels. - Providing an option for users to opt-in or opt-out of email communications, according to data privacy regulations. - Offering a preview of the content, such as a table of contents or a sample chapter, to entice users to complete the form. In the context of a design system, a content download request form is a reusable component that can be integrated into various pages or sections of a website or application. The form's layout, styling, and behavior are consistent across different content types, ensuring a cohesive and familiar user experience. By including the content download request form as part of a design system, designers and developers can save time and effort by reusing existing code and design assets. In conclusion, a content download request form is a UI pattern used to capture user information and preferences for downloading content. Its purpose is to collect the necessary data to provide users with their desired content while minimizing friction and maintaining a consistent user experience. By following best practices and incorporating the form into a design system, designers can create an effective and efficient means for users to engage with and obtain content.>

Content Filtering

Content filtering is a user interface (UI) pattern commonly used in design systems to help users narrow down search results or categorize large amounts of information efficiently. It allows users to apply various filters or criteria to the displayed content, reducing the complexity of navigating and finding relevant information.

Rather than overwhelming users with a long list of unfiltered content, content filtering provides a controlled way for users to select specific attributes, characteristics, or preferences they desire in the content they are seeking. By implementing this UI pattern in design systems, developers offer users a more streamlined and personalized experience.

Content Flagging Form

A content flagging form is a specific type of user interface pattern that is used to allow users to report objectionable or inappropriate content within a digital platform or system. It is typically a form that collects information from the user about the content that they wish to flag, and provides options for categorizing the type of issue or violation. The flagged content can include things like offensive language, hate speech, graphic images, or any other content that goes against the platform's terms of service or community guidelines.

The design of a content flagging form is crucial in order to ensure that users feel empowered to report content that they find objectionable, while also preventing misuse or abuse of the reporting feature. The form should be intuitive and easy to use, with clear instructions and labels to guide the user through the reporting process.

Content Licensing Request Form

A content licensing request form in the context of UI patterns and design systems is a formal document used to obtain permission for the use, distribution, or modification of content that is owned or copyrighted by someone else. It allows individuals or organizations to request authorization to use specific content in their own projects or products. The purpose of the form is to establish a legal and transparent process for requesting content licenses. It typically includes sections for providing information such as the requester's name, contact details, description of the content being requested, intended use of the content, and any proposed modifications or adaptations. By using a content licensing request form, both the content owner and the requester are able to clarify their rights and obligations. The form ensures that the content owner can control the use of their content and properly assess the intended use to determine if it aligns with their terms and conditions. It also provides the requester with a formal and documented way to seek permission and avoid any potential legal issues. Additionally, the form may include terms and conditions that govern the use of the licensed content, such as restrictions on commercial use, attribution requirements, and limitations on distribution or modification. These terms help protect the content owner's rights and ensure that the requester understands and agrees to the conditions under which the content can be used. In a design system or UI patterns context, a content licensing request form is particularly important to ensure that all visual assets, text, icons, and other components used in the design system are properly licensed and authorized for use. This helps maintain consistency, reliability, and legality within the design system, preventing any copyright infringements or unauthorized use of content. Overall, a content licensing request form serves as a formal and structured means of obtaining permission to use copyrighted content within a design system or UI patterns context, promoting legal and transparent content usage for all parties involved.>

Content Marquee

A content marquee is a UI pattern used in web design to display important or attention-grabbing information. It is typically a horizontal scrolling area that showcases content such as news headlines, promotional messages, or featured articles. The content marquee is an effective way to draw users' attention to specific information. It adds visual interest to the user interface and can be an effective tool for communication and engagement. The scrolling motion of the marquee helps to capture the users' attention, making sure that important content is seen even if it is not initially visible on the screen. When designing a content marquee, it is important to consider the content that will be displayed and the overall design system of the website or application. The marquee should blend well with the overall aesthetics and not appear out of place or distracting. It should be visually appealing and easy to read, ensuring that the content is legible and understandable. In terms of implementation, a content marquee can be created using HTML, CSS, and JavaScript. The HTML structure typically consists of a container element that holds the content, and an inner wrapper element that scrolls horizontally within the container. CSS is used to style the marquee, defining properties such as width, height, background color, font size, and text alignment. JavaScript can be used to control the scrolling behavior and timing of the marquee, allowing for smooth and controlled motion. It is important to note that while a content marquee can be a useful design element, it should be used sparingly and purposefully. Too many marquees on a single page can be overwhelming and distracting, diminishing the effectiveness of each individual marquee. Additionally, care should be taken to ensure that the marquee does not negatively impact the overall user experience, such as causing accessibility issues or affecting page load times. In conclusion, a content marquee is a UI pattern used in web design to display important or attention-grabbing information. It is a visually engaging element that can help to communicate and engage with users. When used appropriately and thoughtfully, a content marquee can be an effective tool in enhancing the overall user experience.

Content Removal Request Form

A content removal request form is a user interface pattern commonly used in design systems to provide a structured way for users to request the removal or deletion of specific content from a website or platform. This form allows users to communicate their request and provide necessary details to the relevant administrators or moderators in a clear and organized manner.

The content removal request form typically consists of several input fields and sections to gather relevant information from the users. These fields may include the user's name, contact information, the URL or location of the content in question, a brief description of the content, and the reason for the removal request. Additionally, the form may also include checkboxes or radio buttons to indicate the type of content being reported, such as offensive material, copyrighted content, or personal information.

Content Submission Form

The term UI patterns refers to established solutions or best practices for designing user interfaces. These patterns are reusable and can be applied to different types of interfaces and platforms, providing a consistent and intuitive user experience.

A UI pattern is a general guide or template that helps designers solve common interface design challenges. It offers a proven solution that has been widely accepted and implemented in various applications and websites. By following UI patterns, designers can speed up the design process, improve usability, and enhance user satisfaction.

UI patterns can be categorized into different types, such as navigation patterns, input patterns, layout patterns, and feedback patterns. Navigation patterns, for example, define how users move through an application or website, including methods like menus, tabs, and breadcrumbs. Input patterns, on the other hand, define how users interact with the interface, such as forms, search boxes, and dropdown menus.

A design system, on the other hand, is a collection of reusable components, guidelines, and principles that help ensure consistency and coherency in design across different products or platforms. It acts as a single source of truth for designers and developers, facilitating collaboration and streamlining the design and development process.

A design system typically includes a set of UI patterns, which serve as the building blocks for creating interfaces. These patterns are designed to be modular and flexible, allowing designers to mix and match them to create different layouts and designs. By using a design system, designers can maintain a consistent visual language, improve efficiency, and reduce the risk of inconsistencies and errors in design.

Content Upload Form

A content upload form in the context of UI patterns and design systems refers to a user interface component that allows users to submit and upload content files or data to a website or application. It is a commonly used pattern to enable user-generated content and facilitate data input. The content upload form typically consists of multiple elements and fields that enable users to specify and submit their content. These elements can vary based on the specific requirements of the application but commonly include a file upload button, text input fields, dropdown menus, checkboxes, and radio buttons. The main purpose of the content upload form is to provide a user-friendly and intuitive interface for users to submit their content seamlessly. It helps in streamlining the process of content submission and ensures that the necessary information or files are accurately captured and stored. The file upload button is a crucial element of the content upload form, as it allows users to browse and upload their files from their local system. Upon clicking the file upload button, users are typically presented with a file selection dialog where they can choose the desired file to upload. Once the file is selected, the form should provide clear feedback on the selected file, including the file name and any additional information or restrictions related to the upload. Text input fields are often used in content upload forms to capture metadata or additional details about the uploaded content. These fields can include information such as title, description, tags, or categories. Dropdown menus, checkboxes, and radio buttons are used to provide predefined options or allow users to make selections from a set of choices. Validation and error handling are important aspects of content upload forms. Proper validation should be implemented to ensure that the submitted content meets the required criteria or format. If any errors occur during the submission process, informative error messages should be displayed to guide users in rectifying the issues and resubmitting their content. In conclusion, a content upload form is a fundamental UI component in design systems and UI patterns that enables users to submit their content to a website or application. It streamlines the process of content submission and ensures accurate capture of information or files from users. Properly designed and implemented content upload forms contribute to a seamless user experience and efficient data management.>

Contextual Menus

Contextual menus are a type of user interface pattern commonly used in design systems to provide users with a set of options or actions relevant to the current context or selected item. These menus typically appear upon right-clicking or long-pressing on an item, triggering a menu to display directly adjacent to the item or in a fixed position within the viewport. Contextual menus are designed to provide users with quick and convenient access to a variety of actions or options without cluttering the main interface. They typically list options in a vertical layout, allowing users to scan through the menu easily. Each option in the menu is usually represented by a text label, and occasionally accompanied by an icon to provide a visual cue for the action or option it represents. The content of a contextual menu can vary depending on the context in which it is triggered. It may include options for managing or manipulating the selected item, such as renaming, deleting, duplicating, or sharing. Additionally, contextual menus often provide quick access to advanced functionality or additional information related to the selected item, such as opening a settings dialog or viewing detailed properties. Design systems often provide guidelines and best practices for the design and behavior of contextual menus. These guidelines may include recommendations for visual styling, such as the use of specific colors or typography, to ensure consistency and alignment with the overall system aesthetics. They may also define interaction patterns, such as how the menu should appear and disappear, how options should be selected or activated, and how keyboard navigation should be implemented. Overall, contextual menus are a valuable tool in user interface design, allowing for efficient access to relevant actions or options based on the current context or selected item. By providing users with a concise and easily scannable set of choices, contextual menus enhance user productivity and streamline the user experience.

Contextual menus are a type of user interface pattern used in design systems. They appear upon right-clicking or long-pressing on an item, displaying a menu adjacent to the item or in a fixed position within the viewport. Contextual menus provide quick access to relevant actions or options without cluttering the interface.

Contextual Navigation

Contextual navigation is a user interface pattern that is used in the design system to provide relevant and specific navigation options based on the user's current context or task. It is a technique that helps users quickly and easily find the information or perform the actions they need, without having to navigate through complex hierarchical structures or menus.

In a design system, contextual navigation is typically implemented through the use of menus, tabs, or breadcrumbs. These navigation elements dynamically change based on the user's current location or the task they are trying to accomplish, providing them with options that are relevant and meaningful to their context.

Contextual Search

A contextual search refers to a user interface (UI) pattern and design system that allows users to search for information within a specific context. Instead of performing a general search across all available data or content, a contextual search focuses on retrieving results that are relevant to the current context or scope.

Within the UI, a contextual search typically provides users with a search field or input area where they can enter their search query. Depending on the design system, this search field may be accompanied by a search button or an automatic search function that initiates the search as soon as the user starts typing.

Contextual Tooltips

Contextual tooltips refer to a UI pattern and design system element that provides additional information or guidance to users in a user interface. These tooltips appear when users hover or click on specific elements within the interface, such as buttons, icons, or text links. The purpose of contextual tooltips is to enhance user understanding and provide relevant information about the specific element being interacted with.

Contextual tooltips typically consist of a small pop-up box or bubble that appears near or next to the element of interest. These tooltips often contain concise and relevant text or icons that provide clarifications, instructions, explanations, or warnings related to the element. They serve as a quick reference or reminder of its purpose, functionality, or potential consequences.

Conversation Content Search

A UI pattern, in the context of design systems, refers to a recurring solution to a common user interface problem. It provides a standard way of presenting information or interacting with elements in a user interface. UI patterns help establish consistency and efficiency in the design process, making it easier for users to navigate and understand the interface.

Design systems, on the other hand, encompass a broader set of guidelines, principles, and assets that define how a product's user interface should look and function. They include UI patterns as building blocks, along with typography, color schemes, icons, spacing, and other design elements. Design systems enable a unified and cohesive user experience across different applications or platforms within an organization.

Conversation History

UI patterns refer to commonly used solutions for recurring design problems in user interfaces. These patterns are established conventions that help designers create intuitive and efficient user experiences. A design system, on the other hand, is a set of reusable components, guidelines, and principles that aim to maintain consistency and cohesiveness across a product or platform. UI patterns provide a structured approach to solving user interface challenges. They are tried and tested solutions that have proven to be effective in similar situations. These patterns not only save time and effort for designers but also ensure a familiar and consistent experience for users. By using UI patterns, designers can leverage existing knowledge and best practices to create interfaces that are easy to understand and navigate. A design system, on the other hand, provides a comprehensive set of tools and resources for creating and maintaining a consistent visual language and user experience. It consists of a library of reusable components, style guides, and design principles that guide the creation of new interfaces. A design system ensures that all elements of a product or platform, from buttons to typography, are visually coherent and functionally consistent. A design system promotes collaboration and efficiency among design and development teams. It allows for the rapid creation of new interfaces by providing pre-designed and pre-coded components that can be easily combined and customized. This not only ensures consistency across different parts of a product but also facilitates scalability and future maintenance. In conclusion, UI patterns and design systems are essential elements in creating effective and cohesive user interfaces. UI patterns provide designers with proven solutions for common design challenges, while design systems provide a comprehensive set of tools and resources for maintaining consistency and efficiency. By leveraging UI patterns and following a design system, designers can create interfaces that are not only visually appealing but also intuitive and user-friendly.>

Conversation Personalization

Personalization in the context of UI patterns and design systems refers to the ability to tailor the user experience based on individual preferences, behaviors, and characteristics. It involves creating interfaces that adapt to the unique needs and expectations of each user, providing relevant content, options, and interactions. In the realm of UI patterns, personalization can take various forms. One common approach is to incorporate user preferences into the interface design. This could include allowing users to customize the layout, color scheme, or typography to align with their personal aesthetic preferences. Personalization can also involve adapting the content or functionality of the interface based on the user's past interactions or stated preferences. For example, a news app might prioritize articles on topics that the user has previously shown interest in. Design systems play a crucial role in enabling personalization at scale. They provide a set of reusable components, styles, and guidelines that ensure consistency and efficiency in creating personalized interfaces. By defining a range of customizable options within these design systems, designers and developers can easily incorporate personalization features into their products. To achieve personalization within a design system, components should be designed and developed in a modular and flexible manner. This enables the dynamic assembly of interfaces based on user preferences. Design systems may include components such as user profiles, preference settings, or recommendation engines that enable personalization. In conclusion, personalization in UI patterns and design systems is about creating tailored user experiences based on individual characteristics and preferences. It involves incorporating user choices, adapting content, and providing customizable options within a system of reusable design components. By embracing personalization, designers and developers can enhance user satisfaction, engagement, and overall product success.

Personalization in the context of UI patterns and design systems refers to the ability to tailor the user experience based on individual preferences, behaviors, and characteristics. It involves creating interfaces that adapt to the unique needs and expectations of each user, providing relevant content, options, and interactions.

In the realm of UI patterns, personalization can take various forms. One common approach is to incorporate user preferences into the interface design. This could include allowing users to customize the layout, color scheme, or typography to align with their personal aesthetic preferences Personalization can also involve adapting the content or functionality of the interface based on the user's past interactions or stated preferences. For example, a news app might prioritize articles on topics that the user has previously shown interest in.

Conversation Rating And Feedback

A conversation rating and feedback system in the context of UI patterns and design systems refers to a feature that allows users to provide their feedback and rate their experience with a conversation or interaction. The purpose of a conversation rating and feedback system is to gather valuable insights from users about their experience with a conversation or interaction, which can help in identifying areas of improvement and enhancing user satisfaction. This system typically includes a rating scale or options for users to rate their experience, such as a star rating or a Likert scale. Additionally, it provides a text field or a comment box where users can provide more detailed feedback or share specific suggestions. In the context of UI patterns and design systems, the conversation rating and feedback system is often included in chatbot interfaces, customer support systems, and other interactive components. It helps designers and developers gain a better understanding of user preferences, pain points, and areas of improvement in order to refine and optimize their designs. Implementing a conversation rating and feedback system involves integrating the UI component into the overall design and development workflow. This may require defining and designing appropriate UI elements, such as rating icons, feedback forms, and validation mechanisms for accepting user feedback. Furthermore, it is important to consider the visual consistency and alignment of the conversation rating and feedback UI component with the overall design system. This means ensuring that the colors, typography, and layout of the component are in line with the established design guidelines and patterns. The data collected from the conversation rating and feedback system can be analyzed to track user satisfaction over time, identify patterns or trends in user feedback, and inform decision-making for future design iterations. In conclusion, a conversation rating and feedback system in the context of UI patterns and design systems is a valuable tool for gathering user feedback and rating their experience with conversations or interactions. It helps designers and developers make data-driven decisions to improve the overall user experience.>

Conversation Sorting And Filtering

Conversation sorting and filtering is a UI pattern and design system that allows users to organize and categorize conversations or messages based on specific criteria. It provides users with the ability to efficiently navigate through a large volume of conversations, locate specific messages, and sort them in a way that fits their needs.

Sorting conversations refers to the process of arranging them in a specific order, often based on factors such as date, relevance, or importance. This enables users to prioritize their conversations and easily identify the most recent or significant ones. For example, a sorting option could be implemented to display conversations in chronological order, from the newest to the oldest.

Filtering conversations, on the other hand, allows users to narrow down the displayed conversations by applying specific criteria or conditions. This helps users to focus on a subset of conversations that meet their requirements. Filters can be based on various attributes of a conversation, such as sender, recipient, subject, or status. For instance, a user might apply a filter to display only unread conversations or conversations with a particular sender.

Implementing conversation sorting and filtering in a UI pattern and design system provides several benefits for users. It enhances the user experience by saving time and effort in finding and managing conversations. Users can quickly locate important messages or respond to urgent ones without getting overwhelmed by a large number of conversations. By offering multiple sorting and filtering options, the design system accommodates different user preferences and contexts, improving usability and customization.

In conclusion, conversation sorting and filtering is an essential component of a UI pattern and design system that empowers users to efficiently navigate, organize, and manage conversations. By allowing users to sort conversations based on specific criteria and filter them by relevant attributes, this design pattern enhances the user experience, saves time, and provides greater control over conversations.

Cookie Consent Banner

A Cookie Consent Banner is a user interface element that is commonly used to inform website visitors about the use of cookies on a website and to obtain their consent for their usage. This banner is typically displayed at the top or bottom of a webpage and serves as a notice to comply with various privacy regulations, such as the General Data Protection Regulation (GDPR) in the European Union. The purpose of a Cookie Consent Banner is to provide transparency and control to users by informing them about the types of cookies that may be employed on the website, their purposes, and any third parties that may have access to these cookies. The

41

banner often contains a brief statement explaining the purpose of cookies and providing a link to the website's privacy policy, where users can find more details about how their personal data is being handled. In terms of design, the Cookie Consent Banner should be clearly visible to users without being intrusive or interfering with their browsing experience. It should be easy to dismiss or accept the banner, preferably with a prominently placed "Accept" or "Dismiss" button. The design of the banner should be consistent with the overall look and feel of the website, following the guidelines of the design system in place. From a user experience perspective, the Cookie Consent Banner should be concise and easily understandable, using clear language that avoids technical jargon. It should effectively communicate the relevant information about cookies and obtain explicit consent from users in a non-ambiguous manner. Web developers typically implement the Cookie Consent Banner by adding the necessary HTML, CSS, and JavaScript code to the website's codebase. The banner can be static or dynamic, depending on the requirements and functionalities of the website. It is important to ensure that the banner remains visible and retains the user's preferences even when navigating to different pages within the website. Overall, the Cookie Consent Banner is an essential component of a website's design system, ensuring compliance with privacy regulations, providing transparency to users, and giving them control over their personal data. Its clear and unobtrusive design, along with concise language, contributes to a positive user experience while maintaining the website's legal and ethical responsibilities.>

Copyright Notice

A copyright notice in the context of UI patterns and design system refers to a statement acknowledging the ownership of intellectual property rights, specifically the copyright, for a particular user interface pattern or design element. It serves as a legal declaration that provides information about the exclusive rights and restrictions associated with the use, reproduction, modification, and distribution of the copyrighted material. The copyright notice typically includes the copyright symbol (©), the year of creation or publication, and the name of the copyright owner. It serves as a deterrent against unauthorized use and infringement of the copyrighted material and reinforces the rights of the copyright owner. In the context of UI patterns and design systems, a copyright notice is important to protect the originality and creativity of the design elements or patterns. It informs users, developers, and designers about the ownership of the design and establishes the rights and permissions associated with its usage. By including a copyright notice, designers and creators can assert their rights and protect their work from being copied, reproduced, or used without permission. It also helps in maintaining the integrity and authenticity of the design system or pattern library by preventing unauthorized modifications or alterations. Moreover, a copyright notice also serves as a source of recognition for the creators and designers. It showcases their expertise and originality in the field of UI design, encouraging others to respect their work and seek permission for any usage. Overall, a copyright notice in the context of UI patterns and design systems plays a crucial role in protecting the ownership and rights of the creators. It serves as a legal declaration and deterrent against unauthorized use while also promoting acknowledgment and recognition for the original work.

A copyright notice in the context of UI patterns and design system refers to a statement acknowledging the ownership of intellectual property rights, specifically the copyright, for a particular user interface pattern or design element.

By including a copyright notice, designers and creators can assert their rights and protect their work from being copied, reproduced, or used without permission.

Countdown Timers

Countdown Timers are user interface (UI) patterns commonly used in design systems to create a visual representation of a countdown or timer functionality. They are often used to display the remaining time for certain events or actions to take place. With countdown timers, users can instantly perceive the time left as they visually see the numbers decreasing. They offer a clear and intuitive way to convey temporal information, allowing users to anticipate and plan accordingly. When implemented within a design system, countdown timers follow consistent and standardized rules in terms of appearance, behavior, and interaction. This ensures a cohesive and seamless user experience throughout the application or website. The HTML structure of a countdown timer typically consists of elements such as , , and . The element acts as a container for the countdown timer, providing styling and positioning. Inside the , element is often used to display the numerical values of the countdown, such as hours, minutes, and seconds. The element can be employed to convey the specific time or date the countdown is targeting. To update the countdown timer dynamically, JavaScript is commonly utilized. Through JavaScript, the values displayed within the elements can be modified based on the elapsed time. Additionally, JavaScript allows for smooth transitions and animations, enhancing the visual delight of the countdown timer. Overall, countdown timers play an essential role in UI patterns and design systems, providing users with a visually engaging and informative way to track time. By adhering to the principles of the design system, countdown timers ensure a consistent and intuitive user experience, making them a valuable component within UI designs.

Countdown Timers are UI patterns used to display the remaining time visually.

They follow consistent design system rules and typically consist of

, , and elements in HTML with JavaScript for dynamic updating.

Coupon Code Submission Form

A coupon code submission form is a user interface (UI) pattern and design system element that allows users to input and redeem coupon codes as part of a promotional offer or discount. It typically consists of a text input field where users can type or paste their coupon code, as well as a submit button to process and apply the code. The main purpose of a coupon code submission form is to provide users with a convenient and streamlined way to redeem their coupon codes during the checkout process or at the point of sale. By offering a designated field for coupon code input, it helps ensure that users don't miss out on any discounts or promotions they may be eligible for. From a design perspective, a coupon code submission form should be clear, intuitive, and easy to use. It should prominently display the text input field where users can enter their coupon code, making it visually distinct from other UI elements and easy to locate. Providing a clear label or placeholder text inside the input field can help guide users and clarify the purpose of the form. The submit button is an essential element of the coupon code submission form, as it triggers the redemption process. The button should be visually distinguishable from other buttons on the page to draw attention and encourage user interaction. Its purpose should be clearly conveyed through the label text, such as "Apply" or "Redeem," to ensure users understand its functionality. In terms of functionality, a well-designed coupon code submission form should be responsive and provide immediate feedback to the user. This can be achieved by validating the coupon code on the client side or by performing a server-side validation to ensure the code is valid and applicable. Providing a visual indication, such as a success message or an error message, can help users understand the outcome of their code submission. Overall, a coupon code submission form is a crucial UI pattern and design system element that helps facilitate the seamless redemption of coupon codes. By offering a dedicated and user-friendly input mechanism, it simplifies the process for users to take advantage of promotional discounts and benefits.

A coupon code submission form is a user interface (UI) pattern and design system element that enables users to enter and utilize coupon codes. It typically includes a field for inputting the code and a button to submit it for validation and application. The main aim of this form is to provide a convenient and straightforward way for users to benefit from discounts or promotional offers.

From a design perspective, the coupon code submission form should be visually distinct and intuitive. The field for entering the code should be prominently displayed and accompanied by clear label or placeholder text. The submit button, which triggers the redemption process, should be visually distinguishable and feature descriptive label text. The form should also provide immediate feedback to the user, indicating whether the code has been successfully applied or if there was an error. By implementing a well-designed and responsive coupon code submission form, users can easily redeem their codes and take advantage of discounts or promotional offers.

Course Catalog

A course catalog refers to a user interface pattern and design system that is used to organize and present information about various courses offered by an educational institution or online learning platform. It serves as a comprehensive directory that allows users to search, filter, and navigate through the available courses based on their interests and needs. In terms of UI patterns, a course catalog typically includes a search bar or filter options at the top of the interface, allowing users to enter keywords or select specific criteria such as subject, level, or duration. This helps users narrow down their options and find the courses that align with their preferences. The search results are then displayed in a visually consistent and organized manner, typically in a grid or list format. Each course card or listing within the catalog provides essential details about the course, such as the title, instructor, duration, price, and a brief description. These details are presented in a concise and systematic manner, allowing users to quickly scan and evaluate the courses. Furthermore, a course catalog often includes additional features to enhance the user experience. These may include sorting options to arrange the courses based on relevance, popularity, or price, as well as pagination or infinite scrolling to handle large amounts of course information. Additionally, the catalog may offer links or buttons to enroll in a course or explore more details, enabling users to seamlessly navigate from the catalog to the individual course pages. Design systems play a crucial role in ensuring consistency and coherence within a course catalog. By establishing a set of design guidelines and patterns, a design system ensures that every course listing adheres to a unified visual and interaction style. This consistency enhances the user experience by providing a familiar and intuitive interface, reducing cognitive load and facilitating effortless navigation through the catalog. In conclusion, a course catalog is a UI pattern and design system that organizes and presents information about available courses. Its purpose is to help users explore and select courses based on their interests and needs, while maintaining a consistent and intuitive user experience.>

Credit Card Information Form

A Credit Card Information Form is a user interface (UI) pattern and design system element that allows users to input and submit their credit card details for online transactions. It is commonly used in E-commerce websites, payment gateways, and other digital platforms that require payment processing. The Credit Card Information Form typically consists of several input fields where users can enter their credit card number, expiration date, security code, and name as it appears on the card. It may also include additional fields for billing address and desired payment method. The primary purpose of this form is to securely and efficiently collect the necessary credit card information from users. It follows specific design principles to ensure that users can easily understand and complete the form accurately. Here is an example of how a Credit Card Information Form can be structured in pure HTML:

Card Number:

Expiration Date:

Security Code:

Name on Card:

The form starts with a

tag to provide a logical grouping of the input fields and their associated labels. Each input field has a tag for accessibility purposes, ensuring that screen readers can announce the purpose of each field to the user. The "for" attribute in the tag is linked to the corresponding input field's "id" attribute. The input fields use appropriate type attributes, such as "text" for card number and name, and "password" for security code. The "maxlength" attribute restricts the maximum number of characters users can input to match the card's requirements. The "required" attribute indicates that each field must be filled in before the form can be submitted. Overall, the Credit Card Information Form is a crucial UI element for facilitating secure and efficient credit card transactions on digital platforms. Its design should prioritize usability, accessibility, and security to inspire user confidence and ensure a smooth payment experience.

Custom Fonts And Typography

Custom Fonts and Typography refers to the visual appearance and arrangement of text in a user interface (UI), specifically the use of unique typefaces. In the context of UI patterns and design systems, custom fonts and typography play an essential role in establishing the overall aesthetic and enhancing the user experience. When designing a UI, typography is crucial for readability, hierarchy, and creating a distinct brand identity. Custom fonts allow designers to break free from the limitations of default system fonts and choose typefaces that align with the brand's personality, values, and target audience. By using custom fonts, designers can evoke specific emotions, establish a visual hierarchy, and enhance the overall impact of the UI. A design system provides a set of predefined styles, components, and guidelines to ensure coherence and consistency across a range of interfaces. In the context of custom fonts and typography, a design system defines the primary and secondary typefaces, font sizes, weights, and other typographic attributes to be used consistently across different UI elements. This ensures that all text within the UI adheres to a unified visual language, facilitating brand recognition and creating a cohesive user experience. In HTML, the attributes related to fonts and typography include font-family, font-size, font-weight, line-height, and text-align. These attributes can be applied to different HTML elements such as paragraphs, headings, and blockquotes to achieve the desired visual effect. However, it is important to note that when choosing custom fonts, designers need to consider cross-platform compatibility and web accessibility guidelines to ensure that the text remains legible and accessible across different devices and user contexts. Overall, custom fonts and typography are vital aspects of UI design, serving as powerful tools for brand expression, visual hierarchy, and user engagement. By incorporating custom fonts within a design system, designers can create cohesive and visually appealing interfaces that effectively communicate the brand's message while providing an optimal user experience.

Custom Product Configuration Form

A Custom Product Configuration Form is a user interface pattern that enables users to personalize and customize a product according to their specific needs and preferences. It is commonly used in e-commerce websites where users can create their custom products, such as clothing, furniture, or electronics. The form usually consists of various input fields and options that allow users to select and modify different product attributes. These attributes may include color, size, material, features, and additional upgrades or accessories. Users can make their selections by clicking on radio buttons, checkboxes, drop-down menus, or sliders, depending on the design and functionality of the form. The Custom Product Configuration Form is designed to guide users through the customization process and provide them with a clear overview of their selections and the resulting product. It typically includes visual cues, such as images or thumbnails, to help users visualize their chosen options. Feedback messages or tooltips may also be included to assist users in making informed decisions and avoid potential errors. Once users have completed the customization process, they can review their selections and make any necessary changes before finalizing their order. The form should provide a summary of their selections, including a breakdown of the total cost, expected delivery time, and any additional terms or conditions. To ensure a smooth user experience, the Custom Product Configuration Form should be intuitive, user-friendly, and responsive across different devices and screen sizes. It should also be compatible with assistive technologies, such as screen readers, to cater to users with disabilities. By implementing a Custom Product Configuration Form, businesses can offer a more personalized and engaging shopping experience to their customers. It allows users to create products that meet their unique preferences and requirements, increasing their satisfaction and likelihood of making a purchase.

The Custom Product Configuration Form is a user interface pattern that enables users to personalize and customize a product according to their specific needs and preferences. It offers various input fields and options, allowing users to select and modify different attributes of the product. This form is commonly used in e-commerce websites, guiding users through the customization process and providing them with visual cues and feedback messages. After completing the customization, users can review their selections and finalize their order. The form should be intuitive, user-friendly, responsive, and compatible with assistive technologies to ensure a smooth user experience. By implementing the Custom Product Configuration Form, businesses can offer a personalized and engaging shopping experience to their customers.

Customer Feedback And Loyalty Form

A Customer Feedback and Loyalty Form in the context of UI patterns and design system refers to a standardized interface element that allows customers to provide feedback and express their loyalty towards a product or service. It serves as a means for businesses to gather valuable information and measure customer satisfaction, while also promoting loyalty and enhancing the overall user experience. The Customer Feedback and Loyalty Form typically includes various input fields and options for customers to share their opinions, ratings, and suggestions. It can cover a range of topics such as overall satisfaction, specific features or functionalities, customer service experience, and likelihood to recommend the product or service to others. The form may also include open-ended questions to encourage customers to provide detailed feedback or elaborate on their experiences. One key aspect of designing a Customer Feedback and Loyalty Form is to ensure simplicity and ease of use. It should be visually appealing and intuitive, allowing users to quickly provide feedback without encountering any confusion or frustration. The form's layout and organization should be consistent with the overall design system to maintain a cohesive user experience. To achieve this, UI patterns such as clear labels, concise instructions, and logical grouping of related questions can be employed. The form should be designed to accommodate responsiveness, ensuring it is accessible and user-friendly across different devices and screen sizes. Visual cues such as error messages and validation indicators can also be implemented to guide users through the form and provide a seamless feedback submission process. By incorporating a Customer Feedback and Loyalty Form into a design system, businesses can benefit from consistent and standardized feedback collection methods. This allows for easier analysis of customer responses and enables organizations to make data-driven decisions to enhance their products or services. The form can also serve as a platform for customers to express their loyalty and create a sense of engagement, ultimately fostering a positive relationship between the business and its customers. In conclusion, a Customer Feedback and Loyalty Form in the context of UI patterns and design system is a standardized interface element that facilitates gathering customer feedback and promoting loyalty. It is designed to be user-friendly, visually appealing, and consistent with the overall design system. By utilizing this form, businesses can effectively collect valuable insights, measure customer satisfaction, and make informed decisions to enhance their offerings.>

Customer Journey Maps

Customer journey maps, in the context of UI patterns and design systems, are visual representations that outline the end-to-end experience a customer has while interacting with a product or service. They help to identify and understand the various touchpoints, emotions, and interactions a customer may go through during their journey. The purpose of a customer journey map is to gain insights into the user's perspective, behaviors, and pain points throughout their experience. It provides a holistic view and helps designers and developers align their efforts towards creating a more seamless and satisfying user experience. A typical customer journey map consists of different stages, such as awareness, consideration, purchase, and loyalty. Each stage is represented as a horizontal timeline, with touchpoints along the way. Touchpoints can include website visits, app interactions, customer support calls, social media engagements, and other points of contact. These touchpoints are often accompanied by user goals, motivations, and any emotions they may experience during that stage. Designers use customer journey maps to empathize with users, identify pain points, and find opportunities for improvement. By understanding the user's emotions and mindset at each touchpoint, designers can create meaningful experiences that address specific user needs. It also helps in uncovering any gaps or inconsistencies in the user journey, allowing for targeted improvements in those areas. A customer journey map can be a valuable tool for creating a cohesive design system. By aligning the visual and interaction patterns across different touchpoints, a design system ensures consistency and familiarity for the user. This improves the overall usability of the product or service, as users can easily navigate and understand the interface, regardless of the touchpoint they are using. In conclusion, a customer journey map is a visual representation that outlines the end-to-end experience a customer has while interacting with a product or service. It helps designers and developers gain insights into user perspectives and emotions, identify pain points, and create a more seamless and satisfying user experience. Furthermore, it can contribute to the creation of a cohesive design system by aligning UI patterns and interactions across different touchpoints.>

Customer Reviews Section

A customer reviews section is a UI pattern commonly used in design systems to showcase feedback and testimonials from customers who have used a product or service. It provides valuable social proof and helps potential customers make informed decisions based on the experiences of others.

The customer reviews section typically includes a collection of individual reviews, each consisting of a headline or title, a rating or score, and a brief comment or description. These reviews are often displayed in a grid or card-based layout, allowing users to quickly scan and compare different testimonials.

Customer Support Chatbot

A Customer Support Chatbot is a user interface (UI) pattern and a component of a design system that offers automated assistance and support to customers. It is designed to simulate human-like conversation and provide relevant information or solve customer queries. Customer Support Chatbots are integrated into websites or applications to enhance customer support services and provide immediate responses to common questions or issues. These chatbots use pre-defined responses, machine learning algorithms, or natural language processing techniques to understand and respond to user queries in real-time. The HTML format for a Customer Support Chatbot typically consists of a chat window or dialog box where the user can enter their queries or requests. This chat window is displayed on the interface, allowing customers to communicate with the chatbot seamlessly. The conversation between the customer and the chatbot takes place within this chat window. The chatbot analyzes the customer's input and generates appropriate responses using its pre-programmed knowledge base or AI algorithms. The chatbot's responses are displayed in the chat window, providing information or assistance to the customer. These responses can include text-based answers, links to relevant resources, or instructions to troubleshoot common technical issues. With a well-designed UI, a Customer Support Chatbot provides a user-friendly and intuitive experience for customers seeking support. The chat window should be visually appealing, displaying the chatbot's responses clearly and ensuring easy readability. Furthermore, it is important to consider the overall design system when implementing a Customer Support Chatbot. The chatbot's design elements, such as color schemes, typography, and icons, should align with the existing design system to maintain consistency and branding. In summary, a Customer Support Chatbot is a UI pattern and design system component that automates customer support services by simulating human-like conversation. It offers immediate responses, relevant information, or troubleshooting guidance to customers through a chat window integrated into websites or applications. Its design should be visually appealing and aligned with the overall design system for a seamless user experience.>

Customer Support Links

Customer Support Links refer to a set of user interface (UI) patterns and design system elements that provide customers with access to support resources and assistance, helping them find solutions to their queries or issues related to a product or service. These links assist users in navigating and accessing the support system easily, ultimately enhancing their overall experience. In the context of UI patterns and design systems, customer support links are typically displayed prominently on the website or application interface. These links are strategically placed to ensure maximum visibility and accessibility for users seeking assistance. They are often included within a dedicated support section or menu, and may also be integrated into other relevant areas of the interface to provide seamless access to help and support resources. Customer support links serve as a gateway to a variety of support options, allowing users to choose their preferred method of seeking assistance. Common support options may include FAQs (Frequently Asked Questions), knowledge base articles, user forums, live chat functionality, or contact forms. By providing these options, customer support links cater to a range of user preferences, ensuring that users can access the support resources they need in the most convenient way. Effective customer support links are designed to be intuitive and user-friendly. They feature clear and concise labels or headings that accurately convey the purpose of each link. Additionally, they may utilize recognizable symbols or icons, such as a question mark or a headset, to enhance usability and establish visual consistency with other support-related components. Consistency in design and placement of customer support links is crucial for creating a seamless user experience. It is important to ensure that support links have a consistent appearance throughout the interface, aligning with the overall design system. This consistency helps users easily locate and access these links, regardless of their location within the interface. In conclusion, customer support links play a vital role in UI patterns and design systems by offering users a straightforward means of accessing support resources. By following established design principles and integrating them seamlessly into the interface, these links contribute to an enhanced user experience and promote customer satisfaction.>

Customizable Avatars

Avatars are graphical representations or visual user profiles used in UI (User Interface) design. They serve as a way to personalize and identify users within a system or platform. Customizable avatars are a specific type of avatar that allows users to modify their visual appearance to better reflect their individuality or preferences. Customizable avatars provide users with a range of options to alter various visual attributes such as hairstyle, hair color, facial features, skin tone, clothing, accessories, and more. These options enable users to create a unique and personalized representation of themselves within the system or platform. By offering a selection of customizable features, avatars can better reflect the diversity and creativity of individual users. This can create a more engaging and inclusive user experience, allowing users to express themselves within the digital environment. From a UI patterns and design system perspective, customizable avatars are an essential component that adds an element of personalization and visual appeal. They contribute to the overall aesthetics and brand identity of a platform, while also enhancing the user experience by fostering a sense of ownership, uniqueness, and self-expression. Implementing customizable avatars requires careful consideration of the available options and the technical aspects of the design. Designers need to ensure that the customization process is intuitive, accessible, and responsive across different devices and screen sizes. They should also provide users with meaningful choices that align with their desired level of customization. In terms of design system, customizable avatars may require the creation of a library of visual assets, including different hairstyles, facial features, clothing, and accessories. These assets should be designed consistently, following established design guidelines, to maintain a cohesive and harmonious visual identity. Overall, customizable avatars are a key component of UI design that allows users to personalize their visual representation within a system or platform. They contribute to the overall aesthetics, inclusivity, and engagement of the user experience, while also providing a sense of ownership and individuality.

Customizable Color Themes

Customizable Color Themes refer to a feature in User Interface (UI) patterns and design systems that allows users to customize the color scheme of a digital product or platform according to their preferences. This feature is essential for providing a personalized and visually appealing user experience. In the realm of UI design, color plays a crucial role in creating an interface that is aesthetically pleasing, functional, and consistent. Customizable color themes empower users to modify the default color scheme of an interface, enabling them to tailor it to their liking, brand identity, or accessibility requirements. UI patterns and design systems are frameworks that provide a set of pre-defined design elements, styles, and guidelines to ensure consistency and coherence across an application or system. Customizable color themes are implemented within these established patterns and systems to offer flexibility and enhance the design process. By leveraging these customizable color themes, users can create a personalized look and feel for an interface without having to delve into complex coding or design processes. Instead, they can easily modify preset color palettes or choose their preferred color combinations through a user-friendly interface or configuration tool. Access to customizable color themes is typically integrated into the settings or preferences menu of an application, website, or software. Users may have the option to select from a range of preset themes or define their own custom colors for various UI elements, such as buttons, text, background, and highlights. These themes can be saved and applied throughout the entire system, ensuring a consistent visual experience across different pages or screens. Furthermore, customizable color themes also serve as a valuable tool for branding purposes. Companies can provide their users or clients with the ability to customize the interface colors to align with their brand identity. This feature enhances brand visibility and fosters a sense of ownership for users, as they can effectively integrate the product or platform into their overall brand strategy. In conclusion, customizable color themes in UI patterns and design systems are an essential feature that provides users with the ability to personalize the visual appearance of a digital product or platform. By allowing users to modify the default color scheme, these themes enhance user experience, foster branding opportunities, and promote a visually cohesive interface.

Customizable Dashboards

Customizable Dashboards are a UI pattern and design system element that allows users to personalize and modify the content, layout, and functionality of their dashboard according to their specific needs and preferences. A customizable dashboard provides a range of options and features that enable users to create a tailored and useful workspace. Users can select which data and metrics to display, arrange the components in a desired manner, and adjust the level of detail presented. This flexibility empowers users to design a dashboard that aligns with their unique goals, roles, and workflows. At its core, a customizable dashboard provides a modular layout, enabling users to add, remove, and rearrange various components such as graphs, charts, tables, and widgets. Users can choose from a library of pre-built components or create their own custom components to incorporate into their dashboard. These components can be easily dragged and dropped into specific sections, allowing users to create a personalized view of their data. Furthermore, a customizable dashboard offers users the ability to configure the content and metrics displayed within each component. Users can select specific data sources, define filters and parameters, and choose the visualization style that best suits their needs. This level of customization ensures that users can focus on the most relevant and actionable insights for their specific tasks and responsibilities. Apart from the visual and content customization, a customizable dashboard often includes various interaction options. Users can adjust the time range of the displayed data, drill down into specific details, apply additional filters, and perform other relevant actions to explore and analyze the information further. These interactions provide users with a dynamic and interactive experience, allowing them to dive deeper into their data and uncover meaningful insights. Overall, a customizable dashboard is a crucial element in a modern UI design system. It offers users the ability to design and configure a personalized workspace that meets their unique requirements and preferences. By empowering users to control the content, layout, and functionality, a customizable dashboard enhances usability, productivity, and overall user satisfaction.

Customizable Push Notifications

Push notifications are a crucial component of user interface (UI) patterns and design systems, providing real-time updates and information to users. Customizable push notifications allow users to personalize their notification settings based on their preferences and needs. Customizable push notifications offer users the ability to choose the types of notifications they want to receive, as well as the frequency and delivery methods. By allowing users to customize their notifications, it enhances their overall experience and satisfaction with the application or platform. With customizable push notifications, users can select specific categories or topics that they are interested in and receive notifications related to those areas only. For example, a news application may allow users to choose the types of news they want to be notified about, such as sports, finance, or politics. This ensures that users receive relevant information without being overwhelmed with notifications that are not of interest to them. Furthermore, customizable push notifications enable users to control the frequency of notifications they receive. They may choose to receive notifications in real-time or opt for a less intrusive approach, such as receiving a daily digest or notifications only during specific time frames. Additionally, users can determine the delivery method of push notifications based on their preferences. They may opt to receive notifications via push alerts on their device, email notifications, or through other communication channels like SMS or in-app alerts. From a design system perspective, it is important to provide users with a seamless and intuitive interface for customizing their push notifications. This often involves incorporating clear and concise menus or settings pages where users can easily toggle their preferences on or off. Overall, customizable push notifications empower users to tailor their notification experience to align with their individual needs and preferences. By allowing users to control the types, frequency, and delivery methods of notifications, it enhances their overall satisfaction and engagement with the application or platform.

Customizable Skins/Themes

Customizable Skins/Themes refer to the ability to personalize the visual appearance of a user interface (UI) by allowing users to choose from a range of options or create their own design.

49

This feature is commonly found in UI patterns and design systems, providing users with the flexibility to tailor the look and feel of the application to their preferences or branding requirements. HTML provides several mechanisms to achieve customizable skins/themes. One approach is to utilize Cascading Style Sheets (CSS) to define different styles and apply them dynamically based on user selections. By creating CSS classes for various UI elements, developers can offer users a set of pre-defined styles or themes to choose from. These classes can modify properties such as colors, fonts, borders, and backgrounds to create different visual variations. Additionally, users can have the option to further customize these styles by adjusting individual properties or creating entirely new CSS classes. Another method to enable customizable skins/themes is through the use of variables. CSS variables, defined with the `--` prefix, allow for dynamic changes to be applied globally across the UI. By setting up a set of variables that control colors, font sizes, or other design properties, users can easily modify the entire look of the application by altering these variables. This approach provides a powerful way to customize skins/themes without the need to change individual styles across the entire CSS. To implement customizable skins/themes, developers typically provide an interface or settings panel where users can make their selections or adjustments. This interface should present the available options and provide a way to preview the changes in real-time. Users can then save their preferences, and the chosen skin/theme is applied to the UI accordingly. The customization settings can be stored in a persistent manner, allowing users to revisit their selections every time they use the application. In conclusion, customizable Skins/Themes in the context of UI patterns and design systems refer to the ability to tailor the visual appearance of a UI by offering users a range of pre-defined styles or the option to create their own. This customization is achieved by utilizing CSS and providing an interface for users to make their selections or adjustments. HTML provides the necessary mechanisms to implement flexible and personalized UI designs.

Customizable User Dashboards

A customizable user dashboard refers to a UI pattern and design system that allows users to personalize and modify their dashboard according to their specific needs and preferences. This functionality enables users to arrange, organize, and display relevant information and features in a way that best suits their workflow and goals.

By providing a range of customization options, such as repositioning, resizing, adding, or removing various widgets, users can create a personalized layout that optimizes their productivity and enhances their overall user experience. This level of customization empowers users to have greater control over their dashboard and tailor it to their unique requirements.

Customizable User Profiles

Customizable user profiles refer to a UI pattern and design system that allows users to personalize and modify their own profile within an application or platform. This functionality provides users with the ability to customize and update various aspects of their profile, such as profile picture, name, bio, contact information, and other relevant details.

Within this UI pattern, users typically have access to a settings or profile section where they can manage their profile customization options. This can include uploading and cropping profile pictures, adding or editing personal information, selecting a preferred theme or color scheme, and specifying privacy settings. The design system should provide clear and intuitive controls for these customization features, allowing users to easily make changes to their profile.

Customizable Widgets

A customizable widget refers to a user interface (UI) component that can be modified or personalized to suit the specific needs and preferences of the user. It allows users to adapt the appearance and functionality of the widget within the context of a wider UI system. Typically, customizable widgets are designed as part of a larger design system to ensure consistency and coherence in the overall UI.

These widgets are created with the intention of providing users with flexibility and control over their interactive experiences. By offering customization options, a widget can cater to a diverse range of user preferences, promoting user engagement and satisfaction.

50

Customization Preferences Form

In the context of UI patterns and design systems, a customization preferences form refers to a user interface element that allows users to personalize or modify various settings or features according to their individual preferences. The customization preferences form typically consists of a series of options, checkboxes, radio buttons, sliders, or input fields, along with corresponding labels and descriptions to help users understand and select their preferred settings. These preferences can relate to various aspects of the user interface or application, such as layout, colors, fonts, notifications, privacy settings, and more. The form should be designed in a clear and intuitive manner to ensure easy navigation and understanding for users. It is essential to provide concise and descriptive labels and instructions for each preference option, enabling users to quickly comprehend its purpose and potential impact. Additionally, designing the form with a consistent layout, typography, and visual hierarchy ensures a cohesive and harmonious user experience. To enhance usability, it is recommended to group related preference options together, using headings or sections to create a logical flow and organization within the form. This helps users locate and modify specific preferences more efficiently. Furthermore, considering the principle of progressive disclosure can make the customization preferences form more user-friendly. Rather than overwhelming users with a lengthy form, information can be presented dynamically, revealing additional options or details based on the user's selections or actions. This approach prevents information overload and helps users focus on the options that are relevant to their needs. Accessibility should also be a priority when designing a customization preferences form. Ensuring that all form elements are accessible to users with disabilities, supporting keyboard navigation, and providing appropriate visual cues is crucial for an inclusive user experience. Overall, the customization preferences form plays a significant role in empowering users to tailor their experience and adapt the application or interface to their specific preferences. By prioritizing clarity, consistency, organization, and accessibility, designers can create a user-friendly form that enhances user satisfaction and engagement.

Customization preferences form in the context of UI patterns and design systems refers to a user interface element that enables users to modify various settings or features based on their individual preferences. These settings can pertain to different aspects of the user interface or application.

The form should be designed in a clear and intuitive manner, with concise labels and descriptions for each preference option. Grouping related options together and employing progressive disclosure can enhance usability. Accessible design is also crucial, ensuring that form elements are usable for all users.

Customized Avatars

Customized avatars, in the context of UI patterns and design systems, refer to user profile icons or representations that are personalized and unique to each user. These avatars are typically used in digital platforms, such as social media, messaging apps, or online communities, to visually identify and differentiate users from one another. Avatars are a fundamental component of user interfaces, as they provide a visual representation of each user, making interactions more personal and engaging. Customized avatars take this concept a step further by allowing users to personalize their profile icons according to their preferences, interests, or individuality. Instead of the standard default avatar, which is often a generic silhouette or a randomly generated pattern, customized avatars enable users to express their identity or align with their personal brand. Design systems play a crucial role in the implementation of customized avatars. They provide a set of guidelines, principles, and reusable components that ensure consistency and coherence across different applications or platforms. Within these design systems, specific patterns and guidelines can be established for customized avatars, ensuring a cohesive and streamlined experience for users. When designing customized avatars, various considerations come into play. These include the visual style and characteristics of the avatar, the level of personalization allowed, and the technical constraints of the platform or application. Designers need to strike a balance between offering enough options for customization while maintaining a coherent visual language and ensuring that avatars still serve their primary purpose of user identification. From a technical perspective, customized avatars can be implemented using HTML and CSS. HTML tags, such as or , are utilized to display the avatar image or container,

51

while CSS properties like background-color or border-radius are used to customize its appearance. Additionally, JavaScript can be employed for interactive features, such as allowing users to upload their own images or providing a range of predefined avatar templates. In conclusion, customized avatars in the context of UI patterns and design systems refer to personalized profile icons that allow users to express their individuality or brand. Within design systems, guidelines and patterns are established to create consistent and coherent avatar experiences. Implementation can be achieved using HTML, CSS, and even JavaScript for additional interactivity.>

Customized Product Order Form

A Customized Product Order Form is a user interface pattern and design system that allows users to tailor and personalize their product orders according to their preferences and specifications. It provides a structured and intuitive way for users to select, customize, and submit their requests for customizable products. The Customized Product Order Form typically includes various input fields, checkboxes, dropdown menus, and text areas that enable users to make selections and input their desired specifications. These specifications may include color options, materials, dimensions, engraving or personalization details, and other customizable elements of the product. The form may also include pricing information or dynamic calculations to provide users with real-time feedback on the cost implications of their selections. One of the key principles of the Customized Product Order Form is to make the customization process as user-friendly as possible. This is achieved through a clean and organized layout, logical grouping of options, clear instructions, and visual cues that help users understand the available choices and their corresponding impacts. The form should be easy to navigate, with a logical flow from one customization option to the next, and provide users with the ability to review and modify their selections before finalizing the order. Another important aspect of the Customized Product Order Form is its integration with a backend system that enables the processing and fulfillment of the customized orders. This may involve connecting the form to a database or inventory management system, tracking the status of each order, and generating automated notifications or confirmations for both the user and the seller. By providing users with the ability to customize their product orders, the Customized Product Order Form enhances the overall user experience and empowers users to obtain products that meet their specific needs and preferences. It offers a flexible and convenient way to personalize products, whether it's a customized piece of clothing, a personalized gift item, or even a configurable software package. Overall, the Customized Product Order Form is a valuable UI pattern and design system that enables businesses to offer personalized products while providing users with a seamless and intuitive ordering experience. It combines usability, functionality, and customization options to create a powerful tool for both users and businesses in the realm of e-commerce and product customization.>

DIY And Craft Tutorials

A DIY and Craft Tutorial is a step-by-step guide that provides instructions on how to create various do-it-yourself projects or crafts. It is a systematic and comprehensive approach to enable users to learn and follow a specific process to complete a particular project.

When applied to UI patterns and design systems, DIY and Craft Tutorials can be a useful reference for designers and developers to understand how to implement specific UI patterns and components within a design system. These tutorials can showcase the step-by-step process of creating and integrating UI elements into a design system, ensuring consistency and adherence to the established guidelines.

Dark Mode Toggle

Dark Mode Toggle is a user interface (UI) pattern and design system element that allows users to switch between a light and dark color scheme in an application or website. It provides a toggle switch or button that users can interact with to change the visual appearance of the UI. In the context of UI patterns, a toggle is a UI control element that can be in one of two states: on or off. The Dark Mode Toggle specifically toggles between a light mode and a dark mode. Light mode is characterized by a bright color scheme with light backgrounds and dark text, while dark mode features a dark color scheme with dark backgrounds and light text. The Dark Mode Toggle is an important element in design systems that prioritize accessibility, user preferences, and aesthetic customization. It allows users to choose a color scheme that is more comfortable for their eyes, especially in low-light conditions. Dark mode can also reduce eye strain, save battery life on devices with OLED screens, and provide a unique visual experience. Implementing the Dark Mode Toggle in HTML involves using a toggle switch or button element that triggers a change in CSS styles or classes. When the toggle is in the "on" state, the CSS styles associated with dark mode are activated, resulting in a dark color scheme. Conversely, when the toggle is in the "off" state, the CSS styles associated with light mode are applied, creating a light color scheme. To create the Dark Mode Toggle in HTML, two

tags can be used. The first

contains the label or text description of the toggle, indicating its purpose or functionality. The second

houses the toggle switch or button itself, which users can interact with to switch between light and dark modes. It is important to note that the Dark Mode Toggle should be implemented with consideration for accessibility standards and user preferences. The design should be intuitive and visually distinguishable, providing feedback to users when the toggle state changes. Additionally, the use of appropriate visual cues, such as icons or color indicators, can enhance the user experience and understanding of the Dark Mode Toggle's functionality.>

Dark Mode

Dark Mode is a user interface (UI) design pattern that presents a visual variation of a website, application, or operating system with dark-colored elements instead of the traditional light-colored ones. Also known as night mode or dark theme, Dark Mode aims to improve the user experience by reducing eye strain, saving battery life on devices with OLED screens, and creating a more aesthetically pleasing interface.

Dark Mode typically involves using darker backgrounds, such as black or dark gray, along with lighter text and/or graphical elements that provide sufficient contrast for readability. This design approach is achieved by inverting the color scheme of the traditional light mode, where light backgrounds and dark text are used. The choice of specific colors and contrasts may vary depending on the design system and brand guidelines of the product.

Dashboard Interface

A dashboard interface is a user interface design pattern and component of a design system that provides users with an organized and visually appealing overview of important information and key metrics in a single view. It typically presents data from multiple sources, such as analytics, reports, and other business tools, in a consolidated and easily digestible format. The primary objective of a dashboard interface is to enable users to quickly assess the state of their business or project at a glance. It serves as a central hub for monitoring and tracking performance, identifying trends, and making data-driven decisions. The interface typically consists of various data visualizations, including charts, graphs, tables, and widgets, arranged in a logical and intuitive layout. The design of a dashboard interface should prioritize clarity, simplicity, and efficiency. It should allow users to easily navigate between different sections or modules, customize the displayed data and metrics, and interact with the visualizations to explore more detailed information. The use of color, typography, and icons should enhance visual hierarchy and aid in understanding and interpretation of the data. Important considerations in designing a dashboard interface include selecting the most relevant and actionable metrics to display, providing appropriate levels of detail and context, and ensuring that the interface is responsive and accessible across different devices and screen sizes. It is also important to strike a balance between customization options and maintaining a consistent and coherent design across different user interfaces and experiences. In summary, a dashboard interface is a design pattern and component of a design system that presents key information and metrics in a consolidated and visually appealing manner. It serves as a central hub for monitoring and analyzing data, enabling users to quickly assess the state of their business or project and make data-driven decisions.

The dashboard interface is a user interface design pattern that provides users with an organized and visually appealing overview of important information and key metrics in a single view.

It consists of various data visualizations, such as charts and graphs, arranged in a logical and intuitive layout, allowing users to quickly assess the state of their business or project at a glance.

Dashboard Widgets

Dashboard widgets refer to small, self-contained components or modules within a user interface that provide specific information or functionality. These widgets are typically displayed within a dashboard, a centralized screen or interface that offers an overview of key metrics, data, or features. In the context of UI patterns and design systems, dashboard widgets play a crucial role in improving the usability and user experience of a digital product. They allow users to access and interact with important data and functionality in a concise and convenient manner. By condensing relevant information into small components, dashboard widgets enable users to quickly grasp the current state or trends without overwhelming them with excessive details or complex navigation. HTML provides various elements and techniques to implement dashboard widgets effectively. For instance, dividing content into different sections using elements can help structure the overall widget layout. The use of elements within these sections can allow for the fine-grained styling and alignment of individual elements. To ensure consistency and visual harmony, CSS classes can be applied to the widget elements. By defining and using these classes consistently, designers and developers can establish a cohesive design system that maintains a uniform appearance across multiple dashboard widgets. Furthermore, interactivity and responsiveness are crucial aspects of dashboard widgets. JavaScript can be utilized to add dynamic behavior and enable users to interact with the widgets. For example, click events can trigger additional details or expand the widget to provide more information. Additionally, making the widgets responsive by utilizing responsive design techniques allows them to adapt and display effectively on various screen sizes and devices. Overall, dashboard widgets are essential components in UI design, providing users with essential information and functionality in a compact and user-friendly manner. Through proper structuring and styling, designers can create visually pleasing and consistent widgets that enhance the overall usability and user experience of a digital product.

Dashboard widgets are small modules that condense relevant information and functionality for easy access within a user interface. They improve usability by providing an overview of key metrics and data without overwhelming users with excessive details.

Dashboard

A dashboard in the context of UI patterns and design system refers to a user interface element that presents information in a visual and structured manner, allowing users to quickly and easily access and analyze data or perform actions within a system or application. Dashboards are typically designed to provide an overview or summary of important information, often in the form of widgets or tiles containing data, charts, graphs, or other visual representations. The purpose is to present information in a concise and efficient manner, allowing users to make informed decisions or take appropriate actions based on the insights gained from the displayed data. The design of a dashboard often follows certain principles and guidelines to ensure an intuitive and user-friendly experience. Common elements found in dashboard design include: 1. Widgets or Tiles: These are individual components that display specific data or information. They may include charts, tables, lists, or icons, providing users with quick access to relevant data or actions. 2. Layout and Organization: Dashboards are usually organized in a grid-based layout, with each widget occupying a defined space. This helps maintain consistency and allows users to easily navigate and comprehend the displayed information. 3. Visual Hierarchy: The use of visual cues such as color, size, and typography helps establish a hierarchy of importance within the dashboard. Important or critical information is often highlighted or displayed more prominently. 4. Interactivity: Dashboards may incorporate interactive elements, such as filters, tabs, or drill-down options, allowing users to manipulate and explore the data in more detail. This enhances user engagement and provides a more personalized experience. Overall, a well-designed dashboard should provide users with a clear and comprehensive view of the relevant data, enabling them to monitor performance, identify trends, and make informed decisions. By utilizing visual elements and intuitive interactions, dashboards streamline complex information and empower users to effectively utilize the data at hand for efficient decision-making. In conclusion, a dashboard in the context of UI patterns and design system is a visual and structured user interface element that presents data or information in a concise and efficient manner, allowing users to access, analyze, and take appropriate actions within a system or application.>

Data Export And Download

Data Export and Download is a UI pattern and design system that enables users to retrieve and save data from a web application or software platform onto their local devices. This feature allows users to have a copy of their data for offline use, further analysis, or sharing with others. The Data Export and Download functionality is typically accessed through a user-friendly interface, where users can specify the type and format of data they want to export. The design system ensures that the process is intuitive, consistent, and visually appealing, aligning with the overall user experience of the application. Upon selecting the desired data, users are presented with various export options, such as CSV, Excel, PDF, or other relevant formats. These options cater to the diverse needs of users, accommodating different use cases and allowing seamless integration with external tools and software. Once the export options are chosen, users can initiate the download by clicking on a designated Download button. The system may prompt users to specify a file name and location before commencing the download. This step ensures that users have control over the organization and storage of their exported data. During the export process, the system may display a progress indicator, informing users about the status of their download. This indicator visually reassures users that their data is being prepared and downloaded successfully. To enhance user experience, the design system should also incorporate error handling mechanisms. These mechanisms can include error messages, which are displayed if there are issues with the export process. These messages should be concise and informative, providing users with clear instructions on how to resolve the problem and successfully export their data. Overall, the Data Export and Download UI pattern and design system provides users with the flexibility and convenience of accessing their data offline. By offering a range of export options and maintaining a visually appealing and intuitive interface, the system ensures that users can effortlessly retrieve their data in the desired format, improving their overall experience with the application.>

Data Input Masking

Data Input Masking is a UI pattern and design system technique used to restrict and format the input of data in a specific and consistent manner. It is implemented in forms or input fields to ensure that users enter data in the desired format, following predetermined rules and patterns. Data input masking helps to improve the accuracy and efficiency of data entry by providing real-time guidance to the users. It simplifies the input process by automatically applying the necessary formatting or constraints, reducing errors and ensuring the data is entered correctly. This technique involves using a predefined mask that dictates the format or structure of the data to be input. The mask consists of literal characters and placeholders that represent specific data types, such as dates, phone numbers, social security numbers, credit card numbers, or any other custom format. For example, a phone number input field might have a mask that includes placeholders for the country code, area code, and phone number segments, along with literal characters for parentheses and hyphens. As the user types, the input field applies the mask in real-time, visually indicating the desired format and automatically inserting the literal characters. By enforcing data input rules through masking, users are guided and prompted to enter data correctly without having to refer to separate instructions or validation messages. This reduces cognitive load and eliminates guesswork, providing a more seamless and error-free user experience. Data input masking is especially beneficial for complex data formats or those with specific requirements. It also ensures consistency in the presentation and formatting of data, enhancing the overall visual cohesion of the UI. Overall, data input masking is an effective UI pattern and design system technique that improves data entry accuracy, decreases user errors, and enhances the overall user experience. It simplifies the input process by providing real-time guidance and ensuring data is entered in the desired format or structure.

Data Tables With Sorting

A data table with sorting is a user interface pattern and design system element that displays

55

tabulated data in a structured format, providing the ability for users to sort the data based on specific columns.

A data table is a visual representation of data organized in rows and columns, allowing users to easily scan and analyze information. Each row represents a unique data entry, while each column represents a specific attribute or property of the data. The table enables users to compare and contrast data values across different entries.

The sorting functionality in a data table allows users to organize the data based on their preference or specific criteria. When sorting is applied, the order of the rows is rearranged based on the values in the selected column. This capability is particularly useful when working with large datasets, as it enables users to quickly identify patterns, trends, or outliers.

>

Data Tables

A data table is a UI pattern used in design systems to organize and display tabular data in a structured and user-friendly manner. It consists of rows and columns, with each row representing an individual data entry and each column representing a specific attribute or property of that data.

Data tables are commonly used to present large amounts of data in a concise and structured format, allowing users to easily compare and analyze information. They are particularly useful in applications that require the display of complex data sets, such as financial systems, analytics dashboards, and content management systems.

Data Usage Consent Form

A Data Usage Consent Form is a UI pattern that is used to obtain explicit consent from users for the collection, use, and sharing of their personal data. It is part of a design system that ensures transparency and compliance with data protection regulations.

The Data Usage Consent Form typically consists of clear and concise language that explains what type of data will be collected, how it will be used, and with whom it will be shared. It also informs users about their rights regarding their data and provides options for them to grant or deny consent.

Data Visualization Charts

Data Visualization Charts are graphical representations of data that help users understand, interpret, and analyze information in a visual format. They are commonly used in UI patterns and design systems to present complex data in a concise and intuitive manner.

Data Visualization Charts are an essential component of any user interface as they provide a visual representation of data, allowing users to quickly and easily identify trends, patterns, and relationships. These charts are designed to convey information effectively, facilitating data-driven decision making.

There are various types of Data Visualization Charts, each suitable for different types of data and analytical purposes. Common types include bar charts, line charts, pie charts, scatter plots, and heat maps, among others. These charts are created using HTML, CSS, and JavaScript, allowing for flexibility and customization in terms of appearance and functionality.

UI patterns and design systems often incorporate Data Visualization Charts as standard components, providing users with pre-designed chart templates that can be easily integrated into their applications. These templates typically include a range of styling options, such as color schemes, font sizes, and data labeling, to ensure consistency and cohesiveness within the overall design.

When designing Data Visualization Charts, it is important to consider the target audience and the intended purpose of the chart. The choice of chart type, along with the appropriate labeling and scaling, should be carefully determined to ensure that the data is effectively communicated. Additionally, responsive design principles should be applied to ensure that the charts are optimized for various screen sizes and devices.

In conclusion, Data Visualization Charts play a crucial role in UI patterns and design systems by enabling the effective communication and analysis of complex data. By presenting information visually, these charts enhance user understanding and facilitate data-driven decision making. Incorporating Data Visualization Charts into UI patterns and design systems allows for consistency and customization, ensuring that users can easily interpret and interact with data in a meaningful way.

Dictionary And Translation

A dictionary in the context of UI patterns and design systems refers to a comprehensive collection of predefined design elements, components, and guidelines that are used to create consistent and visually pleasing user interfaces. It serves as a reference guide for designers and developers, providing them with a standardized set of tools and patterns to follow when building digital products.

By using a dictionary, designers can ensure consistency throughout the user interface, making it easier for users to navigate and understand the system. Design elements such as buttons, typography, colors, and layout grids are defined in the dictionary with clear guidelines on their usage and behavior. This helps in creating a cohesive and harmonious design language, enhancing the overall user experience.

Digital Signature Form

A digital signature form refers to a user interface pattern and design system that allows users to digitally sign documents or transactions securely. This form provides a way to authenticate the identity of the signer and ensures the integrity and non-repudiation of the signed content. In the digital world, traditional handwritten signatures are replaced with digital signatures, which are based on cryptographic algorithms and provide a higher level of security. The digital signature form includes various components and interactions to facilitate the signing process: 1. Signer Identification: The form typically requires the signer to input their personal information, such as the full name, email address, and possibly other identification details. This information is used to associate the digital signature with the corresponding signer. 2. Document Selection: The form allows the user to choose the document or transaction that needs to be signed. This could be a PDF file, an online agreement form, or any other type of electronic document. 3. Signature Creation: Once the document is selected, the digital signature form generates a unique signature for the signer. This signature is created using the signer's private key and is specific to the selected document. It ensures that any tampering with the document after signing will be detected. 4. Verification: The digital signature form also includes a verification process to validate the authenticity and integrity of the signed document. This involves verifying the signer's public key, the digital signature itself, and ensuring that the document hasn't been modified since signing. 5. Signature Display: After the signing process is complete, the form may display the signed document and the associated digital signature. This provides a visual confirmation to the signer and other parties involved that the document has been successfully signed. The design system for a digital signature form follows certain guidelines to ensure a consistent and user-friendly experience. It focuses on clear and concise instructions, intuitive navigation, and visually distinct components for each step of the signing process. The use of appropriate colors, typography, and whitespace helps to bring attention to critical elements and minimize user errors. Overall, a digital signature form is a crucial component in secure electronic transactions and document management systems. It ensures the authenticity, integrity, and non-repudiation of signed documents, providing a reliable means of verification in the digital realm.>

Disaster Preparedness

Disaster Preparedness refers to the proactive planning and actions taken to mitigate the impact of a potential disaster or emergency situation. In the context of UI patterns and design systems, disaster preparedness involves designing and implementing features and functionalities that ensure the usability and accessibility of an application or website during and after a disaster or emergency event.

UI patterns and design systems play a crucial role in disaster preparedness by providing consistent and intuitive interfaces that users can easily navigate, even in high-stress or chaotic situations. By adhering to established UI patterns and utilizing a design system, developers can create resilient and scalable user interfaces that allow for efficient interaction with the application or website, regardless of the circumstances.

Document Preview

A document preview in the context of UI patterns and design systems refers to a visual representation or snapshot of a document that is displayed to users before they open or access the actual document. This preview allows users to quickly assess the content, layout, and relevance of the document without having to open it in its entirety. This UI pattern is commonly used in applications or websites that deal with large volumes of documents or files, such as document management systems, file sharing platforms, or email clients. The document preview typically includes key information about the document, such as the title, author, date, and a brief summary or description. This information helps users to quickly determine if the document is what they are looking for or if it is relevant to their needs. The design system for document previews focuses on providing a consistent and intuitive user experience across different devices and platforms. Visual consistency is achieved through the use of standardized templates or layouts for displaying document previews. This ensures that users can easily recognize and understand the preview elements regardless of the specific document being previewed. In addition to visual consistency, the design system also incorporates interactive elements to enhance the usability of document previews. For example, users may be able to zoom in or out, scroll through multiple pages, or access additional options or actions such as downloading or printing the document. The design system also takes into consideration the performance and loading speed of document previews. Documents can often be large and resource-intensive, so the design system may include optimization techniques such as lazy loading or caching to ensure fast and efficient loading of previews. Overall, document previews are a crucial UI pattern and component of design systems for applications or websites that deal with documents or files. They provide users with a quick and convenient way to assess the content and relevance of documents before deciding to open them, ultimately improving the overall user experience and efficiency.

Document Viewer

A Document Viewer is a UI pattern that allows users to view and navigate through documents within a digital application or website. It is commonly used in various contexts such as reading articles, viewing PDF files, or inspecting detailed reports. The Document Viewer typically consists of a main viewing area that displays the content of the document, along with navigation controls or tools to help users navigate through the document. These controls often include features like zooming in and out, scrolling or swiping to move between pages or sections, and searching for specific keywords or phrases within the document. The design system for a Document Viewer should prioritize readability and ease of navigation. The content should be presented in a clear and legible manner, with appropriate typography, line spacing, and contrast. The viewer should provide options for users to customize the layout or appearance of the document, such as choosing different viewing modes (e.g., single page, double page, or continuous scrolling) or adjusting the font size. In terms of interaction design, the Document Viewer should offer intuitive controls that are easy to understand and use. Users should be able to navigate through the document seamlessly, without any confusion or friction. The viewer should provide visual cues or indicators to show users their current position within the document, such as page numbers or a progress bar. Additionally, the viewer may include features like bookmarks or annotations, which allow users to mark specific pages or add notes to the document for future reference. From a technical perspective, the Document Viewer should be optimized for performance and responsiveness, especially when dealing with large or complex documents. It should be able to handle different file formats and render the content accurately, regardless of the device or screen size. The viewer should also support accessibility standards, ensuring that users with disabilities can effectively access and navigate the document. Overall, the Document Viewer UI pattern is a crucial component in any application or website that deals with displaying documents. By providing a user-friendly and efficient way to view and interact with content, the Document Viewer enhances the overall user experience and empowers users to consume information effectively.>

Donation Form

A donation form refers to a user interface (UI) pattern used in the design system of websites or applications to capture information and facilitate the process of accepting monetary contributions or donations from users. It serves as a means for individuals or organizations to support a cause or contribute to a particular initiative by providing their personal details and payment information. In the context of UI patterns, a donation form typically consists of various input fields and components that allow users to enter their personal information, such as name, email address, and mailing address. Additionally, it includes fields for selecting the donation amount or specifying a custom amount, as well as payment options such as credit card details or other online payment methods. The design of a donation form should focus on providing a seamless and intuitive user experience. It should be visually appealing, clear, and easy to navigate, ensuring that users can quickly and effortlessly complete the donation process. The form should also provide feedback and validation to users, guiding them through each step and indicating any errors or missing information. To encourage users to donate, the donation form may include additional features such as suggested donation amounts, options to select different donation frequencies (one-time or recurring), and the ability to allocate donations to specific programs or initiatives. These features aim to enhance user engagement and make the donation process more personalized and meaningful for donors. Moreover, a well-designed donation form should prioritize security and privacy. It should employ best practices for handling sensitive information, such as using secure connections (HTTPS) and implementing encryption techniques to protect users' payment details. Additionally, it should provide reassurance to users by displaying trust seals and indicating the organization's commitment to data protection. By incorporating a donation form into a website or application, organizations can streamline the process of receiving and managing donations. It enables them to efficiently collect valuable funds to support their initiatives, whether they be charitable causes, non-profit organizations, or crowdfunding campaigns. Ultimately, a user-friendly and visually appealing donation form can significantly enhance the effectiveness of fundraising efforts and empower individuals to contribute to causes they care about.

The donation form is a UI pattern that facilitates the acceptance of monetary contributions through a website or application.

It typically includes input fields for personal information and payment details, designed for a seamless and secure user experience.

Downloadable Resources

A downloadable resource, in the context of UI patterns and design systems, refers to any file or document that can be downloaded or saved by a user from a website or application. These resources are typically provided in formats such as PDF, DOC, XLS, PPT, MP3, MP4, ZIP, or any other file type that can be stored on a user's device for offline access or future reference. Downloadable resources are commonly used to offer additional information, guidance, or media content that complements the main content of a website or application. They are often employed to provide users with more in-depth knowledge, user manuals, templates, best practices, or multimedia materials such as images, audio files, or videos. Design systems and UI patterns play a crucial role in the creation and organization of downloadable resources. By adhering to established design guidelines and UI patterns, designers can ensure that these resources are consistent in terms of layout, visual identity, branding, and user experience. This consistency not only enhances the overall look and feel of the downloadable resources but also reinforces the familiarity and usability for users. Design systems also enable designers to create reusable components and modules that can be easily incorporated into the downloadable resources, maintaining a consistent and coherent design language throughout the entire system. This streamlines the development and deployment process, making it more efficient and less time-consuming. Additionally, design systems provide guidelines for the overall structure and navigation of the downloadable resources. By following established UI patterns, designers can ensure that users can easily find and access the resources they need. This includes providing clear labels, intuitive search functionality, well-organized categories or tags, and logical

59

hierarchical structures. In conclusion, downloadable resources in the context of UI patterns and design systems refer to files or documents that users can download and access offline. These resources are often used to provide additional information, guidance, or media content that complements the main content of a website or application. Design systems and UI patterns play a crucial role in creating and organizing these resources, ensuring consistency in terms of design, layout, and user experience.>

Drag And Drop File Upload

A Drag and Drop file upload is a user interface (UI) pattern that allows users to upload files by simply dragging and dropping them from their local file system onto a designated area on a web page or application. This pattern is commonly used in web and mobile applications to provide a more intuitive and seamless file uploading experience for users. The design system for a Drag and Drop file upload typically includes the following elements: 1. Drag and Drop Area: This is the designated area on the web page or application where users can drop their files. It is typically represented by a box or a highlighted section that visually indicates the drop zone. 2. Feedback and Visual Cues: When users drag a file over the designated area, visual cues such as highlighting or changing the appearance of the area provide feedback to the user that they are in the correct drop zone. This helps users understand where they can drop their files. 3. File Previews: As users drag files over the designated area, the system may display file previews or thumbnails to provide users with visual information about the files they are about to upload. This can help users confirm they have selected the correct files before uploading. 4. Progress Indicators: Once users drop their files, a progress indicator may be displayed to show the progress of the upload. This helps users understand the status of their upload and provides feedback on how long it may take to complete. 5. Error Handling: If there are any errors during the upload process, such as unsupported file types or file size limitations, the system should provide clear error messages or visual cues to inform users and allow them to take corrective action. A well-designed Drag and Drop file upload pattern enhances the user experience by simplifying the file uploading process and reducing the number of steps required to upload files. It provides a more natural and intuitive way for users to interact with the system, as dragging and dropping files is a familiar action in modern computing environments. Implementing a Drag and Drop file upload requires HTML, CSS, and JavaScript code. The HTML code defines the structure of the UI elements, such as the drag and drop area and the file previews. The CSS code is used to style these elements to align with the overall design system. JavaScript is used to handle the drag and drop functionality, file validation, and progress tracking. In conclusion, a Drag and Drop file upload is a UI pattern that simplifies the file uploading process by allowing users to drag and drop files onto a designated area on a web page or application. It improves the user experience by providing a more intuitive and seamless way to upload files.

Drag And Drop

A drag and drop UI pattern refers to a user interface design element that allows users to click on an object, hold it, and move it to a different location or drop it onto another object. This intuitive interaction mimics the physical action of picking up an item and moving it elsewhere. Drag and drop is commonly used in various applications and websites to enhance user experience and streamline processes. By enabling users to effortlessly rearrange elements or transfer data, it simplifies complex tasks and makes interactions more efficient. In terms of design systems, drag and drop functionality should be consistent and visually clear to users. It is important to provide appropriate feedback and visual cues to indicate when an object is draggable or droppable. This can be achieved through visual affordances such as hover effects, cursor changes, or highlighting. When implementing drag and drop, it is crucial to ensure accessibility. Users who rely on assistive technologies should have alternative ways to perform the same actions. For example, keyboard shortcuts or a separate interface that allows users to reorder or move elements. To ensure a seamless user experience, designers should consider the context in which drag and drop functionality is used. It should align with the overall user flow and meet user expectations. For instance, in a file management system, users might expect to drag files from one folder to another, whereas in a project management application, they may expect to drag tasks to assign them to different team members. Furthermore, it is essential to provide clear feedback when the drag and drop action is completed. This helps users understand where the object has been dropped and confirms the action they performed. Overall, drag and drop is a valuable UI pattern that simplifies user interactions and improves usability. By incorporating this pattern into design systems, it can enhance the overall user experience and streamline complex tasks.

Draggable Panels

A draggable panel is a user interface pattern commonly used in design systems to allow users to rearrange and customize the layout of panels or modules within a web or mobile application. It provides a flexible and intuitive way for users to organize and prioritize content according to their preferences. Draggable panels typically consist of a header or handle area, which can be clicked and dragged by the user to move the panel around the screen. The panels are usually contained within a larger container or grid system, enabling easy repositioning and resizing. These panels are an effective solution for managing complex interfaces with multiple components, as they enable users to create their own customized layouts based on their specific needs and workflows. They offer a high degree of flexibility and adaptability, allowing users to easily reorder, resize, and hide panels to optimize their workspace. Implementing draggable panels within a design system can greatly enhance the usability and personalization options of an application. By enabling users to rearrange and group panels according to their own preferences, it allows for a more efficient and tailored user experience. To create draggable panels in HTML, the use of external libraries like jQuery UI or interact.js is commonly employed. These libraries provide built-in functionality and event handlers to easily implement draggable behavior. The HTML structure of a draggable panel typically consists of a container element that wraps the panel content, including the header or handle section. However, it is important to consider the accessibility implications when implementing draggable panels. Alternative interaction methods, such as keyboard shortcuts or touch gestures, should be provided to ensure that users with disabilities or limited mobility can still access and interact with the panels effectively. In conclusion, draggable panels are a powerful UI pattern within design systems that allows users to customize and rearrange the layout of content. They offer great flexibility and adaptability, enhancing the user experience and enabling users to create their own ideal workspace. When implementing draggable panels, it is important to consider accessibility and provide alternative interaction methods for users with disabilities or limited mobility.

Dynamic Backgrounds

Dynamic Backgrounds refer to a UI pattern and design system element where the background of a user interface (UI) is characterized by movement, animation, or changing visuals. This pattern enhances the visual appeal and user experience of the UI by creating a more engaging and immersive environment. The primary goal of dynamic backgrounds is to captivate users' attention, increase user engagement, and make the UI more interactive and visually stimulating. This can be achieved through various techniques such as animated gradients, moving patterns, parallax effects, or video backgrounds. Animated gradients utilize color transitions to create a sense of movement within the background. These gradients can be subtle, smoothly transitioning between different shades of the same color, or more vibrant and dynamic, transitioning between contrasting colors. By animating the gradients, a sense of depth and liveliness is added to the UI, making it visually appealing. Moving patterns in dynamic backgrounds involve the repetition or movement of shapes or images. These patterns can be simple and repetitive, creating a rhythmic effect, or more complex and random, generating a sense of curiosity and exploration. The movement of these patterns can be controlled through the use of CSS animations or JavaScript libraries, creating a dynamic and engaging background experience for the user. Parallax effects are another technique used in dynamic backgrounds. By separating the background layers and applying different scrolling speeds to each layer, a 3D-like effect is achieved. This creates an illusion of depth and perspective, making the UI more visually captivating and immersive. Video backgrounds, as the name suggests, involve the use of videos as the background of the UI. These videos can be carefully selected to communicate the brand message or evoke certain emotions. They are played on a loop and can capture users' attention, increase engagement, and create a more memorable user experience. Overall, dynamic backgrounds are an important element in UI design systems as they elevate the visual appeal and help create engaging, immersive, and interactive experiences for users. By utilizing techniques such as animated gradients, moving patterns, parallax effects, or video backgrounds, designers can create visually stunning and captivating UIs that leave a lasting impression on users.

Dynamic Charts And Graphs

Dynamic charts and graphs are UI patterns and design elements that allow users to visually represent and interact with data in a dynamic and intuitive manner. These elements are commonly used in various applications and websites across different industries to display complex data sets in a simplified, easy-to-understand format.

With dynamic charts and graphs, users can easily analyze and interpret data by adjusting and customizing the visual representation. These elements typically provide interactive features such as zooming, panning, filtering, and sorting, which enable users to focus on specific data points or explore the entire dataset comprehensively.

Dynamic Illustrations

Dynamic Illustrations refer to interactive and animated visuals used in UI patterns and design systems. They are employed to enhance user experience and engagement by providing dynamic and visually appealing content. Dynamic illustrations serve as effective communication tools in user interfaces, contributing to the overall design and functionality of the system. They can be found in a wide range of digital products such as websites, mobile applications, and software interfaces. These illustrations are typically designed to demonstrate or represent a certain concept, process, or action. One of the primary goals of dynamic illustrations is to capture the user's attention and guide them through various interactions. They are often used to communicate complex ideas or actions in a more accessible and intuitive manner. By utilizing motion and animation, dynamic illustrations can bring static designs to life, making them more engaging and enjoyable for users. In a UI pattern or design system, dynamic illustrations can be implemented in various ways. They can be used as instructional elements to guide users through a specific task or process. For example, a dynamic illustration can show a step-by-step animation of how to complete a form or navigate through a web page. By visually demonstrating the actions required, users can easily follow along and understand the process. Dynamic illustrations can also be used as feedback mechanisms to provide users with real-time responses to their interactions. For instance, when a user hovers over a button, a dynamic illustration can animate to indicate that it is clickable or provide visual feedback once the button is pressed. Additionally, dynamic illustrations can be used to create visual interest and personality in a design system. By incorporating visually engaging animations and interactions, designers can add a sense of delight and playfulness to the user experience. In conclusion, dynamic illustrations play a crucial role in UI patterns and design systems by enhancing user experience, improving communication, and adding visual interest and engagement. Through their interactive and animated nature, they provide users with intuitive guidance, feedback, and a more enjoyable overall experience.

E-Commerce Categories

In the context of UI patterns and design systems, e-commerce categories refer to the various classifications or groupings of products or services offered in an online store. These categories serve as a way to organize and present the available options to the users, making it easier for them to navigate and find what they are looking for. Each e-commerce platform might have its own specific set of categories based on the types of products it offers. Common categories include clothing, electronics, home appliances, beauty products, books, and many more. These categories can be further divided into subcategories to provide more specific options within a broader category. For example, under the clothing category, there can be subcategories like men's, women's, and children's clothing, and further subdivisions into tops, bottoms, shoes, and accessories. The design of e-commerce categories plays a crucial role in the user experience as it directly influences how easily users can find products and explore different offerings. A well-designed category structure should be intuitive, logical, and easily accessible, allowing users to quickly navigate and filter through the available options. Typically, categories are displayed in a hierarchical manner, where the top-level categories are shown prominently, often in a horizontal navigation bar or menu. This allows users to access the general product groupings with just a click. Subcategories, on the other hand, are usually displayed as drop-down menus or nested within the parent category page. Design systems for e-commerce platforms often include a set of predefined styles and components specifically designed for categories. These components may include header and navigation elements, filters, search bars, and product display grids, among others. By incorporating these design patterns consistently throughout the platform, e-commerce websites can provide a coherent and seamless user experience. In summary, e-commerce categories are the organizational structures used in online stores to group and present products or services to users. They facilitate easy navigation and exploration of offerings, and their design is critical in ensuring a user-friendly experience. The use of design systems and UI patterns enables the consistent and efficient implementation of e-commerce categories across different platforms.>

Education Courses

Education Courses in the context of UI patterns and design system refer to structured and organized learning experiences focused on teaching the principles, techniques, and best practices of designing user interfaces for digital products. These courses aim to equip individuals with the necessary skills and knowledge to create visually appealing, intuitive, and user-friendly interfaces that enhance the overall user experience. The primary objective of education courses in UI patterns and design system is to train students in understanding user behavior, human-computer interaction, and the fundamental principles of design. Participants learn how to create wireframes, develop prototypes, and apply user-centered design methodologies to solve complex design problems effectively. These courses also cover topics such as information architecture, visual design, interaction design, and usability testing. Through a combination of lectures, hands-on exercises, and real-world projects, students gain practical experience and develop a deep understanding of UI patterns and design systems. They learn about the different design patterns and frameworks that can be used to create consistent, scalable, and reusable components. Additionally, education courses in UI patterns and design systems often emphasize the importance of collaboration and effective communication within design teams. Students learn how to work collaboratively with stakeholders, product managers, developers, and other designers to ensure that the design solutions align with the project goals and requirements. Overall, education courses in UI patterns and design system play a crucial role in shaping the next generation of UI designers. By providing a comprehensive understanding of design principles, methodologies, and tools, these courses prepare students to create impactful, user-centered designs that meet the needs and expectations of the target audience. In conclusion, education courses in UI patterns and design system are essential for aspiring designers seeking to enhance their skills and knowledge in creating effective user interfaces. These courses empower students with the ability to create visually appealing, intuitive, and user-friendly designs that improve the overall user experience.>

Email Inbox

In the context of UI patterns and design systems, an email inbox refers to an interface that displays and organizes incoming and outgoing emails in a digital communication platform. It serves as the central hub where users can manage, read, compose, and organize their email messages. The email inbox typically consists of multiple sections and elements that aid in efficient email management. The primary components include: 1. Message List: This area displays a list of emails received by the user, showing key details such as sender name, subject, date, and time. Each email entry in the list is usually represented by a compact preview or summary of the message. 2. Read/Preview Pane: When a user selects an email from the message list, the read or preview pane provides a larger view of the selected message. This pane is used to read the contents of the email in detail, including the sender's name, recipient's name, subject, and the body of the email. 3. Navigation/Filtering Options: To help users manage their emails more effectively, the email inbox often provides various navigation and filtering options. These may include folders, labels, tags, or categories allowing users to organize their emails into specific groups. Additionally, options to filter emails by date, sender, or other criteria further assist users in finding specific messages quickly. 4. Search Functionality: An email inbox typically includes a search bar that enables users to search for specific emails or content within their inbox. This feature facilitates finding messages that may be buried within a large volume of emails. 5. Compose/Reply/Forward: Users can create new emails, reply to received emails, or forward messages using the compose/reply/forward functionality within the email inbox. This feature allows users to initiate new conversations or respond to existing ones. Overall, an email inbox acts as a centralized interface for managing and processing email messages. Its design and layout strive to provide users with a clean, organized, and intuitive experience to efficiently navigate, read, and respond to their emails. Please note that the answer is in plain HTML format within the given constraints, using only two

tags.>

Email Subscription Confirmation Form

A UI pattern refers to a recurring solution used in designing user interfaces. It is a standardized way of organizing and presenting information to users, with the goal of enhancing usability and user experience. A design system, on the other hand, is a comprehensive set of guidelines, components, and standards that ensures consistency and coherence across all user interface elements and interactions within a digital product. The Email Subscription Confirmation Form is a specific UI pattern that is commonly found in email marketing and newsletter subscription processes. Its purpose is to confirm the user's subscription to an email list and obtain their consent to receive future emails. This form typically includes a simple interface that allows the user to enter their email address and submit their subscription confirmation. The design of this form should follow the established design system of the overall product. It should be visually consistent with the rest of the application, using the same color scheme, typography, and overall layout. The form should also adhere to the design system's guidelines for input fields, buttons, and error messages. In terms of layout, the Email Subscription Confirmation Form should be presented in a clear and intuitive manner. The form should be easy to locate and prominently displayed on the page. The user should not have to search for the form or be distracted by other elements on the page. To achieve this, designers often use whitespace and visual cues, such as arrows or icons, to guide the user's attention to the form. When it comes to interaction, the form should provide immediate visual feedback to the user. For example, when the user enters their email address, the form should display a loading or processing indicator to indicate that their request is being handled. Once the subscription confirmation is successfully submitted, the form should display a success message or redirect the user to a confirmation page. It is also essential for the design to consider accessibility principles. The form should be designed in a way that is accessible to users with disabilities, using appropriate HTML elements and attributes, such as labels and ARIA roles. The design should also be responsive and adaptable to different screen sizes and devices. Overall, the Email Subscription Confirmation Form follows the UI pattern of a form and is designed to be user-friendly, visually consistent, and accessible within the context of the established design system.>

Email Subscription Forms

Email Subscription Forms are a common UI pattern and design system component used to collect and manage email subscriptions from users. These forms typically consist of fields where users can enter their email addresses and often include additional options such as checkboxes for subscribing to newsletters or selecting specific topics of interest. Implementing an Email Subscription Form follows a specific design system to ensure consistency and usability across various platforms and devices. The form should have clear labels for each field, providing users with guidance on what information to enter. It should also have validation rules in place to verify the entered email address format and ensure data accuracy. When designing an Email Subscription Form, it is important to strike a balance between collecting necessary user information and ensuring a seamless user experience. Ideally, the form should have a simple and clean layout, avoiding clutter or overwhelming users with too many optional fields. Including a progress indicator or step-by-step process can also help users understand how many steps are required to complete the subscription. To enhance the user experience, Email Subscription Forms can incorporate features such as autocomplete for previously entered email addresses, real-time validation to alert users of any errors, and inline error messages to provide immediate feedback if a field is incorrectly filled. From a design system perspective, Email Subscription Forms should adhere to the overall visual style and branding of the product or website. This includes using consistent typography, colors, and spacing to maintain a cohesive look and feel. The form should be responsive and adapt to different screen sizes and orientations to ensure usability on mobile devices. In terms of accessibility, Email Subscription Forms should comply with WCAG guidelines, which ensure that people with disabilities can use and understand the form. This may involve providing alternative text for form elements, using color contrast that is easy to read, and ensuring that the form can be navigated and filled out using only a keyboard. Overall, Email Subscription Forms are a crucial component of UI design, providing a way for users to voluntarily share their email addresses and opt-in to receive updates and information.

By following design systems and best practices, these forms can offer a user-friendly experience, ensuring successful email subscriptions and minimizing user frustration.

Email Subscription Forms are a common UI pattern and design system component used to collect and manage email subscriptions from users. These forms typically consist of fields where users can enter their email addresses and often include additional options such as checkboxes for subscribing to newsletters or selecting specific topics of interest.

Implementing an Email Subscription Form follows a specific design system to ensure consistency and usability across various platforms and devices. The form should have clear labels for each field, providing users with guidance on what information to enter. It should also have validation rules in place to verify the entered email address format and ensure data accuracy.

Email Subscription Preferences Form

Email Subscription Preferences Form is a user interface (UI) pattern and design system that allows users to manage their email subscription preferences. It is a form that provides users with options to customize the types of emails they would like to receive from a particular website or service. The Email Subscription Preferences Form typically includes a set of checkboxes or toggle switches, each representing a different category or type of email communication, such as newsletters, promotions, notifications, and updates. Users can select or deselect these options based on their preferences. The form may also include additional fields for users to specify their email frequency preferences, such as daily, weekly, or monthly updates. It may also include an option to unsubscribe from all email communications if the user no longer wishes to receive any emails from the website or service. The design of the Email Subscription Preferences Form follows a clear and intuitive layout. Each category or type of email is labeled and accompanied by a checkbox or toggle switch to indicate the user's selection. The form also includes clear instructions, such as "Check the box to receive newsletters" or "Toggle the switch to unsubscribe from promotions." The Email Subscription Preferences Form is an important element of a design system as it provides users with control over their email communications. It allows users to personalize the content they receive, reducing the likelihood of them unsubscribing or marking emails as spam. From a technical standpoint, the form can be implemented using HTML form elements such as checkboxes or toggle switches. Each option can be represented as a separate input element with a corresponding label. The form can be submitted using the HTML `<form>` tag, with the selected preferences sent to the server for processing. In conclusion, the Email Subscription Preferences Form is a UI pattern and design system that empowers users to manage their email subscriptions by providing them with options to customize the types of emails they receive. It is an essential component of a design system that enhances user experience and reduces the risk of unsubscribing or marking emails as spam.

Emergency Alert System

The Emergency Alert System is a UI pattern and design system that facilitates the efficient delivery of critical information to users during emergencies or urgent situations. It is specifically designed to capture the attention of users and effectively communicate important messages to ensure their safety and well-being. This UI pattern typically includes a prominent and noticeable visual component, such as a banner or pop-up, that appears at the top or center of the interface. It uses contrasting colors, bold typography, or other attention-grabbing elements to instantly capture the user's attention. This ensures that the emergency alert stands out from the rest of the content on the screen and is impossible to ignore. The design system for the Emergency Alert System includes consistent visual elements and guidelines that can be applied across different interfaces and platforms. This ensures a seamless and uniform experience for users regardless of the device or application they are using. The design system provides predefined templates, styles, and components that make it easier for designers and developers to implement the emergency alert functionality without compromising the overall user experience. In terms of functionality, the Emergency Alert System allows administrators or authorized users to quickly create and send emergency alerts to all or specific groups of users. It supports various types of alerts, including weather warnings, natural disasters, security threats, or any other critical information that requires immediate attention. The system allows administrators to customize the content, duration, and visibility of the alerts to suit the specific needs of the emergency situation. Users interacting with the Emergency Alert System can typically dismiss the alerts or take appropriate actions based on the instructions provided. The system can include buttons or links that allow users to seek additional information, report their safety status, or perform any other necessary actions. It is essential to ensure that the alert messages are concise, clear, and actionable to enable users to make informed decisions and respond effectively to the emergency situation. Overall, the Emergency Alert System UI pattern and design system play a crucial role in effectively communicating critical information to users in emergencies. By employing attention-grabbing visuals and providing clear instructions, it ensures that users receive and act upon the alerts promptly, enhancing their safety and mitigating potential risks.>

Emergency Contact Form

An emergency contact form is a user interface (UI) pattern commonly used in design systems to collect and display critical contact information in case of emergencies. It is an essential component of a user-friendly and comprehensive emergency preparedness system.

This UI pattern typically consists of a form that prompts users to provide their personal contact information and the contact details of one or more individuals they trust to be contacted in case of emergency situations. The form is designed to be intuitive and easy to fill out, ensuring that users can quickly provide the necessary information during stressful situations.

Key elements of an emergency contact form include fields for entering the user's name, phone number, email address, and address. Additionally, the form includes fields for capturing the name, relationship, and contact information of the emergency contact(s). The UI design of the form should be clear and straightforward, with appropriate labels and placeholders to guide users in filling out the required details. Error handling and validation can also be incorporated to ensure that the provided information is accurate and complete.

Design systems often provide established guidelines and components for emergency contact forms, allowing designers and developers to maintain consistency across multiple digital platforms and applications. These design systems may include pre-designed form layouts, input fields, and error messaging styles that align with the overall visual language and branding of the system.

By incorporating an emergency contact form into a design system, designers can enhance the usability and functionality of their applications by helping users feel supported and secure in emergency situations. This UI pattern promotes proactive emergency preparedness and facilitates effective communication with trusted contacts, offering peace of mind to both users and their emergency contacts.

Emotional Design

Emotional design in the context of UI patterns and design systems refers to the intentional creation of user interfaces that evoke emotional responses in users. It involves considering and incorporating elements of human psychology, such as color, typography, and layout, to create an emotional connection between the user and the interface.

This approach recognizes that users often make decisions based on how they feel rather than purely rational thinking. By tapping into users' emotions, emotional design aims to create a more engaging and memorable user experience.

Emotional Storytelling

Emotional storytelling is a UI pattern and design system that aims to evoke specific emotions and create meaningful connections with users through the use of visual elements, narrative techniques, and user-centered design principles.

This approach recognizes the significant impact emotions have on user experience, enhancing engagement, and promoting a deeper connection between users and the product or service. Emotional storytelling leverages various design elements, such as color schemes, typography, illustrations, animations, and microinteractions, to create a cohesive and immersive experience that resonates with users at an emotional level.

Emotive Icons

Emotive Icons are a type of user interface pattern used in design systems to visually convey emotions or states to users. They are typically represented by small graphical icons or symbols that help to communicate a specific feeling or sentiment in a user-friendly and intuitive way.

These icons are designed to elicit an emotional response from users, providing a more engaging and interactive user experience. By using emotive icons, designers can create a stronger connection between the user and the interface, making the interaction more personal and memorable.

Employee Evaluation Form

Employee evaluation form is a user interface (UI) pattern and design system that provides a structured and intuitive way for employers to assess the performance of their employees. This form allows employers to gather relevant information, provide feedback, and make informed decisions regarding promotion, compensation, and development opportunities. The main purpose of an employee evaluation form is to facilitate a fair and objective evaluation process. It typically includes various sections or fields that cover different aspects of employee performance, such as job knowledge, communication skills, teamwork, problem-solving abilities, and overall effectiveness. The form begins with basic employee information, including their name, department, position, and dates of review. This helps to ensure that evaluations are accurately attributed to the correct employee. Next, the form typically includes a section for rating specific performance criteria. This allows employers to assess the employee's capabilities in different areas and assign scores or ratings accordingly. The criteria can be customized to align with the organization's specific goals and performance expectations. In addition to numerical ratings, the evaluation form also provides a space for written comments or feedback. This allows employers to provide more detailed explanations, suggestions for improvement, and examples of noteworthy accomplishments. The comments section encourages open and constructive communication between employers and employees, fostering a culture of continuous learning and growth. Furthermore, the evaluation form often includes a section for goal setting and development planning. Here, employers and employees can collaboratively identify areas for improvement and establish specific goals and action plans for the future. This supports professional development and ensures that employees are actively engaged in their own growth. From a design system perspective, the employee evaluation form follows a consistent and coherent layout. It utilizes clear headings, labels, and fields to guide users through the form and ensure that all required information is captured effectively. The form's typography, colors, and visual hierarchy are designed to enhance readability and user comprehension. In conclusion, the employee evaluation form is a UI pattern and design system that facilitates a structured and objective assessment of employee performance. It provides employers with a comprehensive and consistent tool to gather information, provide feedback, and develop strategies for employee development. By following a well-designed and intuitive format, this form contributes to a fair and transparent evaluation process within organizations.>

Employee Feedback Form

An Employee Feedback Form is a user interface (UI) pattern and a component of a design system that allows employees to provide feedback on various aspects of their work experience. It is typically used by organizations as a means to gather insights and perspectives from their workforce, facilitating open communication and continual improvement. The Employee Feedback Form follows a structured format, presenting employees with a set of predefined questions or prompts that cover different areas of their job, workplace, or company culture. These questions are carefully crafted to elicit specific feedback and enable organizations to collect relevant and actionable information. The purpose of the Employee Feedback Form is to provide a systematic way for employees to express their thoughts, opinions, and concerns. By offering a standardized format, the form ensures that feedback is collected consistently across the organization, making it easier for managers and decision-makers to analyze and act upon the responses received. The design of the Employee Feedback Form is aimed at enhancing usability and accessibility. It typically features clear and concise instructions, ensuring that employees understand how to complete the form accurately. Additionally, the form may include visual cues, such as progress indicators or required fields, to guide users through the feedback process. When designing the Employee Feedback Form, it is crucial to maintain a balance between simplicity and comprehensiveness. The form should be easy to navigate and complete, yet it should also capture enough information to provide meaningful insights. In this context, the design system provides a set of guidelines, principles, and reusable components that ensure consistency across all forms within the organization. By using an Employee Feedback Form as part of a design system, organizations can promote a culture of transparency and continuous improvement. Feedback becomes a valuable resource for management, enabling them to identify areas of strength and areas that may require attention or action. With the aid of the design system, organizations can consistently collect and analyze feedback, facilitating informed decision-making and fostering a positive work environment. In conclusion, an Employee Feedback Form is a UI pattern and component of a design system that enables organizations to systematically gather feedback from employees. It provides a structured format for employees to express their thoughts and concerns, while ensuring usability and consistency through the use of design system guidelines. This tool promotes transparency, continuous improvement, and informed decision-making within the organization.>

Employee Satisfaction Survey Form

Employee Satisfaction Survey Form is a user interface (UI) pattern that is used to design a system for collecting feedback and measuring the level of satisfaction amongst employees in an organization. It is a structured form that allows employees to provide their opinions, perceptions, and feelings about their work environment, job satisfaction, company policies, communication, teamwork, and other relevant topics. The aim of the survey is to gather insights and data to understand employee experiences and identify areas of improvement within the organization. The Employee Satisfaction Survey Form is typically designed with a clean and intuitive user interface to ensure ease of use and encourage maximum participation. The design should be visually appealing, consistent with the organization's branding, and include appropriate instructions to guide employees through the survey process. The form should also maintain a logical flow, presenting questions in a coherent order and providing clear options for responses. The HTML code for an Employee Satisfaction Survey Form may include various input fields such as radio buttons, checkboxes, dropdown menus, and text fields. These elements allow employees to select their responses or provide written answers based on the provided questions. Additionally, the form may include sections for demographic information, allowing organizations to analyze satisfaction levels based on different employee groups. Using a minimalistic approach, the HTML code for an Employee Satisfaction Survey Form could be structured as follows: ``` <form>

1. On a scale of 1 to 5, how satisfied are you with your work environment?

Answer: 1 2 3 4 5

2. How would you rate your overall job satisfaction?

Answer: 1 2 3 4 5

Submit</button> </form> ``` This HTML code snippet represents a simplified version of an Employee Satisfaction Survey Form. It includes two survey questions, each with a scale of 1 to 5 for employees to provide their responses. The form also includes a submit button for employees to submit their survey answers. Overall, the Employee Satisfaction Survey Form is an essential UI pattern that facilitates the collection of valuable feedback from employees. By designing an intuitive and user-friendly form, organizations can gain valuable insights to make informed decisions and improvements to enhance employee satisfaction and wellbeing.>

Enrollment Form

An enrollment form is a user interface pattern and design system element used to collect information from individuals who wish to sign up or register for a service, program, membership, or any other type of offering.

Enrollment forms typically include fields or sections where users can input their personal details, such as name, contact information, address, and date of birth. They may also include specific questions or prompts related to the purpose of the enrollment to gather additional information relevant to the particular offering.

Error Handling

An error handling is a set of UI patterns and design system practices used to manage and communicate errors, exceptions, and unexpected behaviors effectively to the users.

It involves designing and implementing a consistent and user-friendly approach to handle errors and provide clear instructions or feedback to users on how to resolve the issue or proceed with their tasks. The main goal is to minimize user confusion and frustration while enhancing their overall experience.

Event Details Screen

A event details screen is a user interface (UI) design pattern that displays detailed information about a specific event. It is part of a larger design system that ensures consistency and coherence across the user interface of an application or website. The event details screen typically includes various components such as the event title, date and time, location, description, and possibly additional details like guest speakers, attendees, or related events. It provides users with a comprehensive view of the event, allowing them to quickly understand the key details and make informed decisions. The event title serves as the main focal point of the screen, drawing attention and conveying the core purpose of the event. It is typically displayed prominently at the top of the screen, often in a larger font size or a distinct visual style to create visual hierarchy. The date and time section provides users with specific information about when the event is taking place. It typically includes the date, start time, and end time of the event, allowing users to plan their schedules accordingly. The location component displays the physical or virtual venue where the event is being held. It may include the address, map, or directions to help users navigate to the event location. The description section allows event organizers to provide a detailed overview of what the event is about and what attendees can expect. It offers users a deeper understanding of the event's purpose, goals, and any key information they need to know before attending. Additional details, such as guest speakers or related events, may be included depending on the nature of the event. These details provide users with further information that can help them decide whether the event aligns with their interests and goals. In summary, an event details screen is a UI pattern that presents all the necessary information about a specific event in a cohesive and visually appealing manner. It enables users to understand the event's key details and make informed decisions regarding attending or participating.>

Event Feedback Form

An event feedback form is a user interface pattern used in design systems to collect feedback from individuals who have attended an event. It is a tool that allows event organizers to gather valuable insights and opinions from attendees about their experience. The event feedback form typically consists of a series of questions or prompts that enable participants to provide feedback on various aspects of the event, such as the venue, the content, the speakers, the organization, and any other relevant factors. The form may also include space for attendees to provide additional comments or suggestions. The purpose of the event feedback form is to gather feedback and opinions from attendees in order to assess the success of the event and identify areas for improvement. By collecting feedback, event organizers can gain valuable insights that can help them make informed decisions for future events. The feedback collected through the form can also be used to evaluate the effectiveness of the event in achieving its objectives and meeting the expectations of attendees. When designing an event feedback form, it is important to consider the user experience and ensure that the form is easy to navigate and complete. Clear and concise instructions should be provided to guide users through the form, and the questions should be worded in a way that is easy to understand. Additionally, the form should be visually appealing and consistent with the overall design system to maintain brand identity. In conclusion, an event feedback form is a user interface pattern used in design systems to collect feedback from event attendees. It is a valuable tool that allows event organizers to gather insights and opinions to assess the success of the event and make informed decisions for future events. The design and usability of the form are crucial to ensure a positive user experience.>

Event Feedback Survey Form

Event Feedback Survey Form is a user interface (UI) pattern and design system used to gather feedback from participants attending an event. It serves as a tool to collect valuable insights and opinions about various aspects of the event, such as the organization, content, speakers, venue, and overall experience. The feedback collected through this form helps event organizers understand the attendees' perspectives and make informed decisions for future events. The Event Feedback Survey Form typically consists of a set of questions that participants can answer to provide their feedback. These questions are designed to cover different aspects of the event and can range from multiple-choice questions to open-ended ones. The form is commonly presented to participants through an online platform or a physical form distributed at the event. The purpose of an Event Feedback Survey Form is to gauge the participant's satisfaction level and gather specific feedback on various elements of the event. The questions asked may include topics like the relevance and quality of the content, the effectiveness of the speakers, the organization of the event, the ease of registration and check-in processes, the venue facilities, and any additional feedback the participants may have. By utilizing a UI pattern and design system, the Event Feedback Survey Form ensures consistency and ease of use for participants. The design principles incorporated into the form help create a user-friendly experience, guiding participants through the questions and facilitating their responses. In conclusion, an Event Feedback Survey Form is a UI pattern and design system used to collect feedback from event participants. It helps event organizers understand the strengths and weaknesses of their events and make improvements for future iterations. By utilizing this form, organizers can gather valuable insights to enhance the overall event experience for attendees.>

Event RSVP Form

An RSVP (Répondez s'il Vous Plaît) form is a user interface (UI) pattern and design system that is used to gather responses from individuals who have been invited to a specific event. It allows event organizers to efficiently manage invites and accurately plan for capacity, logistics, and other event-related details. The basic structure of an RSVP form typically consists of several fields and options that users can interact with to respond to the invitation. These fields may include the event details (such as the event name, date, and time), the user's name, and options for their attendance status (such as "Attending," "Not Attending," or "Maybe Attending"). The purpose of this UI pattern is to streamline the RSVP process for both event organizers and attendees. By providing a clear and intuitive form, users can easily indicate their response without any confusion or ambiguity. The design system helps to create a consistent and cohesive experience across different events and ensures that the form is easy to use and understand. In terms of the HTML structure, a basic RSVP form can be implemented using just two

tags. The first

tag can be used to display the event details, such as the event name, date, and time. The second

tag can present the options for the user's attendance status, along with the input fields for their name and any additional details. By utilizing the RSVP form UI pattern and a well-defined design system, event organizers can gather accurate and organized responses from their invitees. This allows them to effectively plan for event logistics, including seating, catering, or any other requirements based on the number of attendees. Furthermore, it ensures that attendees have a seamless experience when responding to the invitation. In conclusion, an RSVP form is a key component of event management, providing an efficient way for event organizers to collect responses and plan accordingly. By following the UI pattern and adhering to a design system, the RSVP form can be user-friendly and consistent across various events, resulting in a smoother and more organized event planning process.>

Event RSVP

70

An event RSVP is a UI pattern and design system component that allows users to respond to an event invitation by indicating whether they will attend, decline, or are undecided about attending. It provides a streamlined and intuitive way for users to communicate their attendance status to event organizers and manage their event schedule.

The event RSVP component typically consists of the following elements:

1. Event Information: This includes details about the event such as the title, date, time, and location. It helps users to quickly recognize the event they are responding to and avoid any confusion.

2. RSVP Options: These are the response options available to the users, typically represented by buttons or checkboxes. The most common options are "Attending," "Not Attending," and "Maybe/Undecided." Users can select their preferred option to indicate their response.

3. Submit or Save Button: This button allows users to submit their RSVP and save their response. It is often placed at the bottom of the RSVP component, indicating the end of the response selection process.

4. Additional Information: In some cases, event organizers may require additional information from the attendees, such as dietary restrictions, availability for specific activities, or any other personalized requests. Depending on the complexity of the event, this additional information section may be included in the RSVP component.

The event RSVP component is crucial for both event organizers and attendees. Organizers can easily keep track of the number of attendees, plan accordingly, and send updates or reminders based on the RSVP responses. Attendees, on the other hand, can manage their schedule effectively, ensure they don't miss important events, and communicate their availability to organizers.

In terms of design system, the event RSVP component should be consistent with the overall UI patterns and styles used in the application or website. It should align with the visual branding guidelines, follow accessibility standards, and be responsive across different devices and screen sizes. The design system should define the styling, layout, and behavior of the event RSVP component to ensure a cohesive user experience.

Event Registration Form

An event registration form in the context of UI patterns and design system is a user interface component that allows individuals to sign up or register for a specific event. It serves as a crucial tool for event organizers in collecting essential information from participants to manage and plan the event effectively.

Typically, an event registration form consists of various input fields and checkboxes to gather relevant details from participants. These fields may include the participant's name, contact information, address, and any additional information required for the event. The form may also include checkboxes or dropdown menus to select event-related options like ticket types, sessions, or guest preferences.

Exit Interview Form

An exit interview form is a structured questionnaire or survey conducted by an organization to gather feedback and insights from employees who are leaving the company. It allows departing employees to provide their thoughts, opinions, and experiences related to their time at the organization.

The purpose of an exit interview form is to understand the reasons for an employee's departure, identify any issues or concerns that may have contributed to their decision to leave, and gather suggestions for improvement. It serves as a valuable source of information for the organization to assess its performance, address any areas of concern, and make necessary changes to retain and attract talent.

Expandable FAQs

Expandable FAQs, also known as collapsible FAQs, are a common UI pattern used in website and application design to provide organized and easily accessible information to users. This design pattern allows users to quickly find answers to their questions without being overwhelmed by a long list of FAQs. In a design system, expandable FAQs are often implemented using HTML and CSS to create a collapsible accordion-style interface. When a user clicks on a question, the corresponding answer expands and is revealed, providing the user with the desired information. This interaction allows for efficient use of space on the page while keeping the content easily scannable and visually organized. When implementing expandable FAQs, it is essential to consider both the user's needs and the design system's guidelines. The questions should be concise and clearly written to help users quickly identify relevant topics. The design system may provide specific guidelines on the spacing, typography, and interaction behavior for the expandable FAQ component. To create an expandable FAQ section in pure HTML, you can utilize the `` and `` elements. The `` element acts as a container for each question and answer pair, while the `` element contains the question itself. By default, the answers are hidden, and users can reveal them by clicking on the question. Here's an example:
```html Question 1

Answer to question 1.

Question 2

Answer to question 2.

``` In the above example, the questions are represented by the `` elements, and the corresponding answers are represented by the `

` tags within each `` element. This structure allows for a clear separation between questions and answers, making it easy for users to navigate and find the information they need. Overall, expandable FAQs are an effective UI pattern that improves the user experience by providing a compact and organized way to present frequently asked questions. By implementing this pattern in a design system using the `` and `` elements, designers can ensure consistency and usability across different applications or websites.>

## Expandable Menus

Expandable menus are a user interface (UI) pattern commonly used in design systems. They allow for the organization and presentation of complex information in a hierarchical structure, making it easier for users to navigate and locate specific content within an application or website. In its simplest form, an expandable menu consists of a primary menu header or label that, when clicked or tapped, expands to reveal additional submenus or options. This expansion can be visualized through the use of animations, such as dropdown or slide-out effects. The primary goal of using expandable menus is to optimize the user experience by providing a clean and intuitive interface. By using expandable menus, designers can effectively manage screen space and showcase a larger amount of content without overwhelming the user. This UI pattern is especially useful in situations where there is a large amount of hierarchical or nested information that needs to be displayed in a structured and easily accessible manner. When implementing expandable menus, designers need to consider several aspects to ensure an optimal user experience. First and foremost, menus should be clearly labeled to provide users with a clear understanding of what information lies within each submenu. Visual cues, such as arrows or icons, can also be used to indicate that the menu is expandable. Additionally, it is important to provide clear visual feedback when menus are expanded or collapsed. This feedback can be achieved through color changes, animations, or even subtle transitions to guide the user's attention and clearly indicate the menu's status. Overall, expandable menus are a valuable UI pattern for designers and developers working on creating intuitive and efficient user interfaces. By effectively managing screen space and organizing complex information in a structured manner, expandable menus enhance the user experience and make applications or websites more user-friendly and accessible. Expandable menus create a hierarchy of information, making it easier for users to navigate complex content. By providing clear labels and visual cues, these menus enhance the user experience and optimize screen space.

## Expense Report Form

The Expense Report Form is a user interface pattern and design system that allows users to input and track their expenses in a structured and organized manner. It provides a consistent and intuitive user experience for users to easily submit their expenses and for administrators to manage and process these expense reports.

The Expense Report Form typically consists of various input fields and sections where users can enter details about their expenses, such as date, description, amount, category, and attached receipts or supporting documentation. Users can also specify additional information related to payment methods, project codes, and any required approvals. The form may also include features such as automatic currency conversion, expense policy compliance checks, and itemized expense breakdowns.

## FAQ Page

A Frequently Asked Questions (FAQ) page is a user interface (UI) pattern commonly found in websites or applications that provides answers to commonly asked questions about a product, service, or topic. It is an essential component of a design system as it helps users quickly find information and solve their queries without the need for direct support.

FAQ pages are designed to provide concise and straightforward answers to the most common user questions. They help improve the user experience by addressing users' concerns and alleviating any uncertainties they may have. By organizing information in a structured and easily navigable manner, FAQ pages streamline the user journey and reduce the need for further assistance.

Typically, FAQ pages consist of a list of questions with corresponding answers. The questions are often displayed as clickable headings or hyperlinks, allowing users to easily navigate to the sections that interest them. The answers are displayed directly below each question, usually in an expanded form, to provide immediate visibility.

When designing an FAQ page, it is crucial to anticipate the most common questions users may have and provide comprehensive yet concise answers. The content should be clear, concise, and easy to understand, avoiding technical jargon or complex terminology. Additionally, it is essential to maintain consistency in formatting and ensure the FAQ page aligns with the overall visual style and design principles of the website or application.

Overall, an FAQ page is a valuable UI pattern that enhances the user experience and promotes self-service by providing quick and accessible answers to frequently asked questions. It empowers users to find the information they need independently, reducing their reliance on support channels and improving overall satisfaction.

## Face Recognition

Face recognition is a UI pattern and design system that utilizes artificial intelligence (AI) algorithms to identify and authenticate individuals based on their unique facial features. It is a technology that can be seamlessly integrated into various applications, websites, and devices to provide secure and convenient access control, identity verification, and personalized user experiences. Face recognition works by capturing and analyzing facial characteristics such as the size and shape of the eyes, nose, mouth, and other facial landmarks. These features are then converted into a digital representation known as a faceprint or facial template. The AI algorithms compare this template with a database of known faces to determine a match. This process happens in real-time, allowing for near-instantaneous identification. In terms of UI patterns, face recognition can be implemented through various user interactions. For example, a login page may offer the option to log in using face recognition instead of a traditional username and password. The user would be prompted to face the device's camera, and the system would capture an image to compare with registered faces. Upon successful recognition, the user would gain access to the application or website. From a design system perspective, face recognition requires careful consideration to ensure a seamless and intuitive user experience. The design should include clear instructions and feedback to guide users through the recognition process.

Visual cues such as highlighting the face or displaying a progress indicator can enhance usability and provide reassurance to the user. Additionally, the design should address potential challenges, such as variations in lighting conditions or user appearance changes (e.g., wearing glasses or facial hair). A robust face recognition system should be able to adapt and accurately identify individuals in different situations. Overall, face recognition offers a secure and efficient method for user authentication and personalized experiences. Its integration into UI patterns and design systems allows for a seamless and intuitive user experience, giving users a convenient and secure way to access applications and websites.>

## Feature Boxes

Feature boxes are a UI pattern used in design systems to highlight and showcase important features or key selling points of a product or service. They are typically used on landing pages or product pages to capture the attention of users and convey the value and benefits of the offering.

Feature boxes are characterized by their box-like structure, which is often outlined or visually differentiated from the surrounding content. They typically contain a combination of text, images, icons, and sometimes interactive elements such as buttons or links to provide a clear and concise overview of the featured information.

## Feature Request Form

A feature request form, in the context of UI patterns and design systems, is a document or interface element that allows users or stakeholders to formally submit their suggestions for new features or improvements to a software application or digital product. The purpose of a feature request form is to provide a structured and organized way for users to communicate their needs and requirements to the development team or product owner. It helps capture all the relevant information about the requested feature, such as the problem it aims to solve, the impact it would have on users, and any specific design or functionality considerations. Typically, a feature request form includes various fields and sections to gather important details. These may include: 1. Title or Brief Summary: A concise and descriptive title that summarizes the feature being requested. 2. Description: A detailed explanation of the feature, including its purpose, benefits, and any relevant examples or use cases. 3. User Impact: Information on how the feature would improve the user experience or address a specific user need. 4. Design Considerations: Any specific design or visual requirements for the feature, such as color schemes, typography, or interaction patterns. 5. Technical Requirements: Any technical considerations or constraints that need to be taken into account while implementing the feature. 6. Priority and Urgency: A way for users to indicate the importance and urgency of their feature request, allowing the development team to prioritize accordingly. 7. Attachments: The option to attach any relevant files, documents, or screenshots that may help illustrate the requested feature. By using a feature request form, product teams can efficiently collect, track, and prioritize user suggestions. It helps avoid misunderstandings and allows stakeholders to provide clear and detailed information about their requested features. This, in turn, facilitates effective communication, collaboration, and decision-making in the development process. Overall, a feature request form serves as a valuable tool in shaping the future direction of a software application or digital product, ensuring that it meets the evolving needs and expectations of its users without compromising the overall design system.>

## Feature Voting Form

A feature voting form is a user interface pattern that allows stakeholders or users to vote or express their preference for certain features or enhancements in a product or service. It is a way to gather feedback and prioritize which features should be implemented or given more attention.

The design system for a feature voting form should provide a clear and intuitive way for users to understand the options and express their preferences. It should include visual cues such as buttons, checkboxes, or icons, and provide a way for users to easily navigate through the options. The form should also provide feedback to the user, such as indicating which features have already been voted on or highlighting the most popular choices.

## Featured Blog Posts

A featured blog post is a prominent and visually appealing article that is showcased on a website or platform to attract the attention of users and encourage them to engage with the content. It is usually positioned in a prominent location on the homepage or a specific section of the website where it is easily visible and stands out from the rest of the content.

The purpose of featuring a blog post is to highlight and promote specific content that is considered important, interesting, or relevant to the target audience. It is often used to showcase popular or trending articles, new product releases, important announcements, or any other content that the website owner or editor wants to draw attention to.

## Feedback Form

A UI pattern refers to a specific, reusable solution design that addresses common user interface challenges. It provides a user-friendly and consistent approach to solving design problems, ensuring a cohesive and intuitive user experience across different screens and interactions.

A design system, on the other hand, is a comprehensive set of guidelines, rules, and components that define the overall look, feel, and behavior of a digital product. It serves as a foundational framework for creating consistent and cohesive visual designs and user experiences.

## Feedback Loops

A feedback loop in the context of UI patterns and design systems refers to the iterative process of gathering user feedback, analyzing it, and incorporating the insights gained into the design and development process. It involves a continuous cycle of understanding user needs, testing design solutions, and refining them based on user input.

Feedback loops provide valuable insights into how users interact with a website or application, allowing designers and developers to make informed decisions and improvements. By incorporating feedback from real users, design teams can create more user-friendly and intuitive experiences.

## Feedback Submission Form

A UI pattern is a recurring design solution that solves a specific user interface problem. It is a proven and tested solution that can be applied to various screens or components within a digital product. UI patterns provide a standard and consistent way of presenting information, structuring content, and guiding user interactions.

Design systems, on the other hand, are a collection of reusable components, styles, guidelines, and documentation that provide a framework for creating and maintaining consistent user interfaces. They encompass both the visual and functional aspects of a product's design, including color palettes, typography, spacing, iconography, and interaction patterns.

## Feedback Survey

UI patterns refer to commonly used design solutions that address specific user interface (UI) challenges. They are predefined interaction and visual design solutions that provide a consistent and user-friendly experience across an application or website. UI patterns are essential components of a design system, which is a collection of reusable UI elements and guidelines that ensure consistency and efficiency in the design and development process. UI patterns are created based on established best practices and user-centered design principles. They serve as a set of guidelines that help designers and developers in making informed decisions about the layout, navigation, and functionality of the user interface. By using UI patterns, designers can provide users with familiar and intuitive interactions, reducing the learning curve and enhancing usability. UI patterns come in different forms, such as navigation patterns, input validation patterns, and data display patterns. Navigation patterns include commonly used elements like menus, tabs, and breadcrumbs, which help users navigate through different sections of an application or website. Input validation patterns provide feedback and validation rules for user inputs, ensuring data accuracy and error prevention. Data display patterns, on the other hand, define the layout and visualization of information, such as tables, lists, and cards. A design system is a broader concept that encompasses UI patterns. It includes a library of UI components, style guidelines, and documentation that define the visual and interaction design of a product. A design system promotes consistency and efficiency by providing a centralized resource for designers and developers. In conclusion, UI patterns are predefined design solutions that address specific UI challenges and contribute to the overall consistency and usability of an application or website. They are an essential component of a design system, which provides a comprehensive set of guidelines and resources for creating cohesive and user-friendly interfaces. By following UI patterns and design system principles, designers and developers can create intuitive and efficient user experiences.

## File Attachments In Conversations

File attachments in conversations refer to the functionality of including and sharing files, such as documents, images, and multimedia, within a user interface (UI) pattern or design system. In the context of UI patterns and design systems, file attachments allow users to exchange files seamlessly during conversations. This functionality enhances communication and collaboration within digital platforms, enabling users to share relevant information and resources. The inclusion of file attachments within conversations provides several benefits. Firstly, it allows users to share and access important information without the need for external platforms or applications. This streamlined approach facilitates efficient communication and reduces the need to switch between different tools or interfaces. Additionally, file attachments offer a means of providing context and supporting content within conversations. Users can attach relevant documents or images that provide additional details or reference points. This feature enhances the understanding of the conversation and allows participants to engage more effectively. Design systems play a crucial role in ensuring the usability and consistency of file attachments within conversations. They define the visual appearance, layout, and behavior of the attachment feature. Consistent design patterns and conventions make it easier for users to understand and interact with the attachment functionality across different conversations and interfaces. When designing file attachments within conversations, it is important to consider accessibility and inclusivity. Providing alternative text for files, ensuring keyboard navigability, and accommodating different file formats are essential aspects of an inclusive UI design. In summary, file attachments in conversations refer to the functionality of incorporating and sharing files within a UI pattern or design system. This feature improves communication and collaboration by allowing users to exchange relevant information seamlessly. Design systems play a critical role in ensuring the consistency and usability of file attachments, while considerations for accessibility and inclusivity are paramount.>

## File Manager

A file manager in the context of UI patterns and design systems refers to a software component or application that allows users to organize, manage, and manipulate files and directories on a computer system. It provides users with a graphical user interface (GUI) to access and interact with the file system. A file manager typically presents a hierarchical representation of the file system, with folders (directories) and files organized in a tree-like structure. Users can navigate through the directory structure by clicking on folders to delve deeper into the file system. The file manager also displays file and folder names, file types, sizes, and other metadata to help users identify and locate specific files. Apart from navigating the file system, a file manager offers various file operations. Users can create new folders and files, rename existing ones, and delete unwanted files and folders. It also allows users to move or copy files and folders to different locations within the file system. Additionally, file managers often include features like search functionality, file sorting and filtering, and the ability to view and modify file properties. To support efficient file management, file managers often provide different viewing modes, such as a list or grid view, which allow users to visualize files and folders in different ways. They may offer customizable views, allowing users to modify the layout and display options according to their preferences. Moreover, file managers may offer various file selection methods, including single file, multiple file, or batch selection, to enable users to perform bulk operations on multiple files. In terms of design system, a file manager adheres to consistent UI patterns and guidelines to ensure a cohesive and intuitive user experience. It follows design principles such as clarity, simplicity, and consistency to provide users with a familiar and predictable interface. A design system may provide standard icons, color schemes, and typography for file managers, ensuring consistency across different applications and platforms. Overall, a file manager is a crucial component of any operating system or software application that deals with file management. It empowers users to efficiently organize, navigate, and manipulate files and directories, ultimately enhancing productivity and ease of use in working with digital content. EOD.>

## File Upload Form

A File Upload Form is a UI pattern designed to allow users to select and upload files from their local devices to a website or application. It serves as an interface for users to provide and transmit files to the server, enabling them to share content or complete specific tasks. This form typically consists of several components: 1. File Input Field: This is the main element where users can select the desired file(s) to upload. It is often accompanied by a "Browse" button that opens a file explorer dialogue for easier file selection. 2. File Type Limitations: Optional instructions or restrictions can be provided to users regarding the supported file types. This can help prevent users from trying to upload incompatible files. 3. Progress Indicator: A progress bar or status message can be displayed to show the uploading progress, providing users with feedback on the file transfer process. 4. Submit Button: A button allowing users to trigger the upload process after selecting the desired file(s). Design systems can play a crucial role in creating an effective File Upload Form by ensuring consistency and coherence across the user interface. By following the established design guidelines and patterns, the form can align with the overall visual language of the system. This includes using standard elements, such as buttons and input fields, which users are familiar with and can easily recognize. In terms of appearance and layout, the form should prioritize clarity and simplicity. The elements should be properly aligned and visually grouped together, enabling users to quickly identify and interact with the necessary components. Consider providing clear instructions or labels to guide users through the file upload process, reducing any potential confusion or errors. Additionally, the form should be designed with accessibility in mind, ensuring it meets the necessary standards for users with disabilities. This can involve incorporating attributes such as proper labeling, ARIA roles, and keyboard navigation support. Overall, the File Upload Form is essential for facilitating the seamless transfer of files between users and a website or application. By adhering to the principles of UI patterns and design systems, the form can provide a consistent and intuitive user experience, enhancing usability and satisfaction.

## Filter Form

A filter form refers to a user interface (UI) pattern and design system that allows users to refine or narrow down their search results by applying various filters. It typically consists of a collection of options, checkboxes, sliders, or inputs that users can select or customize based on their specific preferences. The purpose of a filter form is to enhance the user experience by helping users easily find the information they are looking for within a large dataset or set of search results. It enables users to define their own search criteria and refine the results accordingly, making the process more efficient and tailored to their individual needs. Filter forms are commonly used in various applications and websites, such as e-commerce platforms, search engines, job portals, and online directories. They provide users with the ability to narrow down the available options based on relevant attributes, such as price range, location, category, size, date, or any other relevant data points. When designing a filter form, it is crucial to consider factors such as usability, accessibility, and responsiveness. The form should be intuitive and easy to use, with clear labels and instructions for each filter option. Proper validation should be implemented to prevent any errors or inconsistencies in the user's selections. In terms of UI design, filter forms can be presented in different layouts, depending on the specific requirements and constraints of the application or website. They can be placed in a sidebar, as a dropdown menu, or embedded within the page content. The design should harmonize with the overall aesthetic and branding of the application or website to maintain consistency and enhance the user experience. In conclusion, a filter form is a UI pattern and design system that allows users to refine their search results by applying specific filters. It improves the user experience by enabling users to customize their search criteria and obtain more relevant and focused results. The design of a filter form should prioritize usability, accessibility, and responsiveness to ensure an effective and efficient user experience.

## Filter Tags

Filter tags are a UI pattern commonly used in design systems to allow users to refine or narrow down a set of items or content based on specific criteria or attributes. They provide a way for users to interact with a large amount of information and quickly find relevant results. In the context of UI patterns and design systems, filter tags are typically displayed as clickable or selectable elements that represent different attributes or categories. These tags are often placed above or alongside a collection of items, such as a list or grid, and enable users to specify their preferences or requirements. Filter tags are designed to be easily recognizable and accessible. They generally have a distinctive appearance, such as being visually separated from other elements or having a unique background color. This helps users understand that they can interact with these tags to refine the displayed content. When a user selects a filter tag, it typically triggers a filtering action, which updates the displayed items to only show those that match the selected criteria. This can be done dynamically without requiring a page reload, providing a seamless user experience. Filter tags can be used to filter content based on various attributes, such as categories, tags, dates, locations, or any other relevant criteria. They can also be combined to create more complex filtering scenarios, allowing users to refine the content based on multiple criteria simultaneously. Overall, filter tags are a valuable UI pattern for enhancing the usability and efficiency of search or browsing experiences. By providing users with a visual and interactive way to narrow down large sets of information, they empower users to find the content they are interested in more effectively.

Filter tags are a UI pattern used in design systems to refine or narrow down a set of items based on specific criteria.

They are clickable elements that represent different attributes or categories and trigger a filtering action when selected.

## Filter And Sort Screen

A Filter and Sort screen is a user interface pattern commonly used in design systems to allow users to quickly and efficiently narrow down and organize a large set of data or content based on specific criteria. This pattern typically consists of various filter and sorting options presented in a logical and intuitive layout. The purpose of the Filter and Sort screen is to enable users to easily refine and find relevant information from a vast collection. By presenting them with multiple filter options, users can select and apply specific criteria to refine the data set to their desired subset. These filter options can include checkboxes, radio buttons, dropdown menus, sliders, or text input fields depending on the context and complexity of the data. Users can also combine multiple filters to further refine their search. Sorting options are an essential part of the Filter and Sort screen as they allow users to reorder the filtered results based on different criteria such as alphabetical order, date, popularity, or relevance. The sorting options can be presented as buttons, dropdown menus, or tabs, depending on the design system and screen layout. The Filter and Sort screen is often accompanied by a search bar, which allows users to perform custom searches and further narrow down the results. The search bar provides users with the flexibility to search for specific keywords or phrases within the filtered results. Overall, a well-designed Filter and Sort screen helps users efficiently navigate through a large set of data and find the information they are looking for. It enhances the user experience by providing a flexible and customizable way to interact with complex datasets. By presenting users with clear and intuitive filter options and sorting criteria, the Filter and Sort screen empowers users to quickly and effectively discover the content they need.

Filter and Sort screen is a user interface pattern rapidly used to categorize and organize vast content by applying specific criteria. The main goal of this pattern is to allow users to easily and precisely filter information from a large collection. Filters can be applied individually or in combination to narrow down the data set. Common filter options include checkboxes, radio buttons, dropdown menus, sliders, or text input fields. Sorting options are also provided to reorder the filtered results based on different criteria such as alphabetical order, date, popularity, or relevance. Sorting options can be presented as buttons, dropdown menus, or tabs. The Filter and Sort screen is often accompanied by a search bar to perform custom searches and provide further refinement of results. Overall, a well-designed Filter and Sort screen enhances user experience by facilitating efficient navigation and retrieval of relevant information from complex datasets.

## Filterable Content

Filterable content refers to a user interface pattern and design system that allows users to narrow down or refine the displayed content based on specific criteria or filters. It is a functionality commonly used in various applications and websites to enhance the user experience by providing a more tailored and focused content view. With filterable content, users can selectively view or search for items that match their specific preferences or requirements. This pattern typically involves the use of filter controls, such as checkboxes, drop-down menus, sliders, or search fields, which allow users to specify their desired criteria. Once the filters are applied, the content dynamically updates to display only the items that meet the selected criteria. The main purpose of filterable content is to help users find relevant information more efficiently and effectively. By allowing them to refine their view, it eliminates the overwhelm of large amounts of content and provides a more targeted browsing experience. This pattern is particularly useful in applications or websites that have a vast amount of data or content, such as e-commerce platforms, product catalogs, or data-intensive applications. From a design system perspective, implementing filterable content requires careful consideration of the user interface elements and their visual representation. The design system should provide consistent styles and behaviors for filter controls, ensuring that they are easily recognizable and accessible to users. Additionally, the system should define clear visual cues to indicate the active filters and the applied filtering criteria. In terms of implementation, filterable content often involves a combination of client-side scripting and server-side processing. The client-side scripting is responsible for capturing and interpreting the user's filter selections, while the server-side processing handles the data retrieval and filtering. It is essential to optimize the performance of the filtering mechanism to deliver real-time results and a seamless user experience. In summary, filterable content is a user interface pattern and design system that enables users to refine the displayed content based on specific criteria or filters. It enhances the user experience by allowing users to focus on relevant information, improves efficiency, and reduces information overload. Proper implementation within a design system ensures consistent visual representation and optimal performance.>

## Fingerprint Authentication

Fingerprint authentication is a UI pattern and design system element that allows users to verify their identity by using their unique fingerprint. It is a security feature commonly used in mobile devices, such as smartphones and tablets, as well as in some laptop models. The implementation of fingerprint authentication in a UI pattern involves the use of a fingerprint sensor, which is typically embedded in the device's home button or placed on the back of the device. When a user wants to authenticate their identity, they place their finger on the sensor, and the device captures an image of the fingerprint. The captured fingerprint image is then compared with the fingerprints stored in the device's database. If a match is found, the authentication is successful, and the user is granted access to the device or the specific functionality that requires authentication, such as unlocking the screen, accessing sensitive data, or authorizing a transaction. Fingerprint authentication is a secure and convenient alternative to traditional authentication methods, such as typing a password or PIN. It offers several advantages, including: 1. Security: Since each person's fingerprint is unique, it provides a higher level of security compared to passwords or PINs, which can be easily stolen or guessed. In addition, fingerprints are difficult to replicate, further enhancing the security of the authentication process. 2. Convenience: Fingerprint authentication eliminates the need for users to remember and enter complex passwords or PINs, making the authentication process faster and more convenient. Users can simply place their finger on the sensor, and the device will recognize their identity almost instantly. Overall, fingerprint authentication is an effective and user-friendly UI pattern and design system element that enhances the security of devices and systems while providing a seamless and convenient user experience. Its implementation in various devices and applications has brought about a new era of secure and effortless authentication.>

## Fitness Dashboard

A fitness dashboard is a user interface pattern and design system that provides a visual representation of a person's fitness-related data and activities. It serves as a centralized hub for users to monitor their fitness progress, set goals, track workouts, and analyze various metrics.

The primary purpose of a fitness dashboard is to simplify and streamline the process of managing and tracking fitness activities. It presents information in a clear and organized manner, making it easier for users to understand and make informed decisions about their fitness routines. The design of a fitness dashboard typically includes a range of components such as charts, graphs, and progress bars to display data related to steps taken, calories burned, distance traveled, heart rate, and more. Users can easily track their daily, weekly, or monthly progress and compare it to their set goals. Furthermore, a fitness dashboard often includes features such as goal setting, personalized recommendations, and challenges to keep users motivated and engaged. Users can input their fitness goals and the system provides recommendations and insights to help them achieve those goals. Challenges and achievements are also included to add a gamification element to the fitness experience and foster a sense of accomplishment. In terms of the design system, a fitness dashboard typically follows a consistent and cohesive visual style to provide a seamless user experience. It incorporates key principles of usability, including intuitive navigation, clear labeling, and logical organization of information. The color scheme, typography, and iconography are carefully chosen to enhance readability and convey information effectively. Overall, a fitness dashboard is a valuable tool for individuals looking to lead a healthier lifestyle by providing them with a comprehensive overview of their fitness journey. It empowers users to take control of their physical well-being and make data-driven decisions to optimize their fitness routines.>

## Flashcards

UI Patterns: UI patterns, also known as user interface patterns or design patterns, are predefined solutions to common design problems in user interface design. These patterns provide a set of guidelines and conventions that designers can follow to create a consistent and intuitive user experience. Design System: A design system is a collection of reusable components, guidelines, and documentation that provide a framework for creating and maintaining a consistent visual style and user experience across a product or platform. It helps align the design and development teams by establishing a shared language and set of best practices. Answer:

UI patterns, also known as user interface patterns or design patterns, are predefined solutions to common design problems in user interface design. These patterns provide a set of guidelines and conventions that designers can follow to create a consistent and intuitive user experience.

A design system is a collection of reusable components, guidelines, and documentation that provide a framework for creating and maintaining a consistent visual style and user experience across a product or platform. It helps align the design and development teams by establishing a shared language and set of best practices.

## Flexible Grid Layouts

A flexible grid layout is a user interface (UI) pattern that allows for the organization and placement of content within a design system. It provides a structured framework for arranging elements on a web page or application, ensuring consistency and flexibility across different screen sizes. In the context of UI patterns, a flexible grid layout consists of a set of columns and rows that can adapt and adjust to accommodate various screen sizes and device orientations. It enables responsive design, making it easier for designers and developers to create interfaces that work seamlessly on different devices, such as desktops, tablets, and smartphones. By using a flexible grid layout, designers can create responsive designs that automatically adjust the placement and size of elements based on the available screen real estate. This ensures that the content remains accessible and visually appealing, regardless of the device being used. Implementing a flexible grid layout in a design system involves defining the number of columns and rows and establishing guidelines for how elements should be placed within these grid structures. This helps to maintain consistency and coherence throughout the design system, making it easier for users to navigate and interact with the interface. To create a flexible grid layout, designers and developers can utilize frameworks or CSS grid systems, which provide pre-defined grid structures and classes that can be applied to elements. These frameworks typically include responsive breakpoints that define how the layout should adapt at different screen sizes. In conclusion, a flexible grid layout is an essential element of UI patterns and design systems, enabling responsive design and ensuring consistency across different screen sizes. By implementing a structured framework for arranging content, designers can create interfaces that are visually appealing and accessible on various devices. CSS frameworks and grid systems provide tools and guidelines for effectively implementing flexible grid layouts in design systems, facilitating the creation of responsive and adaptable interfaces.

## Flexible Input Fields

Flexible input fields refer to a UI pattern and design system that allows users to input various types of information in a versatile and adaptable manner. This design approach focuses on providing users with a seamless experience by accommodating different input formats without sacrificing usability or visual consistency. In a flexible input field, the user is presented with a space or box where they can enter information. The field is designed to accept different types of inputs, such as text, numbers, dates, and more. It is capable of adjusting its appearance and behavior based on the type of input required, providing appropriate validation and feedback to the user. The main goal of using flexible input fields is to enhance user experience and simplify the input process. By offering a single, adaptable input field, users don't have to switch between multiple fields or select from a long list of options. This saves time, reduces cognitive load, and minimizes the chances of errors or confusion. To implement a flexible input field in HTML, you can utilize the input element with the type attribute set to "text". This allows users to enter any alphanumeric characters without any specific format restrictions. Additionally, you can use other input types like "number" for numeric input, "date" for date input, or "email" for email address input. For example:

You can further enhance the usability of flexible input fields by providing clear instructions or placeholders within the field to guide users on the expected input format. Moreover, implementing real-time validation or feedback can help users correct any errors or incomplete inputs immediately. By employing flexible input fields in UI patterns and design systems, designers and developers can create more intuitive and user-friendly interfaces that adapt to diverse user needs. This promotes efficiency, reduces user frustration, and improves the overall user experience.

## Flight Search And Booking

A flight search and booking UI pattern is a design system that provides a user-friendly interface to search for flights and make bookings. It consists of various components and elements that allow users to input their travel details, view flight options, and complete the booking process smoothly.

The search functionality is a key component of the flight search and booking UI pattern. It typically includes fields for entering the departure and destination airports, travel dates, number of passengers, and other relevant information. Users can input their travel preferences and refine their search results based on various criteria such as flight duration, layovers, and price range.

Once users have entered their search criteria, the flight search and booking UI pattern displays a list of available flights matching the specified parameters. Each flight option is presented with important details such as the airline, flight times, duration, layovers, and price. Users can compare and select the most suitable flight based on their preferences.

When users have chosen a specific flight, the booking process can begin. The flight search and booking UI pattern provides a clear and intuitive interface for users to input their personal and payment details. Users can securely enter their contact information, passenger details, and payment method in order to complete the booking. Confirmation of the booking is typically provided after successful submission of the required information.

In addition to the core functionality mentioned above, the flight search and booking UI pattern may also include additional features and components to enhance the user experience. For example, it may offer filters to further refine search results, a map that shows the flight route, or a calendar view for easily selecting travel dates. It is essential for this design system to prioritize usability, accessibility, and responsiveness in order to meet the needs of users across different devices and platforms.

## Floating Action Button (FAB)

A Floating Action Button (FAB) is a prominent circular UI element that is used to trigger the primary action or call-to-action on a screen. It is a design pattern commonly used in user interfaces to provide a consistent and intuitive way for users to perform a specific task or action. The FAB is typically represented by a circular button that "floats" above the interface, creating a sense of depth and visual significance. It is usually placed in a fixed position on the screen, often in the bottom right corner, ensuring easy accessibility and visibility. The primary purpose of a FAB is to guide users towards the most important action on a given screen or page. It serves as a visual cue, drawing attention to the primary action and encouraging users to interact with it. The FAB often contains an iconic representation of the action it triggers, such as a plus sign for adding an item or a pencil for editing. Floating Action Buttons can be found in various contexts and applications, including mobile apps, web interfaces, and even desktop applications. They are commonly used for actions that are frequent, essential, or have high priority. In terms of design systems, the FAB is a core component that follows specific guidelines and consistent styling to ensure a cohesive and unified user experience. It adheres to the design principles and visual language of the overall system, maintaining a balance between functionality and aesthetics. The FAB can be customized to match the branding and visual identity of the application or platform it is used in. However, it is important to maintain its recognizable shape and position to ensure familiarity and ease of use for users across different interfaces. In conclusion, the Floating Action Button (FAB) is a crucial UI element in the design of user interfaces. It provides a visually prominent and easily accessible way for users to perform the primary action on a screen. When used effectively and consistently within a design system, the FAB enhances usability and guides users towards key interactions.

## Floating Contact Button

A Floating Contact Button is a user interface (UI) pattern and design element that allows users to easily access a contact option while navigating a website or application. It is typically represented by a small icon that is fixed in position on the screen, often placed in a corner or along one edge. The main purpose of a Floating Contact Button is to provide a convenient and persistent way for users to initiate communication with the website or application owner, such as sending a message, asking a question, or requesting support. The button is designed to be easily noticeable and accessible, encouraging users to engage with the contact option. By using a Floating Contact Button, website and application owners can ensure that important contact information is readily available to users, reducing friction and increasing the likelihood of engagement. It serves as a constant reminder of the available communication channels, enhancing the overall user experience. Floating Contact Buttons are particularly useful when it is crucial for users to have quick and effortless access to communication options. This can be particularly important for businesses and organizations that rely on customer feedback, inquiries, or support requests. The button offers a simple and intuitive way for users to initiate contact without disrupting their current browsing or interaction flow. In terms of design systems, Floating Contact Buttons should follow consistent design guidelines and principles to maintain visual harmony and continuity with the overall UI. This includes adhering to the chosen color palette, typography, and overall style of the application or website. In conclusion, a Floating Contact Button is a UI pattern and design element that provides users with a persistent and easily accessible contact option. Through its fixed position and attention-grabbing iconography, it offers a seamless way for users to initiate communication, contributing to a positive user experience and fostering engagement.>

## Floating Labels In Forms

Floating labels in forms is a UI pattern and design system technique used to enhance the usability and aesthetics of input fields in web forms. In this pattern, the form labels are positioned within the input fields, appearing as placeholders when the fields are empty, and floating or moving up above the fields when the user interacts with them.

This design pattern provides several benefits. Firstly, it saves space and reduces clutter in the form, as the labels are integrated within the input fields. This is especially useful in small or crowded forms where space is limited. Secondly, it improves the user experience by providing context and guidance to the users. The labels are visible at all times, even after the users start entering data, ensuring they always know the purpose and format of the input fields. Lastly, the floating labels add a modern touch to the form design, giving it a sleek and minimalist appearance.

## Floating Labels

Floating labels refer to a UI pattern and design system element that enhances the user experience by providing context and guidance for form fields. In this pattern, when users interact with a form, the label for each input field transitions from a static position above the field to a floating position within the field itself. This transition occurs when the field receives focus (such as when the user clicks or taps on the field) and the user begins to input information. The floating label pattern offers several advantages in terms of usability and aesthetics. Firstly, it provides users with a visual cue as to which field they are currently interacting with, as the label moves inside the field, making it more prominent and easier to identify. This is particularly beneficial when there are multiple form fields on a page, as it helps prevent confusion and enhances form completion efficiency. Additionally, the transition of the label to a floating position conserves screen real estate, allowing for a more compact and visually appealing form design. By integrating the label within the field, unnecessary vertical space is reduced, making the overall form layout more concise and efficient. Furthermore, the floating label pattern eliminates the need for placeholder text in fields, as the label itself serves as a persistent hint or description for the expected input. From a design system standpoint, floating labels can be implemented using HTML and CSS. The label element is positioned above the input field initially, and when the field receives focus, a CSS transition is triggered to move the label inside the field. This transition can be achieved by manipulating the label's position, size, and style properties. Care should be taken to ensure proper accessibility and clear visual distinction between floating labels and placeholder text. In conclusion, floating labels are a UI pattern and design system element that enhances form usability and aesthetics by providing context and guidance within input fields. By transitioning the label from a static position above the field to a floating position inside the field, users are provided with clear indication of the field they are interacting with, while also conserving screen space. When implementing floating labels, it is important to consider accessibility and ensure clear visual distinction.

## Fluid Page Transitions

Fluid Page Transitions refer to a design pattern used in user interface (UI) to create smooth and seamless transitions between different pages or sections within a website or application. This pattern focuses on enhancing the user experience by eliminating abrupt page reloads or jarring transitions, providing a more fluid and cohesive navigation flow. Fluid page transitions aim to create a sense of continuity and visual harmony, allowing users to navigate through different sections or pages with ease and without interrupting their browsing or interaction flow. These transitions typically involve animations, fades, slides, or other visual effects that smoothly guide users from one content area to another. By implementing fluid page transitions, designers can enhance the overall UX by minimizing disruption and providing a more engaging and immersive environment. This pattern not only improves the aesthetic appeal of the UI but also helps users maintain their focus and context, making it easier for them to navigate and find the desired information or complete tasks. To achieve fluid page transitions, designers often utilize technologies such as CSS animations, JavaScript libraries, or frameworks that enable smooth visual effects and transitions. By using these tools, designers can create dynamic transitions that adapt to the user's actions and interactions, providing a more responsive and interactive browsing experience. Overall, fluid page transitions play a crucial role in creating a cohesive and user-friendly UI. By eliminating abrupt breaks and providing smooth transitions, designers can make the browsing experience more enjoyable and intuitive for users, enhancing engagement and encouraging exploration. Fluid page transitions are part of a comprehensive design system that encompasses various UI patterns, guidelines, and principles. By including this pattern in a design system, designers ensure consistency and coherence throughout the entire application or website, keeping the user experience seamless across different pages and sections. In conclusion, fluid page transitions are a UI design pattern that aims to create smooth and seamless transitions between different pages or sections within a website or application. This pattern enhances the overall user experience by minimizing disruption and providing a more engaging and immersive environment. By utilizing technologies such as CSS animations or JavaScript libraries, designers can create dynamic transitions that adapt to the user's actions,

83

providing a smooth and user-friendly browsing experience.

## Flyout Menus

Flyout menus are a prominent UI design pattern used in web and mobile applications to present hierarchical navigation options to users. They typically appear as hidden or collapsible menus that expand or fly out when activated. The primary purpose of flyout menus is to provide a structured and organized way for users to access additional content or functionality without cluttering the main interface. They are especially useful when dealing with complex or extensive navigational systems, as they allow for a more streamlined and efficient user experience. In terms of design systems, flyout menus are an integral part of creating a cohesive and consistent user interface. They contribute to the overall visual and interactive language of an application, ensuring that users can easily navigate through different sections or categories. Furthermore, flyout menus can also enhance the discoverability of features or pages that might otherwise be buried deep within the application's hierarchy. From a technical perspective, flyout menus can be implemented using HTML, CSS, and JavaScript. In HTML, the basic structure of a flyout menu can be achieved using nested and elements, with CSS and JavaScript used to control the display and behavior of the menu. When designing flyout menus, there are several best practices to consider. Firstly, it is important to ensure that the flyout menu is easily accessible and visible to users, either through a visible icon or a clearly signposted trigger. Secondly, the menu should be designed to accommodate different device sizes and screen resolutions, allowing for a responsive and adaptive user experience. Additionally, the use of clear and concise labels or icons within the menu can help users quickly understand the purpose and content of each option. In conclusion, flyout menus are a valuable UI pattern and design system component that enhance the usability and efficiency of web and mobile applications. By providing a structured and organized way to navigate through content or access additional functionality, flyout menus contribute to a more intuitive and enjoyable user experience.

## Follow Us Links

A Follow Us Link is a common UI pattern in web design that provides a way for users to connect and engage with a company or brand through various social media platforms. It is typically displayed as a series of clickable icons or text, each representing a different social media platform.

Follow Us Links are an important component of a design system as they help to create a consistent and cohesive user experience across different pages and platforms. They are often included in the header or footer of a website, allowing users to easily locate and follow the company on social media.

## Followers/Following

Followers/Following refers to a user interface pattern typically used in social media platforms and other online communities. This pattern is commonly used to display information about a user's network and social connections. Followers are individuals who have opted to receive updates and notifications from another user. This could be in the form of subscribing to their posts, activities, or any other content they share on the platform. The number of followers represents the size of the user's audience or network. Following, on the other hand, refers to the act of subscribing to updates and notifications from other users. When a user follows someone, they are essentially expressing interest in the content and activities of that particular user. The number of following represents the size of the user's own subscribed network. In terms of UI design, the followers and following pattern is typically represented by the use of simple numeric counts. These counts are usually displayed prominently on a user's profile or dashboard. The numbers are often accompanied by labels or icons to clarify their meaning. The followers count and following count can be displayed in separate sections or in close proximity to each other. The main purpose is to provide users with a quick snapshot of their network size and engagement. This information can be useful for personal branding, content reach, and overall visibility on the platform. The UI design for followers/following can vary depending on the platform and design system in use. However, it is important to maintain consistency and ensure that the counts are easily readable and accessible to users. The use of contrasting colors, typography, or visual elements can help emphasize the counts and make them stand out. In conclusion, the followers/following UI pattern is a common element in social media platforms and online communities. It provides users with a quick overview of their network size and engagement. The design of this pattern should be consistent, readable, and accessible to enhance the user experience.>

## Food Customization

Food customization refers to the ability for users to personalize their food orders or choices according to their preferences and dietary requirements. In the context of UI patterns and design systems, food customization is a user interface feature that allows users to modify various aspects of their food choices, such as ingredients, toppings, cooking methods, portion sizes, and dietary specifications.

Food customization aims to provide users with control and flexibility over their food selections, enhancing the overall user experience and satisfaction. It allows users to tailor their food orders to suit their unique taste preferences, dietary restrictions, and health concerns. By offering customization options, food-related businesses can cater to a wide range of customer needs, increasing customer loyalty and fostering a sense of personalization.

## Food Delivery Tracking

Food delivery tracking is a user interface (UI) pattern and design system that enables users to track the progress and status of their food delivery orders in real-time. It provides a transparent and efficient way for users to stay informed about their orders and anticipate their arrival.

Through the food delivery tracking UI, users are able to view the current status of their order, such as order confirmed, in preparation, out for delivery, or delivered. It may also display additional information, such as estimated delivery time, delivery person's name or photo, and a live map showing the progress of the delivery. These elements work together to enhance the user experience and keep users engaged and informed.

## Food Ordering

A food ordering UI pattern is a design system that enables users to browse and order food from various restaurants or food delivery services. It provides a seamless and intuitive user experience by showcasing restaurant menus, allowing users to customize their orders, and facilitating the checkout process. The main objective of a food ordering UI pattern is to simplify the food ordering process for users, ensuring that they can easily find and order their desired food items. The design system typically consists of a series of screens or pages that guide users through the ordering process, providing them with relevant information and options at each step. At the core of a food ordering UI pattern is the restaurant menu display. This component presents users with a list of available food items, organized by categories such as appetizers, main courses, desserts, and drinks. Users can browse through the menu, view details about each item, and add their preferred items to their order. To enhance the user experience, the UI pattern often includes features such as search functionality and filter options. Users can search for specific food items or filter the menu based on dietary preferences, cuisines, or pricing. This helps users quickly find the food items they are looking for, improving efficiency and reducing frustration. Once users have selected their desired food items, a food ordering UI pattern provides them with options to customize their order. This may include selecting portion sizes, adding extra toppings, specifying cooking preferences, or leaving special instructions for the restaurant. The customization options cater to users' individual preferences, allowing them to tailor their order to their liking. After finalizing their order, users proceed to the checkout stage. Here, the UI pattern guides users through the process of providing delivery details, selecting payment methods, and reviewing their order summary. The goal is to make the checkout process as simple and straightforward as possible, reducing potential friction points and ensuring a seamless transaction. In conclusion, a food ordering UI pattern is a design system that streamlines the food ordering process for users. By providing an intuitive interface for browsing menus, customizing orders, and completing transactions, it enhances the overall user experience and encourages users to repeatedly engage with the platform.>

## Forgot Password Form

A Forgot Password form is a User Interface (UI) pattern used to provide a way for users to reset or recover their forgotten passwords. It is an essential component of a design system that focuses on user experience and security. The purpose of the Forgot Password form is to assist users who cannot access their accounts due to forgetting their passwords. By providing a simple and secure method for password recovery, it helps users regain access to their accounts efficiently. The Forgot Password form typically consists of two main elements: an input field for the user to enter their email address or username and a button to initiate the password recovery process. -

The first element, the input field, collects the necessary information from the user – their email address or username. This input field can be designed with placeholder text to guide users on what information is required.

-

The second element, the button, triggers the password recovery process. When clicked, it validates the entered information and either sends a password reset link via email or initiates a verification process to confirm the user's identity before allowing them to reset their password.

Furthermore, a Forgot Password form may also provide additional features that enhance usability and security: -

Validation messages: If the user entered information is incorrect or doesn't exist in the system, a validation message can be displayed to guide the user and prompt them to enter valid information.

-

Security measures: To safeguard against unauthorized access to user accounts, Forgot Password forms may incorporate security measures like CAPTCHA or two-factor authentication (2FA) to verify the user's identity before allowing them to reset their password. These measures ensure that the password recovery process is secure and reliable.

In conclusion, a Forgot Password form is a crucial element of a UI pattern and design system, providing users with a straightforward and secure method to recover their forgotten passwords. It follows a well-defined structure with an input field for collecting user information and a button to initiate the password recovery process. Additionally, it may incorporate validation messages and security measures to enhance usability and protect user accounts.

## Form Hints

Form hints are a UI pattern used in design systems to provide additional information or guidance to users when filling out a form. They are typically displayed as short, concise messages that help users understand the purpose or requirements of a particular input field. Form hints are important in providing clarity and reducing friction in the form-filling process. They can be used to explain the expected format of a field, provide examples of valid inputs, or give instructions on what information is required. By offering contextual guidance, form hints can help users correctly fill out a form on their first attempt, saving time and minimizing errors. In terms of design, form hints are usually displayed near or within the input field they relate to. They can be placed below, above, or alongside the field, depending on the layout and visual hierarchy of the form. The text used in form hints should be concise and easy to understand, using plain language instead of technical jargon. When designing form hints, it's important to strike a balance between providing enough information for users to complete the form accurately and avoiding overwhelming them with excessive guidance. Too much text can be overwhelming and may discourage users from filling out the form altogether. On the other hand, too little information can leave users guessing or making unnecessary errors. To implement form hints in HTML, the `

` tag can be used. The hints can be placed within the `

` tags, which will provide proper paragraph structure for the content. It's important to use appropriate CSS styling to differentiate the form hints from the rest of the form elements and make them easily readable. Here's an example of how form hints can be implemented using two

` tags:

Enter your email address:

This field is required and must be a valid email address.

In this example, the first `

` tag provides a label for the email address field, while the second `

` tag serves as the form hint, explaining the requirement and expected format of the input. Including form hints in a design system helps maintain consistency and improves the overall user experience by providing clear and helpful information to users as they fill out forms. By following this UI pattern, designers can ensure that users have a smooth and frictionless form-filling experience.

## Form Validation

Form validation is a crucial aspect of user interface (UI) patterns and design systems that ensures the accuracy and integrity of user-submitted data. It refers to the process of validating and verifying user input within a web form to prevent errors, improve usability, and enhance the overall user experience.

In the context of UI patterns and design systems, form validation involves implementing various validation techniques and feedback mechanisms to guide users in correctly filling out and submitting forms. The main goal is to ensure that the data meets specific requirements, such as format, completeness, and validity, as defined by the application or system.

## Form Wizards

Form Wizards are a user interface pattern and design system element used to guide users through a complex or multi-step form submission process. They provide a structured and step-by-step approach to inputting information, making it easier for users to complete the form accurately and efficiently. A Form Wizard typically consists of multiple sections or steps, with each step representing a different part of the form. It allows users to navigate between these steps in a linear fashion, usually using next and previous buttons, ensuring that they complete all the required fields in a logical order. The main purpose of a Form Wizard is to simplify the overall form submission process by breaking it down into smaller, more manageable parts. By presenting the form in a step-by-step manner, it reduces cognitive load and helps users focus on one section at a time. This can be particularly beneficial for complex forms that require a significant amount of information or involve multiple decision points. Additionally, Form Wizards can provide feedback and validation at each step, notifying users of any errors or missing information before moving on to the next step. This real-time feedback helps users correct mistakes and ensures that the form is completed accurately along the way, reducing the likelihood of errors or frustration. From a design system perspective, Form Wizards often follow consistent visual and interactive patterns to maintain a cohesive and user-friendly experience. They typically feature a progress indicator, indicating the current step and the overall progress through the form. This allows users to understand their position within the form and how much more they need to complete. In summary, Form Wizards are a valuable UI pattern and design system element that simplify complex or multi-step form submission processes. By breaking down the form into smaller sections and guiding users through each step, they enhance usability and accuracy while reducing cognitive load and frustration.

Form Wizards are a user interface pattern and design system element used to guide users through a complex or multi-step form submission process. They provide a structured and step-by-step approach to inputting information, making it easier for users to complete the form accurately and efficiently.

A Form Wizard typically consists of multiple sections or steps, with each step representing a different part of the form. It allows users to navigate between these steps in a linear fashion, usually using next and previous buttons, ensuring that they complete all the required fields in a logical order.

## Forum Thread

A UI pattern refers to a recurring solution to a commonly encountered design problem that occurs in user interfaces. It provides a standard and consistent way of presenting information and interactions to users, ensuring a more intuitive and efficient user experience. UI patterns are essential in design systems, which are comprehensive collections of reusable components, guidelines, and best practices that help maintain consistency and coherence in user interfaces across different platforms and devices. A design system aims to establish a unified visual language and interaction patterns, ensuring a cohesive and user-friendly experience for users. HTML, or Hypertext Markup Language, is the standard markup language for creating web pages and applications. It provides a structured way of organizing content, specifying its meaning and relationships. However, in the provided answer, only two

tags are allowed, and no other HTML tags can be used.

UI patterns are recurring solutions to design problems in user interfaces. They provide a consistent way of presenting information and interactions, enhancing the user experience.

Design systems, on the other hand, are comprehensive collections of reusable components and guidelines that aim to maintain consistency and coherence in user interfaces.

## Friend Requests

A friend request is a UI pattern and design system component that allows users to connect with each other on a social networking platform or application.

When a user wants to connect with someone they know or would like to become friends with, they can send a friend request. This request is typically initiated by clicking on a button or link that is associated with the user they want to connect with. Once the request is sent, the recipient is notified and has the option to accept or decline the request.

Friend requests are an important feature in social networking platforms as they provide a way for users to expand their social network and connect with others who share similar interests or affiliations. It allows users to reach out and establish connections with people they may know in real life or have common connections with.

From a design perspective, friend requests should be visually distinct and easy to locate within the user interface. They are often represented by a specific icon or button that is recognizable and consistent throughout the platform. The design should clearly indicate the status of the friend request, such as whether it is pending, accepted, or declined.

Friend requests should also provide clear and concise messaging to the user, informing them of the action they are taking and the potential consequences. For example, when sending a friend request, the user may be prompted to include a brief message introducing themselves or indicating why they would like to connect. This message should be optional and provide guidance on what is appropriate to include.

In conclusion, friend requests are a fundamental feature in social networking platforms that allow users to connect with others. It is important to design friend request components in a visually distinct and user-friendly manner, providing clear messaging and options for both the sender and recipient of the request.

## Gamification Elements

Gamification elements are design patterns used in user interface (UI) design systems to incorporate game-like features and mechanics in non-game contexts. These elements are implemented to enhance engagement, motivation, and user experiences in various applications and platforms.

Gamification leverages principles and techniques from game design to make activities more enjoyable, increase user participation, and encourage desired behaviors. By incorporating elements such as points, levels, badges, quests, and leaderboards, designers can create a more immersive and rewarding experience for users.

## Gamified Learning

Gamified Learning refers to the incorporation of game elements and mechanics into educational content, platforms, or experiences with the goal of enhancing engagement, motivation, and learning outcomes.

In the context of UI patterns and design systems, Gamified Learning can be implemented through various user interface elements and design strategies. These elements and strategies often aim to provide an immersive and interactive learning environment that encourages active participation, exploration, and skill development.

One common UI pattern used in Gamified Learning is the use of progress indicators. These indicators visually represent the learner's progress, achievements, or goals, providing them with a sense of accomplishment and motivating them to continue their learning journey. For example, a progress bar can be used to show how far the learner has progressed within a course or module.

Another UI pattern that can be used in Gamified Learning is the incorporation of rewards and feedback mechanisms. These can be in the form of badges, points, levels, or virtual currency, which are awarded to learners when they complete tasks, achieve milestones, or demonstrate mastery of certain skills. Rewards and feedback not only provide learners with immediate feedback on their progress but also serve as incentives to encourage further engagement and continued learning.

Furthermore, Gamified Learning can also employ interactive UI elements such as quizzes, puzzles, and challenges. These elements tap into the inherent enjoyment and satisfaction derived from problem-solving and competition. By incorporating these elements into the learning experience, learners are not only motivated to actively engage with the material but also develop and apply their knowledge and skills in a practical and meaningful context.

Overall, Gamified Learning in the context of UI patterns and design systems leverages game elements and mechanics to create engaging and impactful learning experiences. By incorporating progress indicators, rewards and feedback mechanisms, and interactive elements, Gamified Learning enhances motivation, engagement, and knowledge retention, ultimately leading to more effective educational outcomes.

## Gardening Tips And Plant Care

Gardening Tips and Plant Care refers to a set of user interface patterns and design principles that are specifically aimed at enhancing the user's experience with gardening-related websites, applications, or other digital platforms. These patterns and principles are used to create a cohesive and consistent design system that helps users easily navigate and interact with the content, tools, and features related to gardening and plant care.

Within the context of UI patterns and design systems, Gardening Tips and Plant Care focuses on providing users with clear and concise information, guidance, and instructions on various aspects of gardening. This includes tips on how to grow and maintain different types of plants, guidance on selecting the right soil, fertilizers, and watering techniques, as well as advice on pest control and disease prevention.

The design system for Gardening Tips and Plant Care incorporates a range of visual and interaction patterns that aim to facilitate intuitive navigation and enhance the user's understanding of gardening concepts. These patterns include consistent labeling, categorization, and organization of gardening information, the use of visual cues such as icons and imagery to aid comprehension, and the inclusion of interactive elements such as checkboxes or sliders to facilitate user input or customization.

Gardening Tips and Plant Care design principles also emphasize the importance of readability and accessibility. This involves ensuring that the content is presented in a legible and easily comprehensible manner, with appropriate font styles, sizes, and contrast. Additionally, it includes providing alternative text for images and utilizing suitable color palettes and contrast ratios to ensure that the design is accessible to users with visual impairments.

## Geolocation-Based Content

Geolocation-Based Content refers to the display of content on a user interface (UI) that is customized and tailored based on the geolocation information of the user. This UI pattern and design system utilizes the geographical location data of the user to provide relevant and personalized content. The concept behind geolocation-based content is to enhance the user experience by presenting information that is specific to the user's current location. This can be achieved by using various technologies and techniques such as GPS (Global Positioning System), IP address tracking, and Wi-Fi triangulation. By leveraging geolocation data, UI designers can create dynamic content that is location-specific. For example, a weather application can display weather information based on the user's current location. Similarly, a restaurant recommendation app can provide suggestions for nearby restaurants based on the user's geolocation. UI patterns and design systems for geolocation-based content often revolve around the use of interactive maps and location markers. These maps can be integrated into the UI to visually represent the user's location and nearby points of interest. The design of geolocation-based content should prioritize simplicity and ease of use. Users should be able to quickly understand and navigate the interface to access the location-specific information they seek. Clear and intuitive icons, labels, and navigation elements should be used to guide users in interacting with the content. Furthermore, it is important to take into consideration the privacy and security concerns associated with geolocation data. Users should have control over their location information and be provided with clear options to opt-in or opt-out of location tracking. Transparent explanations of how the data is used and protected should be provided to build trust with the user. In conclusion, geolocation-based content is a UI pattern and design system that utilizes the user's geolocation data to personalize and customize the content displayed on the interface. By incorporating interactive maps and location markers, designers can create intuitive and user-friendly interfaces that enhance the user experience. Privacy and security considerations should also be taken into account to ensure user trust and satisfaction with the geolocation-based content.

## Gesture-Based Navigation

Gesture-Based Navigation refers to a user interface pattern and design system that allows users to interact with a digital application or website through gestures, eliminating the need for traditional input methods like mouse clicks or keyboard typing. This approach leverages touch-sensitive screens or other motion-sensing technologies to recognize and interpret hand movements, finger gestures, or body motions as commands or actions in the user interface. Gesture-Based Navigation aims to provide a more intuitive and immersive user experience by mimicking physical interactions with the digital environment. This design pattern offers numerous advantages, including improved accessibility, ease of use, and the potential for more engaging and dynamic interfaces. By relying on gestures, users can interact with the interface naturally, relying on their inherent understanding of physical gestures and movements. Implementing Gesture-Based Navigation requires careful consideration of the specific gestures and corresponding actions that users will perform within the interface. Common examples of gestures include swiping, pinching, tapping, dragging, rotating, and shaking. These gestures can be mapped to various navigation actions, such as scrolling, zooming, selecting, navigating between screens or pages, and triggering specific functionalities. To ensure a seamless and effective user experience, developers and designers need to establish clear and consistent gesture-based interactions. This involves providing visual cues or affordances to help users discover and understand the available gestures. Visual feedback, such as animations, transitions, or changes in interface elements, can enhance the user's perception and comprehension of the gesture-based interactions. Additionally, it is essential to provide alternative methods of navigation for users who may have difficulty performing or interpreting gestures. This can include traditional input methods like keyboard and mouse interactions or voice commands. By accommodating various interaction preferences and abilities, designers can ensure that their interfaces remain accessible and inclusive. In conclusion, Gesture-Based

Navigation is a user interface pattern that enables users to interact with digital applications or websites through gestures, offering a more intuitive and immersive user experience. It requires careful consideration of gestures, clear visual cues, and alternative navigation methods to accommodate diverse user needs. >

## Gesture-Based Interactions

Gesture-based interactions refer to the use of physical movements, gestures, or actions to interact with a user interface (UI) or design system. These interactions are typically performed through touch-sensitive devices or motion-sensing technologies such as smartphones, tablets, touchpads, or motion controllers. In the context of UI patterns and design systems, gesture-based interactions provide a more intuitive and natural way for users to interact with digital interfaces compared to traditional input methods like keyboard and mouse. They allow users to perform actions, navigate, manipulate content, and trigger responses by using gestures commonly associated with real-world physical actions. Gesture-based interactions can include a variety of gestures such as tapping, swiping, pinching, dragging, rotating, or shaking. These gestures can be used in combination or individually to perform different tasks within a UI or design system. For example, a common gesture is the swipe gesture, where users swipe their finger across a touchscreen to scroll through content or switch between pages. Tapping is another common gesture that is used to select items, buttons, or links within an interface. Pinching and spreading gestures are commonly used for zooming in or out on content. These gestures can be applied to images, maps, or other elements that support zoom functionality. Gesture-based interactions can also include more complex gestures or motion-based interactions, such as shaking a device to undo an action or tilting a device to control the movement of objects on the screen. These types of gestures provide a more immersive and interactive user experience. When designing for gesture-based interactions, it is essential to consider the affordances and feedback provided to users. Affordances are visual cues or indicators that suggest the availability of certain gestures or actions. Feedback, such as visual or haptic feedback, confirms to users that their gestures have been recognized and actions have been performed. Overall, gesture-based interactions offer a more engaging, seamless, and intuitive way for users to interact with UIs and design systems. They enhance usability, accessibility, and user satisfaction by leveraging the natural physical actions and behaviors of users, making digital interactions feel more intuitive and effortless.

## Gift Card Redemption Form

A Gift Card Redemption Form is a user interface pattern and design system that allows users to enter their gift card information in order to redeem its value for goods or services. The form typically consists of a set of fields and controls that capture the necessary details, such as the gift card code and the amount to be redeemed. The primary purpose of the Gift Card Redemption Form is to validate and process the gift card information provided by the user. This involves performing checks to verify the authenticity and validity of the gift card code, as well as confirming that the available balance is sufficient to cover the requested redemption amount. The form may also include additional fields or options to enhance the user experience and provide valuable information. For example, it could display the remaining balance of the gift card after the redemption, or offer suggestions for potential purchases based on the gift card's value. In terms of design, the Gift Card Redemption Form should adhere to the overall visual style and branding of the website or application. This ensures consistency and familiarity for the user, reducing any potential confusion or hesitation during the redemption process. To facilitate ease of use, the form should be intuitive and straightforward, with clear instructions and labels for each input field. Validation messages should be provided in real-time or upon form submission to provide immediate feedback to the user if any errors or issues are encountered. Furthermore, the Gift Card Redemption Form should be mobile-responsive, allowing users to redeem their gift cards from any device or screen size. This requires careful consideration of the form's layout and usability to ensure optimal viewing and interaction on different devices. Overall, the Gift Card Redemption Form is an essential component of an e-commerce or service-oriented platform that offers gift cards as a form of payment or gifting. Its purpose is to streamline the redemption process and provide a seamless experience for users, ultimately encouraging the utilization of gift cards and driving customer satisfaction.

The Gift Card Redemption Form is a user interface pattern that facilitates the redemption of gift cards for goods or services.

It encompasses fields and controls for entering the gift card code and redemption amount, as well as validation and error handling to ensure a smooth and accurate redemption process.

## Grid Layout

The Grid Layout is a UI pattern and design system that allows for the creation of responsive and flexible page layouts using a grid-based structure. The Grid Layout provides a way to arrange and align elements on a web page in a consistent and organized manner. It allows for the division of the page into rows and columns, where elements can be placed and positioned based on their relationship to the grid. In the Grid Layout, the page layout is defined by a grid container, which is the parent element that contains all the grid items. The grid container is divided into rows and columns using the grid-template-rows and grid-template-columns properties, respectively. These properties define the size and position of each row and column on the page. Grid items are the individual elements that are placed within the grid. They can be any HTML element, such as headings, paragraphs, images, or other UI components. Grid items are placed within the grid using the grid-row and grid-column properties, which specify the start and end positions of the item within the grid. The Grid Layout provides a powerful set of features for creating responsive and adaptive layouts. Elements within the grid can be aligned and positioned with precision, allowing for complex and flexible page designs. The grid can also adapt to different screen sizes and orientations, making it ideal for creating responsive and mobile-friendly websites. By using a grid-based layout, designers and developers can create visually appealing and consistent page designs. The Grid Layout simplifies the process of creating complex layouts, as it provides a systematic and structured approach to arranging and aligning elements on the page. In conclusion, the Grid Layout is a UI pattern and design system that allows for the creation of responsive and flexible page layouts using a grid-based structure. It provides a systematic and structured approach to arranging and aligning elements on a web page, resulting in visually appealing and consistent page designs.

## Grid View

A grid view is a user interface pattern that presents data or content in a grid-like structure, allowing for organized and efficient display of information. It is typically used in design systems to provide consistent and visually appealing layouts for displaying various types of content.

In a grid view, data is arranged in rows and columns, forming a table-like structure. Each item or element in the grid is displayed in a separate cell, making it easy for users to scan and compare various pieces of information. The grid view can be used to display various types of content, such as images, text, or a combination of both.

## Group Or Community

A group or community in the context of UI patterns and design system refers to a collection of individuals who come together to collaborate, share knowledge, and work towards a common goal of creating and maintaining a set of consistent and user-friendly design patterns and components.

These groups or communities typically consist of designers, developers, and other stakeholders who are responsible for creating the user interface and experience of a product or service. Their main objective is to establish a set of guidelines, standards, and best practices that ensure consistency and coherence across different user interactions and interface elements.

## Grouped Notifications

Grouped Notifications is a UI pattern in which notifications or messages are visually grouped together to provide a more organized and streamlined user experience. It is a design system component that helps users easily identify and manage multiple notifications by presenting them in a cohesive and structured manner.

This UI pattern is particularly useful in scenarios where there are numerous notifications that need to be displayed to the user, such as in messaging apps, email clients, or social media platforms. Instead of presenting each notification individually, Grouped Notifications allows for grouping related messages or notifications into a single container.

## Guest Checkout Form

A Guest Checkout Form is a user interface pattern and design system used in e-commerce websites to facilitate easy and quick purchase transactions for customers who prefer not to create an account or log in. It is designed to provide a seamless and hassle-free checkout experience, allowing users to complete their purchases without the need for any prior registration or account setup. This form typically consists of a series of input fields where customers can provide their contact information and shipping details, along with payment method options. The fields usually include name, email address, phone number, shipping address, and payment details such as credit card information. The form also often incorporates a section for customers to review and confirm their order before finalizing the purchase. The purpose of the Guest Checkout Form is to eliminate any potential friction or barriers that may deter customers from completing their purchase. By allowing users to bypass the registration process, it caters to customers who may be visiting the website for a one-time purchase or are simply hesitant to create an account. From a design system perspective, the Guest Checkout Form prioritizes simplicity, usability, and security. The form's design generally follows a clean and minimalist aesthetic, ensuring that the input fields are easily identifiable and accessible. Clear and concise instructions are provided to guide users through the checkout process smoothly. To ensure a seamless experience, the form often utilizes autocomplete functionality to assist users in filling out the fields quickly and accurately. It may also include real-time validation to minimize errors and provide feedback to users if any required information is missing or invalid. In terms of security, it is essential for the Guest Checkout Form to employ robust encryption technologies to protect users' sensitive information during the transaction process. This includes secure transmission of payment data and adhering to industry-standard security practices. Overall, the Guest Checkout Form is a crucial component of e-commerce websites, providing an efficient and user-friendly option for customers who prefer not to create an account. Its design and functionality aim to streamline the checkout process, minimize friction, and ultimately drive conversions.>

## Hamburger Menu

A hamburger menu is a common user interface (UI) pattern in web and mobile design that provides a menu or navigation system hidden behind a button with three horizontal lines stacked vertically, resembling a hamburger. When the user clicks or taps on the hamburger icon, the menu slides out or expands, revealing a list of options or links that were previously hidden from view.

Originally popularized by mobile applications as a way to conserve screen real estate on smaller screens, the hamburger menu has become ubiquitous across various digital platforms. It allows designers to prioritize content and create a cleaner, less cluttered interface. The visual cue of the three horizontal lines has become widely recognized as a symbol for a hidden menu, reducing the learning curve for users.

## Haptic Feedback

Haptic feedback refers to tactile sensations or vibrations that are provided to users as a response to their interaction with a user interface (UI). It is a design pattern used in UI to enhance the user experience by providing physical or touch-based feedback.

When users interact with digital devices such as smartphones, tablets, or touch screens, they usually expect some form of feedback to confirm that their input has been registered and to guide their actions. Haptic feedback fulfills this need by simulating physical sensations that mimic real-world objects or actions. It aims to create a more engaging and intuitive user experience by bridging the gap between the digital and physical worlds.

## Health Assessment Form

A Health Assessment Form is a user interface (UI) pattern and design system used to gather information about an individual's health for the purpose of evaluation or diagnosis. It offers a structured and systematic approach to collect relevant data, allowing healthcare professionals to assess a person's health status accurately. Through a Health Assessment Form, users can input their personal health information, medical history, current symptoms, and any relevant lifestyle factors. The form may include various sections or fields to cover different aspects of health, such as demographics, medical conditions, medications, allergies, and general health habits. The design of a Health Assessment Form should adhere to principles of usability, accessibility, and visual hierarchy. It should be intuitive and easy to navigate, guiding users through each section of the form. Clear instructions and labels should be provided, ensuring that users understand what information is required. To ensure the privacy and security of users' health information, a Health Assessment Form should comply with legal and ethical regulations, such as data protection laws and HIPAA (Health Insurance Portability and Accountability Act) guidelines. Measures like encryption and data anonymization should be implemented to protect sensitive data. By using a Health Assessment Form within a UI design system, consistency in design elements, typography, colors, and layout can be maintained across different screens or pages. This provides a cohesive and seamless user experience, making it easier for users to interact with the form and enter their health information accurately. Overall, a Health Assessment Form in the context of UI patterns and design systems serves as a vital tool for healthcare professionals to collect essential health data from individuals. By using a well-designed and user-friendly form, it allows for efficient and accurate assessment of a person's health and aids in providing appropriate medical care or recommendations.

A Health Assessment Form is a user interface (UI) pattern and design system used to gather information about an individual's health for evaluation or diagnosis.

It provides a structured approach for users to input their personal health information, medical history, symptoms, and lifestyle factors, ensuring consistent and accurate assessment.

## Health Tracking

A health tracking system refers to a user interface (UI) pattern and design system that allows individuals to monitor and manage their health-related data and activities. It provides a platform for users to record and analyze various aspects of their well-being, such as physical activity, diet, sleep, and vital signs. This system facilitates the tracking of health metrics over time, encouraging users to create healthy habits and make informed decisions regarding their lifestyle and overall wellness. In the context of UI patterns, a health tracking system typically includes a user-friendly dashboard that presents the collected data in a visually appealing and organized manner. This dashboard offers an at-a-glance overview of the user's progress and health trends, presenting the information in a clear and comprehensible way. Users can easily view charts, graphs, and statistics that illustrate their performance and progress towards their health goals. The design system of a health tracking system focuses on simplicity, usability, and accessibility. It ensures that the user interface elements are intuitive and easy to navigate, allowing users to seamlessly record and access their health data on various devices, such as smartphones, tablets, and desktop computers. The design system also emphasizes the use of appropriate color schemes, typography, and iconography to enhance the visual appeal and readability of the interface. Moreover, a health tracking system often incorporates gamification elements to increase user engagement and motivation. It may include features such as goal setting, achievement badges, challenges, and social connectivity, which foster a sense of competition, collaboration, and accountability. By gamifying the experience, users are incentivized to actively participate in tracking their health and maintaining healthy habits. Overall, a health tracking system serves as a valuable tool for individuals who desire to take control of their well-being. It empowers users by providing them with insights and knowledge about their health, enabling them to make informed decisions and take proactive steps towards improving their overall quality of life.>

## Heatmaps

Heatmaps are a visual representation of data that are commonly used in UI patterns and design systems. They display information in a graphical format in order to quickly communicate patterns, trends, and key insights. In the context of UI patterns, heatmaps are often used to analyze user behavior and interactions with a digital product or interface. By tracking and aggregating user data, heatmaps provide designers with valuable insights into how users engage with specific elements or features. Heatmaps are particularly useful in identifying areas of high and low engagement. They use a color gradient scale to represent the intensity of user interactions, with warmer colors (such as red) indicating high levels of activity and cooler colors (such as blue) indicating lower levels. These visual representations help designers make informed decisions when it comes to improving user experience. By identifying the areas where users are most engaged, designers can prioritize enhancements or adjust the layout accordingly. For example, if a heatmap shows that users are not interacting with certain elements, designers may decide to modify their placement, size, or prominence to increase visibility and encourage engagement. Heatmaps can also be used to analyze the effectiveness of specific design elements, such as button placement, menu navigation, or call-to-action buttons. By tracking user interactions, heatmaps can reveal potential areas for improvement or optimization. For instance, if a heatmap indicates that users frequently interact with a particular button, designers can consider making it more prominent or accessible. In the context of design systems, heatmaps can help standardize and streamline user interface elements. By analyzing the usage patterns across different interfaces, designers can identify commonalities and develop consistent components and style guidelines. Heatmaps provide quantitative data that support design decision-making and help prioritize design system improvements. In conclusion, heatmaps are a valuable tool in UI patterns and design systems. They provide designers with insights into user behavior, help improve user experience, and inform the development of consistent design systems. By visually representing data, heatmaps enable designers to make informed decisions based on user interactions and trends.

## Hero Section

A hero section in the context of UI patterns and design systems is a prominently displayed and visually appealing section at the top of a webpage or interface. It is typically the first element that users see when they land on a website or open an application, serving as a focal point to capture their attention and provide an introduction to the content or purpose of the page. The hero section is strategically designed to make a strong impression, often using visually appealing images, compelling copy, and clear call-to-action elements. It sets the tone for the entire user experience and plays a crucial role in establishing brand identity and messaging. In terms of layout, the hero section is usually full-width or covers a significant portion of the screen to maximize its impact. It often incorporates a combination of multimedia elements, such as images or videos, alongside text and interactive elements, if applicable. The primary goal of a hero section is to engage and guide users towards taking specific actions, such as signing up for a service, exploring more content, or making a purchase. It should succinctly convey the intended message and provide a clear value proposition that resonates with the target audience. Design systems play an important role in the creation of hero sections by providing guidelines, patterns, and reusable components. They offer a consistent visual language and ensure a cohesive user experience throughout an application or website. By adhering to design system principles, designers can create visually appealing and effective hero sections that align with the overall design aesthetic and meet the needs of the users. Overall, a hero section serves as the gateway to a webpage or application, capturing users' attention and sparking their interest. It combines compelling visuals, engaging copy, and clear calls to action to create a memorable and effective introduction to the content or purpose of the interface.>

## Home Improvement

A home improvement in the context of UI patterns and design system refers to the process of making enhancements or modifications to the user interface and design elements of a digital product or system.

With the constant advancement in technology and changing user preferences, it is crucial for designers and developers to continuously update and improve the user interface and design system of their digital products. Home improvement in this context involves analyzing and identifying areas of improvement, and implementing changes to enhance the overall user experience.

## Home Screen

The home screen is a fundamental component in the field of user interface (UI) patterns and design systems. It serves as the initial interface that users encounter when launching an application or visiting a website. The home screen acts as a gateway to various features, functionalities, and content that the application or website offers. In a UI pattern or design system, the home screen is typically designed to provide an overview and easy access to key elements of the application or website. It serves as a central hub that allows users to navigate and explore the available options and actions. The purpose of the home screen is to provide a clear and organized interface that helps users understand the overall structure and layout of the system. The home screen often includes a combination of static and dynamic elements. Static elements are those that remain consistent across multiple visits and interactions, providing users with a sense of familiarity and stability. These elements can include logos, branding, navigation menus, and persistent features like search bars or user profiles. On the other hand, dynamic elements are those that change based on user behavior or external factors. These elements provide personalized and relevant content to enhance the user experience. Examples of dynamic elements on a home screen can include personalized recommendations, notifications, recent activity, or trending topics. Additionally, the home screen can also feature interactive elements that allow users to perform actions directly from the initial interface. These elements can include buttons, sliders, input fields, or embedded widgets. Overall, the home screen is a vital component in UI patterns and design systems, as it sets the stage for the user's journey through the application or website. It provides users with orientation, navigation, and access to important features and content. By following established UI design principles and considering user needs and expectations, the home screen can be designed to create a positive and engaging user experience. In conclusion, the home screen plays a crucial role in UI patterns and design systems by serving as the initial interface that users encounter. It provides an overview of the system, access to key elements, and a means to navigate and explore the available options. Through a combination of static and dynamic elements, the home screen aims to create a clear, organized, and personalized user experience.>

## Homework Submission

A UI pattern is a reusable component or set of components used to solve a specific user interface design problem. It provides a consistent and familiar experience for users by following established conventions and best practices. UI patterns can be thought of as pre-designed solutions to common user interface design problems. They are created based on research and analysis of user needs, behaviors, and preferences. By using established patterns, designers can save time and effort in creating intuitive and effective user interfaces. A design system, on the other hand, is a comprehensive set of guidelines, standards, and tools that define how a product's user interface should look, feel, and function. It goes beyond just UI patterns and includes typography, color palettes, layout grids, and other elements that contribute to the overall design language. The design system acts as a single source of truth for the entire product, ensuring consistency across different platforms and devices. It provides clear guidance for designers and developers, ensuring that their work aligns with the product's goals and brand identity. In summary, UI patterns are specific design solutions for common problems, while a design system encompasses a broader set of guidelines and standards for the entire user interface. UI patterns help maintain consistency within a design system, ensuring a cohesive and seamless user experience. By following UI patterns and using a design system, designers can create user interfaces that are intuitive, visually appealing, and align with the overall product goals.>

## Horizontal Navigation

Horizontal navigation refers to a user interface (UI) design pattern that presents navigation elements horizontally on a webpage or application. It is commonly used to provide users with easy access to different sections or pages within a website or app. In this UI pattern, navigation elements are typically displayed in a single line or row along the top, bottom, or sides of the screen. These elements are often represented by text links or icons, which users can click or tap to navigate to different sections or pages. Horizontal navigation can be implemented using HTML and CSS. In HTML, the navigation elements are typically placed within an unordered list () or a series of anchor tags (). The

tags from the requirement limit prompt are not sufficient to write pure HTML, so I will be using tag to break lines between multiple paragraphs for the sole purpose of formatting purposes. For example:

Home About Services Contact

In the above example, each navigation element is wrapped in an (list item) tag, which is nested within the (unordered list) tag. The (anchor) tag is used to create clickable links. To style the horizontal navigation, CSS can be used to define the appearance of the navigation elements and their behavior when interacted with. This can include properties like font size, colors, padding, margins, and hover effects. Horizontal navigation is a popular choice for websites and applications with a limited number of sections or pages to navigate. It offers a clean and intuitive way for users to explore different sections, easily switch between pages, and maintain a consistent user experience. In conclusion, horizontal navigation is a UI pattern that arranges navigation elements horizontally, typically using HTML and CSS, to provide users with easy access to different sections or pages within a website or application. It is a common and effective way to enhance usability and improve the overall user experience.

## Hotel Search And Booking

A hotel search and booking UI pattern refers to a set of design elements and interactive components that allow users to easily search for and book hotels online. It is most commonly used in websites or mobile applications that provide booking services for accommodation.

The design system for a hotel search and booking UI pattern typically includes a range of features and functionalities that enhance the user experience and streamline the booking process. These may include:

1. Search functionality: A search bar or form where users can enter their desired destination, check-in and check-out dates, and other parameters such as the number of guests. The system should provide relevant suggestions as users type, making it easier for them to find their desired location.

2. Filters and sorting options: Users often have specific preferences when looking for a hotel, such as price range, star rating, amenities, or location. The design system should offer filters and sorting options that allow users to refine their search results according to their preferences.

3. Hotel listings: The system should display a list of hotels that match the user's search criteria, with relevant information such as the hotel name, location, price, star rating, and user reviews. Each listing should have a clear call-to-action button that allows users to view more details or proceed with the booking process.

4. Booking process: Once a user selects a hotel, the design system should guide them through the booking process. This may include a step-by-step form where users can enter their personal and payment information, as well as options for adding extras or selecting room types. The system should provide clear instructions and feedback to ensure a smooth booking experience.

Overall, a well-designed hotel search and booking UI pattern should prioritize simplicity, ease of use, and visual clarity. It should provide users with all the necessary information and functionalities they need to make an informed decision and complete their booking without unnecessary complications or confusion.

## Hover Effects

Hover effects refer to the visual changes that occur when a user hovers over an element on a webpage. They are widely used in UI patterns and design systems to enhance the user experience, provide feedback, and add interactivity to the interface. Hover effects play a significant role in improving the usability and intuitiveness of an application. By highlighting interactive elements, they help users understand which elements are clickable or interactive. This feedback fosters a sense of control and engagement while navigating through a website or application. These effects are commonly applied to various UI components such as buttons, links, navigation menus, images, and cards. When a user hovers over any of these elements, the hover effect triggers a change in appearance. This change can take several forms, including color shifts, background changes, animation, or the display of additional information. By visually differentiating the element, hover effects provide users with clear indications of the available actions or the interactive nature of the element. Hover effects also allow designers to incorporate micro-interactions, which are small, subtle animations triggered by user actions. These animations can convey meaningful information or provide a delightful experience for users. For example, when hovering over a button, it may slightly scale up, change color, or display a tooltip – providing instant feedback to the user. Design systems often include pre-defined hover effects as part of their component library. This ensures consistency in the user interface and simplifies the design process by providing ready-to-use styles and animations. Designers and developers can effortlessly apply these predefined hover effects to their UI elements, saving time and effort. In summary, hover effects are essential UI patterns that enhance user experience by providing visual feedback and interactivity. They help users navigate and interact with an interface by indicating clickable or interactive elements. Design systems often offer pre-defined hover effects to ensure consistency and efficiency in the design process.>

## Icon Fonts

Icon Fonts are a popular method of incorporating icons into user interfaces, often used within the context of UI patterns and design systems. They are a collection of scalable vector icons that are converted into font files. These icons can be easily accessed and displayed using a specific HTML character code or CSS class. Using Icon Fonts in UI patterns and design systems offers several advantages. Firstly, they are highly customizable, as they can be resized, colored, and styled with CSS. This allows designers to easily match the icons with the overall aesthetics of the user interface. Secondly, Icon Fonts are lightweight and load quickly, improving the performance of the interface. Unlike rasterized image icons, Icon Fonts are vector-based, which means they can be scaled without losing quality. Additionally, Icon Fonts are easily accessible and compatible with various devices and browsers without the need for additional image files. To use Icon Fonts, designers need to include the required font files in the project and link them in the CSS or HTML. Once the font files are imported, the icons can be accessed and displayed by assigning the appropriate CSS class or using the HTML character code associated with each icon. This makes it easy to add, remove, or modify icons throughout the design system, allowing for consistent icon usage across different UI patterns. In terms of design systems, Icon Fonts are essential for creating a cohesive and unified visual language. By using a consistent set of icons, designers can establish recognizable patterns and improve overall usability. They also contribute to the scalability and maintainability of the design system, as icons can be easily updated or replaced without affecting the layout or structure of the user interface. Additionally, using Icon Fonts encourages reusability, as the same set of icons can be applied across different projects or platforms. In conclusion, Icon Fonts are a versatile and efficient solution for incorporating icons into UI patterns and design systems. Their flexibility, performance, and accessibility make them a popular choice among designers. By utilizing Icon Fonts, designers can create visually appealing interfaces while maintaining consistency and scalability within their design systems.

## Image Annotation

Image annotation refers to the process of adding metadata or additional information to an image. In the context of UI patterns and design systems, image annotation is a technique used to enhance the user experience by providing relevant and descriptive information about an image. One common use case for image annotation is in e-commerce websites, where product images are annotated with details such as price, brand, and availability. This helps users make informed decisions when browsing through products. Another use case is in image galleries or photo sharing platforms, where annotations can be used to provide context or descriptions for the images. For example, in a travel photo gallery, annotations can be used to indicate the location, date, and other details about the photos. Annotations can also be used to highlight specific areas or features within an image. This is commonly seen in educational or scientific applications, where images are annotated to draw attention to important details or to provide explanations. In terms of UI patterns, there are various ways to implement image annotation. One common approach is to display the annotations as tooltips or pop-ups when the user hovers over or clicks on the image. This allows the user to easily access the additional information without cluttering the interface. Another pattern is to display annotations as captions or labels below or beside the image. This is particularly useful when the annotations are short and concise, as it provides a quick overview of the image's content. When implementing image annotation as part of a design system, it is important to consider consistency and usability. The style and placement of annotations should be consistent across the system to ensure a cohesive and intuitive user experience. In conclusion, image annotation is a technique used to enrich the user experience by providing additional information or context to images. This can be achieved through tooltips, captions, or labels, and is commonly used in e-commerce, photo sharing, and educational applications.

## Image Gallery Carousel

A Image Gallery Carousel is a common UI pattern and design system used to display multiple images in a carousel-like format, allowing users to easily navigate and view each image. It is often implemented in websites or mobile applications to showcase a collection of images or photos, providing an interactive and immersive experience for the users. The Image Gallery Carousel typically consists of a central viewport or display area, surrounded by navigation elements such as arrows or dots. These navigation elements enable users to scroll through the images in a sequential or random order. The central viewport shows the current image being viewed, while the navigation elements indicate the total number of images and the current position within the carousel. This UI pattern is designed to enhance the overall user experience by providing an intuitive and visually appealing way to browse through a set of images. Users can simply click or tap on the navigation elements, such as the arrows or dots, to switch between images. The navigation elements also often include additional features, such as hover effects or tooltips, to provide more context or information about each image. Furthermore, the Image Gallery Carousel can incorporate various design elements and animations to create a dynamic and engaging user interface. For example, when transitioning between images, a smooth slide or fade animation can be applied to provide a seamless and visually pleasing experience. Additionally, the carousel can support responsive design, adapting its layout and behavior to different screen sizes and devices, ensuring optimal usability across various platforms. Implementing an Image Gallery Carousel using HTML involves structuring the markup appropriately and utilizing CSS or JavaScript to add functionality and interactivity. HTML elements such as `` tags can be used to create the central viewport and navigation elements, while CSS can be applied to customize the appearance and layout. JavaScript can be used to handle user interactions and enable the scrolling or switching of images within the carousel. In conclusion, the Image Gallery Carousel is a popular UI pattern and design system that offers an intuitive and visually pleasing way to display a collection of images. By incorporating interactive navigation elements and visually appealing animations, it enhances the user experience and allows for seamless browsing and exploration of the images.

## Image Recognition

Image Recognition in the context of UI patterns and design systems refers to the ability of a system or application to automatically identify and categorize images based on their visual content or features.

Image Recognition is a technology that utilizes computer vision and machine learning algorithms to analyze and interpret the visual elements of an image. By extracting features such as colors, shapes, patterns, and textures from an image, the system can compare these features with a pre-trained database or model to determine the most relevant category or label for the image.

## Image Sliders

Image sliders are a commonly used UI pattern in web design that allow users to view multiple images or content pieces in a single component. They are an effective way to display a collection of images or highlight specific content within a given space on a webpage. Image sliders typically consist of a horizontal or vertical sequence of images or content, with only one image or piece of content displayed at a time. They often include navigation controls, such as arrows or dots, that allow users to manually move through the images or content pieces. Some image sliders also include autoplay functionality, where the images or content automatically transition at a preset interval. These components are popular because they provide a visually engaging and space-efficient way to showcase images or content. They are commonly used in photography portfolios, e-commerce product showcases, news articles, and other scenarios where visual representation is important. When designing an image slider, it is crucial to consider usability and user experience. The navigation controls should be intuitive and accessible, allowing users to easily move through the images or content. It is important to ensure that the images or content are displayed clearly and at an appropriate size for the given space. Additionally, the transition between images should be smooth to avoid jarring user experiences. In terms of code implementation, image sliders can be built using HTML, CSS, and JavaScript. HTML provides the structure for the slider, CSS allows for customization and styling, and JavaScript handles the functionality, such as the transition between images and navigation controls. In conclusion, image sliders are a versatile and visually appealing UI pattern that efficiently display multiple images or content pieces within a confined space. They are widely used in web design and can greatly enhance the user experience when implemented effectively.>

## Image Uploading And Cropping

Image Uploading and Cropping is a UI pattern and design system that allows users to upload an image and perform cropping operations on it. This functionality is commonly used in applications that require users to upload and edit images, such as social media platforms, content management systems, and online image editors. The process of image uploading and cropping typically involves multiple steps. First, users are provided with a user-friendly interface to upload an image from their local device. This interface may include a browse button or drag-and-drop functionality to simplify the image selection process. Once an image is uploaded, users are then presented with an interface to crop the image. This interface usually includes a resizable and draggable cropping tool, such as a rectangular or circular frame, that allows users to select the desired portion of the image. This cropping tool is typically overlaid on top of the image, providing a visual representation of the cropped area. Additionally, the image cropping interface may include features such as zooming in and out, rotating the image, and maintaining aspect ratio to give users more control over the cropping process. These features enhance user experience by allowing them to accurately crop the image according to their requirements. After the cropping process is complete, users are given the option to preview the cropped image before confirming their selection. This preview helps users ensure that the cropped image meets their expectations and desired dimensions. From a design system perspective, image uploading and cropping components should be visually consistent with the overall look and feel of the application. This includes adhering to color schemes, typography, and other design guidelines defined by the design system. Consistency across the UI patterns and components within a design system helps maintain a cohesive and professional user experience. In summary, image uploading and cropping is a UI pattern and design system that allows users to upload images and perform cropping operations. It involves multiple steps, including image selection, resizing and dragging the cropping tool, and previewing the cropped image. Consistency with the design system is important to ensure visual harmony throughout the application.

## Image Zoom

The image zoom UI pattern refers to an interactive functionality that allows users to magnify and inspect details of an image. It is commonly used in e-commerce websites, digital galleries, and product catalogs where users need to closely examine specific parts of an image. The image zoom feature enhances the user experience by providing a more detailed view of the image without the need for downloading or opening the image in a separate window. It allows users to examine the image at a higher resolution, enabling them to see intricate details, textures, or fine prints that may not be visible at standard sizes. Typically, image zoom is activated by hovering or clicking on the image, triggering an overlay or an expanded view of the image. The zoomed-in image may appear in a modal window or an enlarged section within the page layout. Users can navigate within the zoomed view by moving their mouse or using touch gestures to pan and focus on different areas of the image. To ensure a seamless zoom experience, designers must pay attention to the quality of the zoomed image. It is essential to provide a high-resolution version of the image or use a progressive loading technique to ensure that the zoomed image appears quickly and in detail. Additionally, designers should consider the performance impact of large images and optimize them accordingly. When implementing image zoom, designers should also consider accessibility guidelines. It is crucial to provide alternative methods for users who may not be able to interact with the zoom feature through mouse or touch gestures. Keyboard support or dedicated controls should be provided to ensure equal access for users of assistive technologies. In conclusion, the image zoom UI pattern is a valuable tool for enhancing the user experience when examining images in more detail. By providing a closer look at an image, users can make more informed decisions, appreciate visual details, and gain confidence in their purchasing choices>

## Immersive Full-Screen Experience

An immersive full-screen experience in the context of UI patterns and design systems refers to a user interface design approach that creates a visually engaging and captivating experience by utilizing the entire screen real estate without any distractions or elements cluttering the interface.

This design pattern aims to deeply immerse users in the content or task at hand by filling the entire screen with the main focus, whether it be an image, video, interactive elements, or other visual elements. It eliminates any unnecessary or extraneous components in the user interface, providing users with a seamless and uninterrupted experience.

## In-App Communities

An in-app community refers to a user interface pattern and design system that facilitates communication, collaboration, and engagement between users within an application. It provides a centralized space where users can interact, share knowledge, and support each other within the app's ecosystem.

The main purpose of an in-app community is to foster a sense of belonging and encourage users to actively participate and contribute to the community. It aims to enhance the overall user experience by providing a platform for users to connect with each other, exchange ideas, ask questions, and provide feedback or support.

## In-App Messages

In-App Messages are a type of user interface (UI) pattern commonly used in design systems to provide real-time communication and important updates to users within a mobile application or web platform. These messages are typically displayed as small pop-up windows or banners that appear within the app's interface. In-App Messages serve as a means of directly interacting with users within the context of the application they are using. They are designed to catch the user's attention and deliver time-sensitive or critical information without interrupting their current workflow. These messages can be used to notify users about new features, updates, promotions, or to deliver personalized content. The design and presentation of In-App Messages are crucial in order to effectively communicate the intended message while maintaining a seamless user experience. The messages should be visually distinct from the rest of the UI to draw the user's attention, but should also blend in harmoniously with the overall design language of the application. Consistency in formatting, typography, and color is essential to ensure a cohesive look and feel. Considering the limited space available within the app's interface, it is important to keep the content of In-App Messages concise and focused. The message should be clear, easy to understand, and actionable. It is recommended to use concise language, avoid jargon, and use plain language that is familiar to the target audience. In terms of interaction design, In-App Messages should provide an option for the user to dismiss or close the message. This allows users to stay in control of their experience and continue using the application without any interruption. The method of dismissal can vary depending on the design, such as a close button or a swipe gesture. However, it is important to ensure that the dismissal action is easy to find and intuitive for users. Additionally, In-App Messages can be enhanced with supporting visual elements such as icons, images, or illustrations to help convey the message or capture the user's attention. These visual enhancements should be used judiciously and in a way that does not overpower the main content or distract the user from the primary task at hand. In conclusion, In-App Messages are an effective UI pattern used in design systems to deliver important information to users within a mobile application or web platform. They serve as a means of real-time communication and rely on concise content, visually distinct design, and intuitive dismissal actions to maintain a seamless user experience.>

## In-Place Editing

In-Place Editing is a UI pattern and design system that allows users to edit content directly within the context of a web page, without needing to navigate to a separate editing interface or page. It provides a seamless, intuitive, and efficient way for users to make changes to text, images, or other types of content without disrupting their workflow or requiring complex interactions.

With In-Place Editing, users can simply click or interact with the content they want to edit, and editable fields or controls become visible, allowing them to input or modify the desired information. This pattern saves users time and reduces cognitive load by eliminating the need to switch between different screens or contexts.

## Inclusive Design

Inclusive Design, in the context of UI patterns and design systems, encompasses designing and creating interfaces that are accessible and usable by a diverse range of users. It focuses on ensuring that all users, regardless of their abilities or disabilities, can interact with and benefit from the digital products or services.

UI patterns are commonly used to provide consistency and familiarity across different components and interactions within a digital interface. When designing UI patterns with an inclusive design approach, it is essential to consider the diverse needs and preferences of all users. This involves recognizing potential barriers and eliminating them through thoughtful design choices and accessible interaction patterns.

## Infinite Scroll With Load More Button

Infinite Scroll with Load More Button is a UI pattern for displaying large amounts of content in a user-friendly and efficient way. It combines the benefits of infinite scrolling and a load more button to provide a seamless and intuitive browsing experience. In this UI pattern, instead of traditional pagination, the content is loaded dynamically as the user scrolls down the page. As the user reaches the end of the current content, more content is loaded below, creating an infinite scrolling effect. This eliminates the need for manual navigation through numbered pages, allowing users to continuously browse without interruption. To enhance usability and control, a load more button is incorporated within the infinite scrolling functionality. This button appears after a certain amount of content is displayed, allowing users to manually trigger the loading of additional content. It acts as a safeguard against excessive scrolling, giving users the option to load more content at their own pace. By using this UI pattern, the design system ensures a smooth and optimal user experience. The infinite scrolling feature eliminates the need for pagination, reducing clutter and simplifying the interface. It enables users to effortlessly explore large collections of content without having to manually click through multiple pages. The load more button introduces an element of control, giving users the ability to manage the pace at which they consume the content. This feature is particularly useful when dealing with lengthy articles, image galleries, or feeds with continuous updates. Users can scroll through the existing content and decide when they want to load more, preventing the feeling of being overwhelmed by an endless scroll. Overall, Infinite Scroll with Load More Button is a UI pattern that seamlessly combines infinite scrolling and manual content loading. It enables users to browse through a large amount of content in a fluid manner, while retaining control over the pace at which they load new content. This UI pattern enhances the design system's usability and creates a more engaging and efficient browsing experience for users. In HTML format:

Infinite Scroll with Load More Button is a UI pattern for displaying large amounts of content in a user-friendly and efficient way.

By using this UI pattern, the design system ensures a smooth and optimal user experience. The infinite scrolling feature eliminates the need for pagination, reducing clutter and simplifying the interface.

## Infinite Scroll

Infinite Scroll is a UI pattern and design system that allows users to continuously load content as they scroll down a web page without the need for pagination or clicking on a "load more" button. It is designed to provide a seamless and uninterrupted browsing experience. When implementing Infinite Scroll, the web page is initially loaded with a predetermined set of content. As the user scrolls down, more content is dynamically fetched and appended to the existing content, creating a smooth scrolling experience. This process is often powered by JavaScript and Ajax, enabling the automatic loading of new content without requiring a page refresh. Infinite Scroll is particularly popular in scenarios where content is continuously generated, such as social media feeds, news articles, or image galleries. It allows users to effortlessly explore a large amount of content without the interruption of having to navigate to a new page or manually load more content. From a design perspective, Infinite Scroll requires careful consideration to ensure a cohesive and user-friendly experience. It is important to provide clear visual cues or feedback, such as a loading spinner or a "loading more" message, to indicate that new content is being fetched. Additionally, it is essential to implement Lazy Loading techniques to optimize performance and prevent unnecessarily loading all content at once. However, it is also crucial to note the potential drawbacks of Infinite Scroll. Since content is constantly loading, users may find it challenging to reach specific items or refer back to previous content. Therefore, it is recommended to include additional navigation or filtering options to mitigate these limitations. In conclusion, Infinite Scroll is a UI pattern and design system that enables dynamic loading of content as users scroll down a web page. It offers a seamless browsing experience and is commonly used in scenarios where content is continuously generated. While it enhances usability, it requires thoughtful implementation and consideration of navigational aids to ensure a positive user experience.

## Insurance Claim Form

A UI pattern is a recurring design solution that can be used to solve a specific user interface problem or provide a certain user experience. It serves as a guide for designers to follow when creating interfaces, ensuring consistency and familiarity for users. In the context of insurance claim forms, a UI pattern refers to the specific design and layout used to capture relevant information from users when filing an insurance claim. This form aims to streamline the process and make it easy for users to provide the necessary details to initiate their claim. A design system, on the other hand, is a comprehensive set of guidelines, components, and resources that are used to create consistent and cohesive user interfaces across different applications or platforms. It defines the overall look and feel, as well as the interaction patterns and visual elements, ensuring a unified and seamless user experience. When designing an insurance claim form, it is important to consider the specific needs and expectations of users in this context. The form should be intuitive and structured in a logical manner, allowing users to easily understand what information is required and how to provide it. The use of well-organized sections and clear labels can help users navigate the form effortlessly. Breaking down the form into smaller subsections, such as personal information, accident details, and supporting documents, can make it less overwhelming and more manageable. Visual cues, such as icons or color coding, can be used to highlight required fields or indicate any errors in the form. Providing helpful hints or tooltips can also assist users in completing the form correctly. Furthermore, incorporating validation checks in real-time can prevent users from submitting incomplete or inaccurate information. This can save users time and frustration by identifying and resolving errors before the form is submitted. Overall, a well-designed insurance claim form follows established UI patterns and adheres to the guidelines set by a design system. It takes into consideration the needs and expectations of users, providing a seamless and efficient experience for submitting insurance claims.

UI patterns for insurance claim forms ensure consistency and familiarity for users, guiding designers in solving design problems.

A design system provides guidelines, components, and resources for creating consistent and cohesive user interfaces, resulting in a unified experience.

## Interactive Buttons In Chat

Interactive buttons in chat refer to a UI pattern and design system that allows users to engage with the chat interface by interacting with buttons that are embedded within the chat conversation. These buttons are typically designed to provide users with various options or actions that they can select or trigger directly from the chat window, enhancing the user experience and making the conversation more intuitive and engaging. HTML provides several ways to create interactive buttons in chat. One common approach is to use the <button> element, which represents a clickable button. The inner text of the <button> element represents the label that appears on the button. By including the necessary event handlers or JavaScript functions, developers can define the desired behavior when the button is clicked. For example, consider a chatbot that offers users a set of predefined options to choose from. Each option is presented as a button within the chat conversation. To implement this using pure HTML, we can use the following code:

Hi there! How can I assist you today? Please select one of the following options:

Option 1</button> Option 2</button> Option 3</button>

In this example, we have a chat message followed by three buttons. Each button is associated with an onclick event that triggers a JavaScript function called optionSelected(), passing the selected option as a parameter. The developer can define the optionSelected() function to handle the user's selection and perform the appropriate action within the chat. By utilizing interactive buttons in chat, designers and developers can create more dynamic and interactive chat experiences. These buttons empower users to easily select options, trigger actions, or navigate through the conversation without having to rely solely on typed commands. The use of interactive buttons not only enhances the usability of the chat interface but also enables more efficient interactions, reducing the cognitive load on users and providing a more intuitive way to engage with the chatbot or application.></button></button>

## Interactive Charts And Graphs

An interactive chart or graph is a visual representation of data that allows users to explore and analyze information in a dynamic and engaging way. It is a user interface (UI) pattern commonly used in design systems to present complex datasets in a clear and concise manner. 1. The Purpose:

The primary purpose of interactive charts and graphs is to present data in a visually appealing and interactive format. By utilizing visual elements such as bars, lines, and pie slices, these UI patterns effectively convey complex information in a digestible and intuitive manner. The interactive nature of these charts and graphs allows users to manipulate and explore the data, enabling them to gain insights and make data-driven decisions. 2. The Functionality:

Interactive charts and graphs offer various functionalities that enhance the user experience and facilitate data analysis. Users can interact with the charts and graphs by hovering over data points to reveal specific values, clicking on elements to display additional information, and zooming or panning to focus on specific areas. These functionalities allow users to explore the data at different levels of granularity, enabling them to discern patterns, trends, and outliers. Additionally, interactive charts and graphs often provide options for customization and personalization. Users can modify the displayed data by selecting different variables or filtering specific criteria, enabling them to tailor the visualizations to their specific needs. This level of flexibility empowers users to manipulate the data to support their analysis and decision-making processes effectively. In conclusion, interactive charts and graphs are valuable UI patterns in design systems that enable the effective visualization and analysis of complex datasets. Through their visually appealing and interactive nature, these UI patterns facilitate data exploration and empower users to derive insights and make data-driven decisions.>

## Interactive Data Visualizations

Interactive Data Visualizations refer to the graphical representations of data that are designed to be interactive and enable users to explore and analyze the information more effectively. In the context of UI patterns and design systems, interactive data visualizations provide a user interface through which users can interact with and make sense of complex data sets. These visualizations typically involve the use of various charts, graphs, maps, and other visual elements to present data in a visually appealing and understandable way. They allow users to explore the data by zooming, panning, filtering, and interacting with the visual components, thereby enabling them to gain insights, identify patterns, and make informed decisions based on the information presented. UI patterns and design systems play a crucial role in the development of interactive data visualizations. They provide a set of standardized design guidelines, components, and patterns that ensure consistency, usability, and visual coherence across the visualizations. Moreover, they help in creating a seamless user experience by guiding the interactions and providing familiar and intuitive controls to manipulate the visual elements. The use of a design system enables designers and developers to create interactive data visualizations that are not only visually pleasing but also functional and user-friendly. By adhering to the design principles and patterns established in the system, they ensure that the visualizations are consistent with the overall user interface and maintain a coherent visual language. Furthermore, design systems help in streamlining the design and development process by providing reusable components and guidelines for creating interactive elements such as tooltips, legends, sliders, and filters. This not only saves time and effort but also ensures that these interactive elements are consistent in terms of appearance and behavior across different visualizations. In summary, interactive data visualizations are graphical representations of data that enable users to explore and analyze information through interactive user interfaces. UI patterns and design systems play a crucial role in ensuring that these visualizations are visually appealing, consistent, and user-friendly. By providing standardized guidelines, components, and patterns, they help in creating seamless user experiences and streamlining the design and development process of interactive data visualizations.

## Interactive In-App Quizzes

Interactive In-app Quizzes refer to a user interface pattern implemented within a design system that allows users to participate in quizzes or surveys directly within a mobile or web application. These quizzes are designed to engage users, collect information, and provide a fun and interactive experience within the app. The design of interactive in-app quizzes typically follows a consistent set of UI patterns and principles defined by the design system. These patterns ensure that the quizzes are visually appealing, easy to navigate, and provide a seamless user experience. The quizzes are usually presented in a structured format with clear instructions, questions, and possible answer choices that users can select. One common design pattern for interactive in-app quizzes is the use of multiple-choice questions. Users are provided with a set of answer choices, and they can select the appropriate option that best fits their response. This pattern allows for quick and easy interaction, and it works well for quizzes with objective questions. Another design pattern is the use of open-ended questions, where users can provide their own answers in text format. This pattern adds an element of user-generated content and allows for more personalized responses. The design system typically includes guidelines on how to display and handle these types of questions. To enhance the user experience, interactive in-app quizzes may also incorporate visual elements such as images, icons, or progress indicators. These visual cues help users understand their progress within the quiz and provide feedback on their answers. Interactive in-app quizzes also adhere to accessibility guidelines defined by the design system. This ensures that all users, regardless of their abilities, can engage with the quizzes effectively. Accessibility considerations may involve providing alternative text for images, using appropriate color contrast, and supporting keyboard navigation. In conclusion, interactive in-app quizzes are a design pattern within a design system that allows users to participate in quizzes directly within a mobile or web application. These quizzes follow consistent UI patterns, provide a visually appealing and engaging experience, and adhere to accessibility guidelines. By integrating interactive quizzes into an app, developers can enhance user engagement, collect valuable data, and create a more interactive and enjoyable user experience.

Interactive In-app Quizzes are a user interface pattern in a design system that allows users to participate in quizzes or surveys directly within the application. The quizzes follow consistent UI patterns, such as multiple-choice or open-ended questions, to provide an engaging and interactive experience. Visual elements and accessibility guidelines are also considered to enhance the user experience and ensure inclusivity.

## Interactive Infographics

Interactive infographics are user interface patterns and design systems that combine visual elements with interactive functionality to convey complex information in a clear and engaging manner. These infographics employ user interaction to enhance comprehension and create a more immersive and dynamic experience for the user. Using interactive elements such as hover

105

effects, clickable areas, and animations, interactive infographics enable users to explore the data or content at their own pace and in a non-linear fashion. This allows users to delve deeper into specific aspects of the information or navigate through different sections based on their interests or needs. By providing this level of interactivity, interactive infographics empower users to uncover insights and understand complex concepts more effectively. In terms of design systems, interactive infographics adhere to established guidelines and best practices to ensure consistency and usability. They utilize a cohesive visual language with clear hierarchies, typography, and color schemes to create a visually appealing and cohesive user interface. By applying these design principles consistently across various interactive elements and screens, interactive infographics enhance the overall user experience and improve user engagement. When designing interactive infographics, designers need to consider both the visual presentation and the interactive functionality. The visual elements should be visually compelling and convey the information in a clear and concise manner, using appropriate charts, graphs, and illustrations to support the content. The interactive functionality should be intuitive and easy to use, allowing users to interact with the infographic seamlessly. In summary, interactive infographics are user interface patterns and design systems that combine visual elements with interactive functionality to create engaging and informative experiences. They enable users to explore and understand complex information effectively by providing interactive elements and adhering to established design systems. By leveraging the power of interactivity, interactive infographics empower users to interact with the data or content at their own pace and uncover insights in a visually compelling manner.

## Interactive Learning Modules

Interactive Learning Modules are self-contained, interactive educational components designed to facilitate the acquisition of knowledge or skills in a user-friendly interface. These modules are commonly incorporated into UI patterns and design systems to enhance the learning experience and promote effective knowledge transfer. In the context of UI patterns, Interactive Learning Modules serve as a means to engage users and encourage active participation. They typically consist of various multimedia elements, such as videos, images, diagrams, and interactive quizzes or exercises, which facilitate the exploration of educational content. By leveraging these modules, designers can create immersive and dynamic learning experiences that cater to a wide range of user preferences and learning styles. Interactive Learning Modules are often designed in a modular manner, enabling easy integration into different UI patterns and design systems. This modular approach ensures consistency and scalability by allowing developers to reuse and adapt these educational components across various interfaces. By adhering to established design guidelines and system-wide standards, designers can maintain visual coherence and ensure a seamless user experience throughout their applications. Furthermore, Interactive Learning Modules contribute to the construction of comprehensive design systems. These systems provide a unified set of principles, guidelines, and reusable components that enable designers to build cohesive and consistent applications. By including interactive learning components within the design system, organizations can foster a culture of continuous learning and knowledge sharing. This approach not only empowers users to acquire new skills but also promotes the adoption and consistent application of design principles across different projects and teams. In conclusion, Interactive Learning Modules are valuable components within UI patterns and design systems, as they facilitate engaging educational experiences, promote knowledge transfer, and contribute to the construction of comprehensive design systems. Their modular nature allows for easy integration and reuse, while adhering to established visual guidelines ensures a cohesive user experience. By incorporating Interactive Learning Modules into their applications, designers can create rich and interactive educational experiences, driving user engagement and fostering continuous learning.

## Interactive Maps With Filters

Interactive Maps with Filters refer to a UI pattern and design system that allows users to explore and navigate maps while applying various filters to refine the displayed information. This pattern maximizes the usability and effectiveness of maps by providing users with the ability to interact with the data and customize their view based on their preferences or specific needs. The main feature of Interactive Maps with Filters is the integration of filter options and controls directly within the map interface. These filters enable users to selectively display or hide specific elements or categories of information on the map. They can include options such as toggling on/off different layers, specifying the time frame or date range, and applying additional criteria like location, type, or rating. The design system for Interactive Maps with Filters should prioritize simplicity, intuitiveness, and accessibility. It should allow users to easily understand and interact with the filters, ensuring a seamless user experience. Clear labeling, visual cues, and consistent design elements should be employed to guide users in effectively navigating and utilizing the available filters. When implementing Interactive Maps with Filters in HTML, it is important to structure the interface in a logical and organized manner. The filters should be prominently displayed and easily accessible, either as a dedicated panel, overlay, or collapsible menu. Grouping related filters together and utilizing headings or section labels can help users quickly identify and understand the purpose of each filter option. Additionally, interactive elements such as checkboxes, sliders, dropdown menus, or search boxes can be used to allow users to interact with and apply the desired filters. These elements should have clear and concise labels to indicate their function and the effects they will have on the displayed map data. Overall, Interactive Maps with Filters provide users with a powerful tool to explore and analyze data visually. By incorporating user-friendly filters directly within the map interface, this UI pattern and design system enhances the usability and flexibility of maps, allowing users to customize their experience and extract relevant information.>

## Interactive Maps

Interactive Maps refer to a user interface pattern and design system that allows users to navigate and explore geographic data in a visual and interactive way. It encompasses a wide range of functions and features that enhance the user's ability to interact with and understand the underlying map data. The main purpose of an interactive map is to provide users with a visual representation of geographic information in a way that is intuitive and easy to comprehend. By displaying data in a map format, users can quickly grasp the spatial relationships and patterns that exist within the data. This can be particularly useful for analyzing data that is geographically distributed, such as population demographics, traffic patterns, or the spread of diseases. One key aspect of interactive maps is their ability to allow users to interact directly with the map itself. This includes the ability to zoom in and out, pan across the map, and interact with individual map features or markers. These interactions can be performed using a variety of input methods, such as mouse clicks, touch gestures, or keyboard controls. By enabling users to interact with the map, they can explore and analyze the data in a more personalized and dynamic manner. In addition to basic navigation and interaction, interactive maps often include a range of additional features to enhance the user experience. These may include the ability to search for specific locations or addresses, overlay different layers of data onto the map, or display additional information when clicking on specific map features. These features can help users to gain deeper insights into the data and customize the map to suit their specific needs. From a design standpoint, interactive maps are typically designed to be visually appealing, with clear and legible map features and intuitive user interface controls. The use of color, typography, and visual hierarchy can help to guide the user's attention and enhance the overall user experience. Design systems are often utilized to ensure consistency and cohesion across different interactive map components and elements. Overall, interactive maps provide a powerful tool for visualizing and exploring geographic data. By combining intuitive navigation, interactive features, and thoughtful design, they can help users to gain valuable insights and make informed decisions based on spatial information.

## Interactive Mood Boards

Interactive Mood Boards are a UI pattern and design system commonly used in the field of user interface design. They provide a platform for designers to collect and organize visual inspiration, as well as to communicate and collaborate on design concepts with team members and clients.

As a UI pattern, Interactive Mood Boards serve as a framework for designers to showcase their creative ideas and gather feedback from stakeholders. They are visual representations of various design elements such as color palettes, typography, imagery, and user interface components. By presenting these elements in a cohesive manner, designers can effectively communicate their vision and design direction.

## Interactive Polls And Surveys

Interactive Polls and Surveys are user interface components designed to gather data and opinions from users through a series of questions and response options. These components are commonly used in websites and applications to engage users and collect valuable insights. In the context of UI patterns and design systems, Interactive Polls and Surveys follow specific guidelines to ensure consistency and usability. These components typically consist of various input elements, such as radio buttons, checkboxes, and text fields, allowing users to select their responses or provide open-ended answers. When designing Interactive Polls and Surveys, it is essential to consider the overall layout and visual hierarchy of the questions and response options. Proper spacing, font choice, and color differentiation can make it easy for users to understand and navigate the survey. Additionally, designers should take into account the flow and logic of the survey. Depending on the purpose of the survey, questions may need to be ordered in a specific sequence or have conditional logic based on previous responses. Validation is another crucial aspect of Interactive Polls and Surveys. It is important to ensure that users provide valid and meaningful responses. Input validation can be implemented through real-time error messages or by preventing users from submitting the survey until all required fields are completed. To increase user engagement and completion rates, Interactive Polls and Surveys can incorporate progress indicators, such as step numbers or a progress bar, to provide users with a sense of progress and encourage them to continue. In terms of accessibility, designers must ensure that Interactive Polls and Surveys are usable by everyone, including individuals with disabilities. This can be achieved by providing alternative text labels for images, using proper color contrast, and ensuring keyboard accessibility for users who cannot utilize a mouse. Overall, Interactive Polls and Surveys play a significant role in gathering user feedback and data. When designed with a clear visual hierarchy, logical flow, proper validation, and accessibility in mind, these components can provide valuable insights to businesses while offering a seamless and engaging user experience.>

## Interactive Product Catalogs

Interactive Product Catalogs are a type of user interface pattern and design system that provides users with a visually appealing and intuitive way to browse and filter through a collection of products or services. It is an effective way to showcase a wide range of offerings and facilitate decision-making for users. In an Interactive Product Catalog, the user is presented with a well-organized and structured layout that allows for easy navigation and exploration. The main goal of this design pattern is to enhance the user experience by providing them with a seamless browsing experience and empowering them to find the products they are looking for quickly and effortlessly. One of the key features of an Interactive Product Catalog is the ability for users to interact with the catalog through various filters and sorting options. Users can refine their search by applying filters based on price, category, brand, size, color, and other relevant attributes. This allows users to narrow down their choices and focus on the products that meet their specific criteria. Another important aspect of an Interactive Product Catalog is the rich visual representation of the products. Each product listing is accompanied by high-quality images, detailed descriptions, and additional information such as availability, ratings, and reviews. This helps users to make informed decisions by providing them with a comprehensive view of the product. The design system of an Interactive Product Catalog should be consistent and cohesive across all pages and elements. It should incorporate a visually pleasing color scheme, typography, and layout that align with the brand identity. Clear and concise labels and navigation elements should be used to guide users through the catalog and help them locate the desired products. Overall, Interactive Product Catalogs are a valuable tool for businesses to showcase their products or services in an engaging and user-friendly manner. By incorporating intuitive navigation, interactive filtering options, and visually appealing product presentations, businesses can effectively enhance the user experience and drive conversions. Interactive Product Catalogs provide an immersive and informative browsing experience, empowering users to explore and find the products they desire.

## Interactive Prototyping

Interactive prototyping refers to the process of creating a dynamic and functional representation of a user interface (UI) pattern or design system. It involves creating a digital simulation that allows users to interact with different components and elements of the UI, providing them with a realistic experience of how the final product will look and behave.

To create an interactive prototype, designers often use specialized prototyping tools that allow them to define and link different UI elements together, adding interactive behaviors and animations. These tools make it easy for designers to demonstrate the flow of user interactions, simulate user input, and show how the UI elements respond to those interactions.

## Interactive Push Notifications

Interactive push notifications are a type of user interface pattern and design system that allow for real-time, interactive communication between a digital platform and its users. These notifications are typically delivered to the user's device, such as a smartphone or computer, and can be triggered by various events or actions. Unlike traditional push notifications, which typically consist of a simple message or alert, interactive push notifications provide users with the ability to directly engage with the content or functionality being presented. This can be achieved through various interactive elements, such as buttons, sliders, or swipe gestures, which allow users to take specific actions or provide immediate feedback. The design and implementation of interactive push notifications follow certain principles to ensure a seamless and intuitive user experience. These include: 1. Clear and concise messaging: Interactive push notifications should deliver brief and focused messages that provide clear information or call-to-action. The content should be easily scannable and understandable at a glance. 2. Visual consistency: Interactive push notifications should adhere to the visual style and branding of the overall user interface and design system. This helps to maintain a cohesive user experience and reinforces the platform's identity. 3. Contextual relevance: Interactive push notifications should be relevant to the user's current context or interests. This can be achieved by leveraging user preferences, behavioral data, or previous interactions to personalize the content and ensure its relevance. 4. Responsiveness and interactivity: Interactive push notifications should be designed to respond quickly and efficiently to user interactions. The user interface elements should be intuitive and responsive, providing immediate feedback to the user's actions. Overall, interactive push notifications enhance user engagement and provide a more personalized and interactive experience. They can be used in various contexts, such as messaging apps, social media platforms, e-commerce applications, and productivity tools, to deliver timely and actionable information to the users. By leveraging the power of real-time communication and user interaction, interactive push notifications contribute to a more immersive and engaging digital experience. Interactive push notifications are a valuable tool in the digital landscape, enabling platforms to communicate with their users in a dynamic and engaging manner. Their effective use requires a user-centric approach, considering the importance of clear messaging, visual consistency, contextual relevance, and responsive interactivity.>

## Interactive Quiz Form

A UI pattern is a reusable design solution that addresses a common interaction or problem within a user interface. It provides a standardized way of presenting and interacting with information and functionality, ensuring consistency and familiarity for users across different interfaces. UI patterns are created with the goal of improving user experience by making interfaces more intuitive, efficient, and enjoyable to use. They are often based on established best practices, research findings, and user feedback. By following established patterns, designers can save time and effort, as well as leverage user familiarity with existing patterns. Design systems, on the other hand, are a collection of reusable components, guidelines, and principles that are used to create a consistent and cohesive visual language for a product or brand. They go beyond user interface patterns and encompass the entire design ecosystem, including color palettes, typography, icons, spacing, and more. A design system serves as a single source of truth for design decisions, ensuring that designers and developers work from the same set of guidelines and standards. This promotes efficiency, collaboration, and scalability, as well as helps maintain a unified and coherent visual experience across different platforms and touchpoints. In summary, UI patterns are predefined solutions for common design problems within a user interface, while design systems encompass a wider range of elements and provide a holistic approach to visual design and interaction. They both play crucial roles in creating effective and user-friendly interfaces, enhancing consistency, and improving overall user experience.

A UI pattern is a reusable design solution that addresses a common interaction or problem within a user interface. It provides a standardized way of presenting and interacting with information and functionality, ensuring consistency and familiarity for users across different interfaces.

Design systems, on the other hand, are a collection of reusable components, guidelines, and principles that are used to create a consistent and cohesive visual language for a product or brand.

## Interactive Reports

Interactive Reports are a user interface pattern and a component within a design system that allows users to explore and analyze data in a visual and interactive manner. These reports provide a convenient and efficient way for users to access and digest information, making data-driven decisions more intuitive and seamless. Through a combination of filtering, sorting, and interactive elements, interactive reports enable users to dynamically manipulate and customize data views according to their specific needs and preferences. Users can interact with the report by selecting filters, sorting columns, or drilling down into the details of specific data points. These interactions provide a sense of control and flexibility, empowering users to uncover insights and discover patterns within the data. The design of interactive reports is centered around providing a clear and organized presentation of data. The layout typically consists of a table or grid structure, where each row represents a data entry and each column represents a data attribute. The headers of the columns often include sort indicators, allowing users to easily sort the data in ascending or descending order. In addition to sorting and filtering capabilities, interactive reports may also include features such as pagination, search functionality, and the ability to export or share the report. Pagination allows users to navigate through large data sets by dividing them into manageable chunks or pages. Search functionality enables users to quickly locate specific data entries by entering keywords or criteria. Export and sharing options enable users to save or distribute the report in different file formats, such as PDF or Excel. The goal of interactive reports is to present data in a concise, organized, and visually appealing manner while allowing users to actively engage with the information. By providing users with the ability to customize and control their data views, interactive reports promote data exploration, analysis, and informed decision-making. In conclusion, interactive reports are a powerful UI pattern within a design system that enables users to dynamically interact with and explore data. Through a combination of filtering, sorting, and interactive elements, these reports empower users to uncover insights and make data-driven decisions efficiently.>

## Interactive Scenario Simulations

Interactive Scenario Simulations refer to a UI pattern that involves presenting users with a series of interactive and dynamic scenarios to simulate real-world situations and gather valuable insights. These simulations serve as an effective tool for training, testing, and learning by providing users with a realistic environment where they can make decisions, face consequences, and learn from their actions.

Designed as a part of a comprehensive design system, Interactive Scenario Simulations offer a structured approach to engage users and facilitate their decision-making process. They can be incorporated into various digital platforms such as e-learning modules, employee training programs, and product demos to enhance user experience and understanding.

## Interactive Story Maps

Interactive Story Maps are a type of user interface (UI) pattern and design system that allows users to navigate and explore content in a visual and immersive way. They are typically used to tell a story or present information in a spatial context, combining maps, images, and textual content. Story Maps can be used in various contexts, such as educational websites, travel guides, news articles, and cultural heritage projects. They provide a dynamic and engaging user experience by enabling users to interact with the content and navigate through different locations or sections of the story. In terms of UI design, Story Maps often consist of a map as the primary visual element, with markers or hotspots indicating points of interest or significant locations within the story. When users click or interact with these markers, additional information such as images, videos, or descriptive text is displayed, offering further context and enhancing the storytelling experience. To ensure a consistent and cohesive user experience, design

110

systems can be applied to Story Maps. A design system encompasses a set of guidelines, principles, and reusable components that maintain visual and interaction consistency across different parts of the application. In the context of Story Maps, a design system may include predefined map styles, standardized marker icons, and consistent typography and layout guidelines. By using a design system, developers and designers can create Story Maps more efficiently, ensuring a coherent visual language and reducing the need to reinvent UI elements. Additionally, design systems promote collaboration and facilitate the scaling of projects by providing a shared set of design assets and guidelines. In summary, Interactive Story Maps are a UI pattern and design system that enable users to explore content in a visual and immersive way. They combine maps, images, and textual content to create a dynamic and engaging user experience. Design systems can be applied to Story Maps to maintain consistency and efficiency in UI design, ensuring a cohesive and scalable project.

## Interactive Storytelling

Interactive storytelling in the context of UI patterns and design systems refers to the use of various elements and techniques to engage users in a dynamic and immersive narrative experience.

It utilizes a combination of text, visuals, animations, and user interactions to create a compelling and interactive story that unfolds in response to user actions. This approach aims to capture and maintain users' attention by offering them an engaging and personalized storytelling experience.

## Interactive Video Tutorials

Interactive Video Tutorials within the context of UI patterns and design systems can be defined as multimedia-based instructional materials that combine video content with interactive elements to deliver engaging and effective learning experiences. These tutorials are designed to provide users with step-by-step guidance and instruction on how to perform specific tasks or use specific features of a product or system. The main objective of interactive video tutorials is to enhance the learning process by providing users with a more dynamic and immersive learning experience. By incorporating interactive elements such as quizzes, assessments, and interactive hotspots, these tutorials encourage active participation and engagement from the learners, facilitating better retention and understanding of the content. In terms of UI patterns and design systems, interactive video tutorials play a crucial role in helping users understand and navigate through complex interfaces or workflows. They provide users with a visual representation of the UI patterns and demonstrate how to effectively use them in real-life scenarios. By presenting the information in a visually appealing and interactive manner, these tutorials not only make the learning process more enjoyable but also enable users to grasp the concepts and functionalities more efficiently. Moreover, interactive video tutorials also contribute to the overall consistency and coherence of a design system. They allow designers and developers to showcase the proper implementation of UI patterns and ensure that the design elements are used consistently across different platforms and devices. By providing users with access to these tutorials, design systems can promote a unified and seamless user experience across various touchpoints. In conclusion, interactive video tutorials, within the context of UI patterns and design systems, are multimedia-based instructional materials that combine video content with interactive elements to deliver engaging and effective learning experiences. They play a crucial role in helping users understand and navigate through complex interfaces, promoting consistency and coherence within a design system.

## Interactive Virtual Tours

Interactive Virtual Tours refer to a design pattern and a component within a larger UI system that enables users to explore a virtual environment or space through an interactive and immersive experience. A virtual tour typically provides users with a dynamic simulation of a physical location, such as a real estate property or a tourist attraction, by utilizing a combination of panoramic images, videos, and interactive elements. The primary goal of an interactive virtual tour is to engage users and enable them to navigate and interact with the virtual environment as if they were physically present. The interactive nature of virtual tours is achieved through various user interface elements and features. These may include hotspots, which are interactive markers placed within the virtual environment that provide additional information or actions when clicked or tapped. Users can interact with these hotspots to access detailed information about specific objects or areas, view related multimedia content, or trigger specific actions like booking a reservation or purchasing tickets. Navigation controls also play a crucial role in interactive virtual tours. Users are provided with intuitive controls to pan, zoom, and rotate the view to explore different angles and perspectives. This navigation functionality enhances the realism and sense of presence within the virtual environment, allowing users to freely move around and examine the surroundings at their own pace. In the context of UI patterns and design systems, interactive virtual tours are designed to be modular components that can be easily integrated within larger interfaces or systems. They typically adhere to established design guidelines and principles, ensuring consistency and usability across different platforms and devices. This adherence to design standards facilitates seamless integration and reduces the cognitive load on users, as they can rely on familiar interactions and visual cues. Whether used for advertising real estate properties, showcasing tourist destinations, or providing an immersive experience for e-commerce products, interactive virtual tours have become increasingly popular and influential in engaging users. By leveraging interactive elements, intuitive controls, and immersive visual content, these tours offer a unique and compelling way for users to explore and experience virtual environments, ultimately enhancing user engagement and satisfaction.

## Interior Design

Interior Design is a specialized field that focuses on creating functional and aesthetically pleasing spaces within buildings. It involves the process of designing, planning, and decorating interior spaces to meet the needs and preferences of the users while considering various factors such as functionality, safety, and visual appeal.

In the context of UI patterns and design systems, interior design refers to the application of design principles and strategies to create visually cohesive and consistent user interfaces. It involves the selection and arrangement of design elements such as colors, typography, imagery, and layout to create an intuitive and engaging user experience.

## Investment Portfolio

An investment portfolio is a collection of investments held by an individual or organization. In the context of UI patterns and design systems, an investment portfolio refers to the visual representation and organization of various investment options and their associated information within a user interface.

The investment portfolio UI pattern is designed to provide users with a comprehensive view of their investments, allowing them to easily track their performance and make informed decisions. This pattern typically includes components such as a dashboard, investment cards, charts, filters, and search functionality.

## Iris Scanning

Iris scanning is a biometric technology that uses the unique patterns found in a person's iris, the colored part of the eye, to authenticate or identify individuals. This technology is often used in user interfaces (UI) patterns and design systems to provide secure and convenient access to various applications and services.

In the context of UI patterns, iris scanning can be implemented as a form of authentication. Users can enroll their iris patterns by capturing high-resolution images of their eyes using specialized cameras. These images are then processed to extract and store the unique information found in the iris. To authenticate, the user simply needs to position their eyes in front of the iris scanner. The scanner captures a live image of the user's eyes and compares it with the enrolled iris patterns stored in the database. If there is a match, the user is granted access to the application or service. Iris scanning offers several advantages in terms of usability and security. Firstly, it eliminates the need for users to remember and enter complex passwords or PINs, reducing the risk of unauthorized access due to weak or stolen credentials. Secondly, the uniqueness and stability of iris patterns make it extremely difficult for impostors to forge or replicate, providing a higher level of security compared to traditional authentication methods. Lastly, iris scanning can be performed quickly and non-intrusively, allowing for a seamless and frictionless user experience. In the design system, iris scanning can be integrated as part of the overall authentication flow. Design guidelines can specify the placement and appearance of the iris scanner UI element to ensure consistency across different applications. For example, the iris scanner can be represented by a circular icon accompanied by clear instructions for users to position their eyes correctly. Visual feedback can also be provided to indicate the progress of the scanning process, such as a loading animation or color changes. Overall, iris scanning in UI patterns and design systems offers a secure and user-friendly method of authentication, leveraging the unique patterns found in the iris to provide seamless access to applications and services.>

## Job Application Form

A job application form is a standardized document or digital interface used by employers to collect relevant information from individuals who are interested in applying for a job within their organization. It serves as the initial step in the hiring process, allowing employers to gather necessary details and assess the suitability of applicants for the available position.

The design of a job application form plays a crucial role in ensuring a seamless and efficient application process. UI patterns and design systems are utilized to create user-friendly interfaces that facilitate the completion of the form. These patterns and systems ensure consistency, ease of use, and accessibility for all applicants.

## Job Posting Form

A job posting form is a user interface element that is used within a design system to allow users to submit information for a job opportunity. It typically consists of a set of input fields and buttons that collect the required data from the user and allow them to submit the form. The purpose of a job posting form is to streamline the application process by providing a standardized way for users to enter their personal information, work experience, and qualifications. It ensures that all necessary details are captured in a structured manner, making it easier for recruiters to review and compare applicants. Typically, a job posting form will include fields for the applicant's name, contact information, and resume. Additional fields may also be included to gather information such as education history, professional licenses or certifications, and a cover letter. Designing an effective job posting form involves considering the principles of usability and accessibility. It should be visually appealing and easy to navigate, with clear labels and input fields that are intuitively arranged. The form should also be responsive, adapting seamlessly to different screen sizes and devices. In a design system, the job posting form should follow established UI patterns and guidelines to ensure consistency across the application. This includes using standardized form elements, typography, and color schemes that align with the overall design system. In summary, a job posting form is a crucial component of a design system that allows users to submit their information for a job opportunity. It provides a structured and standardized way for applicants to input their details, making it easier for recruiters to review and assess candidates. Designing an effective job posting form requires careful consideration of usability and accessibility principles, along with adherence to established UI patterns within the design system.>

## Kinetic Scrolling

Kinetic scrolling is a UI pattern commonly used in modern design systems to enhance the user experience when navigating long lists or content-heavy pages on touch-enabled devices. It allows users to effortlessly scroll through content by simply swiping or flicking their fingers on the screen, simulating the physical motion of scrolling. In a design system, kinetic scrolling is implemented using a combination of JavaScript and CSS. The JavaScript code registers touch events and calculates the velocity and direction of the swipe gestures made by the user. Based on these calculations, the CSS is then manipulated to smoothly animate the scrolling motion, giving the user a sense of momentum and responsiveness. The main goal of kinetic scrolling is to provide a fluid and natural scrolling experience that closely resembles the tactile feedback of physically scrolling on a tactile device. By leveraging the user's intuitive familiarity with this type of interaction, kinetic scrolling improves usability and makes content navigation easier and more enjoyable. When designing for kinetic scrolling, there are a few key considerations. First and foremost, the scrolling motion should be responsive and synchronized with the user's gestures.

113

This means that the scrolling speed should match the velocity of the swipe, and the content should smoothly follow the user's finger movements. Another important aspect is the concept of "over-scrolling" or "rubber-banding." This refers to the behavior where the content temporarily exceeds its boundaries when the user reaches the end of a scrollable area. It provides a visual cue that indicates the end has been reached and adds a natural feel to the scrolling experience. In addition, it is crucial to optimize the performance of kinetic scrolling, especially on mobile devices with limited resources. This can be achieved by employing techniques like lazy loading, where content is loaded on-demand as the user scrolls, rather than all at once. In conclusion, kinetic scrolling is a fundamental UI pattern in modern design systems that brings a sense of realism and fluidity to the scrolling experience on touch-enabled devices. By emulating the physical motion of scrolling, it enhances usability and improves the overall user experience, making content navigation more intuitive and enjoyable.

## Language Learning

A design system is a set of guidelines, components, and rules that ensure consistency and coherence across user interfaces (UI). It provides a structured approach to designing and developing interfaces, and helps maintain a unified design language throughout a project or organization. UI patterns, also known as design patterns, are recurring solutions to common UI design problems. They offer established solutions that have been proven to work effectively and efficiently in various contexts. UI patterns help designers and developers solve problems and make informed decisions by offering solutions to common design challenges. A design system typically incorporates a wide range of UI patterns. These patterns can include navigation patterns, input patterns, layout patterns, feedback patterns, and many others. Each pattern within a design system follows a set of rules and guidelines to ensure consistency both within the pattern itself and in relation to other patterns. By using UI patterns within a design system, designers and developers can create interfaces that are intuitive and familiar to users. This familiarity leads to a more seamless user experience, as users can easily understand and navigate the interface. Furthermore, design systems with UI patterns allow for efficient and scalable design and development processes. Teams can leverage existing patterns and components, which reduces the need for reinventing the wheel and speeds up the design and development cycle. In conclusion, a design system is a comprehensive set of guidelines, components, and rules that ensure consistency and coherence across UIs. UI patterns, on the other hand, are recurring solutions to common UI design problems. By incorporating UI patterns within a design system, designers and developers can create intuitive interfaces that provide a seamless user experience and facilitate efficient design and development processes.>

## Lazy Loading

Lazy loading is a technique used in UI patterns and design systems to improve website performance and user experience by loading content only when it is needed. This approach allows the website to load quickly and display the essential elements to users first, while delaying the loading of non-critical or off-screen elements until the user interacts with or requests them. Lazy loading is particularly beneficial when dealing with large amounts of media such as images, videos, or audio files. Instead of loading all media content upfront, lazy loading enables the website to load only those media files that are visible in the user's viewport or about to become visible as they scroll through the page. This not only reduces the initial load time but also conserves bandwidth, as content that is not immediately required is not downloaded. Implementing lazy loading involves splitting the website's content into different sections or components, each with its own dedicated loading mechanism. When the user arrives on the page, only the essential content is loaded initially, while the remaining content is deferred until necessary. As the user scrolls or interacts with the page, the additional content is loaded dynamically, enhancing the viewing experience. To enable lazy loading, several techniques can be employed. Intersection Observer is a native JavaScript API that can be used to detect when elements enter or leave the viewport, triggering the loading of the desired content accordingly. Another technique involves utilizing placeholder images or low-quality previews that are initially displayed and replaced with the full-resolution images once they are needed. Additionally, lazy loading can be complemented by using progressive rendering techniques. By initially rendering a rough structure or a skeleton of the page, users perceive that the page is loading faster and are less likely to perceive any delays during the loading process. In conclusion, lazy loading is a technique used in UI patterns and design systems to optimize website performance by loading content on-demand. It improves the initial load time, conserves bandwidth, and enhances the user experience by prioritizing and loading only the most essential content, while delaying the loading of non-critical or off-screen elements until they are needed.

## Lecture Viewer

A Lecture Viewer is a user interface pattern and design system that provides users with a structured and intuitive way to view and navigate through lectures or presentations. It is commonly used in e-learning platforms, video lecture websites, and other educational applications. The primary goal of a Lecture Viewer is to enable users to easily access and consume lecture content. It typically consists of a main video or slide viewer, along with various supplemental features such as a table of contents, navigation controls, and annotation tools. The viewer should be visually appealing and provide an immersive experience for users to engage with the lecture material. One of the key features of a Lecture Viewer is the ability to easily navigate through the lecture content. This can be achieved through a table of contents that allows users to jump to specific sections or chapters of the lecture. Additionally, navigation controls such as play, pause, forward, and backward buttons should be available to help users control their viewing experience. Another important aspect of a Lecture Viewer is the inclusion of supplementary materials and features. These may include captions or subtitles for accessibility, related resources or links, and options for taking notes or adding annotations. These additional elements enhance the learning experience and provide users with a more comprehensive understanding of the lecture material. In terms of design system, a Lecture Viewer should follow a consistent and coherent visual style that aligns with the overall branding and user interface guidelines of the platform or application. This includes using a consistent color scheme, typography, and layout throughout the viewer. The design should be intuitive and user-friendly, ensuring that users can easily locate and access the various features and controls. In conclusion, a Lecture Viewer is a user interface pattern and design system that aims to facilitate the consumption and navigation of lecture content. By providing a structured and intuitive interface, along with supplementary materials and features, it enhances the learning experience and enables users to engage with educational material effectively.>

## Lightbox Pop-Up

A lightbox pop-up is a user interface pattern that is commonly used in web and mobile applications to display additional content or functionality without navigating away from the current page. It is a design element that consists of a modal window or dialog box that appears on top of the existing content, dimming the background and focusing the user's attention on the pop-up. The purpose of a lightbox pop-up is to provide contextual information, gather user input, or showcase media content such as images or videos. By overlaying the pop-up on the current page, it allows users to interact with the additional content while maintaining the context of the original page. This pattern is especially useful for presenting important announcements, notifications, or calls to action. The lightbox pop-up typically includes a clear and prominent close button, allowing users to easily dismiss the pop-up and return to the original content. It may also contain other interactive elements such as buttons, forms, or links to perform specific actions or access further information. The design of the lightbox pop-up should focus on simplicity and clarity, ensuring that the additional content or functionality is communicated effectively to the user. To implement a lightbox pop-up in HTML, you can use a combination of HTML, CSS, and JavaScript. The HTML structure of the pop-up can be created using a element with a unique class or ID. You can then style the pop-up using CSS to position it on top of the existing content and apply the desired dimensions, colors, and effects. JavaScript can be used to handle the display and behavior of the pop-up, such as activating it when a specific event occurs or managing user interactions within the pop-up. In summary, a lightbox pop-up is a UI pattern that overlays a modal window or dialog box on the current page to display additional content or functionality. It is an effective way to provide context-specific information or actions without disrupting the user's flow. By implementing a lightbox pop-up using HTML, CSS, and JavaScript, developers can enhance the user experience and improve the usability of their applications.

## List View

A List View is a user interface (UI) pattern commonly used in the design system of web applications and mobile apps. It is used to display a list of items in a structured and visually appealing way, allowing users to easily scan and interact with the content. In a List View, each item is typically represented by a single row or card. The items can be displayed in a vertical or horizontal layout, depending on the design and requirements of the application. The list may contain various types of information, such as text, images, icons, or buttons. The primary purpose of a List View is to present information in a concise and organized manner, making it easy for users to find and access specific items. Users can quickly scan the list to locate the desired item based on its visual representation or associated textual information. List Views often incorporate features to facilitate navigation and interaction. For instance, pagination or infinite scrolling may be implemented to handle large lists by dividing them into smaller, more manageable sections. Filtering and sorting options can be provided to help users narrow down the displayed items based on specific criteria. In addition to supporting content consumption, List Views can also enable various user actions. Common actions include selecting or deselecting items, activating or navigating to item details, and performing bulk operations on selected items. The design of a List View plays a crucial role in ensuring a pleasant user experience. The use of appropriate typography, spacing, and visual hierarchy helps users easily differentiate between items and comprehend the information presented. Consistent styling within the design system ensures a cohesive look and feel across the application. When implementing a List View in HTML, developers can utilize HTML tags such as , , or for creating lists. However, the actual rendering and styling of a List View may require additional CSS classes or custom styling. In summary, a List View is a UI pattern used in the design system of web and mobile applications to present a collection of items in a structured and visually appealing manner. It aims to provide an efficient and user-friendly interface for users to navigate, interact with, and consume the displayed content.>

## Live Chat Support

Live Chat Support is a user interface pattern that is commonly used in design systems to provide real-time assistance and support to users. It is an interactive feature that allows users to communicate with a support representative or a chatbot. The Live Chat Support pattern typically consists of a chatbox or a chat window embedded in a web or mobile application. Users can initiate a conversation by typing a message or selecting predefined options. The chat window displays messages from both the user and the support representative, enabling a seamless and interactive dialogue. The purpose of Live Chat Support is to provide immediate assistance and resolve user queries or issues in a more personal and efficient manner. It offers a convenient alternative to traditional support channels such as phone calls or emails, as users can get instant responses without having to leave the application they are using. From a design system perspective, Live Chat Support involves consistent styling and functionality across different applications or platforms. Design systems provide a standardized set of components, styles, and guidelines to ensure a cohesive user experience. This includes defining the visual appearance of the chat window, the behavior of the chatbox, and the placement of the support button or icon. In terms of UI patterns, Live Chat Support can be implemented using various techniques, such as floating chat icons, slide-out chat panels, or embedded chat windows. The choice of pattern depends on the specific requirements and constraints of the application. Regardless of the implementation, the aim is to make the chat feature easily discoverable, accessible, and visually consistent with the overall design. Live Chat Support is an essential component of modern digital experiences, enabling businesses to provide personalized assistance and support to their users. It promotes engagement, customer satisfaction, and ultimately, enhances the overall user experience. In summary, Live Chat Support is a user interface pattern that facilitates real-time communication between users and support representatives. It is a valuable feature in design systems, offering immediate assistance and resolving user queries efficiently. The consistent implementation of Live Chat Support across different applications ensures a cohesive user experience and enhances customer satisfaction.>

## Live Chat

A UI pattern refers to a recurrent and widely accepted solution to a common user interface design problem. It serves as a guide or blueprint for designing and developing user interfaces that are consistent, intuitive, and efficient. UI patterns are essential components of design systems, which encompass a broader set of guidelines, principles, and design elements. UI patterns help designers and developers create user interfaces that are familiar to users, as they have already encountered similar patterns in other applications or websites. By using established UI patterns, designers can leverage existing user expectations and behavior, reducing the learning curve for users and increasing their overall satisfaction with the interface. UI patterns can range from simple elements like buttons, forms, and navigation menus to more complex patterns like carousels, modals, and content grids. Each pattern has a specific purpose and usage, and it is important to understand when and how to apply them appropriately. Design systems, on the other hand, encompass a wider scope and provide a cohesive set of guidelines, principles, and components for designing and developing user interfaces. They define the overall visual style, typography, color palette, and spacing guidelines, ensuring consistency and coherency across different interfaces and platforms. Design systems often include a comprehensive library or repository of reusable UI components. These components, which may represent individual UI patterns, can be assembled together to create consistent and cohesive user interfaces. They are designed to be modular and versatile, allowing designers and developers to easily customize and adapt them to different contexts and requirements. By leveraging UI patterns within a design system, designers and developers can achieve a more efficient and streamlined design process. They can focus less on reinventing the wheel and more on solving unique design challenges. Additionally, design systems facilitate collaboration and communication between designers and developers, as they provide a shared language and reference point for discussing and implementing UI designs. In summary, UI patterns are recurrent solutions to common design problems, while design systems provide a broader framework of guidelines, principles, and reusable components for creating consistent and coherent user interfaces. Together, they form an essential foundation for effective and efficient UI design and development.

## Live Search

A live search, also known as an instant search or autocomplete search, is a user interface pattern that provides real-time suggestions or results as the user types into a search input field. It is commonly used in search bars or search boxes to enhance the search experience by saving time and effort for the user. When a user starts typing in the search input field, the live search feature immediately starts retrieving relevant suggestions or results based on the entered text. These suggestions or results are dynamically displayed in a dropdown or a list below the search input field, allowing the user to select or explore them further. Live search patterns typically incorporate a design system that ensures consistency and coherence across different elements of the user interface. The design system includes predefined styles, colors, typography, and other visual components that are used consistently throughout the interface. In terms of UI patterns, a live search is beneficial because it offers several advantages. Firstly, it provides instant feedback to the user, helping them refine their search query without having to wait for a page to reload or submit a form. Secondly, it assists users in finding the desired content more quickly by offering predictive suggestions based on their input. Thirdly, it reduces cognitive load by eliminating the need for users to remember or type complicated search queries. From a design system perspective, a live search implementation should align with the overall visual identity of the interface. It should seamlessly integrate with the surrounding elements, such as navigation bars or search filters, to create a cohesive and intuitive user experience. The design system should also prioritize legibility and accessibility, ensuring that the suggestions or results are easy to read and interact with. In conclusion, a live search is a user interface pattern that provides real-time suggestions or results as the user types into a search input field. It enhances the search experience by saving time and effort for users, while a design system ensures consistency and coherence in the overall interface design.

## Live Streaming

Live streaming refers to the real-time transmission of audio and video content over the internet. It allows users to watch and listen to a continuous stream of data as it is being recorded and broadcasted. Live streaming has gained popularity in recent years due to its ability to provide instant and immersive experiences to users.

From a UI patterns perspective, live streaming involves designing interfaces that facilitate the seamless viewing and interaction with live content. The design system for live streaming interfaces focuses on elements and components that enhance the user experience and make it easy for users to access, navigate, and engage with the live content.

## Load More Button

A Load More Button is a user interface (UI) pattern commonly used in web and mobile applications to allow users to retrieve additional content without having to navigate to a new page or refresh the current page. It is a design element that enhances user experience by providing a convenient way to load more items dynamically. The Load More Button is typically placed at the end of a list or grid of content, such as a newsfeed or search results. When clicked, it triggers an event that fetches and displays the next set of items, appending them to the existing content. This pattern is often used in combination with infinite scrolling or pagination to facilitate easy content browsing, especially for long lists or large datasets. From a design system perspective, the Load More Button should adhere to consistent principles and visual styles to ensure a harmonious user experience across the application. It should be easily identifiable and accessible, using appropriate colors, contrast, and typography. As with any UI element, it is crucial to maintain responsiveness and optimal performance, ensuring the button displays and functions appropriately across different devices and network conditions. In terms of HTML implementation, the Load More Button can be created using a <button> element, commonly styled with CSS for a visually appealing appearance. The button should include clear and concise text, such as "Load More" or "Show More," indicating its purpose to the user. Additionally, the button can be associated with JavaScript or other scripting languages to trigger the event that handles the content loading functionality.

<button>Load More</button>

The implementation of the Load More Button should also consider accessibility guidelines to ensure it is perceivable, operable, and understandable for all users, including those with disabilities. This may include providing alternative text for screen readers and keyboard navigation support. To summarize, the Load More Button is a UI pattern that allows users to fetch and display additional content without leaving or refreshing the current page. It is an essential design element in creating seamless browsing experiences, and its implementation in a design system should adhere to consistent principles while considering usability and accessibility requirements.></button>

## Loan Application

A loan application in the context of UI patterns and design systems refers to the user interface design and interaction flow specifically tailored for the process of applying for a loan. It encompasses the visual presentation, layout, and functionality of the loan application form. The loan application form is a crucial component of the overall user experience, as it serves as the primary means for users to provide necessary information and submit their loan request. The form typically includes fields for personal details such as name, contact information, employment information, income details, and loan amount requested. It may also include additional fields depending on the specific requirements of the lending institution, such as credit history, collateral information, and purpose of the loan. Designing the loan application form requires careful consideration to ensure a seamless and intuitive experience for the users. The form should be visually clear and well-organized, with appropriate spacing and alignment to guide the users' attention effectively. The use of labels, placeholders, and instructions can help users understand the purpose and expected format of each form field. To optimize the usability of the loan application form, designers should aim for simplicity and minimize the number of required fields to reduce user effort and completion time. However, it is important to strike a balance between collecting necessary information for loan evaluation and overwhelming users with an excessive number of fields. Designers should also incorporate validation mechanisms to provide users with real-time feedback on the accuracy and completeness of their inputs. Validation can range from simple checks, such as ensuring valid email and phone number formats, to more complex checks such as verifying income details or conducting an automated credit check. In terms of user flow, the loan application should have a logical sequence, guiding users from one stage to the next. Clear indicators of progress, such as progress bars or step indicators, can help users understand their position within the application process. Overall, a well-designed loan application form within a UI pattern and design system ensures an intuitive, efficient, and secure experience for users, leading to increased user satisfaction and a higher completion rate of loan applications.

A loan application in UI patterns and design systems refers to the user interface design and interaction flow specifically tailored for the process of applying for a loan. It encompasses the visual presentation, layout, and functionality of the loan application form.

The loan application form is a crucial component of the overall user experience, as it serves as the primary means for users to provide necessary information and submit their loan request. The form typically includes fields for personal details, employment information, income details, and loan amount requested, while also incorporating validation mechanisms and guiding users through a logical application sequence.

## Local Guides And Recommendations

Local Guides and Recommendations are UI patterns and design system components that provide users with personalized suggestions and advice based on their location and preferences.

Local Guides are user-generated reviews, ratings, and recommendations for local businesses, attractions, and landmarks. These guides are typically created by local residents or frequent visitors of an area who share their firsthand experiences and insights. Local Guides help users discover new places, find popular establishments, and make informed decisions about where to eat, shop, stay, or visit.

## Location Sharing In Chat

Location sharing in chat is a UI pattern and design system feature that allows users to share their current location with others within a chat or messaging interface. This feature enhances communication and enables users to easily convey their geographical whereabouts in real-time. In the context of UI patterns and design systems, location sharing in chat typically consists of a dedicated button or icon that users can select to initiate the sharing process. Upon selection, the user's device utilizes its built-in location services to retrieve the current coordinates or address. The retrieved location information is then displayed within the chat interface, usually as a simple text message or as a map thumbnail. The visual representation provides recipients with a quick overview of the sender's location. To ensure privacy and security, location sharing in chat often includes options for the user to control the level of detail shared. For example, users may have the ability to share only the city or neighborhood, or they may choose to share their precise coordinates. Additionally, design systems often incorporate customization options to match the look and feel of the overall application. This allows for consistent user experiences across multiple platforms and devices. Location sharing in chat can be beneficial in various scenarios. For instance, it can be particularly useful when coordinating meetups with friends or colleagues in a busy or unfamiliar area. It can also aid in emergency situations, where users may need to quickly convey their location to authorities or trusted contacts. Implementing location sharing in chat requires careful consideration of user privacy and data protection. Designers and developers should adhere to best practices in terms of permission management, data encryption, and opt-in/opt-out mechanisms. Providing clear and accessible settings and instructions is crucial to ensure user confidence and control over their shared location information. Overall, location sharing in chat is a valuable UI pattern and design system feature that enhances communication by enabling users to easily share their real-time location with others within a chat interface. By providing this functionality, applications can facilitate coordination and provide additional convenience and safety for their users.>

## Location-Based UI

Location-Based UI is a design pattern that incorporates the use of a user's geographical location to tailor and customize the interface of a digital application or website. It leverages the capabilities of location-based services (LBS) and technologies, such as GPS or IP geolocation, to provide a more relevant and personalized experience to users.

The primary objective of a Location-Based UI is to present information, content, or functionality that is specific to a particular location. This pattern allows developers and designers to enhance the user experience by offering contextually relevant features and content based on the user's current or chosen location.

## Location-Based Content

Location-based content refers to a UI pattern and design system that dynamically adapts and presents information based on the user's geographic location. It involves the use of GPS coordinates or IP address to identify the user's current location and then deliver relevant content that is specific to that location.

By utilizing location-based content, UI designers can provide users with personalized and contextually relevant information. This can enhance the overall user experience by making the interface more intuitive and efficient.

## Login Form

A login form is a user interface (UI) pattern that allows users to log in to a website or application by inputting their credentials, typically a username or email and a password. It is an essential element of any website or application that requires user authentication. The login form serves as the gateway for users to access their personal accounts and the services provided by the website or application. It is a crucial part of the overall user experience (UX) and plays a vital role in ensuring the security and privacy of users' personal information. A well-designed login form should be simple, intuitive, and visually appealing. It should provide clear and concise instructions to users on how to proceed with the login process. The form typically consists of input fields for username/email and password, a "Remember Me" checkbox, a "Forgot Password" link, and a "Sign In" button. The input fields should have appropriate labels and placeholders to guide users in providing the required information. The "Remember Me" checkbox allows users to choose whether to save their login information for future sessions, providing convenience for returning users. The "Forgot Password" link provides a way for users to recover their account if they have forgotten their password. The "Sign In" button is the primary action that triggers the form submission. It should be visually prominent and easily distinguishable from other elements on the page to ensure its discoverability. Upon clicking the "Sign In" button, the form should validate the user's input and authenticate their credentials. In terms of design system, the login form should adhere to the overall visual style and branding of the website or application. This includes consistent typography, colors, and layout. It is important to maintain a cohesive design throughout the entire user journey to establish brand identity and increase usability. Overall, a login form is a fundamental component of a website or application that requires user authentication. Its design and implementation are crucial in providing a seamless and secure login experience for users.

A login form is a UI pattern that allows users to log in to a website or application by inputting their credentials, typically a username or email and a password. It serves as the gateway for users to access their personal accounts and the services provided by the website or application. A well-designed login form should be simple, intuitive, and visually appealing. It should consist of input fields for username/email and password, a "Remember Me" checkbox, a "Forgot Password" link, and a "Sign In" button. The form should adhere to the overall design system and branding of the website or application and provide a seamless and secure login experience for users.

## Login Screen

A login screen is a user interface element that allows users to authenticate themselves before accessing a system or application. It typically consists of an input field for the username or email and a corresponding input field for the password. The login screen provides a secure entry point for users to access protected information or perform specific tasks within a system.

The design of a login screen is an essential aspect of the overall user experience (UX) as it sets the first impression of the application or system. It should align with the overall visual design language, branding, and usability of the system. The login screen typically follows certain UI patterns and design system guidelines to ensure consistency across different platforms and devices.

## Map View

120

A map view is a user interface pattern commonly used in design systems to display geographic information in a visual format. It allows users to interact with and navigate through a map, enabling them to explore and understand spatial data.

The main purpose of a map view is to provide users with a visual representation of geographical locations or areas of interest. It typically includes various elements such as markers, labels, and other graphic elements to indicate points of interest, boundaries, or routes. Users can interact with the map view by zooming in or out, panning, and clicking on markers or other interactive elements to access additional information or perform specific actions.

## Masonry Layout

A Masonry layout is a popular UI pattern and design system used to create visually appealing and dynamic grid-based layouts that can adapt to different screen sizes and orientations. In a Masonry layout, items are arranged vertically in columns, with each item positioned as close to the top of the column as possible. Unlike traditional grid layouts where all items have the same height and width, Masonry layouts allow for varying item heights and widths, resulting in a more fluid and irregular grid appearance. The key characteristic that sets Masonry layouts apart from other grid-based layouts is the ability to fill gaps between items with other items. This feature is particularly useful when dealing with items of varying heights, as it helps to minimize empty spaces and create a visually balanced and responsive layout. To achieve this, Masonry layouts use a technique called "bin-packing," which involves placing items in available spaces within the grid in a way that optimizes the use of space. Implementing a Masonry layout in HTML involves using CSS to define the styling and positioning of the grid items. Each individual item is typically wrapped in a container element, such as a or , and styled using CSS properties such as width, height, margin, and padding. The container elements are then arranged within a parent container that acts as the grid. This parent container can be a or any other suitable container element. To create a Masonry layout, CSS frameworks and libraries such as Masonry.js or Isotope can be used. These libraries handle the complex calculations and animations required to create the fluid grid effect. They also provide additional features such as filtering and sorting of grid items. In conclusion, a Masonry layout is a versatile UI pattern and design system that allows for the creation of visually appealing and responsive grid-based layouts. By dynamically arranging items in a grid and filling gaps between them, Masonry layouts provide a more flexible and engaging user experience.

## Medical History Form

The Medical History Form is a UI pattern and design system component that allows healthcare professionals to gather essential information about a patient's medical background. It typically consists of a series of questions and fields that require the patient to provide details about their medical history, including past illnesses, surgeries, allergies, medications, and family medical history. The purpose of the Medical History Form is to collect accurate and comprehensive information that enables healthcare providers to make well-informed decisions and provide appropriate care to patients. By documenting the patient's medical history, healthcare professionals can identify any underlying conditions, assess the risk of certain treatments or procedures, and tailor their approach to meet the patient's specific needs. When designing the Medical History Form, several considerations need to be taken into account to ensure its effectiveness and usability. The form should be structured logically, with questions and elements organized in a clear and intuitive manner. The use of headings, sections, or tabs can help divide the form into manageable chunks, making it easier for both patients and healthcare professionals to navigate and complete. Additionally, the Medical History Form should be designed with accessibility in mind, ensuring that it can be used by individuals of all abilities. This includes using clear and concise language, providing instructions where necessary, and using form controls that are easily navigable using keyboard-only interactions. It is also important to consider the privacy and security of the data collected through the Medical History Form. Adequate measures should be in place to protect sensitive patient information and ensure compliance with relevant data protection regulations. Overall, the Medical History Form is a crucial component of any healthcare system, allowing healthcare professionals to gather essential information that informs their decision-making process and ultimately improves patient care. By following established UI patterns and design system principles, this form can be developed in a user-friendly and inclusive manner, ensuring that patients can easily provide their medical history, leading to better healthcare outcomes.

The Medical History Form is a UI pattern and design system component that allows healthcare professionals to gather essential information about a patient's medical background. It typically consists of a series of questions and fields that require the patient to provide details about their medical history, including past illnesses, surgeries, allergies, medications, and family medical history.

The purpose of the Medical History Form is to collect accurate and comprehensive information that enables healthcare providers to make well-informed decisions and provide appropriate care to patients. By documenting the patient's medical history, healthcare professionals can identify any underlying conditions, assess the risk of certain treatments or procedures, and tailor their approach to meet the patient's specific needs.

## Medication Reminders

A medication reminder is a user interface pattern and design system element that helps users keep track of their medication schedules and doses. It provides a visual representation of scheduled medication times and notifications to remind users when it's time to take their medication.

The medication reminder typically consists of a list or grid view that displays the name of the medication, the dosage, and the scheduled time for each dose. It may also include additional information such as any specific instructions or precautions for taking the medication. Users can easily navigate through the list or grid to view upcoming doses and mark them as taken once they've been consumed.

## Mega Menu

A mega menu is a type of menu design pattern commonly used in user interface (UI) and web design systems. It is a larger variant of a standard drop-down menu, offering a more extensive and visually rich navigation experience. The mega menu is typically displayed as a horizontal or vertical navigation bar that expands upon hovering or clicking, revealing a grid-like layout of various content categories and subcategories. It provides an efficient and organized way to group a large amount of information, enabling users to quickly find and access the desired content. Unlike traditional menus that often involve multiple levels of nested drop-downs, a mega menu can display more options and information at once. This allows users to have a comprehensive overview of the available sections and easily identify their desired destination within the website or application. The visual design of a mega menu usually incorporates images, icons, and other visual cues to enhance the navigation experience. It aims to create a visually appealing and interactive interface that engages users and encourages exploration. In terms of HTML structure, a mega menu typically consists of nested containers and lists. The outer container holds the entire mega menu, and within it, multiple nested containers are used to organize the different sections or categories of content. Each section is represented by a list, which contains links to the subcategories or specific content items. Attributes like "aria-haspopup" and "aria-expanded" are commonly used to enhance the accessibility of mega menus, allowing screen readers and assistive technologies to provide accurate information to users with disabilities. Overall, the mega menu is an effective UI pattern for websites or applications with complex content structures. It provides a comprehensive navigation solution that optimizes space, improves user engagement, and simplifies the browsing experience for users.>

## Mega Menus

Mega Menus are a type of user interface (UI) pattern commonly used in web design systems. They involve large drop-down menus that provide users with a hierarchical navigation structure and allow them to access a wide range of options and subcategories within a website or application. In terms of HTML, Mega Menus are typically implemented using nested or elements. The main menu is usually represented by a container element, such as a or , which contains the main categories or sections of the website. Each main category is represented by a or element, which can be styled to appear as buttons or links. When a user hovers or clicks on a main category, a dropdown panel is displayed, revealing additional subcategories and options related to that category. These subcategories and options are usually organized in columns or rows to provide a clear and structured presentation. To implement this behavior, the nested subcategories or options are typically placed within a or element that is hidden by default using CSS. When the parent main category is triggered, either through a hover event or a click event, the hidden subcategories are made visible by updating the CSS display property. Mega Menus can be enhanced with additional features such as images, icons, or descriptive texts to provide users with more information and improve the overall user experience. The design and layout of these menus can also be customized to match the visual style of the website or application, making them an integral part of the overall design system. In conclusion, Mega Menus are a powerful UI pattern that allows users to navigate through a complex website or application by providing them with a hierarchical menu structure. By utilizing HTML elements like , , and or , Mega Menus can be easily implemented and customized to fit within a design system.

## Membership Renewal Form

A membership renewal form is a user interface pattern and design system element that is used to collect information and facilitate the renewal process for existing members of an organization or service.

In the context of UI patterns and design systems, a membership renewal form typically consists of a series of fields and prompts that guide the user through the process of renewing their membership. This may include fields for personal information, such as name and contact details, as well as specific membership-related information, such as membership level or duration.

## Mental Health Support

Mental Health Support refers to a set of user interface (UI) patterns and design elements that are specifically developed to create a supportive and inclusive digital environment for individuals facing mental health challenges. These patterns and elements are integrated into a design system, which is a collection of reusable components, guidelines, and documentation that ensures consistency and coherence across various digital products and platforms.

The primary aim of Mental Health Support in the context of UI patterns and design systems is to foster positive user experiences and promote the mental well-being of individuals engaging with digital products. It involves the implementation of design strategies that enhance accessibility, usability, and emotional engagement while addressing the unique needs and sensitivities of individuals with mental health concerns.

## Menu Icons

Menu icons are a set of graphical representations used in user interfaces (UI) to visually represent various menu options or functions available to the user. These icons are typically displayed in a horizontal or vertical bar, commonly known as a menu bar, and are clickable objects that trigger specific actions or display additional submenus when interacted with. In the context of UI patterns and design systems, menu icons serve as visual cues that help users quickly and intuitively navigate through an application or website. They provide a more compact and efficient way to present a range of options and functionalities, especially in situations where space is limited or the menu items are numerous. Design systems provide a consistent and standardized set of menu icons that adhere to the overall visual language and branding of the application or website. These icons are often designed to be simple and easily recognizable, utilizing familiar shapes or symbols that users can easily associate with specific actions or categories. Using menu icons in UI patterns and design systems offers several benefits. Firstly, they enhance the overall user experience by providing a visually appealing and intuitive interface. Icons help users comprehend the available options at a glance, reducing the cognitive load required to process textual information. Secondly, they save space on the screen by condensing menu options into compact graphical representations, allowing for a more efficient use of the available screen real estate. Additionally, menu icons can improve accessibility by providing an alternative means of navigation for users with visual impairments, as they can be paired with appropriate text labels or tooltips. To implement menu icons, HTML can be used to create these graphical representations. For example:

Option 1

Option 2

In this code snippet, the menu icons are represented by the tag, which specifies the image source using the "src" attribute. The "alt" attribute provides alternative text that is displayed if the image fails to load or is inaccessible. The menu option labels are contained within the tags, allowing for the inclusion of accompanying text for improved accessibility. In conclusion, menu icons are graphical representations used in UI patterns and design systems to visually represent menu options or functions. They offer an intuitive and space-saving way to navigate through an application or website, while adhering to the overall visual language and branding. By utilizing HTML, these icons can be easily implemented within the UI, enhancing the user experience and accessibility.

## Menu Selection

Menu Selection: A menu selection is a user interface (UI) pattern that provides users with a list of options or actions to choose from. It is commonly used in various applications, websites, and software systems to enable users to navigate and interact with the interface. The menu selection is typically represented as a dropdown or a list that displays the available options when triggered by the user. This interaction can be initiated by clicking or tapping on a designated area, such as a menu button or icon. Upon activation, the menu expands and reveals the options in a hierarchical or flat structure, depending on the design. The options within a menu selection can vary in nature, ranging from navigation links, settings or preferences, actions, or any other relevant choices for the user. They are usually labeled with concise and descriptive text to ensure clarity and ease of understanding. In some cases, icons or graphics may accompany the text to enhance visual recognition and aid in quick selection. Users can make a selection from the menu by either clicking or tapping on their desired option within the menu. Once a selection is made, the menu typically collapses, and the chosen action or navigation is executed accordingly. However, in certain cases, multi-level menus or sub-menus may be present, allowing users to further explore and choose from nested options. One key aspect of a menu selection is its responsiveness and adaptability. The menu should be designed to work well across different screen sizes and devices, ensuring that users can easily access and make selections regardless of their platform. Additionally, the menu's appearance and behavior should be consistent throughout the application or website, following the established design system to provide familiarity and improve user experience. Overall, the menu selection UI pattern plays a crucial role in enabling users to interact with an interface by providing a structured and intuitive list of options or actions. Its design and implementation should prioritize simplicity, usability, and consistency to enhance user navigation and overall satisfaction.

## Message Copying

Message copying refers to the UI pattern and design system technique that involves replicating or duplicating blocks of text or messages within a user interface. This technique is commonly used in various applications and websites to display consistent and repetitive content across different screens or sections.

By using message copying, designers and developers can ensure a coherent and unified user experience by maintaining consistency in the language, tone, and style of the messages displayed. This pattern is especially useful in scenarios where the same message needs to be presented multiple times to users throughout their interaction with the interface.

## Message Deleting

Message Deleting refers to the act of removing a message or conversation from a user interface (UI). It is a common functionality in various messaging and communication platforms, allowing users to selectively remove unwanted messages or conversations from their view.

In UI patterns and design systems, message deleting is typically implemented using a combination of interactive elements and logical controls. These controls enable users to delete individual messages or entire conversations, providing them with the ability to manage their message history effectively.

## Message Editing

A UI pattern refers to a recurring design solution that solves a specific user interface problem. It serves as a guideline or template for designers and developers to follow when creating consistent and intuitive user experiences within a system.

UI patterns are essential in the development of design systems, which are comprehensive collections of reusable components, guidelines, and rules that ensure a consistent and cohesive design across different products and platforms. A design system provides a set of standard design elements and principles that enable teams to build interfaces efficiently and effectively.

## Message Emojis

Message emojis are graphical representations of emotions, objects, or symbols that are used within user interface (UI) patterns and design systems to enhance communication and expressiveness in digital messaging platforms. They provide a visual element to text-based messages, allowing users to convey their emotions or ideas more effectively.

In the context of UI patterns and design systems, message emojis serve as a form of visual feedback and reinforcement. They can help convey tone, mood, or sentiment that may not be effectively conveyed through text alone. By incorporating emojis into a messaging platform, designers aim to create a more engaging and expressive user experience.

## Message Forwarding

Message forwarding is a UI pattern that allows users to share or redirect a message or information to another recipient or channel. It is a common feature found in messaging applications, email clients, and social media platforms. The purpose of message forwarding is to enable users to easily share content, discussions, or conversations with others. The design system for message forwarding typically includes a straightforward user interface that simplifies the process of selecting a message or conversation and specifying the desired recipient or channel for forwarding. This UI pattern often involves a combination of organizational components, such as lists or grids, and input components, such as text fields or dropdowns, to facilitate the selection and transmission of message content. When implementing message forwarding in a design system, it is crucial to consider key functional requirements and usability considerations. The UI pattern should support the ability to select multiple messages or conversations for forwarding, allowing users to efficiently share multiple pieces of content at once. It is also essential to include options for editing the forwarded message, enabling users to add additional context or commentary before sharing the content. Furthermore, the design system should provide clear visual cues and labels to guide users through the forwarding process. This includes prominently displaying the sender and recipient information of each message, as well as providing intuitive controls for selecting and specifying forwarding recipients. The design system should also support accessibility standards, ensuring that users with disabilities can effectively navigate and use the message forwarding feature. In conclusion, message forwarding is a UI pattern that enables users to share or redirect messages or information to other recipients or channels. When designing this feature as part of a design system, it is important to consider functional requirements and usability considerations, such as the ability to select and forward multiple messages, options for editing forwarded content, and visual cues to guide users through the forwarding process.>

## Message Pasting

Message Pasting refers to the UI pattern used in design systems to allow users to easily share and copy content from a message or notification to another location.

It typically involves providing users with a simple and intuitive way to copy the entire content of a message or notification to their clipboard, so that they can easily paste it into another application or location. This can be particularly useful when users want to share the content of a message with others, or when they need to reference the information in the message elsewhere.

## Message Quotes

Message Quotes in the context of UI patterns and design systems are a design element used to highlight or emphasize important pieces of information within a user interface. They are typically displayed in a contrasting format or style to draw attention to the message they contain.

These quote messages can vary in their appearance depending on the design system or UI pattern being used. They are often presented in a speech bubble or blockquote format, with a distinct background color or border to differentiate them from the surrounding content. The typography used for message quotes is also typically different, often with a larger or bolder font to further emphasize the message.

## Message Reactions

Message reactions refer to a UI pattern and design system that allows users to express their emotions or opinions about a message or conversation by selecting from a set of predefined reactions. These reactions are typically represented by a set of icons or emojis, and clicking on them triggers a visual change in the UI to indicate the selected reaction.

The purpose of message reactions is to provide users with a simple and intuitive way to engage and interact with messages without the need for lengthy replies or comments. They allow users to express their feelings or opinions without the pressure of composing a full response, making conversations more dynamic and engaging.

## Message Translations

A message translation is a UI pattern and design system element that allows for the display of translated messages to be presented in a consistent and user-friendly manner. It is commonly used in applications and websites that have a global user base and need to provide content in multiple languages. The purpose of a message translation is to ensure that users can easily understand and interact with the interface regardless of their language proficiency. It serves as a way to present important notifications, alerts, error messages, confirmation messages, and other types of information in a clear and concise manner. In terms of UI patterns, a message translation typically consists of a container, which can be a box or a bar, that holds the translated message. The container is often styled in a way that stands out from the rest of the interface to draw the user's attention. The message itself is usually displayed in a readable font size and is aligned to maximize legibility. Design systems provide guidelines and components for message translations to ensure consistency across the application or website. They define the color, typography, spacing, and other visual aspects of the message translation to maintain a cohesive user experience. Design systems also facilitate the localization process by providing a framework for translating and incorporating the messages into the interface. Overall, message translations are essential for creating a user-friendly and inclusive experience for users who speak different languages. By implementing this UI pattern and adhering to design system guidelines, organizations can effectively communicate important information to their global user base, fostering understanding and engagement.>

## Message Typing Indicators

Message Typing Indicators are UI patterns and design elements that provide users with real-time feedback on the status of a typing input. These indicators are commonly used in messaging platforms and chat applications to show when someone is actively composing a message or when someone else is typing in a conversation.

When a user starts typing, the typing indicator immediately appears next to their name or profile picture in the chat interface. This informs other participants in the conversation that someone is actively engaged in composing a message. Similarly, when someone else starts typing, their corresponding typing indicator appears in real-time, signaling that they are in the process of sending a message. These indicators help users gauge the responsiveness and engagement of other participants in a conversation, promoting more fluid and interactive communication.

## Messaging Screen

Messaging Screen is a UI pattern that is commonly used in the design of messaging or chat applications. It refers to the user interface and layout of a screen where users can view and interact with their messages and conversations.

The messaging screen typically displays a list of conversations or message threads, each represented by a preview of the most recent message or the participants' names. Users can select a conversation to view its full contents and engage in further conversation.

## Microinteractions

Microinteractions refers to small, contained moments within a user interface (UI) pattern or design system that provide feedback or enable a specific user action. They are typically subtle, often animated, and serve to enhance the overall user experience by creating a sense of control, engagement, and satisfaction.

These interactions can be found in various aspects of a UI, including buttons, checkboxes, sliders, navigation menus, and form fields. They are designed to provide feedback to the user, such as indicating that a button has been clicked, a form has been submitted, or an error has occurred. They can also be used to guide the user through a process, such as showing progress indicators, tooltips, or guidance messages.

## Mixed Reality (MR) Interface

Mixed Reality (MR) Interface refers to a user interface design pattern and a set of design systems that aim to seamlessly blend both virtual and physical elements, providing users with a more immersive and interactive experience.

Unlike Virtual Reality (VR), which creates a completely computer-generated environment, and Augmented Reality (AR), which overlays digital elements on the real world, MR interfaces combine virtual objects with the real world in a way that allows users to interact with and manipulate both. This is achieved by using a combination of cameras, sensors, and display devices, along with sophisticated software algorithms.

The goal of MR interfaces is to create a seamless integration of virtual and physical elements, enhancing the user's perception of reality and enabling them to interact with digital content in a more natural and intuitive manner. This can be achieved through various techniques, such as gesture recognition, voice commands, and haptic feedback.

Designing MR interfaces requires careful consideration of factors such as spatial mapping, object recognition, and user interaction. Spatial mapping involves accurately mapping the physical environment and creating a virtual representation of it, while object recognition helps identify and track physical objects in the real world. User interaction in MR interfaces often involves direct manipulation of virtual objects, either using hand gestures or dedicated input devices.

## Mobile AR Shopping

Mobile AR Shopping refers to a user interface pattern and design system that allows users to experience and interact with virtual products in their physical environment using augmented reality (AR) technology on mobile devices. It combines the convenience of online shopping with the immersive and interactive nature of AR, enabling users to view and evaluate products in real-time, virtually place them in their surroundings, and make informed purchase decisions. This UI pattern incorporates various components and functionalities to enhance the mobile AR shopping experience. One key component is the product catalog, which displays a collection of virtual products available for purchase. Users can browse through the catalog, filter and search for specific items, and access detailed product information such as images, descriptions, and specifications. To visualize how a product would look in their actual environment, users can use the AR view feature. By activating the camera on their mobile device, they can overlay virtual objects onto their surroundings in real-time. This allows them to see how a piece of furniture would fit in their living room, or how a piece of clothing would look when worn. Additionally, users can interact with the virtual objects, rotating them, resizing them, or even trying them on, depending on the type of product. Mobile AR Shopping also includes functionality for

127

personalization and customization. Users can personalize their shopping experience by creating profiles, saving favorite products, and receiving recommendations based on their preferences and previous purchases. They can also customize certain products, such as selecting different colors, materials, or configurations, to meet their specific needs or preferences. A vital aspect of Mobile AR Shopping is the integration of secure and seamless payment options. Users should be able to add items to their shopping cart, view an overview of their selected products, and proceed with the payment process without leaving the AR environment. This integration ensures a fluid and uninterrupted experience, allowing users to easily complete their purchases. In conclusion, Mobile AR Shopping is a UI pattern and design system that leverages AR technology on mobile devices to create an engaging and immersive shopping experience. By combining virtual products with real-world environments, users can make informed purchase decisions, personalize their shopping experience, and enjoy the convenience of online shopping from anywhere.>

## Mobile Accessibility Features

Mobile accessibility features refer to a variety of design elements and functionality within a user interface (UI) that are specifically implemented to enhance the accessibility and usability of mobile applications for individuals with disabilities. These features aim to provide equal access and equal opportunity to individuals with visual, auditory, motor, and cognitive impairments. UI patterns and design systems play a crucial role in the implementation of mobile accessibility features. UI patterns refer to specific design solutions that are commonly used to address user needs and interactions, while design systems are a collection of reusable UI elements, components, and guidelines that ensure consistency and efficiency in the design process. One important aspect of mobile accessibility features is providing alternative ways for individuals with disabilities to navigate and interact with the app. This can be achieved through the use of standard UI patterns such as menus, buttons, and links that are easily recognizable and accessible through various input methods, including touch, gestures, and keyboard navigation. Another key consideration in mobile accessibility is the presentation of content. Design systems can include guidelines for using appropriate font sizes, color contrast, and spacing to ensure that content is legible and perceivable for individuals with visual impairments. Additionally, design patterns such as resizable text and adjustable text spacing can further enhance the readability of content. Mobile accessibility features also encompass the provision of alternative formats for content, such as audio descriptions for images and videos, closed captions for videos, and text-to-speech capabilities for written content. These features ensure that individuals with visual or auditory impairments can access and understand the information presented within the app. Moreover, mobile accessibility features include considerations for motor impairments, such as the ability to navigate through the app using alternative interaction methods like voice commands, gestures, or external devices. Design systems can include guidelines for incorporating sufficient touch target sizes, providing ample spacing between interactive elements, and avoiding time-based interactions that may be challenging for individuals with limited dexterity. In conclusion, mobile accessibility features are indispensable for creating inclusive and user-friendly mobile applications. By incorporating accessible UI patterns and adhering to design systems that prioritize the needs of individuals with disabilities, developers can ensure that their apps are accessible to a wider range of users, fostering equal access and equal opportunity for all.>

## Mobile Accessibility Settings

Mobile Accessibility Settings refers to the set of features, tools, and options available on mobile devices that are specifically designed to enhance the accessibility of the user interface (UI) for individuals with disabilities. These settings encompass various UI patterns and design systems that cater to the needs of users with visual, auditory, motor, or cognitive impairments, ensuring that everyone can effectively use and interact with the device. The Mobile Accessibility Settings typically include options to adjust display settings, such as text size, contrast, and color schemes, to accommodate individuals with visual impairments. Additionally, these settings often offer features like magnification and screen reader compatibility, which enable visually impaired users to navigate the UI and interact with content. Screen readers are assistive technologies that read aloud the text and provide auditory cues, allowing individuals with visual impairments to understand the information presented on the screen. In terms of auditory accessibility, the Mobile Accessibility Settings may provide options for adjusting the volume, pitch, and sound enhancements, ensuring that individuals with hearing impairments can adjust the device to their specific needs. Moreover, captions and subtitles can be enabled for multimedia content, further enhancing the accessibility for users who are deaf or hard of hearing. For individuals with motor impairments, mobile devices may offer accessibility settings that allow them to modify gesture sensitivity, enable switch control, or utilize voice commands. These settings enable users with limited dexterity or motor control to navigate through the UI and interact with the device effectively. Furthermore, Mobile Accessibility Settings may include options for cognitive accessibility, such as simplifying the UI by reducing visual clutter or employing clear and concise language. These settings aim to support individuals with cognitive disabilities, helping them better understand and navigate through the interface. Overall, the Mobile Accessibility Settings form an integral part of inclusive design, promoting equal access and usability for all users, regardless of their abilities. By incorporating such settings into the design system and UI patterns, mobile devices aim to ensure that individuals with disabilities can fully benefit from the features and functionalities offered, enhancing their overall user experience and empowering their digital independence.>

## Mobile Accident Alerts

Mobile Accident Alerts is a UI pattern and part of a design system that provides users with real-time notifications about accidents and incidents related to their mobile devices or services. It aims to enhance the user experience by promptly informing them about any potential issues or dangers they may encounter while using their mobile devices.

The Mobile Accident Alerts pattern consists of various components and functions that work together to deliver timely and relevant information to users. These components typically include an alert notification banner, a concise and informative message, and appropriate action options for the users to take. The design system ensures consistency in the presentation and behavior of the alert across different platforms and devices.

## Mobile Achievements

Mobile Achievements are a UI pattern and design system that aims to incentivize and reward user engagement and progress within mobile applications. It involves the use of visual cues and interactive elements to acknowledge and celebrate specific milestones, accomplishments, or actions performed by the user. Mobile Achievements are typically implemented through badges or icons that are displayed prominently within the user interface. These visual indicators serve as a form of recognition, motivating users to continue engaging with the app and reaching new goals. The achievements may be tied to specific tasks, levels, or achievements within the app, or they can be more general indicators of overall progress. The design of Mobile Achievements should be consistent with the overall visual style and branding of the application. They should be visually appealing and easily distinguishable to ensure clear communication to the user. The size, shape, and color of the achievements can vary depending on the app's design system, but they should always be intuitive and easy to understand. In addition to the visual representation of achievements, Mobile Achievements can also include interactive elements that allow users to view more details about their accomplishments. This can be done through pop-up windows, tooltips, or dedicated achievement screens that provide additional information about the task or action that led to the achievement. The implementation of Mobile Achievements should be thoughtfully designed to avoid overwhelming the user with an excessive number of achievements or notifications. They should be strategically placed within the user interface and triggered at appropriate moments to create a sense of excitement and accomplishment without causing distractions or disruptions. Ultimately, the goal of Mobile Achievements is to create a positive and immersive user experience that encourages users to actively engage with the app, explore its features, and complete desired actions. By rewarding users for their progress and celebrating their accomplishments, mobile applications can foster a sense of satisfaction, motivation, and loyalty, leading to increased user retention and engagement.

Mobile Achievements are a UI pattern and design system that incentivize and reward user engagement and progress in mobile applications. They use visual indicators, such as badges, to recognize accomplishments and motivate users. The design should be consistent with the app's branding and visually appealing. Interactive elements can provide more information about achievements. Careful implementation is important to create a positive experience without overwhelming the user.

## Mobile Air Quality Alerts

Mobile Air Quality Alerts are a user interface (UI) pattern and design system element that provides users with real-time information about the air quality in their current location or specified areas. These alerts are designed to be displayed on mobile devices, such as smartphones or tablets, and are intended to help users make informed decisions about their outdoor activities based on the current air quality conditions. The Mobile Air Quality Alerts UI pattern typically consists of a notification or message that is displayed prominently on the screen of the device. The notification usually includes a brief description of the air quality conditions, such as "Poor," "Moderate," "Good," or "Excellent," along with relevant recommendations or guidelines for users based on the current conditions. These recommendations may include suggestions to limit outdoor activities, use protective measures (e.g., wearing a face mask), or seek shelter in indoor environments. Within a design system, Mobile Air Quality Alerts are usually defined as a specific component or module that can be easily integrated into various mobile applications or websites. This ensures consistency in the visual style, behavior, and accessibility of the alerts across different platforms and applications. The design of Mobile Air Quality Alerts should prioritize clarity and simplicity to ensure that users can quickly and easily understand the information being presented. The alerts should use clear and concise language to describe the air quality conditions and provide relevant guidance to users. Visual cues, such as color-coded indicators or icons, can be used to convey the severity of the air quality conditions at a glance. In terms of interaction, Mobile Air Quality Alerts may include the option for users to dismiss the notification or access more detailed information about the air quality conditions. This additional information may include pollutant levels, a map showing the affected areas, or forecasts for future air quality conditions. Overall, Mobile Air Quality Alerts are an essential component of mobile user interfaces, providing users with timely and critical information to help them navigate the impact of air quality on their daily activities. By incorporating this UI pattern into a design system, developers can ensure a consistent and user-friendly experience across different applications and platforms.

Mobile Air Quality Alerts are a UI pattern and design system element that provides real-time information about air quality to mobile users. The alerts consist of notifications or messages displayed on mobile devices and prioritize clarity and simplicity. They use concise language and visual cues to convey air quality conditions and relevant guidance to users. Mobile Air Quality Alerts are part of a design system to ensure consistency and can include options for dismissal or accessing more detailed information.

## Mobile Alarm Clock

A mobile alarm clock is a user interface (UI) pattern and design system component that allows users to set alarms and manage their wake-up schedule on their mobile devices. It serves the purpose of providing a reliable and customizable alarm system that ensures users are alerted at the desired times. The mobile alarm clock typically consists of a digital or analog clock display, a set alarm time input, and additional functionalities such as snooze, repeat, and customization options for alarm sounds and volume. The UI is designed to be intuitive and easy to use, allowing users to quickly access and modify their alarm settings. When designing a mobile alarm clock, it is crucial to prioritize the usability and accessibility of the interface. The clock display should be highly legible, with clear digits and labels, ensuring that users can effortlessly read the time and alarm settings. Additionally, the UI should provide visual cues, such as color coding, to indicate if an alarm is set or active. An essential aspect of the mobile alarm clock is the alarm management functionality. Users should be able to easily set multiple alarms, modify existing alarms, and enable/disable alarms as per their requirements. It is also common to include the option for users to label their alarms, enabling them to differentiate between various wake-up times or reminders. Furthermore, the mobile alarm clock should offer customization options that cater to individual preferences. This includes the ability to choose from a variety of alarm sounds or even upload custom sounds. The UI should allow users to adjust the volume of the alarm independently from the device's media volume. To enhance the overall user experience, it is advisable to implement features like snooze and alarm repetition. Snooze allows users to temporarily silence the alarm and be reminded again after a specified duration. Alarm repetition ensures that users can set alarms to repeat on specific days or weekdays, providing flexibility for recurring wake-up schedules. In conclusion, a mobile alarm clock is a vital component of mobile device UI patterns and design systems. It facilitates users in managing their wake-up schedule by providing an intuitive and customizable interface. The alarm clock's design and functionality should prioritize usability, legibility, and customization options for a seamless user experience.>

## Mobile Allergy Alerts

Mobile Allergy Alerts is a user interface (UI) pattern and design system that focuses on providing timely and context-aware notifications for individuals with allergies through mobile devices.

The primary goal of Mobile Allergy Alerts is to help allergy sufferers stay informed and manage their allergies more effectively by delivering real-time notifications about relevant allergens in their vicinity. By leveraging location-based services and data from reliable sources such as weather stations, environmental agencies, and pollen counts, this UI pattern aims to deliver accurate and personalized allergy alerts to users.

## Mobile Amber Alerts

Mobile Amber Alerts refer to a specific user interface pattern and design system that is used in mobile applications to notify and alert users about missing children and possible child abduction cases. This pattern aims to leverage mobile devices as a way to rapidly disseminate critical information and engage the community in the search for missing children.

The Mobile Amber Alerts UI pattern typically involves displaying a prominent and visually impactful alert within the mobile application. This alert may include relevant information about the missing child, such as their name, age, physical description, and last known location. It may also provide contact information, such as a dedicated hotline or helpline, for users to report any sightings or provide information related to the case.

## Mobile App Onboarding Tutorial

An onboarding tutorial is a UI pattern used in the design system of a mobile app to guide new users through the app's features and functionalities. It is a series of screens or steps that provide a step-by-step explanation or demonstration of how to use the app. The onboarding tutorial aims to help users quickly understand how to navigate the app and maximize its value.

The onboarding tutorial typically appears when users first install and launch the app. It can also be accessed later through the app's settings or help section for users who want a refresher or missed the initial tutorial. The tutorial screens often include brief and concise text, illustrations, animations, and interactive elements to engage and educate users.

One common approach in implementing an onboarding tutorial is to use a carousel or swipeable screen navigation. Each screen presents a new feature or concept, highlighting its benefits and explaining how to use it. Users can swipe or tap to progress through the tutorial. Alternatively, a linear progression of screens with back and next buttons can be used.

The content of the tutorial screens should be carefully crafted to be clear and easy to understand. It should focus on the core functionalities that users need to know to accomplish important tasks in the app. The text should be concise, using simple language and avoiding technical jargon.

In addition to explaining features, the tutorial can also showcase the app's unique selling points or key differentiators. It can highlight how the app can simplify tasks, save time, or provide unique experiences. This can help create a positive impression and motivate users to continue using the app.

Effective onboarding tutorials take into consideration the user's familiarity with similar apps or existing knowledge of the app's domain. They should strike a balance between providing enough guidance for beginners and not overwhelming experienced users. Options to skip or exit the tutorial should be available to accommodate users who prefer to explore the app on their own.

Overall, a well-designed onboarding tutorial is essential for mobile apps as it improves user engagement, reduces confusion, and increases user retention. By providing a smooth and intuitive introduction to the app, it increases the likelihood of users becoming active and satisfied app users.

## Mobile App Permissions Manager

A Mobile App Permissions Manager is a UI pattern and design system that allows users to manage and control the permissions granted to mobile applications on their devices. This tool provides a centralized location where users can easily review and adjust the permissions that have been granted to different apps. It offers a user-friendly interface which allows users to quickly understand the permissions requested by each app and make informed decisions about whether they want to allow or deny access to specific functions or data. The Mobile App Permissions Manager typically displays a list of installed apps, along with the permissions each app has requested. The list can be sorted and filtered to help users easily find the apps they are looking for. The interface should provide clear, concise descriptions of each permission, so users can easily understand what each permission means and how it may impact their privacy or device functionality. When users interact with the Mobile App Permissions Manager, they should have the ability to selectively enable or disable permissions for each app. This could be done by toggling switches or checkboxes next to each permission. The changes made by the user should be immediately reflected in the app's settings and take effect right away. Appropriate feedback and confirmation messages should be provided to users when they modify permissions. This helps to ensure that users have a clear understanding of the changes they have made and can easily track and manage their preferences. The Mobile App Permissions Manager should also include options for users to revoke or grant permissions globally. For example, users may choose to deny all apps access to their location data at once, or allow all apps to access their camera. These global options can save users time and effort when managing permissions for multiple apps. In conclusion, a Mobile App Permissions Manager is a crucial tool for users to have control over the permissions granted to mobile applications. Its user-friendly interface and intuitive design help users make informed decisions about app permissions and ensure their privacy and device security.>

## Mobile App Permissions

Mobile app permissions in the context of UI patterns and design systems refer to the specific access and capabilities that an application requests from a user's mobile device. When accessing certain features or functionality within a mobile app, the user is often prompted to grant or deny permissions to the app, allowing it to use certain resources or perform certain actions on their device. Permissions can vary depending on the operating system (such as iOS or Android) and the specific capabilities of the device. Examples of common mobile app permissions include: - Camera: This permission allows the app to access the device's camera and capture photos or videos. - Location: This permission allows the app to determine the user's current location using GPS or other location services. - Contacts: This permission allows the app to access the user's contact list and utilize it for features like sharing or connecting with friends. - Microphone: This permission allows the app to record audio using the device's microphone. - Notifications: This permission allows the app to send push notifications to the user's device. - Storage: This permission allows the app to save or access files on the user's device, such as images or documents. - Network access: This permission allows the app to connect to the internet and access online content. Designing the user interface (UI) for app permissions is crucial to ensure a seamless and intuitive user experience. When requesting permissions, it is important to clearly communicate to the user why the app needs the requested access and how it will be used. This can help build trust and increase the likelihood of the user granting the permissions. In terms of UI patterns and design systems, there are a few best practices to consider when dealing with app permissions. These include: 1. Requesting permissions at the right time: Prompting users to grant permissions only when necessary and relevant to the current task can help minimize friction and reduce the likelihood of permission fatigue. 2. Providing clear explanations: Clearly communicate why the app needs each permission and how it will enhance the user experience. Using concise and user-friendly language can help users make informed decisions. 3. Offering granular control: Allow users to grant or deny individual permissions instead of a blanket approval. This gives users more control over their privacy and allows them to customize their app experience. 4. Ensuring transparency: Displaying a link or button to the app's privacy policy or terms of service can provide additional transparency and help users understand how their data will be used. By following these best practices and considering the user's needs and expectations, designers can create a seamless and user-friendly experience when it comes to app permissions.>

## Mobile App Theme Store

A Mobile App Theme Store is a user interface pattern and design system that provides a collection of pre-designed themes for mobile applications. It allows developers and designers to choose from a variety of ready-made visual styles, color schemes, and typography options that can be easily applied to their app's user interface. The main purpose of a Mobile App Theme Store is to provide a convenient and efficient way for app creators to enhance the visual appeal and user experience of their mobile applications. By offering a range of pre-designed themes, it eliminates the need for developers to start designing from scratch and allows them to quickly apply a cohesive and visually pleasing style to their app. In a Mobile App Theme Store, themes are typically organized into categories based on their visual style, such as minimalistic, material design, or flat design. Each theme within a category may have different variations or customization options, providing further flexibility for app creators to tailor the visual style to their specific needs. Once a theme is selected from the Mobile App Theme Store, it can be easily integrated into the design system of the mobile application. The design system usually includes a set of style guidelines, reusable UI components, and design principles that ensure consistency and coherence throughout the app's interface. By adhering to the design system, app creators can maintain a unified look and feel across different screens and functionalities of the application. In terms of implementation, a Mobile App Theme Store could be a standalone web-based platform or a feature integrated into a mobile development framework or tool. It may offer previews of themes, allowing developers to see how a specific theme will look like in their app before making a final selection. In conclusion, a Mobile App Theme Store is a valuable resource for mobile app developers and designers, providing a curated collection of pre-designed visual styles that can be easily applied to enhance the aesthetics and user experience of their applications.>

## Mobile Art Gallery

A Mobile Art Gallery is a user interface pattern and design system specifically created for mobile devices, such as smartphones and tablets, to showcase and navigate through a collection of artwork or other visual content. It provides a visually appealing and interactive experience for users to explore and appreciate various art pieces in a digital environment. The user interface of a Mobile Art Gallery consists of a series of screens or views that allow users to browse through the collection of artwork. The main screen typically presents a grid or list view of thumbnails representing the different art pieces available. Users can scroll vertically or horizontally to navigate through the collection and select a specific artwork to view in more detail. When a user taps on a thumbnail, a new screen or modal view opens, displaying the selected artwork prominently. This screen provides a larger and more detailed view of the artwork, allowing users to fully appreciate its beauty and details. It may also include additional information about the artwork, such as the artist's name, title, medium, and any relevant descriptions or captions. To enhance the user experience, a Mobile Art Gallery often incorporates various touch gestures and interactions. Users can swipe horizontally to switch between different artworks, swipe vertically to view additional information or related content, and pinch-to-zoom to inspect finer details of the artwork. These gestures enable users to explore the artwork intuitively and at their own pace, creating a more engaging and immersive experience. In terms of design, a Mobile Art Gallery follows a consistent visual language and layout to maintain coherence and usability. It may use a minimalistic and clean design aesthetic to focus attention on the artwork itself, with subtle use of colors and typography to complement and enhance the viewing experience. The overall design should prioritize legibility, ease of navigation, and accessibility to ensure that users can easily browse and enjoy the art collection. By providing a mobile-friendly and visually appealing interface, a Mobile Art Gallery allows art enthusiasts to access and appreciate a diverse range of artwork conveniently and on-the-go. Whether it is a curated collection or a platform for artists to showcase their work, a Mobile Art Gallery enables users to explore, discover, and engage with art in a digital environment.>

## Mobile Audiobook Player

A mobile audiobook player refers to a user interface (UI) design pattern and a component of a design system specifically tailored for the purpose of listening to audiobooks on mobile devices. Its primary function is to provide a sleek and user-friendly interface for users to conveniently access and control their audiobook playback.

The design of a mobile audiobook player typically revolves around a minimalistic and intuitive approach, focusing on key features and functionalities while avoiding unnecessary clutter. The player is designed to fit seamlessly within the overall design system of the application or platform it is a part of, maintaining consistency in visual and interactive elements.

## Mobile Avalanche Alerts

Mobile Avalanche Alerts are a user interface pattern and design system specifically designed for mobile devices to provide users with timely and critical information about avalanches.

These alerts aim to increase user awareness and safety by notifying them about potential avalanche risks in their current location or any specific areas of interest. The primary goal of this UI pattern is to help users make informed decisions and take necessary precautions when traveling or engaging in outdoor activities in avalanche-prone regions.

## Mobile Background Wallpaper

A mobile background wallpaper refers to the visual image or design that serves as the backdrop or the decorative element on the screen of a mobile device. It is a pattern or image that is displayed behind all other graphical elements on the screen, providing a visually appealing and personalized experience for the user. In the context of UI patterns and design systems, mobile background wallpapers play a crucial role in enhancing the overall aesthetic appeal and user experience of a mobile application. They serve as a means to reflect the brand identity, convey the app's theme, or simply provide a visually pleasing backdrop. The use of a well-designed and carefully chosen mobile background wallpaper can create a cohesive and harmonious visual experience, aligning with the app's color palette, typography, and overall UI design. It can also provide differentiation and uniqueness, making the app stand out among its competitors. Additionally, mobile background wallpapers can contribute to the overall usability of the application by enhancing the legibility of the content displayed on the screen. When chosen wisely, the contrast between the background wallpaper and the text or other graphical elements can improve readability and ensure optimal user interaction. Design systems in mobile app development often include a set of pre-designed and standardized mobile background wallpapers. These wallpapers follow specific guidelines, such as aspect ratios, resolutions, and file formats, to ensure seamless integration into the app's UI. To implement a mobile background wallpaper in HTML, the "style" attribute can be used within the "body" tag. This attribute allows the inclusion of CSS properties to set the desired background image. For example: ```html

This is the content of the mobile app.

``` In this example, the "url('path-to-image.jpg')" represents the path to the desired image file that will serve as the mobile background wallpaper. The content within the "

" tags represents the actual content of the mobile app, which will appear on top of the background wallpaper. In conclusion, a mobile background wallpaper is a visual element that serves as the backdrop or decorative element on the screen of a mobile device. It contributes to the overall aesthetic appeal, brand identity, and user experience of a mobile application, while also enhancing usability and content legibility.>

## Mobile Barcode Scanner

A mobile barcode scanner is a user interface (UI) pattern and design system component that allows users to scan barcodes using their mobile device camera. It is commonly used in applications and websites that require efficient and accurate barcode scanning for various purposes, such as product lookup, inventory management, ticketing, and loyalty program integration.

The mobile barcode scanner UI pattern typically consists of a designated scan button or area,
```

which triggers the camera to open and initiates the barcode scanning process. The user aims the camera at the barcode they wish to scan, and the scanner detects and captures the barcode image. It then decodes the barcode data and provides the relevant information to the user or performs the intended action, such as searching for product details or adding an item to a shopping cart.

Mobile Battery Saver Mode

Mobile Battery Saver Mode is a user interface pattern and design system feature that helps conserve and optimize the device's battery life. When enabled, it allows the device to limit various background processes and functionalities that consume excessive power, thus extending the battery's overall longevity.

Typically, Mobile Battery Saver Mode plays a significant role in maintaining battery performance during low-power situations, such as when the battery level is critically low or when the user needs their device to last for an extended period without access to a power source. It achieves this by intelligently adjusting settings and reducing power-hungry activities, such as reducing the device's screen brightness, disabling push notifications, restricting background data synchronization, and limiting CPU performance.

Mobile Battery Usage

Mobile Battery Usage refers to the amount of power consumed by a mobile device's battery while it is in use. It is an important aspect to consider in UI patterns and design systems as it directly impacts the user experience and functionality of the device.

Efficient battery usage is crucial for mobile devices as they are often used on-the-go and may not have access to a power source for extended periods of time. Therefore, UI patterns and design systems should aim to optimize battery usage to enhance the user's overall experience and ensure that the device remains functional for longer periods of time.

Mobile Bike Sharing

A mobile bike sharing system is a user interface (UI) pattern and design system that provides a convenient and accessible way for users to rent bicycles using their mobile devices. This system allows users to locate nearby bike stations, easily check bike availability, and make reservations or unlock bikes using their smartphones.

The mobile bike sharing UI pattern typically includes the following key features:

- Map Integration: The system integrates with a map interface that displays the locations of nearby bike stations. Users can easily view the available bikes at each station and their distance from their current location.

- Bike Reservation: Users can reserve bikes in advance through the mobile app. This ensures that a bike will be available for them when they arrive at the station. The reservation feature allows users to select a specific bike station and reserve a bike for a defined period of time.

- Bike Unlocking: Once a bike is reserved, users can unlock it using their mobile devices. This is typically done by scanning a QR code or entering a unique code provided by the system. After unlocking the bike, users can start using it for their desired duration.

- Trip Tracking: The mobile bike sharing system may also include a feature that allows users to track their trip in real-time. This feature may provide information such as distance traveled, duration, calories burned, and other useful data.

The design system for mobile bike sharing should prioritize simplicity and ease of use. It should have a clean and intuitive user interface, with clear navigation and prominently displayed information. The color scheme and visual elements should be consistent with the branding of the bike sharing service to create a cohesive user experience.

Overall, a mobile bike sharing system offers users an efficient and flexible way to access and use bicycles. Its user-friendly interface and well-designed features make it easy for users to find, reserve, and use bikes, enhancing the overall user experience.

Mobile Biometric Authentication

Mobile biometric authentication refers to the use of unique human characteristics, such as fingerprints, facial recognition, or voice patterns, to verify the identity of a user on a mobile device or application. This technology provides an additional layer of security and convenience by replacing or supplementing traditional login methods, such as passwords or PINs.

By leveraging the built-in sensors and cameras of mobile devices, biometric authentication offers a seamless and user-friendly way to access and authenticate personal information or perform secure transactions. Users can simply scan their fingerprint, look at the camera, or speak a passphrase to gain access to their device, apps, or specific features within an app.

Mobile Bluetooth Settings

Mobile Bluetooth Settings refer to the user interface (UI) patterns and design system that allow users to manage and control the Bluetooth connectivity of their mobile devices. In the context of UI patterns, Bluetooth settings typically appear as a dedicated section within a mobile device's system settings. This section provides users with various options and controls to enable or disable Bluetooth, pair their device with other Bluetooth-enabled devices, and manage the connections. The Bluetooth settings UI is designed to be intuitive and user-friendly. It usually consists of a toggle switch at the top, enabling users to easily turn their device's Bluetooth on or off. Below the toggle switch, there is commonly a list of paired and available devices, along with options to search for new devices to connect with. Within the Bluetooth settings, users can typically perform the following actions: 1. Enable or Disable Bluetooth: The toggle switch prominently placed at the top of the settings allows users to easily enable or disable Bluetooth connectivity on their mobile device. 2. Pairing with Devices: Users can initiate a search for Bluetooth devices available in the vicinity, enabling them to pair their mobile device with them. Upon selecting a device to pair with, the UI may prompt for authorization or PIN entry, if required. 3. Manage Paired Devices: Once paired, the UI often provides options to manage the list of paired devices. Users can view detailed information about each paired device, including its name, type, status, and the option to disconnect or forget the device. 4. Additional Settings: Some devices offer additional settings within the Bluetooth settings section, allowing users to customize their Bluetooth experience. These settings may include options like visibility, device name, and connection preferences. The design system for Bluetooth settings focuses on ensuring consistency and clarity across various mobile platforms. It employs standardized icons and intuitive navigation to enhance user understanding and ease of use. Overall, the UI patterns and design system for mobile Bluetooth settings aim to provide users with an easily accessible and straightforward means of managing and controlling the Bluetooth connectivity of their mobile devices.>

Mobile Boarding Pass

A mobile boarding pass is a digital ticket that allows passengers to check-in for a flight and access their boarding pass directly from their mobile device. It is a user interface (UI) pattern and element within a design system that aims to streamline the travel experience and eliminate the need for a physical boarding pass.

Mobile boarding passes are typically presented in the form of a digital barcode or QR code that can be scanned at various checkpoints throughout the airport, including security, boarding gates, and even duty-free shops. This digital format makes it convenient for passengers to have all their flight information readily accessible on their mobile devices.

Mobile Car Maintenance Tracker

A Mobile Car Maintenance Tracker is a user interface pattern and design system that allows users to keep track of their car maintenance and service records using a mobile application. It provides a convenient and organized way for users to monitor and manage their vehicle's maintenance needs.

The primary goal of a Mobile Car Maintenance Tracker is to help users stay on top of their car's maintenance requirements and ensure the longevity and optimal performance of their vehicle. The app enables users to easily record and track essential maintenance tasks such as oil changes, tire rotations, fluid checks, and filter replacements. By capturing this information in a centralized database, users can conveniently refer back to it whenever necessary.

The design system of a Mobile Car Maintenance Tracker typically includes various screens and features that facilitate seamless user interactions. It often incorporates intuitive navigation menus, allowing users to access different sections of the app effortlessly. These sections can include a dashboard displaying upcoming maintenance tasks, a history tab for reviewing past services, and settings to customize reminders and notifications.

Additionally, a Mobile Car Maintenance Tracker often utilizes input forms and data entry fields to capture relevant information about each maintenance task. These forms may include fields for entering the date of the service, mileage at the time of maintenance, the type of service performed, and any additional notes or details. Users can also set reminders based on mileage or time intervals to ensure timely service scheduling. Moreover, the app may provide visual indicators or progress bars to help users visualize the completion status of scheduled or overdue tasks.

The UI pattern and design principles of a Mobile Car Maintenance Tracker prioritize simplicity, ease of use, and clear visual hierarchy. The interface typically includes minimalistic and consistent styling, employing a user-friendly color palette and typography. It aims to streamline the user experience by prioritizing essential information and minimizing visual clutter. The app may also feature intuitive gestures or interactions, such as swipe actions to mark tasks as completed or to navigate between different screens.

Mobile Carpooling

Mobile Carpooling is a mobile application feature or functionality that allows users to share rides with others who are traveling in the same direction or have similar destinations. This concept aims to reduce traffic congestion, carbon emissions, and the need for individual vehicles by promoting the sharing of vehicles among users.

In terms of UI patterns and design systems, Mobile Carpooling typically consists of several key elements:

1. User Profiles: Each user has a profile that includes information about their preferences, commute details, and personal information (such as name, profile picture, and contact information). This information helps in determining suitable matches for carpooling.

2. Ride Listings: Users can create listings for their upcoming rides, specifying the pickup location, destination, and other relevant details (such as the departure time, vehicle type, or any special requirements). These listings are visible to other users who may be interested in joining the same ride.

3. Ride Matching: The mobile carpooling app uses algorithms to match users based on their location, destination, and other preferences. The app suggests potential matches to users who are looking for carpool partners, considering factors such as proximity, route compatibility, and user ratings/reviews.

4. Communication and Coordination: Once a match is made, users can communicate within the app to discuss specific details or coordinate logistics. This may involve messaging, notifications, or even in-app calling features to facilitate communication between the driver and passengers.

5. Ratings and Reviews: After each ride, users have the opportunity to rate and review their experience with their carpooling partner. These ratings and reviews help in building a trusted community and improving user safety.

Overall, the design of Mobile Carpooling applications should focus on simplicity, ease of use, and clear communication. The interface should enable users to easily navigate through the various features, view relevant information, and interact with potential carpooling partners effectively.

Mobile Checkout Process

Mobile Checkout Process refers to the series of steps that a user follows to complete a purchase on a mobile device. This process involves a set of carefully designed user interface (UI) patterns and a coherent design system to ensure a seamless and efficient checkout experience for the user. The mobile checkout process typically starts with a clear and visible "Checkout" button or call-to-action (CTA) that prompts the user to proceed to the next step. Once the user clicks on the checkout button, they are taken to a dedicated checkout page or a modal overlay, where they can review their cart items, add or remove items, and proceed to the payment step. In the payment step, the user is presented with different payment options, such as credit card, Paypal, or mobile payment providers. The UI should clearly display the available payment options, ensuring that they are easy to select and understand. It is crucial to minimize the steps required to input payment information to reduce friction and provide a smooth checkout experience. After selecting the preferred payment method, the user is prompted to enter their payment details. The UI should provide clear form fields for the user to input their credit card information or other necessary payment details. It's important to keep the form fields concise, intuitive, and easy to fill in on a mobile device. Additionally, real-time validation can be implemented to help the user input accurate information and avoid errors. Once the payment information is successfully entered, the user is then prompted to review their order details, including shipping address and any applied discounts or promotions. They should also have the option to edit or update these details if necessary. Clear and concise summaries of the order and associated costs should be provided to ensure transparency. After reviewing the order, the user can proceed to the final confirmation step, where they are presented with a "Place Order" or similar CTA. On clicking this button, the user's order is confirmed, processed, and a confirmation message is displayed. Additionally, an order summary or receipt should be sent to the user's email address or available in their user account for future reference. In conclusion, the mobile checkout process is a crucial part of any e-commerce application, and its effectiveness heavily relies on well-designed UI patterns and a consistent design system. By providing clear prompts, intuitive payment options, concise form fields, and transparent order summaries, the mobile checkout process ensures a seamless and efficient purchasing experience for users on mobile devices.>

Mobile Closed Captions

Mobile Closed Captions: Mobile Closed Captions refer to a user interface pattern and design system that displays text-based transcriptions or descriptions of audio content on mobile devices. This feature is primarily designed to assist individuals who are deaf or hard of hearing in understanding and engaging with multimedia content on their mobile devices. The primary purpose of Mobile Closed Captions is to provide an inclusive user experience by ensuring that individuals with hearing impairments can fully comprehend audio content. By displaying synchronized captions alongside audio or video content, Mobile Closed Captions enable users to read the dialogue, sound effects, and other relevant auditory information. This allows them to effectively follow and engage with the content, enhancing their overall multimedia experience. In terms of UI patterns, Mobile Closed Captions typically appear as a dedicated area within the mobile app or media player interface. The captions are often displayed in a legible font and contrasting color to ensure readability. They may be positioned at the bottom or top of the screen, providing a visually distinct separation from the visual content. Design systems for Mobile Closed Captions should include guidelines for formatting, styling, and caption placement to ensure consistency across different mobile devices and applications. These design systems should consider factors such as font size, colors, text alignment, and background opacity to optimize accessibility and readability. Implementing Mobile Closed Captions in an HTML format can be achieved using various techniques. Developers can include the element within the or tag to define the caption data. This allows mobile devices to recognize and display the captions accordingly. Additionally, CSS styling can be applied to customize the appearance of the captions to meet the design system requirements. In conclusion, Mobile Closed Captions are an essential feature in mobile UI patterns and design systems that prioritize accessibility and inclusivity. By providing synchronized text-based transcriptions of audio content, Mobile Closed Captions enable individuals with hearing impairments to fully engage with multimedia experiences on their mobile devices. Implementation of Mobile Closed Captions in HTML involves the use of the element and CSS styling to ensure consistent formatting and user experience.>

Mobile Color Inversion

Mobile color inversion is a UI pattern and design system that enables users to change the color scheme of a mobile application or website by inverting the colors. This pattern is typically used to enhance accessibility and improve visibility for users with visual impairments or other conditions that may affect their ability to perceive colors accurately. In a color inversion design system, the traditional color scheme of an application is reversed, with light elements becoming dark and vice versa. For example, a white background would become black, black text would become white, and colors would be inverted accordingly. This creates a high contrast between text and background, making it easier for users to read and interact with the content. The purpose of mobile color inversion is to make digital content more accessible and inclusive. By providing users with the option to invert colors, designers can accommodate a wider range of visual needs. This pattern can benefit users with conditions such as color blindness, low vision, and sensitivity to bright or dark colors. Implementing color inversion in a design system requires careful consideration of various UI elements. The system should ensure that the inverted colors maintain legibility, readability, and visual clarity across all components, including text, icons, buttons, and images. It is important to avoid scenarios where the inverted colors create visual confusion or reduce the usability of the application. From a technical standpoint, mobile color inversion can be achieved by using CSS and JavaScript. CSS can be used to apply the inverted color scheme to different elements, while JavaScript can be used to toggle between the original and inverted color schemes based on user preferences. In conclusion, mobile color inversion is a UI pattern and design system that allows users to change the color scheme of a mobile application or website by inverting the colors. It is used to enhance accessibility and improve visibility for users with visual impairments or other specific needs. By considering the legibility, readability, and visual clarity of the inverted colors, designers can create a more inclusive and user-friendly interface.>

Mobile Commenting System

A mobile commenting system is a user interface pattern and design system that enables users to engage in discussions, share their thoughts, and provide feedback on mobile platforms. It allows users to write comments, reply to existing comments, and interact with other users in a structured and organized manner. The mobile commenting system typically consists of a comment input field where users can enter their comments. The input field may also provide options for formatting text, adding emojis, and attaching media files such as images or videos. Once a comment is posted, it is displayed along with other comments in a hierarchical structure. Each comment may have a timestamp indicating when it was posted and the name or username of the commenter. Users can then read and review comments by scrolling through the comment section. To enable discussions and interactions, the mobile commenting system also provides features such as reply functionality. Users can reply to a specific comment by clicking on a reply button or a designated area next to the comment. This helps to maintain the context of the conversation and allows for nested comments. In addition to commenting and replying, the mobile commenting system often includes features for upvoting or downvoting comments. This allows users to express their agreement or disagreement with a particular comment. The comment with the highest number of upvotes is typically displayed at the top of the comment section or using other visually distinctive elements. The design of a mobile commenting system should prioritize readability and usability. Clear typography, appropriate spacing, and legible font sizes are important considerations to ensure that users can easily read and comprehend comments. The system should also incorporate responsive design principles to adapt to different screen sizes and orientations. In conclusion, a mobile commenting system is a UI pattern and design system that facilitates user engagement, discussion, and feedback on mobile platforms. It allows users to post comments, reply to existing comments, and interact with other users in a structured and organized manner. By providing a user-friendly and visually appealing interface, the mobile commenting system enhances user experience and promotes meaningful conversations.>

Mobile Community Safety Alerts

Mobile Community Safety Alerts are a UI pattern and design system feature that provides real-

139

time, location-based notifications to mobile users in order to enhance community safety and security. Safety alerts can include a wide range of information, such as emergency alerts, severe weather warnings, crime reports, traffic accidents, and other relevant updates that may impact the well-being of individuals within a specific geographic area. These alerts are typically triggered by authoritative sources, such as law enforcement agencies, weather services, or other trusted organizations responsible for public safety. In terms of the UI pattern, the Mobile Community Safety Alerts feature typically consists of a notification system integrated into a mobile app or platform. When a new alert is issued, it is displayed as a prominent and attention-grabbing notification directly on the user's mobile device. This ensures that individuals quickly receive and acknowledge the alerts, helping them to stay informed and potentially take appropriate action to protect themselves and others. The design system for Mobile Community Safety Alerts focuses on ensuring that the alerts are highly visible, easily distinguished from other notifications or app content, and presented in a format that provides essential information at a glance. This includes elements such as vibrant colors, clear typography, and concise messaging that delivers the necessary details without overwhelming the user. Additionally, the design system may incorporate features that allow users to customize the types of alerts they wish to receive or tailor the notification settings based on their preferences. This allows users to filter out irrelevant or non-essential alerts, ensuring they only receive information that is relevant to their immediate safety and well-being. In summary, Mobile Community Safety Alerts are a UI pattern and design system that leverages real-time, location-based notifications to enhance community safety and security. By providing timely and relevant information to mobile users, these alerts empower individuals to make informed decisions and take appropriate action in emergency situations or when potential threats arise.>

Mobile Construction Zone Alerts

The Mobile Construction Zone Alerts UI pattern is a design system component that provides real-time notifications to mobile users about ongoing construction zones or roadwork in their vicinity.

These alerts are designed to enhance user safety and improve their overall mobility experience by providing relevant information about potential delays, detours, or hazards due to construction activities.

Mobile Cooking Tutorials

Mobile Cooking Tutorials refer to a user interface pattern and design system that focuses on providing step-by-step instructional content for cooking recipes on mobile devices. This design concept aims to offer a seamless and engaging user experience by using mobile-friendly layouts and interactive features.

With Mobile Cooking Tutorials, users can easily navigate through recipe instructions and visually follow each step in the cooking process. The user interface typically incorporates clear and concise text instructions, accompanied by visually appealing images and videos to enhance comprehension and facilitate the cooking process. The design system ensures consistency in the visual style, typography, and color scheme of the tutorials across different recipes, creating a cohesive and recognizable brand identity.

Mobile Currency Converter

A Mobile Currency Converter is a user interface pattern and design system that allows users to easily convert between different currencies on their mobile devices. It provides a convenient tool for travelers, online shoppers, and anyone who needs to quickly convert currency values. The Mobile Currency Converter typically consists of a simple and intuitive interface that allows users to input the amount they want to convert and select the currencies they wish to convert between. The design is often minimalistic, focusing on usability and clarity. It may include visual cues such as flags or currency symbols to help users quickly identify the currencies they are working with. The design system ensures consistency across different screens and contexts within the currency converter. It includes a set of predefined styles, colors, and typography that remain consistent throughout the application. This creates a unified and coherent user experience. The user interface pattern and design system of the Mobile Currency Converter also takes into consideration the principles of responsive design. It is optimized for various screen sizes and orientations, providing a seamless experience across different mobile devices. The Mobile Currency Converter allows users to obtain real-time conversion rates, ensuring accurate and up-to-date calculations. It may also provide additional features such as the ability to save and manage favorite currencies or view historical exchange rates. These functionalities enhance the overall usefulness and convenience of the mobile currency converter. In conclusion, a Mobile Currency Converter is a user interface pattern and design system that enables users to perform currency conversions easily on their mobile devices. It offers simplicity, clarity, and responsiveness, providing a seamless experience for users who need to convert currencies on the go.>

Mobile DIY And Crafts

Mobile DIY and Crafts refers to a design system that provides a collection of UI patterns and guidelines for creating mobile applications with a focus on do-it-yourself (DIY) projects and crafts. This design system is specifically tailored for mobile platforms and aims to provide a consistent and user-friendly experience for users engaged in DIY activities.

The Mobile DIY and Crafts design system includes a set of predefined UI patterns and components that can be used to build mobile applications related to various DIY and craft projects. These patterns and components cover a wide range of functionalities and features, including project galleries, step-by-step instructions, material lists, shopping carts, and social sharing options.

Mobile Dark Mode

Mobile dark mode is a user interface (UI) pattern and design system that provides a dark color scheme for mobile applications and websites. It is specifically tailored for mobile devices, such as smartphones and tablets, to enhance the viewing experience in low-light environments and reduce eye strain.

Dark mode replaces the traditional light-colored background with a dark or black background, and the text, icons, and other user interface elements are displayed in light colors or shades to ensure readability. This UI pattern is becoming increasingly popular as it offers a sleek and modern aesthetic while also conserving power on devices with OLED or AMOLED displays, as these screens do not require backlighting for black pixels.

Mobile Dashboard

A mobile dashboard is a user interface pattern and design system that provides a consolidated view of important information and functionality on a mobile device. It is a visual representation of key data and tasks that allows users to quickly access and interact with various features and tools. The primary goal of a mobile dashboard is to provide users with an at-a-glance overview of important metrics, trends, and insights. It can help users monitor performance, track progress, and make informed decisions in a timely manner. A well-designed mobile dashboard should prioritize relevant information and make it easily accessible. It should use visual elements such as charts, graphs, and progress bars to display data in a clear and concise manner. The layout should be intuitive, with a logical organization of content and a consistent design language. Key features of a mobile dashboard include customizable widgets or modules that allow users to personalize the dashboard according to their needs and preferences. Users should be able to rearrange, add, or remove modules based on the information they find most valuable. Navigation within a mobile dashboard should be seamless, with clear pathways to deeper levels of data or functionality. It should provide intuitive search and filtering capabilities to help users find specific information or perform specific actions efficiently. In terms of design system, a mobile dashboard should adhere to established visual and interaction patterns to ensure consistency across different screens and devices. It should incorporate responsive design principles to adapt to various screen sizes and orientations. The use of color, typography, and iconography should be consistent with the overall branding of the application or platform. Overall, a mobile dashboard plays a crucial role in providing users with actionable insights and facilitating effective decision-making. It allows users to stay informed, track performance, and manage tasks efficiently, all within the limited real estate of a mobile device.>

Mobile Data Backup And Restore

Mobile Data Backup and Restore is a UI pattern and design system that allows users to save, transfer, and restore their personal data from one mobile device to another. This feature is particularly useful when users upgrade to a new device, switch to a different operating system, or need to restore their data after a software or hardware failure.

With Mobile Data Backup and Restore, users can securely back up their contacts, messages, photos, videos, documents, and other important data to a cloud storage platform or a local storage location. The backup process ensures that users' data is protected and easily accessible whenever needed. Additionally, this feature provides users with the flexibility to restore their data selectively, only restoring the specific files or information they require, rather than having to restore their entire backup.

Mobile Data Usage Tracker

A Mobile Data Usage Tracker is a user interface (UI) pattern and component of a design system that enables mobile users to monitor and manage their data consumption. It provides users with valuable insights and controls over their mobile data usage, helping them to stay within their data limits and avoid unexpected charges. The Mobile Data Usage Tracker typically consists of visuals, graphs, and statistics that depict the user's data consumption in a clear and easily comprehensible manner. Users can see their data usage trends over a selected period, which can be daily, weekly, monthly, or custom time frames. The graphical representation allows users to quickly understand their usage patterns, such as peak usage times or days. This information empowers users to make informed decisions about their data usage and adjust their behavior accordingly. In addition to visual representation, the Mobile Data Usage Tracker also includes numerical data, such as the total amount of data used, data usage per app, or data used on a particular day. This detailed breakdown helps users identify the apps or activities that consume the most data, enabling them to make informed choices about which apps to use or how to optimize their data consumption. The Mobile Data Usage Tracker design system ensures a consistent and seamless user experience across different devices and platforms. It follows established UI patterns and guidelines, such as using intuitive icons for actions like refreshing data or toggling between time frames. It also incorporates responsive design principles to adapt to various screen sizes and orientations. Furthermore, the design system supports customization options, allowing users to set their data limits, receive notifications when approaching their limit, or even set data usage restrictions for specific apps or time frames. These customizable features provide users with greater control and flexibility over their data usage, helping them to manage their resources efficiently. In conclusion, a Mobile Data Usage Tracker is a UI pattern and design system component that helps mobile users monitor and manage their data usage. It presents data consumption in visual and numerical formats, empowering users to make informed decisions about their data usage. It follows established UI patterns and supports customization options for a seamless and personalized user experience.>

Mobile Data Usage

Mobile Data Usage refers to the amount of data consumed by a mobile device while connected to a cellular network. It is measured in megabytes (MB) or gigabytes (GB) and represents the total amount of data transmitted to and from the device over the network.

In the context of UI patterns and design systems, Mobile Data Usage pertains to the presentation and management of data consumption information within a mobile application or interface. This information is crucial for users to understand and monitor their data usage, particularly in scenarios where data plans may have limitations or costs associated with exceeding certain thresholds.

Mobile Device Administration

Mobile Device Administration refers to the process of managing and controlling mobile devices, such as smartphones and tablets, within an organization. It involves implementing policies, configurations, and security measures to ensure the proper functioning and security of these devices.

In the context of UI patterns and design systems, Mobile Device Administration focuses on creating user interfaces and interactions that allow administrators to efficiently manage and control mobile devices. The main goal is to provide a seamless experience for administrators, enabling them to easily navigate and perform their tasks.

Mobile Device Information

A mobile device information refers to the details and specifications of a mobile device, such as smartphones or tablets, which are used to inform the user about the device's capabilities, features, and technical specifications. In the context of UI patterns and design systems, mobile device information plays a vital role in ensuring that the user interface is optimized and tailored to the specific device being used.

UI patterns and design systems involve creating consistent and intuitive user experiences across different devices and screen sizes. Mobile device information helps designers and developers understand the limitations and capabilities of a particular device, allowing them to implement appropriate UI patterns and design elements. For example, if a mobile device has a smaller screen size, the design system may recommend using a collapsible menu or a vertical scrolling layout to accommodate the limited screen real estate. This ensures that the user can navigate the interface easily and efficiently.

Mobile Disaster Preparedness

Mobile Disaster Preparedness refers to the design and implementation of user interface (UI) patterns and design systems specifically tailored for mobile devices to assist users in preparing for and responding to natural disasters, emergencies, and other crisis situations.

These UI patterns and design systems aim to provide users with easily accessible and user-friendly mobile applications or websites that help them effectively plan, organize, and manage their disaster preparedness efforts. By leveraging the unique capabilities of mobile devices, such as GPS, notifications, and real-time data, these design solutions enable users to receive timely updates, access relevant information, and communicate with emergency services or other users during times of crisis.

Mobile Disaster Recovery

Mobile Disaster Recovery refers to the design and implementation of user interface (UI) patterns and a cohesive design system specifically tailored for the recovery and restoration of mobile applications and services in the event of a disaster or disruption.

When a disaster or disruption occurs, such as a natural calamity or a technical failure, the availability and functionality of mobile applications and services are often severely impacted. Mobile Disaster Recovery aims to minimize the downtime and ensure a seamless user experience by providing a set of pre-defined UI patterns and a comprehensive design system that can be quickly implemented to restore critical mobile functionalities.

Mobile Document Scanner

A mobile document scanner is a user interface (UI) pattern and design system used to capture and digitize physical documents using a mobile device, such as a smartphone or tablet. It leverages the device's camera to take a photo or scan a document, and then processes the image to enhance the quality and extract relevant information.

With a mobile document scanner, users can easily convert physical documents into digital format, making them easier to store, organize, and share. This UI pattern typically consists of the following components:

1. Camera and capture controls: The UI provides a live preview from the device's camera, allowing users to properly align and capture the document. Capture controls, such as a shutter button or gesture, enable users to take the photo or start the scanning process.

2. Document alignment and edge detection: To ensure high-quality scans, the mobile document

143

scanner offers visual guidance and tools to align the document within the camera preview. It also employs edge detection algorithms to automatically crop and straighten the document, eliminating any unnecessary background or skewed angles.

3. Image processing and enhancement: Once the document is captured, the mobile document scanner applies image processing techniques to enhance the scanned image. This may involve adjusting brightness, contrast, and sharpness, as well as removing shadows or noise to improve legibility.

4. Document cropping and editing: After processing the image, users can further fine-tune the scanned document by manually cropping or adjusting its borders. This ensures that only the relevant content is retained and any unwanted portions are removed.

5. Export and sharing options: Once the document is digitized, the mobile document scanner provides various options for exporting and sharing it. This typically includes saving the document as a PDF or image file, sending it via email or messaging apps, or uploading it to cloud storage services.

Overall, a mobile document scanner simplifies the process of digitizing physical documents, offering a convenient and efficient way to capture and manage paperwork using a mobile device. It streamlines workflows, reduces clutter, and promotes a paperless approach to document handling.

Mobile Dynamic Themes

Dynamic themes in the context of UI patterns and design systems refer to a feature or functionality that allows users to change the visual appearance of a mobile application or website. These themes provide the ability to modify elements such as color schemes, typography, iconography, and other visual elements to suit the user's personal preferences or the context in which the application is being used. By implementing dynamic themes, designers and developers can create a more personalized and accessible user experience. Users can choose from a variety of pre-defined themes or customize the visual style according to their preferences. This flexibility enhances user satisfaction and engagement, as it enables them to interact with the application in a way that is visually pleasing to them. A design system is a collection of principles, guidelines, and components that are used to create consistent and cohesive user interfaces. It provides a framework for designers and developers to work together efficiently and ensures that the end product is aesthetically pleasing, usable, and accessible. Dynamic themes can be a part of the design system, allowing for the implementation and management of various visual styles within the system. From a technical standpoint, dynamic themes are often implemented using CSS variables or through the use of a theming library or framework. CSS variables allow for the creation of re-usable styles that can be easily modified at runtime. By defining variables for colors, typography, and other design elements, developers can create a set of themes that can be dynamically applied to different parts of the user interface. In conclusion, dynamic themes provide users with the ability to customize the visual appearance of a mobile application or website according to their preferences. They are a key component of a design system, enabling the implementation and management of various visual styles. By using CSS variables or theming libraries, developers can create a flexible and personalized user experience that enhances user satisfaction and engagement.>

Mobile E-Wallet Management

A mobile e-wallet management system refers to the user interface patterns and design system used for creating and managing electronic wallets on mobile devices.

E-wallets, also known as digital wallets or mobile wallets, are virtual wallets that allow users to store, manage, and secure digital payment information such as credit card details, bank account information, and loyalty cards. With the increasing popularity of mobile payment services, e-wallets have become an integral component of the digital economy.

The user interface (UI) patterns and design system for mobile e-wallet management should prioritize simplicity, efficiency, and security. The design should provide users with intuitive

144

navigation and easy access to their e-wallets, enabling them to perform essential tasks effortlessly. The design should also incorporate strong security measures to protect users' financial information and prevent unauthorized access.

Mobile Earthquake Alerts

Mobile Earthquake Alerts is a UI pattern and design system that provides real-time notifications of earthquake events on mobile devices. It is designed to deliver timely and relevant information to users, helping them stay informed and take appropriate actions in response to seismic activities.

The key objective of Mobile Earthquake Alerts is to serve as an efficient and effective means of communicating critical earthquake information to mobile users. This pattern incorporates various design elements and strategies to ensure that earthquake notifications are delivered promptly, displayed prominently, and easily comprehensible. The system aims to strike a balance between delivering accurate information and minimizing user anxiety or panic.

Mobile Educational Courses

A mobile educational course refers to a digital learning experience that is designed specifically for mobile devices, such as smartphones and tablets. It encompasses a wide range of instructional materials and educational content that can be accessed on-the-go, allowing learners to engage in self-paced learning anytime and anywhere.

UI patterns and design systems play a significant role in shaping the user experience of mobile educational courses. UI patterns refer to recurring design solutions that solve common user interface problems, while design systems provide a set of cohesive elements, guidelines, and principles for creating consistent and user-friendly interfaces.

Mobile Emergency Alerts

Mobile Emergency Alerts are a user interface pattern specifically designed to notify mobile device users about critical or potentially life-threatening situations. These alerts are implemented in the form of push notifications, which appear directly on the user's mobile device screen regardless of the current application or setting. Mobile Emergency Alerts are an essential component of a comprehensive emergency management system. They allow governmental agencies, emergency services, and other authorized organizations to quickly and efficiently communicate vital information to the public during emergencies such as natural disasters, terrorist threats, or other significant events. These alerts typically include concise and direct messages that inform users about the situation at hand, provide instructions on how to stay safe, and may also include details regarding relevant actions or precautions that need to be taken. The content of the alerts is carefully crafted to ensure clarity and avoid panic or confusion among recipients. Mobile Emergency Alerts may also include links to additional resources or emergency contact information to offer further assistance. In terms of design, Mobile Emergency Alerts adhere to specific UI patterns and principles to ensure their effectiveness and usability in critical situations. They typically take advantage of high-contrast colors and easily legible typography to ensure readability, especially in challenging or stressful conditions. The alerts also employ familiar visual cues, such as icons or symbols, to convey the nature of the emergency quickly. To ensure accessibility, Mobile Emergency Alerts are designed to be compatible with a wide range of mobile devices and operating systems. They are built using standard HTML and CSS, allowing for consistent rendering across various platforms. In conclusion, Mobile Emergency Alerts are a crucial aspect of a well-designed emergency management system. Their implementation follows established UI patterns and design principles to effectively and efficiently deliver critical information to mobile device users during emergencies. Proper design and adherence to accessibility standards ensure that these alerts reach and inform as many people as possible, potentially saving lives and minimizing harm in times of crisis.>

Mobile Emergency Contacts

Mobile Emergency Contacts refer to a UI pattern and design system that provides users with a quick and efficient way to access and contact emergency services or important contacts in case of emergencies. This feature is commonly found in mobile applications and user interfaces, aimed at enhancing user safety and security. In the context of UI patterns and design systems, Mobile Emergency Contacts typically consist of a designated area or screen within the mobile application where users can enter and store the contact information of emergency services such as police, ambulance, fire department, or any other relevant emergency numbers. Additionally, users can also add the contact information of their trusted family members, friends, or local authorities who can be contacted during emergencies. The design of Mobile Emergency Contacts focuses on simplicity, ease of use, and accessibility. It typically includes clear and visible sections for adding and managing emergency contact information. The user interface should provide input fields for entering contact names, phone numbers, and any additional details or instructions. Additionally, a visual indicator, such as an icon or label, is often included to clearly distinguish these emergency contacts from regular contacts. When a user encounters an emergency situation, they can easily access the Mobile Emergency Contacts screen or feature and quickly initiate a call or message to the desired emergency service or contact. This can be done by tapping on the respective contact's information, which is typically displayed in a clean and visually prominent format. Design systems for Mobile Emergency Contacts should follow established design principles, guidelines, and best practices to ensure consistency and intuitive user experiences across different mobile applications or platforms. These principles include proper spacing, color contrast, typography, and the use of familiar UI elements such as buttons, icons, or dropdown menus. In summary, Mobile Emergency Contacts are a crucial feature of mobile applications that prioritize user safety and security. By providing a dedicated and accessible area to store and contact emergency services or important contacts, these UI patterns and design systems enhance the overall usability and user experience of mobile applications, helping users to swiftly respond to emergency situations and seek assistance when needed.>

Mobile Emergency Services

Mobile Emergency Services are a set of UI patterns and design system elements specifically designed for mobile applications that provide emergency assistance. These services focus on ensuring fast and efficient access to emergency help in critical situations, such as medical emergencies, accidents, natural disasters, and personal safety concerns. The main objective of Mobile Emergency Services UI patterns and design system is to enable users to swiftly and easily communicate their emergency situations and receive appropriate assistance in a timely manner. These services aim to minimize the time required for users to access emergency contacts or call emergency services, as well as provide essential information to emergency responders. The UI patterns and design system for Mobile Emergency Services typically include the following elements: 1. Emergency Contact Information: This pattern provides a dedicated section within the application to store emergency contact details. It allows users to add and manage contacts such as ambulance services, hospitals, police, and other emergency service providers. The design system ensures that this information is easily accessible and prominently displayed within the application interface. 2. SOS Button: This pattern involves the inclusion of a prominent SOS button within the application, which users can tap or press in emergency situations. When activated, this button triggers an immediate alert to emergency services or designated contacts with the user's location information, enabling quick response. The design system ensures the SOS button stands out and is easily distinguishable from other interface elements. 3. Emergency Alerts and Notifications: This pattern involves the use of alerts and notifications to keep users informed about local emergency situations. These notifications can include information about natural disasters, severe weather conditions, or any other emergencies that might affect the user's safety. The design system ensures that these alerts are attention-grabbing and clearly convey the urgency of the situation. 4. Location Tracking: This pattern enables the application to track the user's location during an emergency to provide accurate information to emergency responders. The design system ensures that the location tracking feature is privacy-conscious and transparent, with clear notifications and controls. In conclusion, Mobile Emergency Services UI patterns and design system are essential components of mobile applications that aim to provide quick, efficient, and reliable emergency assistance. These patterns and elements ensure that users can access emergency contacts, trigger alerts, and share their location effectively, helping to save lives and improve overall emergency response.>

146

Mobile Emergency Shelter Locator

A Mobile Emergency Shelter Locator is a user interface pattern and design system that aims to provide a comprehensive and efficient solution for finding and accessing emergency shelters in a mobile application or website. The primary goal of this UI pattern is to assist individuals in locating and obtaining essential information about emergency shelters in their area during times of crisis or natural disasters. By presenting the relevant information in a clear and intuitive manner, this design system supports users in making timely and informed decisions about their safety and well-being. The Mobile Emergency Shelter Locator typically includes the following key elements: 1. Interactive Map: The user interface incorporates an interactive map that allows users to visualize the locations of emergency shelters in their vicinity. The map may be zoomable and draggable, enabling users to explore different areas. It may also display additional contextual information, such as nearby roads, facilities, or hazards. 2. Search Functionality: The design system provides a search functionality that allows users to enter specific criteria or keywords to filter the available emergency shelters. This may include options such as searching by location, capacity, availability, or specific services offered. 3. Shelter Details: When a user selects a specific shelter from the map or search results, the UI pattern displays detailed information about that particular emergency shelter. This may include its address, contact information, opening hours, available amenities, occupancy status, and any specific instructions or guidelines. 4. Accessibility Features: The design system ensures that the UI pattern is accessible to a wide range of users, including those with disabilities or limited vision. This may involve using color contrast, large fonts, alternative text for images, and keyboard navigation support. 5. Notifications and Updates: In times of crisis, it is crucial to keep users informed about any changes or updates regarding the availability or accessibility of emergency shelters. The Mobile Emergency Shelter Locator may incorporate push notifications or real-time updates to ensure that users receive the most current information. Overall, the Mobile Emergency Shelter Locator UI pattern and design system provides a user-friendly and reliable solution for individuals seeking emergency shelter assistance during critical situations. By leveraging intuitive navigation, comprehensive information display, and accessibility features, this design system aims to prioritize user safety and peace of mind.>

Mobile Evacuation Routes

Mobile Evacuation Routes are UI patterns and design system components specifically designed for mobile applications and websites to provide users with clear and intuitive routes to evacuate or exit a certain location in case of emergency situations. These components aim to ensure user safety and improve user experience by visually and functionally guiding them towards the nearest and safest exit points. The key purpose of Mobile Evacuation Routes is to provide users with easily accessible and quickly understandable directions to evacuate a building or area, with the primary objective of minimizing panic and confusion during emergency scenarios. By implementing these UI patterns and design system components, designers can effectively communicate vital information to users in a concise and user-friendly manner. Mobile Evacuation Routes typically include elements such as directional arrows, symbols, and textual instructions displayed on a map or floor plan of the premises. These components help users orient themselves and navigate through the environment to reach designated evacuation points. Additionally, interactive features like real-time updates on evacuation routes, alternate paths, or emergency exit availability can provide users with the most accurate and up-to-date information, ensuring their safety during critical situations. When designing Mobile Evacuation Routes, it is important to consider the specific needs of mobile users, such as limited screen size, touch-based interactions, and potential distractions during emergencies. Therefore, designers should prioritize simplicity, clarity, and ease of use, making sure that the evacuation routes are easily distinguishable and function optimally on mobile devices. In conclusion, Mobile Evacuation Routes are essential UI patterns and design system components that enhance user safety and experience in emergency situations. Through clear visual cues, intuitive navigation, and real-time updates, these components help users evacuate or exit a location efficiently and effectively, ensuring their well-being during critical scenarios.>

Mobile Event Ticketing

Mobile Event Ticketing is a user interface pattern and design system that allows users to easily purchase, manage, and display event tickets on a mobile device. It provides a seamless and convenient way for users to find and attend events, while also offering organizers a streamlined solution to sell and distribute tickets.

The mobile event ticketing user interface pattern is designed to be user-friendly, intuitive, and visually appealing. It incorporates best practices in mobile design to ensure a smooth and effortless ticketing experience for users. The design system includes consistent visual elements, color schemes, typography, and iconography that creates a cohesive and recognizable ticketing app.

One key feature of mobile event ticketing is the ability to search and discover events. Users can browse through various categories, such as concerts, sports events, or theater shows, and easily filter the results based on location, date, or genre. The search results provide essential information, including event details, ticket prices, and availability.

Once users find an event they are interested in, they can view more details about the event, such as the venue, date, time, and seating plan. The seating plan allows users to select their preferred seats or sections, and the ticketing system automatically updates the availability in real time. Users can then proceed to purchase the tickets securely through integrated payment gateways.

After purchasing the tickets, users can access and manage their tickets directly within the app. The tickets are typically stored digitally as QR codes or barcodes, which can be easily scanned at the event venue for entry. Users can also transfer or sell their tickets to others through a secure and verified system, ensuring a safe and reliable ticket exchange between users.

In addition to ticket management, mobile event ticketing apps may provide additional features, such as event reminders, personalized recommendations, and social sharing options. These features enhance the overall user experience and encourage users to engage with the app beyond just ticket purchases.

In conclusion, mobile event ticketing is a user interface pattern and design system that enables users to easily search, purchase, manage, and display event tickets on their mobile devices. It provides a seamless and convenient ticketing solution for both users and event organizers, offering a user-friendly interface and a visually cohesive design system.

Mobile File Manager

A Mobile File Manager is a user interface pattern and design system that allows users to manage and organize files and folders on a mobile device. It provides a user-friendly and intuitive interface that enables users to perform various file-related operations such as viewing, renaming, moving, copying, deleting, and sharing files. The purpose of a Mobile File Manager is to simplify the file management process on a mobile device, making it easier for users to access and manipulate their files. It typically consists of a navigation panel, a file and folder listing, and a set of action buttons. The navigation panel in a Mobile File Manager allows users to browse through different storage locations such as internal storage, external SD card, and cloud storage services. It provides a hierarchical structure that represents the file system, allowing users to navigate through folders and subfolders with ease. The file and folder listing in a Mobile File Manager displays all the files and folders within the selected storage location or directory. It presents the files in a visually appealing and organized manner, often using icons, file names, file sizes, and file types for easy identification. Users can tap on a file or folder to open it or perform various actions on it. A Mobile File Manager also includes a set of action buttons or contextual menus that allow users to perform operations on files and folders. These actions may include renaming a file, moving or copying a file to a different location, deleting a file, sharing a file through various platforms, or compressing files into a zip archive. Furthermore, a Mobile File Manager may also provide additional features such as file search, sorting and filtering options, file preview, and integration with cloud storage services. It aims to provide a comprehensive and efficient file management experience for users on their mobile devices. In conclusion, a Mobile File Manager is a user interface pattern and design system that facilitates file management on mobile devices. It enables users to organize, manipulate, and interact with files and folders through an intuitive and user-friendly interface.>

Mobile Fitness Challenges

A mobile fitness challenge in the context of UI patterns and design system refers to a feature or component that is integrated into a mobile fitness application or platform, aimed at engaging users in various physical activities and promoting a healthy lifestyle. These challenges are designed to spark motivation and encourage users to set and achieve fitness goals, making their fitness journey more enjoyable and interactive.

Mobile fitness challenges generally take the form of virtual competitions or goal-oriented activities that users can participate in individually or as part of a group or community. They often incorporate social aspects, allowing users to connect with friends, family, or fellow fitness enthusiasts, and compete or collaborate with them towards achieving specific milestones or targets.

Mobile Fitness Tracker

A mobile fitness tracker is a user interface (UI) pattern and design system that allows users to track their physical activities, health metrics, and fitness goals using a mobile device. The main purpose of a mobile fitness tracker is to help users monitor and analyze their daily physical activities. It typically includes features such as step counting, distance tracking, calorie counting, heart rate monitoring, sleep tracking, and goal setting. These features aim to provide users with an overview of their health and fitness progress, as well as motivate and encourage them to achieve their personal fitness goals. In terms of UI patterns, a mobile fitness tracker usually consists of a dashboard or home screen that displays an overview of the user's daily activity and vital health metrics. This screen often includes visual representations such as charts or graphs to help users easily understand their progress. The design system of a mobile fitness tracker focuses on delivering a clean and intuitive user experience. It typically follows a minimalistic design approach, with simple and straightforward navigation and interaction. The use of icons and visual cues is common to facilitate quick comprehension and ease of use. Additional features of a mobile fitness tracker may include community forums or social sharing capabilities, allowing users to connect with others and share their progress or compete in challenges. Integration with external devices, such as heart rate monitors or smartwatches, is also common to enhance tracking accuracy and expand functionality. Overall, a mobile fitness tracker is a UI pattern and design system that assists users in monitoring and managing their physical activities and health metrics. Through its intuitive interface and comprehensive features, it empowers users to take control of their fitness journey and make informed decisions towards a healthier lifestyle.

A mobile fitness tracker is a UI pattern and design system that enables users to track physical activities on a mobile device. It incorporates features like step counting, calorie counting, heart rate monitoring, and sleep tracking. The design focuses on a minimalistic approach with clean navigation and visual cues for ease of use. It may also include social sharing capabilities and integration with external devices.

Mobile Flashcards

Mobile flashcards refer to a user interface (UI) pattern and design system that is specifically designed for mobile devices. They offer a concise and efficient way to present information in a question-and-answer format. Mobile flashcards are often used in educational applications, where they serve as a tool for self-paced learning and memorization. In terms of UI patterns, mobile flashcards generally consist of two main components: a question and an answer. The question is typically displayed on one side of the card, while the answer is hidden or revealed upon user interaction. This interaction can be a tap, a swipe, or any other gesture that the mobile device supports. When the user reveals the answer, the card flips over to display the answer side. The user then has the option to mark their understanding of the question as correct or incorrect, and the app progresses to the next card in the set. The design system for mobile flashcards encompasses various elements and principles to ensure an intuitive and engaging user experience. The cards themselves are typically visually appealing, utilizing colors, typography, and imagery to capture the user's attention. The question and answer text is usually displayed in a legible and easy-to-read manner, allowing users to quickly process the information. Navigation within the flashcard set is also an important aspect of the design system.

149

Users should be able to easily move forward and backward through the cards, as well as navigate to specific cards within the set. Additionally, a progress indicator may be included to show the user's current position within the set and the overall progress. Furthermore, mobile flashcards often provide additional features to enhance the learning experience. These features may include the ability to create custom card sets, import or export card sets, track learning progress, and receive reminders or notifications for regular practice. In conclusion, mobile flashcards are a UI pattern and design system specifically tailored for mobile devices. They offer a concise and efficient way to present information in a question-and-answer format, making them valuable tools for educational apps. Through visually appealing design, intuitive navigation, and additional features, mobile flashcards provide an engaging and effective learning experience on mobile devices.>

Mobile Flight Booking

Mobile Flight Booking refers to the process of selecting and purchasing flight tickets through a mobile application or website. It involves a user-friendly interface that allows users to search for flights, compare prices, choose their preferred airline, select dates and times, and make payments securely.

The UI patterns and design system for Mobile Flight Booking should focus on providing a seamless and efficient experience for users. This can be achieved by incorporating the following key elements:

1. Clear and intuitive navigation: The UI should have a visually appealing and easy-to-navigate layout. Users should be able to find the flight search feature prominently displayed, allowing them to start their booking process without any confusion. The navigation should be minimalistic and provide clear paths to search, compare, and book flights.

2. Advanced search filters: The flight search feature should include advanced filters to help users narrow down their options. These filters can include preferences for non-stop flights, specific airlines, departure times, price ranges, and more. The UI should provide interactive sliders, checkboxes, or dropdown menus to easily apply these filters and refine search results.

3. Quick access to pricing information: Users should be able to quickly view the prices for different flights based on their search criteria. The UI should display prices clearly and prominently, helping users compare options and make informed decisions. Additionally, the UI should provide a breakdown of the total cost, including any additional fees or taxes, to avoid any surprises during the payment process.

4. Seamless booking process: The UI should guide users through a smooth and hassle-free booking process. It should allow users to select their preferred flight, enter passenger details, and securely make payments. The UI should also provide users with the option to save their payment and personal information for future bookings, making the process even more convenient.

Overall, Mobile Flight Booking UI patterns and design systems should prioritize simplicity, ease of use, and efficiency. By incorporating clear navigation, advanced search filters, transparent pricing information, and a seamless booking process, users will have a positive experience while planning and booking their flights on mobile devices.

Mobile Flood Alerts

Mobile Flood Alerts are a UI pattern and design system specifically developed for mobile devices to provide users with timely and critical information about potential or ongoing floods in their area. The main purpose of the Mobile Flood Alerts is to ensure the safety of users by alerting them to potential threats and allowing them to take necessary precautions. In terms of UI patterns, Mobile Flood Alerts typically consist of a notification system that delivers push notifications to users' mobile devices. These notifications are triggered based on real-time data from a reliable source, such as a national weather service or a local emergency management agency. The alerts are designed to be highly visible and attention-grabbing, ensuring that users notice and respond to them promptly. The design system for Mobile Flood Alerts focuses on

150

delivering information in a clear and concise manner, considering the limited screen space available on mobile devices. The alerts usually include a brief description of the flood threat, such as the severity level, expected duration, and affected areas. The information is presented in a well-structured format, allowing users to quickly understand the situation and make informed decisions. To support accessibility, Mobile Flood Alerts often incorporate visual cues, such as color coding, to convey the severity level of the flood threat. For example, a red color might indicate a high-severity alert, while yellow could represent a moderate-severity alert. These visual cues enable users to quickly assess the urgency of the situation, even if they are unable to read the text due to location or visual impairments. Additionally, Mobile Flood Alerts may include interactive features that allow users to access more detailed information about the flood threat. This could include a link to a dedicated webpage or a map that shows the affected areas and potential evacuation routes. By providing access to relevant resources, Mobile Flood Alerts empower users to effectively respond to the flood threat and mitigate potential risks. In conclusion, Mobile Flood Alerts are a UI pattern and design system specifically designed for mobile devices to deliver timely and critical information about potential or ongoing floods. Through attention-grabbing push notifications and clear, concise information presentation, Mobile Flood Alerts help users make informed decisions and take necessary precautions to ensure their safety.>

Mobile Font Customization

Mobile font customization refers to the ability to modify the appearance of text on a mobile device's user interface (UI) in a way that aligns with specific design patterns and a design system. It involves tailoring the font styles, sizes, and other attributes to create a cohesive and visually appealing user experience. In the context of UI patterns, font customization can help establish consistency across different screens and interactions within a mobile app or website. It allows designers to adhere to established guidelines, ensuring that the font choices are in line with the overall visual language and branding. Font customization is an essential aspect of a design system as it allows for easy integration and scalability. Design systems provide a set of predefined styles and components, including fonts, which can be customized to suit the needs of a specific application. This customization ensures that the fonts used in the UI are not only visually pleasing but also highly readable on mobile devices of varying screen sizes and resolutions. When customizing fonts for a mobile UI, designers consider factors such as legibility, readability, and accessibility. They choose font families that are easy to read, even at smaller sizes, and ensure appropriate line heights and letter spacing to enhance legibility. By providing options for font size adjustments, users with visual impairments or different preferences can customize the UI to meet their specific needs. HTML provides several ways to customize fonts. The CSS (Cascading Style Sheets) properties such as "font-family," "font-size," and "line-height" allow for precise control over the appearance of text. Designers can define font stacks, which are fallback options if the preferred font is not available on the target device. Additionally, they can specify font weights, styles, and variations to create a hierarchy within the text and emphasize important content. In summary, mobile font customization is the process of adapting font styles, sizes, and other attributes within a mobile device's UI to align with established design patterns and a design system. It ensures consistency, legibility, and scalability while allowing for user customization. Through CSS properties, designers can customize fonts to enhance the user experience and reflect the visual language of the application or website.>

Mobile Food Diary

A mobile food diary is a user interface (UI) pattern and design system that allows users to conveniently track and record their food consumption and related activities using a mobile device. It provides a structured and organized way for individuals to monitor and analyze their dietary habits, promoting healthy eating and overall well-being. The mobile food diary typically consists of various screens or sections that enable users to input and view their food and drink intake, as well as other relevant information such as the time and location of consumption. Users can track their meals throughout the day, including breakfast, lunch, dinner, and snacks, by selecting or inputting specific food items or by searching an extensive database of foods. The diary may also offer the option to record additional details such as portion sizes, ingredients, and preparation methods. In addition to tracking meals, a mobile food diary may feature sections for recording physical activities, water intake, and other lifestyle factors that can impact one's overall

151

health. This holistic approach provides users with a comprehensive overview of their daily habits, allowing them to identify patterns, set goals, and make informed decisions to improve their dietary choices. The design system of a mobile food diary focuses on ensuring an intuitive and user-friendly experience. It employs consistent visual design elements, such as color schemes, typography, and iconography, to create a cohesive interface. Clear and concise labeling of buttons and input fields helps users quickly understand their purpose and functionality. The diary's layout is optimized for small screens, with easy-to-navigate menus and screens that allow for seamless interactions. Usability is a key consideration in the design of a mobile food diary. The system should provide users with quick and effortless ways to enter and retrieve information. Auto-suggestions and predictive text can be employed to expedite the process of adding items to the diary. Users can also be offered the ability to customize and save their frequently consumed meals for faster entry in the future. Furthermore, a mobile food diary may incorporate features like data visualization and analysis. Graphs, charts, and summaries can be generated to present users with a comprehensive overview of their dietary patterns, nutrient intake, and progress towards their goals. These visual representations can help users gain insights into their eating habits and encourage positive changes. Overall, a mobile food diary is an efficient and user-friendly solution for individuals seeking to maintain a balanced and healthy diet. By providing a structured way to track consumption and analyze data, it empowers users to make informed decisions and adopt healthier eating habits.>

Mobile Fuel Price Finder

A Mobile Fuel Price Finder is a user interface (UI) pattern and design system that provides a convenient and efficient way for users to find and compare fuel prices on their mobile devices. It is specifically designed for mobile platforms to ensure optimal user experience and accessibility.

The Mobile Fuel Price Finder typically includes a search bar where users can input their location or select from a list of nearby locations. This provides users with accurate and up-to-date fuel prices based on their current or desired location. The search functionality can also include filters, such as fuel type or brand, to further refine the results and meet users' specific needs.

The UI design of the Mobile Fuel Price Finder focuses on simplicity and usability. It employs a clean and intuitive layout with clear navigation options. The use of responsive design ensures that the interface adapts seamlessly to different screen sizes and orientations, providing an optimal viewing experience for users on various mobile devices.

One common feature of the Mobile Fuel Price Finder is the ability to view detailed information for each fuel station, including address, contact information, and hours of operation. This allows users to make informed decisions and easily plan their fuel purchases based on convenience and pricing.

To enhance the user experience, the Mobile Fuel Price Finder may also incorporate additional features such as user reviews and ratings, directions to the fuel station using built-in navigation systems, and the option to save favorite fuel stations for future reference.

The design system of the Mobile Fuel Price Finder defines a consistent set of visual elements, typography, and iconography to maintain a cohesive and recognizable brand identity. This ensures a seamless and familiar experience for users across different screens and interactions within the app.

In summary, the Mobile Fuel Price Finder is a mobile-centric UI pattern and design system that provides users with a convenient way to find and compare fuel prices. Its user-friendly interface, responsive design, and detailed information empower users to make informed decisions and optimize their fuel purchasing experience.

Mobile GPS Location

The Mobile GPS Location is a UI pattern and design system that allows mobile applications to access and display the current geographical location of the user. It enables the application to provide location-based services and features to enhance the user experience.

Developers can integrate the Mobile GPS Location feature into their mobile applications by utilizing the built-in GPS (Global Positioning System) technology available on modern smartphones and tablets. The GPS system uses satellite signals to determine the device's precise location, providing accurate latitude and longitude coordinates.

Through the Mobile GPS Location UI pattern, users can benefit from various location-based functionalities, such as finding nearby places, tracking routes, and navigating directions. These features are particularly useful in applications related to maps, transportation, travel, and social networking.

Designing the UI for Mobile GPS Location involves presenting the user's location in a visually informative and user-friendly manner. Typically, the location is displayed using a map interface, including markers or pins to indicate the user's position. The map may also show other relevant information, such as nearby points of interest or the user's movement trajectory.

Additionally, the design should consider providing controls or options to allow users to interact with the location information. This could include zooming in or out of the map, toggling between different views (e.g., satellite, terrain), and enabling additional functionalities like searching for specific addresses or landmarks.

To adhere to design system principles, the Mobile GPS Location UI pattern should follow consistent visual styles, typography, and color schemes used across the application. It should also consider responsive design to ensure optimal display and functionality across different screen sizes and orientations.

In summary, the Mobile GPS Location UI pattern and design system enable mobile applications to access and display the user's current geographical location. By integrating this feature, developers can provide enhanced location-based services, while adhering to consistent design principles ensures a cohesive and intuitive user experience.

Mobile GPS Navigation

A mobile GPS navigation refers to a user interface (UI) pattern and design system that provides real-time navigation and route guidance on a mobile device. It allows users to navigate to different locations, view maps and directions, and receive voice prompts and turn-by-turn instructions to reach their desired destinations.

Through the use of GPS (Global Positioning System) technology, a mobile GPS navigation system tracks the user's current location and provides accurate directions to their selected destination. The UI pattern of a mobile GPS navigation typically includes various features and elements to enhance the user experience and facilitate efficient navigation.

Mobile Gamepad Integration

Mobile gamepad integration refers to the implementation of user interface patterns and design systems that accommodate the use of gamepads in mobile applications. It involves creating a seamless and intuitive experience for users who prefer to play games using external controllers on their mobile devices. One of the key aspects of mobile gamepad integration is ensuring that the gamepad controls align with the user's expectations. This includes mapping the different buttons and axes of the gamepad to specific actions within the game or application. The design system should provide clear instructions on how to connect and configure the gamepad, as well as display relevant information such as battery status or connection stability. In terms of UI patterns, the integration should allow for both on-screen touch controls and gamepad-based controls. This can be achieved by providing a toggle or switch in the settings menu to enable gamepad support. When the gamepad is connected, the UI should adapt accordingly, hiding on-screen controls and displaying gamepad-specific instructions or prompts. Design consistency is crucial in mobile gamepad integration. The design system should maintain a cohesive visual language across all screens, ensuring that gamepad-supported features seamlessly blend with the rest of the user interface. This includes consistent iconography and color schemes that convey the same meaning regardless of the input method used. Accessibility is another important consideration. The design system should provide options to customize gamepad controls, such as button remapping or sensitivity adjustments, to accommodate different user preferences. Additionally, the UI should always provide alternative navigation methods for users who do not have a gamepad or prefer other input methods. Mobile gamepad integration requires thorough testing to ensure compatibility with a wide range of gamepad models and brands. The design system should account for different button layouts, as well as the capabilities of the gamepad's analog sticks or triggers. It should also consider the possibility of simultaneous input from both the gamepad and touch screen, allowing users to seamlessly switch between the two without disruptions. In conclusion, mobile gamepad integration is a design system that supports and enhances the use of external controllers in mobile applications. It focuses on creating a consistent and intuitive user experience, allowing users to easily connect and configure their gamepads, providing clear instructions and prompts, maintaining design consistency, ensuring accessibility, and thorough compatibility testing.>

Mobile Gamification Elements

UI patterns are recurring solutions to common design problems. They provide a set of rules and guidelines that help designers create consistent and user-friendly interfaces. Design systems, on the other hand, are a collection of reusable components, guidelines, and standards that ensure a cohesive and efficient design process. Gamification elements in mobile UI patterns and design systems refer to the incorporation of game-like mechanics and techniques into non-game applications. These elements are used to enhance user engagement, motivation, and enjoyment. By leveraging these elements, designers can create a more immersive and rewarding experience for users. One commonly used gamification element is the use of points, badges, and leaderboards. Points are awarded to users for completing certain tasks or achieving specific milestones. Badges are visual representations of accomplishments or achievements, which can be displayed on a user's profile. Leaderboards show the rankings of users based on their performance or progress, encouraging competition and social interaction. Another gamification element is progress bars or visual indicators. These elements provide users with a sense of accomplishment and progress as they complete tasks or move forward in their journey. Progress bars can be used to show the completion status of a task or the overall progress of a user's profile. Challenges and quests are also commonly used gamification elements in mobile UI patterns. Challenges are specific tasks or goals that users can complete within the application. Quests, on the other hand, are a series of interconnected challenges that users can undertake to earn rewards or unlock new content. In addition to these elements, mobile UI patterns and design systems often incorporate rewards and incentives. Rewards can be in the form of virtual goods, discounts, or special privileges. Incentives can be used to encourage users to take certain actions or engage with specific features of the application. Overall, gamification elements in mobile UI patterns and design systems aim to create a more enjoyable and motivating user experience. By leveraging game-like mechanics and techniques, designers can increase user engagement, promote desired behaviors, and enhance overall satisfaction with the application.

Gamification elements in mobile UI patterns and design systems refer to the incorporation of game-like mechanics and techniques into non-game applications to enhance user engagement and motivation.

These elements include points, badges, leaderboards, progress bars, challenges, quests, rewards, and incentives.

Mobile Gardening Tips

Mobile Gardening Tips are a set of UI patterns and design system guidelines specifically created for the mobile platform. These tips ensure that the design of mobile applications or websites related to gardening is user-friendly, visually appealing, and efficient in conveying information. The first tip is to prioritize simplicity and minimalism in the design. Mobile screens have limited space, and cluttered interfaces can make it difficult for users to navigate and find the information they need. By using clean layouts, minimal color palettes, and concise text, mobile gardening apps can provide a seamless experience to users. Another important aspect is the use of intuitive navigation patterns. Mobile gardening apps should have easily accessible menus, clear navigation labels, and consistent placement of navigation elements. This allows users to easily explore different sections of the app and find the desired information quickly. The third tip is to use appropriate typography and font sizes. Mobile screens are smaller than desktop screens, so it's important to use fonts that are easily readable on mobile devices. To enhance readability, designers should opt for fonts with simple structures and avoid using small font sizes that could strain the user's eyes. Mobile gardening apps should also make effective use of visuals. High-quality images and illustrations related to gardening can engage users and enhance their experience. However, it's crucial to optimize these visuals for mobile devices to ensure fast load times and smooth scrolling. Furthermore, mobile apps should consider the context in which they are used. For example, it's important to design with touch interactions in mind. Providing large, tappable buttons and ensuring that interactive elements have adequate spacing can prevent accidental taps and improve overall usability. Lastly, mobile gardening apps should be responsive and adaptable to different screen sizes and orientations. Designers should consider the various devices and orientations users may have and ensure that the app's layout remains usable and visually appealing across all scenarios. In summary, Mobile Gardening Tips are a set of UI patterns and design system guidelines aimed at creating user-friendly and visually appealing mobile applications or websites related to gardening. By prioritizing simplicity, intuitive navigation, appropriate typography, optimized visuals, touch interactions, and responsive design, these tips can ensure a seamless and enjoyable user experience in the mobile gardening space.>

Mobile Gestures Cheat Sheet

Gestures are a fundamental aspect of mobile user interfaces (UI). They refer to the physical actions or movements users make on a mobile device's screen, typically using their fingers or thumbs, to interact with the interface and perform various actions or tasks. Mobile gestures play a vital role in enabling users to navigate through apps, access features, and manipulate content, enhancing the overall user experience and usability of a mobile application.

There are several commonly used mobile gestures that have become widely adopted and established as standard UI patterns and design system elements. These gestures help users interact with and control mobile apps in an intuitive and efficient manner. Understanding and implementing these gestures in mobile app design is crucial for creating a seamless and familiar user experience.

Mobile Gestures

Mobile gestures refer to the specific hand movements or actions that users perform on a mobile device's touch screen interface to interact with the user interface (UI) elements and navigate through the application or website. In the world of UI patterns and design systems, gestures play a vital role in enhancing the user experience by providing intuitive and efficient ways of engaging with the content. Tap Gesture: The tap gesture is one of the fundamental gestures in mobile design. It is performed by touching the screen briefly with a single finger. Tapping is used to select an item, activate an element, or trigger an action. For example, tapping on a button performs the associated action, tapping on a link opens a new page, and tapping on an image may enlarge or zoom it. Double Tap Gesture: The double tap gesture involves rapidly tapping the screen twice with a single finger. This gesture is often used to perform specific actions, such as zooming in or out on an image or text. For example, double tapping on an image may zoom in, and double tapping again may zoom out. Swipe Gesture: The swipe gesture is performed by quickly moving the finger across the screen in a specific direction, usually horizontally or vertically. Swiping is commonly used for scrolling, navigating between pages, or revealing hidden menus or options. For instance, swiping left or right on a list allows the user to browse through various items, and swiping down on a screen may refresh the content. Pinch Gesture: The pinch gesture involves using two fingers to zoom in or out on the screen. The user places two fingers on the screen and then pinches them together or spreads them apart. This gesture is primarily used to scale or resize elements like images or maps. For example, pinching out on an image enlarges it, while pinching in reduces its size. Long Press Gesture: The long press gesture is performed by pressing and holding a finger on a specific area of the screen for an extended period. It triggers additional options or context-specific actions. For instance, long-pressing on a text message may reveal options to copy, delete, or forward it. These mobile gestures are essential components in designing intuitive and user-friendly mobile interfaces. By incorporating these gestures into a design system, developers can ensure a smooth and enjoyable user experience, enabling users to interact effortlessly with the app or website.

Mobile Habit Tracker

A mobile habit tracker is a user interface pattern that is used in the design system of mobile applications to help users track and analyze their habits. It provides a visual representation of user habits, allowing them to set goals, track their progress, and make informed decisions about their behavior.

The mobile habit tracker typically consists of a calendar or timeline view, where users can see their daily, weekly, or monthly habits at a glance. Each habit is represented by a color-coded icon or indicator, making it easy for users to identify and differentiate between different habits. Users can interact with the habit tracker by tapping on a specific day or habit, which opens a detailed view or menu where they can add or edit their habits, set reminders, or view statistics and progress charts.

One of the key features of a mobile habit tracker is the ability to set goals and reminders. Users can define specific goals for each habit they want to track, such as exercising for 30 minutes a day or drinking 8 glasses of water. The habit tracker then sends reminders and notifications to help users stay on track and meet their goals. By providing visual feedback and reminders, the habit tracker encourages users to form positive habits and stick to their routines.

In addition to tracking habits, a mobile habit tracker can also provide insights and analytics to help users understand their behavior patterns. It can generate reports and charts that show trends, progress, and correlations between different habits. This data-driven approach empowers users to make informed decisions and identify areas for improvement.

The design of a mobile habit tracker should be intuitive, minimalistic, and visually appealing. It should be easy for users to navigate, add or edit habits, and view their progress without feeling overwhelmed. The use of color, icons, and typography should be consistent with the overall design system of the mobile application, ensuring a seamless and cohesive user experience.

In conclusion, a mobile habit tracker is a user interface pattern designed for mobile applications to help users track, analyze, and improve their habits. It provides a visual representation of habits, allows goal setting and reminders, and offers insights and analytics to empower users in making positive changes.

Mobile Health Advisory Alerts

Mobile Health Advisory Alerts are user interface (UI) patterns and design system elements that provide important and timely notifications to users in the context of mobile health applications. These alerts serve as a means to inform users about critical health-related information such as medication reminders, appointment notifications, and important health tips. They are designed to capture the user's attention and convey the message clearly and concisely. Mobile Health Advisory Alerts typically appear as small pop-up windows or banners that overlay the main content of the mobile health application. They can be triggered based on specific conditions, such as a scheduled medication time or an upcoming medical appointment. Once triggered, these alerts appear on the user's screen, ensuring that the important information is easily accessible and cannot be missed. The design of these alerts follows a consistent and standardized approach to maintain a cohesive user experience. They are typically styled using colors and typography that align with the overall design system of the mobile health application. This helps users quickly recognize and associate the alerts with the app, increasing their usability and ensuring a seamless and intuitive experience. In terms of interaction, Mobile Health Advisory Alerts often provide users with clear actions to take in response to the notification. This could include dismissing the alert, snoozing it for a later time, or taking immediate action, such as marking medication as taken or confirming an appointment. The use of Mobile Health Advisory Alerts in UI patterns and design systems is crucial for ensuring that users receive important health-related information in a timely manner. By effectively capturing the user's attention and providing clear actions, these alerts contribute to improved patient engagement, medication adherence, and overall healthcare outcomes. In conclusion, Mobile Health Advisory Alerts are UI patterns and design system elements that play a vital role in delivering important health-related notifications to users in mobile health applications. They are designed to capture attention, convey messages clearly, and provide users with actionable options. Implemented within a cohesive design system, these alerts enhance the overall user experience and contribute to improved healthcare outcomes.>

Mobile Health Diagnostics

Mobile Health Diagnostics refers to a system that enables the delivery of healthcare services, particularly diagnostic tests and results, through mobile devices such as smartphones and tablets. It involves the integration of technology, healthcare, and user interface design to provide a seamless and user-friendly experience for both healthcare professionals and patients.

The UI patterns and design system for Mobile Health Diagnostics aim to ensure intuitive navigation, clear presentation of information, and easy interaction for users. The design elements are carefully selected and arranged to optimize usability, accessibility, and visual consistency across different mobile devices and platforms.

Mobile Health Monitoring

Mobile Health Monitoring is a user interface (UI) pattern and design system that focuses on the seamless integration of health monitoring features into mobile devices. This design approach aims to provide convenient and user-friendly access to health-related information and services through mobile applications. At its core, Mobile Health Monitoring revolves around the concept of using mobile devices, such as smartphones or tablets, as a means to monitor various aspects of an individual's health. This could include tracking vital signs, measuring physical activity, monitoring sleep patterns, or managing chronic conditions, among other health-related functionalities. The UI patterns within Mobile Health Monitoring typically involve the use of intuitive and visually appealing interfaces that allow users to easily navigate and access the desired health monitoring features. These interfaces may display real-time data, such as heart rate, blood pressure, or steps taken, in a clear and concise manner. Graphs and charts may be utilized to present trends and patterns over time, enabling users to monitor their progress and make informed decisions about their health. Additionally, Mobile Health Monitoring also incorporates features for data input, allowing users to manually enter information such as symptoms, medication intake, or dietary details. This input can be beneficial for individuals who want to keep track of their overall health and share relevant data with healthcare professionals. The design system aspect of Mobile Health Monitoring ensures consistency and cohesiveness across different mobile applications and platforms. It provides a unified set of UI components, typography styles, color schemes, and iconography that maintain a cohesive visual language throughout various health-related apps. A well-defined design system allows for easy scalability and customization of UI elements, providing a seamless experience for both developers and end-users. In conclusion, Mobile Health Monitoring is a UI pattern and design system that enables the integration of health monitoring features into mobile devices. Through intuitive interfaces and consistent design principles, this approach aims to enhance user experience and facilitate the management of personal health information on-the-go.>

Mobile Health Records

Mobile Health Records (MHR) refer to the digitalization and accessibility of individuals' personal health information through mobile devices such as smartphones and tablets. In the context of UI patterns and design systems, MHR focuses on optimizing the user experience for accessing, managing, and interacting with health records on mobile platforms.

The design of mobile health records aims to provide a user-friendly and intuitive interface that allows individuals to easily navigate through their medical information, including medication history, lab results, appointments, and other relevant data. The UI patterns and design system for MHR should take into consideration the unique characteristics and constraints of mobile devices, such as smaller screen sizes, touch-based interactions, and varying network connectivity.

Mobile Hearing Aid Compatibility

Mobile Hearing Aid Compatibility refers to the capability of a mobile device to work effectively with hearing aids. It encompasses both software and hardware aspects to ensure seamless communication between the mobile device and the hearing aid. From a UI patterns and design system perspective, Mobile Hearing Aid Compatibility requires the implementation of specific user interface elements and guidelines to support individuals with hearing loss. These elements aim to enhance accessibility, usability, and user experience for those who rely on hearing aids to communicate and interact with mobile devices. To achieve Mobile Hearing Aid Compatibility, designers need to consider several key factors: 1. Volume control: Mobile devices should provide a range of volume levels, allowing users to adjust the sound output to their individual needs. The volume control should be intuitive, easy to access, and accurately reflect the changes made by the user. 2. Hearing aid compatibility ratings: Mobile devices should display clear and standardized hearing aid compatibility ratings. These ratings help users identify which devices are suitable for their specific hearing aids and ensure compatibility. 3. Telecoil mode: Telecoil technology enables hearing aids to magnetically receive sound signals from compatible devices, such as mobile phones. Designing for a telecoil mode involves providing an option to switch to this mode for improved sound quality and reduced background noise. 4. Visual indicators: Mobile devices should incorporate visual indicators to inform users about device status, such as incoming calls, messages, or alarms. These visual cues help individuals with hearing loss stay informed and not solely rely on auditory notifications. 5. Captioning and subtitles: Providing options for captions and subtitles in multimedia content (such as videos) can significantly improve accessibility for individuals with hearing loss. Designers should include controls and settings to enable or disable captions based on user preferences. The implementation of these UI patterns and design system elements fosters inclusivity and enables individuals with hearing loss to fully utilize mobile devices. By adhering to Mobile Hearing Aid Compatibility principles, designers contribute to a digital environment that embraces diversity and accessibility. Overall, Mobile Hearing Aid Compatibility involves designing mobile device interfaces that accommodate the unique needs of individuals with hearing loss. It requires consideration of volume control, hearing aid compatibility ratings, telecoil mode, visual indicators, and options for captioning and subtitles. By incorporating these elements, designers enhance the usability and accessibility of mobile devices for individuals with hearing aids.>

Mobile High Contrast Mode

Mobile High Contrast Mode refers to a user interface (UI) pattern and design system specifically designed for mobile devices to enhance readability and accessibility for users with visual impairments or specific requirements related to contrast sensitivity. It aims to provide a high level of contrast between text, images, and background colors to ensure that content is legible and easily understandable. In Mobile High Contrast Mode, the UI elements, such as text, buttons, icons, and backgrounds, are carefully designed to have a distinct contrast with each other. This helps users with reduced vision or sensitivity to perceive and distinguish between different elements on the screen. The color combinations are chosen based on accessibility guidelines that prioritize contrast and readability. To achieve Mobile High Contrast Mode, the design system typically includes a set of predefined color palettes. These palettes consist of a limited number of colors that have been tested for their contrast ratio and legibility. The colors are selected to create a clear distinction between elements while minimizing confusion and visual distractions. In practice, when a user enables the Mobile High Contrast Mode on their mobile device, the system applies the predefined color palettes to various UI components. For example, text might be displayed in a high-contrast combination of black and white, ensuring maximum readability. Backgrounds may have a dark color to create a sharp contrast with the text and other graphic elements. One of the distinctive features of Mobile High Contrast Mode is its adaptability to different devices and platforms. Regardless of the specific mobile operating system, the design system provides a consistent and accessible UI experience across various devices, including smartphones and tablets. By implementing Mobile High Contrast Mode, designers aim to ensure that information and user interfaces are accessible and usable for a wide range of users, including those with visual impairments or contrast sensitivity issues. This design pattern contributes to an inclusive and user-friendly mobile experience where users can effortlessly interact with content and navigate through applications. In conclusion, Mobile High Contrast Mode is a UI pattern and design system specifically developed for mobile devices to enhance accessibility and readability for users with visual impairments. It utilizes predefined color palettes and carefully designed contrast ratios to ensure that content is legible and easily distinguishable on mobile screens.>

Mobile Home Renovation Planner

158

A Mobile Home Renovation Planner is a user interface pattern and design system specifically developed for mobile applications that facilitate the planning and organization of home renovation projects. It provides users with a structured and intuitive way to manage all aspects of their renovation, from initial inspiration and design ideas to budgeting, scheduling, and tracking progress.

This UI pattern and design system is designed to be responsive and user-friendly, ensuring seamless navigation and a visually appealing experience on mobile devices. It incorporates familiar mobile app conventions and adheres to industry best practices for mobile UI design, ensuring a smooth and intuitive user experience.

Mobile Home Security Control

A Mobile Home Security Control is a user interface pattern that is used in the design system of a mobile application to provide users with a centralized control panel for managing the security and smart home devices in their mobile homes. It allows users to conveniently and efficiently monitor and control various aspects of their home security, such as alarm systems, door locks, surveillance cameras, and smart home devices.

The Mobile Home Security Control pattern typically includes a dashboard or home screen that provides an overview of the current status of the home security system, including any triggered alarms or detected anomalies. This screen also displays the status and controls for individual devices, such as the ability to arm or disarm the alarm system or lock and unlock doors. Users can easily navigate between different sections or screens to access specific device controls or view detailed information about security events or device history.

Mobile Home Workout Videos

Mobile Home Workout Videos refer to a collection of video content within a mobile application that is specifically designed to guide users through exercise routines and workouts. This user interface (UI) pattern provides users with a convenient and accessible way to engage in fitness activities without the need for expensive equipment or a gym membership. The videos are typically organized and categorized based on different types of workouts, such as cardio, strength training, yoga, or pilates.

The design system for Mobile Home Workout Videos aims to deliver an intuitive and user-friendly experience. The UI elements and interaction patterns are optimized for mobile devices, ensuring that users can easily access and navigate through the workout videos. The home screen of the application serves as the central hub where users can browse and discover new workout videos. It may feature a carousel or a grid layout showcasing curated or trending videos, which helps users quickly find content that matches their interests and goals.

Mobile Hotel Booking

A mobile hotel booking UI pattern refers to a set of design elements and guidelines used to create a seamless and user-friendly experience for hotel booking applications on mobile devices. It involves the layout, navigation, and interaction patterns that enable users to easily search for, select, and book hotel rooms using their smartphones or tablets.

The mobile hotel booking design system aims to ensure consistency and efficiency across all the screens and interactions within the application. It focuses on creating a visually appealing and intuitive interface that aligns with the users' expectations and needs.

Mobile Hotspot Settings

The Mobile Hotspot Settings refer to the user interface (UI) elements and design system that allow users to configure and manage the settings related to their mobile hotspot functionality.

Mobile hotspots are devices or features that enable users to share their cellular data connection with other devices, such as smartphones, tablets, or laptops. The Mobile Hotspot Settings provide users with a way to control various aspects of their hotspot, including its name, password, security settings, and connected devices.

Mobile Hurricane Alerts

A mobile hurricane alert is a user interface (UI) pattern and design system that provides timely and relevant information about hurricanes and impending weather conditions. It is specifically designed for mobile devices, providing a seamless and user-friendly experience for users who need to stay informed during hurricane events.

The mobile hurricane alert UI pattern typically includes the following components:

1. Alert notifications: The design system incorporates a push notification feature that sends real-time alerts to users about hurricane updates, as well as any related warnings or advisories. These alerts immediately grab the user's attention, ensuring they are aware of the latest information.

2. Weather information: The design system displays comprehensive weather information, including the storm's current location, intensity, and predicted path. Visual representations such as maps, radar images, and satellite imagery may be used to enhance the user's understanding of the situation.

3. Emergency contacts: The UI pattern provides quick access to emergency contact numbers, such as local authorities, utility providers, and emergency services. This allows users to easily contact the relevant parties in case of an emergency or if they require immediate assistance.

4. Preparedness resources: The design system also includes a section dedicated to providing users with essential preparedness resources. This may include checklists, survival guides, evacuation routes, and information on emergency shelters, helping users effectively plan and prepare for a hurricane event.

The mobile hurricane alert UI pattern, when implemented effectively, serves as a vital tool for users to stay informed and makes it easier for them to take necessary actions to protect themselves and their loved ones during hurricane events. The emphasis on real-time updates, intuitive design, and readily accessible resources ensures that users have the information they need at their fingertips, even in high-stress situations.

Mobile In-App Purchases

In the context of UI patterns and design systems, mobile in-app purchases refer to the ability for users to make purchases from within a mobile application. These purchases typically involve buying additional content, features, or functionality that enhance the user's experience within the app. Mobile in-app purchases are an important revenue stream for mobile app developers, as they provide a way to monetize their applications beyond the initial download cost. This business model allows developers to offer their apps for free or at a reduced cost, while still generating income from users who choose to make in-app purchases. From a design perspective, mobile in-app purchases need to be seamlessly integrated into the user interface to ensure a smooth and efficient purchasing process. Designers must consider factors such as placement, visibility, and ease of use to maximize the likelihood that a user will complete a purchase. Key UI patterns and design principles for mobile in-app purchases include: 1. Clear Call to Action: The purchase option should be prominently displayed and easily identifiable to users. This can be achieved through the use of buttons or visual cues that clearly indicate the availability of additional content for purchase. 2. Consistency: The design of the in-app purchase process should align with the overall visual style and branding of the application. This creates a cohesive and familiar experience for users, reducing confusion and increasing trust in the purchasing process. 3. Transparency: Users should have clear information about the cost and benefits of the in-app purchase before making a decision. This can be achieved by displaying the price, a description of what is being purchased, and any applicable terms and conditions. 4. Security: Mobile in-app purchases involve the handling of sensitive user information, such as credit card details. Designers need to ensure that the purchasing process is secure and that users' personal and financial information is protected. In conclusion, mobile in-app purchases are a fundamental aspect of monetizing mobile applications. Designing an intuitive and seamless user interface for in-app purchases is crucial for maximizing conversion rates and ensuring a positive user experience.>

160

Mobile Interior Design

Mobile Interior Design refers to the process of designing visually appealing and user-friendly user interfaces (UI) for mobile applications. It involves the creation of consistent and cohesive design patterns and a well-defined design system that provides a seamless experience for users across different screens and devices.

The goal of Mobile Interior Design is to enhance the usability and accessibility of a mobile application by focusing on the arrangement, organization, and presentation of its visual elements. It encompasses the selection of appropriate color schemes, typography, icons, and imagery to create an intuitive and engaging interface.

Mobile Investment Portfolio

A mobile investment portfolio is a user interface pattern and design system specifically tailored for investment mobile applications. It provides users with a consolidated view of their investment accounts, allowing them to track and manage their investment portfolios on the go.

This design system focuses on delivering a seamless user experience by organizing and presenting investment-related information in a clear and intuitive manner. It prioritizes simplicity, efficiency, and accessibility, enabling users to easily access critical investment data and take informed actions.

Mobile Invoice Payment

Mobile Invoice Payment refers to a user interface pattern and design system that allows users to conveniently and securely pay their invoices using their mobile devices. This feature is specifically designed to enhance the user experience by streamlining the payment process and providing a user-friendly interface.

The Mobile Invoice Payment design system typically consists of a series of screens or steps that guide the user through the payment process. These screens are intuitively designed to ensure that users can easily understand and complete each step, minimizing confusion and errors.

Mobile Invoice Viewing

A mobile invoice viewing UI pattern refers to the design and layout of a user interface for displaying invoices on a mobile device. It is a crucial component of a comprehensive design system that ensures consistency and harmonious user experiences across various screens and platforms.

The mobile invoice viewing pattern typically includes elements such as the invoice number, date, billing address, a list of line items including their descriptions, quantities, rates, and totals, as well as any applicable taxes, discounts, and a grand total. The design system ensures that these elements are displayed in a clear, concise, and visually appealing manner.

Mobile IoT Device Control

Mobile IoT Device Control refers to a user interface pattern and design system that allows users to remotely monitor and control Internet of Things (IoT) devices through their mobile devices. It provides a convenient and intuitive way for users to access and interact with their IoT devices, enabling them to manage various aspects of these devices without the need for physical proximity. The main purpose of Mobile IoT Device Control is to empower users with the ability to monitor and control their IoT devices from anywhere at any time. By leveraging the power and ubiquity of mobile devices, users can easily check the status of their devices, adjust settings, receive notifications, and perform other actions to ensure efficient operation. Mobile IoT Device Control typically includes a range of features and functionalities designed to enhance the user experience. These may include real-time data visualization, intuitive controls and gestures, push notifications, scheduling capabilities, and integration with other mobile apps or services. When designing the user interface for Mobile IoT Device Control, it is important to prioritize simplicity and ease of use. The interface should provide clear and concise information about the status of the IoT devices, as well as intuitive controls for managing the devices. Visual cues such as

161

icons, colors, and typography can be used to convey important information and guide user actions. In terms of design system, consistency is crucial to ensure a seamless and cohesive user experience across different devices and platforms. Common UI patterns, such as navigation menus, control panels, and card-based layouts, can be employed to create familiarity and align with established design conventions. Overall, Mobile IoT Device Control offers users a convenient and efficient way to monitor and control their IoT devices from their mobile devices. By providing a user-friendly interface and leveraging mobile technology, it enables users to seamlessly manage their IoT devices and ensure optimal performance and functionality.>

Mobile Language Courses

Mobile Language Courses are a set of user interface (UI) patterns and design system specifically tailored for learning languages on mobile devices. These patterns and design elements aim to enhance the overall user experience by providing an intuitive and optimized interface for language learning. The main focus of Mobile Language Courses is to present language content in a clear and organized manner, making it easy for users to navigate and comprehend. The design system ensures consistency across the app, providing a familiar and predictable experience for learners. One prominent UI pattern in Mobile Language Courses is the use of tabs or navigation bars to allow users to switch between different sections of the app, such as lessons, quizzes, and vocabulary. This enables learners to easily access the specific content they want to study, enhancing their learning experience. Another common design element is the use of progress indicators to track the user's language learning journey. These indicators can be in the form of a progress bar or a completion percentage, giving learners a sense of accomplishment and motivating them to continue their studies. Mobile Language Courses also incorporate interactive elements, such as swipe gestures or tap actions, to make the learning experience more engaging. For example, users can swipe left or right to move between flashcards or tap on a word to see its translation or pronunciation. These interactive features help to reinforce language learning and make it more enjoyable for users. In terms of visual design, Mobile Language Courses often utilize a clean and minimalist aesthetic. This helps to reduce visual clutter and allows the content to take center stage. Appropriate use of fonts, colors, and icons further enhance the overall clarity and readability of the language materials. In conclusion, Mobile Language Courses are a comprehensive set of UI patterns and design elements that are specifically designed for language learning on mobile devices. By providing a user-friendly and visually appealing interface, these courses aim to optimize the learning experience and facilitate language acquisition.>

Mobile Language Learning

Mobile Language Learning is a user interface pattern and design system specifically designed for mobile devices to facilitate language learning. It provides a structured and intuitive learning experience through interactive features and accessible design elements. The UI pattern of Mobile Language Learning focuses on delivering a seamless and engaging learning experience. It employs a minimalist design approach, with a clean and uncluttered layout that allows users to easily navigate through the app and focus on the language learning content. The use of subtle animations and transitions enhances the user experience and adds a touch of interactivity. The design system of Mobile Language Learning is based on the principles of simplicity, consistency, and accessibility. It is developed with a mobile-first approach, ensuring that the app is optimized for small screen sizes and touch interactions. The typography is carefully chosen to be legible and easily readable on mobile devices. The use of colors is purposeful, with a visually appealing palette that aids in content comprehension and encourages engagement. The Mobile Language Learning design system incorporates various interactive elements to facilitate language learning. These include vocabulary exercises, flashcards, quizzes, and audio/video lessons. These interactive features are designed with a focus on usability, making it easy for users to interact with the app and track their progress. Additionally, the system provides feedback and recommendations based on user performance, allowing learners to assess their strengths and weaknesses and improve accordingly. Mobile Language Learning also includes features that promote a personalized learning experience. It allows users to set learning goals, track their progress, and customize the app settings according to their preferences. The system supports multiple languages, providing learners with the flexibility to learn a language of their choice. In summary, Mobile Language Learning is a user interface pattern and design system that enables language learning on mobile devices. It employs a minimalist design approach, provides a seamless and engaging learning experience, and incorporates interactive features and personalization options to enhance the learning process.>

Mobile Language Selection

Mobile Language Selection refers to the user interface pattern that allows users to choose the desired language for the content or interface of a mobile application or website. It is an important feature in a globalized world where people from different regions and cultures access digital platforms.

Implementing a Mobile Language Selection UI pattern involves providing users with a list or dropdown menu of available languages. Users can then select their preferred language, and the application or website dynamically updates the content to display in the chosen language.

Mobile Large Text Mode

Mobile Large Text Mode is a UI pattern and design system that caters to users with visual impairments or those who prefer larger text sizes on mobile devices. It is implemented to enhance readability and accessibility in mobile applications, ensuring that text content is easily legible without causing strain or discomfort to users.

In this mode, all the text elements within the mobile interface are presented in a larger font size than the default, making it easier for users with visual limitations to read and understand the content. The increased font size helps in improving the visibility and legibility of the text, reducing the need for users to strain their eyes or zoom in to read the content.

Mobile Leaderboards

Mobile Leaderboards are a UI pattern commonly used in mobile applications and websites to display and rank a list of users or entities based on certain criteria or scores. This design element plays a vital role in engaging users and creating competition.

Mobile Leaderboards typically consist of a vertical list with user avatars or entity names along with their corresponding scores or rankings. The list is usually scrollable for accommodating a large number of entries. The leaderboard displays the highest-ranking individual or entity at the top, with descending ranks as the list progresses down.

The design of Mobile Leaderboards should prioritize providing clear and concise information to the users. The use of typography, colors, and graphics can be employed to emphasize important information such as top-ranked users or entities. Additionally, it is important to consider the space available on mobile screens, as the leaderboard should be easily readable without compromising the usability of other elements within the mobile application or website.

Mobile Loan Calculator

A Mobile Loan Calculator is a user interface (UI) pattern and design system that allows users to calculate and estimate the cost and expenses associated with a loan, specifically tailored for mobile devices. It provides an intuitive and efficient way for users to determine the loan amount, interest rate, loan term, and other relevant factors that influence the monthly installment and total repayment amount. The Mobile Loan Calculator typically consists of a clear and structured layout that displays input fields for the necessary loan parameters, such as loan amount, interest rate, and loan term. The UI should include appropriate labels and placeholders to guide users in accurately entering the required information. Additionally, it may incorporate sliders or number inputs with predefined ranges to aid users in setting values within acceptable limits. Once the user has provided all the required input, the Mobile Loan Calculator immediately computes and displays the resulting monthly installment and total repayment amount. The UI should present this information clearly and prominently to ensure easy comprehension for the user. It is essential to format the calculated amounts consistently and concisely for optimal readability, typically by utilizing a currency symbol, decimal separator, and appropriate number of decimal places. To enhance usability, a Mobile Loan Calculator should also provide additional features such as an amortization table, which shows the breakdown of each monthly payment's principal and interest components. This functionality allows users to gain further insights into the loan's progress and make informed decisions about potential early repayments or refinancing options. Moreover, a Mobile Loan Calculator can integrate other value-added features such as the ability to choose between different repayment frequencies (e.g., monthly, bi-weekly) or to visualize the loan repayment graphically through charts or graphs. These features further enhance the user experience by providing additional flexibility and empowering users to visualize the impact of their decisions on the loan repayment process. In conclusion, a Mobile Loan Calculator is a UI pattern and design system that simplifies and streamlines the process of calculating and estimating loan costs on mobile devices. By providing a user-friendly interface, clear and intuitive inputs, and instant calculation results, it enables users to make informed decisions regarding their loans and better manage their finances.>

Mobile Magnifier

A mobile magnifier is a user interface (UI) pattern that is commonly used in mobile applications and design systems to allow users to zoom in and magnify the content displayed on their mobile devices.

The mobile magnifier typically consists of a magnifying glass icon or button that users can interact with, either by tapping or pressing and holding. When activated, the magnifier expands a portion of the screen, making the content within that area larger and easier to view. This can be especially useful for users with visual impairments or for situations when small text or images need to be examined more closely.

In terms of design system considerations, the mobile magnifier should be visually consistent with the overall UI and adhere to the established design principles and guidelines. It should seamlessly integrate into the mobile application or system without causing any disruptions or inconsistencies in the user experience.

When implementing the mobile magnifier, there are a few key aspects to consider:

First, it is important to ensure that the magnifier is easily discoverable and accessible to users. It should be placed in a prominent location within the UI, such as the toolbar or a contextual menu, and its icon or button should have clear visual cues to indicate its purpose.

Second, the magnifier should provide a smooth and responsive user experience. The magnified content should be rendered quickly and accurately, without any noticeable lag or pixelation. Users should be able to interact with the magnified content effortlessly, such as scrolling or zooming within the magnified area.

Lastly, it is crucial to provide clear and intuitive controls for users to navigate within the magnified content. This can include options to pan or adjust the magnification level, as well as the ability to exit the magnifier and return to the regular view of the screen.

In conclusion, a mobile magnifier is a UI pattern and design system component that enables users to zoom in and magnify content on their mobile devices. When implementing a mobile magnifier, it is important to consider its visibility, responsiveness, and navigation controls in order to provide a seamless and meaningful user experience.

Mobile Medication Reminder

A mobile medication reminder is a user interface (UI) pattern and design system component that aids in managing medication schedules. It provides users with a convenient and accessible way to keep track of their medications, ensuring they take the right dosage at the right time.

The mobile medication reminder typically consists of a set of features and functionalities that help users stay organized and adhere to their medication regimens. These include:

1. Medication Schedule: The UI pattern displays a visual representation of the user's medication schedule, showing the specific medications they need to take and when. It allows users to view their daily, weekly, or monthly medication plans, including dosage instructions and any specific notes provided by their healthcare providers.

164

2. Reminders and Notifications: The design system component sends timely reminders and notifications to the user's mobile device, alerting them when it's time to take their medication. It can use various interaction patterns like push notifications, pop-up alerts, or audible alarms to ensure users don't miss their doses.

3. Medication Details: The UI pattern provides a way for users to access detailed information about their medications directly within the app. This includes the medication name, dosage, frequency, side effects, and interactions with other drugs. Users can consult this information to ensure they are fully informed about their prescriptions.

4. Tracking and Logging: The design system component allows users to track their medication intake by recording when they have taken each dose. It provides a log or history of past medication events, giving users a sense of accomplishment and helping them remember if they have taken their medication as prescribed.

5. Refill and Pharmacy Integration: The mobile medication reminder can integrate with pharmacy systems and services to facilitate medication refills. It can provide options for users to order their prescriptions online or in-app, helping them stay on top of their medication supply.

Overall, the mobile medication reminder UI pattern and design system component aim to improve medication adherence and overall health outcomes for users. By providing a user-friendly and intuitive interface, it helps individuals stay organized and on track with their medication schedules, reducing the risk of missed doses and medication errors.

Mobile Meditation Timer

A Mobile Meditation Timer is a user interface (UI) pattern that is part of a design system specifically created for mobile applications to assist users in practicing meditation. It is a tool that aids in maintaining focus and practicing mindfulness during meditation sessions. This UI pattern typically consists of a timer that displays the remaining duration of the meditation session. It may include a start button to initiate the timer and a pause button to temporarily stop the session if needed. The timer is presented in a visually pleasing and calming manner, often using soothing colors and minimalist design elements to promote a peaceful ambiance. In addition to displaying the remaining time, a Mobile Meditation Timer may also provide audio cues at specific intervals. These audio cues can help guide the user through their meditation practice, signaling the end of one phase or prompting them to transition into another state of mindfulness. The inclusion of audio cues can enhance the user experience by providing additional guidance and support during the meditation session. The design of a Mobile Meditation Timer should prioritize a clean and uncluttered interface to minimize distractions and create a calming atmosphere. It should have easily accessible controls, such as intuitive buttons for starting, pausing, and resetting the timer. The visual and auditory elements should be carefully chosen to align with the user's meditation goals and preferences. A Mobile Meditation Timer can be integrated as a standalone feature within a mobile app or as part of a broader meditation or wellness app. It should be designed to seamlessly blend with the overall visual and interaction design of the app, adhering to its established design system and UI patterns. By providing a Mobile Meditation Timer as part of a mobile app's design system, developers and designers can offer users a valuable tool to support their meditation practice. This UI pattern assists users in maintaining focus, improving their mindfulness, and enabling a more immersive meditation experience through visually and audibly guided sessions. A well-designed Mobile Meditation Timer is an essential component of a mobile app's design system, promoting a more mindful and calm user experience.>

Mobile Memory Usage

Mobile Memory Usage refers to the amount of memory that is consumed by a mobile application or system when it is in use. In the context of UI patterns and design systems, it is essential to consider the memory usage of a mobile application to ensure optimal performance and user experience. When designing UI patterns and implementing a design system, it is crucial to prioritize efficiency and minimize the memory footprint of the application. Bloated and memory-intensive applications can lead to slow performance, sluggish user interfaces, and potentially cause the application to consume excessive battery power. To achieve efficient memory usage, UI patterns and design systems should focus on the following aspects: 1. Optimized Asset

Management: Efficiently managing assets such as images, videos, and audio files is critical for minimizing memory consumption. This can be achieved through techniques such as lazy loading, using appropriate file formats, compression, and caching. 2. Streamlined Data Processing: Processing large amounts of data can significantly impact memory usage. Design systems should optimize data operations by minimizing redundant computations, utilizing data structures that are memory-efficient, and implementing lazy loading or pagination for large datasets. 3. Effective Memory Allocation: Allocating and releasing memory resources appropriately is essential to minimize memory leaks and optimize performance. Proper garbage collection techniques should be employed to ensure timely and efficient memory reclamation. 4. Responsiveness and Performance: UI patterns and design systems should prioritize swift and responsive user interfaces. This includes optimizing animations, transitions, and other interactive elements to minimize memory usage and ensure smooth user experiences. 5. Testing and Profiling: Regular testing and profiling of mobile applications are crucial to identify memory-intensive operations, memory leaks, and potential performance bottlenecks. This can be done through tools and techniques such as memory profilers, stress testing, and performance monitoring. By considering these aspects and incorporating efficient memory usage strategies into UI patterns and design systems, mobile applications can deliver optimal performance, reduce battery consumption, and provide a seamless user experience across devices with varying memory capacities.>

Mobile Mental Health Support

Mobile Mental Health Support refers to a user interface (UI) pattern and design system that aims to provide accessible and effective support for mental health through mobile applications. This design system encompasses a range of components and guidelines that ensure consistency, usability, and emotional well-being. The UI pattern of Mobile Mental Health Support is designed to address the unique challenges faced in providing mental health support through mobile applications. It takes into consideration the limited screen space, touch-based interactions, and the need for privacy and security. The design system provides a framework for creating user-centered interfaces that promote a positive user experience and encourage engagement with mental health resources. The components of Mobile Mental Health Support design system include user interface elements, such as buttons, navigation menus, and forms, that are optimized for mobile devices. These components are designed to be intuitive, easy to understand, and visually appealing, promoting a sense of calm and trust. The design system also includes typography and color guidelines that are carefully chosen to create a soothing and supportive atmosphere. Accessibility is a key consideration in the Mobile Mental Health Support design system. It ensures that the interface is easy to use for all users, regardless of their abilities or disabilities. This includes providing options for customizable font sizes and color schemes, as well as ensuring that the app is compatible with screen readers and other assistive technologies. The design system also incorporates evidence-based practices for mental health support. This includes incorporating principles from cognitive-behavioral therapy, mindfulness, and other therapeutic approaches into the design and content of the app. The content is presented in a clear and concise manner, making it easy for users to understand and apply in their daily lives. In summary, Mobile Mental Health Support is a UI pattern and design system that aims to provide accessible and effective support for mental health through mobile applications. It encompasses a range of components and guidelines that promote consistency, usability, and emotional well-being. By incorporating evidence-based practices and considering the unique challenges of mobile devices, this design system provides a user-centered interface that encourages engagement and support for mental health.>

Mobile Mind Mapping

A mobile mind mapping is a user interface (UI) pattern and design system used to visually organize and structure information in a hierarchical and interconnected manner on a mobile device. It allows users to capture, explore, and expand their thoughts, ideas, and concepts in a flexible and interactive way. Typically, mobile mind mapping employs a tree-like structure, where the main idea or concept is placed at the center of the screen, known as the central topic. From the central topic, users can create branches that represent related sub-topics or sub-ideas. These branches can be further expanded into more detailed levels, forming a multidimensional and interconnected map of thoughts. To interact with a mobile mind mapping interface, users usually employ touch and gesture-based interactions. They can tap on the central topic to add content or create new branches, swipe or pinch to navigate and zoom in or out of the map, and drag and drop elements to rearrange and reorganize the information. This intuitive and tactile interaction allows users to quickly capture and visually structure their thoughts, making it a powerful tool for brainstorming, note-taking, organizing projects, and managing information. In terms of design system, mobile mind mapping often follows principles of simplicity, clarity, and flexibility. The interface should provide a clean and uncluttered canvas for users to focus on their ideas without unnecessary distractions. It also needs to support various visual elements, such as text, icons, colors, and shapes, to assist users in expressing their ideas in a visually meaningful way. Furthermore, a mobile mind mapping design system should provide a range of customization options, enabling users to personalize the appearance of their mind maps to suit their preferences and style. This can include options to change the color theme, font styles, and line thickness. By offering customization possibilities, the design system allows users to create mind maps that are not only informative but also visually appealing and engaging. Overall, a mobile mind mapping UI pattern and design system offers a versatile and dynamic method for users to capture, organize, and explore their thoughts on mobile devices. By leveraging touch interactions and providing a flexible design system, it empowers users to visually structure information and foster creativity in a mobile context.>

Mobile Museum Guides

A mobile museum guide refers to a user interface pattern and design system specifically designed for museum applications on mobile devices. It aims to provide users with a seamless and intuitive experience while navigating and exploring various exhibits and collections within a museum. The mobile museum guide typically consists of a set of interactive screens and features that allow users to access information about the museum, its exhibits, and additional contextual content. The UI pattern focuses on simplicity, clarity, and ease of use, ensuring that visitors can effortlessly explore the museum and locate desired information. The design system of a mobile museum guide incorporates visual elements, such as icons and typography, that maintain consistency and create a cohesive visual language throughout the application. These elements are carefully chosen to enhance readability and aesthetics, ensuring that users can easily distinguish and interpret different types of content and interactive elements. The mobile museum guide interface utilizes responsive design techniques, enabling it to adapt efficiently to different screen sizes and orientations. This ensures that the application remains accessible and functional on a wide range of mobile devices, including smartphones and tablets. Through the UI pattern, a mobile museum guide typically offers features like interactive maps, allowing users to locate themselves within the museum and navigate to different exhibits. It may also include search functionality, enabling visitors to find specific exhibits or types of content. Additionally, the guide often provides multimedia content, such as images, videos, and audio clips, allowing users to delve deeper into the museum's collections and related information. Overall, a mobile museum guide serves as a digital companion for museum visitors, offering an engaging and informative experience. Its UI pattern and design system focus on intuitive navigation, clarity of information, and visual consistency to ensure that users can interact seamlessly with the application while exploring the museum's exhibits and collections.

A mobile museum guide refers to a user interface pattern and design system specifically designed for museum applications on mobile devices. The guide aims to provide users with a seamless and intuitive experience while navigating and exploring various exhibits and collections within a museum.

The mobile museum guide typically consists of interactive screens and features that allow users to access information about the museum, exhibits, and additional contextual content. It incorporates visual elements, such as icons and typography, to maintain consistency and enhance readability. The guide utilizes responsive design techniques to ensure compatibility with different screen sizes and orientations, and often includes features like interactive maps, search functionality, and multimedia content to facilitate exploration and engagement for museum visitors.

Mobile Music Player

A mobile music player is a user interface (UI) pattern and design system specifically designed for accessing and playing music on a mobile device. The main purpose of a mobile music player is to provide users with a convenient and intuitive way of managing and listening to their music collections on their mobile devices. It typically includes features such as browsing and searching for songs, creating and managing playlists, and controlling playback. In terms of UI patterns, a mobile music player typically utilizes a tab-based navigation system to allow users to switch between different sections of the app, such as the library, playlists, and settings. This ensures that users can easily access their music collection and desired features without feeling overwhelmed or confused by a cluttered interface. In addition to tab-based navigation, a mobile music player often incorporates a menu or drawer component that provides quick access to additional options and settings. This allows users to customize their music playback experience by adjusting settings such as shuffle, repeat, and equalizer settings. From a design system perspective, a mobile music player follows consistent visual and interaction patterns to create a cohesive and familiar user experience. It typically leverages common design principles such as hierarchy, contrast, and readability to ensure that users can easily navigate and interact with the app. Within the app's screens, a mobile music player often features a cover art display, song information, and playback controls. These elements are typically arranged in a clear and organized manner, using typography and visual cues to convey important information and guide user interactions. Overall, a mobile music player provides a streamlined and enjoyable way for users to access and play their music on a mobile device. It incorporates intuitive UI patterns and design system principles to create a cohesive and user-friendly experience, ensuring that users can easily manage their music collections and enjoy their favorite songs wherever they go.>

Mobile Neighborhood Watch

A Mobile Neighborhood Watch is a UI pattern and design system that is specifically designed for mobile applications aimed at creating safer neighborhoods and communities.

This design system incorporates a range of features and functionalities that enable users to participate in the promotion of safety and security within their immediate surroundings. It provides a platform where community members can collaborate and share information to help prevent and address any suspicious activities or incidents.

Mobile Network Usage

The mobile network usage refers to the amount of data consumed by a user while utilizing their mobile device on a cellular network. This includes data usage for activities such as browsing the internet, streaming videos, downloading files, sending and receiving emails and messages, using social media applications, and making voice or video calls. In the context of UI patterns and design systems, mobile network usage is an important aspect to consider when creating user interfaces for mobile applications. Designers need to take into account the varying data consumption patterns of users and ensure that the app's interface is optimized for efficient data usage. When designing interfaces, it is crucial to provide users with clear and concise information about their mobile network usage. This can include displaying the amount of data consumed in a specified time period, such as daily, weekly, or monthly, as well as providing insights into how the data was used (e.g., browsing, video streaming, app usage). To effectively communicate mobile network usage information, UI patterns and design systems can employ data visualization techniques. This can include the use of charts, graphs, or progress bars to visually represent the data usage, allowing users to quickly understand and assess their consumption. Designers should also consider offering features that allow users to manage and control their mobile network usage. This can involve providing options to set data usage limits, receive notifications when reaching certain thresholds, or even offering suggestions on how to optimize data consumption. Overall, incorporating mobile network usage considerations into UI patterns and design systems helps ensure that the user interfaces are user-friendly, informative, and efficient in providing users with the necessary information to manage and understand their data consumption. By designing interfaces that efficiently communicate mobile network usage, designers can help users make informed decisions about their data usage and ultimately enhance their mobile experience.>

Mobile News Feed

A Mobile News Feed refers to a user interface (UI) pattern and design system commonly found in mobile applications or responsive websites. It is specifically designed to display a continuous stream of news articles, blog posts, social media updates, or any other type of content in a compact and scannable manner on mobile devices.

The Mobile News Feed typically follows a vertical scrolling layout, allowing users to easily swipe or scroll through the content. Each item in the feed is presented as a card or tile, containing a headline, a brief summary or excerpt, and often a thumbnail image or an avatar representing the source. The cards are arranged in reverse chronological order, with the most recent content appearing at the top.

Mobile Note-Taking

Mobile note-taking is a user interface design pattern that allows users to create, store, and organize notes on their mobile devices. It is a part of a comprehensive design system that provides a consistent and intuitive user experience across different mobile applications.

This pattern typically consists of a note-taking app or feature that provides users with a minimalistic and user-friendly interface for capturing and managing their notes. Users can create new notes, edit existing notes, and delete notes as needed.

Mobile note-taking often includes features such as text formatting options (e.g., bold, italic, bullet points), the ability to attach images or files to notes, and synchronization across multiple devices or platforms. These features are designed to enhance the functionality and versatility of note-taking apps, allowing users to create and access their notes anytime, anywhere.

In terms of design, mobile note-taking follows the principles of simplicity, clarity, and efficiency. The user interface is typically clean and uncluttered, with a focus on the content and functionality of the app. The use of intuitive icons, buttons, and gestures enables easy navigation and interaction with the note-taking app.

The design system for mobile note-taking encompasses a set of standardized components, styles, and guidelines that ensure consistency and cohesion across different apps and platforms. It includes elements such as typography, color schemes, icons, and layouts, which help create a unified and cohesive visual language for note-taking apps.

Overall, mobile note-taking is an essential UI pattern and design system for mobile devices, providing users with a convenient and efficient way to capture, organize, and access their notes on the go.

Mobile Notifications Settings

Mobile notifications settings refer to the user interface (UI) patterns and design system that allow users to manage and customize the notifications they receive on their mobile devices. Notifications are messages or alerts sent by applications to notify users about important information or events.

The mobile notifications settings typically provide users with options to enable or disable notifications for specific apps, as well as the ability to customize the type and frequency of notifications they wish to receive. These settings are usually accessed through the device's system settings or within the individual app settings. Within the mobile notifications settings, users can often find various options to control the behavior of notifications. Some common settings include:

- Enabling or disabling notifications for specific apps: Users can choose which apps are allowed to send notifications to their mobile device. By enabling notifications for an app, users will receive alerts whenever that app has important updates or new information. Disabling notifications for an app will prevent the app from sending any alerts or messages.

- Customizing notification types: Users can define the type of notifications they want to receive for each app. This can include options such as receiving a pop-up message, a sound alert, or a vibration when a notification is received. Users can also choose to receive notifications silently, meaning they will only appear in the notification center without any additional alerts.

- Managing notification priority: Some mobile operating systems offer the ability to prioritize certain notifications over others. This means that important notifications will appear more prominently, while less important ones may be grouped or hidden. Users can customize these settings to ensure they don't miss out on critical information.

- Setting notification schedules: Mobile notifications settings may provide users with the option to define specific times when they want to receive notifications. This can be useful, for example, to avoid being disturbed during sleep or important meetings. Users can define these schedules based on their own preferences and needs.

In conclusion, mobile notifications settings in the context of UI patterns and design systems allow users to have control over the notifications they receive on their mobile devices. By customizing these settings, users can ensure they receive relevant and timely alerts while minimizing distractions.

>

Mobile Nutrition Tracking

Mobile Offline Mode

Mobile Offline Mode is a user interface pattern and design system feature that allows a mobile application to function even when there is no internet or network connectivity available. In this mode, the application provides limited functionality and displays information that has been previously downloaded or cached on the device.

When a mobile device is in Offline Mode, the application's user interface is designed to provide a seamless and uninterrupted user experience. The design system ensures that the user is aware of the offline status by displaying appropriate visual cues, such as a different color theme or an indication in the top navigation bar. This helps the user to easily recognize the current mode and adapt accordingly.

Mobile Order Tracking

Mobile Order Tracking is a UI pattern and design system that allows users to track their orders directly from their mobile devices. It provides a seamless and intuitive experience for users to stay up-to-date with the status and location of their orders throughout the entire delivery process.

The Mobile Order Tracking user interface typically consists of several key components, including:

A status indicator: This component visually represents the current status of the order, such as "Order Confirmed," "Being Prepared," "In Transit," or "Delivered." It provides a quick and clear way for users to understand the progress of their order at a glance.

Timeline or progress bar: This component displays a visual representation of the order's progress through various stages of the delivery process. It may include timestamps or estimated delivery times to give users a sense of the timeline for their order.

Order details: This component provides users with access to detailed information about their order, such as the items purchased, delivery address, and contact information for the delivery provider. Users can easily reference this information as needed to ensure accuracy and make any necessary updates or changes.

Interactive map: In many Mobile Order Tracking implementations, an interactive map is included to visually display the current location of the delivery provider and the user's delivery address. This provides an additional layer of context and helps users anticipate the arrival time of their order.

Notifications: Mobile Order Tracking often includes push notifications or other types of notifications to keep users informed about status updates and important milestones in the delivery process. These notifications can be customized based on user preferences and settings to ensure they receive the most relevant and timely information.

In conclusion, Mobile Order Tracking is a powerful UI pattern and design system that enhances the overall user experience of tracking orders on mobile devices. By providing clear status indicators, timelines, detailed order information, interactive maps, and timely notifications, Mobile Order Tracking helps users stay informed and engaged throughout the delivery process.

Mobile Parking Finder

A Mobile Parking Finder is a user interface pattern and design system that enables users to easily locate and navigate to available parking spaces using their mobile devices.

This pattern typically consists of a mobile app or a website that provides real-time information about parking availability, rates, and any additional details such as hours of operation or payment methods. The goal of this pattern is to assist users in finding convenient parking options quickly and efficiently, enhancing their overall parking experience.

Mobile Payment Confirmation

A mobile payment confirmation refers to the step in a user interface (UI) pattern or design system where a user is presented with confirmation of a mobile payment transaction. It is an essential part of the payment process that helps users verify the success or failure of their payment.

Typically, the mobile payment confirmation appears after a user has completed the necessary steps to make a payment, such as entering payment details and confirming the transaction. The confirmation message provides crucial information about the payment, including the payment amount, payment method used, and any additional details specific to the transaction or the app. It also reassures the user that their payment has been successfully processed or alerts them to any issues that may have occurred.

Mobile Payment Options

Mobile payment options are a set of user interface patterns and design elements that provide users with the ability to make payments using their mobile devices. These options are a part of a larger design system that aims to create a consistent and intuitive experience for users when it comes to making payments through their mobile devices. The first mobile payment option is the digital wallet. A digital wallet is a secure application that stores a user's payment information, such as credit card details, in a virtual form. When using a digital wallet, users can make payments by simply selecting the desired payment method stored in their wallet. This eliminates the need for users to manually enter their payment information each time they make a purchase. Digital wallets often utilize technologies such as Near Field Communication (NFC) or QR codes to enable contactless payments in physical stores. The second mobile payment option is mobile banking. Mobile banking refers to the ability to perform banking activities, including making payments, using a mobile device. This option typically involves accessing a mobile banking application provided by a bank or financial institution. Users can link their bank accounts or credit cards to the mobile banking app and make payments directly from their accounts. Mobile banking apps often offer additional features such as transaction history, bill payment, and money transfers. Both digital wallets and mobile banking options provide users with a convenient and secure way to make payments using their mobile devices. These options aim to streamline the payment process by eliminating the need for physical cash or traditional payment methods such as credit cards. In addition, they offer added security measures such as encryption and authentication to protect users' payment information. In conclusion, mobile payment options are an essential part of a design system for mobile applications. They provide users with convenient and secure ways to make payments using their mobile devices. The digital wallet and mobile banking options are two common patterns in mobile payment design, offering users the ability to store and access their payment information easily and make payments with just a few taps on their screens.>

Mobile Personal Finance Dashboard

A Mobile Personal Finance Dashboard is a user interface pattern and design system that provides a visually appealing and intuitive way for users to manage their personal finances on a mobile device. The primary goal of a Mobile Personal Finance Dashboard is to present financial information in a clear and organized manner, allowing users to easily track their income, expenses, savings, and investments. The dashboard typically consists of various modules or widgets that display different aspects of the user's financial data, such as account balances, transaction history, budgets, and financial goals. The design of a Mobile Personal Finance Dashboard follows established principles of mobile app design, with a focus on simplicity, efficiency, and ease of use. The interface is usually composed of clean and minimalistic elements, with a limited color palette and restrained use of graphics or animations to avoid clutter and distractions. The layout of the dashboard is carefully designed to ensure optimal visibility and usability on a small screen, with key information and actions placed within easy reach of the user's thumb. The use of intuitive icons and labels helps users quickly understand the purpose and functionality of different dashboard components. Interaction and navigation within a Mobile Personal Finance Dashboard are typically implemented using common mobile UI patterns, such as swiping, tapping, and scrolling. Users can easily switch between different sections of the dashboard, access detailed information about their accounts or transactions, and perform actions like adding or editing transactions, setting budget limits, or defining financial goals. In order to enhance the user experience and provide additional value, a Mobile Personal Finance Dashboard may also offer features like personalized financial recommendations, spending analysis, goal tracking, or integration with external financial services or institutions. Overall, a Mobile Personal Finance Dashboard serves as a practical and convenient tool for individuals to gain a comprehensive overview of their financial status and make informed decisions about their money, all within the convenience of their mobile device. It empowers users to take control of their finances and work towards their financial goals, ultimately leading to improved financial well-being. >

Mobile Personalization Options

Mobile personalization options refer to the various features and customization settings available to users on a mobile device's user interface (UI). These options allow users to modify the appearance, functionality, and content of their mobile experience to align with their individual preferences and needs.

To enhance user satisfaction and usability, mobile personalization options should be designed in consideration of UI patterns and design systems. UI patterns refer to recurring solutions to common design problems, while design systems provide guidelines and principles for consistent and cohesive design. By aligning personalization options with UI patterns and design systems, the overall user experience remains intuitive and cohesive across different customization choices and screens.

Mobile Podcast Player

A mobile podcast player is a user interface pattern and design system that is specifically designed and optimized for accessing and consuming podcasts on a mobile device. This type of player provides a seamless and intuitive experience for users to browse, discover, and play podcast episodes on their smartphones or tablets.

A key characteristic of a mobile podcast player is its simplicity and user-friendly design. It typically features a clean and minimalistic interface that eliminates clutter and enhances ease of use. The player often utilizes a card-based layout, where podcast episodes are visually presented as individual cards, displaying relevant information such as episode titles, artwork, and duration.

In terms of functionality, a mobile podcast player offers various features that cater to the unique needs of podcast listeners. These include a comprehensive search function, allowing users to easily find and filter podcasts based on specific criteria such as genre, host, or keyword. The player also enables users to subscribe to their favorite podcasts, creating a personalized library of subscribed shows for easy access.

Additionally, a mobile podcast player offers seamless playback controls, allowing users to play, pause, rewind, and fast forward podcast episodes with ease. It may provide playback speed options, enabling users to adjust the speed at which episodes are played to suit their preferences. The player often includes a progress bar that indicates the current playback position, enabling users to easily navigate through episodes and pick up where they left off.

Furthermore, a mobile podcast player may incorporate social sharing features, allowing users to easily share their favorite episodes or recommend podcasts to their friends and followers on social media platforms. It may also provide options for offline listening, allowing users to download episodes and listen to them without an internet connection.

In conclusion, a mobile podcast player is a specialized user interface pattern and design system that provides a seamless and user-friendly experience for accessing and consuming podcasts on a mobile device. It offers a range of features and functionalities tailored to the unique needs of podcast listeners, ensuring a convenient and enjoyable podcast listening experience.

Mobile Police Activity Alerts

Mobile Police Activity Alerts is a user interface (UI) pattern and design system that is intended to provide real-time notifications to users regarding police activities and incidents happening in their location. This system aims to keep users informed and aware of any relevant law enforcement activities and events occurring in their area, utilizing their mobile devices.

The UI pattern of Mobile Police Activity Alerts typically includes elements such as push notifications, badges, pop-ups, and alerts within a mobile application or website. These alerts are triggered based on various criteria, such as the user's current location, proximity to ongoing police operations, or specific areas of interest defined by the user.

This UI pattern is designed to provide users with important information related to police activities, including crime incidents, emergencies, traffic disruptions, and community outreach initiatives. By delivering these alerts to users' mobile devices, they can stay updated and make informed decisions based on real-time data.

The design system of Mobile Police Activity Alerts focuses on ensuring a user-friendly and clear presentation of information. It employs intuitive visual cues and clear language to convey the nature of the police activity, urgency, and any relevant instructions or recommendations for the users. The alerts are designed to be concise yet informative, allowing users to quickly grasp the necessary details without overwhelming them with excessive information.

The Mobile Police Activity Alerts design system also emphasizes user engagement and interaction. It often includes features like interactive maps, allowing users to visualize the location and extent of ongoing police activities. Users may also have the option to customize their alert settings, specify their areas of interest, or provide feedback to further optimize the system.

Overall, the Mobile Police Activity Alerts UI pattern and design system serve two primary purposes: keeping users informed about police activities happening in their vicinity and promoting community engagement with law enforcement efforts. By implementing this UI pattern and design system, mobile applications and websites can effectively contribute to enhancing public safety, promoting transparency, and fostering a sense of connection between law enforcement agencies and the communities they serve.>

Mobile Pollen Alerts

Mobile Pollen Alerts are a user interface pattern and design system element that provides users with real-time notifications about the presence of pollen in their current location. These alerts are designed to help users who are allergic or sensitive to pollen to stay informed about the pollen levels in their area, allowing them to take necessary precautions to minimize their exposure and manage their symptoms.

Implemented as part of a mobile app or website, Mobile Pollen Alerts typically consist of a small, unobtrusive notification or message that appears on the user's device screen. The alert may include information such as the current pollen levels (low, moderate, high), pollen types (e.g., grass, tree, weed), and any specific recommendations or actions users can take to reduce their exposure to pollen, such as wearing a mask or avoiding outdoor activities during peak pollen times.

Mobile Power Outage Alerts

Mobile Prescription Refill

Mobile Prescription Refill is a user interface pattern and design system that facilitates the process of refilling prescription medications using a mobile device or app. This pattern streamlines the prescription refill process by providing a simple and intuitive user interface, allowing users to easily submit their prescription refill requests without the need for a traditional paper-based workflow.

The Mobile Prescription Refill pattern typically consists of multiple screens or views that guide the user through the refill process. These screens are designed to be easy to navigate and understand, providing clear instructions and prompts to the user at each step of the process.

The first screen of the Mobile Prescription Refill pattern usually prompts the user to input their prescription information, such as the medication name, dosage, and quantity. This information can often be entered manually, or the pattern may provide the option to scan the medication label or barcode using the mobile device's camera. The pattern may also offer autocomplete or search functionality to help the user quickly find their medication in a database.

Once the user has entered or scanned their prescription information, the Mobile Prescription Refill pattern typically guides the user to the next screen, where they can review and confirm the details of their refill request. This screen presents the medication details in a clear and concise manner, allowing the user to verify that the information is correct before submitting the request.

After confirming the refill request, the Mobile Prescription Refill pattern may prompt the user to choose their preferred pharmacy for pickup or delivery. This screen typically presents a list of nearby pharmacies, along with relevant information such as distance, operating hours, and contact details. The user can then select their desired pharmacy and proceed to the final step.

The last screen of the Mobile Prescription Refill pattern serves as a confirmation and summary of the refill request. It may include a unique order or prescription number, estimated pickup or delivery date, and any additional instructions or information. The user can easily access this summary screen at any time to review the status of their refill request.

Mobile Privacy Screen Protectors

Mobile privacy screen protectors are a category of protective accessories designed to prevent unauthorized viewing of the content on a mobile device's screen. They are typically made of thin, adhesive film that can be easily attached and removed from the device's screen. Privacy screen protectors are engineered to limit the viewing angle of the screen, making it difficult for anyone other than the device user to see the display clearly. These screen protectors work by employing micro-louver technology, which consists of tiny vertical blinds that are incorporated into the film material. When the protector is attached to the screen, the micro-louvers allow light to pass through in a specific direction, limiting the field of view. This means that by adjusting the orientation of the device, the user can control who can see the screen. When viewed from a certain angle, the screen appears dark and distorted to anyone trying to look at it from the side, while the user sees the content clearly when viewing from the front. Privacy screen protectors are particularly useful in situations where the user needs to protect sensitive information from prying eyes, such as when using mobile banking apps, viewing confidential documents, or entering personal passwords. By limiting the viewing angle, these protectors help prevent shoulder surfing and increase the overall privacy and security of the device. From a UI pattern and design system perspective, privacy screen protectors require careful consideration to ensure a consistent and optimal user experience. Designers need to take into account the limited viewing angles and potential distortion of the screen when creating user interfaces. This may involve adjusting font sizes, icon placements, and other UI elements to ensure readability and usability within the restricted field of view. Additionally, designers may need to address the challenge of accommodating different screen sizes and resolutions while maintaining the effectiveness of the privacy screen protector. This could involve conducting usability testing and adapting the UI patterns and design system to ensure compatibility across various devices. In summary, mobile privacy screen protectors are accessories that limit the viewing angle of a mobile device's screen to protect sensitive information from being visible to unauthorized individuals. They use micro-louver technology to restrict lateral visibility, ensuring that the screen remains visible only to the device user. Designers must consider the constraints and limitations of these protectors when creating UI patterns and design systems to ensure a consistent user experience.>

Mobile Profile Dashboard

A Mobile Profile Dashboard is a user interface pattern and design system specifically designed for mobile devices. It serves as a centralized hub for users to access and manage their personal information and settings. The Mobile Profile Dashboard typically consists of multiple sections or cards, each representing a specific category or aspect of the user's profile. These sections can include personal information, preferences, account settings, and other related details. The dashboard provides users with a quick and convenient way to view and update their profile information without having to navigate through different screens or menus. The design of the Mobile Profile Dashboard follows a clean and intuitive layout, optimized for small screens and touch interactions. It utilizes a responsive design approach to ensure that the dashboard adapts seamlessly to different screen sizes and orientations. This allows users to access their profile information on various mobile devices such as smartphones and tablets. The Mobile Profile Dashboard is characterized by its simplicity and ease of use. It employs clear and concise labels, icons, and navigation elements to guide users through the different sections and options available. The use of minimalistic design principles helps to reduce cognitive load and improve the overall user experience. Additionally, the Mobile Profile Dashboard often incorporates interactive elements such as collapsible sections, expandable cards, and inline editing to enhance usability. These features enable users to quickly access and modify their profile information, providing a seamless and efficient user experience. Overall, the Mobile Profile Dashboard is a vital component of mobile applications and websites where users need to manage their personal information and preferences. It provides a consolidated view of profile-related data and serves as a central hub for users to control their account settings and update relevant information. Its simplicity, responsiveness, and user-friendly design make it an essential pattern in mobile user interface design.>

Mobile Programming Courses

Mobile programming courses are educational programs aimed at teaching individuals the necessary skills and knowledge to develop mobile applications. These courses focus on providing learners with a comprehensive understanding of mobile programming languages and frameworks, as well as best practices in user interface (UI) patterns and design systems. UI patterns refer to commonly used solutions to design problems that occur during the development of mobile applications. They are essentially pre-established design templates that developers can follow to create intuitive and user-friendly interfaces. UI patterns help maintain consistency throughout an app and ensure a seamless user experience. Examples of popular UI patterns include tab navigation, cards, and sliders. Design systems, on the other hand, go beyond UI patterns and encompass a set of guidelines, principles, and components that define the visual and interactive aspects of an application. A design system provides a framework for creating uniformity and cohesion in mobile app designs, making it easier for developers and designers to collaborate and maintain brand consistency. Mobile programming courses cover the principles and practices of UI patterns and design systems, equipping learners with the knowledge of how to effectively apply these concepts in their app development projects. Students will learn how to identify and implement appropriate UI patterns based on user needs, industry standards, and design principles. Furthermore, these courses focus on teaching learners how to develop and integrate design systems into their mobile applications. This includes understanding typography, color schemes, iconography, and other design elements. Students will also gain hands-on experience in using tools and software to create, manage, and iterate on design systems. By taking mobile programming courses that cover UI patterns and design systems, individuals can enhance their ability to create visually appealing, intuitive, and consistent mobile applications. These skills are crucial for success in the ever-evolving mobile app development industry, as they directly impact user satisfaction and engagement. Overall, mobile programming courses provide learners with the necessary knowledge and skills to develop mobile applications, with a specific focus on UI patterns and design systems. By mastering these concepts, developers can create mobile apps that are not only visually appealing but also user-friendly and efficient.>

Mobile Progress Tracking

Mobile Progress Tracking refers to the user interface pattern and design system that allows users to keep track of their progress in a mobile application or website. This pattern provides a visual representation of the user's progress in completing a task or reaching a goal, enabling them to easily understand where they are in the overall process. In this pattern, the progress is typically shown through a progress bar that visually represents the completion status. The progress bar may be displayed horizontally or vertically, depending on the design and layout of the mobile application or website. The progress bar is divided into segments or steps, indicating the different stages or milestones in the process. Each segment represents a specific task or goal that the user needs to complete. The progress bar may also include labels or numbers to indicate the percentage of progress achieved or the number of steps completed. This provides users with a clear understanding of how far they have come and how much more they need to accomplish. Mobile Progress Tracking also incorporates interactive elements that allow users to navigate back and forth between different steps or stages. This enables users to easily review their previous progress or jump ahead to a later step if needed. The design system for Mobile Progress Tracking focuses on providing a consistent and intuitive user experience across different devices and platforms. It includes guidelines for the placement, size, and visual style of the progress bar, as well as the labels and interactive elements. In conclusion, Mobile Progress Tracking is a user interface pattern and design system that allows users to visually track their progress in a mobile application or website. It provides a clear representation of the completion status and allows users to navigate between different steps or stages. The design system ensures consistency and ease of use across different devices and platforms.>

Mobile Property Finder

A Mobile Property Finder is a user interface pattern and design system specifically developed for mobile devices, aimed at assisting users in finding properties. It provides a seamless and intuitive experience for users to search for and explore various properties such as houses, apartments, and commercial spaces. The Mobile Property Finder typically comprises a set of interactive components and features designed to cater to the specific needs of mobile users. These components and features include search filters, property listings, map integration, saved searches, and notifications. The search filters allow users to refine their property search based on criteria such as location, price range, property type, and amenities. Users can easily select and adjust these filters using simple touch gestures or buttons, making it effortless to find the properties that meet their requirements. The property listings display relevant information about each property, including details like price, location, size, and number of bedrooms. Users can browse through these listings using touch gestures like swiping or scrolling, enabling them to quickly compare and evaluate different properties. Map integration is a key feature of the Mobile Property Finder, allowing users to view properties on a map. This feature provides a visual representation of the properties' locations, giving users a better understanding of the surrounding area and proximity to amenities or points of interest. Saved searches enable users to save their preferred search criteria for easy access in the future. This feature eliminates the need to re-enter search parameters each time, saving time and effort for frequent property searches. Notifications inform users about new properties or updates that match their saved searches or preferences. This ensures that users stay informed and don't miss out on potential opportunities. The design system for the Mobile Property Finder follows mobile-first principles, prioritizing usability, simplicity, and responsiveness. It incorporates a clean and intuitive interface, optimized for touch interactions and small screen sizes. Consistent typography, color schemes, and iconography enhance the overall visual aesthetic and contribute to a cohesive user experience. In conclusion, a Mobile Property Finder is a specialized user interface pattern and design system that enhances the property search experience on mobile devices. It provides a range of features and components tailored to the needs of mobile users, ensuring a seamless and efficient property search process.>

Mobile Public Transportation

176

Mobile Public Transportation is a user interface (UI) pattern and design system that focuses on providing efficient transportation services to users through a mobile application. The primary goal of this design system is to enhance the user experience by making it easy for users to navigate, plan, and access public transportation options directly from their mobile devices. The Mobile Public Transportation design system typically consists of various screens and components that are specifically designed to cater to the needs of commuters using public transportation. These screens and components are designed to be intuitive, user-friendly, and visually appealing with a focus on providing quick and convenient access to relevant information. One of the key features of the Mobile Public Transportation design system is the ability to view real-time information about transit routes, schedules, and arrival times. This feature ensures that users can plan their journeys effectively and stay informed about any delays or disruptions. Additionally, the design system may also include features such as ticket purchasing, fare information, and integration with mobile payment systems to streamline the ticketing process. Furthermore, the design system may include features that facilitate navigation and wayfinding, such as interactive maps, route planning, and GPS tracking. These features help users easily identify the nearest bus or train stops, select the most efficient routes, and track their progress during the journey. The Mobile Public Transportation design system also emphasizes the importance of accessibility. It ensures that the application is usable by individuals with disabilities and provides features such as text-to-speech functionality, screen magnification, and customizable font sizes to accommodate different user needs. In summary, the Mobile Public Transportation design system is a UI pattern that aims to provide a seamless and convenient experience for users accessing public transportation services through a mobile application. By incorporating features such as real-time information, ticketing functionality, navigation assistance, and accessibility options, this design system enhances the overall user experience and promotes the use of public transportation as a sustainable and efficient mode of travel.>

Mobile QR Code Scanner

A mobile QR code scanner is a user interface pattern and design system element that allows users to scan and read information from Quick Response (QR) codes using their mobile devices.

QR codes are two-dimensional barcodes that can store various types of data, such as URLs, text, contact information, or app downloads. They are widely used in marketing, advertising, and retail to provide convenient access to information or engage users in interactive experiences.

Mobile Real Estate Listings

A mobile real estate listings UI pattern refers to the design and layout used to display property listings on a mobile device. It is a user interface (UI) pattern specifically tailored for viewing real estate listings on smartphones or tablets.

The design system for mobile real estate listings focuses on creating a visually appealing, easy-to-navigate, and user-friendly interface that allows users to search, browse, and view property details seamlessly on their mobile devices. The use of responsive design principles ensures that the listings can be accessed and displayed effectively across different screen sizes and orientations.

Mobile Recipe Builder

A mobile recipe builder is a user interface pattern and design system specifically designed for mobile devices that allows users to easily create and customize their own recipes.

It provides a user-friendly and intuitive way for users to input and organize ingredients, instructions, cooking times, and other details in a step-by-step format. The recipe builder includes a variety of pre-designed templates and layouts that users can choose from to create their recipes.

Mobile Remote Control

A Mobile Remote Control is a UI pattern and design system that enables users to control and interact with a remote device or application using their mobile devices. It provides a seamless and intuitive way for users to navigate, operate, and manage the remote device or application. The Mobile Remote Control design system focuses on creating a user-friendly interface that is optimized for mobile devices, ensuring a smooth and responsive user experience. It encompasses various UI components and interactions to enable users to remotely control and monitor the target device or application. The design system adopts a minimalist and clean approach, prioritizing simplicity and ease of use. The interface typically consists of a central control panel with essential buttons and controls, enabling users to perform basic functions such as power on/off, volume adjustment, playback control, and navigation. To enhance usability, the Mobile Remote Control design system leverages intuitive gestures and interactions. For example, users can swipe or tap to switch between different control modes or screens, making it quick and easy to access different features and settings. In addition to basic controls, the Mobile Remote Control design system allows users to access advanced functionalities or settings through contextual menus or overlays. These menus provide additional options and customization, allowing users to personalize their control experience based on their specific preferences. Consistency and visual hierarchy play a crucial role in the design system. The interface follows established mobile design guidelines, ensuring that users can easily recognize and interpret the controls and their corresponding actions. Clear labeling and visual cues help users understand the purpose and functionality of each control element. Overall, the Mobile Remote Control UI pattern and design system aim to provide an intuitive and efficient way for users to remotely control and interact with a target device or application using their mobile devices. By simplifying the control process and optimizing the user experience, it enhances convenience and accessibility, ensuring a seamless and enjoyable user journey.>

Mobile Rental Car Reservation

A mobile rental car reservation refers to the process of reserving a car for a specific period of time through a mobile application or website. This UI pattern and design system allows users to easily search for, select, and book a rental car using their mobile device. The mobile rental car reservation system typically consists of various interactive components and screens that guide users through the reservation process. It starts with a search screen where users can input their pickup and drop-off locations, as well as the desired dates and times. This information is then used to display relevant search results on a results screen. The results screen presents users with a list of available rental car options, along with their details such as the car category, price, and features. To help users make a decision, thumbnail images and brief descriptions may be included. Users can explore more information about a specific car by tapping on it, which takes them to a detailed car information screen. In the detailed car information screen, users can view comprehensive details about the selected car, including images, specifications, and any additional fees or requirements. From this screen, users can customize their reservation by selecting optional extras such as GPS, child seats, or additional drivers. The screen also displays the total estimated cost of the reservation. Once users are satisfied with their selection, they can proceed to the reservation confirmation screen. This screen summarizes all the details of the reservation, including the pickup and drop-off locations, dates and times, selected car, optional extras, and total cost. Users may be required to provide their personal information, such as name, phone number, and payment details, to complete the reservation. Finally, users can review and confirm their reservation by accepting the terms and conditions and tapping the "Book Now" button. In conclusion, a mobile rental car reservation system is a UI pattern and design system that enables users to easily search, select, and book a rental car through a mobile application or website. It includes screens for search, results, detailed car information, and confirmation, providing a seamless and convenient experience for users to reserve their desired rental car.>

Mobile Ride-Sharing

Ride-sharing is a mobile application service that allows users to request a ride and be matched with a nearby driver who can transport them to their desired destination. The user interface (UI) patterns and design systems play a crucial role in ensuring a seamless and intuitive ride-sharing experience.

UI patterns in a ride-sharing app typically include elements such as a map interface displaying the user's current location, destination input fields, and a confirmation button to initiate a ride request. Design systems help maintain consistency across the app by providing guidelines for colors, typography, and overall visual aesthetics.

Mobile Road Closure Alerts

Mobile Road Closure Alerts are a UI pattern and design system that provides users with notifications and information regarding road closures and disruptions on mobile platforms.

This pattern is designed to enhance user experience and ensure safety by delivering real-time updates on road closures, construction sites, accidents, and other events that may impact travel routes. Through a clear and intuitive interface, users can quickly and easily access relevant information, plan alternative routes, and avoid delays and congestion.

Mobile Screen Reader

A mobile screen reader is a software application designed to assist individuals with visual impairments to interact with user interfaces (UI) on mobile devices. It reads out the content on the screen and provides auditory feedback, enabling people with visual impairments to navigate and use mobile applications effectively.

Mobile screen readers are an essential component of UI patterns and design systems, ensuring accessibility for all users. They help create an inclusive user experience by enabling individuals with visual impairments to access the same information and functionalities as sighted users.

Mobile Severe Weather Alerts

Mobile Severe Weather Alerts refer to the notifications or warnings issued to mobile device users to inform them about impending severe weather conditions in their area. These alerts are part of a user interface pattern and design system that aims to provide timely and relevant information to users, ensuring their safety and well-being during extreme weather events.

The design of Mobile Severe Weather Alerts follows a set of guidelines to ensure consistency and effectiveness. These alerts typically appear as notifications on the user's mobile device, accompanied by a distinct sound or vibration to grab their attention. The notification usually includes a brief and concise message that describes the type of weather event, its severity level, and its potential impact on the user's location.

Mobile Shopping Cart

A mobile shopping cart is a user interface element that allows users to view, modify, and complete their purchase transactions on a mobile device. It is an essential component of any e-commerce platform's design system. The mobile shopping cart provides users with a summary of the items they have added to their cart, including product names, quantities, prices, and any selected options or variations. Users can easily navigate between the cart and the rest of the website or app, allowing them to continue shopping, update quantities, or remove items as needed. In addition to displaying the contents of the cart, the mobile shopping cart also provides users with options to modify their order. This may include the ability to enter coupon codes or promotional offers, select shipping options, update quantities, or choose different variations of a product. A well-designed mobile shopping cart should have a clear and intuitive layout that makes it easy for users to understand and interact with. It should display relevant information such as product images, descriptions, and prices, while also providing clear navigation and controls for modifying the order. The mobile shopping cart should also be responsive, adapting to different screen sizes and orientations to provide a consistent and seamless user experience. It should be optimized for touch interactions, allowing users to easily scroll, tap, and swipe to navigate and interact with the cart. In terms of UI patterns, the mobile shopping cart may incorporate elements such as tabs or collapsible sections to organize and present information in a compact and structured manner. It may also employ modal dialogs or overlays to display additional details or prompts without redirecting the user away from the shopping cart. Overall, a well-designed mobile shopping cart is essential for ensuring a smooth and enjoyable user experience in mobile e-commerce. It not only allows users to easily view and modify their orders but also facilitates the completion of their purchase transactions, ultimately contributing to the success of an e-commerce platform.

A mobile shopping cart is a critical component of any e-commerce platform's design system that allows users to view, modify, and complete their purchase transactions on a mobile device. It provides a summary of the items in the cart, allowing users to easily navigate, update quantities, and remove items. The mobile shopping cart should have a clear and intuitive layout, displaying relevant information and providing responsive and touch-optimized interactions. It may incorporate elements such as tabs, collapsible sections, modal dialogs, or overlays to organize and present information efficiently. A well-designed mobile shopping cart contributes to a smooth user experience and the overall success of an e-commerce platform.

Mobile Sketching And Drawing

Mobile sketching and drawing is a fundamental technique used in the context of UI patterns and design systems to create and visualize user interface designs for mobile applications. It involves the use of hands-on sketching and drawing tools to quickly explore and communicate design ideas, interactions, and screen layouts. Mobile sketching and drawing serves as a crucial step in the design process, allowing designers to rapidly iterate, refine, and validate design solutions before moving into more detailed digital designs. It is a versatile and flexible approach that helps bridge the gap between initial conceptualization and final implementation. In the realm of UI patterns, mobile sketching and drawing enables designers to brainstorm and explore different design options, considering factors such as usability, visual hierarchy, and information architecture. By sketching out different screens and interactions, designers can easily visualize the flow and structure of the app, making informed decisions on navigation, content placement, and user interactions. When working with a design system, mobile sketching and drawing helps designers maintain consistency and coherence across different screens and interactions. By sketching different components and layouts, designers can ensure that they adhere to the established design principles, style guides, and brand guidelines. This ensures a seamless and cohesive user experience throughout the mobile app. The use of hands-on sketching and drawing tools, such as paper, pencils, and markers, offers a tangible and intuitive way for designers to explore their design ideas. This physical interaction allows for a deeper connection and understanding of the design concepts, enabling designers to think creatively and experiment freely. Overall, mobile sketching and drawing is an essential technique in the realm of UI patterns and design systems. It empowers designers to quickly ideate, iterate, and communicate design ideas for mobile applications. By leveraging this technique, designers can create intuitive, visually appealing, and user-centered mobile experiences. >

Mobile Sleep Tracker

A mobile sleep tracker is a user interface (UI) pattern and design system used in mobile applications to monitor and track a user's sleep patterns and quality of sleep. It provides users with insight and analysis of their sleep behavior, helping them make informed decisions to improve their overall sleep health.

The mobile sleep tracker typically consists of various components and features that enable users to record and analyze their sleep habits. These components include:

1. Sleep Recording: The sleep tracker allows users to start and stop a sleep recording session. This feature often includes options for setting sleep goals and reminders to help users establish healthy sleep routines.

2. Sleep Analysis: After a sleep session, the tracker provides users with a detailed analysis of their sleep patterns. This analysis may include information such as total sleep time, time spent in different sleep stages (e.g., deep, light, REM), and interruptions during sleep. Graphs and visualizations may be used to present this information in a user-friendly manner.

3. Sleep Trends: Over time, the mobile sleep tracker accumulates data and generates trends to showcase the user's sleep habits and progress. It may offer insights on sleep quality, consistency, and the correlation between sleep and other factors, such as stress or exercise.

4. Sleep Recommendations: Based on the recorded data and analysis, the sleep tracker may offer personalized recommendations and suggestions to improve sleep hygiene. This could include advice on adjusting bedtime routines, creating a sleep-friendly environment, or adopting

relaxation techniques.

Overall, a well-designed mobile sleep tracker aims to enhance users' sleep awareness and help them establish healthy sleep habits. It can empower individuals to take control of their sleep health, leading to improved overall well-being.

Mobile Smart Home Integration

Mobile Social Sharing

Mobile Social Sharing refers to the feature or functionality within a mobile application or website that allows users to share content or information from the app or website to their social media networks or other communication channels.

Mobile social sharing is an essential component of modern user interface (UI) patterns and design systems. It enables users to easily share interesting or relevant content with their friends, followers, or connections, extending the reach and impact of the app or website and promoting user engagement and interaction.

Mobile Speech-To-Text

The mobile speech-to-text user interface pattern is a design system that allows mobile users to convert spoken words into written text by using their device's built-in speech recognition technology. This feature is commonly implemented through a microphone symbol or button that users can activate to start dictating their words.

Speech-to-text technology has become increasingly popular as it offers users a more convenient way to input text on their mobile devices, especially for tasks such as composing messages, taking notes, or performing internet searches. By enabling users to speak naturally instead of typing, it can enhance productivity and accessibility for individuals who have difficulty with physical keyboards or those in situations where typing is not feasible.

Mobile Speed Trap Alerts

Mobile Speed Trap Alerts are a user interface (UI) pattern and design system that provides real-time notifications to mobile users about the location of speed traps or areas where law enforcement officers are monitoring the speed of vehicles.

Speed trap alerts are typically displayed as pop-up messages or notifications on a mobile device's screen. The alerts notify drivers in advance about the presence of speed traps in their vicinity, allowing them to adjust their driving behavior accordingly and avoid potential speeding tickets or other penalties.

Mobile Stock Market Tracker

A Mobile Stock Market Tracker is a user interface (UI) pattern and design system that provides users with a mobile application to track and monitor stock market activity. The primary purpose of the Mobile Stock Market Tracker is to give users real-time access to stock market data, enabling them to follow the fluctuations and trends of various stocks and financial instruments. This UI pattern typically includes features such as stock price charts, news updates, portfolio management tools, and customizable alerts. The design system of the Mobile Stock Market Tracker focuses on providing an intuitive and user-friendly experience. The UI elements are carefully crafted to present the relevant information in a clear and concise manner. This includes using visual cues, such as colors and icons, to highlight important data points, trends, and events. The layout of the Mobile Stock Market Tracker is designed to optimize the display of information on a mobile device. The UI patterns prioritize the most relevant and timely information, such as current stock prices and portfolio performance. This ensures that users can quickly access the data they need without unnecessary distractions or clutter. In terms of functionality, the Mobile Stock Market Tracker allows users to personalize their experience by customizing the data they receive and how it is presented. This includes the ability to select stocks to track, set up alerts for price changes or other events, and organize their portfolio in a way that suits their investment strategy. Overall, the Mobile Stock Market Tracker is a powerful tool for investors and anyone interested in staying informed about the stock market. Its UI patterns and design system are carefully crafted to provide a seamless and efficient experience, enabling users to make informed decisions about their investments.>

Mobile Storage Usage

The mobile storage usage refers to the functionality and display of the storage space available on a mobile device within the context of user interface (UI) patterns and design systems. It provides users with information about the amount of storage used and available on their mobile devices, allowing them to manage and optimize their storage usage effectively. In UI patterns and design systems, mobile storage usage is typically represented visually using a graph or progress bar. This visual representation provides users with a quick overview of their current storage status, indicating how much storage space is being used and how much is still available. It allows users to easily assess whether they need to delete or manage files to free up space. Furthermore, the mobile storage usage UI pattern can also include additional features and functionalities. For example, it may include detailed breakdowns of storage usage by file types, such as photos, videos, music, and apps. This breakdown enables users to identify which types of files are taking up the most space on their devices and take appropriate actions to optimize their storage. Design systems often provide guidelines for designing mobile storage usage interfaces that are consistent and aligned with the overall visual design language. These guidelines may include aspects such as color schemes, typography, and iconography used to represent storage usage. In summary, the mobile storage usage UI pattern and design system provide users with a clear and accessible way to understand and manage the storage space on their mobile devices. It ensures that users are aware of their storage usage, helping them make informed decisions about how to optimize their device's storage and maintain its performance.>

Mobile Task Manager

A Mobile Task Manager is a user interface (UI) pattern and design system that allows users to efficiently organize, track, and manage their tasks on mobile devices. It provides a visual representation of tasks, enabling users to easily prioritize and complete them. A Mobile Task Manager typically consists of a main task list, where users can view and access all their tasks at a glance. Each task is displayed as a separate item, containing key information such as the task title, due date, and priority. Users can tap on a task to view more details or mark it as completed. This UI pattern often includes features like task categorization, where users can group similar tasks together for better organization. It may also offer filtering and sorting options, enabling users to focus on specific tasks or view them in a particular order. In addition to the task list, a Mobile Task Manager may incorporate features like task creation and editing. This allows users to easily add new tasks or make changes to existing ones. Users can typically input task details such as title, due date, priority, notes, and attachments. Mobile Task Managers often provide users with the ability to set reminders for tasks, helping them stay on track and meet deadlines. These reminders can be customized to suit individual preferences, such as through push notifications or email alerts. The design of a Mobile Task Manager follows a consistent set of visual elements and interactions, adhering to a design system. This ensures a cohesive and intuitive user experience across different screens and devices. Common design elements include clear typography, concise icons, well-defined spacing, and a balanced color palette. Overall, a Mobile Task Manager is a purpose-built UI pattern and design system that empowers users to efficiently manage their tasks on mobile devices. By providing an organized and visual approach, it simplifies the complex task management process and helps users stay productive while on the go.>

Mobile Telemedicine

Mobile Telemedicine refers to the use of mobile technology to provide medical care remotely. It involves the use of smartphones, tablets, or other mobile devices to connect patients with healthcare professionals, allowing for virtual consultations, diagnosis, and treatment. In the context of UI patterns and design system, Mobile Telemedicine relates to the development of user interfaces and design principles specifically tailored for mobile telemedicine applications. It focuses on creating intuitive and user-friendly interfaces that enable seamless communication and interaction between patients and healthcare providers. Mobile telemedicine UI patterns prioritize accessibility and ease of use, taking into consideration the limitations and unique characteristics of mobile devices. The design system incorporates responsive layouts, clear navigation, and concise content presentation to ensure a smooth and efficient user experience. Effective UI patterns for mobile telemedicine often include features such as: 1. Registration and Authentication: Streamlined and secure processes for users to create accounts, log in, and verify their identities. 2. Patient Profiles: Comprehensive profiles that allow users to manage personal information, medical history, and preferences. 3. Appointment Scheduling: Intuitive calendars or booking systems that enable patients to request or schedule virtual consultations with healthcare professionals. 4. Video Consultations: Seamless integration of video conferencing capabilities for real-time remote consultations with healthcare providers. 5. Messaging and Notifications: Efficient communication channels that facilitate messaging between patients and doctors, as well as push notifications for appointment reminders or other important updates. 6. Prescriptions and Medical Records: Secure digital systems for managing prescriptions, medical records, and the sharing of important documents between patients and healthcare professionals. A comprehensive design system for mobile telemedicine should prioritize user-centered design principles, ensuring that the interface is intuitive, visually appealing, and accessible to a wide range of users. It should also consider factors such as data privacy and security, adhering to industry standards and regulations to protect sensitive patient information. By leveraging UI patterns and adhering to a well-defined design system, mobile telemedicine applications can offer a seamless and reliable healthcare experience for patients, enhancing accessibility and convenience while promoting efficient communication and remote medical care.>

Mobile Text-To-Speech

Mobile Text-to-Speech (TTS) refers to the functionality of converting written text into spoken words using a mobile device. It is a feature that can be implemented in user interface (UI) patterns and design systems to enhance accessibility and provide an alternative method of consuming textual content. TTS enables users with visual impairments or reading difficulties to access information on a mobile device without relying on visual cues. By converting text into spoken words, TTS allows these users to interact with content and navigate through applications in a way that suits their needs. In UI patterns, TTS can be integrated as a tool or option that users can activate to listen to the text on the screen. It can be incorporated as an icon or button that triggers the TTS functionality. This allows users to choose when and how they want to use TTS, providing them with greater control over their interactive experience. When designing a system that includes TTS, it is important to consider factors such as voice quality, speed, and pause functionality. Voice quality refers to the clarity and naturalness of the synthesized speech. Speed control allows users to adjust the rate at which the text is spoken, while pause functionality enables users to halt the speech as needed. These considerations ensure that TTS is optimized for accessibility and usability. In terms of user experience, TTS can significantly improve the accessibility of mobile applications. By providing an alternative method of consuming content, it empowers users with different abilities to access information and interact with digital interfaces. It can also support multitasking by allowing users to listen to text while performing other tasks, such as driving or exercising. Overall, mobile Text-to-Speech is a valuable feature that enhances accessibility and inclusivity in UI patterns and design systems. By converting written text into spoken words, it enables users with visual impairments or reading difficulties to access content and interact with digital interfaces in a way that suits their needs.>

Mobile Theme Customization

Mobile theme customization refers to the process of modifying the visual appearance and behavior of a mobile application or website to align with a specific brand identity or user preferences. It involves adjusting various elements, such as colors, fonts, layout, and interactive components, to create a cohesive and personalized user interface (UI). In the context of UI patterns and design systems, mobile theme customization is essential to create a consistent and recognizable experience for users. UI patterns serve as reusable solutions to common design challenges, while design systems provide a comprehensive set of guidelines and assets for maintaining a unified look and feel across different platforms and devices. Customizing the mobile theme starts with understanding the brand identity and user expectations. The designer or developer must consider the target audience, the purpose of the application or website, and any specific requirements or constraints. By aligning the visual elements with the brand's colors, typography, and style, the customization aims to establish a strong visual identity and reinforce the brand image. Colors play a crucial role in mobile theme customization. They can evoke emotions, establish hierarchy, and provide visual cues to guide users. The customization process involves selecting a color palette that aligns with the brand and ensuring proper contrast and readability. This may involve adjusting the background, text, button, and link colors. Consistency is key, and the chosen colors should be consistently applied throughout the UI. Typography customization focuses on selecting appropriate fonts and adjusting their size, weight, and spacing. The goal is to create a harmonious and readable text hierarchy that complements the overall design. The designer may also customize interactive components, such as buttons, forms, and navigation menus, to create a visually coherent experience that aligns with the brand's visual language. Layout customization involves arranging the different UI elements in a logical and user-friendly manner. This includes defining the grid system, spacing, and alignments. The customization aims to create a balance between aesthetics and functionality, ensuring that the user can easily navigate and interact with the mobile application or website. In conclusion, mobile theme customization is a crucial aspect of UI design, enabling the creation of a visually appealing and user-friendly mobile experience. By aligning the visual elements with the brand's identity and user expectations, customization ensures consistency and enhances the overall user experience.>

Mobile Therapy Sessions

Mobile Therapy Sessions is a UI pattern and design system that provides a user-friendly and visually appealing interface for conducting therapy sessions through mobile devices. It offers a seamless and convenient way for therapists and clients to communicate and engage in therapeutic interventions remotely.

With Mobile Therapy Sessions, therapists can create and schedule virtual therapy sessions, invite clients to join, and securely conduct video or text-based therapy sessions from anywhere. The design system ensures a consistent and intuitive user experience, promoting accessibility and ease of use for both therapists and clients.

Mobile To-Do List

A mobile to-do list is a user interface pattern and design system component that allows users to create, manage, and track their tasks and activities on a mobile device. It provides a structured and organized way for users to keep track of their daily, weekly, or long-term tasks, ensuring that important tasks are not forgotten or overlooked. The mobile to-do list typically consists of a list of tasks, with each task represented by a checkbox or toggle button indicating its completion status. Users can easily add new tasks by tapping on a designated area or using a dedicated button, and can also edit or delete existing tasks as needed. The list is usually scrollable and can be sorted or filtered based on different criteria, such as due date, priority, or category. In terms of design, the mobile to-do list should be visually appealing and intuitive to use. It should follow the overall design system of the mobile application, ensuring consistency in colors, typography, and layout. The list should be easy to read, with clear and legible text, and should not overwhelm the user with too much information or cluttered design elements. To enhance usability, the mobile to-do list may include additional features such as reminders, notifications, or the ability to set deadlines and priorities for tasks. Users should be able to easily distinguish between completed and incomplete tasks, and may have the option to mark tasks as important or urgent. Overall, the mobile to-do list is a crucial component of many mobile applications, helping users stay organized, manage their time effectively, and achieve their goals. By providing a user-friendly and visually appealing interface, it allows users to easily track their tasks and activities, improving productivity and reducing stress.

A mobile to-do list is a user interface pattern and design system component that allows users to create, manage, and track their tasks on a mobile device. It follows the design system of the mobile application, providing a structured and organized way for users to keep track of their daily, weekly, or long-term tasks. In terms of design, the mobile to-do list should be visually appealing, easy to read, and intuitive to use. It may include additional features such as reminders and notifications to enhance usability. Overall, the mobile to-do list helps users stay organized, manage their time effectively, and achieve their goals.

Mobile Tornado Alerts

Mobile Tornado Alerts are user interface (UI) patterns and design system elements that are utilized in mobile applications to provide alert notifications related to tornado warnings and safety measures. These alerts are crucial in ensuring the safety and well-being of users who may be located in areas prone to tornadoes. The primary objective of Mobile Tornado Alerts is to effectively communicate essential information about tornado warnings and associated actions that need to be taken by individuals or communities. This includes notifying users about the presence of tornado warnings in their vicinity, providing recommendations for immediate actions to ensure safety, and conveying relevant updates or instructions from emergency management authorities. In terms of UI patterns, Mobile Tornado Alerts typically consist of visually distinct elements that draw attention to the alert message. These elements may include prominent banners or notifications displayed at the top or bottom of the mobile screen, use of attention-grabbing colors or icons, and concise yet informative text content. The design system ensures consistency and familiarity across various mobile applications by providing guidelines on the visual appearance and behavior of these alerts. The UI patterns of Mobile Tornado Alerts are carefully designed to prioritize key information and actions, enabling users to quickly understand the severity of the situation and take appropriate measures. The alerts convey the urgency of the tornado warning, advising users to seek shelter, evacuate if necessary, or follow specific safety procedures. They may also provide real-time updates on the tornado's path, potential impact areas, and estimated arrival times, empowering users to make informed decisions. To enhance the effectiveness of Mobile Tornado Alerts, the design system may incorporate features such as persistent alerts that remain visible until the threat has passed or is no longer relevant. This ensures that users do not miss critical information even if they are momentarily away from their mobile devices. In summary, Mobile Tornado Alerts are UI patterns and design system elements utilized in mobile applications to provide timely and essential notifications related to tornado warnings and safety measures. They are designed to effectively communicate the severity of the tornado warning and empower users with necessary information and actions to ensure their safety.>

Mobile Traffic Alerts

A mobile traffic alert is a user interface pattern and design system that provides real-time information about traffic conditions on mobile devices. It is designed to help users navigate through congested areas, avoid traffic jams, and reach their destinations more efficiently.

Mobile traffic alerts typically include the following information:

- Current traffic conditions: This includes the overall traffic flow, indicating whether it is congested, moderate, or clear. It may also provide information about any accidents, road closures, or construction activities that may be impacting the traffic. - Estimated travel time: Mobile traffic alerts provide users with an estimate of how long it will take to reach their destination based on the current traffic conditions. This helps users plan their travel accordingly and make informed decisions about when to leave. - Alternative routes: In case of heavy traffic or road blockages, mobile traffic alerts suggest alternative routes that users can take to avoid congestion and reach their destination faster. These alternative routes are dynamically updated based on the current traffic conditions. - Incident alerts: Mobile traffic alerts notify users about any incidents on their route, such as accidents, road closures, or weather conditions that may impact their travel. This allows users to be aware of any potential disruptions and plan their journey accordingly.

Mobile traffic alerts are typically displayed on a map interface, which provides a visual representation of the traffic conditions. The alerts may be represented using different colors or symbols to indicate different levels of traffic congestion or incidents. Users can zoom in and out of the map to view traffic conditions at different locations.

Overall, mobile traffic alerts help users make informed decisions about their travel by providing real-time information about traffic conditions. By using this design system, users can navigate through congested areas more efficiently, save time, and have a smoother travel experience.

Mobile Traffic Updates

A mobile traffic update refers to a feature or component in a user interface (UI) pattern or design system that provides real-time information and updates about the current status and conditions of mobile traffic. This feature is typically found in applications or websites that offer navigation or transportation-related services.

The purpose of a mobile traffic update is to help users make informed decisions about their travel routes and plans by providing them with up-to-date information on traffic flow, congestion, accidents, road closures, and other relevant data. This information is often sourced from various reliable and authoritative data providers, such as government transportation agencies, traffic management systems, or crowd-sourced reports from users.

Mobile Travel Itinerary

A mobile travel itinerary refers to a user interface (UI) pattern and design system used in mobile applications to help travelers keep track of their travel plans and arrangements. It provides a visually organized and structured view of all the important aspects of a trip, such as flights, accommodation, activities, and transportation. The primary purpose of a mobile travel itinerary is to assist travelers in easily accessing and managing their travel details while on the go. It offers a comprehensive overview of the trip's schedule and relevant information, allowing users to conveniently access and update their itinerary as needed. The design of a mobile travel itinerary typically consists of a list or card-based layout. Each section of the itinerary represents a different aspect of the trip, presented in a logical order. Within each section, important details such as departure and arrival times, reservation numbers, and locations are displayed. The itinerary may also include additional features, such as maps, directions, and contact information, to further enhance the user experience. These features provide travelers with quick access to essential information, allowing them to navigate their destination and easily communicate with service providers when necessary. To ensure a user-friendly experience, a mobile travel itinerary often incorporates intuitive navigation and interaction patterns. This includes the ability to add or remove items, edit details, and customize the view according to personal preferences. Furthermore, a mobile travel itinerary is typically integrated with other travel-related services and platforms, encouraging users to explore additional functionalities. For example, users may be able to book flights, make hotel reservations, or discover local activities directly from their itinerary. Overall, a mobile travel itinerary is a vital tool for both leisure and business travelers to organize, manage, and access their travel information conveniently. Its design system and UI patterns prioritize clarity, simplicity, and efficiency to streamline the travel planning process and enhance the overall travel experience.>

Mobile Tsunami Alerts

A mobile tsunami alert is a user interface pattern and design system that provides a method for alerting mobile device users about an incoming tsunami. It focuses on delivering crucial information quickly and efficiently to ensure the safety of individuals in affected areas.

The design system for mobile tsunami alerts typically incorporates a set of guidelines and principles that dictate the visual and interactive aspects of the user interface. This ensures consistency and usability across different mobile devices and platforms.

Mobile UV Index Alerts

Mobile UV Index Alerts are a UI pattern and design system that provide users with timely notifications and information regarding the UV index levels in their current location. The purpose of these alerts is to raise user awareness about the potential harmful effects of UV radiation and assist them in taking appropriate measures to protect themselves from sun damage.

Implemented as a component of a mobile application or website, Mobile UV Index Alerts utilize real-time data from weather APIs or other reliable sources to calculate and display the UV index levels for the user's specific location. These alerts typically include a visual indicator, such as a color-coded scale or icon, to represent the current UV index level. This visual representation helps users quickly and easily understand the potential risk associated with the current UV index.

Mobile VPN Settings

A mobile VPN (Virtual Private Network) setting is a feature in a user interface (UI) design system that allows users to configure and manage their VPN connections on their mobile devices. A VPN is a secure network connection that encrypts the user's internet traffic and routes it through a remote server, providing privacy, anonymity, and security.

The mobile VPN settings UI pattern typically includes options for enabling or disabling the VPN connection, selecting the server location or protocol, and managing any advanced settings. In the UI design system, these settings are organized in a logical and intuitive way to make it easy for users to understand and make changes to their VPN configuration.

Mobile VR/AR Headset Support

Mobile VR/AR headset support refers to the functionality and design considerations in creating user interfaces (UI) for virtual reality (VR) and augmented reality (AR) experiences on mobile devices. UI patterns for mobile VR/AR headsets are specifically tailored to work seamlessly on a wide range of mobile devices, including smartphones and tablets. These patterns aim to optimize the user experience by leveraging the unique capabilities of these devices, such as their motion sensors, touchscreens, and high-resolution displays. A well-designed UI for mobile VR/AR headsets focuses on providing an immersive and intuitive experience for users. This involves utilizing a combination of visual elements, interaction patterns, and navigation techniques that are optimized for the limited screen real estate and the 3D space of the VR/AR environment. One key aspect of UI design for mobile VR/AR headsets is the concept of gaze-based interaction. This involves tracking the user's head movements and using that information to determine where they are looking in the virtual environment. By using the user's gaze as an input, UI elements can be dynamically displayed, hidden, or activated, resulting in a more natural and intuitive interaction. In addition to gaze-based interaction, UI patterns for mobile VR/AR headsets also make use of touch-based interactions. This allows users to interact with UI elements directly using their fingers on the device's touchscreen. These touches can trigger specific actions, such as selecting and dragging objects, scrolling through content, or activating various UI controls. To ensure a consistent and coherent user experience across different VR/AR applications, a design system can be implemented. A design system provides a set of guidelines, patterns, and reusable components that help maintain design consistency and speed up the UI development process. By adhering to a design system, UI designers and developers can create visually appealing and functional interfaces that align with the overall visual language and brand identity. In conclusion, mobile VR/AR headset support involves designing and implementing UI patterns and a design system specifically for mobile devices. These designs aim to provide an immersive and intuitive user experience by leveraging the unique capabilities of mobile devices and optimizing the UI for the 3D space and limited screen real estate.>

Mobile Video Streaming Quality Control

Mobile Video Streaming Quality Control is a user interface pattern and design system that enables users to manage and optimize video streaming quality on their mobile devices. It allows users to customize the video streaming experience by providing options to adjust quality settings, such as resolution, bit rate, and buffering. The goal of Mobile Video Streaming Quality Control is to provide users with the ability to tailor the video streaming quality to their specific preferences and network conditions, ensuring a smooth and enjoyable viewing experience.

The Mobile Video Streaming Quality Control UI pattern typically consists of a settings menu or panel that can be accessed within the video streaming application or platform. Within this settings menu, users can find options related to video quality control. These options may include the ability to select the desired video resolution, adjust the bit rate allocation, and enable or disable automatic buffering. Users can choose their preferred settings based on their device capabilities, network conditions, and personal preferences. By providing these customization options, Mobile Video Streaming Quality Control empowers users to optimize their video streaming experience according to their specific needs and limitations.

Mobile Virtual Closet

A Mobile Virtual Closet is a user interface pattern and design system that allows users to virtually organize and manage their clothing and accessories collections on mobile devices. In a

Mobile Virtual Closet, users can create a digital representation of their physical wardrobe by adding images or descriptions of their clothing items and accessories. This digital closet serves as a convenient way to keep track of their clothing inventory, plan outfits, and make more informed purchasing decisions. The design of a Mobile Virtual Closet typically consists of a grid-like layout, where each item is represented by a thumbnail image or a text description. Users can easily navigate through their collection by scrolling or using filtering and sorting options. Additionally, the pattern includes features such as the ability to tag items with categories or keywords, add notes or comments, and create outfits by combining different pieces. One of the key benefits of a Mobile Virtual Closet is its ability to help users better organize their clothing and accessories. By visually seeing their collection in one place, users can easily identify items they no longer need or haven't worn in a while, promoting decluttering and more sustainable consumption habits. Furthermore, the virtual aspect of the closet allows users to access their wardrobe anytime, anywhere, and eliminates the need for physical storage space. To enhance the user experience, Mobile Virtual Closets often integrate with other services or features. For instance, users may be able to import or sync their closet data with online shopping platforms, allowing for seamless outfit planning and shopping. Additionally, users might be able to share their favorite outfits or individual items with friends or on social media platforms. In conclusion, a Mobile Virtual Closet is a user interface pattern and design system that offers a convenient and organized way for users to digitally manage and explore their clothing and accessory collections on mobile devices. It provides users with a visual representation of their wardrobe, promotes sustainable consumption, and offers additional features to enhance the overall experience.>

Mobile Virtual Tours

A Mobile Virtual Tour is a user interface pattern and design system that allows users to experience a virtual tour on a mobile device. It provides an interactive and immersive experience by combining multimedia content such as images, videos, and audio with user-interactions.

The Mobile Virtual Tour pattern consists of various components and features that enhance the user experience. These include:

1. Navigation: The Mobile Virtual Tour provides intuitive and easy-to-use navigation options. Users can navigate through different points of interest in the virtual tour using gestures such as swiping, tapping, and pinch-to-zoom. The navigation is designed to be smooth and seamless, providing a sense of continuity throughout the tour.

2. Multimedia Content: The Mobile Virtual Tour incorporates various multimedia elements to engage users and provide a rich and immersive experience. This can include high-quality images, videos, 360-degree panoramas, and audio narrations. The multimedia content is carefully curated to provide relevant and informative context to the user.

3. Interactive Hotspots: The Mobile Virtual Tour allows users to interact with specific points of interest within the tour through interactive hotspots. These hotspots can be represented as clickable icons, labels, or markers that provide additional information or trigger specific actions when tapped. This allows users to explore and learn more about different areas or objects within the virtual tour.

4. Annotations and Descriptions: The Mobile Virtual Tour provides annotations and descriptions for different points of interest within the tour. These annotations can include text, images, or multimedia content that provides detailed information or storytelling elements. Users can access this information by tapping on specific hotspots or by a swipe gesture.

Overall, a Mobile Virtual Tour is designed to provide an immersive and interactive experience for users on mobile devices. It allows users to explore various locations or objects through multimedia content and interactive elements, providing a unique and engaging way to discover and learn.

Mobile Voice Alerts

Mobile Voice Alerts are a UI pattern and design system element that are used to notify users about important events or updates through voice messages on mobile devices. They provide auditory feedback instead of visual alerts, allowing users to receive information without having to look at the screen. Voice alerts are designed to be concise and clear, delivering the necessary information in a succinct and understandable manner. They can be used in a variety of situations, such as incoming calls or text messages, low battery warnings, or system notifications. The purpose of using voice alerts is to enhance the user experience by providing an alternative way of delivering information. They can be particularly useful in situations where users may not be able to or prefer not to look at their screens, such as while driving or when their hands are occupied. Voice alerts are typically triggered by specific events or actions, and are accompanied by appropriate sounds or tones to capture the user's attention. The content of the voice message should be carefully crafted to convey the necessary information concisely and effectively. When designing voice alerts, it is important to consider the context in which they will be used. Factors such as the urgency of the information, the target audience, and the device's capabilities should be taken into account. Voice alerts should be easily distinguishable from other sounds or noises that the user may encounter on their mobile device. In terms of visual design, voice alerts can be represented by simple icons or symbols to indicate the type of alert, but these visual cues should not rely on color alone, as colorblind users may have difficulty distinguishing them. Additionally, text captions can be provided to complement the voice message, especially for users who are deaf or hard of hearing. In conclusion, mobile voice alerts are a UI pattern and design system element that deliver important information to users through voice messages on mobile devices. They enhance the user experience by providing an alternative way of receiving information, particularly in situations where visual feedback may not be possible or preferred. Considerations should be made for the context, content, and visual representation of voice alerts to ensure they are effective and accessible to all users.>

Mobile Voice Assistant

A mobile voice assistant is a user interface pattern and design system that enables users to interact with their mobile devices using voice commands. It provides a more natural and convenient way for users to access information, perform tasks, and control various features and functions of their mobile devices.

With a mobile voice assistant, users can perform a wide range of actions simply by speaking to their devices. They can ask questions, make requests, give instructions, and receive spoken responses or visual feedback on the screen. This allows users to perform tasks hands-free and without the need for complex navigation or input methods.

Mobile Voice Commands

A mobile voice command is a user interface pattern and design system that allows users to interact with their mobile devices by giving spoken commands rather than using traditional touch or keystroke inputs.

By leveraging speech recognition technology, mobile voice commands enable users to perform a variety of tasks, such as opening apps, initiating phone calls, composing messages, setting reminders, playing media, and controlling device settings, simply by speaking their requests aloud.

Mobile Voice Confirmations

Mobile Voice Confirmations are a UI design pattern and component in a design system that allows users to confirm and verify their actions or selections using voice commands on mobile devices.

With the rise of voice assistants and voice recognition technology, Mobile Voice Confirmations provide an alternative method of interaction that can enhance usability and accessibility for mobile users. This pattern is particularly useful in scenarios where users may have limited physical dexterity or prefer hands-free interactions.

Mobile Voice Control

Mobile Voice Control is a user interface pattern and design system that allows users to interact with mobile devices using their voice as the primary input method. It enables users to perform various actions and tasks on their mobile devices without the need to use touch or physical buttons.

This UI pattern leverages voice recognition technology to interpret and understand spoken commands from users. The design system encompasses the visual and functional components that make up the Mobile Voice Control interface. It includes the layout, typography, colors, icons, and other visual elements, as well as the interaction and behavior guidelines for voice-based interactions.

Mobile Voice Dialing

Mobile Voice Dialing is a user interface pattern and design system that allows users to initiate phone calls using voice commands on their mobile devices. It is a feature that utilizes speech recognition technology to interpret and convert spoken words into text, enabling users to perform phone call actions hands-free. The primary objective of Mobile Voice Dialing is to provide a convenient and efficient way for users to make phone calls without having to manually type or search for contacts. By using their voice, users can simply say the name or number of the person they wish to call, and the mobile device will process the command and initiate the call. In terms of UI patterns, Mobile Voice Dialing typically involves a dedicated button or an activation phrase that triggers the voice recognition feature. Once activated, users are prompted to speak their desired command, such as "Call John Smith" or "Dial 123-456-7890". The mobile device's speech recognition system then transcribes the spoken words into text, verifies the command, and proceeds to connect the call. Design systems for Mobile Voice Dialing focus on providing clear and concise voice command instructions to users. This includes ensuring that the system is trained to recognize different accents, speech patterns, and variations in pronunciation. Additionally, design considerations are made to minimize background noise interference and account for possible speech recognition errors. Mobile Voice Dialing is a valuable feature for users with limited manual dexterity or those who require a hands-free experience while using their mobile devices. It offers convenience, accessibility, and promotes safe phone usage while driving or performing other tasks that require hands-on attention. Overall, Mobile Voice Dialing enhances the user experience by providing a seamless and intuitive way to initiate phone calls through voice commands. By incorporating this UI pattern and design system, mobile devices become even more versatile and user-friendly for a broader range of users.>

Mobile Voice Dictation

Mobile voice dictation is a user interface (UI) pattern and design system that allows users to input text into a mobile device by speaking rather than typing. It provides users with the convenience of verbalizing their thoughts or messages, which are then converted into written text by the device's speech recognition technology.

With mobile voice dictation, users can simply tap on a designated microphone icon on the mobile interface to activate the speech recognition feature. As they speak into the device's microphone, their words are translated into text in real-time, appearing on the screen. This permits users to bypass the need for traditional typing, saving time and effort.

Mobile Voice Feedback

Mobile Voice Feedback is a user interface (UI) pattern and design system that enables users to provide feedback or input through voice commands on mobile devices. It allows users to interact with the system by speaking instead of typing or using traditional touch gestures. One way Mobile Voice Feedback is implemented is through voice recognition technology, which converts spoken words into text. This text can then be used as input for various actions within the application or system. For example, users can dictate messages, perform searches, or navigate through menus and options using their voice. Mobile Voice Feedback is designed to enhance the user experience by providing an alternative input method that can be more efficient and convenient in certain scenarios. It is particularly useful in situations where typing on a small mobile keyboard may be difficult or inconvenient, such as when the user is on the move or has limited dexterity. The design system for Mobile Voice Feedback typically includes a set of guidelines and best practices for integrating voice commands into the user interface. These guidelines help ensure a consistent and intuitive voice interaction experience across different parts of the system. In terms of UI patterns, Mobile Voice Feedback may involve the use of voice-enabled buttons or icons that users can tap or click to activate voice input. Once activated, the system may provide visual feedback, such as a microphone icon or animation, to indicate that it is ready to accept voice commands. Mobile Voice Feedback can also be combined with other UI patterns and design elements, such as natural language processing and intelligent voice assistants. These technologies allow the system to understand and respond to users' commands in a more intelligent and conversational manner. In conclusion, Mobile Voice Feedback is a UI pattern and design system that enables users to provide feedback or input through voice commands on mobile devices. It enhances the user experience by offering an alternative input method that is convenient and efficient, particularly in scenarios where typing may be challenging. The design system includes guidelines for integrating voice commands into the user interface and can be combined with other technologies to create a more intelligent and interactive voice interaction experience.>

Mobile Voice Memos

A mobile voice memo is a user interface pattern and design system component that allows mobile users to record and save audio messages or notes. It provides a convenient way for users to capture and store audio content on their mobile devices.

The mobile voice memo UI pattern typically consists of a button or icon that initiates the recording process when pressed. Once activated, the user's voice is captured and converted into a digital audio file. The user can then save the recorded memo, attach a title or description, and organize it within the system.

Mobile Voice Messaging

Mobile Voice Messaging is a UI pattern and design system element that allows users to send and receive voice messages through a mobile device. It provides a convenient and alternative method of communication compared to traditional text-based messaging.

Mobile Voice Messaging typically consists of a user interface with a microphone button or icon that users can tap to start recording their voice message. Once the recording is complete, users can send the message to their desired recipient or recipients. The message is then delivered to the recipient's device, where they can listen to it at their convenience.

Mobile Voice Navigation

The Mobile Voice Navigation UI pattern refers to the design and implementation of a user interface that allows users to navigate through a mobile application or website using voice commands. It is an alternative to traditional touch-based navigation and provides an intuitive way for users to interact with the system. The Mobile Voice Navigation design system encompasses various components and visual styles that are used to create a consistent and seamless experience for users. This includes the design of voice command prompts, feedback mechanisms, and error handling. Voice commands are recognized and processed by the system using speech recognition technology. These commands can be simple phrases or keywords that trigger specific actions or navigate to different sections of the application or website. For example, a user can say "Open settings" to navigate to the settings page or say "Search for hotels" to perform a search operation. The Mobile Voice Navigation UI pattern requires a clear and concise voice command prompt to guide users and ensure successful interaction. This prompt should be displayed prominently on the screen and provide a visual indication of the system's readiness to receive voice commands. It is also important to provide visual feedback to users, such as highlighting the recognized command or displaying a loading indicator during processing. Error handling is another crucial aspect of the Mobile Voice Navigation design system. If the system fails to understand a command or encounters an error, it should provide users with clear and specific instructions or suggestions for correcting the input. This helps users understand how to properly use voice commands and reduces frustration. In conclusion, the Mobile Voice Navigation UI pattern offers an alternative way for users to navigate through a mobile application or website using voice commands. It is important to design and implement this pattern as part of a comprehensive design system that includes voice command prompts, feedback mechanisms, and error handling.>

Mobile Voice Notes

Mobile Voice Notes are a user interface (UI) pattern and design system that allows users to record and store audio notes on their mobile devices. This feature provides users with the ability to quickly capture and save important information or ideas by simply speaking into their devices. The Mobile Voice Notes UI pattern typically consists of a microphone icon or button that users can tap to begin recording their voice. Once the recording is complete, the audio file is saved and can be accessed later for playback or further actions. Users may also have the option to add titles or tags to their voice notes for easier organization and retrieval. In terms of the design system, Mobile Voice Notes often follow a consistent visual style and layout across different screens or interfaces. This helps users recognize and understand the functionality of the feature, as well as provides a seamless and cohesive experience. The design system may include guidelines for the placement and appearance of the microphone icon or button, as well as the overall layout of the voice note interface. In HTML format:

Mobile Voice Notes are a UI pattern and design system for recording and storing audio notes on mobile devices. It allows users to capture important information by speaking into their devices.

The Mobile Voice Notes UI pattern includes a microphone icon or button for recording, with options for saving, playback, and organization. The design system ensures a consistent and intuitive user experience across different screens and interfaces.

Mobile Voice Notifications

Mobile Voice Notifications refer to a user interface pattern and design system used to present information in a spoken format on mobile devices. This pattern utilizes voice-based notifications as a means to deliver important updates, alerts, or messages to users. Unlike traditional text-based notifications, mobile voice notifications rely on speech synthesis technology to convert written text into audible messages. These notifications follow a specific design system that includes guidelines for voice messaging and audio cues. The goal is to ensure consistency and provide a seamless user experience across different mobile applications. The design system includes considerations for the tone, pacing, and volume of the voice messages, as well as guidelines for the use of background sounds or music. The mobile voice notifications pattern can be used in various scenarios, such as: 1. Alerts and emergency notifications: In situations that require immediate attention, mobile voice notifications can convey critical information to users verbally. For example, in the event of a natural disaster or security breach, the system can issue voice-based alerts to inform users and provide instructions. 2. Reminders and calendar events: Mobile voice notifications can also be used to remind users about upcoming events, appointments, or deadlines. Instead of relying solely on text-based reminders, the system can read out the details of the event to ensure that users are aware of their schedules. 3. Application updates and status notifications: When there are important updates or changes to an application, voice notifications can inform users about the new features or bug fixes. These notifications can include audio cues to indicate success or failure, allowing users to understand the status of their requests. Mobile voice notifications aim to enhance user accessibility and engagement by providing an alternative method of communication. By utilizing voice-based technology, these notifications cater to users who may have visual impairments or prefer a hands-free approach to receiving information. Additionally, voice notifications can capture users' attention more effectively compared to traditional text-based notifications, as they can be heard even when the device is not within immediate sight. In summary, mobile voice notifications are a user interface pattern and design system that utilize spoken text to convey important information, alerts, and reminders to users. These notifications follow specific guidelines for voice messaging and audio cues, aiming to provide a consistent and accessible user experience.>

Mobile Voice Prompts

Mobile voice prompts refer to the auditory cues provided by a user interface (UI) system in mobile devices. These prompts are designed to guide and inform users through various actions and interactions within the UI. Voice prompts are an essential component of a well-designed UI as they provide audio feedback to users, aiding in the navigation and comprehension of the system. They are particularly useful in mobile devices where visual attention and physical interaction may be limited. Voice prompts are used in conjunction with other UI elements such as buttons, menus, and icons to enhance the user experience. They can be triggered at specific points in the interaction flow, such as when a button is pressed or when a certain action is completed. The primary goal of mobile voice prompts is to provide users with clear and concise instructions or status updates. For example, when a user taps on a button, a voice prompt may say "Select an option" to guide the user further. In case of an error or invalid input, the voice prompt may notify the user by saying "Please enter a valid value". Voice prompts should be designed to be easily understood and recognized by users. They should use simple and familiar language, avoid jargon or technical terms, and be spoken at an appropriate pace. Tone of voice and clarity of pronunciation also play a significant role in ensuring that the prompts are informative and intelligible. Design systems play a crucial role in the creation and implementation of mobile voice prompts. They provide a set of guidelines and standards for the visual and auditory components of the UI. These guidelines ensure consistent and cohesive voice prompts across the entire system, contributing to the overall usability and user satisfaction. In conclusion, mobile voice prompts are audio cues that guide and inform users within a mobile UI. They are an integral part of a well-designed UI, providing clear instructions and feedback to enhance the user experience. Through the use of design systems, voice prompts can be developed consistently and effectively, ensuring their usability and usefulness.>

Mobile Voice Recorder

A mobile voice recorder is a UI pattern and design system that allows users to record, store, and manage audio recordings on their mobile devices. It provides a simple and intuitive interface for capturing audio using the device's microphone and offers options for playback, editing, and organizing recorded files. The mobile voice recorder typically consists of a primary recording screen where users can start and stop recording, and view visual feedback such as waveform or audio levels to monitor the recording. The screen may also display controls for adjusting microphone sensitivity or enabling features like noise cancellation. Once a recording is complete, the mobile voice recorder offers options for playback, allowing users to listen to the recorded audio to ensure its quality. Users can also use the playback feature to review recordings or transcribe audio content. In some cases, the voice recorder may offer playback controls such as play, pause, fast forward, and rewind to facilitate easy navigation through recorded files. To enhance usability and organization, the mobile voice recorder may incorporate features for file management. This can include the ability to name or rename recordings, add tags or labels for easier categorization, and organize recordings into folders or playlists. Additionally, users may be able to delete or archive recordings they no longer need, freeing up storage space on their devices. To provide a seamless and consistent user experience, the mobile voice recorder follows a design system that adheres to UI guidelines, ensuring that the interface elements such as buttons, icons, and typography are consistent and visually appealing across different screens and devices. The design system also facilitates easy navigation and accessibility, allowing users to quickly accomplish their tasks without confusion or frustration. In conclusion, a mobile voice recorder is a UI pattern and design system for recording, managing, and organizing audio recordings on mobile devices. It offers features such as recording, playback, editing, and file management, providing users with a user-friendly and consistent interface to capture and manage audio content effectively.>

Mobile Voice Reminders

Mobile Voice Reminders are a UI pattern and design system feature that allows users to set and receive audio notifications or reminders on their mobile devices.

These reminders are designed to be interacted with using voice commands, eliminating the need for users to manually input reminders or check notifications visually. The voice reminders can be set for specific times, events, or even recurring intervals.

Mobile Voice Search

Mobile Voice Search is a user interface pattern and design system that enables users to interact with a mobile device by speaking commands or queries instead of typing or tapping on the screen. It leverages speech recognition and natural language processing technologies to convert spoken words into readable and actionable text.

In a mobile voice search system, the user initiates the interaction by activating the voice assistant feature on their mobile device, such as Siri, Google Assistant, or Alexa. The device's microphone captures the user's spoken words, which are then processed by the voice recognition software to transcribe the speech into text. The system then uses natural language processing algorithms to understand the user's intent and context, extracting keywords and meaningful information from the transcribed text.

This extracted information is then used to perform various actions or provide relevant search results. For example, the user can ask the voice assistant to make a phone call, send a text message, search for information on the internet, play music, set reminders, or control smart home devices. The voice assistant interacts with different apps and services on the device to fulfill the user's request.

Mobile voice search offers several benefits to users. Firstly, it provides a more convenient and hands-free way of interacting with mobile devices, especially in situations where manual input is difficult or not practical, such as when driving or cooking. Secondly, it can save time and effort by directly speaking commands or queries instead of typing them out. Additionally, it can improve accessibility for users with disabilities or physical limitations.

In terms of design, a mobile voice search interface should be visually minimalistic and unobtrusive, as the primary mode of interaction is through speech. The interface should provide clear and concise feedback to the user, indicating that their voice input has been recognized and processed. It should also offer suggestions or prompts to guide the user in formulating their commands or queries, helping them navigate the voice interface effectively.

In conclusion, mobile voice search is a user interface pattern and design system that enables hands-free and convenient interaction with mobile devices by converting spoken commands or queries into readable and actionable text. It leverages speech recognition and natural language processing technologies to understand user intent and perform various actions or provide relevant search results.

Mobile Voice Translation

Mobile Voice Translation is a UI pattern and design system that enables users to easily translate spoken language from one language to another using a mobile device. This feature is particularly useful for users who need to communicate with others who speak different languages, especially in situations where written translation may not be practical or feasible.

The Mobile Voice Translation design system typically includes several key components. First, there is a speech recognition module that listens to the user's spoken language and converts it into text. This module uses advanced algorithms and machine learning techniques to accurately transcribe the user's speech, taking into account factors such as accents and background noise.

Second, there is a translation module that takes the transcribed text and translates it into the desired language. This module may rely on pre-defined language models or rely on online translation services such as Google Translate or Microsoft Translator. The translation module ensures that the translated text is accurate and conveys the intended meaning from the original spoken language.

Finally, there is a text-to-speech module that converts the translated text into spoken language. This module uses synthesized voices or recordings of native speakers to provide a natural-sounding output. The text-to-speech module ensures that the translated text can be easily understood by the recipient, bridging the language barrier and facilitating effective communication.

The Mobile Voice Translation UI pattern typically consists of a clear and intuitive user interface that guides the user through the translation process. This may include prompts and instructions to help the user speak clearly and choose the desired languages. The UI may also include real-time feedback, such as showing the transcribed text as the user speaks, to ensure accuracy and prompt correction if needed.

In summary, Mobile Voice Translation is a UI pattern and design system that leverages speech recognition, translation, and text-to-speech technologies to enable users to easily communicate in different languages using their mobile devices. It enhances user experience by providing a convenient and efficient means of overcoming language barriers, promoting inclusivity and enabling effective communication in diverse settings.

Mobile Volcano Alerts

Mobile Volcano Alerts is a user interface pattern designed for mobile devices that provides timely and relevant information about volcanic activity. It is part of a comprehensive design system that aims to ensure the safety and well-being of users in areas prone to volcanic eruptions.

This UI pattern is specifically developed to deliver volcanic alerts to mobile users in a clear and concise manner, keeping them informed about any potential hazards or safety precautions they need to take. The design system behind Mobile Volcano Alerts focuses on providing a seamless and intuitive user experience while prioritizing critical information.

Mobile Volunteer Opportunities

A mobile volunteer opportunity in the context of UI patterns and design systems refers to a specific task or assignment that is aimed at improving the user experience and interface design of a mobile application or website through the collaborative efforts of volunteers.

Mobile volunteer opportunities typically involve individuals with skills and knowledge in user interface (UI) design, user experience (UX) design, graphic design, and front-end development. These opportunities allow volunteers to contribute their expertise and creativity to the improvement of mobile applications and websites, making them more user-friendly, visually appealing, and efficient.

Mobile Wallet Integration

Mobile Wallet Integration refers to the process of incorporating a mobile wallet feature within a user interface (UI) pattern or design system. It involves the seamless integration of a digital wallet functionality, allowing users to make secure payments, store payment information, and access loyalty programs or rewards directly from their mobile devices. Mobile wallet integration aims to simplify transactions and enhance the user experience by eliminating the need for physical payment methods such as credit cards or cash. By integrating mobile wallets into UI patterns and design systems, businesses can provide a convenient and efficient way for users to make purchases, manage their finances, and track their transactions. In the context of UI patterns, mobile wallet integration typically involves the incorporation of specific UI elements and components. These may include dedicated wallet buttons or icons, streamlined checkout processes, and clear indicators of available wallet options. These UI patterns enable users to easily identify and utilize mobile wallet functionalities throughout their interactions with an application or website. From a design system perspective, mobile wallet integration necessitates the establishment of cohesive visual and interaction guidelines. This ensures consistency across various touchpoints, such as mobile apps, websites, or even physical point-of-sale systems. Design systems play a crucial role in creating a unified experience, enabling users to seamlessly transition between different platforms while accessing their mobile wallets. To summarize, mobile wallet integration within UI patterns and design systems allows for the incorporation of convenient and secure payment options into digital experiences. With the increasing popularity of mobile payments, businesses can leverage mobile wallet integration to enhance user satisfaction, streamline transactions, and drive customer loyalty. Overall, mobile wallet integration within UI patterns and design systems enhances the user experience by seamlessly incorporating digital payment options into various platforms.>

Mobile Wallet Passes

Mobile Wallet Passes are digital representations of physical membership cards, tickets, coupons, or other forms of identification, stored on a mobile device to simplify transactions and streamline user experiences. They are designed to mimic the functionality of traditional physical passes like paper tickets or plastic loyalty cards, but with the added convenience of being easily accessible, easily shareable, and digitally customizable.

As part of a UI pattern or design system, Mobile Wallet Passes provide a consistent and intuitive user interface for interacting with these digital passes. They typically feature a card-like design, resembling the physical passes they are designed to replace, and may include details such as pass name, logo, expiration date, barcode, and other relevant information. The design system ensures a cohesive visual language and consistent user experience across different types of passes and mobile wallet platforms.

Mobile Wardrobe Planner

A Mobile Wardrobe Planner is a UI pattern and design system that allows users to efficiently plan and organize their wardrobe using a mobile device. It provides a user-friendly interface for users to manage and coordinate their clothing items, accessories, and outfits in a digital format. With a Mobile Wardrobe Planner, users can keep track of their entire wardrobe, including clothing pieces, shoes, bags, and other accessories. They can easily add new items to their collection and classify them based on different categories such as type, color, season, and occasion. This categorization helps users quickly locate and select the appropriate items when planning outfits. The design system of a Mobile Wardrobe Planner ensures a cohesive and consistent user experience across all screens and interactions. It utilizes intuitive navigation and clear visual hierarchy to guide users through the process of managing their wardrobe. The system employs a minimalistic and clean design aesthetic, with emphasis on readability and usability. The Mobile Wardrobe Planner also offers features that allow users to create outfits for specific occasions or events. Users can mix and match different clothing items and accessories to experiment with various combinations and styles. The planner provides a seamless way to save and access these outfit combinations for future reference. Furthermore, the Mobile Wardrobe Planner includes functionalities that enable users to plan their outfits in advance for specific days, weeks, or trips. It integrates with a calendar or scheduling system, allowing users to assign outfits to different dates and receive reminders for upcoming events. This feature helps users stay organized and prepared for different occasions. In conclusion, a Mobile Wardrobe Planner is a UI pattern and design system that provides users with a mobile-friendly tool to efficiently manage and plan their wardrobe. It offers features such as categorization, outfit creation, and scheduling to enhance the user experience and help users make better use of their clothing items.>

Mobile Weather Alerts

Mobile Weather Alerts are a user interface pattern and design system element that provide timely and relevant information about weather conditions through mobile applications. These alerts are designed to grab the user's attention and provide important updates about severe weather events, such as hurricanes, thunderstorms, or blizzards, directly on their mobile devices.

Mobile Weather Alerts typically appear as a notification or pop-up message within the mobile application, and may also be accompanied by a distinct sound or vibration to further capture the user's attention. The content of the alert includes key details about the weather event, such as the type of event, severity level, location, and time duration. This information allows users to quickly assess the potential impact of the weather event and take appropriate actions.

The design of Mobile Weather Alerts follows established best practices to ensure that the alert is noticeable, easy to read, and quickly comprehensible. These design principles include high contrast between the text and background, legible font size, and clear visual hierarchy. The use of icons or visual indicators may also be employed to enhance the quick understanding of the alert's content.

Mobile Weather Alerts are an important element of mobile weather applications, as they serve to keep users informed and safe during severe weather conditions. By providing real-time updates and actionable information, these alerts empower users to make informed decisions regarding their safety and well-being. The inclusion of Mobile Weather Alerts in a design system ensures consistency and usability across different mobile applications, allowing users to easily understand and interact with the alerts regardless of the specific weather application they are using.

Overall, Mobile Weather Alerts enhance the user experience by providing timely and relevant weather information directly on mobile devices. Their inclusion in a design system ensures consistency and usability, while their design principles facilitate quick comprehension and action by the users. By effectively communicating severe weather events, Mobile Weather Alerts contribute to the safety and well-being of the users.

Mobile Weather Widget

A Mobile Weather Widget is a user interface (UI) pattern and a component of a design system that provides users with real-time weather information on mobile devices. It is commonly used in mobile applications or home screen widgets to display weather conditions, temperature, and forecast data in a compact and visually appealing manner. The purpose of the Mobile Weather Widget is to enable users to quickly access and glance at the current weather conditions without the need to open a dedicated weather application or navigate through multiple screens. This widget provides a seamless and convenient experience for users who want to stay informed about the weather in their location or other specified locations. The Mobile Weather Widget typically consists of a small rectangular box or card that appears on the home screen or within a mobile app. It includes essential weather information such as the current temperature, weather icon, and a brief description of the weather conditions (e.g., sunny, cloudy, rainy). Additionally, it may display additional data such as the high and low temperatures for the day, humidity, wind speed, and a multi-day forecast. To ensure a consistent and intuitive user experience, the Mobile Weather Widget follows standard design principles and practices. It often adopts a minimalist and clean design approach, using simple icons, clear typography, and a limited color palette. The weather icon represents the current weather condition at a glance, allowing users to quickly interpret the information without the need to read the text. Furthermore, the widget employs responsive design techniques to optimize its appearance and layout across different screen sizes and orientations. Users can interact with the Mobile Weather Widget by tapping or clicking on it, which can lead to a more detailed weather forecast or other related information. This allows users to access more comprehensive data if they desire a deeper understanding of the weather conditions. Overall, the Mobile Weather Widget plays an essential role in providing users with accessible and concise weather information directly on their mobile devices. Its design and functionality aim to enhance the user experience by offering convenience, simplicity, and immediate access to up-to-date weather data.>

Mobile Wi-Fi Settings

Mobile Wi-Fi settings refer to the configuration and management options available for mobile Wi-Fi networks on a device. It allows users to control various aspects of their Wi-Fi connections, including network selection, password management, signal strength monitoring, and other related settings. In the context of UI patterns and design systems, mobile Wi-Fi settings follow a standardized layout and structure to ensure consistency and ease of use across different devices and operating systems. The goal is to provide users with a clear and intuitive interface that simplifies the process of managing their Wi-Fi connections. The design of mobile Wi-Fi settings typically includes a top-level menu or tab that allows users to access different sections or categories of settings. These sections may include basic network information, advanced settings, security options, and more. Each section focuses on a specific aspect of Wi-Fi management to help users navigate and find the desired options quickly. Within each section, the settings are presented in a structured manner, often organized in a list or grid-like format. This allows users to scan and locate the specific settings they want to modify easily. Additionally, clear labels and concise descriptions are used to assist users in understanding the purpose and functionality of each setting. Mobile Wi-Fi settings may include various options and features, such as: 1. Network selection: Users can view available Wi-Fi networks, choose the network they want to connect to, and manage saved networks. 2. Password management: Users can enter or modify Wi-Fi passwords, enable password protection, or view saved passwords. 3. Signal strength monitoring: Users can check the current signal strength of their Wi-Fi connection and troubleshoot any issues. 4. Advanced settings: Users can access additional configuration options, including proxy settings, DNS settings, IP address settings, and more. 5. Security options: Users can enable or disable security features like WPA2 encryption,

MAC filtering, or network visibility options. 6. Notifications and alerts: Users can customize notifications for Wi-Fi events such as successful connections, network disconnections, or low signal strength. By following established UI patterns and design systems, mobile Wi-Fi settings provide a consistent and user-friendly experience across different devices and platforms, allowing users to manage and customize their Wi-Fi connections effortlessly.

Mobile Wi-Fi settings refer to the configuration and management options available for mobile Wi-Fi networks on a device. It allows users to control various aspects of their Wi-Fi connections, including network selection, password management, signal strength monitoring, and other related settings.

In the context of UI patterns and design systems, mobile Wi-Fi settings follow a standardized layout and structure to ensure consistency and ease of use across different devices and operating systems. The goal is to provide users with a clear and intuitive interface that simplifies the process of managing their Wi-Fi connections.

Mobile Wildfire Alerts

A mobile wildfire alert refers to a user interface (UI) pattern that is designed to provide timely and relevant information about wildfires to mobile device users. It is part of a larger design system that aims to deliver crucial notifications and alerts to individuals in areas affected by wildfires, allowing them to take appropriate action to ensure their safety.

This UI pattern typically features a prominent and attention-grabbing display of wildfire alerts on the mobile device's screen. The design follows established UX principles to create a clear and intuitive layout that effectively communicates the urgency and importance of the information being presented.

Mobile-Friendly Design

Mobile-Friendly Design is a UI pattern and design system that aims to optimize the user experience on mobile devices by providing a layout and interaction that adapts to smaller screens and touch-based input.

This design approach takes into consideration the unique constraints and capabilities of mobile devices, such as limited screen real estate, different form factors, and interactive gestures. By adopting mobile-friendly design principles, websites and applications can ensure that they are accessible and usable for mobile users.

Modal Pop-Up

A modal pop-up is a UI design pattern that is commonly used to present important information or actions that require the user's attention and interaction. It is a type of overlay that appears on top of the main content of a webpage or application, temporarily interrupting the user's flow and focusing their attention on the specific task or message at hand. Modal pop-ups are typically used for tasks such as displaying notifications, asking for user input, displaying additional information, or confirming actions. They are designed to be visually distinct from the rest of the page, appearing as a floating element with a darkened background to emphasize their importance and create a sense of hierarchy. One key characteristic of modal pop-ups is that they disable interactions with the underlying content while they are displayed. This ensures that the user's attention is fully focused on the modal, preventing them from accidentally interacting with elements outside of the modal. This behavior is achieved through techniques such as preventing scrolling, disabling keyboard input, or applying an overlay that captures all user input until the modal is dismissed. Modal pop-ups typically include a clear call-to-action, such as buttons or links, to guide the user towards the desired action or response. They should provide concise and relevant information, allowing the user to make an informed decision or complete a task without overwhelming them with unnecessary details. The content and design of modal pop-ups should be consistent with the overall visual style and branding of the application, ensuring a cohesive user experience. When designing modal pop-ups, it is important to consider the user's context and flow. They should be used sparingly and only when necessary, as frequent or overly intrusive use can disrupt the user's experience and create frustration. It is also important to provide clear and intuitive ways to dismiss the modal, such as a close button or a gesture, to ensure that the user can easily exit the modal and return to their previous task. In conclusion, a modal pop-up is a UI design pattern used to display important information or actions that require user attention and interaction. They are visually distinct, temporarily interrupt the user's flow, and disable interactions with underlying content until they are dismissed. Modal pop-ups should be used sparingly, provide clear and concise information, and be consistent with the overall design and branding of the application.

Multi-Level Dropdowns

Multi-Level Dropdowns are a type of user interface pattern commonly used in web design systems. They are designed to provide a hierarchical structure for organizing and accessing content or options in a user-friendly and efficient manner. Multi-Level Dropdowns consist of a series of nested menus or lists that expand or collapse as the user interacts with them. The top-level menu serves as the primary navigation component, while each subsequent level represents sub-categories or options related to the parent item. The key feature of Multi-Level Dropdowns is the ability to drill down into deeper levels of the hierarchy without leaving the current page. This allows users to access specific content or perform actions without the need for multiple page loads or excessive scrolling. The hierarchy within Multi-Level Dropdowns is typically represented by indentation or nesting, making it visually clear which items are sub-categories or options of others. Each level may also feature visual cues such as arrows or icons to indicate expandable or collapsible elements. The interaction with Multi-Level Dropdowns involves hovering or clicking on a parent item to reveal its sub-categories or options. This interaction can trigger animations or transitions to provide a smooth and intuitive experience for the user. Sub-levels can be displayed either by expanding vertically or horizontally, depending on the design preferences and space constraints. Multi-Level Dropdowns are particularly useful for websites or applications with a large amount of content or complex navigation structures. They help to simplify the user experience by breaking down information into manageable chunks and reducing cognitive load. In summary, Multi-Level Dropdowns are a UI pattern that facilitates navigation and access to content by organizing it hierarchically and allowing users to drill down into deeper levels without leaving the current page. Their use in design systems helps create consistency and efficiency in user interfaces.

Multi-Step Conversation Flow

A multi-step conversation flow is a UI pattern that guides users through a series of sequential steps or stages within a design system. It is commonly used in user interfaces to break down complex processes, allowing users to easily understand and complete tasks. This conversation flow typically includes a series of screens or pages that users navigate through, with each step providing specific instructions or requesting information from the user. The flow is designed to be linear, meaning users must complete one step before moving on to the next. The primary purpose of using a multi-step conversation flow is to simplify complex processes and make them more manageable for users. By breaking tasks into smaller steps, it reduces cognitive load and helps prevent users from feeling overwhelmed. This pattern is particularly useful for processes that involve multiple decision-making points or require users to input a significant amount of information. In terms of design system implementation, a multi-step conversation flow can be achieved through various UI elements and components. For example, a progress indicator is commonly used to visually represent the current step and overall progress within the flow. This helps users understand where they are in the process and how much more they need to complete. Furthermore, clear and concise instructions or labels should be provided on each step to guide users through the flow. This helps users understand the purpose of each step and what is expected from them. Additionally, appropriate input fields or controls should be used to collect user input, ensuring that the flow is intuitive and effortless to follow. By implementing a multi-step conversation flow within a design system, designers can create a seamless and engaging user experience. It simplifies complex processes, improves usability, and increases the likelihood of successful task completion.>

Multi-Language Selection Form

A multi-language selection form is a user interface pattern used in design systems to allow users to choose their preferred language for the content displayed on a website or application. This form typically consists of a dropdown menu or a list of clickable options that represent different language options. When a user interacts with the form, they can select the desired language, and the content is then translated or displayed in the chosen language.

The multi-language selection form is an essential component of a design system as it allows websites and applications to cater to a diverse range of users who may speak different languages. By providing multiple language options, developers and designers can create a more inclusive and accessible user experience.

Multimodal UI

A multimodal user interface (UI) refers to a design system that allows users to interact with a digital system or application through multiple input modes. These input modes can include touch, gestures, voice commands, and other forms of input. The goal of a multimodal UI is to provide a more flexible and intuitive user experience by accommodating different user preferences and contexts. A typical multimodal UI design system consists of various components and patterns that support different input modes. These components can include buttons, sliders, forms, and other interactive elements that can be activated through touch or gestures. In addition, the design system should provide support for voice input, allowing users to interact with the application using natural language commands or queries. When designing a multimodal UI, it is important to consider the different capabilities and limitations of each input mode. For example, touch input may be more suited for quick actions and navigation, while voice input can be useful for complex queries or tasks that require hands-free interaction. The design system should provide appropriate feedback and guidance to the user to ensure a smooth and seamless interaction across different input modes. In order to maintain consistency and coherence across the different input modes, a multimodal UI design system should adhere to established UI patterns and guidelines. These patterns define the visual and interaction design for various components and provide a unified experience for the user. By following these patterns, designers can ensure that the application is intuitive and easy to use, regardless of the input mode. Overall, a multimodal UI design system aims to enhance the user experience by providing a flexible and adaptable interface that accommodates different input modes. By considering the capabilities and limitations of each input mode and adhering to established UI patterns, designers can create intuitive and engaging applications that seamlessly integrate touch, gestures, and voice commands. >

Multistep Forms

A multistep form is a user interface pattern commonly used in design systems to break down lengthy or complex forms into multiple smaller steps or sections. This approach helps to improve usability by reducing cognitive load and preventing users from feeling overwhelmed or discouraged by a large amount of information or tasks to complete. With a multistep form, the user is guided through the form in a step-by-step manner, where each step represents a logical chunk of information or a specific task. Typically, a progress indicator is provided to give users a sense of their progress and the total number of steps remaining. Each step in a multistep form is usually presented on a single screen or page, allowing users to focus their attention on a specific set of inputs or actions. By breaking down the form into smaller sections, users are more likely to complete the form as they can accomplish each step at a time, which feels less overwhelming. From a design system perspective, multistep forms are often implemented using a combination of HTML, CSS, and JavaScript. HTML is used to structure the form elements and steps, CSS is used for styling and layout, and JavaScript is used to handle the logic and navigation between steps. In terms of HTML structure, each step of the form is typically contained within a separate section or div element, with each input field wrapped inside a label element. Using the appropriate HTML attributes such as 'for' and 'id' helps to establish the association between labels and inputs for improved accessibility and usability. Additionally, semantic HTML tags like 'fieldset' and 'legend' can be used to group related fields together and provide a meaningful description or title for each step. In conclusion, multistep forms are a valuable UI pattern in design systems that help improve the usability of lengthy or complex forms. By breaking down the form into smaller sections and guiding users through a step-by-step process, multistep forms reduce cognitive load and enhance the overall user experience.

Museum Exhibits

A museum exhibit in the context of UI patterns and design systems refers to a specific display or presentation of information, artifacts, or interactive elements within a museum setting. It is a curated and organized arrangement of objects, illustrations, multimedia content, or interactive components designed to communicate a specific theme, concept, or story to museum visitors.

Museum exhibits, in the context of UI patterns and design systems, typically follow certain established patterns and guidelines to create cohesive and consistent experiences for visitors. These patterns often involve the use of consistent visual styles, layouts, and interactions across different exhibits within a museum or across multiple museums in a network.

Music Player

A Music Player is a user interface (UI) component dedicated to playing audio files, such as songs or podcasts. It is a key element in music-related applications and websites, providing controls for playback, volume adjustment, song selection, and other related features. The Music Player typically consists of a compact and intuitive design that allows users to easily navigate and control their audio experience. It often includes standard controls, such as play, pause, next, previous, repeat, and shuffle buttons. These buttons enable users to start, stop, skip to the next or previous track, as well as control the playback order. Volume control is another essential feature of a Music Player, allowing users to adjust the sound level. It can include a volume slider or buttons to increase or decrease the volume. Additionally, users may have the option to mute or unmute the audio. In addition to the basic controls, a Music Player may display relevant song information, such as the title, artist, album, and track length. This information helps users identify and select the desired audio file. It may also include visual feedback, such as a progress bar, indicating the current position within the track. To enhance the user experience, a Music Player can provide additional functionality. For example, it may include a search bar that allows users to find specific tracks or artists quickly. It could also offer playlist management features, enabling users to create, edit, and delete playlists, as well as add or remove songs from existing playlists. Furthermore, a Music Player might incorporate a favorites or favorites-like feature. This feature allows users to mark specific tracks or artists as their favorites, making them easily accessible from a dedicated section or playlist. Design systems ensure consistency and cohesiveness across various UI components, including the Music Player. A design system can define the visual appearance, interaction behaviors, and underlying coding guidelines for the Music Player, promoting a seamless and uniform user experience across different screens and platforms. In conclusion, a Music Player is a UI component that provides controls for playing audio files. It includes features such as playback controls, volume adjustment, song selection, and additional functionalities like search, playlists, and favorites. Design systems ensure consistency and cohesiveness across the Music Player and other UI components.>

Navigation Drawer

A Navigation Drawer is a user interface pattern commonly used in web and mobile applications to provide easy access to application features and settings. It is a panel that slides in from the side of the screen when triggered and contains a list of options or links for users to navigate through different sections or perform various actions within the application. The Navigation Drawer is typically represented by an icon or button called the "hamburger menu" that consists of three horizontal lines. When the user clicks or taps on the hamburger menu, the Navigation Drawer slides in covering a part of the screen, temporarily displacing the main content of the application. This interaction allows users to focus on their current task while providing a convenient way to navigate and access additional functionality. Inside the Navigation Drawer, the options or links are usually presented as a vertical list or grouped into categories. Each option or link can lead to a different page or perform a specific action within the application. Users can easily browse through the options and select the one they desire, triggering the appropriate action or transition to the corresponding page. The Navigation Drawer is a widely adopted UI pattern due to its effectiveness in organizing and simplifying complex applications with multiple features and settings. It saves screen space by hiding these options until needed, providing a clutter-free and focused interface. Additionally, it enhances discoverability by exposing secondary features that might otherwise be buried in menus or settings screens. When implementing a Navigation Drawer, it is important to take into account the visual design consistency and user experience guidelines specific to the platform or operating system being used. This ensures a seamless and familiar interaction for users across different applications. In conclusion, the Navigation Drawer is a user interface pattern that enables easy access to application features and settings by sliding in a panel from the side of the screen. It enhances navigation, organization, and discoverability within complex applications, providing a clutter-free and focused user experience.>

Near Field Communication (NFC)

Near Field Communication (NFC) is a technology that enables short-range communication between devices, allowing them to exchange data wirelessly. It uses radio frequency identification (RFID) and operates within a range of a few centimeters.

NFC has become particularly popular in the context of UI patterns and design systems, as it offers a convenient and intuitive way for users to interact with digital interfaces. By simply bringing their NFC-enabled devices close to one another, users can engage in a variety of actions without the need for physical contact or cumbersome setups.

Neumorphism

Neumorphism is a UI design trend and pattern that has emerged in recent years. It is a combination of skeuomorphism, which is the design technique that mimics real-world objects, and flat design, which focuses on minimalism and simplicity.

Neumorphism aims to create user interfaces that have a three-dimensional appearance, as if they are extruded from the screen. This is achieved by using subtle gradients and shadows to create soft, pillowy edges and surfaces.

Neumorphic design relies heavily on the use of light and shadow to create depth and realism. The UI elements appear to be slightly raised from the background, giving them a tactile and interactive feel.

To achieve the neumorphic effect, designers use light sources to cast shadows or gradients on the interface elements. This creates a sense of depth and helps users understand the hierarchy of the different elements on the screen.

The color palette used in neumorphic design is generally muted and pastel, with light and dark shades of the same hue. This further enhances the softness and realism of the interface.

The use of neumorphism in a design system can provide a visually pleasing and intuitive user experience. It can make the user interface more engaging and inviting, as it mimics real-world objects, which users are already familiar with.

However, it is important to use neumorphism sparingly and with care. Overuse or misuse of the technique can make the interface visually overwhelming or confusing. It is crucial to strike a balance between aesthetics and usability.

News Feed

A news feed is a UI pattern and design system component commonly seen in social media platforms and content aggregators. It presents a continuous stream of updates, posts, or articles, arranged in reverse chronological order with the most recent content appearing at the top.

The primary purpose of a news feed is to provide users with a convenient and efficient way to consume and engage with a large volume of content. It serves as a central hub or dashboard where users can easily discover, browse, and interact with various types of information, such as news articles, blog posts, social media updates, or multimedia content.

Newsletter Signup Form

A newsletter signup form is a user interface element commonly found in websites and applications that allows users to voluntarily provide their email address and subscribe to receive updates or information from the organization or company. This form is typically used to collect user data for marketing purposes and can be an essential part of building a subscriber list. The design of a newsletter signup form is an important aspect of the overall user experience. It should be visually appealing, easy to understand, and encourage users to sign up. A well-designed form can help increase conversion rates and attract more subscribers. There are several key elements that make up a newsletter signup form. The first is a clear and concise headline or title that explains the purpose of the form. This helps users understand what they are signing up for and sets expectations. Next, there should be a clear input field where users can enter their email address. This field should be prominently displayed and invite users to take action. The design should also provide visual feedback, such as a blinking cursor or highlighting effect, to indicate that the field is interactive. To further encourage signups, a call-to-action button should be placed near the input field. The button should use persuasive language, such as "Subscribe" or "Sign up now," and stand out from the rest of the form. It is important to use contrasting colors and visual cues, such as arrows or icons, to draw attention to the button. In addition to the input field and call-to-action button, a newsletter signup form may also include other elements to gather additional information from the user. This could include fields for the user's name, company, or interests. However, it is important to strike a balance between collecting enough information to personalize the newsletter content and making the signup process too lengthy or intrusive. Lastly, a well-designed newsletter signup form should provide clear feedback to the user after they submit their information. This could be in the form of a success message, a confirmation email, or a redirect to a thank-you page. Feedback reassures users that their signup was successful and helps build trust. Overall, a newsletter signup form is a crucial tool for businesses and organizations to gather email addresses and communicate with their audience. Its design should prioritize user experience, making it easy and inviting for users to subscribe.

Newsletter Signup Pop-Up

A Newsletter Signup Pop-up, in the context of UI patterns and design systems, refers to a user interface element that appears as a separate window or overlay on a website or application with the purpose of encouraging users to subscribe to a newsletter. This design pattern is commonly used to capture the attention of website visitors and entice them to subscribe by offering various incentives such as exclusive content, deals, or updates. The pop-up typically includes a form where users can enter their email address and sometimes additional information, such as their name or preferences. The Newsletter Signup Pop-up is an effective way for businesses and organizations to grow their subscriber base and establish a direct line of communication with their audience. When strategically placed and designed, it can significantly increase conversion rates and facilitate lead generation. To ensure a seamless user experience, it is important to carefully consider the timing, placement, and design of the pop-up. Timing is crucial as it should not disrupt the user's attention or hinder their interaction with the website. Implementing a delay or triggered action, such as scrolling, can help address this concern. Placement should also be strategic, taking into account the user's focus and the prominence of the pop-up within the overall page layout. In terms of design, the pop-up should align with the overall branding and visual style of the website or application. This helps establish trust and maintain a cohesive user experience. The form fields should be clear and easy to understand, with concise and persuasive copy that highlights the benefits of subscribing. It is important to consider the frequency and targeting of the pop-up as well. Bombarding users with frequent or irrelevant pop-ups can lead to frustration or even deter visitors from engaging with the website. Implementing targeting based on user behavior, such as exit intent or engagement levels, can help make the pop-up more relevant and effective. In conclusion, a Newsletter Signup Pop-up is a user interface element that aims to capture user email addresses by offering incentives for subscribing. By strategically considering timing, placement, design, and targeting, businesses and organizations can maximize the effectiveness of this design pattern and grow their subscriber base.>

Newsletter Subscription Preferences Form

A newsletter subscription preferences form is a user interface pattern and design system element that allows users to specify their preferences and settings for receiving newsletters. It typically includes a set of options or checkboxes for different types of newsletters or content categories, as well as other relevant settings such as frequency and language. The newsletter subscription preferences form serves as a tool for the user to communicate their newsletter preferences to the website or application. By providing these preferences, users can tailor their experience and receive only the content they are interested in, avoiding information overload and enhancing their overall satisfaction with the platform. The form is usually designed in a clear and concise manner, making it easy for users to understand and interact with. It should provide a straightforward layout that allows users to quickly scan and select their preferred options. The use of checkboxes is a common approach in these forms, as they allow users to select multiple options at once. To enhance the usability of the newsletter subscription preferences form, it is important to categorize and label the options clearly. This can be done through the use of headings or section titles for different types of newsletters or content categories. Additionally, providing brief descriptions or summaries for each option can help users make informed decisions. Furthermore, the form may offer additional settings beyond just the content preferences. For example, users may be able to specify the frequency at which they wish to receive newsletters (e.g., daily, weekly, monthly) or choose the language in which they want to receive the content. Overall, the newsletter subscription preferences form is an important element in the user experience of websites and applications that offer newsletter subscriptions. By allowing users to customize their preferences, it empowers them to receive relevant content and maintain control over their inbox. This not only improves the user experience but also increases the likelihood of engagement and retention.>

Note-Taking Screen

A Note-Taking Screen refers to a user interface pattern and design system that provides users with a designated space to create and organize textual notes. It typically consists of a blank canvas or input area where users can enter and edit their notes, along with various tools and features to help manage and enhance the note-taking experience. The primary purpose of a Note-Taking Screen is to facilitate the capture and storage of information in a digital format. It enables users to jot down thoughts, ideas, reminders, and other important details, serving as a virtual replacement for traditional pen and paper. This pattern is particularly useful for individuals who need to regularly document and reference information or maintain a digital record of their thoughts and observations. In terms of design, a Note-Taking Screen typically features a simple and intuitive layout that allows users to focus on their writing. It may include options to adjust the formatting and style of the text, such as changing fonts, colors, and alignment. Additionally, it may offer tools for organizing and categorizing notes, such as creating folders or tags, to facilitate better information retrieval. To enhance the functionality of a Note-Taking Screen, designers often incorporate additional features. For example, users may have the ability to insert images, add attachments, or embed links within their notes. Some design systems also provide collaboration capabilities, allowing multiple users to access and edit the same set of notes simultaneously, promoting teamwork and knowledge sharing. The overall goal of a Note-Taking Screen is to provide a user-friendly and efficient tool for capturing and managing textual information. It should be easy to navigate, provide quick access to important functions, and support seamless integration with other applications or platforms. By leveraging this pattern, users can conveniently and effectively organize their thoughts and access their notes whenever and wherever needed. In conclusion, a Note-Taking Screen is a user interface pattern and design system that offers users a digital space for capturing, organizing, and managing textual notes. It provides a flexible and customizable platform for users to document their thoughts, ideas, and observations, with various tools and features to enhance the note-taking experience.>

Notification Badges

A notification badge, in the context of UI patterns and design systems, is a visual indicator that notifies the user about certain events or activities within an application or website. It is typically displayed as a small badge overlaid on top of an associated icon or element, such as a menu item or a user profile picture. The main purpose of a notification badge is to grab the user's attention and inform them about new or unread content, updates, notifications, or any other relevant activities that require their attention.

The notification badge is commonly used in various applications, especially those with real-time features or social functionalities. By providing a glimpse of the current status or pending actions, these badges help users keep track of important information without having to navigate through multiple screens or menus.

Notification Banners

Notification Banners refer to a common user interface pattern used in the design and layout of websites and applications. They are elements that are typically displayed at the top or bottom of a screen, providing important information or alerts to users without interrupting their current tasks.

Notification Banners are designed to be attention-grabbing, easily noticeable, and quickly dismissible. They may appear as a narrow horizontal bar or a small rectangular box, often contrasting with the rest of the interface to ensure visibility. The content of a Notification Banner can vary, ranging from informational messages, warnings, reminders, to notifications of completed actions or system updates.

Notification Center

A notification center is a UI pattern or design system component that provides users with a centralized location to view and manage notifications or alerts in a digital application or platform.

When it comes to user interface design, notifications play a crucial role in keeping users informed about important events, updates, or actions within the application. However, bombarding users with constant pop-up notifications can easily lead to frustration and cognitive overload.

A Notification Center addresses this issue by providing users with a dedicated space or panel where they can access and manage notifications in a more organized and non-intrusive manner. Instead of interrupting the user flow with pop-up alerts, the Notification Center accumulates notifications and allows the user to review them at their own convenience.

The Notification Center typically includes visual indicators to show the number of unread notifications, making it easy for users to quickly gauge the urgency or importance of the notifications waiting for their attention. Users can typically navigate to the Notification Center through a designated icon or shortcut, such as a bell or envelop icon, positioned somewhere within the user interface.

Once inside the Notification Center, users can view a list or stack of notifications, usually sorted by recency. Each notification may include relevant information, such as a brief summary, source, timestamp, and any associated actions or options. Users can interact with individual notifications, such as marking them as read, dismissing them, or clicking on them to perform a specific action or view more details.

Some Notification Centers also provide filtering or sorting capabilities, allowing users to manage and organize their notifications based on their preferences or priorities. This helps users stay organized and focus on the notifications that are most relevant to them.

In conclusion, a Notification Center acts as a centralized hub for managing notifications in an application, providing users with a convenient and organized way to stay informed without interrupting their workflow. By adopting this UI pattern or design system component, designers and developers can enhance the user experience by promoting better notification management and reducing the potential for user frustration or cognitive overload.

Notification Pop-Ups

A notification pop-up is a user interface element that presents important information or alerts to the user in a temporary and visible manner. It is typically used to capture the user's attention and prompt them to take a specific action or provide important information without interrupting their current workflow.

When a notification pop-up appears, it is commonly displayed as a small window or overlay that appears on top of the current screen content. It may contain text, icons, images, or other multimedia elements to convey the message effectively. The duration of the pop-up's visibility can vary, from a few seconds to longer periods, depending on the urgency and significance of the information being presented.

Notification Preferences Form

A notification preferences form is a user interface element that allows users to customize their preferences for receiving notifications within an application or system. It is a structured form that presents a set of options and settings related to notifications, typically organized into categories or sections. The purpose of a notification preferences form is to empower users with control over their notification experience. By providing a clear and organized interface, users can easily navigate through the available options and make selections based on their preferences and needs. The form typically consists of a series of checkboxes, radio buttons, or toggles that represent specific notification settings. Each option is labeled with a clear and concise description that communicates the purpose and impact of the corresponding setting. The form may also include additional elements to enhance usability and accessibility. For example, it may provide filters or search functionality to help users quickly find specific notification settings. It may also include tooltips or informative text to provide additional context or guidance for users who are uncertain about certain settings. Additionally, a notification preferences form may include sections or categories to organize the available settings. This helps users locate and understand related options more easily. For example, notifications may be grouped into categories such as "Account", "Activity", or "Promotions", allowing users to quickly find and adjust settings based on their interests or preferences. The design of a notification preferences form should prioritize simplicity and clarity. It should use a consistent and visually distinguishable style for the different elements, ensuring that users can quickly scan and understand the available options. The form should also provide clear feedback to users when they make changes, such as displaying a confirmation message or an updated summary of their selected preferences. Overall, a well-designed notification preferences form promotes user control and personalization, allowing users to tailor their notification experience according to their individual needs and preferences. This can help improve user satisfaction and engagement with the application or system.

Notification Settings

A notification settings UI pattern refers to a design system that allows users to configure their preferences for receiving notifications from an application or system. This pattern typically includes a variety of options that enable users to control the types and frequency of notifications they receive, as well as the channels through which they are delivered. The notification settings pattern is an essential component of any user interface, as it empowers users to tailor their notification experience to their individual needs and preferences. By providing users with the ability to customize their notification settings, designers can ensure that their application or system delivers relevant and timely information without overwhelming the user with unnecessary or excessive notifications. In the context of a design system, the notification settings pattern should be consistently implemented across different interfaces and platforms to maintain a cohesive and intuitive user experience. This involves establishing a common set of options and controls that can be easily understood and interacted with by users across different devices and operating systems. The notification settings pattern often includes options such as enabling or disabling notifications, selecting the types of notifications to receive (e.g., email, push notifications, in-app notifications), choosing the specific categories of content to be notified about, and setting the frequency or urgency of notifications. Additional features may involve choosing the time frames during which notifications are allowed, configuring sound or vibration settings, or specifying preferences for displaying notifications on the lock screen. To ensure a user-friendly notification settings UI, designers should organize the options in a clear and logical manner, using appropriate labels and descriptions to assist users in understanding each setting. They should also provide helpful tooltips or contextual prompts to guide users through the customization process. The interface should offer feedback to users when changes are made, allowing them to preview the effects of their settings before finalizing them. Overall, the notification settings UI pattern plays a crucial role in enhancing the user experience by giving users control over their notification preferences. By implementing this pattern consistently within a design system, designers can create a seamless and intuitive notification customization experience for users across different platforms and interfaces. >

Notification Sounds

Notification sounds are auditory cues used in user interfaces to provide users with timely

206

information or updates. They are an integral part of UI patterns and design systems as they help to enhance the user experience by notifying users of important events or actions. Notification sounds serve multiple purposes in UI design. They alert users to new messages, notifications, or events that require their attention. By providing an auditory cue, notification sounds can effectively grab the user's attention even if they are not actively looking at the interface. This ensures that users are informed about important updates or events in a timely manner. Design systems often include a range of predefined notification sounds that adhere to the overall visual and auditory style of the interface. These sounds are carefully designed to be distinctive, recognizable, and appropriate for different types of notifications. For example, a short and subtle chime may be used for less critical notifications, while a more attention-grabbing sound can be used for urgent alerts. In addition to their functional role, notification sounds also contribute to the overall user experience and branding of an interface. They can help create a sense of consistency and familiarity across different parts of an application or website. By using consistent sounds, users can quickly associate specific sounds with certain actions or events, which enhances their overall understanding and navigation of the interface. When designing notification sounds, various factors need to be considered. The volume and duration of the sound should be appropriate to avoid being too intrusive or too subtle. The tone and pitch of the sound should align with the purpose and urgency of the notification. Additionally, it is important to ensure that the sound is distinguishable from other sounds in the environment and does not cause confusion or interference. In conclusion, notification sounds play a crucial role in UI patterns and design systems by providing users with auditory cues for important events and updates. They enhance the user experience, facilitate timely notifications, and contribute to the overall branding and consistency of the interface. Carefully designed notification sounds can effectively grab the user's attention and help them stay informed in an intuitive and engaging manner.

On/Off Toggles

On/Off Toggles are a UI pattern commonly used in design systems to provide users with a binary control input for switching between two states. They are often utilized for enabling or disabling a specific feature or setting within an application or website. In terms of design, On/Off Toggles typically consist of a labeled toggle switch that can be activated or deactivated by the user. The switch represents the current state, with "On" indicating that the feature is enabled or active, while "Off" indicates that it is disabled or inactive. These toggles are designed to be intuitive and visually distinct so that users can easily understand and interact with them. They are commonly used for settings that require quick user actions or have a direct impact on the UI or functionality of the system. From a UX perspective, On/Off Toggles offer a clear and concise way for users to control specific features without the need for complex menus or options. They provide a sense of direct control and can improve the overall user experience by reducing the number of steps required to change a setting. In terms of accessibility, it is crucial to ensure that On/Off Toggles are properly labeled so that screen readers can accurately convey the current state to visually impaired users. ARIA (Accessible Rich Internet Applications) attributes can be utilized to provide additional information and context to assistive technologies. When implemented in a design system, On/Off Toggles should adhere to the system's established visual and interaction guidelines. Consistency in both appearance and behavior is important to ensure a seamless experience across different screens and contexts. In terms of HTML implementation, On/Off Toggles can be created using a combination of HTML, CSS, and JavaScript. The exact implementation may vary depending on the specific design system or framework being used. However, the basic structure typically involves a labeled `<input>` element of type "checkbox" or "radio" and associated CSS to style the toggle switch. Overall, On/Off Toggles are a versatile and widely used UI pattern in design systems. They provide a straightforward and efficient way for users to control specific features or settings, contributing to a more intuitive and streamlined user experience.

Onboarding Wizard

A onboarding wizard is a UI pattern and design system component that guides users through a step-by-step process to familiarize them with a new system or feature. It is commonly used to introduce users to a product or service, helping them understand its functionalities and how to make the most out of it. The onboarding wizard typically consists of a series of sequential steps, each containing relevant information and necessary actions for users to complete. Each step is presented in a clear and concise manner, ensuring that users can easily comprehend the provided information and execute the suggested actions. The onboarding wizard is designed to provide a smooth and engaging user experience. It often includes visual elements, such as images or icons, to enhance understanding and make the process more visually appealing. The use of clear and concise language is crucial to ensure that users can easily follow along and complete each step without confusion. To further enhance user engagement, the onboarding wizard may also include interactive elements, such as progress indicators or tooltips, to provide real-time feedback and guidance. These elements can help users track their progress and understand their location within the overall onboarding process. By breaking down complex information into bite-sized steps, the onboarding wizard allows users to gradually familiarize themselves with the system or feature, reducing potential overwhelm or confusion. It enables users to build confidence and proficiency as they progress through the onboarding process, ultimately leading to a better user experience and increased adoption of the product or service. In summary, the onboarding wizard is a UI pattern and design system component that facilitates the introduction and familiarization of users with a new system or feature. Through a series of sequential steps, it guides users and provides clear instructions and actions to ensure a smooth onboarding experience. By breaking down complex information and utilizing visual and interactive elements, the onboarding wizard enhances user engagement and comprehension, leading to a positive user experience.>

One-Handed Mode

One-Handed Mode is a user interface pattern and design system feature that provides an optimized layout and functionality for users who primarily operate their device with one hand. This mode aims to enhance the usability and accessibility of a user interface, particularly for devices with larger screens that may be difficult to operate with one hand alone.

In One-Handed Mode, the user interface is adapted to accommodate the limited range of motion and reachability of a single hand. This typically involves resizing and repositioning elements within the interface to make them more easily reachable. For example, buttons, menus, and other interactive elements may be shifted to one side of the screen, closer to the user's thumb or fingers. This allows users to perform actions and navigate through the interface more comfortably and efficiently.

Order Confirmation Screen

A Order Confirmation Screen is a user interface pattern that is typically displayed after a user has completed an online purchase or placed an order. It serves as a formal confirmation of the user's purchase, providing important details such as order summary, delivery information, and payment details. The Order Confirmation Screen plays a crucial role in reassuring users that their order has been successfully processed and serves as a reference point for future communication or support regarding their purchase. It should be designed to be informative, clear, and visually appealing. Typically, an Order Confirmation Screen includes the following elements: 1. Order Summary: This section provides a detailed summary of the items or services that the user has ordered. It should include product names or descriptions, quantities, prices, and any applicable discounts or promotional offers. 2. Delivery Information: This section displays the user's shipping address and any relevant delivery instructions or preferences, such as estimated delivery dates or tracking information. It should clearly state where the order will be delivered and if there are any additional charges or requirements. 3. Payment Details: This section confirms the user's chosen payment method, such as credit card details or payment gateway information. It should provide a summary of the payment amount, any applied discounts, and the final total. If there are any additional charges or fees, they should be clearly stated. 4. Confirmation Messages: This section should include a prominent message or heading stating that the order has been successfully placed or completed. It should be concise and displayed in a visually distinct manner, such as using larger or bolded text. 5. Contact Information: This section typically includes the retailer's contact information, such as customer support email address or phone number. It can also provide links to additional resources or FAQs that may address common questions or concerns related to the order. 6. Order number and reference: This section provides a unique order identifier or number that the user can reference in any future communication regarding their purchase. It is important to clearly display this information so that users can easily retrieve it when needed. Overall, the Order Confirmation

Screen is a critical component of an online shopping experience, as it provides users with the necessary information and reassurance that their order has been successfully processed. It should be designed to be visually appealing, easy to understand, and accessible on various devices and screen sizes.>

Order Form

An order form is a UI pattern and design system component that enables users to provide and submit their information to initiate a purchase or request a service. It typically consists of various input fields, checkboxes, drop-down menus, and buttons that facilitate the collection of relevant information from the user. The primary purpose of an order form is to streamline the ordering process and make it more efficient for both the user and the business. It ensures that all necessary information is captured accurately and in a structured manner, reducing the likelihood of errors or missing details. Order forms are designed to be intuitive, user-friendly, and visually appealing. They often follow a consistent design system that aligns with the overall look and feel of the product or website. The layout and organization of form elements are carefully considered to optimize clarity and usability. Input fields are used to collect essential information such as the user's name, shipping address, contact details, and payment information. These fields are typically labeled or accompanied by placeholder text to provide context and guidance to the user. Some fields may have specific formatting requirements or validation rules to ensure the accuracy and completeness of the entered data. Checkboxes and radio buttons allow users to select from available options or make choices based on their preferences. They are commonly used for selecting product variations, delivery options, or additional services. These options are typically presented in a clear and concise manner to avoid overwhelming the user with unnecessary information. Drop-down menus are used when there is a long list of options to choose from, such as selecting a country or a product category. They help conserve space and provide a more condensed view of available choices. Users can click or tap on the dropdown menu to reveal the options and make their selection. Buttons play a crucial role in order forms, particularly the submit and cancel/reset buttons. The submit button is responsible for validating the entered information and initiating the order placement process. On the other hand, the cancel/reset button allows users to discard their progress and start over if needed. Overall, an order form is an essential component of any e-commerce platform or service-oriented website. It aims to simplify the purchasing process, gather accurate information, and enhance user satisfaction. By adhering to UI patterns and design systems, order forms can provide a consistent and cohesive user experience across different products and platforms.

Overlay Menus

Overlay menus are a type of user interface (UI) pattern used in website and application design systems. They are created to provide users with a convenient and accessible way to navigate different sections and content within a website or application. Overlay menus typically appear as a transparent or semi-transparent layer that is superimposed over the main content of a webpage or application. When activated, usually by clicking on a specific button or icon, the overlay menu slides or fades into view, temporarily covering the underlying content. These menus often offer a simplistic and minimalist design, with a focus on user-friendly navigation options. They commonly display a list of links or buttons that enable users to access different pages, sections, or features of a website or application. Overlay menus can be categorized into two main types: full-screen overlay menus and partial-overlay menus. Full-screen overlay menus cover the entire screen, blocking the view of the underlying content entirely when activated. They are particularly useful when there is a need to display a comprehensive menu with numerous options, or when the menu design is an integral part of the overall user experience. On the other hand, partial-overlay menus partially cover the screen, allowing users to still see some of the underlying content while navigating the menu. These menus are commonly used when there is a need to provide quick access to specific options or when the menu design aims to prioritize the visibility of the underlying content. Both types of overlay menus are often accompanied by animation effects to enhance the user experience. The animations can include transitions, such as sliding or fading, to make the menu's appearance and disappearance more seamless and visually appealing. Overlay menus are an effective UI pattern for organizing and presenting navigation options without cluttering the main content. They offer a way for users to focus on the menu options without being overwhelmed by excessive visual elements on the screen. Additionally, overlay menus can contribute to a consistent and cohesive design system by utilizing the same style and interaction patterns across different pages or sections within a website or application. In conclusion, overlay menus are a popular UI pattern used to create accessible and user-friendly navigation systems in website and application design. They provide a convenient way for users to access different sections or features without disrupting the overall user experience.

Page Title

A page title in the context of UI patterns and design systems refers to the main heading or name given to a specific page within a website or application. It serves as a brief summary or descriptor of the content found on that particular page.

The page title is important for several reasons. Firstly, it provides users with a clear and concise indication of what they can expect to find on the page. This helps users quickly determine if the page is relevant to their needs or interests. Additionally, when users bookmark or save a webpage, the page title is often used as the default name for the saved link, making it easier for users to identify and find the page again in the future.

Page Transitions

Page transitions are UI patterns and design systems that enable smooth and fluid animations when navigating between different pages or sections within a website or application. These transitions play a vital role in enhancing the user experience by providing visual cues and feedback, making the navigation more engaging and intuitive. In HTML, page transitions can be achieved using various techniques like CSS animations, transitions, and JavaScript animations. CSS animations allow you to apply different animation effects to HTML elements, while CSS transitions provide a way to smoothly animate property changes over a specified duration. To create a page transition using CSS animations, you can define keyframes that specify the intermediate states of an element during the animation. By animating properties such as opacity, transform, or position, you can create effects like fade-ins, slide-ins, and rotations. CSS transitions, on the other hand, allow you to smoothly animate property changes without specifying intermediate states. You can define the start and end states of an element's properties and set the transition duration, timing function, and delay. This way, when a property is changed (e.g., on a hover or click event), the transition effect will be applied automatically. JavaScript animations provide more flexibility in creating page transitions. By using frameworks like jQuery or GSAP, you can control and manipulate the animations programmatically. These libraries offer advanced features like easing functions, timeline control, and sequence management, allowing for complex and customized page transitions. When implementing page transitions, it's essential to consider the overall design system and maintain consistency throughout the website or application. The transitions should complement the visual style and purpose of the site, enhancing the user's understanding of the navigation flow. In conclusion, page transitions are UI patterns and design systems that add fluid and engaging animations when navigating between pages or sections. They can be implemented using CSS animations, transitions, or JavaScript animations, depending on the complexity and desired effects. By incorporating well-designed and thoughtful transitions, you can improve the user experience and make the navigation more intuitive and enjoyable. >

Pagination

Pagination is a UI pattern and design system element used to break down a large set of content into multiple pages for better usability and navigation. It allows users to access content in a structured and organized manner, enhancing the overall user experience. The primary purpose of pagination is to divide a lengthy or extensive piece of content into smaller, more manageable sections. By doing so, users can easily navigate through different pages and locate specific information without feeling overwhelmed. Pagination provides a systematic structure to the content, facilitating quick access to desired data. From a design perspective, pagination is typically represented by a series of numbered buttons, usually placed at the bottom of the page or at the end of a content section. These numbered buttons signify the various pages available within the content set. Users can click on these buttons to move between pages and explore additional information. In addition to numbered buttons, pagination may also include navigation arrows to navigate to the previous or next page. These arrows offer an alternative method of moving through the content, particularly useful when the number of pages is extensive. Pagination is commonly used in various scenarios, such as search result pages, article archives, product listings, and other content-heavy sections. It helps avoid clutter and overload by presenting content in manageable chunks. It is especially beneficial when dealing with large datasets or when it is necessary to display content incrementally. When implementing pagination, it is crucial to consider the user's context and provide intuitive cues. Clear labels and indicators should be used to guide users through the available pages. It is also essential to incorporate responsive design principles to ensure that pagination remains accessible and functional across different devices and screen sizes. Overall, pagination is an integral part of UI patterns and design systems. It allows users to navigate through content efficiently, breaks down information into easily digestible chunks, and improves the overall user experience by providing a more organized and structured interface.

Parallax Scrolling

Parallax scrolling is a UI pattern commonly used in web design that creates an illusion of depth by animating different layers of content at different speeds as the user scrolls down a webpage. This technique is often employed to enhance the visual experience and engagement of users. In a parallax scrolling design, the webpage is divided into multiple sections, each containing various elements such as images, text, and graphics. As the user scrolls, the elements within these sections move at different speeds, giving the impression of a three-dimensional space. This movement is achieved by manipulating the CSS property called "transform" with the "translate" function. The primary purpose of parallax scrolling is to make websites more visually appealing and interactive. By creating a dynamic and immersive experience, it captivates users and encourages them to explore the content further. Additionally, parallax scrolling is often utilized in storytelling websites or marketing campaigns to convey a narrative or evoke emotions. Implementing a parallax scrolling effect requires careful consideration of both design and performance aspects. It is important to strike a balance between aesthetics and usability, ensuring that the scrolling experience remains smooth and easy for users. Excessive or poorly implemented parallax scrolling can result in slower page loading times and negatively impact user experience, especially on mobile devices with limited resources. From a design system perspective, parallax scrolling is considered a design choice rather than a foundational component. It can be incorporated into a design system by defining guidelines and best practices for its usage within specific contexts. This may involve providing recommendations on the number of layers, animation duration, and types of elements suitable for parallax scrolling. In conclusion, parallax scrolling is a UI pattern used in web design that creates a sense of depth and interactivity by animating different layers of content at different speeds as the user scrolls. It enhances the visual experience and engagement, making websites more captivating and immersive. However, careful consideration should be given to ensure optimal performance and usability.

Password Change Form

A password change form is a user interface (UI) pattern and design system element that allows users to update their current password and set a new one. It typically includes fields for the current password, new password, and confirm password, along with a submit button to initiate the password change process. The purpose of a password change form is to provide a secure and convenient way for users to update their passwords, whether it's due to a security incident, password expiration, or simply a desire for a stronger password. By providing a dedicated form for this task, it helps to streamline the process and ensure that users can easily modify their passwords without confusion or error. In terms of UI design, a password change form should follow certain usability and accessibility guidelines to provide a seamless user experience. It should be visually consistent with the overall design system of the application or website, using appropriate typography, color palettes, and spacing to maintain visual harmony. The form should include clear and concise labels for each input field, communicating what type of information is required. It is essential to provide clear instructions on password requirements, such as minimum length, character requirements, and whether special characters or numbers are necessary. This helps users understand the criteria for a valid password and minimizes potential errors during the password change process. To enhance the security of the form, it is common to mask the characters of the current and new password fields, displaying bullets or asterisks instead of the actual characters. This ensures that passwords are not visible to others who may

211

be nearby. Additionally, using encryption protocols, such as HTTPS, is crucial to safeguard the transmission of sensitive data when the form is submitted. Overall, a well-designed password change form ensures that users can easily and securely update their passwords. By adhering to design system principles and usability guidelines, it facilitates a positive user experience and boosts confidence in the security of the application or website.

A password change form is a user interface (UI) pattern and design system element that allows users to update their current password and set a new one. It includes fields for the current password, new password, and confirm password, along with a submit button.

The form should be visually consistent with the design system, have clear labels, provide instructions on password requirements, mask characters in password fields, and use encryption protocols to ensure security.

Password Recovery Form

A Password Recovery Form is a user interface element that provides a means for users to regain access to their account by resetting their password. It is an essential component in any authentication system, as it helps users who have forgotten their passwords or suspect that their accounts have been compromised.

The Password Recovery Form typically consists of a simple and intuitive layout, designed to guide the user through the process of resetting their password. It should be easy to find and access, typically located on the login page or within the user account section of a website or application.

Upon clicking on the Password Recovery Form, users are usually prompted to provide some form of identification to verify their account ownership. This may include their registered email address or username. The form should clearly indicate the required fields and provide appropriate error messages in case of invalid input.

Once the identification step is completed, users are typically sent an email with a link or a temporary password to finalize the password recovery process. The form should provide clear instructions on what to expect after submitting the identification information and how to proceed with the next steps.

The design of the Password Recovery Form should prioritize usability and security. It should have a clean and uncluttered layout, with prominent fields for identification and clear instructions. Additionally, it is crucial to implement security measures to prevent unauthorized access to user accounts. This may include the use of CAPTCHA, email verification, or multi-factor authentication.

Password Reset Request Form

The Password Reset Request Form is a user interface (UI) pattern that is commonly used in design systems to enable users to request a new password in case they have forgotten their existing one. This form provides a straightforward and secure way for users to regain access to their account without compromising account security. In terms of UI design, the Password Reset Request Form typically includes the following elements: 1. Username or email field: This is where the user enters their username or email associated with their account. It is used to identify the user and send a reset link to their registered email address. 2. Submit button: Once the user has entered their username or email, they click on the submit button to initiate the password reset process. This action triggers an email to be sent to the user's registered email address with further instructions. To create a Password Reset Request Form in pure HTML format, you can use the following code:

Username or Email:

Submit</button>

In the first paragraph, we provide a brief definition of the Password Reset Request Form in the context of UI patterns and design systems. We explain its purpose and note that it allows users to request a new password if they have forgotten their existing one. In the second paragraph, we describe the common elements of the Password Reset Request Form, including the username or email field and the submit button. Finally, we provide the HTML code for creating a Password Reset Request Form using two

tags. The first

tag contains a label and an input field for the username or email, while the second

tag includes a submit button to initiate the password reset process. By following this design pattern and utilizing a Password Reset Request Form, designers can ensure a smooth and secure user experience when it comes to account password retrieval.>

Password Reset

A password reset refers to a user interface pattern and design system that allows users to regain access to their accounts when they forget their passwords. It is a crucial feature in many web applications, ensuring that users can easily recover their accounts and continue using the platform without requiring direct support. The password reset process typically follows a series of steps. First, the user realizes they have forgotten their password and clicks on the "Forgot password" link or button on the login page. This action triggers the initiation of the password reset flow. The user is then prompted to provide their email address or username associated with their account. Once the user submits their email address or username, the system validates their input and checks if it matches any registered accounts. If a match is found, the user is sent an automated email containing a unique link or a temporary password. This email serves as a security measure to verify the user's identity and prevents unauthorized access to their account. After receiving the email, the user clicks on the link provided or uses the temporary password to access a dedicated password reset page. This page typically prompts the user to enter a new password that meets certain security requirements such as minimum length and a combination of uppercase and lowercase letters, numbers, and special characters. Once the user submits their new password, the system updates it and confirms the password reset process. It is crucial to design the password reset flow with a focus on usability and security. Clear and concise instructions should be provided at each step to guide users through the process. Additionally, measures such as email validation and the requirements for a strong password help ensure the security of the account. Overall, the password reset feature is essential for web applications to provide a seamless and secure experience for users. By implementing this UI pattern and design system effectively, developers can enable users to regain access to their accounts while reducing the need for direct support.>

Password Strength Indicator

The Password Strength Indicator is a UI pattern and design system component that provides users with visual feedback on the strength of their chosen password. This feature typically appears on registration or password reset forms to assist users in creating secure passwords. The Password Strength Indicator assesses the strength of a password based on various criteria such as length, complexity, and combination of different character types (e.g., uppercase letters, lowercase letters, numbers, and special characters). The algorithm used to determine the strength can vary depending on the specific implementation and the desired level of security. The visual representation of password strength helps users make informed decisions when setting their passwords. Typically, the Password Strength Indicator consists of a progress bar or a color-coded indicator, which visually illustrates the strength level of the entered password. The progression or color change reflects the improvements in strength as the user creates a password that meets the desired criteria. For example, a weak password might be represented as a short progress bar or displayed in red, indicating that it does not meet the minimum requirements for security. As the user adds complexity to their password (e.g., by including numbers, special characters, or a mix of uppercase and lowercase letters), the progress bar grows longer or changes color to indicate a stronger password. The Password Strength Indicator helps users understand the impact of their password choices in terms of security. By providing real-time feedback, it encourages users to make stronger passwords that are more resistant to unauthorized access. This feature is especially important in the context of data breaches and growing concerns about online security. In summary, the Password Strength Indicator is a UI pattern and design system component that provides users with visual feedback on the strength of their chosen password. By visually representing the strength level, this feature helps users create secure passwords and enhance their account security.

Passwordless Authentication

Passwordless authentication refers to a method of user verification and access control that does not rely on traditional passwords. It is a UI pattern and design system that aims to simplify and enhance the authentication experience for users. In passwordless authentication, users are authenticated through alternative means, such as email, SMS, or biometrics, without the need for remembering and entering passwords. This approach eliminates the inconvenience and security risks associated with passwords, such as weak passwords, password reuse, and the need for regular password updates. The UI pattern for passwordless authentication typically involves the following steps: 1. User Initiation: Instead of entering a password, the user initiates the authentication process by providing their email address or phone number. 2. Verification Code: Once the user initiates the process, a unique verification code is generated and sent to the provided email address or phone number. The code serves as a temporary access token. 3. Code Entry: The user receives the verification code and enters it into a designated input field within the authentication UI. 4. Verification: The entered code is verified against the generated code to confirm the user's identity. 5. Access Granted: If the verification is successful, the user is granted access to the system or application. By implementing passwordless authentication as a design system, organizations can provide a more seamless and secure user experience. This design system should adhere to the following principles: 1. Simplicity: The design should be intuitive and easy to understand, ensuring that users can effortlessly complete the authentication process. 2. Accessibility: The UI should be accessible to users with disabilities, providing support for alternative input methods and assistive technologies. 3. Security: Although passwordless authentication reduces reliance on traditional passwords, it should still ensure the security of user accounts. Strong encryption and protection against common attack vectors, such as phishing, should be implemented. 4. Customization: The design system should be customizable to fit the organization's branding and visual identity. Passwordless authentication offers numerous benefits, including improved user experience, reduced support costs related to forgotten passwords, and enhanced security. By adopting this UI pattern and design system, organizations can provide a more secure and user-friendly authentication process.

Patient Registration Form

A patient registration form in the context of UI patterns and design systems is a structured system of input fields and instructions that allows a user to input and submit their personal and medical information in order to register as a patient with a healthcare provider or facility. The form typically follows a standardized design and layout that is consistent with the overall UI patterns and design system of the healthcare provider or facility's website or application.

The patient registration form is an essential component of the user experience when interacting with a healthcare provider or facility's website or application. It serves as the primary method for users to provide their personal information, such as name, date of birth, address, contact details, and insurance information, as well as their medical history and any relevant medical conditions or allergies.

Payment Information Form

A Payment Information Form is a user interface (UI) pattern that is used in design systems to collect and validate payment details from users during an online transaction. It is an essential component of e-commerce websites and applications, and it ensures the secure and efficient processing of payments. The Payment Information Form typically consists of various fields that require the user to input their payment details. These fields include the cardholder's name, card number, expiration date, and CVV or security code. Additionally, the form may also include fields for the billing address, email address, and phone number. Each field is labeled to provide clear instructions to the user and to improve the usability of the form. The design of the Payment Information Form is crucial as it directly impacts the user experience and the trust users place in the system. It is essential to employ best practices for layout, styling, and validation to ensure ease of use and security for the users. The layout of the Payment Information Form should be intuitive and visually pleasing. Using a single-column layout ensures that users can easily navigate through the form and complete it without confusion. Fields should be well-spaced to prevent accidental inputs and to improve readability. Styling the form with a consistent and easily recognizable color scheme helps users identify important elements such as required fields and error messages. Providing clear and concise error messages is essential, as it helps users rectify mistakes and verify the accuracy of their inputs. Validation plays a critical role in the Payment Information Form. It helps users input accurate and valid payment details, reducing the chances of transaction failures or fraud. Real-time validation can be implemented to provide immediate feedback on the entered card number, expiration date, and CVV. This feedback can include visual indicators such as green checkmarks or red crosses to indicate success or failure. To enhance security, it is recommended to implement encryption and SSL protocols to protect the user's payment information during transmission. Additionally, the design should include an option for users to securely save their payment details for future transactions, allowing for a convenient and time-saving experience. In conclusion, the Payment Information Form is a crucial UI pattern in design systems for collecting and validating payment details. By following best practices in layout, styling, and validation, the form can ensure a seamless and secure payment process for users in e-commerce applications.

Payment Method Selection Form

A Payment Method Selection Form is a user interface (UI) pattern that allows users to choose from a variety of payment methods when making a purchase or payment. It is an essential component of a design system that ensures consistency and usability across different interfaces and platforms. The Payment Method Selection Form typically includes a list of available payment options, such as credit/debit cards, mobile wallets, bank transfers, or alternative payment methods. Each payment method is presented as a selectable item, usually represented by an icon or logo, along with a label or description. The form may also include additional fields or options related to the selected payment method. For example, if the user chooses to pay with a credit card, they may be required to enter their card details, such as the card number, expiration date, and security code. Alternatively, if the user selects a mobile wallet like Apple Pay or Google Pay, they might be prompted to authenticate their payment using their device's biometric authentication. The Payment Method Selection Form should be designed in a way that is intuitive and accessible to all users. It should follow established UI design principles, such as using clear and descriptive labels, providing visual feedback on user interactions, and ensuring that the form is easy to navigate and complete. To achieve consistency and maintain a unified design language, it is important to incorporate the Payment Method Selection Form into the overall design system. This design system should include guidelines, components, and patterns for all aspects of the user interface, including typography, colors, spacing, and interaction behaviors. By adhering to the design system, designers and developers can ensure that the Payment Method Selection Form aligns with the overall brand identity and provides a seamless user experience across different devices and platforms. In conclusion, a Payment Method Selection Form is a crucial component of a design system that enables users to choose from various payment options when making a purchase. By following established UI patterns and integrating it into a cohesive design system, designers can create a user-friendly and consistent payment experience for their users.

Payment Plan Selection Form

A Payment Plan Selection Form is a user interface (UI) pattern that allows users to choose a payment plan option for a particular product or service. It is a part of a larger design system that ensures consistency and ease of use across different interfaces within an application. The Payment Plan Selection Form typically consists of a series of options presented to the user, along with relevant information such as the price, duration, and any additional benefits associated with each plan. The user can select one option from this list based on their preferences and requirements. The form should be designed in a clear and organized manner to facilitate easy decision-making for the user. Each plan option should be presented in a concise manner, using minimal text to convey the essential details. The use of concise language helps to keep the form visually appealing and prevents overwhelming the user with excessive information. A well-designed Payment Plan Selection Form should also incorporate visual cues to assist users in understanding the available options. This can be achieved through the use of clear headings, contrasting colors, and appropriate spacing between different elements. Visual cues allow users to quickly scan the available options and make an informed decision without much effort. Furthermore, the form should provide a clear call to action, such as a button labeled "Select Plan" or "Continue," that guides users to the next step in the payment process. This button should be visually distinct from other elements on the page, making it easy for users to identify and interact with. In summary, a Payment Plan Selection Form is an essential component of a design system that enables users to choose a payment plan for a product or service. It should be designed with clarity, simplicity, and visual cues to facilitate easy decision-making for users.>

Payment Screen

A payment screen is a crucial part of a user interface that is designed to facilitate the process of making payments for goods or services. It is a dedicated screen where users enter their payment details, such as credit card information, in order to complete a transaction. The payment screen is typically designed to be intuitive and user-friendly, with clear instructions and prompts to guide the user through the payment process. It may include fields for entering payment card details, such as the card number, expiration date, and security code, as well as options to select the billing address and payment method. In addition to the basic payment fields, the screen may also include additional features to enhance the user experience and security. This can include features like autofill for card details, real-time validation to ensure the entered information is correct, and secure encryption to protect sensitive payment data. The design of the payment screen is an important consideration in creating a consistent and cohesive user experience. It should align with the overall design system and user interface patterns to ensure that the payment process feels seamless and integrated with the rest of the application or website. Key principles in designing a payment screen include clarity, simplicity, and trustworthiness. The screen should clearly communicate what information is needed from the user and how to properly enter it. It should be designed in a simple and straightforward manner, avoiding unnecessary complexity or distractions. Additionally, the screen should instill a sense of trust and security in the user, through the use of recognizable payment icons, secure connection indicators, and clear privacy policies. Overall, a well-designed payment screen is crucial for a positive user experience and successful completion of transactions. It should strive to streamline the payment process, provide clear instructions and guidance, and inspire trust and confidence in the user. By following established UI patterns and design system guidelines, designers can create an effective and user-friendly payment screen.>

Personalization Widgets

Personalization Widgets refer to user interface (UI) components or elements that are specifically designed to provide customized and tailored experiences to users. These widgets are an integral part of UI patterns and design systems, enabling the creation of personalized interfaces that cater to the unique preferences and needs of individual users. The main purpose of Personalization Widgets is to enhance the user experience by presenting relevant content, features, and recommendations based on user data, behavior, and preferences. These widgets allow users to feel more engaged and connected with the application or website they are interacting with, as they receive personalized and curated information that is specifically tailored to their interests. Personalization Widgets can take various forms and can be implemented in different parts of the user interface. These may include personalized product recommendations based on previous purchases, personalized news feeds that display content based on user preferences, personalized advertisements that align with user interests, and personalized search suggestions that anticipate user intent. Design systems play a crucial role in the implementation and consistency of Personalization Widgets. By establishing a set of standardized UI elements and components, design systems ensure that Personalization Widgets are seamlessly integrated into the overall user interface. This consistency not only enhances the visual appeal of the interface but also contributes to a more intuitive and user-friendly experience. Furthermore, Personalization Widgets should be designed with careful consideration for user privacy and data protection. Collecting and utilizing user data for personalization purposes should be done transparently, with clear consent from the user and adherence to relevant regulations and best practices for data privacy and security. In conclusion, Personalization Widgets are UI components that enable the creation of personalized and customized experiences for users. By leveraging user data and preferences, these widgets provide tailored content and recommendations, enhancing user engagement and satisfaction. Design systems

216

play a vital role in ensuring the seamless integration and consistency of Personalization Widgets within the overall user interface.

Photo Gallery

A photo gallery is a user interface (UI) pattern commonly used in website and application design systems to display a collection of images. It provides a visually appealing and organized way to showcase multiple images in a single location. The main purpose of a photo gallery is to allow users to browse through and view images conveniently. It typically consists of a grid or a series of thumbnails representing each image. When a thumbnail is clicked or tapped, a larger version of the image is displayed, either in a modal window or within the same screen. In addition to viewing images, a photo gallery may offer additional functionality to enhance the user experience. This can include features such as zooming in on an image, navigating between images using navigation arrows or swipe gestures, and even providing options to share or download the images. These additional features contribute to the overall usability and user satisfaction of the photo gallery. When designing a photo gallery, it is important to consider various aspects to ensure an optimal user experience. This includes selecting an appropriate layout to display the images, choosing the right thumbnail size and aspect ratio, and implementing responsive design techniques to ensure the gallery scales well across different devices and screen sizes. Furthermore, accessibility should also be considered when designing a photo gallery. Providing alternative text for each image enables users with visual impairments to understand the content of the images. Keyboard navigation and clear focus states should also be implemented to ensure that users who rely on assistive technologies can navigate and interact with the gallery effectively. Overall, a photo gallery is an essential component of UI patterns and design systems. It provides a visually pleasing and user-friendly way to showcase a collection of images. By considering layout, responsiveness, accessibility, and additional functionality, designers can create a photo gallery that enhances the overall user experience and effectively presents the images to the audience.>

Podcast Player

A podcast player is a user interface (UI) pattern and component within a design system that allows users to discover, play, and manage audio content, specific to podcasts. It provides a dedicated space for users to engage with their favorite podcast shows, listen to episodes, and control various playback functionalities.

The primary function of a podcast player is to provide a seamless and intuitive user experience for consuming audio content. It typically consists of a prominent display area for podcast artwork, episode titles, and additional metadata such as duration and release date. This helps users quickly identify and select their desired podcast and episode to play.

Playback controls are an essential part of a podcast player. These controls, such as play, pause, rewind, fast forward, and skip, allow users to control the audio playback according to their preferences. Additionally, a progress bar or timeline provides a visual representation of the current position within the episode and allows users to navigate to specific moments in the content.

A well-designed podcast player also incorporates features that enhance the user experience. These include the ability to adjust playback speed, download episodes for offline listening, subscribe to new episodes, and create playlists or queues for continuous listening. Furthermore, it may offer options for sharing episodes with others or integrating with social media platforms.

In terms of UI design, a podcast player typically follows the design system's guidelines and principles to maintain consistency and accessibility across different platforms and devices. It should have a clear hierarchy of information, use appropriate typography, and employ visual cues such as icons or indicators to communicate various states and actions.

Overall, a podcast player is an integral component of a design system and is an essential tool for users to discover, listen, and engage with podcast content. Its purpose is to provide an intuitive and enjoyable experience, allowing users to easily navigate through episodes, control playback, and engage with additional features that enhance their overall listening experience.

217

Polls And Surveys

Polls and surveys are UI patterns commonly used in design systems to gather information and feedback from users. These patterns provide a structured and systematic approach to collect data by presenting a series of questions or statements for users to respond to.

A poll typically consists of a single question with multiple answer choices, allowing users to select one option that best represents their opinion or preference. The purpose of a poll is to quickly gather a snapshot of user sentiment or insights on a specific topic. Polls are often used to gauge public opinion, conduct market research, or make informed decisions based on user feedback.

On the other hand, a survey is a more comprehensive and in-depth form of data collection. It generally consists of multiple questions, varying in format and complexity, to collect detailed information on a specific topic or user experience. Surveys can include different types of questions such as multiple-choice, open-ended, rating scales, and more. They provide a more thorough understanding of user preferences, behaviors, and demographics.

When designing polls and surveys as part of a design system, it is important to consider several factors. Firstly, the questions should be clear, concise, and relevant to the purpose of the poll or survey. Unclear or ambiguous questions can lead to incorrect or inconsistent responses, affecting the validity of the collected data.

Secondly, the user interface and interaction design should be intuitive and user-friendly. Users should be able to navigate through the questions easily, understand the available response options, and provide their answers without confusion or frustration. Proper visual hierarchy, consistent styling, and logical flow are essential in ensuring a smooth user experience.

Lastly, consideration should be given to data privacy and ethics. Polls and surveys often involve the collection of personal or sensitive information. Designers should implement appropriate measures to protect user privacy, ensure informed consent, and adhere to relevant data protection regulations.

By incorporating polls and surveys into a design system, organizations and designers can gather valuable insights, feedback, and data to inform decision-making, improve user experiences, and drive innovation.

Pop-Out Navigation

The Pop-Out Navigation is a UI pattern commonly used in web design to present a set of navigation links or menu options in a compact and unobtrusive manner. It typically appears as a small button or icon that, when clicked or hovered over, expands into a panel or overlay displaying the navigation items. The main purpose of a Pop-Out Navigation is to declutter the interface and provide a more focused and immersive user experience. By hiding the navigation options until they are needed, this pattern helps free up screen real estate and avoids overwhelming the user with a large number of options at once. When implemented effectively, a Pop-Out Navigation can enhance usability by allowing users to quickly access the desired content or functionality without interrupting their workflow. It provides a hierarchical organization of options, enabling users to navigate through different levels or categories. This pattern is particularly beneficial for websites or applications with complex information architectures or extensive menu structures. From a design system perspective, the Pop-Out Navigation should maintain consistency with the overall visual language and branding of the interface. It should align with the chosen color scheme, typography, and iconography to create a seamless and cohesive experience. Additionally, the behavior of the pop-out panel, such as animation or transition effects, should be thoughtfully designed to ensure a smooth and intuitive interaction. In terms of implementation, a Pop-Out Navigation can be created using various front-end technologies such as HTML, CSS, and JavaScript. The HTML structure typically consists of a container element that holds the navigation button/icon and the hidden panel. CSS is then used to style the elements and control their positioning and visibility. JavaScript is often employed to add interactivity, handling the toggle or expansion of the navigation panel when the button/icon is interacted with. In conclusion, the Pop-Out Navigation is a UI pattern that offers a compact and space-saving way to present navigation options in web interfaces. It helps enhance the user experience by organizing the menu hierarchy and keeping the interface clutter-free. Following the principles of a design system, the implementation of this pattern should align with the overall visual language and functionality of the interface.

Portfolio Showcase

A portfolio showcase refers to a collection of design projects, typically presented in a visually appealing and organized manner with the goal of highlighting the skills, creativity, and expertise of the designer or design team. It serves as a representation of their past work and serves as a tool to demonstrate their abilities to potential clients or employers. In the context of UI patterns and design systems, a portfolio showcase can be seen as an integral part of showcasing the application of various UI patterns and the consistency of a design system. It allows designers to present their work systematically and emphasizes their ability to create coherent and user-friendly interfaces. A portfolio showcase often includes screenshots or images of the design projects, detailed descriptions of each project, and sometimes additional information such as the design process, challenges faced, and solutions implemented. By including projects that cover a wide range of industries and design challenges, the showcase demonstrates the designer's versatility and adaptability. A well-organized portfolio showcase follows a clear structure and layout, making it easy for viewers to navigate through the projects and find the information they are looking for. It should feature a visually appealing design that reflects the designer's branding and aesthetic preferences, while also ensuring that the focus remains on the showcased projects rather than overwhelming visual elements. Furthermore, a portfolio showcase should effectively communicate the designer's thought process, problem-solving abilities, and attention to detail. It should provide insights into the rationale behind design decisions and demonstrate the designer's understanding of user-centered design principles. In summary, a portfolio showcase in the context of UI patterns and design systems is a curated collection of design projects that serves as a visual representation of a designer's skills and expertise. It allows designers to demonstrate their ability to apply UI patterns and maintain consistency within a design system. A well-organized and visually appealing portfolio showcase effectively communicates the designer's thought process, problem-solving abilities, and attention to detail.>

Prescription Request Form

A Prescription Request Form is a UI pattern that allows users to request medication prescriptions from healthcare providers. It is commonly used in online healthcare platforms or websites where users can schedule appointments, communicate with healthcare professionals, and request prescription refills. The Prescription Request Form typically consists of several input fields and options that users need to fill out in order to submit their prescription request. These fields often include personal information, such as name, date of birth, and contact information, as well as specific details about the medication needed, such as the drug name, dosage, and quantity. The design of the Prescription Request Form follows a formal and structured approach to ensure accuracy and efficiency in the prescription request process. The form is typically divided into sections or steps, guiding the user through the required information. This helps to prevent errors or omissions and allows healthcare providers to gather all necessary details in a systematic manner. The overall layout of the Prescription Request Form is carefully designed to be user-friendly and accessible. Clear labels and instructions are provided for each input field, ensuring that users understand what information is required. Additionally, the form may include validation methods to ensure that the entered information meets the necessary criteria, such as proper formatting for phone numbers or email addresses. In terms of aesthetics, the Prescription Request Form often adopts a clean and minimalist design, focusing on simplicity and clarity. This helps users to easily locate the required fields and complete the form without any distractions or confusion. Furthermore, the Prescription Request Form is typically integrated into a larger design system or user interface (UI) pattern, maintaining consistency with the overall visual style and interaction patterns of the platform or website. This ensures a seamless and cohesive user experience, as users navigate between different sections of the platform, such as appointment scheduling or messaging with healthcare providers. Overall, the Prescription Request Form is an essential UI pattern in online healthcare platforms, facilitating the process of requesting medication prescriptions from healthcare providers. Its structured and user-friendly design ensures accuracy and efficiency, while integration into a larger design system maintains visual consistency and a cohesive user experience on the platform.

A Prescription Request Form is a UI pattern that allows users to request medication prescriptions from healthcare providers.

The form follows a formal and structured approach with input fields for personal information and medication details, ensuring accuracy and efficiency. It is integrated into a larger design system, maintaining visual consistency and a seamless user experience.

Press Mentions

Press Mentions are references or citations of a company, product, or service in various media outlets such as newspapers, magazines, websites, and blogs. These mentions can include articles, reviews, interviews, and other forms of coverage that discuss or highlight the entity in question. In the context of UI patterns and design systems, press mentions refer to the recognition and acknowledgment received by a company or its design system in the media.

Press mentions in the realm of UI patterns and design systems can serve multiple purposes. They can help raise awareness and visibility of a company's design system, demonstrating its value and relevance to the broader design community. Press mentions can also validate the quality and effectiveness of a design system as they are often the result of positive reviews or endorsements by industry experts or influential designers.

Pricing Tables

Pricing Tables are a UI pattern that are commonly used in design systems to present various pricing options for products or services in a structured and visually appealing manner. They are typically displayed as a grid or a list, with each option organized in a separate column or row. The purpose of Pricing Tables is to provide users with an easy-to-understand comparison of different pricing plans or packages, enabling them to make an informed decision based on their needs and budget. Each option within the table includes key features, benefits, and pricing details, allowing users to evaluate the value they would receive for each plan. Pricing Tables often include the following elements: 1. Plan Name: This is the name or label for each pricing option, typically indicating different tiers or levels of service. The plan names should be clear and concise, reflecting the distinguishing features of each package. 2. Features: The features section outlines the key functionalities or services provided in each plan. It is important to highlight the unique features and benefits of each package, emphasizing what sets them apart from one another. 3. Pricing Details: This section displays the pricing information for each plan, including the cost, payment frequency (e.g., monthly or annually), and any additional charges or discounts. It is essential to clearly present the pricing structure and any limitations or restrictions associated with each plan. 4. Call-to-Action (CTA): Each pricing option should include a prominent CTA button or link that encourages users to take action. The CTA might say "Choose Plan," "Buy Now," or "Sign Up," directing users to the next step in the conversion process. By implementing Pricing Tables in a design system, designers and developers can ensure consistency in the presentation of pricing information across different products or services. This allows users to easily compare options and make a confident decision, ultimately increasing conversions and customer satisfaction. Overall, Pricing Tables serve as a practical and effective tool for presenting pricing plans and options in a user-friendly way. Their structured format and clear information hierarchy help users make informed decisions when selecting the best package for their needs.>

Privacy Policy Acceptance Form

The Privacy Policy Acceptance Form is a UI pattern used to present users with a clear and concise summary of the privacy policy of a website or application, and to obtain their explicit consent to proceed. This form is an essential part of any design system as it ensures that users are informed about the data collection, usage, and sharing practices of a platform before they engage with it.

The Privacy Policy Acceptance Form typically includes key sections such as a brief introduction explaining the purpose of the form, a summary of the main points of the privacy policy, and a statement asking users to indicate their agreement. It may also include links to the full privacy policy document for users who wish to review it in detail.

Privacy Policy Link

A Privacy Policy Link is a user interface element and an essential part of a design system for a website or application. It is a formal statement or document that informs users about how their personal information is collected, used, and shared by the website or application. The Privacy Policy Link is typically placed in the footer or header of the user interface for easy access.

The purpose of the Privacy Policy Link is to provide transparency and establish trust between the platform and its users. It helps users understand how their personal data will be treated and gives them control over their privacy. The link should be easily visible and accessible to users, allowing them to review the privacy policy at any time.

Privacy Settings

Privacy settings refer to the options and controls offered to users within a user interface (UI) to manage their personal information, visibility, and data security. These settings are an essential part of the design system and UI patterns to ensure that users have control over their privacy and can customize their experience based on their preferences. UI patterns are predefined solutions to common design problems that provide a consistent and familiar experience for users. In the context of privacy settings, UI patterns are used to present and organize the available options in a logical and easy-to-understand way. These patterns help users navigate and configure their privacy settings efficiently while maintaining clarity and transparency. Design systems, on the other hand, are a collection of reusable components, guidelines, and rules that govern the visual and functional aspects of an interface. Privacy settings are a crucial part of a design system, as they need to be consistent across different screens and platforms to provide a cohesive user experience. The design system ensures that privacy settings are implemented consistently and adhere to the overall aesthetics and usability of the UI. The purpose of privacy settings is to empower users to control their privacy and make informed decisions about the information they share. These settings typically include options such as managing visibility, controlling data collection and usage, and choosing sharing preferences. By offering these settings, UI patterns and design systems ensure that users feel confident and in control of their personal information within the interface. To implement privacy settings in a UI, designers need to consider the following principles: 1. Transparency: Clear and concise descriptions should be provided for each setting, explaining the implications and consequences of selecting a particular option. Users should have a clear understanding of what they are consenting to. 2. Granularity: Privacy settings should offer a range of options, allowing users to customize their preferences to the level of detail that suits them. For example, users might want to specify the visibility of certain information to specific groups or individuals. By adhering to these principles, privacy settings within UI patterns and design systems offer users the necessary control over their privacy while ensuring a consistent and intuitive user experience. They contribute to building trust and confidence in the interface, enabling users to engage with the system in a manner that aligns with their individual privacy needs and preferences.>

Product Cards

Product Cards are a commonly used UI pattern in web design systems that aim to showcase information and details about specific products in a visually appealing and organized manner. These cards provide a consistent and structured layout that enables users to quickly understand and compare different products. The main purpose of product cards is to provide an overview and highlight the key features of a product, making it easier for users to make informed decisions. Each product card typically contains a combination of text, images, and occasionally interactive elements such as buttons or dropdowns. In terms of structure, product cards usually consist of a fixed container with a defined width and height, creating a grid-like layout when multiple cards are displayed side by side. This helps maintain a consistent and balanced arrangement of content across different screen sizes. The visual design of product cards often follows the brand's guidelines and visual identity. Color schemes, typography, and imagery are carefully chosen to create a cohesive and visually appealing user interface. The use of whitespace, borders, and shadows helps separate different sections within the card, providing a clear visual hierarchy and aiding in content organization. Product cards typically include essential information such as the product name, price, rating, and a brief description. These details are often accompanied by visually appealing images that showcase the product from

221

different angles or in various contexts. Additionally, some product cards may include user reviews or ratings to provide social proof and build trust. To enhance the user experience, product cards may incorporate interactive elements such as buttons for adding products to a shopping cart or wishlist. These buttons often use familiar icons or labels to clearly indicate their purpose and functionality. In summary, product cards are a fundamental UI pattern used in design systems for displaying and organizing information about products. They provide a visually appealing and structured layout that allows users to quickly evaluate and compare different products based on key features and details. Creating consistent and visually engaging product cards can significantly enhance the overall user experience and contribute to a successful design system.

Product Cards are a commonly used UI pattern in web design systems that aim to showcase information and details about specific products in a visually appealing and organized manner. These cards provide a consistent and structured layout that enables users to quickly understand and compare different products.

The main purpose of product cards is to provide an overview and highlight the key features of a product, making it easier for users to make informed decisions. Each product card typically contains a combination of text, images, and occasionally interactive elements such as buttons or dropdowns.

Product Comparison Form

The Product Comparison Form is a UI pattern and design system component that allows users to compare multiple products side by side based on various features, specifications, and attributes. This form provides a structured and organized layout for presenting product information in a clear and visually appealing manner. The main purpose of the Product Comparison Form is to help users make informed decisions by easily comparing the key characteristics and details of different products. It assists users in evaluating and selecting the most suitable option that meets their needs and preferences. The form typically consists of a table-like structure where each row represents a specific feature or attribute, and each column corresponds to a different product. The top row usually displays the product names or images, while the leftmost column contains the feature labels or descriptions. The cells in the intersection of rows and columns contain the relevant information or data associated with each feature for each product. The Product Comparison Form provides a consistent and systematic arrangement of information, allowing users to quickly scan and compare the product details. It enables users to easily identify similarities and differences between the products, facilitating effective decision-making. This UI pattern often includes interactive elements such as checkboxes or radio buttons to allow users to select the products they want to compare. Users can choose specific products from a list or search for them using a search bar or dropdown menu. This flexibility in product selection enhances usability and customization. Additionally, the Product Comparison Form may include sorting or filtering options to help users prioritize and organize the information based on their needs. Users can sort the products based on specific features or criteria, such as price, ratings, or availability. Overall, the Product Comparison Form is a valuable component of UI patterns and design systems that simplifies the decision-making process for users. Its structured layout, interactive elements, and sorting options enable users to efficiently compare and evaluate multiple products, ultimately leading to a more informed purchasing decision.

The Product Comparison Form is a UI pattern and design system component that allows users to compare multiple products side by side based on various features, specifications, and attributes. The form provides a structured and organized layout for presenting product information in a clear and visually appealing manner. It helps users make informed decisions by easily comparing the key characteristics and details of different products. The form consists of a table-like structure where each row represents a specific feature or attribute, and each column corresponds to a different product. The top row displays the product names or images, while the leftmost column contains the feature labels or descriptions. Interactive elements such as checkboxes or radio buttons enable users to select the products they want to compare, and sorting or filtering options help users prioritize and organize the information based on their needs.

Product Comparisons

Product comparisons in the context of UI patterns and design systems refer to the visual representation and arrangement of information to enable users to analyze and contrast multiple products or options. In a design system, product comparisons typically involve the use of consistent and standardized components and layouts to present key details and features of different products side by side. These components may include tables, cards, or grids that display relevant information such as product names, descriptions, prices, ratings, and specifications. The purpose of product comparisons is to aid users in making informed decisions by allowing them to easily understand the similarities and differences among different options. By presenting information in a structured and visually organized manner, users can quickly scan and analyze the features of each product, enabling them to determine which one best meets their needs. HTML is a powerful tool for creating product comparison interfaces within design systems. One approach to representing product comparisons in HTML is to create a table structure. Each row of the table represents a different product, while each column corresponds to a specific attribute or feature. The table can be styled using CSS to enhance readability and ensure consistency with the overall design system. Here is an example of how a simple product comparison table can be created using HTML:

Product Comparison Table:

Product 1 | Product 2 | Product 3

Feature 1 | Feature 1 | Feature 1

Feature 2 | Feature 2 | Feature 2

Feature 3 | Feature 3 | Feature 3

Price | Price | Price

Rating | Rating | Rating

In this example, three products are compared based on three features: Feature 1, Feature 2, and Feature 3. The table also includes information on the price and rating of each product. The use of horizontal lines helps to visually separate the different sections of the table, making it easier for users to comprehend and navigate the comparison. By leveraging HTML to structure and organize product comparisons, design systems can provide users with a clear and concise overview of different options, facilitating their decision-making process.>

Product Configuration Form

A Product Configuration Form is a user interface pattern and design system used to collect and organize user input for customizing and personalizing a particular product or service. This form allows users to select different options or configurations based on their preferences or specific requirements. The primary purpose of a Product Configuration Form is to guide users through the process of customizing a product, ensuring that they provide all necessary information and make informed choices. It serves as a medium for capturing user preferences and specifications, guiding them towards their desired outcome. A Product Configuration Form typically consists of various input fields, checkboxes, dropdown menus, or other interactive elements to allow users to select or enter their desired options. These input fields are organized and grouped logically to enhance usability and maintain a clear flow of information. The form may also include labels, tooltips, or help text to provide additional context or guidance to the users. This helps them understand the purpose of each input and make informed decisions. Validation and error messages are included to ensure that users enter valid and complete information, reducing the likelihood of errors. In terms of design, a Product Configuration Form adheres to the overall design system or visual language of the product or service it represents. It maintains consistency in terms of visual elements such as colors, typography, and layout to ensure a seamless user experience. Furthermore, a Product Configuration Form can be responsive, adapting to different screen sizes and devices to ensure accessibility across platforms. It should be designed with a focus on usability and accessibility, ensuring that users with disabilities can also interact with it effectively. In summary, a Product Configuration Form is a user interface pattern and design system that allows users to customize and personalize a product or service. It guides users through the process of selecting options, capturing their preferences, and ensuring a seamless and user-friendly experience.>

Product Configurators

Product Configurators are UI patterns and design systems that allow users to customize and personalize products according to their specific preferences and requirements. A product configurator typically consists of a set of interactive elements and controls, such as dropdown menus, checkboxes, sliders, and input fields. These elements are designed to give users a wide range of options for customizing various aspects of a product, such as color, size, material, features, and more. The purpose of a product configurator is to simplify the customization process for users, making it easy and intuitive for them to choose the exact specifications they desire. By providing a dynamic and interactive interface, product configurators enable users to visualize the changes they make in real-time, ensuring a seamless and enjoyable user experience. Design systems play a crucial role in the development of product configurators. They provide a consistent and cohesive set of design elements, patterns, and guidelines that ensure a harmonious and visually appealing interface. Design systems also facilitate scalability and maintainability, as they define reusable components and patterns that can be easily extended and updated. When designing a product configurator, UI designers should consider several factors to optimize usability and effectiveness. These include: 1. Clear and intuitive navigation: The configurator should have a clear and logical flow, guiding users through the customization process step by step. It should be easy for users to understand their current progress and navigate back and forth between different customization options. 2. Visual feedback: Real-time visual feedback is essential to help users understand the impact of their customization choices. For example, when a user selects a different color option, the configurator should show the product image or representation with the updated color. 3. Error prevention and validation: The configurator should include proper error prevention and validation mechanisms to ensure that users input valid and acceptable values. Clear error messages and prompts should be provided to help users correct any mistakes or inconsistencies. In conclusion, product configurators are powerful tools that allow users to personalize and customize products according to their preferences. By incorporating design systems and adhering to established UI patterns, product configurators can provide a seamless and visually appealing user experience.>

Product Detail Screen

The Product Detail Screen is a user interface pattern that provides detailed information about a specific product within a design system. It typically displays all the relevant details, features, specifications, and images related to the product in a structured and organized manner.

This screen serves as a central hub for users to gather comprehensive information about the product before making a purchase decision. It helps users evaluate the product's suitability, performance, and quality based on their specific needs and preferences.

Product Feedback Form

A product feedback form is a user interface (UI) pattern that allows users to provide feedback on a product or service. It is an essential component of a design system, which is a collection of reusable UI elements, patterns, and guidelines that helps maintain consistency and improves the user experience across different products and platforms. The feedback form typically consists of a set of fields where users can enter their feedback, along with additional fields to capture relevant information such as their name, email address, and the specific product or feature they are providing feedback on. The form may also include optional fields to gather more detailed information or allow users to upload screenshots or other supporting files. The main purpose of a product feedback form is to gather valuable insights and opinions from users, which can be used to improve the product or service. By providing a structured way for users to share their thoughts and concerns, the feedback form ensures that important feedback is captured in a systematic manner. In terms of UI design, the feedback form should be easy to find and access within the product or website. It should have a clear and intuitive layout that guides users through the process of providing feedback. The form should use appropriate labels and placeholders to clearly indicate what information is required in each field. To ensure a positive user experience, it is important to keep the feedback form simple and concise. Avoid overwhelming users with too many fields or complex questions. Instead, focus on capturing the most relevant information that will help address the user's feedback. In conclusion, a product feedback form is a UI pattern that allows users to provide feedback on a product or service. It is an integral part of a design system, ensuring consistency and improving the user experience. The form should be easily accessible, have a clear and intuitive layout, and gather relevant information while keeping it simple and concise.>

Product Highlight Reels

Product Highlight Reels are UI patterns commonly used in design systems to showcase the key features or highlights of a product or service. They effectively communicate the core offerings and benefits to users in a visually appealing and concise manner. The Product Highlight Reels design pattern typically consists of a series of cards or tiles that display a short description or title, accompanied by an image or icon representing the product feature. Each card is usually arranged in a grid or carousel format, allowing users to easily navigate through the different highlights. These reels are designed to capture the attention of users and provide a quick overview of the product's key features. They serve as a visual summary, enticing users to explore further or consider purchasing the product. By condensing the information into bite-sized chunks, Product Highlight Reels effectively communicate the main selling points and advantages of the product, making it easier for users to understand its value proposition. The design of Product Highlight Reels is often kept clean, with minimal text and a focus on eye-catching visuals. The use of images or icons that represent each feature helps users quickly grasp the main ideas without getting overwhelmed by text-heavy descriptions. The reel format allows for easy scrolling or swiping, enhancing the user experience and enabling effortless navigation through the different features. From a design system perspective, Product Highlight Reels offer consistency and coherence across different pages or sections of a product website or application. They provide a standardized way of presenting information, ensuring that users have a familiar and intuitive experience regardless of where they encounter the highlights. This contributes to a cohesive and seamless overall design, enhancing brand recognition and trust. In conclusion, Product Highlight Reels are UI patterns that effectively showcase the key features and benefits of a product or service. Through visually appealing and concise presentations, they capture user attention and communicate the core offerings. Incorporating these design patterns in a design system allows for consistency and coherence, creating a seamless and intuitive experience for users.

Product Recall Request Form

A Product Recall Request Form is a user interface (UI) pattern and design system that allows users to request the recall of a specific product. This form is typically used by customers who have purchased a product that is faulty, defective, or poses a risk to their health or safety. The main purpose of a Product Recall Request Form is to provide a structured and efficient way for customers to report any issues they have encountered with a product. This form helps to streamline the recall process for both the customers and the company by collecting all the necessary information in a standardized format. The design of a Product Recall Request Form should be user-friendly and intuitive, helping customers easily navigate through the form and provide the required information. It is important to make the form visually appealing and accessible to all users, including those with disabilities. Typically, a Product Recall Request Form includes fields to capture the following information: 1. Contact Information: This section requires users to enter their full name, phone number, email address, and sometimes their physical address. This information is essential for the company to contact the customer and communicate any updates or resolutions regarding the product recall. 2. Product Details: This section requires users to provide specific details about the product, including its name, model number, date of purchase, and any other relevant information. This helps the company identify the affected product and take appropriate actions. Additionally, a Product Recall Request Form may include optional fields for users to provide additional details or describe the issue they have encountered. It may also include a text box for users to attach any supporting documents or images related to the product recall request. In conclusion, a Product Recall Request Form is a

UI pattern and design system that enables customers to report issues and request the recall of a faulty or defective product. It helps streamline the recall process by collecting all the necessary information in a structured and user-friendly manner.>

Product Recommendation Engine

A Product Recommendation Engine is a user interface (UI) pattern that allows a system to suggest relevant products to users based on their preferences, behavior, or characteristics. It is an integral part of a design system and can greatly enhance the user experience by providing personalized recommendations. The purpose of a Product Recommendation Engine is to assist users in discovering products they may be interested in, increasing the likelihood of conversions and customer satisfaction. This engine utilizes algorithms that analyze user data, such as browsing history, purchase history, and demographic information, to generate recommendations that are tailored to the individual user. In terms of UI patterns, a Product Recommendation Engine is typically integrated into the product listing or detail pages of an e-commerce website or application. It can be showcased in various formats, such as a "Recommended for You" section, a "Customers also bought" carousel, or a personalized homepage showcasing relevant products. A well-designed Product Recommendation Engine should have a visually appealing and intuitive user interface. It should seamlessly blend with the overall design system and maintain consistency with other UI elements. The product recommendations should be displayed in a clear and organized manner, ensuring that users can easily differentiate between various suggestions. The design system for a Product Recommendation Engine should focus on maintaining a balance between providing relevant recommendations and avoiding overwhelming the user with too many choices. It should also prioritize displaying products that are most likely to engage the user and align with their preferences. To achieve a cohesive user experience, the design system should consider factors such as color schemes, typography, and layout consistency across different devices and screen sizes. In conclusion, a Product Recommendation Engine is a UI pattern that aims to enhance the user experience by suggesting relevant products to users based on their preferences. It is an integral part of a design system and requires careful consideration of UI elements to ensure usability, coherence, and effectiveness.>

Product Return Request Form

A Product Return Request Form is a user interface (UI) pattern and design system that allows users to request the return of a product they have purchased from a company. This form serves as a standardized way for users to communicate their desire to return a product and provides the necessary fields and information for the company to process the request efficiently. The form consists of various input fields, checkboxes, and text areas to capture the required information from the user. This may include the user's contact details, order information, reason for the return, and any additional comments or instructions. The design of the form should be clean, organized, and intuitive, guiding the user through the process seamlessly. The UI pattern should adhere to established design principles and best practices to ensure usability and accessibility for users. It should have clear labels and instructions for each field, using descriptive and concise language to avoid confusion. The form should also provide informative error messages if the user fails to complete the required fields correctly or if there are any issues with the submission. The design system for the Product Return Request Form should align with the overall branding and visual identity of the company. This includes the use of consistent typography, color schemes, and imagery. The form should be responsive and adaptable to different screen sizes and devices, allowing users to complete the request on desktop computers, laptops, tablets, and mobile phones. The form should have a clear submission button that is prominently displayed and labeled appropriately, such as "Submit" or "Request Return." Once the user submits the form, they should receive a confirmation message indicating that their request has been received and is being processed. Overall, the Product Return Request Form is an essential component of any e-commerce or customer service-oriented website. It provides a straightforward and user-friendly way for users to initiate the return process and ensures that the company can efficiently handle these requests.>

Product Review Form

A product review form is a common UI pattern used in design systems to collect feedback and

226

opinions from users about a specific product. It provides a structured way for users to share their experiences, thoughts, and ratings regarding the product. The form typically includes various fields and components such as text inputs, rating scales, checkboxes, and text areas. These elements allow users to provide specific details about different aspects of the product, such as its usability, functionality, design, and overall satisfaction. By collecting this information, businesses and product teams can gain valuable insights into user opinions and preferences, helping them make informed decisions for future improvements or updates. In terms of design, product review forms should be visually appealing, intuitive, and easy to navigate. The layout should be well-organized and clearly indicate the purpose of each field or component. Labels and placeholder text can be used to guide users in providing the required information. Additionally, proper validation should be implemented to ensure that the data entered is accurate and complete. Furthermore, it is essential to consider the mobile responsiveness of the product review form. As a growing number of users access websites and applications from their mobile devices, having a form that adapts seamlessly to different screen sizes and resolutions is crucial for a positive user experience. Overall, a well-designed product review form is a valuable tool in gathering user feedback, which can be used to improve and enhance products. By implementing this UI pattern as part of a design system, businesses can maintain consistency and ensure that users have a seamless experience across different platforms and touchpoints.

A product review form is a structured UI pattern that collects user feedback about a specific product. It includes various fields and components like text inputs, rating scales, and checkboxes. The form helps businesses gain insights into user opinions and preferences, aiding in future improvements. The design should be visually appealing, intuitive, and responsive for different devices.

Product Support Form

A Product Support Form is a user interface pattern that is part of a design system commonly used in websites and applications. It serves as a means for users to reach out for assistance or to report issues they may be encountering with a particular product or service. The purpose of a Product Support Form is to facilitate communication between users and product support teams. It typically consists of a set of input fields where users can provide their contact information, describe the problem they are facing or the question they have, and submit the form for further processing. The design of a Product Support Form aims to offer a simple and intuitive user experience. It should be easy to locate and navigate to the form, ensuring that users can quickly access the support they need. The form itself should be visually appealing, with clear labels and descriptive placeholders for each input field. To enhance usability, a Product Support Form may include validation mechanisms to ensure that users provide the necessary information in the correct format. Error messages can be displayed inline or below the respective input field, helping users identify and correct any mistakes they have made before submitting the form. Once a user completes and submits a Product Support Form, the information entered is typically sent to a support team for further review and action. Depending on the system and workflow in place, the submission may trigger an automatic acknowledgement email, redirect users to a confirmation page, or display a success message within the form itself. In conclusion, a Product Support Form is an essential component of a design system that allows users to seek assistance or report issues they may be experiencing with a particular product or service. It serves as a bridge between the users and the support team, enabling efficient communication and problem resolution.

A Product Support Form is a UI pattern used for users to reach out for assistance or report issues with a product or service.

It allows users to provide their contact information, describe the problem, and submit the form for review by the support team.

Product Thumbnails

Product thumbnails refer to small images or representations of products that are typically displayed in a consistent manner within a user interface (UI). They are commonly used in e-commerce websites and other digital platforms to provide a visual preview of products to users. These thumbnails are an integral part of UI patterns and design systems as they help users quickly browse and evaluate products. They serve as an entry point for users to engage with individual products and are designed to capture their attention. The main purpose of product thumbnails is to entice users to click on them for further information or to make a purchase. In terms of UI patterns, product thumbnails are commonly used in grid layouts or carousels, where they are organized in a systematic and visually appealing manner. They are often displayed in a consistent aspect ratio and size to create a cohesive and organized user experience. The placement of product thumbnails within a UI is essential for guiding users' attention and ensuring easy navigation. Design systems play a crucial role in determining the visual style and elements of product thumbnails. They define the specific guidelines for image sizes, shapes, and aspect ratios to maintain consistency throughout the interface. Consistent styling and placement of product thumbnails enhance the overall visual appeal of the UI and contribute to the recognition and familiarity of the brand. Product thumbnails should be visually appealing, high-quality images that accurately represent the product. They should showcase the key features and details of the product, such as its color, design, or packaging. Additionally, thumbnails may also include additional information, such as the product name, price, or rating, to help users make informed decisions. Overall, product thumbnails are essential UI elements that provide users with a preview of products within an interface. They serve as visual cues that entice users to click and explore further, making them an integral part of effective e-commerce and other digital platforms. Product thumbnails enhance the user experience and help users make informed decisions by providing a visual preview of products within an interface. They are a crucial component of UI patterns and design systems, ensuring consistency and visual appeal throughout the interface.>

Product Warranty Registration Form

A product warranty registration form is a user interface pattern or design system component that allows users to register their purchased products in order to activate and/or extend the warranty period.

This type of form typically contains a set of fields that users need to fill out, such as their personal information (name, contact details), the product details (model, serial number), purchase information (date, location), and any other relevant information required by the warranty provider. Users may also be prompted to attach proof of purchase, such as a scanned receipt or invoice.

The purpose of the product warranty registration form is twofold. Firstly, it allows users to easily provide the necessary information to the warranty provider, ensuring that their product is officially registered and eligible for warranty coverage. Secondly, it helps the warranty provider to gather important data about their customers and products, including purchase trends, product performance, and customer satisfaction.

The design of a product warranty registration form should prioritize simplicity and ease of use. It should be visually appealing and clearly communicate the purpose of each field. The form should be logically structured, with related fields grouped together and labeled clearly. It is also important to minimize the number of mandatory fields to avoid overwhelming the user with unnecessary requirements.

Additionally, the form should provide helpful instructions and guidance to assist users in filling out the required information accurately. This can be achieved through the use of placeholder text, tooltips, or inline help text. Error checking should be implemented to validate user inputs in real-time and provide meaningful error messages to assist users in correcting any mistakes.

Furthermore, it is recommended to leverage autocomplete or autofill functionality to streamline the data entry process for returning customers, reducing the effort required to complete the form.

In conclusion, a product warranty registration form is an important component of a user interface pattern or design system that facilitates the registration of purchased products for warranty purposes. By ensuring a user-friendly design and providing clear instructions, this form enhances the user experience and helps warranty providers collect valuable data.

Profile Cards

Profile Cards are a common UI pattern used in design systems to display information about a specific entity or user. They are typically used in social media platforms, online communities, or websites with user profiles. Profile Cards serve as a concise and organized way to showcase key details or attributes of a person, company, or any other entity. They provide a snapshot of relevant information that allows users to quickly get a sense of who or what they are viewing. In terms of design, Profile Cards usually consist of a compact, rectangular container that contains several fields or sections. The card might include an avatar or profile picture, along with the name or username of the entity being displayed. Additional information can also be shown, such as a short bio, location, job title, or any other relevant details. When it comes to the HTML structure of a Profile Card, it is important to maintain a consistent and semantic markup. The main container div of the card can have a class or id for easy styling purposes. Each section within the Profile Card can be wrapped in a paragraph tag, allowing for a clean and straightforward structure. Using semantic HTML elements like paragraph tags ensures that the content is properly structured and accessible. This helps search engines interpret and index the information accurately, improving the overall SEO performance of the website. Profile Cards can be styled using CSS to align with the overall design system or branding guidelines. The layout, typography, color scheme, and spacing should be consistent with the rest of the user interface for a cohesive and harmonious look. In conclusion, Profile Cards are a key component of user interface design systems, providing a concise and visually appealing way to present information about a specific entity. By utilizing semantic HTML and consistent styling, Profile Cards not only enhance the user experience but also contribute to the overall accessibility and findability of the digital product.

Profile Completion Progress

Profile completion progress refers to the visual representation of the user's progress in completing their profile information or tasks within a user interface (UI) pattern or design system. It provides a clear indication of how much of the profile is complete and encourages users to fill out the necessary information or complete the required tasks. In UI patterns, profile completion progress bars or indicators are commonly used to show users the percentage of their profile that is complete. The progress bar is typically displayed either at the top or in a side panel of the profile page, providing a visual representation of the user's progress. The bar is divided into segments representing different sections or tasks that need to be completed. Design systems play a crucial role in implementing and maintaining consistency and efficiency across different UI patterns or platforms. They provide a set of guidelines, standards, and reusable components that help streamline the design and development process. When it comes to profile completion progress, design systems ensure that the visual representation and interaction design of the progress bar align with the overall user experience and branding. The profile completion progress bar serves multiple purposes. Firstly, it acts as a motivator for users by highlighting the remaining tasks or information required to complete their profile. This visual feedback encourages users to take action and complete their profiles, as seeing progress can be satisfying and create a sense of accomplishment. Secondly, the progress bar provides users with a clear overview of the profile completion process. By dividing the progress into segments, users can easily identify which sections they have completed and which are still pending. This allows them to prioritize the areas that need attention, making the overall process more efficient. Lastly, the profile completion progress bar sets user expectations by providing a clear indication of the effort required to complete their profile. Users can estimate the time and effort needed to finish the remaining tasks based on the percentage displayed in the progress bar. This helps manage user expectations and reduces any potential frustration or confusion. In conclusion, the profile completion progress in UI patterns and design systems serves as a visual representation of the user's progress in completing their profile. It motivates users, provides an overview of the completion process, and sets expectations regarding the effort required. Design systems ensure consistency and efficiency in implementing these progress indicators by providing clear guidelines and reusable components for maintaining a cohesive user experience.>

Profile Edit Form

A Profile Edit Form is a user interface (UI) pattern that allows users to modify their personal information or settings within a system or application. It is an essential feature in platforms that require user profiles, such as social media networks, online marketplaces, and productivity tools. The purpose of a Profile Edit Form is to provide a structured and intuitive way for users to update their profile information according to their preferences. It typically includes fields for personal details like name, email address, phone number, location, and profile picture. Additionally, it may include optional sections for privacy settings, preferences, or additional information such as a bio or job title. Profile Edit Forms should adhere to the overall design system of the application or website, ensuring consistency in terms of layout, styling, and interaction patterns. Designers typically create a standardized template for Profile Edit Forms that can be reused across different screens and platforms. This helps to maintain a cohesive and familiar user experience. In terms of layout, Profile Edit Forms can be organized in a single vertically scrolling page or divided into multiple tabs or sections. Using tabs or sections can help to group related information, making it easier for users to navigate and update their profile in a focused manner. The fields in a Profile Edit Form should be labeled clearly, indicating the type of information required. Ideally, the form should provide clear instructions or hints to assist users in filling out each field, especially if certain formatting rules or limitations apply. Error messages should also be displayed if any information entered is incorrect or missing. To enhance usability, Profile Edit Forms may include additional features such as auto-suggestions, input validation, or real-time feedback to provide users with instant confirmation or suggestions for their inputs. Additionally, they should be responsive and adaptable to different screen sizes and devices to cater to the increasing number of mobile users. Overall, a well-designed Profile Edit Form streamlines the process of updating personal information within an application or system. It ensures that users can easily manage their profiles, providing them with a personalized experience and allowing them to maintain accurate and up-to-date information.

Profile Edit Form is a UI pattern that enables users to modify their personal information or settings within an application or system.

The form should adhere to the overall design system, provide clear labels and instructions for each field, and include features like auto-suggestions and input validation to enhance usability.

Profile Page

A Profile Page is a UI pattern and a part of the design system that provides a comprehensive overview of an individual, presenting relevant information and allowing users to view and interact with the person's details and content. A Profile Page typically includes various sections, such as a profile picture, personal information, contact details, a brief bio or description, and social media links. It may also incorporate additional components like a timeline of activities, a gallery of images or videos, and tabs for different types of content or settings. The profile picture is a visual representation of the person and usually displayed at the top of the page. It helps users identify the individual at a glance and creates a personal connection. The personal information section provides essential details such as the person's name, title, organization, location, and any other pertinent information that helps users understand who they are. Contact details enable users to get in touch with the person, typically including email address, phone number, and links to social media profiles or personal websites. These contact options allow users to initiate communication or follow the person's online presence. The bio or description section allows the individual to provide a brief overview of themselves, highlighting their expertise, interests, or accomplishments. This section serves as an introduction and can be used by users to quickly assess the person's background and professional focus. A timeline or activity feed may be included to showcase the individual's recent or significant activities. This could involve displaying posts, updates, or events related to the person, presenting a dynamic view of their ongoing contributions or interactions. A gallery component may be used to display images or videos that are relevant to the person's profile or achievements. This visual representation can provide additional context or showcase the person's work in a more engaging way. Tabs are commonly utilized to organize different types of content or settings within the Profile Page. For instance, an individual may have separate tabs for their bio, work history, projects, or preferences. This helps users navigate through the various sections and locate specific information or functionalities. In conclusion, a Profile Page is a crucial component in UI design and serves as a central hub for presenting and interacting with an individual's information and content. It incorporates essential sections like personal information, contact details, bio, timeline, gallery, and tabs to create a comprehensive and visually appealing user experience.>

Profile Photo Upload Form

A profile photo upload form is a user interface (UI) pattern and design system element that allows users to upload or change their profile picture. It typically consists of a form or input field where users can select an image file from their device storage or take a photo using their device's camera. The profile photo upload form follows a simple and intuitive design to ensure a seamless user experience. It typically includes a "Choose File" or "Upload Photo" button that users can click on to access their device's file manager and select the desired image file. Additionally, some forms may offer the option to take a photo directly from the user's device camera. Once the user selects or takes a photo, the form may display a preview of the chosen image. This preview allows users to verify that they have selected the correct photo before finalizing the upload. It may also provide an option to make any necessary adjustments or edits, such as cropping or rotating the image. The design of the profile photo upload form should be consistent with the overall UI patterns and design system of the application or website. This ensures a cohesive and familiar experience for users. The form should be visually pleasing, easy to understand, and accessible to all users, including those with disabilities. In terms of HTML structure, a profile photo upload form can be created using basic HTML elements. The form element should have an action attribute specifying the server-side script that handles the file upload process. It should also have an enctype attribute set to "multipart/form-data" to allow the form to handle binary files like images. Inside the form, an input element of type "file" is used to create a file browse button. This input element allows users to select an image file from their device. The form may also include a preview element, such as an img element, where the selected or captured image will be displayed. Here is an example of a profile photo upload form created using HTML:

Choose a photo: </form>

Profile Privacy Settings Form

A Profile Privacy Settings Form is a user interface (UI) pattern and design system component that allows users to customize the visibility and accessibility of their profile information on a platform or website. The form typically consists of a set of options or checkboxes that enable users to control what information is visible to others and what actions can be performed on their profile. This form is commonly used in social networking platforms, online communities, and websites where users have personal profiles. By providing users with granular control over their profile privacy settings, this form empowers individuals to manage their online presence and protect their personal information. Users can choose to make their profile completely public, visible only to friends or connections, or restrict access to specific pieces of information or actions. The Profile Privacy Settings Form is designed to be intuitive and user-friendly, with clear labels and tooltips that explain the purpose of each option. It should also include contextual help or links to further information to assist users in making informed decisions about their privacy settings. When designing the layout of the form, it is important to consider the sequence and grouping of options. Similar settings should be grouped together to facilitate easy scanning and selection. For example, options related to profile visibility should be grouped separately from settings related to actions or access control. Additionally, the form should include clear instructions on how to save and apply the changes made to the privacy settings. This can be achieved through prominent buttons or call-to-action elements that indicate the next steps. Overall, the Profile Privacy Settings Form is an essential component in any platform or website that prioritizes user privacy and control. By providing users with the ability to define their own boundaries and choose who can access their profile information, this form enhances the user experience and builds trust with the platform or website.

A Profile Privacy Settings Form is a UI pattern used to customize the visibility and accessibility of profile information on a platform or website. It enables users to control what information is visible to others and what actions can be performed on their profile. The form consists of options or checkboxes that allow users to make their profile public, visible to friends, or restrict access to specific information or actions. It is designed to be intuitive and user-friendly, with clear labels and tooltips. The form's layout should group similar settings together and provide instructions on how to save and apply changes. The Profile Privacy Settings Form empowers users to manage their online presence and protect their personal information.

Profile Setup Screen

A Profile Setup Screen is a user interface pattern and design system component that allows users to set up and update their profile information within a digital platform. It serves as a centralized hub where users can input, edit, and manage various aspects of their profile, such as personal details, contact information, preferences, and preferences. The Profile Setup Screen is designed with a clear and intuitive layout to make it easy for users to navigate and update their profile information. It typically consists of different sections or tabs, each corresponding to a specific category or type of information. This segmentation helps to organize and streamline the profile setup process, allowing users to focus on individual sections without feeling overwhelmed. Within each section, users are provided with input fields, checkboxes, dropdown menus, and other interactive elements to input or select their desired details. These elements are labeled clearly to provide guidance and context to users, ensuring they understand what information is being requested or updated. To enhance the user experience and minimize errors, the Profile Setup Screen often includes validation mechanisms. These mechanisms can include real-time error checking, such as highlighting incomplete or incorrect fields, providing suggestions or error messages, and enforcing any necessary input formats or restrictions. By implementing these validation mechanisms, the Profile Setup Screen helps users to input accurate and valid information, reducing the likelihood of errors or data inconsistencies. In addition to inputting profile information, the Profile Setup Screen may also include features for uploading profile pictures, managing privacy settings, connecting social media accounts, and other related profile management tasks. These supplementary features further enhance the usability and functionality of the Profile Setup Screen, giving users more control over their digital presence and identity. Overall, the Profile Setup Screen is an essential component of any digital platform that requires user profiles. It provides users with a convenient and streamlined interface for setting up and managing their profile information, ensuring accuracy, consistency, and control over their digital identity. >

Progress Bars

A progress bar is a graphical user interface (UI) pattern used to visually represent the progress or completion of a task. It is a design element commonly found in software applications, websites, and other digital interfaces. A progress bar typically consists of a horizontal bar that fills up gradually from left to right, accompanied by a textual or numerical representation of the progress percentage. It serves as a visual feedback indicator for the user, providing them with an estimation of how much of the task has been completed or how far it has progressed. The primary purpose of a progress bar is to enhance the user experience by keeping them informed and engaged during lengthy or time-consuming processes. It helps to manage user expectations, alleviate uncertainty, and reduce frustration by providing a sense of control and transparency. In addition to indicating progress, a progress bar may also include other relevant information, such as the remaining time or the number of steps completed out of the total. These additional details can further enhance the user's understanding of the ongoing process and help them make informed decisions or take appropriate actions. From a design system perspective, progress bars are an integral part of creating a consistent and cohesive UI. They provide a standardized approach for representing progress across different screens, modules, or components within an application or website. By adhering to a predefined design system, progress bars can maintain visual harmony and ensure a seamless user experience. In terms of HTML implementation, a progress bar can be created using the

tags and appropriate CSS styling. The

tags can be used to contain the textual representation of the progress, while CSS can be applied to define the width and appearance of the progress bar itself. For example:

50% completed

In the above HTML snippet, the first

tag represents the textual representation of the progress, indicating that 50% of the task is completed. The second

tag is styled using CSS to define the width as 50% and set the background color as a blue shade (#007bff), representing the progress visually. Overall, progress bars serve as instrumental elements in UI design, providing users with a clear indication of ongoing processes and facilitating a more efficient and satisfactory user experience.

Progressive Disclosure

Progressive disclosure refers to a design principle used in user interfaces (UI) and design systems to manage complexity and enhance user experience by presenting information gradually and only when necessary.

It involves breaking down complex tasks or information into manageable chunks and presenting them to users in a way that guides them through the interaction or decision-making process.

Progressive Web App (PWA) Features

A Progressive Web App (PWA) refers to a web application that employs modern web technologies to deliver a user experience similar to native mobile applications. PWAs combine the reach of the web with the performance and functionality of native apps, making them an ideal choice for mobile and desktop platforms. One of the key features of PWAs is their ability to work offline or in unstable network conditions. By utilizing service workers, PWAs can cache essential resources and provide offline functionality. This means that users can continue using the app even without an internet connection, enhancing their experience and productivity. Another notable feature of PWAs is their ability to be installed on the user's device, similar to native apps. This allows users to access the app from their device's home screen, making it easily accessible and providing a seamless user experience. Furthermore, PWAs can send push notifications to users, enabling them to stay engaged and receive timely updates even when the app is not actively being used. PWAs offer a responsive design, adapting to different screen sizes and orientations. This ensures that the app looks and functions well across various devices, including mobile, tablet, and desktop. By utilizing responsive design techniques, PWAs provide a consistent and optimized user interface, regardless of the device being used. Additionally, PWAs are designed to be fast and performant. They utilize techniques like lazy loading, which allows resources to be loaded only when needed, resulting in faster load times and improved performance. PWAs also leverage caching and pre-fetching strategies to minimize network requests and provide a smooth user experience. In terms of UI patterns, PWAs often follow the principles of Material Design or other design systems to ensure a cohesive and familiar user interface. These design systems provide guidelines for layout, typography, color schemes, and more, which helps establish a consistent and intuitive user experience. Overall, Progressive Web Apps offer a range of features that enhance the user experience and provide a powerful alternative to traditional web applications. By leveraging modern web technologies and adhering to UI patterns and design systems, PWAs bring the best of both web and native apps, resulting in engaging and efficient user experiences.

Property Comparison

Property Comparison is a process of analyzing and evaluating different properties or attributes within UI patterns and design systems. It involves assessing the characteristics and features of these properties to determine their suitability, effectiveness, and applicability in a given context. In the realm of UI patterns and design systems, various properties play a crucial role in determining the overall user experience and visual aesthetics. These properties encompass a wide range of aspects such as layout, color, typography, spacing, interaction, and accessibility. The comparison of properties entails a systematic examination of their strengths, weaknesses, and potential trade-offs. This evaluation helps designers and developers make informed decisions regarding the selection and implementation of specific properties to achieve the desired user interface outcome. One aspect of property comparison involves considering the scalability and adaptability of properties. Scalability refers to the ability of a property to maintain its effectiveness and performance across varying screen sizes and devices. Whereas adaptability focuses on how well a property can be adjusted and tailored to meet specific design requirements and user needs. Another critical facet of property comparison is accessibility. This involves assessing whether a property adheres to established accessibility guidelines and standards in order to ensure inclusive and equal access for all users. Accessibility considerations encompass factors such as contrast ratios, text legibility, keyboard navigability, and the appropriate use of alternative text for non-text elements. Additionally, property comparison involves evaluating the impact of properties on the overall coherence and consistency of the user interface. Consistency ensures that similar elements or actions are presented in a uniform manner throughout an application or website, enhancing user familiarity and reducing cognitive load. Coherence, on the other hand, focuses on the harmonious integration of various properties to create a visually cohesive and aesthetically pleasing user interface. In conclusion, property comparison within the context of UI patterns and design systems is a critical process that involves analyzing and evaluating different properties to make informed decisions regarding their selection and implementation. This evaluation helps ensure the creation of scalable, adaptable, accessible, and visually cohesive user interfaces, ultimately enhancing the overall user experience.>

Property Details

A property details UI pattern refers to the design and layout of the information and elements displayed for a specific property or item. It is commonly used in various digital platforms, including websites and mobile applications, to present comprehensive details about a particular product, service, or real estate listing.

This UI pattern typically includes essential information such as the property's name, description, images, location, amenities, pricing, and other relevant details. The goal is to provide users with a clear and organized presentation of the property's features and specifications, enabling them to make informed decisions or take further actions.

Property Management

Property management in the context of UI patterns and design systems refers to the practice of organizing and maintaining a collection of reusable components, styles, and guidelines that streamline the development and maintenance of consistent user interfaces.

A property management system serves as a centralized repository for UI assets and serves as a reference for designers and developers to ensure visual and functional consistency across an application or website.

Pull-To-Load

Pull-to-Load is a UI pattern and design system element commonly used in mobile applications, specifically in list views or scrollable content areas. It allows users to load additional data or refresh the existing data by pulling down on the screen. When implemented within a mobile app, Pull-to-Load provides an intuitive and interactive way for users to retrieve more content without explicitly tapping on a button or navigating to a different page. The pattern leverages the natural scrolling and touch gestures of mobile devices to enhance the user experience and improve overall usability. To initiate a Pull-to-Load action, users place their finger or thumb on the screen and then drag it downwards, typically with a certain amount of resistance. As the user pulls down, a visual indicator, such as a loading spinner or a progress bar, appears to provide feedback that the action is being recognized. Once the user releases their finger, the app responds by executing the designated behavior, either loading additional content or refreshing the existing content. This behavior is specified by the app's logic and can vary depending on the context. For example, in a social media app, pulling down on the home feed might trigger a refresh to display the latest posts, while pulling down on a list of messages could load older messages. Pull-to-Load is often used in conjunction with pagination, where content is loaded in smaller chunks to improve performance and reduce data usage. By enabling users to pull down to load more content, it eliminates the need for additional navigation or pagination controls, providing a seamless and continuous browsing experience. From a design system perspective, Pull-to-Load should adhere to the app's overall visual language, including colors, typography, and brand guidelines. The visual indicator and animation used during the pull-down gesture should be consistent with the app's design philosophy. In conclusion, Pull-to-Load is a UI pattern that enhances mobile app usability by allowing users to load additional content or refresh existing content through a pull-down gesture. Its implementation should align with the overall design system of the app, maintaining consistency in visual elements and animations.

Pull-To-Refresh

Pull-to-Refresh is a UI pattern and design system used in web and mobile applications to enable users to manually refresh the content of a page or view. It provides an intuitive and engaging way for users to update the displayed information without having to navigate or perform additional actions. This pattern typically consists of a scrollable container, such as a list or a feed, where the user can pull the content downwards to trigger a refresh. When the pulling action reaches a predefined threshold, a visual indicator is displayed to inform the user that a refresh is about to occur. Upon releasing the content, the system performs a refresh operation, fetching updated data from the server or refreshing the displayed information in real-time. By incorporating Pull-to-Refresh, users are provided with a direct and interactive way to update content without relying on traditional buttons or menus. This interaction paradigm is not only visually appealing, but it also enhances the overall user experience by providing immediate feedback to the user's actions. When utilizing Pull-to-Refresh in a design system, it is essential to maintain consistency across different platforms and applications. This includes establishing a clear visual cue for the refresh indicator and ensuring that the refresh operation is performed smoothly and efficiently. Additionally, providing informative messages or feedback during the refresh process can help manage user expectations and prevent confusion or frustration. To implement Pull-to-Refresh in HTML, you can use JavaScript or a library that supports this functionality. Here is an example:

In this example, the first `

` tag represents the scrollable container, which may contain the content that the user wants to refresh. The second `

` tag with the class "refresh-indicator" is used to display the visual cue indicating the refresh operation. The specific styling and behavior of these elements can be customized according to the design requirements. Pull-to-Refresh is a widely adopted UI pattern due to its simplicity and effectiveness in enabling users to update content with a natural gesture. By incorporating this pattern into a design system, users can enjoy a seamless and engaging user experience while interacting with web and mobile applications.

Purchase Request Form

A Purchase Request Form is a standardized user interface (UI) pattern used within a design system to facilitate the process of making a purchase request. It is designed to gather necessary information from the user and serve as a communication tool between the user and the organization responsible for fulfilling the request. The purpose of a Purchase Request Form is to streamline and simplify the purchase request process. It helps ensure that all required information is collected, reducing the chances of errors or missing information. By following a consistent form layout and design, users can easily understand and navigate the form, increasing efficiency and reducing the time spent on completing the request. The structure of a Purchase Request Form typically includes fields for capturing essential details such as the requester's name, contact information, the item or service being requested, quantity, budget allocation, and any relevant additional details or attachments. These fields are carefully arranged in a logical order, ensuring that all necessary information is captured without overwhelming the user with too many inputs. The design of a Purchase Request Form within a design system adheres to the overall visual language and style of the system. This consistency in design elements, such as colors, typography, and spacing, helps users easily recognize and interact with the form. Additionally, the use of clear labels, instructional text, and validation messages ensures that users understand the purpose of each field and can provide accurate information. An effective Purchase Request Form also incorporates error handling and validation to guide users and prevent submission of incomplete or erroneous requests. Real-time validation alerts or error messages are displayed if the user enters incorrect information or leaves required fields empty, guiding them towards the necessary corrections. In summary, a Purchase Request Form is a standardized UI pattern used within a design system to facilitate the process of making a purchase request. It ensures that all necessary information is collected in a streamlined manner, adheres to the design system's visual guidelines, and incorporates error handling and validation for a seamless user experience.

A Purchase Request Form is a standardized UI pattern used within a design system to facilitate the process of making a purchase request. It ensures efficient and accurate gathering of necessary information from users and serves as a communication tool between the user and the organization responsible for fulfilling the request.

Structured with carefully arranged fields and designed with consistency in visual elements, a Purchase Request Form ensures a streamlined and user-friendly experience. It incorporates error handling and validation to guide users and prevent submission of incomplete or erroneous requests. By following the guidelines of the design system, this UI pattern ensures consistent visual language and style throughout the form.

QR Code Scanning

QR Code scanning is a user interface pattern and design system that allows users to easily scan QR (Quick Response) codes using their mobile devices or other scanning devices. QR codes are two-dimensional barcodes that can be quickly scanned and decoded to access information or perform specific actions.

The QR Code scanning pattern is designed to provide a seamless and efficient way for users to interact with QR codes. It typically includes the following components:

1. QR Code Display: This is where the QR code is shown to the user. It can be displayed on a variety of mediums such as webpages, mobile apps, or physical objects. The QR code is designed in a way that makes it easy to scan and interpret.

2. Scanning Interface: The scanning interface is the area where the user can scan the QR code. It is usually represented by a camera icon or a designated scanning button. When the user taps or clicks on this icon, their device's camera is activated to scan the QR code.

3. Feedback and Results: Once the scanning process is initiated, the user receives feedback on the scanning status. This can include visual cues such as a scanning animation or progress bar. Once the QR code is successfully scanned, the user is presented with the decoded information or the action associated with the QR code.

The design system for QR Code scanning focuses on providing a clear and intuitive user experience. It prioritizes legibility and ease of use to ensure that users can quickly and accurately scan QR codes. The design system also takes into account different devices and screen sizes, adapting the scanning interface to optimize user interaction.

Overall, QR Code scanning UI patterns and design systems enable users to easily scan and decode QR codes, facilitating access to information and actions in a fast and efficient manner.

Quick Actions

Quick Actions refer to a common user interface pattern and design system element that provides users with quick and easy access to commonly performed actions within an application or website. It is a way to streamline and simplify the user experience by presenting commonly used actions prominently and making them easily accessible. Quick Actions are typically displayed as a set of buttons or icons, often located in a toolbar or a designated area within the user interface. They are meant to be highly visible and easily identifiable, allowing users to quickly find and execute the desired action without having to navigate through multiple menus or screens. The primary purpose of Quick Actions is to enhance efficiency and convenience for users by reducing the number of steps or clicks required to perform a specific task or action. This is particularly useful in situations where certain actions are performed frequently or are critical to the user's workflow. Quick Actions can be customized to suit the specific needs and context of the application or website. They can include a wide range of actions, such as creating a new item, saving changes, deleting an item, sharing content, printing, or sending a message. The specific actions included in Quick Actions should be based on user research, identifying the most commonly used functionalities. In terms of design system, Quick Actions should adhere to the overall visual and interaction guidelines of the system. They should have consistent styling, such as size, color, and typography, to maintain a cohesive and intuitive user experience. The position and placement of Quick Actions within the user interface should also be consistent across different screens or contexts to ensure familiarity and ease of use. In summary, Quick Actions are a common UI pattern and design system element that provides users with quick and easy access to commonly performed actions. They enhance efficiency and convenience by reducing the number of steps required to perform a task and should adhere to the overall design system guidelines to maintain consistency and coherence in the user experience.

Quick Replies

Quick Replies are a UI pattern used in conversational interfaces to offer users a set of predefined responses or actions to choose from. They are commonly used in chatbots, messaging apps, and voice assistants to streamline the conversation flow and provide users with prompt and easy-to-select options. Quick Replies serve as shortcuts for users to respond or interact with the system without having to type or speak out their responses. They are usually displayed as a horizontal list of buttons or text options, placed within the user interface to enable quick selection. By presenting users with a limited number of pre-defined choices, Quick Replies help guide the conversation and reduce cognitive load. This pattern can be particularly useful in scenarios where the possible user inputs or system responses are limited and predictable, streamlining the interaction process and ensuring a more efficient user experience. Quick Replies are designed to be concise, clear, and relevant to the conversation context. They should reflect the possible user intents or actions that align with the system's capabilities. The options provided should be mutually exclusive and collectively exhaustive to cover a wide range of potential user responses. Implementing Quick Replies in a design system involves creating a consistent visual style and interaction behavior. The buttons or text options should follow the overall design language of the system, including typography, colors, and spacing. The selected option should provide visual feedback to indicate the user's choice, such as highlighting or changing color. In terms of HTML implementation, Quick Replies can be represented using the `<button>` element for each option. The textual content of the button represents the available response or action. The buttons can be placed within a `

` tag to maintain a clear and concise structure. For example:

<button>Yes</button> <button>No</button> <button>Maybe</button>

<button>Accept</button> <button>Decline</button>

Note that this HTML implementation is just an example, and the actual styling and behavior may vary depending on the design system and requirements of the conversational interface. Overall, Quick Replies provide a convenient way for users to interact with conversational interfaces by reducing the effort required to input responses. They contribute to a more efficient and user-friendly experience by offering predefined options that match the system's capabilities and conversation context.></button>

Quick Settings Panel

A Quick Settings Panel is a user interface component that provides easy access to a set of frequently used settings or controls within an application or operating system. It offers a convenient way for users to configure or toggle specific features without navigating through multiple menus or screens. The Quick Settings Panel is typically displayed as a compact, expandable panel that can be accessed with a single tap or click. It is often represented by an icon or a button located in a prominent area of the user interface, such as the top or bottom of the screen. Upon activation, the panel expands to reveal a set of quick settings options. The panel usually organizes the settings in a visually appealing and intuitive manner, often using icons or short labels to represent each setting or control. This helps users quickly identify and locate the desired option. The settings are typically grouped into categories or sections, such as connectivity, display, sound, and notifications, in order to provide a well-organized and easy-to-navigate interface. Within the Quick Settings Panel, users can directly interact with the settings by tapping or clicking on the corresponding options. Depending on the nature of the setting, this interaction may trigger an action or present additional options or information. For example, tapping on the Wi-Fi icon may toggle the Wi-Fi connectivity on or off, while tapping on the battery icon may display the battery percentage or power-saving options. The Quick Settings Panel is designed to enhance the user experience by providing quick access to commonly used settings, improving overall efficiency and convenience. It is particularly useful in scenarios where users frequently switch between different settings or need to access certain controls on a regular

237

basis. In conclusion, the Quick Settings Panel is a UI component that offers a simplified way for users to access frequently used settings or controls within an application or operating system. It provides a compact, expandable panel that organizes settings into categories and allows for direct interaction with the options. By offering quick and easy access to common settings, it enhances the usability and efficiency of the overall user experience.>

Quiz And Exam

UI patterns refer to recurring design solutions that solve specific user interface and experience problems. These patterns provide a set of guidelines and solutions that address common challenges in user interface design, such as navigation, inputs, and interactions. They help designers create consistent and predictable interfaces that are intuitive and easy to use. A design system, on the other hand, is a comprehensive set of guidelines, components, and assets that define the visual and behavioral aspects of a product's user interface. It provides a consistent and cohesive design language that ensures a unified user experience across different platforms and devices. A design system typically includes guidelines for typography, color, spacing, and other visual elements, as well as reusable UI components and patterns. In the context of UI patterns, a quiz pattern is a commonly used design solution for presenting a series of questions or prompts to the user. It typically consists of a sequential or non-linear flow where each question is presented one at a time. The user can select an answer or input a response, and then proceed to the next question. The quiz pattern often includes features such as progress indicators, feedback on correct or incorrect answers, and a final score or result summary. An exam pattern, on the other hand, is a more formal and structured version of the quiz pattern. It is commonly used for assessment purposes, such as in educational or certification settings. The exam pattern typically includes a set of questions that are timed and graded. It may also include features such as question randomization, multiple choice options, and scoring algorithms. The exam pattern provides a standardized way of evaluating the user's knowledge or skills in a specific area. In conclusion, UI patterns and design systems play a crucial role in creating effective and user-friendly interfaces. They provide designers with a set of proven solutions and guidelines that help ensure consistency and usability. The quiz pattern and exam pattern are two examples of commonly used UI patterns for presenting interactive questions and assessments to users. By following these established patterns and utilizing a design system, designers can create interfaces that are intuitive, visually pleasing, and easy to use.>

Quote Request Form

A UI pattern is a reusable solution or design element that addresses a common interaction or visual problem in user interface design. It is a best practice or proven way to solve a particular design challenge, making it easier for users to understand and navigate through an interface. UI patterns can be applied to various components of a user interface, such as navigation menus, input forms, search bars, and buttons. They provide a consistent look and feel across different sections of a website or application, making it more intuitive for users to interact with the interface. A design system, on the other hand, is a set of guidelines, rules, and principles that define the overall visual and interaction design of a product or platform. It includes the UI patterns, components, and design assets that can be used to create a cohesive and user-friendly interface. By using a design system, designers and developers can ensure consistency in the visual appearance and behavior of a product's interface. It provides a shared language and framework for designing and developing new features or pages, enabling teams to work more efficiently and maintain a coherent design language. The primary goal of UI patterns and design systems is to enhance the user experience by reducing cognitive load and making the interface more intuitive. They help users understand how to interact with the interface by following commonly recognized and established design patterns. Additionally, UI patterns and design systems promote scalability and flexibility in the design process. By reusing existing patterns and components, designers and developers can save time and effort in creating new interfaces. They also create a shared understanding and consistency among different teams working on the same product. In conclusion, UI patterns and design systems play a crucial role in user interface design by providing best practices, reusable solutions, and consistent design elements. They improve the usability and user experience of a product or platform while promoting efficiency, scalability, and collaboration in the design process. >

238

Radial Menu

A radial menu is a user interface (UI) pattern and design system that presents options or actions in a circular layout. It is commonly used in touchscreen devices or applications where space is limited but a comprehensive set of choices need to be displayed. The radial menu consists of a central hub or pivot point with radial spokes or sectors that radiate outward from the hub. Each spoke or sector represents a different option or action that users can select. When activated, the radial menu expands to reveal additional sub-options or detailed information related to the selected option. Users can interact with the radial menu by tapping or clicking on the desired spoke/sector or by dragging their finger or cursor across the screen to rotate the menu. The benefits of using a radial menu include efficient use of screen space, easy access to a large number of options, and intuitive interaction. It allows for quick navigation and selection without the need for multiple nested menus or excessive scrolling. The circular layout also provides a visual hierarchy, with primary options closer to the central hub and secondary options farther away. Radial menus can be customized to fit the specific needs of an application or system. They can be single-level or multi-level, depending on the complexity of the options. The menu items can be text-based, icon-based, or a combination of both. Customizable features may include the size, color, and arrangement of the spokes/sectors, as well as animation effects for menu expansion and collapse. When designing a radial menu, usability considerations are crucial. The menu should be easy to understand and navigate, with clear labels or visual cues for each option. The spacing between spokes/sectors should be sufficient to prevent accidental selection. Visual feedback, such as highlighting or animation, can help users understand their interactions with the menu. In conclusion, a radial menu is a UI pattern and design system that presents options or actions in a circular layout. It offers an efficient and intuitive way for users to interact with a touchscreen device or application. By leveraging the advantages of the circular layout, radial menus provide a visually appealing and easy-to-use interface for accessing a wide range of options.

Radial Progress Bars

Radial progress bars are graphical elements used in user interface (UI) design to visually represent the completion or progress of a particular task or process. They are commonly employed in design systems as part of a cohesive visual language to provide users with a clear understanding of their progress in a dynamic and engaging manner. These UI elements consist of a circular shape that is divided into segments or arcs, each representing a portion of the overall progress or completion. The filled portion of the circle corresponds to the amount of progress made, while the empty portion signifies the remaining work to be done. A radial progress bar typically features additional visual cues such as color gradients or animations to enhance the user experience and provide a sense of interactivity. For example, the filled portion of the circular shape may start as a solid color and gradually transition to a different color as the progress increases, providing a more intuitive representation of completion. Design systems often incorporate radial progress bars to maintain consistency in the UI across different applications or components. By using the same visual language, these design patterns help users easily recognize and understand their progress in various contexts. Radial progress bars can be effectively used in a wide range of applications, including goal tracking, file uploads, form completion, and download indicators. Their circular shape can be easily understood and visually appealing to users, making them a versatile choice for conveying progress in UI design. In conclusion, radial progress bars are UI elements used to visually represent the progress or completion of a task or process. They consist of circular shapes divided into segments, with the filled portion indicating progress made and the empty portion indicating remaining work. By incorporating visual cues and animations, radial progress bars enhance the user experience and provide a consistent visual language within design systems.

Rate And Review System

A Rate and Review System is a UI pattern and design system that allows users to provide feedback and ratings on products, services, or any other type of content. It is commonly used in e-commerce websites, mobile apps, and other platforms where users can express their opinions and share their experiences. The primary goal of a Rate and Review System is to enable users to rate and review items in a quick and easy manner, while also allowing other users to browse and make informed decisions based on the collective feedback. This system provides value by

239

giving users the ability to contribute their own insights, as well as benefit from the experiences of others. The design of a Rate and Review System typically includes elements such as a star rating scale, a text input area for writing a review, and options for submitting the feedback. The star rating scale is a visual representation of a numerical rating, usually ranging from one to five stars. Users can select the number of stars that best represents their opinion of the item. The text input area allows users to further elaborate on their rating by writing a review, sharing their thoughts, and providing specific feedback. In addition to the basic rating and review functionality, a Rate and Review System often includes features such as sorting options, filtering options, and the ability to flag or report inappropriate content. Sorting options allow users to view reviews based on criteria such as most recent, highest rated, or most helpful. Filtering options allow users to narrow down the reviews based on specific characteristics or criteria. The flag or report feature allows users to bring attention to reviews that violate guidelines or contain offensive content. A well-designed Rate and Review System takes into consideration factors such as usability, accessibility, and moderation. Usability ensures that the system is intuitive and easy to use, allowing users to navigate and interact with the rating and review elements effortlessly. Accessibility ensures that the system is inclusive and can be used by all users, including those with disabilities. Moderation ensures that the system maintains a high quality of feedback by monitoring and managing the reviews to prevent spam, fraudulent content, or abusive behavior. In conclusion, a Rate and Review System is a UI pattern and design system that enables users to provide feedback and ratings on products or services. It is a valuable tool for users to share their experiences and make informed decisions, while also promoting user engagement and trust in a platform.

Rating Form

A UI pattern is a reusable solution that addresses a specific design problem in user interface development. It provides guidance for the arrangement and interaction of elements within a user interface, aiming to improve usability and user experience. UI patterns help designers and developers create consistent, predictable, and familiar interfaces by following established best practices. Design systems, on the other hand, are a collection of UI patterns, components, guidelines, and assets that work together to create a cohesive and scalable design language. They provide a set of rules and constraints that ensure consistency and coherence across different products or interfaces. Design systems can include various elements such as colors, typography, spacing, icons, and more. UI patterns and design systems are complementary. UI patterns serve as building blocks within a design system, while design systems provide the framework and structure for implementing UI patterns consistently. When designing user interfaces, it is important to consider the context in which UI patterns and design systems are used. Context refers to the specific environment and requirements of the product or interface being designed. The context may include factors such as the target audience, the platform or device, the purpose of the interface, and the business goals. By leveraging UI patterns and design systems, designers and developers can create interfaces that are not only visually pleasing but also intuitive and user-friendly. Consistency and familiarity are key when it comes to user interface design, and UI patterns and design systems help ensure that users can quickly understand and interact with an interface without confusion or frustration. Overall, UI patterns and design systems are essential tools in the world of user interface design. They provide a foundation for creating effective and efficient interfaces, promoting a positive user experience and ultimately driving the success of a product or service.

UI patterns are reusable solutions for design problems, guiding the arrangement and interaction of elements in user interfaces.

Design systems consist of UI patterns, components, guidelines, and assets that create a cohesive and scalable design language.

Rating And Feedback

UI patterns refer to a set of established design elements and interactions that are commonly used in user interfaces. These patterns serve as a guide for designers and developers, providing them with a framework that helps create consistent and intuitive user experiences. A design system, on the other hand, is a more comprehensive set of guidelines and documentation that encompasses UI patterns as well as other design elements such as colors, typography, icons, and more. It serves as a single source of truth for all design-related decisions, ensuring that all products and services within an organization maintain a cohesive visual language. UI patterns are important because they provide users with familiarity and predictability. When users encounter a familiar pattern, they can quickly understand how to interact with the interface, reducing the learning curve. Consistency in design also helps build trust and credibility with users, as it gives off a sense of professionalism and reliability. Design systems are beneficial for both designers and developers. For designers, a design system provides a centralized repository of design assets and guidelines, allowing them to work more efficiently and consistently across projects. For developers, a design system offers pre-built components and code snippets, reducing the need for custom development and saving time. By using UI patterns and design systems, organizations can create harmonious and efficient user interfaces. These systems help streamline design and development processes, resulting in products and services that are visually appealing, easy to use, and aligned with the organization's brand identity. In conclusion, UI patterns are individual design elements and interactions that are commonly used in user interfaces, while design systems are comprehensive guidelines that encompass UI patterns and other design elements. Together, they ensure consistency and familiarity, making interfaces more intuitive and user-friendly. They also provide efficiency and scalability for designers and developers, allowing for faster and more consistent design and development processes.>

Read Receipts

A read receipt is a UI pattern used in design systems to indicate whether a message or notification has been read by the recipient. It serves as a mechanism to provide feedback to the sender, confirming that their message has been viewed.

To implement read receipts in a UI, a system needs to track the status of the message, i.e., whether it has been read or not. This information could be stored server-side or locally on the recipient's device. Once a message has been viewed, the UI should visually indicate this status to the sender.

Real Estate Listings

A Real Estate Listings UI pattern is a design element or module commonly used in websites or applications that display a collection of real estate properties available for sale or rent.

This UI pattern typically includes a grid or card layout with each property listing represented by a thumbnail image, title, location information, price, and other relevant details. It allows users to quickly browse through a large number of properties and easily access more information about each one.

Real-Time Updates

Real-Time Updates refer to a UI pattern and design system that allows for the immediate and automatic display of information without the need for manual refreshing or page reloading. This pattern is commonly used in web applications, dashboards, and mobile apps to provide users with real-time information and enhance their overall experience. Real-Time Updates enable data to be displayed on the user interface as soon as it becomes available, eliminating the need for the user to manually refresh the page or trigger an action to retrieve updated information. This can be particularly useful in scenarios where time-sensitive or dynamic data is involved, such as stock market updates, news feeds, instant messaging, or collaborative editing platforms. By employing Real-Time Updates, designers can create interfaces that keep users constantly informed and up to date, minimizing the risk of them missing important or newly available information. This pattern leverages technologies such as AJAX (Asynchronous JavaScript and XML) or WebSockets, which enable the seamless exchange of data between the server and the client-side, facilitating real-time updates. In terms of design system, Real-Time Updates call for careful consideration to ensure a seamless and visually comprehensible experience for users. Animation and visual cues can be utilized to signify that new information has arrived or to indicate that the UI is actively updating in real-time. This can include subtle changes in color, icons, or progress indicators. However, designers should exercise caution to avoid overwhelming the user with excessive or distracting animations, as this may result in a negative experience. Real-Time Updates are a valuable UI pattern and design system element, delivering timely information to users and facilitating dynamic interactions. By implementing this pattern in an intuitive and visually appealing manner, designers can offer a more engaging and efficient user experience, enhancing the usability and effectiveness of their applications or platforms.

Real-Time Collaboration

Real-time Collaboration in the context of UI patterns and design systems refers to the ability of multiple users to work together simultaneously on a shared project or document. It allows for synchronous communication and cooperation, enhancing productivity and efficiency in remote team settings.

Real-time collaboration is a fundamental aspect of modern design systems, as it enables designers, developers, and other stakeholders to collaborate seamlessly throughout the design process. By eliminating the need for manual file sharing and version control, real-time collaboration streamlines the workflow and ensures that everyone is working on the latest version of the project.

Recent Blog Posts

UI patterns and design systems are essential tools in creating cohesive and user-friendly interfaces. One common element found within these systems is the concept of blog posts. In the context of UI patterns, blog posts refer to a standardized format for displaying articles or updates on a website or application. Blog posts typically consist of a title, a date or timestamp, and the content of the article. The title usually serves as a clickable link that redirects users to the full article. The content of the blog post may include text, images, and other multimedia elements. Design systems provide guidelines and components for the consistent styling and structure of blog posts. These guidelines ensure that blog posts across a website or application have a consistent look and feel, making it easier for users to navigate and consume content. Design systems dictate the typography, color palette, spacing, and overall layout of blog posts within the interface. When designing blog posts within a UI pattern or design system, it is important to consider the following principles: 1. Consistency: Blog posts should follow a standardized format across the interface. The title, date, and content should be consistently styled and positioned to ensure familiarity and ease of use for the user. 2. Readability: The typography and layout of blog posts should prioritize readability. Clear and legible fonts, appropriate line heights, and well-structured paragraphs make it easier for users to consume the content. 3. Visual Hierarchy: Design systems often define a visual hierarchy for blog posts, helping users quickly identify the most important information. This hierarchy can be achieved through the use of headings, subheadings, color contrast, and visual cues. 4. Responsiveness: In today's multi-device world, blog posts should adapt to different screen sizes and orientations. Responsive design ensures that the content is accessible and legible across a range of devices, from desktops to mobile phones. By adhering to the guidelines set by UI patterns and design systems, designers can create visually consistent and user-friendly blog posts. These standardized formats not only enhance the overall aesthetics of the interface but also improve the user experience by making it easier for users to navigate and consume content.

In the context of UI patterns and design systems, blog posts refer to a standardized format for displaying articles or updates on a website or application. They typically consist of a title, date, and content, and are designed to be visually consistent and user-friendly.

Design systems provide guidelines for the consistent styling and structure of blog posts, ensuring that they have a cohesive look and feel across the interface. These guidelines cover elements such as typography, color palette, spacing, and layout. By following these guidelines, designers can create visually appealing and easy-to-read blog posts that enhance the overall user experience.

Recipe Search And Cooking

A Recipe Search and Cooking UI pattern and design system provides users with a platform to search for various recipes and assist them in the process of cooking. This pattern typically includes a search bar and filters to allow users to search for specific recipes based on their preferences and dietary restrictions. Additionally, it also offers features such as recipe collection, meal planning, and step-by-step instructions to guide users through the cooking process.

The Recipe Search and Cooking UI pattern is designed to be intuitive and user-friendly, enabling users to easily discover and access a wide range of recipes. The search bar allows users to enter specific keywords or ingredients to search for relevant recipes, while filters enable them to narrow down their search based on various criteria such as meal type, cuisine, or difficulty level. These features help users find recipes that align with their preferences and dietary needs.

Once users have found a recipe they are interested in, the UI pattern provides them with detailed information about the recipe, including ingredients, cooking time, and serving size. Some patterns may also include user ratings and reviews to provide additional insights and help users make informed decisions about which recipes to try. Users can easily add the recipe to their collection or meal plan for future reference, and they can also print or share the recipe with others.

During the cooking process, the Recipe Search and Cooking UI pattern provides users with step-by-step instructions, including images or videos, to guide them through each stage of the recipe. This assists users in following the recipe accurately and achieving the desired outcome. The pattern may also offer features such as timers and measurement converters to make the cooking process more convenient for users.

Referral Program Signup Form

A referral program signup form is a user interface (UI) pattern and a component of a design system that allows users to sign up for a referral program. The form typically consists of fields and elements that collect the necessary information from users in order to join the referral program. The referral program signup form is designed to be concise and intuitive, making it easy for users to complete the process and provide the required information. The form usually includes fields such as name, email address, and optionally, any additional information that may be required for the referral program. The purpose of the referral program signup form is to capture the necessary details and validate the user's eligibility for the referral program. The form may also include terms and conditions, privacy policy, or other relevant information that users need to be aware of before signing up. To ensure a positive user experience, it is important to design the referral program signup form in alignment with the overall UI patterns and design system of the application or website. This ensures consistency in visual style, typography, colors, and other UI elements, which creates a cohesive and seamless experience for users. By adhering to the design system, designers can maintain a unified look and feel across different components and pages of the application or website. This consistency not only enhances the overall aesthetics but also helps users navigate and interact with the referral program signup form more easily. When designing the referral program signup form, it is important to consider accessibility standards and best practices to ensure that the form is usable by all users, including those with disabilities. This may include using proper contrast between text and background colors, providing clear and concise instructions, and using correct labeling for form fields. In conclusion, a referral program signup form is a UI pattern and component of a design system that enables users to sign up for a referral program. It is designed to be user-friendly, consistent with the overall design system, and accessible to all users. By following these guidelines, designers can create a seamless and efficient user experience for signing up for referral programs.>

Refund Request Form

A refund request form is a standardized user interface (UI) pattern and element of a design system that allows users to submit a formal request for a refund of a product or service they have purchased. The refund request form typically consists of a set of fields and inputs where users are required to provide specific information related to their purchase. This may include details such as the order number, product name, purchase date, and reason for the refund. The purpose of the refund request form is to streamline the refund process and ensure that all necessary information is gathered from the user to facilitate the refund request. By following a standard form structure, the form provides a consistent and familiar user experience, making it easier for users to understand and complete the refund request. In terms of UI design, the refund request form should be visually distinct from other elements on the page, usually by using a specific form layout or styling. This helps users easily identify and locate the form on the website or application. Furthermore, the design of the refund request form should prioritize usability and accessibility. It should be intuitive and responsive, allowing users to easily navigate through the form fields. Clear and concise error messages should be provided to guide users in case any required information is missing or improperly entered. Additionally, a well-designed refund request form should provide users with feedback and confirmation once the form has been successfully submitted. This helps to instill confidence in users that their request has been received and is being processed. To summarize, a refund request form is a standardized UI pattern and design system element that allows users to formally request a refund. Its purpose is to streamline the process by gathering necessary information in a consistent and familiar manner. The form should be visually distinct, prioritize usability and accessibility, and provide feedback to users upon submission.>

Registration Form

A registration form is a UI pattern and design system element that allows users to create a new account or join an existing platform or service. It typically consists of a series of fields that users need to fill out with their personal information, such as name, email address, password, and additional details that may be required. The purpose of a registration form is to collect necessary information from users in order to establish their identity and provide them with access to the platform or service. By requiring users to provide their personal information, the form helps to ensure the security and integrity of the system by preventing unauthorized access or fraudulent activity. Registration forms are an important component of any user interface (UI) pattern and design system as they provide a consistent and standardized way for users to sign up for a service. By following a common set of design principles and guidelines, registration forms can be easily recognized and understood by users, leading to a more intuitive and efficient user experience. In terms of HTML structure, a registration form can be created using form elements such as input fields, checkboxes, and buttons. The form element acts as a container for all the input fields and controls within the registration form. Each input field is typically enclosed within a label element, which provides a clear description of what information is expected from the user. For example, a basic registration form may include the following fields:

<form> Name: Email: Password: Confirm Password: </form>

In this example, the user is required to provide their name, email address, password, and confirm the password for registration. The "required" attribute is used to enforce the mandatory fields. Overall, a registration form is a crucial element in UI patterns and design systems as it allows users to sign up for a platform or service, ensuring authenticity and security while providing a standardized user experience.

Related Articles Section

The Related Articles section is a UI pattern commonly used in websites and applications to provide users with additional content that is relevant to the current article or page they are viewing. This section aims to enhance user engagement and provide a seamless browsing experience by offering related articles that may be of interest to the user. In a design system, the Related Articles section is an important component that follows certain guidelines and principles to ensure consistency and cohesiveness in the overall user interface. It is crucial to establish a clear hierarchy and visual consistency within this section to make it easily distinguishable from the main content but still visually connected to the overall design. When implementing the Related Articles section in HTML, it is important to structure the content properly to ensure accessibility and improve search engine optimization. It is recommended to use semantic HTML tags such as headings, paragraphs, and anchor tags to provide a clear and meaningful structure to the content. Typically, the Related Articles section is represented as a group of article preview cards, each containing a title, short description, and a thumbnail image. These cards are typically displayed in a grid or a list format, depending on the design and layout requirements of the website or application. To implement this section in HTML, you can use the

tag to represent the title and description of each related article. Additionally, you can use the tag to wrap the title, creating a clickable link to the full article. The thumbnail image can be added using the tag along with appropriate alt text to improve accessibility. Here is an example of how the Related Articles section can be implemented in pure HTML using only two

tags:

Title of Related Article 1 Short description of Related Article 1

Title of Related Article 2 Short description of Related Article 2

In this example, the

tag is used to wrap the title and description of each related article. The tag is used to create a clickable link for the title, directing the user to the full article. The tag is used to create line breaks and improve readability. By following these guidelines and properly structuring the content, the Related Articles section can greatly enhance user experience and encourage further exploration of the website or application.>

Related Products/Posts

A related product or post is a UI pattern commonly used in design systems to display additional items that are related to the current product or post being viewed. It provides users with a way to explore similar or relevant content, ultimately enhancing the overall user experience.

In terms of the design system, a related product or post component is typically a visually consistent module that can be easily incorporated into different pages or screens. It typically includes a thumbnail image or icon, a title or headline, and sometimes a brief description. The module is often clickable, allowing users to navigate to the related content they are interested in.

Report Abuse Form

A Report Abuse Form is a user interface pattern and a key component of a design system that allows users to report any content or behavior that is deemed inappropriate, offensive, or harmful within a digital platform or application. It is an essential feature for maintaining a safe and respectful environment for all users. The main purpose of a Report Abuse Form is to provide an accessible and straightforward way for users to report problematic content or actions that violate community guidelines, terms of service, or acceptable use policies. It enables users to flag content that may include hate speech, harassment, spam, nudity, or any other type of explicit or inappropriate material. The Report Abuse Form typically consists of a set of fields and elements that allow users to provide relevant information regarding the reported content or action. It typically includes the following components: 1. Description: A text box or area where the user can enter a detailed description of the issue they are reporting. This allows users to explain the problem in their own words and provide additional context if necessary. 2. Category: A dropdown menu or selection of predefined categories to classify the nature of the reported issue. This helps to categorize and prioritize the reported incidents for the platform administrators. 3. Attachments: An option to include any supporting evidence such as screenshots, photos, or videos related to the reported content or action. This allows users to provide visual proof to support their claims. 4. Personal Information: An optional section where users can provide their contact details (such as name and email address) if they wish to receive updates or follow-up regarding the reported incident. This provides transparency and allows administrators to communicate with the user if necessary. By utilizing a Report Abuse Form, digital platforms can ensure that user reports are efficiently collected and reviewed by administrators or moderators. This helps in identifying and resolving issues promptly, taking appropriate actions such as removing offensive content, warning or banning users involved, or implementing preventive measures to deter future violations. Overall, a Report Abuse Form plays a vital role in maintaining a positive and secure user experience within digital platforms by empowering users to actively contribute to the enforcement of guidelines and the overall well-being of the online community.>

Request For Assistance Form

A UI pattern is a reusable solution that designers and developers can use to solve common design problems in user interfaces. It provides a standard way of addressing a particular interaction or layout challenge, making it easier to create consistent and intuitive experiences for users. UI patterns are typically based on best practices and user research, allowing designers to leverage tested and proven solutions. They help ensure that the interface is easy to understand and navigate, reducing the learning curve for users. By following established patterns, designers can focus on customizing the interface to meet the specific needs of their product or brand, rather than reinventing the wheel. A design system, on the other hand, is a comprehensive set of rules, guidelines, and reusable components that define the visual and functional aspects of a user interface. It provides a cohesive and consistent experience across different platforms and products, ensuring that the interface looks and behaves in a familiar way regardless of the context. A design system typically includes a variety of UI patterns, as well as style guides, brand guidelines, and other design assets. It helps ensure that the interface is visually appealing, accessible, and aligned with the overall brand identity. It also promotes collaboration and efficiency among designers and developers, as they can easily reuse and remix existing components and patterns. In summary, UI patterns and design systems are essential tools in the field of user interface design. They provide designers and developers with standardized solutions and guidelines for creating effective and user-friendly interfaces. By leveraging these patterns and systems, designers can streamline their workflow, improve consistency, and ultimately deliver better user experiences.>

Request For Information (RFI) Form

A Request for Information (RFI) form is a tool used in user interface (UI) patterns and design systems to gather specific information or clarifications from stakeholders or users. It is a formal document that helps in planning, designing, and implementing UI elements effectively. The RFI form consists of structured questions that aim to collect details about requirements, preferences, expectations, and specific aspects related to the UI design. These questions can cover various areas such as user experience, functionality, aesthetics, accessibility, and technical considerations. The form typically starts with general information about the project or design system, followed by specific queries to gather the necessary information. The questions can be open-ended, multiple-choice, or require simple yes/no answers, depending on the context and goals. By using an RFI form, designers and developers can ensure that they have a clear understanding of the requirements and constraints before starting the UI design process. It helps in avoiding misunderstandings, streamlining communication, and ensuring that all stakeholders are on the same page. The RFI form can be shared electronically or in a printable format, depending on the convenience of the stakeholders. It should have a clear and concise format, making it easy for respondents to understand and answer the questions accurately. The answers provided in the RFI form serve as valuable inputs for the UI design process. They help the design team to make informed decisions, prioritize features, and create a user-centered design. The form also acts as a reference document throughout the design process, allowing designers to align their efforts with the expectations and requirements of the stakeholders. In conclusion, an RFI form is a formal document used in UI patterns and design systems to gather specific information and clarifications from stakeholders. It plays a vital role in ensuring effective communication, understanding requirements, and enabling the creation of user-centered designs.>

Request For Proposal (RFP) Form

A Request for Proposal (RFP) form is a formal document used to solicit proposals or bids from potential vendors or contractors for a particular project or service. In the context of UI patterns and design systems, an RFP form is designed to gather information and specifications from various vendors or agencies for the development or enhancement of a user interface (UI) or design system. The RFP form serves as a means to communicate the project requirements, goals, and expectations to potential bidders. It typically includes sections such as project background, scope of work, deliverables, timeline, budget, evaluation criteria, and submission requirements. The purpose of an RFP form is to provide a clear and structured framework for vendors to submit their proposals, allowing for an objective evaluation process. It enables the organization to compare and assess different proposals based on specific criteria and select the most suitable vendor for the project. The RFP form should contain detailed information about the desired UI patterns and design system. This can include the desired visual style, color palette, typography, iconography, and layout guidelines. It should also specify the behavior and interaction patterns required for different components or elements of the UI. Additionally, the

RFP form may request information on the vendor's experience and expertise in UI design and development, their approach to usability and accessibility, and their understanding of the target audience and business goals. By using an RFP form, organizations can ensure that they receive comprehensive and comparable proposals from different vendors, facilitating a fair and transparent selection process. It helps to establish clear expectations and requirements upfront, reducing the risk of misunderstandings or delays during the project execution phase. In summary, an RFP form in the context of UI patterns and design systems is a formal document that facilitates the solicitation and evaluation of proposals from potential vendors or agencies. It outlines the project requirements and expectations, allowing organizations to select the most suitable vendor for their UI design and development needs.>

Request For Quote (RFQ) Form

A Request for Quote (RFQ) form is an essential component of UI patterns and design systems. It is a formal document or webpage where customers can request quotes for products or services they are interested in purchasing. The RFQ form serves as a means of communication between the customer and the company, providing specific details about the desired products or services, and allowing the company to provide accurate pricing information. The RFQ form typically includes fields for the customer to input their contact information, such as name, email address, and phone number. It also includes fields for the customer to specify the quantity and type of product or service they are interested in. Additionally, the form may include fields for the customer to provide any specific requirements or preferences they have. The purpose of the RFQ form is to streamline the process of requesting quotes. By providing a structured format for customers to submit their requests, it allows companies to efficiently gather the necessary information to provide accurate and timely quotes. This helps to avoid misunderstandings and ensures that the quotes are tailored to the customer's needs. In terms of UI patterns and design systems, the RFQ form should adhere to the overall design aesthetic and principles of the interface. This includes consistent branding, typography, and color schemes. It should be visually appealing and easy to navigate, with clear instructions and intuitive input fields. To create a RFQ form in pure HTML format, you can utilize the <form> element to create the overall structure of the form. Within the form, you can use the <input> element to create the necessary text fields for the customer to input their contact information, quantity, type, and any specific requirements. Additionally, you can use the element for larger text inputs, such as a comments or additional information field. It is important to ensure that the RFQ form is accessible and responsive, meaning it can be easily used and viewed on different devices and screen sizes. This can be achieved by using CSS media queries and responsive design techniques. Overall, a well-designed RFQ form is an essential component of UI patterns and design systems. It provides a streamlined and efficient way for customers to request quotes, while also ensuring that companies have the necessary information to provide accurate pricing information and meet customer needs.></form>

Resource Booking Form

A Resource Booking Form is a user interface pattern and design system used for reserving or booking resources such as rooms, facilities, equipment, or services. It provides a structured and intuitive way for users to select and confirm their desired booking details. The form typically includes a series of input fields and interactive elements that guide users through the booking process. These elements may include fields for selecting the date and time of the booking, specifying the duration or quantity of the resource, and providing any additional information or preferences. Users are often presented with a calendar or date picker component to easily choose the desired date for their booking. This helps prevent errors and ensures accurate and consistent input. Time selectors may also be included to allow users to specify the start and end time of their reservation. To enhance usability, the Resource Booking Form may include validation mechanisms to ensure that the inputs are valid and within the acceptable range. This may involve checking for conflicts in scheduling, availability of resources, or any business rules or constraints associated with the booking process. In addition to input fields, the form may also display informative labels, instructional text, or tooltips to guide users and provide context for the booking process. Clear and concise error messages can be shown if users submit invalid or incomplete information, helping them to resolve any issues and complete the booking successfully. Once all the necessary details have been provided, users can submit the form to confirm their booking. A confirmation message or summary of the booking details may be displayed for users to review and ensure the accuracy of their reservation. Overall, a well-designed Resource Booking Form makes it easy and efficient for users to book the desired resource. It promotes a seamless user experience by providing a structured and intuitive interface for selecting and confirming reservations, reducing errors, and improving overall usability.

The Resource Booking Form is a user interface pattern and design system used for reserving or booking resources such as rooms, facilities, equipment, or services.

It includes a series of input fields and interactive elements for selecting and confirming the desired booking details, along with validation mechanisms, instructional text, and confirmation messages to enhance usability and guide users through the booking process.

Resource Download Form

A resource download form is a user interface pattern that enables users to request or access downloadable resources, such as documents, files, or media content, from a website or digital platform. This form typically includes fields or elements where users can provide their contact information, select the desired resource, and submit their request.

The purpose of a resource download form is to facilitate the distribution of valuable content or materials to users while also collecting important user information for marketing or communication purposes. By offering downloadable resources, businesses and organizations can provide valuable information, tools, or educational materials to their audience, which can help establish credibility, generate leads, or nurture existing relationships.

Resource Reservation Cancellation Form

A Resource Reservation Cancellation Form is a user interface (UI) pattern and component of a design system that allows users to cancel or modify their previously made reservations for resources or services. This form provides a structured way for users to request the cancellation or modification of their reservations, ensuring efficient and clear communication between the user and the system. The Resource Reservation Cancellation Form typically includes various fields and options that the user needs to fill out in order to successfully cancel or modify their reservation. These fields may include information such as the user's name, contact details, reservation ID, and a reason for cancellation or modification. The form may also offer additional fields or options depending on the specific requirements of the reservation system. The purpose of the Resource Reservation Cancellation Form is to streamline and standardize the process of cancelling or modifying reservations for both the user and the system. By providing a dedicated form for this purpose, users can easily communicate their request without the need for direct contact with customer support or administrative staff. This reduces the burden on customer support teams and allows for efficient processing of cancellation or modification requests. The design of the Resource Reservation Cancellation Form should adhere to the established design system guidelines to ensure consistency and familiarity for users. This includes using appropriate typography, color schemes, and layout patterns that are consistent with the overall design system. Clear and concise labels should be used for each form field, and validation should be implemented to ensure that the user provides all necessary information accurately. Overall, the Resource Reservation Cancellation Form is an essential component of a design system that facilitates the cancellation or modification of reservations in a user-friendly and efficient manner. By providing a standardized form, users can easily communicate their requests, saving time and effort for both the user and the system.>

Resource Reservation Form

A Resource Reservation Form is a UI pattern that allows users to reserve or book a specific resource or service within a given system. It is commonly used in various industries such as hotels, restaurants, event management, and transportation. The purpose of a Resource Reservation Form is to provide a structured and user-friendly way for users to request and secure a resource or service. The form typically consists of input fields and options that allow users to specify the details of their reservation, such as date, time, duration, quantity, and any additional requirements or preferences. By using a Resource Reservation Form, users can easily communicate their booking needs and preferences to the system or provider. This helps streamline the reservation process, reduce errors or miscommunications, and ensure a smooth and enjoyable experience for both the user and the service provider. In terms of design system, a Resource Reservation Form should follow the overall UI design guidelines and visual identity of the system. This includes using consistent typography, colors, and spacing to ensure a cohesive and harmonious appearance. The form should be visually appealing and easy to understand, with clear labels and intuitive input fields. From a technical perspective, a Resource Reservation Form can be implemented using HTML form elements such as `<input>`, ``, and ``. These elements allow users to input and select the necessary details for their reservation. Additionally, client-side validation can be applied to ensure that the inputs are valid before submitting the form. Overall, a Resource Reservation Form plays a crucial role in facilitating the booking process and improving the user experience. It helps users easily communicate their reservation needs and preferences, while also providing a clear and structured way for service providers to manage bookings. By adhering to the design system guidelines, a Resource Reservation Form can seamlessly integrate with the overall user interface and provide a visually consistent and user-friendly experience. >

Resume Submission Form

A UI pattern is a pre-designed solution for a commonly occurring user interface problem or challenge. It is a template or blueprint that defines the structure, behavior, and visual presentation of a user interface element or a set of elements. UI patterns are developed to provide a consistent and intuitive user experience across different devices, platforms, and applications.

UI patterns serve as a guide for designers and developers to create user interfaces that are both aesthetically pleasing and functional. They are based on industry best practices, user research, and usability principles, and are aimed at improving usability, discoverability, and efficiency in digital products.

Return Authorization Form

A Return Authorization Form is a user interface pattern that facilitates the process of returning a product or request for a refund or exchange. It is an essential component of a design system that aims to provide clarity, efficiency, and consistency in handling returns, reducing customer confusion and dissatisfaction.

Typically, a Return Authorization Form includes fields and sections that collect necessary information such as order details, reason for the return, desired outcome (refund, exchange, store credit), and contact information of the customer. It may also include specific instructions and guidelines on how to complete the form accurately.

Returns And Refunds

The Returns and Refunds UI pattern refers to the design system and interaction patterns used to facilitate the process of returning or refunding products or services. It is a crucial component of e-commerce platforms and other transactional websites, aiming to provide a seamless and intuitive experience for users who wish to return or get a refund for their purchases.

The Returns and Refunds UI pattern typically includes the following elements:

1. Return Policy: It is essential to clearly communicate the return policy to users upfront. This includes information about the timeframe within which returns are accepted, any conditions or restrictions, and how refunds are processed.

2. Return Initiation: Users should be able to initiate a return or refund request easily. This can be achieved through a dedicated "Returns" or "Refunds" section within their account or order history, where they can select the item(s) they want to return and provide a reason for their decision.

3. Return Instructions: Clear instructions should be provided to guide users through the return process. This may include information on how to package the item, where to send it, and any

required documentation or labels.

4. Return Status Tracking: Users should be able to track the status of their return or refund request. This can be accomplished by providing updates at each stage of the process, such as when the item is received, when the refund is initiated, and when it is completed.

5. Refund Options: Users should have options for how they receive their refund, such as store credit, original payment method, or a combination of both. The UI should clearly present these options and allow users to make their preference known.

By following this Returns and Refunds UI pattern, designers can ensure that the return and refund process is transparent, efficient, and user-friendly, leading to higher customer satisfaction and loyalty.

Review Submission Form

A UI pattern, in the context of design systems, refers to a reusable and standardized solution to a commonly occurring design problem in a user interface. It serves as a guideline for designers and developers to create consistent and coherent user experiences across different applications or websites. UI patterns are an essential component of design systems as they help establish a unified visual language and improve user familiarity and usability. They streamline the design and development process by providing pre-defined solutions to common design challenges, reducing the time and effort required to create new interfaces.

A design system, on the other hand, is a comprehensive set of guidelines, principles, and reusable components that define the overall design and user experience of a digital product. It encompasses a wide range of elements, including typography, color palettes, iconography, spacing, and layout patterns, to ensure consistency in both visual appearance and interaction behavior. A design system serves as a central resource for designers and developers, providing them with the necessary tools and assets to create on-brand and cohesive interfaces.

Rewards And Loyalty

Rewards and loyalty are UI patterns and design system components that are utilized to encourage users to engage with a product or service frequently and consistently. These patterns are designed to foster a sense of appreciation and value towards the user, ultimately leading to increased retention and customer satisfaction.

Rewards can take various forms such as points, badges, or virtual currency, which are earned by users for completing specific actions or milestones within the product or service. These rewards act as incentives, motivating users to continue using the product and exploring its features. They create a sense of achievement and progress, as users can track their accumulation of rewards over time.

Loyalty, on the other hand, focuses on building long-term relationships with users. It involves recognizing and rewarding users for their continued support and loyalty to the product or service. Loyalty programs often include tiered membership, where users can unlock additional benefits and privileges as they move up the loyalty ladder. These benefits can include exclusive offers, early access to new features, or personalized recommendations.

When designing rewards and loyalty components, it is essential to consider the target audience and align the rewards with their motivations and goals. The rewards should be meaningful and valuable to users, providing a sense of tangible benefit or recognition. Additionally, the design of these components should be visually appealing and intuitive, ensuring that users can easily understand how to earn and redeem rewards.

By implementing rewards and loyalty patterns effectively, product designers can create a positive user experience that encourages continued engagement and fosters a sense of loyalty towards the product or service. These patterns can contribute to increased user retention, satisfaction, and ultimately, the overall success of the product or service.

Rich Media Galleries

Rich Media Galleries are a UI pattern that allows users to view and interact with a collection of multimedia content, such as images, videos, and audio, in a visually appealing and immersive way.

These galleries are designed to provide an engaging and interactive experience for users by presenting the content in a dynamic and interactive manner. They often include features such as zooming, rotating, and panning functionality, as well as autoplay and fullscreen capabilities. Users can navigate through the gallery by swiping, clicking on navigation buttons, or using keyboard shortcuts.

Rich Media Messages (Images, Videos)

Rich Media Messages refer to the use of images and videos in user interface (UI) patterns and design systems. These elements are utilized to enhance user experience and convey information in a visually appealing manner.

Images are static visual representations that can effectively communicate concepts, emotions, or information. They can be used to illustrate a point, showcase products, or add visual interest to the user interface. Images can be displayed within a design system using various formats such as JPEG, PNG, or GIF, and can be incorporated into UI patterns such as hero banners, thumbnails, or avatar icons.

Rich Snippets

Rich Snippets are a UI pattern and component of a design system that enhances search engine results by providing additional information and structured data to users. They help users easily understand and navigate search results by displaying concise and relevant information directly on the search page. Rich Snippets are typically used for search results related to businesses, events, products, recipes, reviews, and other structured content. They utilize schema markup, a standardized vocabulary of tags, to add context and meaning to the content displayed in search results. When search engines detect this markup, they are able to interpret and display the information in a more visually appealing and organized manner. By incorporating Rich Snippets into a design system, websites can take advantage of the additional visibility and attract more targeted organic traffic. These snippets act as a preview of the website's content, showcasing key information such as ratings, prices, availability, and descriptions, directly on the search results page. This allows users to quickly assess the relevance and credibility of the search result before clicking on it. To implement Rich Snippets in HTML, the schema.org vocabulary is used to define the structured data. Various schema.org types, such as LocalBusiness, Product, Recipe, and Review, can be utilized depending on the nature of the content being marked up. The specific properties and values provided in the schema markup will determine what information is displayed in the Rich Snippet. To give an example, if a website is listing a local business, the schema markup may include properties such as name, address, telephone, and website. This information, when structured using schema.org vocabulary, can be displayed in a Rich Snippet as a summary card with the business's name, address, and contact details directly on the search results page. In summary, Rich Snippets are a UI pattern and component of a design system that use schema markup to enhance search engine results. They provide users with concise and structured information directly on the search page, making it easier to assess the relevance and credibility of search results. By incorporating Rich Snippets into their websites, businesses can increase their visibility and attract more targeted organic traffic.>

Rich Text Editing

Rich Text Editing refers to the ability to format and manipulate text in a user interface (UI) using various editing tools and options. It is a critical component in UI design patterns and design systems, as it provides users with the ability to create and edit text content with different styles, fonts, colors, sizes, and other formatting options.

A design system is a collection of reusable components, patterns, and guidelines that ensure consistency and efficiency in UI design and development. It provides a set of predefined styles, behaviors, and interactions that designers and developers can use to create consistent and cohesive user experiences. Rich Text Editing is an important part of a design system, as it allows for the standardization of text formats, ensuring that text content follows a predefined set of rules and styles.

Room Reservation Form

A Room Reservation Form is a user interface pattern and design system used to gather the necessary information from users in order to book a room or space for a specific date and time. The form typically consists of a series of input fields and checkboxes that collect the necessary details such as the user's name, contact information, desired date and time of reservation, and any additional requirements or special requests. The form may also include a calendar widget or date picker for easy selection of the desired reservation date. The purpose of this form is to streamline the booking process, making it easy and efficient for users to reserve a room or space. By providing all the necessary information upfront, the form eliminates the need for back-and-forth communication and allows the reservation to be confirmed quickly. The Room Reservation Form follows certain design principles and best practices to ensure a smooth and user-friendly experience. It should have a clear and intuitive layout, with labels for each input field to indicate the required information. The form should also provide helpful error messages or validation feedback if users enter incorrect or incomplete information. In terms of aesthetics, the form should adhere to the overall visual design system of the application or website it is a part of. This includes consistent use of colors, typography, and spacing to maintain a cohesive look and feel. The form should also be responsive and adaptable to different screen sizes and devices, ensuring a seamless experience for users regardless of the device they are using. Overall, a well-designed Room Reservation Form is an essential component for any application or website that offers room or space booking services. It provides a simple, efficient, and visually appealing way for users to reserve rooms, making the entire process convenient and hassle-free.

Safety Instructions

A safety instruction in the context of UI patterns and design systems is a set of guidelines or recommendations aimed at ensuring the secure and proper use of the system or application.

These instructions are typically provided to users or developers and serve as a reference for understanding the potential risks and mitigating measures associated with the system. They outline best practices and precautions to prevent accidents, errors, or unintended consequences.

Screen Mirroring

Screen Mirroring is a UI pattern and design system that allows the user to display the content of one screen onto another screen. It enables the user to replicate the screen of a device onto a larger display, such as a television or a projector. The primary use case for screen mirroring is to enhance the user experience by providing a bigger and clearer view of the content from the primary device. This is particularly useful when sharing multimedia content, such as photos, videos, or presentations with a larger audience or when engaging in activities that require a larger screen, such as gaming or video conferencing. Screen mirroring can be achieved through various technologies, such as wired connections (e.g., HDMI, DisplayPort) or wireless connections (e.g., Wi-Fi, Bluetooth). The choice of technology depends on the specific device and its capabilities. In terms of design, screen mirroring should provide a seamless and intuitive experience for the user. The user should be able to easily initiate the mirroring process and switch between devices without encountering any difficulties. The UI should be simple and straightforward, allowing the user to quickly understand how to use the feature. Additionally, it should provide clear feedback to the user regarding the status of the mirroring process, such as indicating when the connection is established or when there is an error. A design system for screen mirroring should provide guidelines and components that can be easily implemented in various applications and platforms. It should include standardized visual and interaction patterns that ensure consistency and familiarity for the user. The design system should also consider the different devices and screen sizes that may be involved in the mirroring process and provide adaptable components that can be used across different contexts. Overall, screen mirroring is a powerful UI pattern and design system that enhances the user experience by allowing the content from one screen to be displayed on another. It provides a seamless and intuitive way to share and enjoy content on a larger display, contributing to a more engaging and immersive user experience.>

Screen Recording

A screen recording is a digital process that captures and records the visual display of a device's user interface (UI) patterns and design system. It allows for the creation of video recordings that showcase the interaction between users and the interface, serving as a valuable tool in analyzing and communicating UI design. By recording the screen, designers and developers can demonstrate the functionality and behavior of their UI patterns and design system in action. This allows for a more comprehensive understanding of how users interact with the interface, identifying any issues or areas for improvement. Screen recordings are commonly used in usability testing, where participants' interactions with the interface are captured for analysis. By observing real user interactions, designers can gain insights into how users navigate through the UI, interact with different elements, and complete tasks. This information can be invaluable for refining the design and improving the overall user experience. In addition to usability testing, screen recordings are also useful for documenting and communicating UI patterns and design guidelines within a design system. By recording the intended interactions and behaviors, designers can provide visual examples that help ensure consistent implementation across different projects and teams. Screen recordings can be created using various software and tools specifically designed for this purpose. They typically enable users to select the screen area to be recorded, choose the desired frame rate and video quality, and specify audio settings if required. The resulting video file can then be edited and shared as needed. In conclusion, a screen recording is a digital process that captures and records the visual display of a device's UI patterns and design system. It serves as a valuable tool in usability testing, allowing designers to observe and analyze user interactions with the interface. Additionally, screen recordings aid in documenting and communicating UI patterns within a design system, ensuring consistency across different projects and teams.>

Screenshot Capture

Screenshot Capture refers to a user interface (UI) pattern and design system element that allows users to capture screenshots or screen recordings of their device screen, commonly used in software applications, operating systems, or websites. It is designed to provide a convenient and easy way for users to capture and save a visual representation of the current display on their device.

Screenshot Capture typically consists of a button or an icon that triggers the screenshot capturing functionality. When users interact with this button or icon, the system captures a screenshot of the current screen and saves it in a specific format or location, depending on the implementation. Some systems also offer additional options such as capturing a specific area of the screen or recording a video of the screen. The purpose of Screenshot Capture is to enable users to visually capture and share information or moments from their device screen. It can be used for various purposes, including documenting software issues or glitches, sharing interesting content or moments with others, or simply keeping a record of important information displayed on the screen. In terms of UI design, Screenshot Capture should have a visually distinguishable button or icon that represents the screenshot capturing functionality. It should be easily accessible and placed in a prominent position within the user interface, ensuring that users can quickly locate and utilize it when needed. Clear and concise labels or tooltips can also be provided to guide users on how to use the Screenshot Capture feature. Furthermore, it is important to consider the user experience when implementing Screenshot Capture. The capture process should be fast and seamless, minimizing any disruption to the user's workflow. After capturing the screenshot, users should be provided with clear feedback, such as a notification or preview of the captured screenshot, and options for saving or sharing it. In conclusion, Screenshot Capture is a UI pattern and design system element that allows users to capture screenshots or screen recordings of their device screen. It provides a straightforward and convenient way for users to visually capture and share information or moments from their screen. Implementing Screenshot Capture involves designing a visually distinguishable button or icon, ensuring easy accessibility, and providing a seamless capture process with clear feedback to enhance the user experience.

253

Scroll Hijacking

Scroll hijacking is a UI pattern in web design where the scrolling behavior of a webpage is altered or manipulated to deviate from the default browser behavior. This is done by intercepting the scroll event and implementing custom scrolling effects or animations that override the natural scrolling behavior. By default, scrolling allows users to navigate through the content of a webpage vertically or horizontally using a mouse wheel, trackpad, or touch gestures. However, with scroll hijacking, the natural scrolling experience is disrupted, causing confusion and frustration for users. This technique is often used to create unique and visually appealing interactions, such as parallax scrolling or animated transitions between sections of a webpage. It aims to enhance the user experience by providing engaging visual effects. However, scroll hijacking can also have negative effects on usability and accessibility if not implemented carefully. One common approach to scroll hijacking is to split the content of a webpage into distinct sections, and then use JavaScript to control the scrolling behavior between these sections. Each section is given a fixed position on the page, and when the user scrolls, the website animates to the next section instead of smoothly scrolling through the content. While scroll hijacking can be visually impressive, it often comes at the expense of user control. Users may find it difficult to navigate the page at their own pace or scroll back to a previous section. It can also impact users who prefer to use alternative input devices or assistive technologies for scrolling. When implementing scroll hijacking, designers should consider the usability and accessibility implications. Providing clear visual cues and intuitive navigation controls can help mitigate the negative effects of scroll hijacking. Additionally, it is important to ensure that the custom scrolling effects do not interfere with the overall responsiveness and performance of the webpage. In conclusion, scroll hijacking is a UI pattern used in web design to alter or manipulate the scrolling behavior of a webpage. While it can create visually appealing interactions, it should be implemented with caution and consideration for usability and accessibility.

Scroll Progress Bar

A scroll progress bar is a UI element that visually indicates the user's progress through a webpage or document by displaying the amount of content that has been scrolled through.

It is typically represented as a horizontal bar or line that appears at the top or bottom of the viewport, parallel to the direction of scrolling. The length or width of the bar is directly proportional to the amount of content that has been scrolled through. As the user scrolls through the content, the progress bar fills up or advances, providing a visual representation of their position within the page.

Scroll-To-Top Button

A scroll-to-top button is a UI pattern designed to allow users to easily navigate back to the top of a webpage without having to manually scroll. It is a small, fixed-position button typically placed in the lower right or left corner of the screen. When clicked or tapped, the scroll-to-top button instantly scrolls the page vertically to the top, providing a smooth and effortless user experience. The main purpose of a scroll-to-top button is to enhance the usability and accessibility of long webpages. As users scroll down a page, the button remains visible, serving as a constant reminder that they have the option to return to the top with a single click. This eliminates the need for repetitive scrolling or the use of keyboard shortcuts, saving time and effort for the user. Scroll-to-top buttons are a common component in design systems, as they provide a consistent and intuitive means of navigation across different websites and applications. They are often included as part of a user-friendly interface, contributing to a positive overall user experience. To implement a scroll-to-top button in pure HTML, only two paragraphs are required. The first paragraph can be used to describe the purpose and functionality of the button, while the second paragraph can provide an example of the HTML code needed to create it:

A scroll-to-top button is a UI pattern that allows users to navigate back to the top of a webpage with a single click. It is a fixed-position button placed at the bottom of the screen and remains visible as users scroll down. When clicked, the button instantly scrolls the page to the top, improving usability and accessibility.

To create a scroll-to-top button in HTML, the following code can be used:

Search Autocomplete

An autocomplete search is a user interface (UI) pattern that allows users to quickly find and select a desired item or input by suggesting possible matches as they type in a search field. It enhances the user experience by providing real-time suggestions that anticipate and narrow down search results, reducing the need for manual input and improving efficiency. Autocomplete search is commonly used in various applications, websites, and design systems to improve search functionality and speed up user interactions. It is particularly useful in situations where the search input has a large number of options or a complex hierarchy, making it difficult for users to find the desired item by scrolling or navigating through a list. The autocomplete functionality typically starts providing suggestions after the user has entered a certain number of characters or triggers the search by pressing the Enter key or clicking a search button. The suggestions are dynamically generated based on pre-existing data sources, including databases, API calls, or predefined lists. The suggestions are usually displayed in a dropdown menu or a list below the search input field, allowing users to visually scan and select their desired option. The suggestions provided by autocomplete search are based on the characters entered by the user and can be ranked by relevance or popularity. This helps users find their desired item quickly and easily without having to type the entire search query. The suggestions are updated in real-time as the user continues to type or modify their search input. Autocomplete search can be further enhanced by incorporating additional features or filters to refine the search results. This can include options such as filtering by category, geography, or date, as well as displaying additional information or previews for each suggestion to aid in decision-making. Overall, autocomplete search is a powerful UI pattern and design system element that significantly improves search usability and efficiency. By providing real-time suggestions and reducing manual input, it allows users to find and select their desired items more quickly and effortlessly.

Autocomplete search is a UI pattern that suggests possible matches as users type in a search field.

It enhances user experience, improves efficiency, and reduces manual input by providing real-time suggestions based on pre-existing data sources.

Search Bar

A search bar is a user interface (UI) pattern commonly used in design systems to provide users with a way to enter keywords or queries to search for specific content within an application or website. It typically consists of a text input field and an associated button or icon that triggers the search functionality.

Search bars are an essential component of many applications and websites as they allow users to find information quickly and efficiently. They are especially useful in content-heavy platforms such as e-commerce websites, news aggregators, and social media networks, where users often need to search for specific items, articles, or user profiles.

Search Form

The search form is a UI element used in user interfaces to allow users to input search queries and submit them to retrieve relevant information or search results. It is a commonly used UI pattern and a fundamental component of many design systems. The search form typically consists of a text input field where users can enter their search query and a submit button to initiate the search. Depending on the complexity of the search functionality, additional features like filters, advanced options, or auto-suggestions can be included. The design of the search form should prioritize usability and clarity. It should be easily recognizable as a search input, typically through the use of a search icon or a label. The input field should have clear and concise placeholder text that provides guidance on what users should enter. It is important to ensure that the input field has sufficient width to accommodate longer search queries without truncating the text. Furthermore, the search form should adhere to accessibility standards to ensure that it is usable for all users, including those with disabilities. This includes providing descriptive labels for screen readers and ensuring proper keyboard navigation. In terms of placement, the search form is commonly positioned prominently in the header or navigation bar of a website or application. This ensures that it is easily accessible from anywhere within the interface and allows users to quickly initiate a search. When designing a search form, it is important to consider the context in which it will be used. This includes understanding the specific needs and expectations of users, as well as the type of content or data being searched. The design should be consistent with the overall UI of the system and maintain a cohesive aesthetic. Overall, the search form is an essential UI pattern that allows users to search for specific information within a system. By implementing it effectively, designers can enhance the usability and accessibility of their interfaces, providing users with a seamless search experience.

Search Results Screen

A search results screen is a user interface pattern and design system element that presents a list of search results to the user. It is commonly used in search engines, e-commerce platforms, and other applications where users search for specific information or items. The search results screen typically consists of multiple search results displayed in a structured grid or list format. Each search result usually includes a title, a brief description, and other relevant information such as images, ratings, or prices. The search results are often presented in a scrollable view, allowing users to easily browse through the list. The primary purpose of the search results screen is to provide users with a clear and concise overview of the search results. It allows users to quickly scan and evaluate the available options, helping them make informed decisions based on their search query. The design of the search results screen should be intuitive and user-friendly, enabling users to easily navigate through the list and access more detailed information if needed. To enhance the usability of the search results screen, design systems often include additional features and elements. For example, a filtering or sorting mechanism can be incorporated to help users refine their search and narrow down the results. Pagination or infinite scrolling can be implemented to accommodate large sets of search results without overwhelming the user with too much information on a single page. Furthermore, the design of the search results screen should align with the overall visual language and branding of the application. Consistent use of typography, colors, spacing, and other design elements ensures a cohesive and visually pleasing user experience. In conclusion, a search results screen is an essential component of UI patterns and design systems that presents a list of search results to the user. It aims to provide users with a clear and concise overview of the available options, enabling them to make informed decisions based on their search query. Proper design and implementation of the search results screen enhance user experience and improve the overall usability of the application.>

Security And Privacy Settings

Security and privacy settings refer to the features and options within an interface that allow users to control and protect their personal information and ensure the safety of their digital activities.

These settings typically include various configurations and preferences that users can customize based on their needs and preferences. They are designed to offer users granular control over their privacy and security, enabling them to decide what information they want to share, who can access it, and what level of protection they desire.

From a UI design system perspective, security and privacy settings should be easily accessible, straightforward, and intuitive. They should be prominently displayed within the interface and integrated seamlessly into the overall design. By following established UI design patterns for security and privacy settings, designers can ensure that users can easily locate and modify these settings without confusion or frustration.

Some common UI patterns for security and privacy settings include:

1. Account Protection Settings: These settings allow users to enable two-factor authentication, change their password, or set up security questions to protect their account from unauthorized access.

2. Privacy Preferences: This pattern enables users to define their privacy preferences by controlling what information is shared or made public. It may include options to manage visibility

of personal data, control targeted advertising, or choose which third-party apps have access to their data.

3. Notification Management: This pattern allows users to customize their notification preferences, including opting in or out of certain types of notifications, choosing notification channels, or setting quiet hours.

By implementing these UI patterns and ensuring the clear communication of security and privacy settings, designers can empower users to take control of their digital presence and protect their personal information effectively.

Service Cancellation Form

A service cancellation form is a UI pattern and design system component used to facilitate the process of canceling a service or subscription. It provides a structured and standardized way for users to request the termination of their account or membership.

When designing a service cancellation form, it is important to consider the following key components:

1. Heading and Introduction: The form should include a clear and concise heading that indicates its purpose, such as "Service Cancellation Form." An introduction paragraph can be added to provide additional context or instructions for users.

2. User Information: The form should include fields for users to provide their personal information, such as name, email address, and account ID. This information is crucial for the service provider to identify and process the cancellation request.

3. Reason for Cancellation: To gather valuable feedback, including a dropdown or radio button options for users to select their reason for canceling the service is recommended. This information can help the service provider to better understand user needs and potentially improve their offerings or address any issues.

4. Confirmation and Submit: After users have filled out all the necessary information, a confirmation section can be added to summarize their cancellation request. This section should include a checkbox or a statement that confirms users understand the consequences of canceling their service. Finally, a submit button enables users to complete the cancellation process.

A well-designed service cancellation form greatly enhances the user experience by providing a straightforward and efficient way for users to terminate their service. By adhering to established UI patterns and design system guidelines, the form can maintain consistency with other components and ensure a seamless experience for users across the platform.

Session Timeout Handling

Session timeout handling is a crucial aspect of user interface (UI) patterns and design systems. It refers to the implementation of features that effectively manage user sessions and provide a smooth user experience when a session expires or becomes inactive.

Sessions are temporary data storage mechanisms that allow websites and applications to maintain user-specific information for a certain period of time. However, these sessions have a limited lifespan, and if users remain inactive for an extended period of time, their session may expire. This can occur due to various reasons such as security concerns, resource allocation, or simply to improve system performance.

When a session timeout occurs, it is essential to handle it in a user-friendly and intuitive manner. Users should be provided with clear notifications and instructions on how to proceed. The primary goal is to ensure that they do not lose any unsaved work or feel frustrated by the interruption.

One common approach to session timeout handling is to display a timed-out message on the UI.

257

This message typically informs users that their session has expired and provides options to either log in again or continue as a guest. By presenting these choices, users can easily decide whether to resume their session or perform actions as a guest without logging in.

In addition to the timed-out message, it is important to offer a proactive warning to users before their session expires. This warning can be in the form of a pop-up or a notification at the top of the screen. By providing users with advance notice, they have the opportunity to extend their session or save their work before it is lost.

Furthermore, it is good practice to include an auto-logout feature that automatically redirects users to a login page upon session expiration. This ensures that users are securely logged out and prevents unauthorized access to their accounts. Additionally, it helps maintain the privacy and security of sensitive user information.

Overall, session timeout handling plays a vital role in maintaining a positive user experience. By implementing clear notifications, proactive warnings, and secure logout mechanisms, users can seamlessly navigate through a system even when their sessions expire or become inactive.

Settings Screen

A Settings Screen is a user interface element that provides access to various customizable options and preferences within an application or system. It is a central hub for managing the configuration settings of the software or device.

The Settings Screen is typically organized in a hierarchical structure, with different categories or sections representing different areas of customization. Each section contains a set of related options or settings that users can modify according to their preferences. These settings can range from basic functionalities like language preference and display settings to more advanced options such as account settings, notification preferences, and privacy settings.

Shake To Undo

Shake to Undo is a UI pattern and design system feature that allows users to undo an action by physically shaking their device. It is primarily used in mobile applications and provides a unique and intuitive way to reverse a recent action. The Shake to Undo feature is based on the principle of gesture-based interaction, where users can perform a specific physical movement to trigger an action. In this case, shaking the device serves as the gesture to initiate the undo action. Implementing Shake to Undo requires integrating the device's accelerometer, which detects and measures motion, into the application's code. When the user shakes their device, the accelerometer detects the movement and triggers the undo action. The Shake to Undo pattern is designed to enhance the user experience by providing a quick and convenient method to reverse an action. It eliminates the need for complex navigation or searching for an undo button, as the gesture itself serves as the direct command for undoing the previous action. This UI pattern is particularly useful in cases where users may make accidental mistakes or want to quickly revert a recent change without going through multiple steps. By shaking the device, they can easily undo the action and return to the previous state. However, it is essential to consider potential challenges and limitations when implementing Shake to Undo. For instance, the feature should be implemented in a way that avoids accidental triggers, as users may inadvertently shake their device while performing other actions. Furthermore, it is crucial to provide clear feedback to the user when the shake gesture is recognized and the undo action is triggered. In summary, Shake to Undo is a UI pattern and design system feature that allows users to reverse an action by physically shaking their device. It enhances the user experience by providing a quick and intuitive method to undo recent changes, without the need for complex navigation or searching for an undo button. By integrating the device's accelerometer, the shake gesture is recognized and triggers the undo action, offering a convenient way to revert an accidental mistake or quickly return to the previous state.

Shipping Address Form

A shipping address form is a user interface (UI) pattern that collects information about where a package or shipment should be delivered. It is an essential component of e-commerce websites and shipping applications, enabling users to provide accurate and complete delivery details.

The shipping address form typically consists of various input fields and labels that prompt users to enter their name, address, city, state/province, postal code/ZIP code, country, and contact information. These fields are designed to capture all the necessary information required to deliver a package successfully. Depending on the design, additional fields may be included to accommodate specific shipping requirements or preferences.

Shipping Method Selection Form

A shipping method selection form is a UI pattern and design system component that allows users to choose from various shipping options during the checkout process. It provides users with a clear and intuitive way to select their preferred shipping method, enabling them to make an informed decision based on their specific needs and preferences. The shipping method selection form typically consists of a list or multiple radio buttons, each representing a different shipping option. The form may also include additional information and details about each shipping method, such as estimated delivery times, shipping fees, and any other relevant details that can help users make an informed decision. To use the shipping method selection form, users simply need to click on the radio button corresponding to their desired shipping option. The selected shipping method is then highlighted or visually indicated to provide feedback to the user. Upon submitting the form, the selected shipping method is communicated to the backend system for further processing and fulfillment. The shipping method selection form is designed to be user-friendly and efficient, ensuring a smooth and seamless checkout experience. It should be visually appealing and accessible, with clear and concise labels for each shipping option. The form should also be responsive and adaptable, allowing it to be easily viewed and used across different devices and screen sizes. As part of a design system, the shipping method selection form should adhere to established design guidelines and principles, ensuring consistency and coherence with the overall user interface. It should align with the branding and visual identity of the website or application, providing a cohesive and unified experience for users. In conclusion, a shipping method selection form is a crucial component of the checkout process, providing users with the ability to choose their preferred shipping option. It should be designed to be user-friendly, visually appealing, and consistent with the overall design system. By incorporating this UI pattern, businesses can enhance the user experience and streamline the shipping process.

Shipping And Delivery

A shipping and delivery UI pattern is a design pattern used in user interface (UI) design systems to provide a seamless and intuitive experience for users when ordering products or services online and tracking their delivery progress.

It typically consists of multiple components and features that work together to guide users through the entire shipping and delivery process, from selecting shipping options to tracking their package's status.

Shopping Cart

A shopping cart is a user interface pattern commonly used in e-commerce websites and applications, as part of the overall design system. It serves as a virtual container that allows users to collect and manage items they wish to purchase. The shopping cart acts as an intermediary between the user and the checkout process, enabling users to add, remove, and modify the quantity of items they want to buy. It provides a visual representation of the current state of the user's selected items, including their names, prices, and quantities. In addition, it may display relevant information such as estimated delivery dates, promotional offers, and total cost. The design of a shopping cart typically includes consistent visual elements and functionality to ensure a seamless user experience. It usually features key components such as product thumbnails, item descriptions, pricing details, quantity selectors, and remove buttons. A shopping cart may also incorporate additional features like saved items for later, wishlists, or the ability to compare items. When users interact with the shopping cart, they can easily add items to it by pressing an "Add to Cart" button or a similar call-to-action. They can then view the contents of the cart at any time, prior to proceeding to the final checkout step. They have the flexibility to update the quantity of individual items or remove them altogether. Furthermore, users may be prompted to provide additional information, such as selecting preferred variations or specifying customization options, depending on the product and website or application requirements. From a design system perspective, the shopping cart pattern ensures consistency and cohesiveness in the overall user interface. Its appearance, behavior, and functionality should align with the established visual guidelines and user interaction principles. It may inherit styles and components from the design system, such as color schemes, typography, and form elements, to create a cohesive and familiar experience for users. Overall, the shopping cart pattern serves as an integral component of an e-commerce website or application, facilitating users in managing their selected items before proceeding to the checkout process. Its design and implementation should prioritize usability, functionality, and consistency to enhance the overall user experience and drive successful conversions.

A shopping cart is a user interface pattern commonly used in e-commerce websites and applications, as part of the overall design system. It serves as a virtual container that allows users to collect and manage items they wish to purchase.

The shopping cart acts as an intermediary between the user and the checkout process, enabling users to add, remove, and modify the quantity of items they want to buy. It provides a visual representation of the current state of the user's selected items, including their names, prices, and quantities.

Sidebar Navigation

The sidebar navigation is a user interface pattern commonly used in design systems to provide an organized and efficient way for users to navigate through an application or website. It typically appears as a vertical column on one side of the screen and contains a list of links or icons that represent different sections or pages within the interface.

Users can interact with the sidebar navigation by clicking on the links or icons, which then take them to the corresponding section or page. This navigation pattern is especially useful for applications or websites with a large amount of content or complex information architecture, as it allows users to quickly and easily access different sections without the need for excessive scrolling or searching.

Sign-Up Screen

A sign-up screen is a UI pattern and design system component that allows users to create a new account or register for a service or platform. It typically consists of a form with fields for entering personal information such as username, email address, password, and other required data. The primary purpose of a sign-up screen is to collect the necessary information from users to create their account and grant them access to the service or platform. It serves as the initial interaction point between the user and the system, enabling a smooth onboarding process. The sign-up screen is designed to be user-friendly and intuitive, guiding users through the registration process in a clear and concise manner. It should provide clear instructions on how to fill out the form fields and include any necessary validation to ensure the accuracy and completeness of the entered data. In terms of design, the sign-up screen should align with the overall visual identity and branding of the platform or service. This includes using consistent colors, typography, and graphical elements to create a cohesive and engaging user experience. The layout should be responsive and adaptable to different screen sizes and devices, ensuring that users can easily access the sign-up screen regardless of their preferred device. To enhance usability, it is important to limit the number of required form fields and only request the essential information needed to create the account. Providing optional fields for additional information can be beneficial, but should not be overwhelming or create friction in the sign-up process. Additionally, incorporating password strength indicators and real-time feedback during form input can help users create secure passwords and reduce errors. Implementing measures such as CAPTCHA or email verification can also help prevent spam or fraudulent registrations. In conclusion, a sign-up screen is a crucial component of any UI pattern and design system, serving as the gateway for users to join and interact with a platform or service. It should be designed with a focus on simplicity, usability, and security, ensuring a smooth and seamless registration process for users.>

Site Map

A site map is a visual representation of the structure and organization of a website. It acts as a navigation tool for users to understand the hierarchy and relationships between different pages and sections of a website. A site map typically consists of a hierarchical diagram or list of all the pages on a website, organized in a logical order. Site maps are an important part of user interface (UI) patterns and design systems as they provide a clear overview of the website's content and structure. They help users quickly find and navigate to the desired information, improving the user experience and reducing frustration. Site maps are especially useful for large and complex websites with multiple levels and sections. In UI design, site maps serve as a blueprint for organizing the content and functionality of a website. They help designers and developers understand the scope of the website and plan the user flow accordingly. By visualizing the relationships between different pages and sections, designers can determine the best layout and navigation patterns to ensure a seamless user experience. Additionally, site maps are useful for content strategy and information architecture. They assist in identifying any gaps or redundancies in the website's content, making it easier to create a cohesive and well-structured user experience. Content creators can refer to the site map to ensure that all relevant information is included and easily accessible to the users. In summary, a site map is a visual representation of the structure and organization of a website, serving as a navigation tool for users to understand the hierarchy and relationships between different pages and sections. It is an essential component of UI patterns and design systems, aiding in the organization of content, planning of user flows, and improvement of the overall user experience.>

Skeleton Screens

Skeleton screens are a UI pattern and design system element commonly used in web and mobile applications. They are designed to improve user experience by providing a visual placeholder during the loading process of content, giving users a sense of progress and reducing perceived wait time. In the context of UI patterns, skeleton screens are used as a temporary visual representation of the final content that is yet to be loaded. They are typically displayed in place of actual content, giving the illusion of an empty or incomplete interface. By displaying a rough outline of the expected content, skeleton screens provide users with a visual cue that the page is loading and help to manage their expectations. As a part of a design system, skeleton screens are often built to adhere to specific brand guidelines and overall visual style. They may incorporate the same colors, typography, and layout principles as the final design, ensuring a consistent and seamless experience for users. When it comes to implementation, skeleton screens are typically constructed using HTML and CSS. The HTML structure usually consists of div elements that represent the different sections or components of the page. These div elements are often given class names that correspond to the type of content they will eventually hold, such as "header", "sidebar", or "product-card". The CSS styles applied to these div elements define the visual appearance of the skeleton screens, including colors, borders, and spacing. In terms of user perception, skeleton screens provide a sense of continuity between the loading state and the final content state. This transition from skeleton screens to full content is smoother and less jarring compared to traditional loading spinner or blank screens. Users are able to anticipate the layout and structure of the content, which can make the waiting experience more tolerable. Overall, skeleton screens are a valuable tool in the UI designer's toolkit. They not only improve perceived performance and reduce user frustration but also contribute to a more polished and professional user experience. By incorporating skeleton screens into a design system, designers can ensure consistency and brand alignment across different parts of an application.

Skeuomorphic Design

Skeuomorphic design is a UI pattern and design system that mimics the aesthetic elements and textures of real-world objects and materials. It is characterized by the use of realistic and familiar visual cues, such as shadows, gradients, and textures, to create a sense of familiarity and intuitiveness in digital interfaces. In the context of user interface design, skeuomorphism aims to bridge the gap between the physical and digital worlds by simulating the look and feel of physical objects. This design approach leverages people's existing knowledge and familiarity with physical objects to create a more intuitive and user-friendly experience. One of the key principles of skeuomorphic design is the replication of real-world objects in their entirety, including their visual properties and interaction behaviors. For example, a skeuomorphic design for a note-taking app may feature a virtual notepad that displays realistic lined paper texture and a virtual pen that simulates writing movements. This design approach creates a sense of tangibility and familiarity, making it easier for users to understand and interact with the digital interface. Skeuomorphic design was particularly popular in the early days of digital interfaces when technology limitations made it challenging to create complex and visually appealing designs. Designers used skeuomorphism to make digital interfaces more relatable and accessible to users who were accustomed to physical objects. However, as technology advanced and user expectations evolved, flat design and minimalism gained prominence in UI design. Skeuomorphic design fell out of favor as it was seen as outdated and often resulted in cluttered and visually heavy interfaces. Flat design, on the other hand, emphasized simplicity and clean aesthetics with the absence of shadows, gradients, and textures. Nevertheless, skeuomorphism continues to be used in certain contexts where it enhances the user experience. For example, in gaming interfaces, skeuomorphic elements may be employed to simulate real-life game controllers or recreate familiar game environments. In productivity apps, skeuomorphic elements may be used to replicate the appearance of physical tools and instruments, such as a calculator interface resembling a physical calculator. Overall, skeuomorphic design is a design approach that utilizes visual cues from the physical world to create a sense of familiarity and intuitiveness in digital interfaces. While it has lost popularity in recent years, it still has its place in certain contexts where recreating physical elements enhances the user experience.

Slide-Out Menus

Slide-out menus, also known as off-canvas menus, are a user interface pattern commonly used in web and app design systems. They provide a versatile and space-efficient way to display navigational options and additional content, while preserving the primary focus on the main screen. Slide-out menus are typically hidden from view until triggered by the user, often through a hamburger icon or a swipe gesture on touch-enabled devices. When activated, the menu slides out from the edge of the screen, partially or completely overlaying the main content. This allows users to access secondary options, such as navigation links, settings, or additional actions, without cluttering the user interface. From a design system perspective, slide-out menus contribute to a consistent and intuitive user experience across different pages or screens of a website or application. By keeping the menu hidden, valuable screen real estate is preserved for the main content, enhancing its visibility and focus. Additionally, slide-out menus can also enhance mobile responsiveness, as they can adapt to different screen sizes and orientations. To implement a basic slide-out menu in HTML, the following code example can be used:

First, create a container element for the slide-out menu:

```
<div id="slide-out-menu">
```

Next, populate the menu with navigation links or other options:

```
<a href="#">Home</a> <a href="#">About</a> <a href="#">Services</a> <a href="#">Contact</a>
```

Finally, style the container element and add event listeners to trigger the slide-out effect. This can be achieved with CSS and JavaScript or modern frameworks and libraries, depending on the specific implementation requirements.

Slideshow Carousel

A slideshow carousel is a user interface pattern and design system commonly used to display a series of images or content in a sequential and interactive manner. It consists of a container element that holds multiple slides and provides controls for users to navigate through the slides. The slideshow carousel typically comprises of a main display area where the current slide is shown, and navigation controls that allow users to move to the next or previous slide. These controls can be in the form of clickable buttons (commonly represented by arrows) or indicators (such as dots or numbers) that visually represent the number of slides and the user's current position within the slideshow. In terms of implementation, the slideshow carousel relies on the use of HTML, CSS, and JavaScript to create the desired functionality and visual appearance.

The HTML structure usually involves a container element that wraps around individual slide elements. Each slide element contains the content to be displayed, such as images, text, or multimedia. Styling the slideshow carousel involves applying CSS styles to the container and slide elements to control their positioning, size, and transition effects. This includes techniques like using CSS flexbox or grid for layout, applying animations for slide transitions, and customizing the appearance of the navigation controls. The interactive behavior of the slideshow carousel is typically achieved using JavaScript. This includes adding event listeners to the navigation controls to trigger the slide transitions, updating the current slide based on user input, and implementing any additional functionalities like autoplay or pause on hover. When designing a slideshow carousel, it is important to consider factors such as the size and aspect ratio of the content to ensure optimal display on different devices and screen sizes. Additionally, accessibility features like keyboard navigation, screen reader compatibility, and responsive design should also be taken into account to provide an inclusive user experience. In summary, the slideshow carousel is a versatile UI pattern and design system that allows for the organized presentation of multiple images or content in a visually appealing and interactive way. It is a popular choice for showcasing portfolios, product galleries, and other visual-centric content on websites and applications.

Sliding Panels

Sliding Panels in the context of UI patterns and design systems refer to a user interface component that allows for the presentation of content in a sliding manner, typically to reveal additional information or functionality. This pattern is commonly used in websites and applications to optimize space and improve user experience by minimizing clutter and providing a seamless transition between different sections of content.

The basic structure of a sliding panel consists of a main container, which holds the primary content, and a sliding panel that is initially hidden from view. The sliding panel can be triggered to slide in or out through various user interactions, such as a click or swipe gesture. When the sliding panel is activated, it smoothly slides into view, either from the side or from the top/bottom, revealing additional content or functionality.

Social Media Feed

A social media feed is a user interface (UI) pattern commonly used in design systems to display and organize content from multiple users or sources in a chronological order. It allows users to view and interact with posts, updates, and other forms of media shared by their connections or subscribed accounts.

A social media feed serves as a central hub where users can quickly and easily consume a vast amount of information in a single platform. It condenses and presents diverse content, such as text, images, videos, and links, in a structured manner for efficient browsing and engagement.

Typically, a social media feed is designed to accommodate continuous scrolling, allowing users to effortlessly navigate through a virtually endless stream of content. As users scroll down, additional posts dynamically load to provide a fluid and uninterrupted browsing experience. This infinite scrolling feature eliminates the need for manual pagination and enables users to access older posts without disruption.

Designing an effective social media feed requires careful consideration of various elements. The layout should prioritize the display of content, with each post structured in a way that harmonizes text, media, and associated metadata. Visual cues, such as avatars or profile pictures, facilitate user recognition for different accounts. Timestamps help users easily identify the recency of posts and can indicate activity levels on the platform.

Social media feeds often incorporate engagement features to encourage user interaction. Buttons or icons for "likes," comments, and shares enable users to express their reactions, provide feedback, and propagate content across the platform. These features foster community engagement and virality, allowing content to spread beyond immediate connections.

Users may also have the ability to customize their social media feed, organizing content by relevancy, topic, or specific user preferences. This personalization enhances the user experience by tailoring the feed to individual interests and providing a more curated content consumption experience.

In conclusion, a social media feed is a UI pattern that aggregates and displays user-generated content in a structured manner, enabling efficient browsing, engagement, and interaction within a social media platform. It offers a continuous scrolling experience, incorporates visual cues and timestamping, and includes engagement features to boost user interactivity and content dissemination.

Social Media Sharing Buttons

The Social Media Sharing Buttons are a UI pattern commonly used in website design systems to enable users to easily share content on various social media platforms. These buttons are typically placed on web pages or articles, allowing users to quickly and conveniently share the content with their social networks. The Social Media Sharing Buttons usually consist of icons or logos of popular social media platforms, such as Facebook, Twitter, Instagram, Pinterest, and LinkedIn, among others. When users click on one of these buttons, they are redirected to the respective social media platform, where they can post the content or share it with their connections. These buttons are an important element of any website or online content because they help increase the reach and visibility of the content. By providing users with a seamless way to share content on their preferred social media platforms, these buttons encourage more people to engage with and distribute the content, ultimately driving more traffic to the website or article. From a design system perspective, the Social Media Sharing Buttons can be implemented using HTML and CSS. The icons or logos can be added as images or by utilizing icon fonts, enabling the buttons to be easily resized and customized. Additionally, CSS styles can be applied to the buttons to match the overall visual design of the website or application. To ensure accessibility, it is important to include alternative text for the Social Media Sharing Buttons, allowing screen readers to convey the purpose of the buttons to visually impaired users. This can be achieved by using the "alt" attribute in the HTML img tag. In conclusion, Social Media Sharing Buttons are a UI pattern that allows users to easily share content on social media platforms. They are an essential component of a design system and can be implemented using HTML and CSS. By incorporating these buttons into a website or application, content can be effectively distributed and shared, ultimately increasing its visibility and reach.>

Social Sharing Buttons

Social sharing buttons refer to a set of interactive elements in a user interface (UI) that allow users to easily share content on various social networking platforms. These buttons are designed to facilitate the sharing process by providing a simple and visually appealing way for users to interact with social media. In the context of UI patterns and design systems, social sharing buttons are an established and common pattern used to encourage and facilitate social sharing. They are typically placed on web pages, blog posts, or other types of content to give users the ability to share that specific piece of content with their social media networks. Social sharing buttons are essential in today's digital landscape, as they enable users to amplify and distribute content they find interesting or valuable. By incorporating social sharing buttons in a UI, designers are able to harness the power of social media platforms to increase the reach and visibility of their content. These buttons are often displayed as a row or cluster of icons, each representing a different social media platform. Common examples include icons for Facebook, Twitter, LinkedIn, Pinterest, and Instagram. When a user clicks on one of these icons, they are typically prompted to log in to their social media account (if they haven't already) and presented with a pre-populated message or post containing a link to the content they wish to share. The user can then personalize or customize the message before finally posting it to their chosen social media platform. The design and placement of social sharing buttons play a crucial role in their effectiveness. It is important to position them prominently within the UI, ensuring they are easily visible and accessible to users. Additionally, the buttons should be visually consistent with the overall design system of the UI to maintain a cohesive and polished look. In summary, social sharing buttons are UI elements used to encourage users to share content on social media platforms. They are designed to facilitate the sharing process by providing an intuitive and visually appealing way for users to interact with social media. By incorporating social sharing buttons in a UI, designers can empower users to amplify and distribute content, thereby increasing its reach and visibility.

Sort Form

UI Patterns: UI patterns, also known as user interface patterns or design patterns, are recurring solutions to common design problems or challenges encountered in user interface design. These patterns capture best practices and provide guidelines for creating efficient and effective user interfaces. UI patterns help designers and developers by taking advantage of proven design solutions, reducing the need for trial and error, and improving the usability and user experience of an application or website. They are commonly used in the design of websites, web applications, mobile apps, and other digital interfaces. Design System: A design system is a collection of reusable components, guidelines, and principles that helps ensure consistency and coherence in the design of a product or system. It provides a set of rules, styles, and patterns that define how elements within the design should look and behave. A design system promotes efficient and consistent design and development by offering pre-designed and pre-tested components that can be easily reused across different projects. It facilitates collaboration between designers, developers, and other stakeholders, ensuring that everyone is aligned and working towards a common goal. Design systems typically include a visual style guide, which outlines the visual design elements such as color palette, typography, and icons. They also often include a component library, which provides a catalog of pre-built UI elements like buttons, forms, and navigation bars. Additionally, a design system may include documentation and guidelines on interaction patterns, accessibility requirements, and user research findings. By using a design system, teams can save time and effort in the design process, reduce inconsistencies and improve the overall quality of the user interface. It allows for scalability and flexibility, enabling teams to iterate and evolve the design over time without starting from scratch. Overall, a well-designed and implemented design system contributes to a more efficient and coherent user experience. In conclusion, UI patterns and design systems are important tools in user interface design. UI patterns provide solutions to common design problems, while design systems ensure consistency and efficiency in the design process. By utilizing these tools, designers and developers can create user-friendly and visually appealing interfaces.

Splash Screen

The splash screen is a UI pattern commonly used in design systems to provide an initial visual experience for users when they launch an application or website. It is typically a full-screen image or animation that is displayed for a short period of time before the main content of the application is loaded. The purpose of a splash screen is to engage users and create anticipation while the application's resources are being loaded in the background. It provides a visual cue that the application is being loaded and helps to prevent users from perceiving any delay as a problem with the application. The splash screen often includes branding elements such as the application or company logo, as well as a loading indicator to inform users that the application is still loading. Some splash screens may also include a brief slogan or tagline to further reinforce the brand image. In terms of design system considerations, the splash screen should follow the established visual language and style of the overall design system. This includes using the same color palette, typography, and graphic elements to ensure a cohesive and consistent user experience. From a technical perspective, the splash screen should be optimized for fast loading times to minimize any delay experienced by users. This may involve compressing the image or optimizing the animation to reduce file size. Additionally, the splash screen should be designed to be responsive and adaptive, ensuring it looks and functions well across different devices and screen sizes. Overall, the splash screen is an important UI pattern that not only serves a practical purpose of informing users about the loading process but also contributes to the overall brand experience and enhances the aesthetics of the application. By incorporating the splash screen into a design system, designers can ensure a consistent and engaging user experience across different applications and platforms.>

Split Screen Layout

A split screen layout is a user interface pattern that divides the screen into two or more equal or proportional sections, allowing different types of content to be displayed side by side. This layout is commonly used in web and mobile applications, creating a visually balanced and organized interface.

In a split screen layout, each section typically contains independent content or functionalities, providing users with the ability to interact with different elements simultaneously. This pattern is especially useful when presenting contrasting or complementary information, enabling users to compare and analyze data more efficiently.

Stepper Form

A stepper form is a user interface (UI) pattern and design system that guides users through a multi-step process, ensuring a clear and structured workflow. It is commonly used when the information or task at hand requires several distinct stages or inputs that need to be completed in a specific order. In a stepper form, each step represents a separate section of the process, allowing users to focus on one task at a time while providing a clear visual indication of their progress. Typically, the steps are displayed as sequential numbers or labels, accompanied by relevant icons or brief descriptions. The primary purpose of a stepper form is to break down complex tasks into smaller, more manageable steps, enhancing user experience by reducing cognitive load and preventing information overload. By presenting the steps in a logical order, the user is guided through the process, knowing exactly what is expected at each stage. Stepper forms can be particularly valuable in scenarios where users may feel overwhelmed by a large number of fields or complex inputs. By dividing the task into smaller parts, users can focus on individual sections, resulting in a more efficient and effective completion of the form. Another significant advantage of stepper forms is that they allow for error prevention and validation at each step. By validating user input in real-time, errors or incomplete information can be identified and addressed promptly, preventing users from encountering issues or having to redo substantial portions of the form. Furthermore, stepper forms often include clear navigation options, such as previous and next buttons, enabling users to move forward or backward in the process. This flexibility allows users to review and modify their inputs before finalizing the form. Overall, a stepper form is a valuable UI pattern and design system that enhances the user experience by breaking down complex tasks into smaller, more manageable steps. It offers clear guidance, validation, and navigation, ensuring a seamless and efficient completion of multi-step processes.

A stepper form is a UI pattern that guides users through a multi-step process, breaking it down into smaller, more manageable steps.

It provides a clear and structured workflow, preventing information overload and enhancing the user experience.

Stepper Interface

A stepper interface is a UI pattern commonly used in design systems to guide users through a sequential process or task with multiple steps. It is typically presented in the form of a horizontal bar or a series of vertical steps, allowing users to easily track their progress and navigate between steps. The main purpose of a stepper interface is to break down complex processes or tasks into smaller, more manageable steps, making them easier for users to understand and complete. It provides a clear visual indicator of the user's current step and the steps remaining, helping to reduce confusion and improve overall user experience. In a design system, a stepper interface is often designed to be consistent and reusable across different applications or platforms. It usually includes standard interaction behaviors, such as highlighting the active step and disabling or hiding subsequent steps until the current step is completed. This ensures that users follow a predefined flow and prevents them from skipping important steps. To enhance usability, a stepper interface may also include additional features such as optional steps, error handling, and contextual guidance. Optional steps allow users to skip certain steps if they are not relevant to their specific situation, while error handling helps users identify and correct any mistakes before proceeding. Contextual guidance can be provided at each step to clarify the purpose of the step or provide additional instructions. Overall, a stepper interface is an effective UI pattern for guiding users through complex processes or tasks with multiple steps. It simplifies the user journey by breaking it down into smaller, manageable steps and provides a visual indicator of progress. By using a consistent design and incorporating additional features as needed, a stepper interface can greatly improve the user experience and ensure successful task completion.

266

A stepper interface is a UI pattern used in design systems to guide users through a sequential process or task with multiple steps. It breaks down complex processes into smaller, manageable steps for easier completion. The interface usually consists of a horizontal bar or vertical steps. Its main purpose is to provide a clear visual indicator of the current step and the remaining steps, ensuring users follow a predefined flow and preventing them from skipping important steps. A stepper interface is designed to be consistent and reusable across different applications, and often includes features like optional steps, error handling, and contextual guidance. Overall, a stepper interface enhances usability and improves the user experience by simplifying complex processes and providing clear progress indicators.

Sticky Footer

A sticky footer is a user interface pattern and design system element that allows for consistent placement of content at the bottom of a webpage, regardless of the page's content height. It "sticks" to the bottom of the viewport or the bottom of the content, ensuring that it remains visible even when scrolling. Traditionally, footers have been placed at the bottom of the content, typically after the main area of a website or application. However, in cases where the content on a page is not enough to fill the entire viewport, the footer can appear halfway down the page, leaving empty space at the bottom. This can create a disjointed and unbalanced visual experience for the user. A sticky footer solves this issue by staying fixed to the bottom of the viewport or the bottom of the content, regardless of the amount of content present. This means that even if there is limited content on a page, the footer will still be positioned at the bottom, creating a consistent and pleasing design. To achieve a sticky footer, CSS is typically used along with HTML. By setting the CSS position property to "fixed" or "sticky" and the bottom property to 0, the footer will remain fixed at the bottom of the viewport or the content. The content area will then expand to fill the remaining space, ensuring that the footer stays at the bottom. Using a sticky footer not only improves the visual appeal of a webpage, but it also enhances user experience. It provides a sense of balance and completion to the design, creating a more polished and professional aesthetic. Additionally, it ensures that important information, such as contact details or navigation links, is always accessible to the user. In conclusion, a sticky footer is a UI pattern and design system element that allows for consistent placement of content at the bottom of a webpage. It ensures that the footer remains visible even when scrolling, creating a balanced and visually appealing design. By using CSS to position the footer, it stays fixed at the bottom of the viewport or content, providing a seamless user experience.

Sticky Navigation

A sticky navigation refers to a user interface (UI) pattern that keeps the navigation menu fixed at the top of the screen as the user scrolls down the page. This design element ensures that important navigation options are always easily accessible, improving the overall user experience.

Implementing a sticky navigation involves using CSS positioning techniques to fix the menu to the top of the viewport, regardless of scrolling. By doing so, the navigation menu remains visible and accessible at all times, eliminating the need for the user to scroll back to the top of the page to access it.

Stock Market Dashboard

A Stock Market Dashboard is a user interface (UI) pattern and design system that provides a centralized platform for visualizing and interacting with stock market data. It is designed to facilitate informed decision-making and analysis for investors and traders. The primary goal of a Stock Market Dashboard is to present a comprehensive view of stock market information, allowing users to monitor the performance of different stocks and gain insights into market trends. The dashboard typically displays various financial metrics, such as stock prices, market indices, trading volumes, and market capitalizations. These metrics are often accompanied by visual representations, such as charts and graphs, to help users understand and interpret the data more easily. A well-designed Stock Market Dashboard follows the principles of a good UI pattern and design system. It emphasizes simplicity, efficiency, and clarity by organizing information in a structured and intuitive manner. The layout is often divided into different sections or modules, each providing specific information or functionality. For example, there may be separate sections for displaying portfolio performance, stock watchlists, or news updates. In terms of visual design, a Stock Market Dashboard uses appropriate colors, typography, and spacing to ensure legibility and visual hierarchy. The use of meaningful icons and intuitive symbols helps users quickly identify and understand different elements and actions within the dashboard. Interactivity is a crucial aspect of a Stock Market Dashboard, allowing users to personalize their experience and explore relevant data. Users can customize the dashboard based on their preferences, such as selecting specific stocks to track or adjusting the time range for data visualization. Interactive features like filters, sorting options, and data export functionalities enable users to analyze the data in multiple ways and derive meaningful insights. Overall, a Stock Market Dashboard serves as a valuable tool for investors and traders to monitor and analyze stock market data effectively. Its well-organized layout, visual representations, and interactive features make it easier for users to make informed decisions and stay updated with the latest market trends.>

Storytelling Layout

A storytelling layout is a user interface pattern and design system that aims to enhance user engagement and comprehension by presenting information in a narrative and visually appealing manner.

It is designed to mimic the structure of traditional storytelling, which consists of a clear beginning, middle, and end. This layout breaks down information into smaller, digestible chunks and presents them sequentially, guiding the user through a linear flow of content.

Structured Data

A structured data is a systematised way of arranging and presenting information in a user interface (UI) pattern and design system. It involves organising data into a cohesive and logical structure that can be easily comprehended and interacted with by users.

The primary goal of using structured data in UI patterns and design systems is to enhance usability and optimize the user experience. It allows users to quickly find, understand, and navigate through the information presented, leading to improved efficiency and satisfaction.

Subnavigation

Subnavigation refers to a type of user interface (UI) pattern commonly used in web design systems. It is typically a set of links or buttons placed horizontally or vertically, often appearing below a primary navigation menu. The purpose of subnavigation is to provide users with additional pathways to access content within a website or application. The subnavigation is designed to complement the primary navigation by organizing related links into logical groups or categories. It allows users to navigate to specific sections or subsections of the website with ease. By utilizing subnavigation, designers aim to improve the overall user experience by reducing friction and facilitating quick access to desired information or functionality. In terms of its visual presentation, subnavigation is usually presented as a compact set of links or buttons, often in the form of text labels or icons. It is typically placed within a distinct area of the user interface, separate from the primary navigation menu, to distinguish it as a secondary navigation option. The selection of links or buttons included in the subnavigation is based on the overall information architecture and content hierarchy of the website or application. It is important to organize the links in a logical and intuitive manner, ensuring that users can easily find what they are looking for. The labels used for the subnavigation should be concise and clear, conveying the purpose or destination of each link. In terms of implementation, subnavigation can be created using HTML and CSS. In HTML, the subnavigation links can be contained within a or element, with each link represented by an element. CSS can be used to style the subnavigation, including its position, size, colors, and typography, to ensure it aligns with the overall design system. Overall, subnavigation is a key component of UI patterns and design systems, providing users with an additional layer of navigation options to access specific content or functionality. Its purpose is to enhance the overall user experience by facilitating easy and efficient navigation within a website or application.

Subscription Cancellation Form

A Subscription Cancellation Form is a user interface (UI) pattern used in design systems to provide users with a structured and easy-to-use method for canceling their subscriptions. It typically consists of a form with several fields and options that allow users to input the necessary information to cancel their subscription. The purpose of the Subscription Cancellation Form is to streamline the cancellation process and ensure that users have a clear and straightforward way to end their subscription without any hassle. By following a standardized design pattern, it helps to improve the overall user experience and minimize user frustration. The Subscription Cancellation Form is designed to be intuitive and user-friendly. It often includes fields for users to input their account information such as their name, email address, and subscription ID. Additionally, it may include checkboxes or dropdown menus that allow users to specify the reason for canceling, such as cost, lack of use, or dissatisfaction with the service. To guide users through the cancellation process, the form should include clear instructions and tooltips that provide additional information where needed. It is also important to include a confirmation step where users can review their cancellation details before finalizing the cancellation. In terms of visual design, the Subscription Cancellation Form should align with the overall aesthetics of the design system. It should be visually consistent with other forms and components, using a clean and minimalist style. Important elements such as the cancellation button or confirmation message should be highlighted to ensure they stand out and are easily recognizable. Overall, the Subscription Cancellation Form is a crucial component of a design system that focuses on providing a smooth cancellation experience for users. By adhering to established UI patterns, it helps to simplify the cancellation process and minimize user frustration.>

Subscription Downgrade Form

A subscription downgrade form is a user interface pattern and design system element that allows users to request a decrease in their subscription level or plan. It is commonly used in subscription-based services or platforms where users have the flexibility to choose different subscription tiers or options. The subscription downgrade form typically consists of a set of fields or input elements that collect relevant information from the user who wants to downgrade their subscription. These input fields may include the user's name, email, current subscription level, desired downgrade level, reason for downgrade, and any additional notes or comments. Upon submission of the form, the information is sent to the service provider or platform's backend system. The backend processes the request and performs the necessary adjustments to the user's subscription level in accordance with the request. This may involve changing the subscription plan, adjusting pricing, or modifying features and access rights associated with the user's subscription. The subscription downgrade form follows the principles of a good user interface design system. It should have a clear and intuitive layout that guides users through the downgrade process, making it easy for them to understand and fill out the necessary information. The form should also provide appropriate error handling and validation, ensuring that users provide accurate and required information before submitting the form. In addition, the subscription downgrade form should be designed in a way that maintains consistency with the overall design language of the platform or service. This means adhering to established color schemes, typography, and visual elements. Consistency makes the form feel familiar and cohesive within the larger user interface, creating a smooth and seamless user experience. Overall, the subscription downgrade form serves as a crucial tool for users to communicate their desire for a lower subscription level. By providing a well-designed and user-friendly interface, the form streamlines this process, making it straightforward and efficient for both users and service providers.>

Subscription Form

A subscription form is a user interface (UI) pattern that is used in design systems to collect information from users who wish to subscribe to a service or receive updates from a website or application. It typically consists of input fields and a submission button, allowing users to enter their contact details or preferences and then submit the form. The subscription form is an important component of a design system as it allows websites and applications to gather user data in a structured manner. By providing a designated form for users to subscribe, websites and applications can ensure that the data collected is accurate, relevant, and consistent. When designing a subscription form, it is essential to consider the usability and accessibility of the

269

form. The form should be visually appealing, with clear and concise instructions that guide users in completing the required fields. Additionally, the form should be accessible to users with disabilities, ensuring that it can be easily understood and filled out using assistive technologies. To create a subscription form using pure HTML, the <form> element can be used to define the form and its attributes such as the action and method. Within the <form> element, the <input> element can be used to create input fields for users to enter their contact details or preferences. The type attribute of the <input> element can be set to "text" for textual inputs, "email" for email addresses, or "checkbox" for checkboxes. The <button> element can be used to create a submission button for users to submit the form. In the above example, the form action attribute is set to "/subscribe" to specify the URL where the form data will be submitted. The method attribute is set to "POST" to indicate that the form data should be sent using the HTTP POST method. By utilizing a subscription form in a design system, websites and applications can streamline the process of collecting user information and improve the overall user experience.

Subscription Pause Form

A Subscription Pause Form is a user interface pattern and design system component that allows users to temporarily suspend or pause their subscription to a service or product. This form provides a structured and consistent way for users to request a pause in their subscription, giving them control over their payment schedule and service usage. The Subscription Pause Form typically includes a set of input fields and options that allow users to specify the duration of the pause and provide any additional information or comments. The form may also include a confirmation section that displays the details of the request before submission. The primary objective of the Subscription Pause Form is to simplify the process of requesting a pause in the subscription by guiding users through a clear and intuitive interface. This helps to reduce friction and confusion, ensuring that the user's intent is accurately captured and communicated to the service provider. By incorporating this pattern into a larger design system, organizations can maintain consistency across different interfaces and platforms. This consistency helps to build trust and familiarity with users, as they can expect a similar experience when interacting with various parts of the system. In terms of HTML implementation, a Subscription Pause Form can be created using basic form elements such as text inputs, checkboxes, and radio buttons. Additionally, labels can be used to provide context and guidance for each input field. The form should include a submit button that triggers the submission of the pause request. It is essential to validate the user's input before submission to ensure that all required fields are filled correctly. Overall, the Subscription Pause Form is a valuable component in user interface design. It allows users to maintain control over their subscriptions while providing a seamless and familiar experience. Whether it is incorporated into a larger design system or used as an individual component, the Subscription Pause Form contributes to an overall user-friendly and efficient service.>

Subscription Renewal Form

A subscription renewal form is a user interface (UI) pattern within a design system that allows users to renew their subscription or membership to a service or product. It provides a structured and intuitive way for users to extend or continue their access to a particular offering.

In the context of UI patterns and design systems, a subscription renewal form typically consists of a series of form fields and interactive elements that guide users through the renewal process. This may include fields for entering personal information, selecting a subscription plan or term, and providing payment details.

Subscription Upgrade Form

A subscription upgrade form in the context of UI patterns and design system refers to a user interface element or component that enables users to upgrade their existing subscription plan to a higher or more advanced level. It provides a streamlined and intuitive way for users to easily opt for additional features, benefits, or increased usage limits by upgrading their current subscription.

The subscription upgrade form typically includes various elements such as a summary of the user's current subscription plan, details of the upgraded plan, and the associated cost or pricing

270

information. It may also include options or checkboxes for selecting additional features or add-ons that are available with the upgraded plan. Additionally, the form usually includes a call-to-action button or link for users to proceed with the upgrade process.

Suggested Actions

Suggested actions are a type of user interface (UI) pattern commonly used in design systems. They are designed to provide users with a clear and concise set of options or actions that they can take within an application or website. Suggested actions are typically displayed as a series of buttons or links that are visually distinct from other elements on the page. These buttons or links are usually labeled with short and descriptive text, providing users with a clear understanding of the action they will be taking. The purpose of suggested actions is to guide users towards completing specific tasks or actions within the application or website. By presenting users with a set of predefined options, suggested actions help to simplify the decision-making process and reduce cognitive load. Suggested actions are often used in scenarios where there are multiple possible actions but a clear and preferred option exists. For example, in a messaging app, when a user receives a message, suggested actions may be displayed below the message, offering options such as "Reply," "Forward," or "Delete." In terms of design system implementation, suggested actions can be defined using HTML. The HTML markup for suggested actions can vary depending on the specific design and styling needs, but generally, it involves using the

tag to define each action option. For example:

Reply

Forward

Delete

In this example, each suggested action is represented by a separate

tag. The text within each

tag represents the action label, such as "Reply," "Forward," or "Delete." It's important to note that while the provided HTML example demonstrates the basic structure for implementing suggested actions, the specific styling and interaction details would need to be customized based on the design system and UI requirements of the application or website. Overall, suggested actions are a valuable UI pattern that helps to enhance the user experience by providing clear and actionable options for completing tasks. When used effectively within a design system, suggested actions can improve usability and guide users towards desired actions.>

Suggested Searches

A UI pattern is a reusable solution to a common design problem that occurs in user interfaces. It serves as a proven best practice that helps designers and developers create a consistent and efficient user experience across different applications or websites.

A design system, on the other hand, is a comprehensive set of guidelines, components, and rules that define the visual and interaction patterns of an interface. It provides a centralized resource for designers and developers to ensure consistency and coherence in the design and development process.

Suggestion Box Form

A suggestion box form is a user interface pattern commonly used in design systems to provide a structured way for users to offer suggestions, feedback, or opinions. It typically consists of a form where users can input their ideas or suggestions, and a submit button to send their input. The primary purpose of a suggestion box form is to gather user feedback and suggestions, which can be valuable for improving products, services, or overall user experience. By providing a dedicated space for users to share their thoughts, businesses can gain insights into users' needs, preferences, and pain points. This, in turn, helps businesses make informed decisions

271

and prioritize enhancements or new features. The design of a suggestion box form should be intuitive and user-friendly to encourage users to provide their input. It should have clear instructions on how to use the form and what types of suggestions are welcome. Including descriptive labels for each input field can help users understand what kind of information is expected from them. In terms of functionality, a suggestion box form should include appropriate validation to ensure that users provide necessary information and to prevent spam or irrelevant suggestions from being submitted. Basic validation checks, such as required fields and length limits, can help ensure that the inputs are relevant and meaningful. Design systems often incorporate suggestion box forms as a standard UI pattern to maintain consistency and improve efficiency across various user interfaces. By adopting a consistent design for suggestion boxes, businesses can streamline the process of collecting and analyzing user suggestions. This not only saves time and effort for designers and developers but also provides a seamless user experience when users encounter suggestion boxes in different contexts. In conclusion, a suggestion box form is a UI pattern and component commonly used in design systems. It serves as a structured input mechanism for users to provide feedback, suggestions, or opinions. By incorporating a suggestion box form into a design system, businesses can gather valuable insights from users and improve their products or services accordingly.>

Support Request Form

UI patterns or design patterns refer to commonly used solutions or approaches to design and format user interfaces (UIs) in a consistent and efficient manner. These patterns provide guidance and best practices for designers and developers to create intuitive and user-friendly interfaces. A design system, on the other hand, is a comprehensive set of guidelines, rules, and components that define the visual and functional aspects of a product or brand. It includes UI patterns as one of its key elements but also encompasses typography, color schemes, iconography, spacing, and other design elements. Design systems promote consistency and efficiency by providing a shared language and resources for designers and developers. They ensure that all elements across the product or brand are consistent, enabling users to have a familiar and coherent experience. By utilizing UI patterns within a design system, designers can leverage existing design solutions and avoid reinventing the wheel. UI patterns can be standard components such as navigation menus, search bars, forms, or more complex interactions like sliders or carousels. These patterns follow established principles and best practices, allowing designers to focus on the usability and functionality of the UI without having to start from scratch. Design systems and UI patterns also benefit developers by providing them with pre-built components and templates. This saves time and effort, as they can reuse code to implement UI patterns consistently and efficiently. In summary, UI patterns are specific design solutions that address common user interface challenges. They are an integral part of a design system, which provides comprehensive guidelines and resources for designing and implementing UI in a consistent and efficient manner. (Please note that the following is a pure HTML format of the answer, using only two

tags as requested in the prompt):

UI patterns are commonly used solutions or approaches to design and format user interfaces (UIs) in a consistent and efficient manner. These patterns provide guidance and best practices for designers and developers to create intuitive and user-friendly interfaces.

A design system is a comprehensive set of guidelines, rules, and components that define the visual and functional aspects of a product or brand. It includes UI patterns as one of its key elements but also encompasses typography, color schemes, iconography, spacing, and other design elements.

Survey Form

UI patterns, also known as user interface patterns or design patterns, refer to reusable solutions for common design problems that occur in user interface design. They provide a set of best practices and guidelines that help designers create intuitive and user-friendly interfaces. UI patterns aim to improve the usability and overall user experience of a system by offering standardized solutions to recurring design challenges. These patterns are developed based on extensive user research and feedback, and they have proven to be effective in solving specific design problems. By using UI patterns, designers can save time and effort by not reinventing the wheel for each new project. A design system, on the other hand, is a complete set of design guidelines, components, and assets that define and govern the visual and interactive elements of a product or brand. It provides a unified and consistent look and feel across different platforms and touchpoints, ensuring a coherent user experience. A design system typically includes various UI patterns, which serve as building blocks for creating consistent and cohesive interfaces. The main purpose of a design system is to establish a common language and visual identity that guides the design and development process. It helps maintain consistency across different teams and projects, facilitating collaboration and scalability. By using a design system, organizations can streamline the design process, improve efficiency, and ensure a cohesive user experience across their products and services. In summary, UI patterns are reusable solutions for common design problems in user interface design, while a design system is a comprehensive set of design guidelines and assets that define the visual and interactive elements of a product or brand. Both UI patterns and design systems play a crucial role in creating intuitive, user-friendly, and visually consistent interfaces.

Swipe Down To Refresh

Swipe Down to Refresh refers to a user interface (UI) pattern and design system that allows users to update or refresh the content of a page or application by swiping their finger downward on a touch screen device. This interaction is commonly used in mobile apps and websites to provide an intuitive and convenient way for users to see the latest content or updates without having to navigate to a different page or manually refresh the page. When a user performs a swipe down gesture on a screen, the UI responds by visually indicating that the content is being refreshed. This can be achieved through various visual cues, such as showing a loading spinner or a progress bar. The refresh action typically triggers a backend request to fetch the latest data, which is then asynchronously updated on the screen when the response is received. Swipe Down to Refresh is particularly useful in scenarios where the content is dynamic and frequently updated, such as in social media feeds, news articles, or email applications. Instead of relying on manual refresh buttons or periodic auto-refresh, users can simply swipe down at their own discretion to stay up to date with the latest information. This UI pattern promotes a more seamless and interactive user experience. In terms of implementation, developers can use JavaScript or specific libraries to recognize the swipe down gesture and trigger the refresh action. Additionally, using CSS animations or transitions can enhance the visual feedback during the refresh process, providing a smooth and engaging user experience. However, it is important to note that the Swipe Down to Refresh pattern may not be suitable for all types of applications or content. For instance, in cases where the content does not require frequent updates or the refresh action could cause data loss, alternative UI patterns or mechanisms should be considered. It is essential to analyze the specific requirements and user needs to determine if Swipe Down to Refresh is the appropriate solution. In conclusion, Swipe Down to Refresh is a UI pattern and design system that allows users to update or refresh the content of a page or application by swiping their finger downward on a touch screen device. This pattern provides a simple and intuitive way for users to stay up to date with dynamic content, enhancing the overall user experience.

Swipe Gestures

Swipe gestures refer to the action of swiping a finger across a touch-sensitive surface, such as a smartphone or tablet screen, to perform certain actions or navigate through an interface. This UI pattern has gained significant popularity in recent years due to its intuitive and engaging nature. Swipe gestures are an essential part of mobile and touch-based user interfaces, allowing users to interact with content in a fluid and natural way. They enable users to easily navigate through a series of screens or pages by swiping left or right, providing a seamless browsing experience. In terms of design systems, swipe gestures are often included as a standard interaction pattern. They can be used to trigger actions such as navigating to the next or previous item, dismissing or closing a modal, revealing hidden content, or switching between different views or tabs. By incorporating swipe gestures into the design system, consistency and familiarity can be maintained across different applications or interfaces. When implementing swipe gestures, it is important to consider the following guidelines: 1. Clear feedback: Provide visual or haptic feedback to indicate that a swipe gesture has been recognized and registered. This feedback can include animations, color changes, or subtle vibrations, ensuring that users are aware that their action has been acknowledged. 2. Gesture recognition: Implement swipe gesture recognition algorithms that can accurately detect and interpret user input. This involves distinguishing between intentional swipes and accidental touches or taps. 3. Accessibility: Keep in mind that not all users may be able to perform swipe gestures. Provide alternative methods of interaction (e.g., buttons or menus) for users who have disabilities or difficulties performing swipe gestures. 4. Contextual relevance: Ensure that swipe gestures are used in a meaningful and logical manner within the interface. They should align with the user's mental model and serve a specific purpose, enhancing the overall usability of the application. In conclusion, swipe gestures are a key component of modern user interfaces, particularly in mobile and touch-based environments. By incorporating swipe gestures into the design system and adhering to design principles, developers can create intuitive and engaging interfaces that enhance user interactions.

Swipe To Confirm

Swipe to Confirm is a user interface pattern in which users can confirm an action by performing a swiping gesture on the screen. This pattern is commonly used in mobile applications and allows for a more intuitive and engaging user experience. In a typical Swipe to Confirm implementation, users are presented with a prompt or a dialog box that requires their confirmation to proceed with a certain action. Instead of using traditional buttons or checkboxes, users can simply swipe their finger across the screen in a specific direction to confirm their decision. The Swipe to Confirm pattern leverages the touch gestures and capabilities of mobile devices to enhance the usability and interactivity of the interface. By incorporating swiping as a confirmation mechanism, it eliminates the need for users to tap on small buttons or navigate through multiple screens, making the confirmation process faster and more efficient. When designing a Swipe to Confirm interaction, it is crucial to provide visual cues and instructions to guide users on how to perform the swiping gesture. This can be achieved through animations, tooltips, or even subtle hints within the user interface. Additionally, it is important to consider the accessibility aspect of this pattern by providing alternative methods of confirmation for users who may have difficulty performing swipe gestures. From a design system perspective, Swipe to Confirm can be incorporated as a predefined component or interaction that follows consistent visual and interaction guidelines. This ensures that the swipe gesture is recognizable and consistent across different parts of the application, providing users with a sense of familiarity and ease of use. In conclusion, Swipe to Confirm is a user interface pattern that enables users to confirm actions through swiping gestures on mobile devices. By leveraging the touch capabilities of mobile devices, this pattern enhances the interactivity and efficiency of the confirmation process. When implementing Swipe to Confirm, it is important to provide clear instructions and consider accessibility requirements.

Swipe To Delete

Swipe to Delete is a UI pattern commonly used in mobile and touch-based interfaces to delete or remove an item from a list or grid by swiping the item in a specific direction, usually sideways. This interaction is primarily facilitated through a touch gesture where the user places their finger on the screen and moves it horizontally across the item they want to delete. The Swipe to Delete pattern offers a convenient and intuitive way for users to remove unwanted or unneeded items quickly without the need for additional taps or buttons. It enhances the user experience by eliminating the need for confirmation dialogues or multiple steps, thus streamlining the deletion process. This pattern is especially useful in mobile applications where screen real estate is limited, and simplifying interactions is vital for usability. Implementing Swipe to Delete requires careful consideration of design and coding. The pattern typically involves the creation of a draggable element within the item, allowing users to perform the swipe gesture on that specific area. The element should be visually differentiated to provide a clear indication of its purpose, often through visual cues like a trash bin icon or a color change. Additionally, animations can be employed to enhance the UX, such as revealing the deleted item partially before completely swiping it away. Design systems play a crucial role in implementing Swipe to Delete consistently across an interface. A well-established design system provides standardized guidelines for the visual and interactive components involved in this pattern. It ensures that the swipe gesture works consistently throughout the application, reducing confusion and improving the overall user experience. In summary, Swipe to Delete is a UI pattern frequently employed in mobile and touch-based interfaces to enable users to delete or remove items from a list or grid effortlessly. It simplifies the deletion process, enhances usability, and provides a convenient way for users to manage their content. Implementing the pattern requires thoughtful design and coding, while a robust design system ensures consistency and reinforces the overall user experience.

Swipe To Dismiss

Swipe to Dismiss is a user interface pattern utilized in design systems to enable users to dismiss or remove elements, such as notifications or items, by swiping them off the screen. It allows users to seamlessly interact with the interface by providing a natural gesture-based method of interaction. In this pattern, a swipe gesture is performed by dragging the element horizontally across the screen, typically in the direction opposite to its initial appearance or expansion. Once the element is dragged to a certain threshold or off the screen entirely, it is considered dismissed and is removed from the user's view. The Swipe to Dismiss pattern improves the user experience by providing a simple and intuitive way to remove temporary or unwanted content without relying on traditional buttons or menus. It offers a sense of direct manipulation, mimicking real-world actions while reducing cognitive load. Implementing Swipe to Dismiss involves several key considerations. Firstly, the element being swiped should have a clear visual indication that it is dismissible, often through the use of visual cues like icons or animations. Additionally, it is crucial to define the area in which the swipe action can be initiated, ensuring it is large enough for users to perform the gesture comfortably. The behavior of the element upon dismissal should also be taken into account. Depending on the context, it can simply disappear, animate off the screen, or reveal additional options or confirmation dialogs. Regardless of the specific behavior, it must align with the user's mental model and provide visual feedback to indicate successful dismissal. To implement Swipe to Dismiss in HTML, it requires leveraging JavaScript or libraries specifically designed for this purpose. By capturing touch or swipe events and updating the position of the element accordingly, the swipe gesture can be detected and the necessary actions can be triggered programmatically. In summary, Swipe to Dismiss is a UI pattern that allows users to easily dismiss elements by performing a swipe gesture. It enhances the overall user experience by providing a natural and intuitive method of interaction, improving the efficiency of content management in various contexts.

Swipe To Like

Swipe to Like is a user interface pattern and design system element commonly used in mobile applications and websites for allowing users to express positive feedback or interest by swiping a card or image in a specific direction. The swipe gesture is widely recognized as an intuitive and natural interaction method, particularly on touch-enabled devices. In this UI pattern, a series of cards or images is presented to the user one at a time, often in a stack or carousel-like manner. The user can then swipe left or right on each card to either like or dislike the content. The direction in which the swipe is performed typically corresponds to the action being taken, with right indicating a like or positive response, while left signifies a dislike or negative response. The Swipe to Like pattern not only offers a visually engaging way for users to interact with content but also provides several advantages from a design perspective. Firstly, it simplifies the user experience by reducing the number of explicit buttons or controls required, allowing for a more streamlined and minimalistic interface. Additionally, the swipe gesture leverages the intuitive nature of touch-based interactions, making it more natural and effortless for users to express their preferences. From a usability standpoint, Swipe to Like offers several benefits. The pattern encourages quick decision-making by presenting content to users in a rapid, swipeable manner. This can be especially useful in scenarios where the user needs to review a large amount of content efficiently, such as in dating apps or image-based social media platforms. Moreover, Swipe to Like allows for a more inclusive and accessible design. The gesture-based interaction provides an alternative approach for users who may have difficulty with small buttons or precise taps, making the action more accessible to a wider range of users. When implementing Swipe to Like, it is essential to provide visual cues and feedback to guide user interaction. Animations and transitions can be used to communicate the swipe action and provide immediate feedback on the outcome of the gesture. For example, when a user swipes right to like a card, a visual cue such as a heart icon or color change can signify the successful action. In conclusion, Swipe to Like is a UI pattern that enables users to express positive feedback or interest by swiping cards or images in a specific direction. Its intuitive and gesture-based interaction makes it an effective design element for engaging mobile applications and websites, offering a visually appealing and inclusive user experience.

Swipe To Share

Swipe to Share is a user interface pattern that allows users to share content or information through a swipe gesture on a touch screen device. It is a popular design element used in mobile applications and websites to enhance user engagement and simplify the sharing process.

The Swipe to Share pattern typically involves a swipe gesture, usually in a horizontal direction, that triggers a sharing menu or options overlay. This menu may include various sharing options such as social media platforms, messaging apps, email, or other communication channels. The user can then choose the desired sharing option by either tapping on it or continuing the swipe gesture in the corresponding direction.

Swipe-Up Menu

A swipe-up menu is a user interface pattern and design system element that provides a hidden or additional set of options, content, or actions within a mobile app or website. It is commonly used when there is a need to display a larger number of elements or content that cannot fit on the main screen without cluttering the interface. The swipe-up menu is triggered by a swipe gesture from the bottom of the screen upwards, typically starting from a designated handle or indicator. The menu then slides into view, revealing its contents, and can be swiped back down to hide it. This interaction commonly follows the natural scrolling behavior found on touchscreens, providing a smooth and intuitive user experience. The swipe-up menu is often used to present secondary actions or features that are not immediately necessary or frequently used. It allows users to access these options without cluttering the main screen or overwhelming the primary user flow. This helps to keep the interface clean, organized, and focused on the main tasks or content. The content of a swipe-up menu can vary based on the specific application or website. It can range from a simple list of additional options or actions to more complex and nested menus. The menu items can be textual, graphical, or a combination of both, depending on the design and visual style of the overall interface. The menu can also contain navigation elements, allowing users to switch between different sections or screens within the app or website. Swipe-up menus are a popular choice for mobile design due to the limited screen real estate on smartphones and tablets. They offer a space-efficient and user-friendly method of incorporating additional functionality without sacrificing usability or overwhelming the user with too many options at once. Overall, the swipe-up menu is a versatile UI pattern and design system element that provides a hidden or supplementary set of options, content, or actions within mobile apps and websites. It enhances the user experience by enabling a clean and organized interface while still allowing access to important secondary features or information.

Swiping Carousel

A swiping carousel is a user interface (UI) pattern commonly used in web design to showcase multiple content items, such as images or cards, within a confined space. It allows users to horizontally swipe or scroll through the content, providing an interactive and engaging experience. The swiping carousel is typically displayed as a horizontal row, with each content item occupying a single pane. The content items can be images, cards with text and images, or any other type of visual content. The carousel may also include indicators, such as dots or thumbnails, to provide a visual representation of the number of content items and the user's current position. Users can interact with the swiping carousel by clicking or tapping on the content items to view more details or by swiping or scrolling horizontally to move through the items. On touch-enabled devices, users can also swipe the carousel using touch gestures, such as dragging or flicking. From a design system perspective, a swiping carousel can be customized to fit the overall UI and brand guidelines. The size, spacing, colors, and typography of the carousel can be adjusted to match the design system's visual language. Additionally, the behavior and animation of the carousel can be tailored to align with the system's interaction patterns. To implement a swiping carousel using pure HTML, you can start by defining a container element with a fixed width and height to contain the carousel. Within the container, individual panes can be created for each content item using HTML elements like

. Styling can be applied to the panes to set their width, height, and positioning within the container. JavaScript or CSS can be used to handle the swiping or scrolling functionality, allowing users to interact with the carousel. In conclusion, a swiping carousel is a UI pattern that enables users to interactively navigate through multiple content items within a confined space. It provides a visually appealing and engaging way to display and browse through content, enhancing the overall user experience.

Tabbed Content

Tabbed content refers to a user interface pattern commonly used in web design and interface development to organize and present information or functionality in a visually appealing and intuitive manner. It is a design system that allows users to navigate between different sections or categories of content within a single page or interface, using a set of tabs or buttons.

With tabbed content, users can easily switch between different sections of content without having to navigate to separate pages or reload the entire page. Each tab represents a specific category or section, and when clicked, it reveals the content associated with that category while hiding the content of other categories. This helps in organizing a large amount of information into easily digestible chunks and improves the overall user experience.

Tabbed Navigation

Tabbed navigation refers to a user interface (UI) pattern commonly used in design systems to organize and navigate content within a website or application. It provides a visually intuitive way for users to switch between different sections or pages without the need for excessive scrolling or searching through menus. In tabbed navigation, a horizontal row or vertical column of tabs is presented at the top or side of the interface. Each tab represents a distinct section or category of content. When a user clicks or taps on a tab, the corresponding content is displayed below or alongside the tabs, replacing the previous content. Tabbed navigation is particularly useful when there is a limited amount of screen space available and when users need to switch between different contexts or tasks within the same interface. It helps to keep the interface organized and allows users to quickly access the information they need. The design of tabbed navigation should be consistent and visually distinguishable, making it easy for users to identify and understand the available options. Tabs are typically styled as clickable elements with clear labels or icons to represent their associated content. Active tabs are often highlighted to indicate the section or page currently being viewed. It is important to note that tabbed navigation should be used judiciously and only when it enhances the user experience. When there are too many tabs to fit within the available space, it can become overwhelming and lead to a cluttered interface. In such cases, alternative navigation patterns like dropdown menus or accordion menus may be more appropriate. When implementing tabbed navigation in HTML, the structure can be achieved using HTML and CSS. Each tab can be represented by a `<button>` element, with the active tab having an additional class or attribute to indicate its current state. The associated content for each tab can be placed within separate `` elements and hidden or shown based on the active tab. Overall, tabbed navigation is a useful UI pattern that allows users to easily navigate between different sections or pages within an interface. By organizing content and providing a clear structure, it improves the usability and accessibility of websites and applications.

Table Of Contents

A table of contents is a navigational element commonly used in UI patterns and design systems to provide users with an overview of the content and structure of a document or website. It typically appears at the beginning of a document or as a sidebar in a website layout.

The table of contents organizes the sections or pages of a document or website into a hierarchical structure, allowing users to easily navigate to specific parts of the content. It is especially useful for long documents or websites with multiple sections, as it provides a quick way for users to find and access the information they need.

Tabs Interface

A tabs interface is a common UI pattern and design system component that is used to organize and present a set of related content or options in a compact and visually appealing manner. It

277

provides a way for users to switch between different sections or categories of information or functionality within a single screen or layout.

The tabs interface is typically displayed as a horizontal or vertical list of tab headers, with each tab representing a distinct section or category. When a tab is selected or clicked, the corresponding content or options associated with that tab are displayed in the main area of the interface, while the other tabs remain visible but inactive.

Tag Clouds

Tag clouds, also known as word clouds or weighted lists, are a UI pattern commonly used in design systems to visually represent the frequency or popularity of words or tags in a collection of content. They are essentially a graphical representation of textual data, where words or tags are shown in varying font size or color based on their importance or occurrence. In the context of UI patterns, tag clouds are used to give users a quick visual summary or overview of the content available on a website or application. They are often placed on the sidebar, footer, or header of a webpage, and are typically presented as a cloud-like cluster of words or tags. The size or color of each word represents its frequency or relevance within the content. Larger or bolder words indicate higher frequency or importance, while smaller or lighter words indicate lower frequency or importance. Tag clouds are interactive elements that allow users to filter or navigate content by clicking on specific words or tags. When a user clicks on a word or a tag within the cloud, it typically leads to a page or a collection of content related to that specific tag. This helps users quickly find and explore relevant content based on their interests or preferences. Tag clouds are an effective way to present large amounts of information in a compact and visually appealing manner. They provide a glimpse into the content available on a website or application, allowing users to discover popular topics or themes. Additionally, they can serve as a navigational aid, allowing users to explore related content easily. To implement a tag cloud in HTML, the basic structure involves placing the cloud of words or tags within a container element, usually a

tag. Each word or tag is enclosed within a tag, and its style, such as font size or color, can be defined using CSS. For example:

Word Tag Cloud

In this example, the word "Word" is displayed with a larger font size of 18 pixels, while the word "Tag" is displayed with a font size of 14 pixels, and the word "Cloud" is displayed with a font size of 10 pixels. This visual variation in font sizes helps users quickly identify the importance or relevance of each word within the tag cloud. In conclusion, tag clouds are a useful UI pattern in design systems for visually representing the frequency or popularity of words or tags. They provide users with a quick overview of the content available and allow for easy navigation and exploration based on user interests.

Tagging Form

Tagging form is a UI pattern and design system element that allows users to assign one or more predefined labels or categories to a specific item or piece of content. It is commonly used in applications or websites where users need to organize and filter information, such as in task management systems, e-commerce websites, or content management systems. The tagging form consists of an input field, where users can type in the labels or categories they want to assign, and a list of predefined tags that can be selected with a single click. The predefined tags can be displayed as a dropdown menu or as a list of checkboxes, depending on the design and functionality of the system. When users start typing in the input field, the tagging form provides suggestions based on previously used tags or existing tags in the system. This auto-suggest feature helps users to select the appropriate tags quickly and ensures consistent tagging across the system. Once the user selects or types in the desired tags, they are displayed as visually distinct elements, usually enclosed within colored rectangles or circles. This visual representation of the tags enhances their visibility and makes it easier for users to quickly identify and edit them if needed. The tagging form also allows users to remove tags that have been assigned by mistake or are no longer relevant. This can be done by either clicking on a small 'x' button next to the tag or using a delete key on the keyboard. The use of tagging form in a design system ensures consistency and improves the efficiency of data organization and retrieval for both the users and the system administrators. By using predefined tags, the design system can provide a more structured and cohesive way of categorizing information, reducing the risk of inconsistent or duplicate tags. In conclusion, tagging form is a UI pattern and design system element that enables users to assign labels or categories to items or content. It provides auto-suggestions, visual representation, and easy editing or removal of tags. The use of tagging form enhances data organization, consistency, and user efficiency in applications or websites where information filtering and categorization are crucial.

Tagging System

A tagging system is a UI pattern commonly used in design systems to categorize and organize content. It allows users to add descriptive keywords or labels, called tags, to items or pieces of content, making it easier to find and filter information within a system.

The tagging system consists of several key components:

The first component is the tag input field, where users can enter keywords or labels. This field may provide autocomplete suggestions based on previously used tags or available options from a predefined tag list. Users can enter multiple tags separated by commas or other delimiters.

The second component is the tag display area, which shows the tags that have been added by the user. Each tag is typically displayed as a colored pill-shaped button with the tag label inside. Users can remove tags by clicking on a small "x" icon associated with each tag.

The third component is the tag list or tag cloud, which displays all available tags in a visually appealing format. This can be represented as a cloud-like visual with different tag sizes based on usage frequency, or as a simple list of tags. Clicking on a tag from the tag list or cloud usually filters the content to display only items associated with that tag.

The tagging system can be used in various contexts, such as organizing files or documents, categorizing products in an e-commerce platform, or filtering content in a blog or news website. It provides a flexible and user-friendly way to label and manage content, improving search and navigation within the system.

Tagging And Labeling Systems

Tagging and labeling systems are UI patterns and design systems used to organize and classify content in a structured and efficient manner. They play a crucial role in enhancing the usability and navigation of websites and applications. Tags provide a descriptive keyword or phrase that helps users easily understand and categorize the content. They can be applied to a wide range of elements such as articles, products, images, or videos, enabling users to search, filter, and retrieve information effortlessly. Tags are typically displayed as clickable links or buttons, allowing users to easily select or deselect them to refine their search results. Labeling, on the other hand, refers to the act of assigning descriptive text or symbols to user interface elements. Labels provide clarity and help users understand the purpose or function of a particular element, such as buttons, form inputs, or navigation menus. They facilitate quick comprehension and interaction with the interface. In UI patterns and design systems, tagging and labeling systems are commonly used together to create a cohesive and intuitive user experience. By employing a consistent and standardized set of tags and labels, designers can establish a clear and predictable structure that users can easily understand and navigate. When implementing tagging and labeling systems, it is important to consider several factors. First, tags and labels should be concise and meaningful to ensure they accurately represent the content or functionality they are associated with. Furthermore, they should be organized in a logical hierarchy, allowing users to easily navigate and explore related content. In terms of design, tags and labels should be visually distinguishable from other elements on the page to draw attention and aid in scanning. Colors, typography, and icons can be used to differentiate tags and labels from regular text or other UI elements. Overall, tagging and labeling systems are essential components of UI patterns and design systems, providing a structured and efficient way to classify and navigate content. By employing these systems effectively, designers can greatly enhance the usability and accessibility of websites and applications, resulting in a more satisfying user experience.>

Task Details Screen

A Task Details Screen in the context of UI patterns and design systems refers to a user interface component that provides an overview and information about a specific task or item. It is commonly used in applications or software where users need to manage or track different tasks or projects. The Task Details Screen typically includes various sections or elements to display relevant information related to the task at hand. These elements may include: 1. Task Title: This is a clear and concise heading that represents the task or item being viewed. It should be descriptive enough to convey the purpose or nature of the task. 2. Description: A brief but comprehensive description of the task is included to provide users with more context or details. This section should explain the purpose, requirements, or any specific instructions related to the task. 3. Status: The current status of the task is displayed to inform users about its progress. This could include labels such as "In Progress," "Completed," or "Pending" to indicate the stage the task is in. 4. Assigned To: The name or username of the person responsible for completing the task is mentioned here. This section helps to assign accountability and keeps team members informed about who is responsible for the task. 5. Due Date: A deadline or due date for the completion of the task is included to ensure timely execution. This section helps users prioritize their tasks and stay organized. 6. Attachments: If applicable, there may be a section to display any files, documents, or images related to the task. Users can access these attachments to review or utilize them while working on the task. 7. Comments/Notes: A dedicated space for users to leave comments or notes about the task is provided. This encourages collaboration and enables users to communicate with each other regarding specific details or progress updates. The Task Details Screen provides a comprehensive view of a specific task, allowing users to understand its purpose, progress, and relevant details. By presenting information in a structured and organized manner, users can easily access and reference the necessary information to complete their tasks effectively.>

Task List

In the context of UI patterns and design system, a task list refers to a structured and organized set of tasks or actions that need to be completed within a user interface. It provides users with a clear overview of the tasks that they need to accomplish and allows them to track their progress. A task list typically consists of individual items, each representing a specific task or action. These items are displayed in a sequential order, often accompanied by additional information such as due dates, priorities, or progress indicators. Users can interact with the task list to mark tasks as completed, postpone or reschedule tasks, or add new tasks. Task lists are commonly used in various applications and systems to enhance productivity and streamline workflow management. They are particularly valuable in scenarios where there are multiple tasks or activities that need to be completed within a certain timeframe. By providing a centralized and organized view of tasks, users can prioritize their work and ensure that nothing gets overlooked. Design systems play a crucial role in shaping the visual representation and interaction patterns of task lists. They provide a set of guidelines, components, and design principles that ensure consistency and coherence across different interfaces and platforms. In the context of task lists, design systems define the visual appearance of task items, the layout of the list, and the interaction behaviors associated with each task. They help maintain a unified experience for users, regardless of the specific application or device they are using. Overall, task lists are powerful tools that improve efficiency and help users stay organized. By providing a clear structure and visual representation of tasks, they enable users to manage their workload effectively and prioritize their actions. Through the integration of design systems, task lists can achieve a consistent and user-friendly design that enhances usability and overall user experience.>

Tax Declaration Form

A Tax Declaration Form is a user interface pattern and design system used to collect and record information related to an individual's or organization's tax obligations. It serves as a standardized means for taxpayers to provide accurate and complete details to tax authorities, facilitating the process of tax assessment and compliance. The Tax Declaration Form typically consists of a set of clearly labeled fields and sections that prompt users to enter specific pieces of information, such as personal details, income sources, deductions, and tax liability calculations. These fields are designed to accommodate a variety of data types, including text, numbers, and dates, and often incorporate validation rules to ensure accurate and consistent entries. The design of the Tax Declaration Form follows established principles of user-centered design, aiming to make the information collection process as efficient and user-friendly as possible. The form's layout is carefully structured to guide users through each section, with clear instructions and guidance provided when necessary. The use of appropriate spacing, typography, and color schemes helps to enhance readability and distinguish different sections. To improve the user experience, the Tax Declaration Form may include interactive elements, such as drop-down menus, checkboxes, and radio buttons, allowing users to select from predefined options rather than manually entering data. This reduces the likelihood of errors and speeds up the completion process. In addition to the core functionality of data collection, the Tax Declaration Form may incorporate supplementary features to further assist users. These can include contextual help tooltips, inline error messages, and progress indicators to provide guidance and feedback throughout the form-filling process. By adhering to a consistent design system, Tax Declaration Forms promote a cohesive and familiar user experience across different tax forms and related interfaces. This facilitates seamless navigation and reduces cognitive load, allowing users to focus on providing accurate and comprehensive tax information. Ultimately, the Tax Declaration Form is an essential component of tax administration, ensuring that accurate and complete tax information is obtained from taxpayers in a standardized and efficient manner. Its user-friendly interface and adherence to design system principles contribute to a positive user experience, resulting in increased compliance rates and improved efficiency for both taxpayers and tax authorities.>

Team Member Profiles

A team member profile, in the context of UI patterns and design systems, refers to a standardized representation of an individual team member's information and attributes. It is typically used to showcase the expertise, skills, and roles of team members within an organization or project.

The team member profile is an important component of a design system as it allows for consistent presentation of team members' details across different interfaces or platforms. It provides an organized and uniform way of displaying information such as the team member's name, position, bio, contact details, and social media links.

Terms And Conditions Acceptance Form

A Terms and Conditions Acceptance Form in the context of UI patterns and design systems refers to a formal agreement wherein a user acknowledges and agrees to abide by the terms and conditions set forth by a website, application, or system.

When users interact with a platform or service, it is necessary to establish clear guidelines and regulations to protect both the user and the organization providing the service. The Terms and Conditions Acceptance Form serves as a legally binding contract that outlines the rights, responsibilities, and limitations for both parties involved.

Terms And Conditions Link

A terms and conditions link refers to a clickable element within a user interface (UI) pattern or design system that directs users to a separate page containing the terms and conditions (T&C) of a service or product. The T&C page outlines the legal agreement between the user and the company or organization operating the service or providing the product, establishing the rights, responsibilities, and limitations of both parties.

The purpose of including a terms and conditions link in a UI pattern or design system is to ensure that users are aware of and have access to the legal terms that govern their use of the service or product. By clicking on the link, users can review the T&C before proceeding with their engagement, whether it be creating an account, making a purchase, or using certain features.

Testimonial Carousel

A testimonial carousel is a UI pattern and design system element commonly used on websites to display customer testimonials or reviews in an interactive and visually pleasing way. It is a
281

dynamic component that allows the user to view multiple testimonials within a confined space without overwhelming the page with excessive content. The testimonial carousel typically consists of a horizontal or vertical scrolling container that contains individual testimonial cards. Each card displays a short quote or excerpt from a customer testimonial, along with relevant information such as the customer's name, job title, and company. The purpose of the testimonial carousel is to showcase positive feedback and endorsements from satisfied customers or users. It adds credibility and social proof to the website, helping to build trust and confidence in the products or services being offered. The carousel design allows for easy navigation and exploration of multiple testimonials. Users can interact with the carousel by clicking or tapping on navigation arrows or indicators to scroll through the testimonials. Some carousels may also include autoplay functionality, automatically cycling through the testimonials at a predetermined interval. By using a carousel, websites can effectively present a variety of testimonials in a limited amount of space, making it ideal for landing pages or product pages where space is at a premium. The dynamic nature of the carousel also adds visual interest and engagement to the page, keeping users interested and encouraging them to stay on the website longer. In terms of design system, the testimonial carousel should adhere to consistent visual styling and branding guidelines. This includes using the same typography, color scheme, and layout as other components within the design system. The testimonial cards should be designed to be easily scannable and readable, with clear contrast between the text and background. Overall, the testimonial carousel is a valuable UI pattern and design system element that helps websites effectively showcase customer testimonials in an engaging and visually appealing way, enhancing the credibility and trustworthiness of the brand or product.>

Text-To-Speech Interface

A Text-to-Speech Interface is a user interface pattern and design system that converts written text into spoken words, allowing users to listen to the content instead of reading it. This interface enables accessibility by providing an alternative way to consume textual information for individuals with visual impairments or reading difficulties. In the context of UI patterns and design systems, a Text-to-Speech Interface should adhere to certain design principles to ensure usability and inclusivity. It should seamlessly integrate into the overall user interface and be easily discoverable for users who may benefit from this feature. The Text-to-Speech Interface typically consists of a playback control that allows the user to play, pause, and stop the speech output. The playback control may be represented by icons or labeled with text, ensuring clarity and understanding for all users. Additionally, it should provide an option to adjust the speech rate, allowing users to personalize the experience to their preferences. When implementing a Text-to-Speech Interface, it is essential to consider the design system of the application to maintain consistency. The interface should use typography that is legible and suitable for screen reading. It should also follow the color scheme and visual hierarchy established by the design system. To support internationalization and multilingual users, the Text-to-Speech Interface should provide language options when applicable. This ensures that users can listen to the content in their preferred language, improving accessibility and inclusion. Furthermore, the Text-to-Speech Interface should be responsive and adapt to different screen sizes and orientations. This ensures that users can access the speech functionality on various devices, such as mobile phones, tablets, or desktop computers. In conclusion, a Text-to-Speech Interface is a design pattern and system that enables users to listen to written content through spoken words. It should adhere to design principles and seamlessly integrate into the overall user interface, ensuring accessibility and inclusivity for individuals with visual impairments or reading difficulties.

Thumbnail Preview

A thumbnail preview is a user interface pattern commonly used in design systems to display a smaller version of an image or media file, often used as a preview or teaser before the full content is accessed or viewed. It is a compact representation that allows users to quickly assess the content and make a decision on whether to engage further or not.

The thumbnail preview typically consists of a small square or rectangular container that holds the image or media file. It is designed to be visually appealing, ensuring that the content is clear and recognizable at a smaller size. The thumbnail preview is usually accompanied by additional information such as a title, description, or metadata, giving users more context about the content before they engage with it.

Time Entry Form

A time entry form is a user interface pattern used in design systems that allows users to input and submit time-related data. It provides a structured and intuitive way for users to enter specific information such as hours, minutes, and possibly additional details like dates or time zones.

The purpose of a time entry form is to simplify the process of collecting time-related data from users. By providing a standardized layout and input fields, it ensures consistency and reduces user errors while entering time. The design of the form typically includes labels for each input field, indicating the type of information required, as well as placeholders or examples to guide users on how to input the data correctly.

Timed Progress Indicator

A Timed Progress Indicator is a user interface (UI) pattern that provides users with a visual representation of the progress and duration of a timed task or process. It is a component commonly used in design systems to enhance the user experience and improve usability. The Timed Progress Indicator typically consists of a progress bar or a countdown timer, accompanied by relevant labels or notifications, to keep users informed about the ongoing process and the remaining time. It serves as a feedback mechanism, giving users visibility into the progress and duration of the task, enabling them to manage their time effectively and set expectations. In terms of UI design, a Timed Progress Indicator is crucial in scenarios where time is a critical factor, such as file uploads, downloads, installations, or any other process that may take a significant amount of time. By incorporating this pattern into a design system, designers can ensure consistency and familiarity across different applications or interfaces, promoting seamless experiences for users. The HTML implementation of a Timed Progress Indicator can be achieved using the

tag as follows:

The Timed Progress Indicator is a UI pattern that visualizes the progress and duration of a timed task or process. It utilizes a progress bar or countdown timer, along with accompanying labels or notifications, to keep users informed.

Incorporating the Timed Progress Indicator into a design system improves usability and allows for consistent experiences. It is particularly valuable in scenarios where time is a critical factor, ensuring users can effectively manage their time.

In conclusion, the Timed Progress Indicator is an essential UI pattern used in design systems to provide users with real-time feedback on the progress and duration of timed tasks or processes. By utilizing a progress bar or countdown timer, along with informative labels or notifications, designers can enhance the user experience and enable efficient time management. Incorporating this pattern into HTML-based interfaces ensures consistency and familiarity for users across various applications or platforms.

Timeline Interface

A Timeline Interface is a UI pattern that is commonly used to display a collection of events or activities in chronological order. It allows users to easily navigate and explore a series of events or milestones over time. The main purpose of a Timeline Interface is to provide a visual representation of the sequence of events, allowing users to understand the order and duration of each event. Typically, a timeline consists of a horizontal axis that represents time and markers or points that indicate the occurrence of events at specific points on the axis. In terms of design systems, a Timeline Interface follows certain principles to ensure consistency and usability. It often takes into consideration factors like font size, spacing, colors, and icons to create a cohesive and user-friendly experience. Additionally, it may incorporate responsive design techniques to adapt to different screen sizes and orientations. When designing a Timeline Interface, it is important to consider the content and context in which it will be used. The timeline should provide enough information about each event, such as a title, date, and description, to enable users to understand the significance of each milestone. Interaction elements like navigation controls, zoom in/out functionality, or filters can also enhance the user experience.

From a coding perspective, creating a Timeline Interface can involve the use of HTML, CSS, and JavaScript. HTML is used to structure the content and define the timeline elements, CSS is used to style the layout, colors, and typography, and JavaScript is used to handle any interactivity or animation effects. In conclusion, a Timeline Interface is a UI pattern that is commonly used to visualize and navigate a series of events or activities in chronological order. It plays a crucial role in conveying a sense of time and context to users, enabling them to understand the sequence and duration of events. When designing and coding a Timeline Interface, it is important to consider the content, context, and principles of a design system to create a consistent and user-friendly experience.

Timeline Section

A timeline section is a user interface (UI) pattern that displays a chronological sequence of events or actions. It is commonly used in websites and applications to showcase the progress or history of a particular process or story. A timeline section typically consists of a linear representation of time, with each event or action depicted as a point or a milestone along the timeline. These points are often accompanied by brief descriptions or labels to provide context and information to the user. In terms of design system, a timeline section is a predefined component that follows a set of consistent visual and interaction patterns. It helps maintain a unified look and feel across different parts of a website or application, ensuring a cohesive user experience. HTML is commonly used to structure and present the content of a timeline section. Here's an example of how it can be implemented using only 2

tags:

2005 - Company founded Lorem ipsum dolor sit amet, consectetur adipiscing elit.

2010 - Product launched Lorem ipsum dolor sit amet, consectetur adipiscing elit.

In the above example, the tag is used to highlight the year or date, while the tag is utilized to provide a description of the event or action associated with that particular timeline point. By using HTML to structure the timeline section, developers can easily manipulate and style the content using CSS. This allows for a consistent presentation across different devices and screen sizes. In conclusion, a timeline section is a UI pattern commonly used to present a chronological sequence of events or actions. It provides users with a visual representation of progress or history, and can be implemented using HTML and styled according to the design system of a website or application.>

Toggle Switches

A toggle switch is a common UI element used in both web and mobile applications to enable or disable a specific feature or setting. It presents a binary choice to the user, allowing them to toggle between two options, typically represented by a "on" and "off" state.

In terms of design systems, toggle switches often adhere to established conventions to ensure consistency across the interface. They are characterized by their simple, compact layout and clear visual indicators of the selected state. While the exact appearance of toggle switches may vary depending on the design system being used, they generally consist of a rectangular container, a handle, and labels for the "on" and "off" positions.

Tooltips

Tooltips are a common user interface pattern used in design systems to provide additional information or context to users when interacting with various elements in a digital interface.

They typically appear as small, contextual dialog boxes that are triggered by specific user actions, such as hovering over or clicking on an element. Tooltips often contain brief snippets of text or visual cues that help users understand the purpose, function, or meaning of an element.

Track Order

A "Track Order" feature is a UI pattern implemented within a design system that allows users to track the progress and status of their orders. This feature provides valuable information to users and helps them stay informed about the whereabouts of their package or the fulfillment process. Typically, the "Track Order" feature is prominently placed on an e-commerce website or mobile application, ensuring easy access for users who want to check the status of their purchases. Upon clicking or tapping on the "Track Order" button or link, users are directed to a dedicated page or screen that provides detailed information regarding their order. The track order page displays important details such as the current order status, estimated delivery date, and any available tracking numbers or links provided by the shipping carrier. It may also include details about the items included in the order, as well as any relevant updates or notifications related to the order's progress. The design system for the track order feature should prioritize clear and concise presentation of information to enhance the user experience. In terms of UI design, it is important to use a clean and uncluttered layout, with intuitive navigation and easy-to-read typography. The use of informative icons or visual indicators can also help users quickly grasp the status of their order. Additionally, the design system should ensure that the track order feature is responsive and accessible across different devices and screen sizes. This allows users to comfortably track their orders on desktop computers, smartphones, and tablets. By implementing a track order feature within a design system, businesses can enhance customer satisfaction by providing transparency and visibility into the order fulfillment process. This feature helps users minimize any anxieties surrounding their purchases, and it ultimately contributes to a positive user experience within the e-commerce platform.

A "Track Order" feature is a UI pattern that allows users to track the progress and status of their orders. It is prominently placed on an e-commerce website or mobile application, providing easy access for users to check the status of their purchases. Upon clicking or tapping on the "Track Order" button or link, users are directed to a dedicated page that displays important details such as the current order status, estimated delivery date, and any available tracking numbers or links. The design system for the track order feature prioritizes clear and concise presentation of information, with a clean and uncluttered layout, intuitive navigation, and informative icons or visual indicators. It is responsive and accessible across different devices and screen sizes. This feature contributes to a positive user experience by providing transparency and visibility into the order fulfillment process.

Travel Booking

A travel booking refers to the process of making arrangements for transportation, accommodations, and other travel-related services. In the context of UI patterns and design systems, a travel booking interface is a user interface that enables users to search, compare, and book travel services such as flights, hotels, car rentals, and tours. The travel booking interface typically consists of various components, including search forms, search results, booking forms, and payment forms. The user starts by entering their travel details, such as the destination, travel dates, and preferences. The search form usually includes input fields, dropdown menus, and checkboxes to capture this information. Once the user submits the search form, the system retrieves relevant results from a database or an API and displays them in the search results section. The search results typically show a list of options, sorted by relevance or price. Each option usually includes details such as the name of the service provider, the price, and a brief description. Users can further filter and sort the results to find the most suitable option. When the user selects a specific option, the booking form appears, allowing them to provide their personal details, such as their name, contact information, and payment method. The booking form may also include additional options or upgrades for the selected service. After completing the booking form, the user proceeds to the payment form, where they enter their payment details, such as credit card information. The payment form may also include additional security measures, such as CAPTCHA, to prevent fraudulent transactions. Once the user submits the payment form, the system processes the payment, confirms the booking, and provides a confirmation page or email with the booking details. Users may also have the option to print or save the booking confirmation for future reference. In summary, a travel booking interface in the context of UI patterns and design systems is a user interface that enables users to search, compare, and book travel services. It consists of components such as search forms, search results, booking forms, and payment forms, allowing users to enter their travel details, view and select options, provide personal and payment information, and receive a confirmation of their booking.>

Travel Itinerary Form

A travel itinerary form is a specific UI pattern and design system that allows users to input and organize their travel plans and details in a structured and efficient manner. It provides a well-defined layout and set of fields for users to fill in relevant information about their trip, such as destination, dates, transportation, accommodation, and activities.

This type of form typically consists of various form fields and components that users can interact with to input their travel information. These may include input fields for text, selections from dropdown menus, checkboxes for selecting optional items, and date pickers for selecting travel dates. The form may also include buttons for adding or removing items or for submitting the completed form.

Travel Itinerary

A travel itinerary, in the context of UI patterns and design systems, refers to a structured and organized representation of travel plans that includes essential details arranged in a clear and intuitive manner. It is a user interface element designed to provide users with a comprehensive overview of their travel arrangements, allowing them to easily understand and manage their trip. The primary purpose of a travel itinerary is to present information in a way that is easily digestible and accessible to users. It typically includes important details such as flight and hotel reservations, transportation information, activities and events, and other relevant information regarding the trip. A well-designed travel itinerary follows certain design principles and UI patterns to enhance user experience. It should be visually appealing, using appropriate fonts, colors, and spacing to ensure readability and clarity of information. Consistency in layout and formatting is crucial to provide a seamless experience across different screens and devices. The structure of a travel itinerary may vary depending on the complexity of the trip and the target audience. However, it generally consists of distinct sections for different aspects of the journey. Each section may contain relevant sub-sections to further organize and categorize the information. To aid user comprehension, a travel itinerary often incorporates visual cues and navigational elements. For example, using icons or symbols to represent different types of activities or modes of transportation can quickly convey information at a glance. Interactive elements such as collapsible sections or expandable details can further enhance the user experience by providing additional information on demand. In a design system, a travel itinerary is considered a reusable component or pattern that can be applied consistently across different interfaces and platforms. It should adhere to the overall visual and interactive guidelines of the design system, ensuring a cohesive and unified user experience. By providing users with a well-designed travel itinerary, designers aim to simplify the process of trip planning and management. Users can easily refer to and navigate through their itinerary, making informed decisions and adjustments when necessary. This ultimately enhances user satisfaction and reduces potential confusion or frustration associated with travel arrangements. In conclusion, a travel itinerary in the context of UI patterns and design systems is a carefully designed and structured representation of travel plans that offers users a clear and organized overview of their trip. It follows specific design principles, incorporates visual cues and navigational elements, and is considered a reusable component in a design system.>

Tree View

A Tree View is a user interface pattern that displays hierarchical data in a structured manner, resembling a tree structure. It allows users to navigate through and interact with the different levels or branches of the hierarchy, making it easier to visualize and understand the relationships between the data elements. A Tree View typically consists of parent nodes, child nodes, and leaf nodes. Parent nodes function as containers for child nodes, and child nodes can have their own child nodes, creating a nested structure. Leaf nodes, on the other hand, represent the end points or final data elements in the hierarchy. In terms of design, a Tree View is often represented by a vertical or horizontal list of nodes, with indentation or icons to indicate the level of hierarchy. By clicking or expanding the parent nodes, users can reveal or collapse the child nodes, allowing them to navigate through the different levels of the hierarchy. Tree Views are commonly used in applications and systems dealing with hierarchical data, such as file explorers, project management tools, organizational charts, and knowledge bases. They provide a convenient and efficient way to browse, search, or modify hierarchical information.

When implementing a Tree View, it is important to consider the usability and user experience. Providing clear labels, appropriate icons, and visual cues will help users easily understand the structure and navigate through the hierarchy. Additionally, incorporating features like drag-and-drop functionality or context menus can enhance the interaction and make it easier for users to perform actions on the nodes. In conclusion, a Tree View is a user interface pattern that displays hierarchical data as a tree structure, allowing users to navigate and interact with the different levels of the hierarchy. It is a widely used pattern in various applications and should be carefully designed to ensure usability and a seamless user experience.

Troubleshooting Form

A troubleshooting form is a user interface pattern and a component of a design system that allows users to report and resolve issues or problems they encounter while using a product or service. It provides a structured and systematic approach to problem-solving by guiding users through a series of steps to identify and resolve the issue. The main purpose of a troubleshooting form is to gather specific information from users in order to understand and diagnose the problem more effectively. This helps support teams and technical staff in providing targeted solutions and support. A typical troubleshooting form consists of several elements: 1. Title or heading: This provides a clear indication that the form is for troubleshooting purposes and sets the context for users. 2. Description or instructions: A brief description or instructions guide users on how to approach the troubleshooting process. It may include information on what type of problems to report, what details to provide, and any specific requirements. 3. Steps or checklist: A series of steps or a checklist is provided to help users systematically identify and understand the problem. This can include questions about the specific issue, details about any error messages or warning signs, or requests for additional information like screenshots or log files. 4. Input fields: Users are presented with input fields or text areas to provide relevant information or details about the issue. This may include fields for the user's name, contact information, product version, and a description of the problem. 5. Submit or send button: Once users have provided all the necessary information, they can submit the form by clicking on a submit or send button. This triggers the form to be sent to the appropriate support team or technical staff for review and resolution. Overall, a well-designed troubleshooting form enhances the user experience by providing a structured and user-friendly approach to problem-solving. It helps users articulate their issues more clearly and assists support teams in providing targeted and efficient solutions.

A troubleshooting form is a user interface pattern and a component of a design system that allows users to report and resolve issues or problems they encounter while using a product or service.

It provides a structured and systematic approach to problem-solving by guiding users through a series of steps to identify and resolve the issue.

Two-Factor Authentication (2FA) Setup Form

Two-Factor Authentication (2FA) is a security measure implemented within user interface (UI) patterns and design systems to provide an additional layer of security for user login processes. It is commonly used to protect sensitive user information, such as financial or personal data, from unauthorized access.

In the context of UI patterns and design systems, a 2FA setup form is a user interface element that allows users to configure and enable two-factor authentication for their accounts. This form typically includes fields and options for users to enter their account credentials, select a preferred method of authentication, and set up or link their secondary authentication device.

UI Pattern

A UI pattern, also known as a user interface pattern, is a recurring solution to a common user interface (UI) problem. It is a proven design solution that addresses a specific interaction or interface challenge in a consistent and effective way. UI patterns are commonly used in the development of user interfaces for websites, web applications, and mobile apps.

287

A design system, on the other hand, is a comprehensive set of guidelines, rules, and components that define the visual and interaction design of a product. It provides a unified and consistent experience across different platforms and devices. A design system helps designers and developers work efficiently by providing a library of reusable UI elements, typography, colors, and other design assets.

User Account Dashboard

A User Account Dashboard is a user interface (UI) pattern and design system that provides users with a centralized location to access and manage various aspects of their account. It serves as a control panel where users can view and customize their account settings, manage personal information, track activity and usage, and access features and functionalities associated with their account. The User Account Dashboard typically consists of different sections or modules, each dedicated to a specific area of account management. These sections may include: 1. Profile and Personal Information: This section allows users to view and update their personal details, such as name, contact information, and profile picture. Users can make changes to their information and save the updates for future reference. 2. Account Settings: This section provides users with the ability to customize and configure account settings according to their preferences. Users can modify options such as password, security settings, notification preferences, and privacy settings. 3. Activity and Usage: This section presents users with a summarized overview of their account activity and usage. It may include information such as login history, recent transactions, usage statistics, and any important notifications or alerts related to their account. 4. Billing and Payment: This section allows users to manage their billing and payment information. Users can view invoices, update payment methods, and make payments for any subscribed services or products associated with their account. 5. Support and Help: This section provides users with access to support resources and assistance. Users can find FAQs, contact customer support, submit feedback or inquiries, and seek help for any issues or concerns related to their account. Overall, the User Account Dashboard offers a centralized and efficient way for users to interact with their accounts and perform necessary actions. It streamlines the account management process, ensuring that users can easily navigate and access the various components of their account in a user-friendly and intuitive manner.>

User Account Deletion Request Form

A user account deletion request form is a specific user interface pattern that allows users to request the deletion of their account within a digital platform or service. This form is typically part of a larger design system, which governs the visual and interactive elements of the user interface. The user account deletion request form is a formal and structured component, adhering to the overall design system's principles and guidelines. The purpose of this form is to provide users with a clear and straightforward process for deleting their accounts, while also ensuring that the platform or service maintains proper workflow and security measures. The form typically consists of input fields and explanatory text to guide users through the account deletion process. Users are prompted to provide their account details, such as username or email address, and may also be asked to confirm their decision or provide additional feedback regarding their reason for deleting the account. The design of the form should prioritize simplicity and clarity. Form fields should be clearly labeled and arranged in a logical order, enabling users to quickly and accurately input their information. Additionally, concise and informative instructions or tooltips may be provided to resolve any potential confusion or uncertainty for users. Furthermore, to ensure the security and validity of the account deletion request, the form should include appropriate measures such as password authentication or CAPTCHA verification. These measures help prevent unauthorized deletion requests and maintain the integrity of the platform or service. By implementing this user interface pattern, platforms or services can effectively handle account deletion requests while respecting user privacy and providing a seamless user experience. The form serves as a vital component within the design system, ensuring consistency and usability for all users who wish to delete their accounts.

A user account deletion request form is a formal and structured interface pattern that allows users to request the removal of their account within a digital platform or service. The form adheres to the overall design system's principles and guidelines, prioritizing clarity and simplicity. It typically includes input fields for account details, as well as instructions and security measures to validate the request. This UI pattern ensures a seamless user experience while maintaining the platform's integrity.

User Account Lock Request Form

A User Account Lock Request Form is a UI pattern or design system element that allows users to submit a request to have their account locked. This form is typically used in systems where the user account can be temporarily locked or disabled, such as in online banking or social media platforms.

The purpose of the User Account Lock Request Form is to provide a secure and convenient way for users to suspend their account temporarily. There may be various reasons why a user may want to lock their account, such as to prevent unauthorized access in case of a security breach or to take a break from using the platform.

User Account Merge Request Form

The User Account Merge Request Form is a UI pattern and design system element used to consolidate multiple user accounts into a single account. It provides users with a streamlined and simple process to combine their accounts, eliminating the need to manage multiple sets of credentials and improving the overall user experience.

By utilizing the User Account Merge Request Form, users can select the accounts they wish to merge and provide any necessary information or documentation to verify their ownership. The form should include clear instructions and guidance to assist users in understanding the process and requirements.

User Account Reactivation Form

A User Account Reactivation Form is a UI pattern and design system element used to allow users to reactivate their previously created or inactive accounts. This form typically includes a series of input fields and options that the user needs to complete in order to initiate the reactivation process. The purpose of the User Account Reactivation Form is to provide a straightforward and user-friendly way for users to regain access to their accounts. This form is especially useful for users who have forgotten their password or let their account become inactive for an extended period of time. The form usually starts with a heading or title indicating that it is a reactivation form. It may also include a brief explanation of the reactivation process or any specific requirements. This helps users understand the purpose of the form and what they need to do to reactivate their account. Next, the form typically includes a series of input fields where users can enter their account information. This may include fields for the user's username, email address, or any other identifying information associated with their account. These fields should be clearly labeled and may include placeholder text or examples to guide the user in entering the correct information. Additionally, the form may include optional checkboxes or radio buttons for the user to indicate their preferences or specific actions they want to take during the reactivation process. For example, users may be able to choose whether they want to reset their password or update their account information. Once the user has completed all the required fields and options, they can click a submit button to initiate the reactivation process. This button should be clearly labeled and visually distinct to indicate that it is the final step in completing the form. In summary, a User Account Reactivation Form is an important UI pattern and design system element that allows users to easily and effectively reactivate their previously created or inactive accounts. By providing clear instructions, well-labeled fields, and intuitive options, this form helps users regain access to their accounts in a user-friendly manner.

A User Account Reactivation Form is a UI pattern and design system element used to allow users to reactivate their previously created or inactive accounts.

Next, the form typically includes a series of input fields where users can enter their account information. This may include fields for the user's username, email address, or any other identifying information associated with their account. These fields should be clearly labeled and may include placeholder text or examples to guide the user in entering the correct information.

User Account Recovery Form

A User Account Recovery Form is a specific UI pattern and design system component that allows users to regain access to their accounts when they have forgotten their login credentials or their accounts have been compromised. It serves as a user-friendly and secure way for users to reset their passwords or retrieve their account information. This form typically includes several input fields such as email address or username and may also include additional security measures like CAPTCHA or two-factor authentication. The purpose of these input fields is to collect the necessary information from the user in order to verify their identity and proceed with the account recovery process. Once the user has entered their information, they can submit the form, triggering a series of backend processes that verify the provided information and perform the account recovery steps. These processes typically include sending an email to the user's registered email address with a password reset link or providing a temporary password directly on the form. The UI design of a User Account Recovery Form should adhere to established design system guidelines to ensure consistency and usability across different interfaces and devices. It should have clear labels and explanatory text to guide the user through the process and provide informative error messages if there are any issues with the submitted information. Additionally, the form should be designed with security in mind, protecting user data and preventing unauthorized access. This may include measures such as encrypting the user's information during transmission, utilizing secure protocols, and implementing rate limiting or other security checks to prevent abuse. In summary, a User Account Recovery Form is a UI pattern and design system component that facilitates the process of account recovery for users who have lost access to their accounts. It collects the necessary information from the user, verifies their identity, and provides appropriate account recovery options. The design of the form should prioritize user experience, security, and adherence to established design system guidelines.>

User Account Suspension Request Form

A User Account Suspension Request Form is a UI pattern used in the design system of a website or application to provide users with a means to request the suspension or temporary deactivation of their account. This form typically consists of a series of input fields and checkboxes, allowing users to provide the necessary information to initiate the account suspension process. The form may include fields such as the user's name, email address, and account username, as well as a text area for users to provide a reason for their suspension request. The purpose of the User Account Suspension Request Form is to streamline the account suspension process and ensure that users have a clear and structured way to communicate their intention to temporarily discontinue their account usage. By providing this form, the website or application can have a standardized procedure for handling account suspension requests, reducing the need for back-and-forth communication or manual intervention from support staff. When designing this form, it is important to consider the user experience and make the process as user-friendly as possible. The form should have clear and concise instructions, guiding users through the necessary steps to submit their request. It should also include validation rules to ensure that users provide all the required information before submitting the form. In addition, it is crucial to prioritize the security of user data and account suspension requests. Implementing robust security measures, such as encryption and authentication protocols, can help protect sensitive user information during the form submission process. Overall, the User Account Suspension Request Form is an essential UI pattern in the design system of websites and applications that allows users to request the temporary deactivation of their accounts. By providing this form, businesses can ensure a streamlined account suspension process while prioritizing user experience and data security.

A User Account Suspension Request Form is a UI pattern used in the design system of a website or application to provide users with a means to request the suspension or temporary deactivation of their account.

This form typically consists of a series of input fields and checkboxes, allowing users to provide the necessary information to initiate the account suspension process. The form may include fields such as the user's name, email address, and account username, as well as a text area for users to provide a reason for their suspension request.

User Account Termination Form

A User Account Termination Form is a UI pattern and design system component that allows users to terminate or delete their account or profile on a website or application. It provides a structured and easy-to-use interface for users who want to discontinue their relationship with the platform.

The User Account Termination Form typically includes a set of fields and options that users need to complete in order to successfully terminate their account. These fields may include a confirmation statement, password verification, and a reason for leaving. The form may also include a checkbox or radio button to confirm that the user understands the consequences of account deletion, such as losing all data and access to the platform's features.

User Account Unlock Request Form

A User Account Unlock Request Form is a UI pattern and design system used to facilitate the process of unlocking a user's account in an application or system. It is a form that allows the user to request the unlocking of their account by providing necessary information and submitting the request.

The User Account Unlock Request Form typically includes fields for the user to enter their username or email address associated with the account, along with any additional required information such as security question answers or a verification code. The form may also include a message or instructions to inform the user about the process and any requirements or limitations.

The primary objective of a User Account Unlock Request Form is to provide a straightforward and efficient way for users to regain access to their locked accounts. By following a standardized design system, the form ensures consistency and familiarity for users, thereby reducing confusion and improving the overall user experience.

When designing a User Account Unlock Request Form, it is important to consider usability and accessibility. The form should have clear and concise labels for each field, providing hints or examples when necessary. Error handling and validation should be implemented to alert users about any issues with their input and guide them towards successful submission.

Additionally, the User Account Unlock Request Form should align with the overall visual design of the application or system to maintain a cohesive user interface. Consistent use of colors, typography, and layout should be followed to establish a sense of brand identity and familiarity.

User Activity Feeds

User activity feeds are a UI pattern commonly used in design systems to display a chronological list of activities or events performed by users within a digital platform or application. They provide a way to present real-time updates or historical information in a condensed and organized manner.

The purpose of user activity feeds is to keep users informed and engaged by exposing them to the actions and interactions happening within the system. This can include activities such as creating new content, sharing, commenting, following, liking, or any other user-generated actions.

Activity feeds typically consist of a single column or a grid-like layout, where each activity is represented as a compact card or item. These cards typically show relevant information about the user who performed the activity, the type of action taken, and a brief description or preview of the related content.

Design systems often provide predesigned templates for activity feeds to ensure visual consistency and usability across different components and layouts. By utilizing a design system, developers and designers can easily implement and customize activity feeds to fit the specific needs and branding of a digital platform.

291

In terms of user interaction, activity feeds may allow users to perform actions directly from the feed, such as liking or commenting on an activity. They may also provide filters or sorting options to allow users to customize the content they see based on their preferences or interests.

Overall, user activity feeds are an effective way to showcase user interactions and keep users engaged by providing real-time updates on relevant activities within a digital platform or application. They are a valuable component in UI design patterns and design systems, offering a streamlined and user-centric way to present and consume information.>

User Agreement Acceptance Form

A User Agreement Acceptance Form is a component of a user interface pattern or design system that is used to obtain the informed consent of users when they interact with a digital product or service. It serves as a formal agreement between the user and the provider, outlining the terms and conditions that govern the use of the product or service.

The User Agreement Acceptance Form typically includes a summary of the key terms and conditions, such as the user's rights and responsibilities, intellectual property rights, privacy and data protection, and dispute resolution mechanisms. It may also include a statement of the user's acknowledgment and acceptance of these terms, often through the use of checkboxes or buttons to indicate consent.

User Assistance Requests

A user assistance request refers to a specific action or feature within a user interface that allows users to seek help or guidance when using a system, application, or website. It is a part of UI patterns and design systems aimed at improving the user experience by providing useful information, instructions, or support to users in an easily accessible manner.

User assistance requests typically take the form of prompts, icons, or clickable elements that users can interact with to access helpful resources, such as tutorials, documentation, FAQs, or support channels. These features are commonly designed to be intuitive and prominently placed within the interface, ensuring that users are aware of and can easily find the assistance they need.

User Authentication In Chat

User Authentication in Chat is a UI pattern and design system that provides a secure way for users to access and interact with a chat application or platform. It involves the process of verifying the identity of the user before granting access to the chat system.

Authentication is essential in chat applications to ensure that only authorized users can access the platform and engage in conversations. It helps protect sensitive information, maintain privacy, prevent unauthorized access, and establish trust among users.

User Avatars

User Avatars are graphical representations of individual users within a digital interface, typically used to provide a visual identity and enhance the user experience. Avatars can be customized to reflect the user's characteristics, such as profile pictures, initials, or even abstract designs.

Implemented as a UI pattern, user avatars contribute to a consistent and recognizable design system. They serve multiple purposes, including personalization, identification, and visual hierarchy. Avatars help users quickly identify and differentiate between different individuals, especially in collaborative or social platforms where multiple users are present.

User Badges And Achievements

User badges and achievements are UI elements that are designed to visually represent and acknowledge specific accomplishments or milestones that a user has achieved within a digital platform or application. They serve as a form of recognition and encouragement for users to engage and explore various features or functionalities within the system. These badges and achievements are typically displayed prominently within a user's profile or public profile within the platform.

In terms of UI patterns and design systems, user badges and achievements can be considered as elements of gamification, rewarding users for their participation and progress within the system. They often utilize visual cues such as icons or graphical representations to symbolize the specific accomplishment or achievement. For example, a badge could be represented by a trophy icon to signify winning a competition or completing a challenging task. When designing user badges and achievements, it is important to consider the overall visual consistency and hierarchy within the UI. They should be distinguishable from other UI elements without overwhelming the overall design. Users should be able to easily understand the meaning and significance of each badge or achievement without additional explanation. Furthermore, user badges and achievements should be meaningful and attainable, providing users with a sense of progression and accomplishment. They should align with the goals and objectives of the platform, encouraging users to engage in desired behaviors or explore specific features. In this sense, they can serve as motivational tools to drive user engagement and retention. Overall, user badges and achievements are valuable components of UI patterns and design systems, as they not only enhance the visual appeal of the platform but also contribute to a sense of community and accomplishment among users. When implemented effectively, they can incentivize users to explore and engage with the system, ultimately leading to a more fulfilling and satisfying user experience.

User Block And Unblock

User Block and Unblock is a UI pattern and design system feature that allows administrators or users with certain privileges to suspend or restore a user's access and functionality within a platform or application. This functionality is commonly found in social media platforms, content management systems, and online communities.

When a user is blocked, their ability to interact with the platform is restricted. They are typically prevented from logging in, posting content, commenting, messaging other users, or accessing certain features or sections of the platform. This action is often taken as a result of a violation of terms of service, inappropriate behavior, or other actions that are deemed to be disruptive or against the platform's policies.

Unblocking a user effectively reverses the block, restoring their access and functionality to the platform. This allows the user to log in again, resume posting content, interacting with others, and accessing previously restricted features or sections.

From a design perspective, the User Block and Unblock pattern typically involves the use of a control or button within the user's profile or account settings. This control allows administrators or users with the appropriate privileges to initiate the block or unblock action. The design should make it clear to the user what action is being taken and provide the necessary confirmation or feedback to prevent accidental or unintended blocking or unblocking.

In a design system, the User Block and Unblock pattern should have consistent styling and behavior across different platforms or applications. This helps to ensure a cohesive user experience and makes it easier for users to understand and interact with the functionality. The pattern should also be flexible enough to accommodate different levels of blocking or restrictions, allowing administrators to choose the appropriate level of restriction based on the severity of the behavior or violation.

User Consent Management

User consent management refers to the system and interface design patterns that are used to gather, organize, and store user consent for the collection and processing of their personal data. It plays a crucial role in ensuring compliance with data protection regulations, such as the General Data Protection Regulation (GDPR). In the context of UI patterns, user consent management typically involves the display of clear and easily understandable consent requests to users in a way that allows them to make informed decisions regarding the use of their personal data. These patterns often include the following key elements: 1. Consent gathering:

293

User consent is typically obtained through the use of checkboxes or similar input mechanisms. The checkboxes are presented alongside concise and explicit explanations of what data is being collected and how it will be used. Users are also provided with the option to opt out or withdraw their consent at any time. 2. Consent organization: The design system ensures that user consent information is stored and organized in a way that is easily accessible and searchable. This includes maintaining records of when consent was given, what specific consent options were chosen by the user, and any subsequent updates or withdrawals of consent. 3. Granularity of consent: To comply with data protection regulations, user consent management should allow for granular control over the types of data being collected and processed. This means giving users the ability to selectively consent or opt out of specific data collection practices, rather than providing a single, all-or-nothing consent option. 4. Transparency: User consent management should prioritize transparency by clearly communicating to users how their personal data will be used and shared. This may include terms and conditions, privacy policies, or links to further information. By implementing user consent management design patterns and adhering to design system principles, organizations can create interfaces that respect user privacy rights and help to build trust with their audience. Effective user consent management is essential for staying in compliance with data protection regulations and maintaining a positive user experience.

User Context Retention

User Context Retention refers to the practice of maintaining and preserving a user's context and state within a user interface (UI) pattern or design system. It involves ensuring that a user can seamlessly transition between different screens, components, or interactions without losing their progress, data, or customization settings.

This retention of user context is crucial for creating a consistent and fluid user experience, as it reduces frustration and cognitive load by eliminating the need for users to re-enter information or navigate back to their original state. It enhances efficiency and productivity, particularly in complex or multi-step workflows.

User Data Access Logs

User Data Access Logs refer to a feature in UI patterns and design systems that allow for the tracking and monitoring of user interactions and activities within an application or website. These logs provide a detailed record of when and how users access, edit, and interact with their data.

By capturing user data access logs, designers and developers can gain insights into the usage patterns, preferences, and behaviors of their users. This information can be invaluable in improving the overall user experience and tailoring the application or website to better suit the needs and expectations of the users.

User data access logs typically include information such as the date and time of the access, the user's unique identifier or username, the specific action performed (e.g., view, edit, delete), the type of data accessed, and any related metadata. This log data is often stored in a centralized database or log file, where it can be easily analyzed and queried.

From a design perspective, user data access logs can inform important decisions regarding the layout, organization, and functionality of an application or website. For example, by analyzing the logs, designers may discover that certain features or sections of the interface are rarely used or difficult to access, prompting them to redesign or reposition these elements for improved usability.

In addition, user data access logs can also help in identifying and resolving any potential security or privacy concerns. By carefully monitoring and auditing user interactions, designers and developers can detect and respond to any suspicious or unauthorized activities, ensuring the integrity and confidentiality of user data.

Overall, user data access logs play a crucial role in the iterative design process by providing valuable data on user behaviors, preferences, and usage patterns. By analyzing this data, designers and developers can make informed decisions to create more efficient, intuitive, and user-centric interfaces.>

User Data Access Request Form

A User Data Access Request Form is a UI pattern and design system element that allows users to request access to their personal data held by an organization. This form typically provides a structured way for users to submit their data access requests, guiding them through the necessary information and steps to complete the request.

When designing a User Data Access Request Form, it is important to consider the following key elements:

1. Clear and concise instructions: The form should provide clear and straightforward instructions on how to complete the request. This may include information on what types of personal data can be requested, any specific requirements for verification, and how long the process is expected to take.

2. Required fields: The form should clearly indicate which fields are mandatory to complete the request. This helps to ensure that users provide all the necessary information for their request to be processed effectively.

3. Privacy and security considerations: The form should address privacy and security concerns by clearly outlining how the user's personal data will be handled and protected during the request process. This may include information on encryption, data storage, and any applicable legal regulations.

4. Progress indication: If the User Data Access Request Form consists of multiple steps or sections, it is helpful to provide a progress indication to let users know how far they have progressed in the process. This can be achieved through visual indicators or a step-by-step timeline.

Overall, a well-designed User Data Access Request Form creates a user-friendly experience by guiding users through the process of requesting access to their personal data. By providing clear instructions, required fields, addressing privacy concerns, and using progress indication, this form helps to ensure that users can easily exercise their rights to access their personal data.

User Data Anonymization Request Form

A User Data Anonymization Request Form is a user interface pattern and design system element that allows users to easily request the anonymization of their personal data. It provides a systematic and standardized way for users to exercise their rights to data protection and privacy.

The form typically includes fields for users to provide their identifying information, such as their name, email address, and any other relevant details necessary to locate and process their data. It may also include optional fields for users to specify the scope or reasons for their request.

User Data Anonymization

Data anonymization refers to the process of transforming personal data into a form that does not allow the identification of individuals. This is done to protect the privacy and confidentiality of users' information while still allowing for data analysis and the development of user interface (UI) patterns and design systems.

In the context of UI patterns and design systems, data anonymization plays a crucial role in ensuring that sensitive user data is not exposed or identifiable. By anonymizing the data, designers and developers can create reusable UI patterns and design systems that can be used across different applications without compromising the privacy of users.

User Data Compliance

User Data Compliance refers to the adherence to legal and ethical guidelines in handling and protecting user data within the context of UI patterns and design systems.

In order to ensure proper compliance, designers and developers must take into consideration various factors. First and foremost, obtaining explicit consent from users is essential. This involves clearly communicating the purpose for which the data is being collected, how it will be used, and any potential third-party involvement. Transparency is crucial in this process to establish trust and give users the opportunity to make informed decisions about sharing their personal information.

To further ensure compliance, UI patterns and design systems should prioritize data minimization. This means only collecting the data that is necessary for the intended purpose and avoiding the collection of sensitive or unnecessary information. Designers should closely evaluate the data fields and forms they create, aiming for simplicity and relevance, without burdening users with excessive requests for personal details.

Data security is another fundamental aspect of compliance. Implementing appropriate security measures, such as encryption and access controls, is crucial to safeguard user data from unauthorized access or breaches. UI patterns and design systems should incorporate best practices for data protection, such as secure storage and transmission protocols, to mitigate potential risks and ensure the privacy of user information.

Maintaining compliance also involves providing users with the ability to exercise their rights over their personal data. This includes allowing users to easily access, modify, or delete their information as well as providing mechanisms for addressing any concerns or complaints. Design systems should facilitate these processes by including intuitive interfaces that enable users to manage their data effectively.

Furthermore, compliance requires ongoing monitoring and assessment of data handling practices. Regular reviews and audits should be conducted to ensure alignment with evolving legal and regulatory requirements. Designers and developers need to remain up-to-date with relevant privacy standards and adapt their UI patterns and design systems accordingly.

In conclusion, User Data Compliance in the context of UI patterns and design systems encompasses obtaining explicit consent, data minimization, data security, user rights, and ongoing monitoring. By incorporating these principles into their designs, designers can create user-centered experiences that prioritize privacy and comply with legal and ethical requirements.

User Data Consent API

User Data Consent API is a set of UI patterns and design system that provides a formal definition for obtaining user consent for data processing. This API aims to ensure transparency and compliance with data protection regulations by allowing users to provide informed consent for the collection, use, and sharing of their personal data.

The User Data Consent API follows a standard set of guidelines and best practices for implementing consent mechanisms in user interfaces. It provides a consistent and intuitive user experience across different platforms and applications. The API offers a range of customizable UI components, such as consent dialogs, checkboxes, and consent banners, to seamlessly integrate consent collection into the user interface.

User Data Consent Agreements

A user data consent agreement is a formal agreement between an organization and its users, outlining the terms and conditions for the collection, use, and storage of user data. It is an essential component of a user interface (UI) pattern and design system, as it promotes transparency, trust, and compliance with data protection regulations.

The purpose of a user data consent agreement is to ensure that users are fully informed about how their data will be used and to obtain explicit consent from them before collecting any personal information. This agreement typically includes details such as the types of data being collected, the purpose of data collection, the duration of data storage, and mechanisms for user control and consent withdrawal.

User Data Consent Assessment

User Data Consent Assessment refers to the process of obtaining user consent for the collection, storage, and use of their personal data in a digital platform or application. It involves providing users with clear and transparent information about how their data will be processed, and giving them the choice to provide or withhold their consent.

In the context of UI patterns and design systems, User Data Consent Assessment aims to ensure that the interface and presentation of data consent requests are user-friendly, accessible, and compliant with legal and privacy regulations. It involves designing and implementing intuitive and visually appealing components that enable users to easily understand and manage their data privacy settings.

User Data Consent Audit Reports

User Data Consent Audit Reports refer to a collection of records and documents that provide a comprehensive overview of the user data consent process within a system or platform. These reports aim to document and track how user data is collected, stored, and used, ensuring compliance with relevant privacy laws and regulations. In the context of UI patterns and design systems, User Data Consent Audit Reports serve as a crucial tool for designers and developers to evaluate and improve the user experience related to data consent. These reports assist in identifying areas of the user journey where data collection occurs, helping to enhance transparency, trust, and control for users. User Data Consent Audit Reports typically include information such as the types of data collected, the purpose of data collection, the legal basis for processing, and any third parties with whom the data is shared. They may also outline the methods used to obtain user consent, such as checkboxes, pop-ups, or explicit agreements. By analyzing these reports, UI designers and developers can better understand the user flow and identify opportunities for optimization. For example, they may find instances where the consent process is overly complex or lacks clarity, leading to a cumbersome user experience. In such cases, they can make informed decisions to simplify the consent process, provide clearer explanations, or offer more granular options for data control. Moreover, User Data Consent Audit Reports are essential for ensuring compliance with privacy regulations, like the General Data Protection Regulation (GDPR) in the European Union. These reports demonstrate the organization's commitment to transparency and accountability, providing evidence that data protection measures are in place and being actively monitored and reviewed. In summary, User Data Consent Audit Reports play a critical role in evaluating and refining the user experience surrounding data consent. By enabling informed decision-making, fostering transparency, and ensuring compliance with privacy regulations, these reports contribute to building user trust and confidence in the system or platform.>

User Data Consent Audit Trails

A user data consent audit trail is a UI pattern and design system that provides a concise and structured representation of a user's consent activities and interactions within a digital platform or application. It serves as a visual record or log that helps users navigate and understand their data privacy choices, as well as the subsequent actions taken by the platform based on those choices.

This design system typically includes a chronological display of key events related to the user's data consent, such as when consent was given or revoked, specific data categories or purposes that were consented to, and any changes or updates made to the consent settings. The audit trail may also include information about the legal basis for processing the data, the duration of consent, and any third parties involved in data sharing.

User Data Consent Auditing

User Data Consent Auditing is a crucial component of UI patterns and design systems that ensures the ethical and compliant handling of user data. It involves both the technical and legal aspects of collecting, storing, and processing personal data in a digital product or service.

The purpose of User Data Consent Auditing is to provide transparency, accountability, and control over the use of user data. It involves implementing mechanisms to obtain explicit and informed consent from users for data collection and processing activities. This includes informing users about the type of data being collected, how it will be used, and any third parties it will be shared with.

User Data Consent Best Practices

User Data Consent Best Practices, in the context of UI patterns and design systems, refer to established guidelines and recommendations for designing consent flows in a user interface. These best practices focus on ensuring that users have clear and accessible information about how their data will be collected, used, and shared, and that they have the ability to make informed decisions and provide their consent. One important aspect of user data consent best practices is transparency. This means presenting clear and concise information to users about what data will be collected, how it will be used, and who it will be shared with. The information should be easily understandable and avoid complex legal jargon, enabling users to make informed decisions about sharing their data. Another key aspect is granularity. Designers should provide users with granular control over their data, allowing them to choose which specific types of data they are comfortable sharing. This can be achieved by offering customizable consent options or toggle switches for different data categories or purposes. In addition, user data consent best practices emphasize the importance of providing users with options to manage their consent preferences. This includes offering simple and accessible ways for users to change or withdraw their consent at any time. Designers should ensure that the interface makes it clear how users can access and modify their consent settings. Furthermore, it is essential to make the consent flow accessible to all users. This involves using clear and concise language, avoiding the use of technical or ambiguous terms, and providing appropriate visual cues and feedback. Designers should also consider the needs of users with disabilities by following accessibility standards and guidelines. Designers are encouraged to keep the consent flow unobtrusive and avoid interrupting the user experience unnecessarily. It is important to strike a balance between providing necessary information and requesting consent without overwhelming or frustrating the user. Finally, user data consent best practices promote privacy by default. This means that, whenever possible, designers should design interfaces that prioritize privacy and minimize the collection of personal data. Default settings should align with user privacy expectations and only request additional data when necessary. By following these user data consent best practices, designers can create interfaces that respect users' privacy, empower them to make informed decisions, and enhance their overall user experience.>

User Data Consent Certification

User Data Consent Certification is a UI pattern and design system that focuses on obtaining explicit consent from users for the collection, storage, and usage of their personal data. It ensures that users fully understand and agree to how their data will be handled by an application or service. This pattern is crucial in today's digital landscape, where privacy and data protection are paramount concerns. User data consent certification ensures that businesses and organizations adhere to legal and ethical standards by obtaining user consent in a transparent and user-friendly way. The design system for user data consent certification includes various components and guidelines to create a seamless and informative user experience. It includes clear and concise explanations of what data is being collected, how it will be used, and who it will be shared with. The design system also emphasizes providing users with granular control over their data, allowing them to easily opt-in or out of specific data collection and usage scenarios. One key element of the design system is the use of prominent and easy-to-understand visuals. This includes the use of clear labels, checkboxes, and toggles to visually represent data collection and usage options. The design system also includes the use of colors and iconography to convey the importance and sensitivity of user data. In addition to visuals, the design system emphasizes the use of plain and jargon-free language. This ensures that users, regardless of their technical knowledge, can fully understand the implications of consenting to data collection and usage. The language used in the consent certification process should be respectful, informative, and concise. Overall, user data consent certification is a critical aspect of UX design in today's data-driven world. It helps to build trust between users and businesses by ensuring transparency, control, and informed decision-making regarding personal data. By following the guidelines and principles of this design system, businesses and organizations can obtain user consent in a respectful and user-friendly manner, while also complying with legal and ethical requirements.

298

User Data Consent Compliance Assessments

A user data consent compliance assessment is a framework used in UI patterns and design systems to evaluate the compliance of a user interface with data protection regulations and guidelines regarding obtaining and managing user consent for data collection and processing.

The purpose of a user data consent compliance assessment is to ensure that the design and functionality of the user interface accurately reflect the requirements and intentions of data protection laws, such as the General Data Protection Regulation (GDPR). It involves a systematic evaluation of the user interface, its components, and interactions to determine if they support and align with the principles and obligations of user consent under applicable regulations.

User Data Consent Compliance Automation

User Data Consent Compliance Automation refers to the implementation of a user interface (UI) pattern and design system that allows developers and designers to easily incorporate user consent features into their applications while ensuring compliance with data protection regulations.

This pattern and design system streamline the process of obtaining and managing user consent, providing developers with standardized components, guidelines, and best practices. It aims to strike a balance between user privacy and business needs by giving users control over their data while ensuring that organizations can still collect and utilize user information for legitimate purposes.

User Data Consent Compliance Best Practices

The User Data Consent Compliance Best Practices refer to guidelines and recommendations for ensuring that user data is collected, processed, and stored in compliance with applicable data protection regulations and user privacy preferences.

When designing user interfaces and implementing design systems, it is important to consider these best practices to ensure that the user's consent is obtained transparently and effectively. This helps to establish trust with users and demonstrates a commitment to data privacy.

User Data Consent Compliance Certification

User Data Consent Compliance Certification is a formal acknowledgment or confirmation issued to show that a user or organization complies with the regulations and requirements pertaining to the collection, use, storage, and sharing of user data. It is an essential component of user interface (UI) patterns and design systems, as it ensures that the design and functionality of digital products or services adhere to legal and ethical guidelines. The User Data Consent Compliance Certification is typically implemented within the UI of an application or website to inform users about the data practices and obtain their consent. This certification signifies that the platform has taken appropriate measures to protect and respect user privacy rights. It demonstrates transparency in data practices and empowers users with control over their personal information. In a UI pattern, the User Data Consent Compliance Certification is often displayed prominently on the interface, either as a banner, popup, or notification. Its design should clearly communicate the purpose of the certification, emphasize the importance of user consent, and provide easy-to-understand options for users to grant or revoke consent. To ensure compliance with UI design systems, the User Data Consent Compliance Certification should adhere to a consistent visual style and placement across the entire product or service ecosystem. It should be seamlessly integrated into the overall design, maintaining harmony with other UI elements and branding guidelines. The User Data Consent Compliance Certification UI pattern should include essential information such as the purpose of data collection, the types of data being collected, how the data will be used, who will have access to the data, and any relevant third-party integrations. Clear and concise language should be used to convey this information, avoiding jargon or complex legal terms. Additionally, the User Data Consent Compliance Certification UI pattern should provide visible and accessible options for users to manage their consent preferences. This may include options to enable or disable specific data processing activities, adjust privacy settings, or request the deletion of personal data. In summary, the User Data Consent Compliance Certification is a crucial element of UI patterns and design systems. It ensures that digital products or services comply with data protection regulations and empowers users with control over their personal information. By implementing this certification within the UI, platforms demonstrate their commitment to privacy and foster trust with users.

User Data Consent Compliance Checks

User Data Consent Compliance Checks refer to a set of UI patterns and design system guidelines that ensure the proper handling and display of consent information in user interfaces. These checks are necessary to comply with data protection regulations and to enhance the user experience by providing transparency and control over the use of their personal information. The primary objective of User Data Consent Compliance Checks is to obtain explicit consent from users before collecting, processing, or using their personal data. This involves presenting clear and concise information regarding the purpose, scope, and duration of data collection, and enabling users to make informed decisions. To achieve compliance, designers and developers should follow best practices when implementing consent-related user interfaces. This includes: 1. Clear and Legible Presentation: Consent information should be displayed in a way that is easy to read and understand. It should be presented prominently on the screen, using a legible font size and color contrast that ensures readability for all users. 2. Unambiguous Language: Consent requests should use simple and concise language that avoids technical jargon or ambiguous terms. The purpose of data collection and any potential impacts on the user should be clearly explained. 3. Granular Options: Users should be provided with granular options to consent or withhold consent for different types of data processing. This allows users to have control over the specific categories of personal data they are comfortable sharing. 4. Default Settings and Pre-Ticked Boxes: Consent checkboxes or switches should not be pre-selected or pre-ticked by default. Users should actively make a choice to provide consent, rather than having to opt-out of data collection. 5. Accessible Design: Consent-related UI elements should be accessible to all users, including those with disabilities. Designer should ensure that screen reader support, keyboard navigation, and alternative text are implemented properly. By adhering to these User Data Consent Compliance Checks, designers and developers can ensure that their user interfaces are in compliance with data protection regulations, and provide users with a transparent and controllable experience when it comes to sharing their personal information.

User Data Consent Compliance Consultation

User Data Consent Compliance Consultation refers to the process of ensuring that user data is collected, stored, and processed in accordance with applicable data privacy laws and regulations, such as the General Data Protection Regulation (GDPR) in the European Union.

In the context of UI patterns and design systems, user data consent compliance consultation involves designing and implementing user interface elements and patterns that enable users to provide informed consent for the collection and processing of their personal data. This includes obtaining clear and unambiguous consent from users, providing them with transparent and easily understandable information about the purpose and use of their data, and giving them control over their data through privacy settings and preferences.

User Data Consent Compliance Controls

User Data Consent Compliance Controls are UI patterns and design system components that allow users to provide their informed consent for the collection, processing, and storage of their personal data in compliance with regulatory requirements and industry best practices. These controls ensure transparency and empower users to make informed decisions about their personal data. They typically include the following elements: 1. Consent Request: A clear and concise statement explaining the purpose and scope of the data collection. It should include details about the data being collected, how it will be used, and any third parties it may be shared with. 2. Granularity: The ability for users to provide consent at different levels of detail, depending on their preferences. For example, users may be able to grant consent for specific types of data processing or limit their consent to certain channels or purposes. 3. Opt-in/Opt-out Mechanisms: Clear and unambiguous options for users to either provide or withdraw their consent. This could be in the form of checkboxes, toggle switches, or buttons with clear labels, such as "Yes, I agree" or "No, I do not consent". 4. Information Access: Users should have easy access to information about their consent settings and the personal data that has been collected and stored. This can include a dedicated consent management interface where users can review and update their preferences. 5. Explanations and Clarifications: Supplementary information, such as tool-tips or contextual help, should be provided to help users understand the implications of their choices and the consequences of withholding or withdrawing consent. 6. Retention Period: Users should be informed about how long their data will be retained and provided with the option to set an expiration date for their consent. 7. Revocation and Deletion: Users should have the ability to revoke their consent at any time and request the deletion of their personal data. This can be provided through a clear and easily accessible mechanism, such as a "Delete my data" button or a contact form. These compliance controls should be designed with the user experience in mind, ensuring that they are intuitive, accessible, and easy to understand. They should be consistent across different touchpoints, such as websites, mobile apps, and third-party services, to provide a seamless and coherent user experience. By implementing User Data Consent Compliance Controls, organizations can demonstrate their commitment to user privacy and data protection, building trust and fostering positive relationships with their users.>

User Data Consent Compliance Dashboards

User Data Consent Compliance Dashboards refer to UI patterns and design systems that facilitate the management and tracking of user data consent in compliance with relevant regulations and policies.

These dashboards are typically designed to provide a visual representation of the different stages of the consent lifecycle, allowing users to easily understand and manage the consent status for their collected data. They aim to enhance transparency and user control over their personal information, promoting trust and compliance with data protection protocols.

User Data Consent Compliance Documentation

The User Data Consent Compliance Documentation is a comprehensive set of guidelines and requirements regarding the collection, use, and storage of user data within a UI pattern or design system. Its purpose is to ensure that the user's privacy is protected and that the system is in compliance with relevant laws and regulations.

This documentation includes all the necessary information and instructions for designers, developers, and other stakeholders to understand and implement the required data consent features and functionality. It outlines the specific data that is being collected, the intended purpose of collection, and how the data will be stored and used.

User Data Consent Compliance Frameworks

A User Data Consent Compliance Framework is a set of guidelines and principles that outline the requirements and best practices for obtaining and managing user consent for the collection and processing of personal data within a user interface (UI) pattern or design system.

These frameworks are designed to ensure that organizations comply with relevant data protection regulations, such as the General Data Protection Regulation (GDPR) in the European Union, and provide clear and transparent consent options for users.

User Data Consent Compliance Guidelines

User Data Consent Compliance Guidelines refer to a set of rules and regulations that govern the way user data is collected, used, and stored in accordance with legal requirements and user preferences. These guidelines ensure that businesses and organizations implement transparent and user-friendly user consent mechanisms to enable users to make informed decisions about their data. In the context of UI patterns and design systems, User Data Consent Compliance Guidelines provide a framework for designing and implementing consent dialogs and interfaces that respect user privacy. These guidelines aim to strike a balance between preserving user control over their data and providing a seamless user experience. To comply with User Data Consent Compliance Guidelines, designers should consider the following key principles: 1.

301

Transparency: Consent dialogs should clearly articulate why user data is being collected, how it will be used, and with whom it will be shared. Designers should provide succinct and easily understandable explanations, avoiding technical jargon or ambiguous language. 2. Granularity: Consent options should be presented to users in a granular and explicit manner. Users should be able to selectively grant or deny consent for specific data processing activities. Designers should avoid pre-ticked checkboxes or bundled consent requests, ensuring that users have control over each data processing activity. 3. Simplicity: Consent dialogs should be designed to be concise and easy to understand. Complex or lengthy explanations can overwhelm users and hinder their ability to make informed decisions. Designers should use clear and concise language and provide additional information only when necessary. 4. Control: Consent dialogs should provide users with options for managing their data preferences. Users should be able to easily access and update their consent settings at any time. Designers should provide clear instructions and intuitive controls for opting in or out of data processing activities. 5. Accessibility: Consent dialogs should be designed with accessibility in mind, considering users with different abilities. Designers should use appropriate color contrasts, provide alternative text for images, and ensure that consent dialogs are navigable using keyboard-only interactions. By adhering to User Data Consent Compliance Guidelines, designers can contribute to building trust with users by providing them with control and transparency over their personal data. Following these guidelines not only ensures compliance with legal requirements but also enhances the user experience by empowering users to make informed decisions about their data.

User Data Consent Compliance Laws

User Data Consent Compliance Laws refer to the regulations and guidelines that govern how companies and organizations collect, use, and protect the personal data of their users or customers. These laws are designed to ensure that individuals have control over their personal information and are informed about how it is being used. Compliance with these laws is crucial for companies to maintain trust and transparency with their users, avoid legal penalties, and uphold ethical practices.

When it comes to UI patterns and design systems, it is essential for designers and developers to consider these laws and incorporate appropriate features and elements that facilitate compliance. This includes providing clear and concise information to users about what data is being collected and for what purposes, as well as obtaining explicit consent from users before collecting or processing their personal information. Designers should aim to make these consent requests easily noticeable and understandable, ensuring that users have a clear understanding of what they are agreeing to.

User Data Consent Compliance Management

User Data Consent Compliance Management is a UI pattern and design system that focuses on facilitating and ensuring compliance with data protection regulations by obtaining and managing user consent for the collection and processing of their personal information.

With increasing concerns around privacy and data security, organizations need to implement robust mechanisms to obtain user consent and demonstrate compliance with relevant regulations such as the General Data Protection Regulation (GDPR). The User Data Consent Compliance Management pattern provides a framework for designing user interfaces that enable organizations to achieve these objectives.

This pattern typically includes a series of screens or dialogs that guide users through the process of granting consent for the collection and processing of their personal data. These screens are designed to be clear, transparent, and easy to understand, ensuring that users are fully informed about how their data will be used and allowing them to make informed decisions.

The User Data Consent Compliance Management pattern also includes features for managing and documenting user consent. This may involve implementing mechanisms for storing and retrieving consent records, providing users with the ability to review and update their consent preferences, and facilitating the withdrawal of consent if desired.

In addition to these functional components, the design system associated with User Data Consent Compliance Management focuses on aesthetics and usability. It provides guidelines and best practices for creating visually appealing and intuitive user interfaces that enhance the user experience and encourage user engagement with the consent management process.

Overall, User Data Consent Compliance Management is essential for organizations operating in environments where data protection regulations are in place. By adopting this UI pattern and design system, organizations can ensure that they handle user data in a responsible and compliant manner, building trust with their users and minimizing the risk of legal and reputational issues.

User Data Consent Compliance Monitoring

User Data Consent Compliance Monitoring is a UI pattern and design system that ensures compliance with data privacy regulations by monitoring and tracking user consent for the collection and processing of personal information.

With the increasing focus on data privacy and protection, organizations need to implement mechanisms to obtain and manage consent from users regarding the usage of their personal data. User Data Consent Compliance Monitoring provides a solution to address this requirement.

The pattern involves the implementation of a user interface that enables users to easily view and manage their consent preferences. This interface typically includes options for users to grant or revoke consent for specific data collection and processing activities. Users can also access information about the purpose and scope of data usage, the entities involved, and the rights they have regarding their personal information.

In addition to the user-facing interface, the design system behind User Data Consent Compliance Monitoring includes back-end processes and workflows that handle the storage, retrieval, and monitoring of user consent data. This design system ensures that user preferences are consistently and accurately recorded and applied across the organization's systems and processes.

By implementing User Data Consent Compliance Monitoring, organizations not only demonstrate their commitment to data privacy but also provide users with transparency and control over the usage of their personal information. This pattern helps organizations build trust and maintain compliance with data protection regulations.

User Data Consent Compliance Notifications

User Data Consent Compliance Notifications refer to a design pattern or system in the user interface (UI) that prompts users to grant or deny their consent for their personal data to be collected, processed, or shared by an application or website in compliance with applicable data protection regulations and policies. These notifications typically appear as pop-ups or banners, prominently displayed within the UI, to inform users about the purpose and scope of data collection and request their explicit consent to proceed. The notifications are designed to be clear, concise, and easy to understand, ensuring that users are fully informed about their data privacy rights and the implications of granting or withholding their consent. Key components of User Data Consent Compliance Notifications include: 1. Clear and Concise Explanation: The notification should provide a clear and concise explanation of why the user's data is being collected and how it will be used. It should avoid technical jargon or complex language, ensuring that users can easily comprehend the purpose and implications of data collection. 2. Opt-In/Opt-Out Options: The notification should include clear options for users to either grant or deny their consent. The options should be easy to distinguish and accompanied by explicit labels, such as "Accept" and "Decline," to ensure users can make an informed decision based on their preferences. 3. Granular Consent: If the data collection involves multiple purposes or types of data, the notification should allow users to provide granular consent by selecting or deselecting specific data categories or purposes. This allows users to have more control over their personal information and consent to only what they are comfortable with. 4. Link to Privacy Policy: The notification should provide a prominent link to the app or website's privacy policy, where users can find detailed information about data handling practices, retention periods, and their rights as data subjects. This link ensures transparency and enables users to make an informed decision based on the full context. 5. Clear Dismissal Option: It is important to provide users with a clear and easily accessible option to dismiss the notification without providing consent. This respects the user's autonomy and allows them to continue using the app or website without being compelled to share their personal data. By implementing User Data Consent Compliance Notifications in the UI, organizations demonstrate their commitment to user privacy and comply with legal and ethical obligations regarding data protection. These notifications empower users by providing them with the necessary information and control over their personal data, fostering trust and transparency in digital interactions.

User Data Consent Compliance Officers

User Data Consent Compliance Officers

User Data Consent Compliance Officers are individuals or teams responsible for ensuring that a system's user interface (UI) patterns and design system align with data privacy regulations and obtain appropriate user consent for data collection and processing. They play a crucial role in safeguarding user privacy and ensuring ethical data practices.

In the context of UI patterns and design systems, User Data Consent Compliance Officers primarily focus on implementing and maintaining features that adhere to data protection regulations, such as the General Data Protection Regulation (GDPR) or the California Consumer Privacy Act (CCPA). These officers work closely with UX designers, developers, and legal teams to ensure that user data is handled in a compliant and transparent manner.

The main responsibilities of User Data Consent Compliance Officers include:

1. Reviewing and updating UI patterns and design system components to incorporate data privacy requirements.

2. Collaborating with UX designers to create user-friendly interfaces for consent management, making sure that users can easily understand and control the data they share.

3. Ensuring that all necessary consents and acknowledgments are obtained from users, especially when sensitive data is involved.

4. Conducting regular audits and assessments to identify and address potential compliance gaps in the UI patterns and design system.

5. Keeping up-to-date with changes in data protection laws and regulations to ensure ongoing compliance.

6. Working closely with the legal team to interpret and implement legal requirements related to user data consent in the UI patterns and design system.

By fulfilling these responsibilities, User Data Consent Compliance Officers contribute to building a trustful relationship between users and the system by demonstrating a commitment to protecting user privacy and complying with data protection regulations.

User Data Consent Compliance Programs

User Data Consent Compliance Programs are UI patterns and design systems that ensure websites and applications are in compliance with data privacy regulations by implementing a clear and transparent consent process for collecting and using user data.

These programs typically consist of a set of standardized visual and interactive elements that prompt and obtain user consent, provide information about data collection and usage, and enable users to manage their data preferences. The goal is to empower users with control over their personal information while still allowing businesses to collect and utilize data for legitimate purposes.

User Data Consent Compliance Regulations

User Data Consent Compliance Regulations refer to the set of rules and guidelines that govern the collection, storage, and usage of personal data by organizations. These regulations aim to protect the privacy and rights of individuals by ensuring that their personal information is handled in a transparent and secure manner.

In the context of UI patterns and design systems, complying with user data consent regulations is crucial. It involves designing and implementing user interfaces that provide clear and concise information to users about how their data will be collected, used, and shared. It also requires obtaining explicit consent from users before collecting their personal information.

User Data Consent Compliance Reporting

User Data Consent Compliance Reporting is a UI pattern and design system that facilitates the reporting of compliance with data consent regulations. It provides a standardized and user-friendly way of presenting information related to the collection, storage, and usage of user data in accordance with legal requirements and best practices.

The main goal of User Data Consent Compliance Reporting is to enhance transparency and accountability in data processing activities. It allows users to understand what data is being collected, how it is being used, and who has access to it. This helps to build trust between users and organizations by empowering users with the knowledge and control over their personal information.

User Data Consent Compliance Standards

User Data Consent Compliance Standards

User Data Consent Compliance Standards refer to a set of guidelines and regulations implemented to ensure that user data is collected, processed, and stored in a manner that respects individuals' privacy and complies with applicable data protection laws. These standards are designed to provide transparency and control to users over their personal information and require organizations to obtain explicit consent from individuals before collecting or using their data.

In the context of UI patterns and design systems, compliance with user data consent standards is crucial for creating interfaces that prioritize user privacy and data protection. Designers and developers must consider these standards when designing and implementing features that involve data collection or processing, such as sign-up forms, cookie consent notifications, or data sharing prompts.

User Data Consent Compliance Support

User Data Consent Compliance Support refers to a feature or functionality provided in a user interface (UI) pattern or design system that helps ensure compliance with data protection regulations and guidelines by obtaining and managing user consent for the collection, processing, and storage of personal data.

In the context of UI patterns and design systems, User Data Consent Compliance Support typically includes a set of components, templates, and guidelines that are designed and implemented to facilitate the implementation of data consent mechanisms within an application or website and to support the presentation and management of user consent information.

User Data Consent Compliance Technology

User Data Consent Compliance Technology refers to a framework or system that enables businesses to gather and manage user data in compliance with relevant privacy regulations and laws. This technology helps organizations obtain proper consent from users before collecting, using, or sharing their personal information.

The UI patterns and design system of User Data Consent Compliance Technology focus on facilitating transparent and user-friendly experiences for obtaining consent. The primary goal is to ensure that users are well-informed about the data being collected and how it will be used. The design system aims to provide clear and concise explanations of data collection practices, as well as options for users to grant or revoke consent.

The UI patterns in User Data Consent Compliance Technology often include informative pop-ups or banners that explicitly state the purpose of data collection and how it will be used. These patterns typically provide users with a choice to either grant or deny consent, along with options to learn more about their rights and the organization's privacy policy.

The design system of User Data Consent Compliance Technology also incorporates features like granular consent management, allowing users to select specific categories or types of data they are comfortable sharing. This level of control helps build trust and gives users confidence in the organization's commitment to privacy.

Furthermore, User Data Consent Compliance Technology may include mechanisms for recording and storing consent records to ensure compliance with regulations such as the General Data Protection Regulation (GDPR). These mechanisms may involve secure storage of consent timestamps and associated user preferences.

In summary, User Data Consent Compliance Technology focuses on implementing UI patterns and design systems that enable organizations to obtain informed consent from users regarding data collection and comply with privacy regulations. The technology aims to provide transparent and user-friendly experiences, giving users control over their personal information and fostering trust between businesses and their users.>

User Data Consent Compliance Tools

A User Data Consent Compliance Tool is a UI pattern or design system that helps organizations ensure compliance with applicable data protection laws and regulations by providing a user-friendly way for individuals to grant or revoke consent for the collection, use, and sharing of their personal data.

These tools typically consist of a user interface (UI) component or set of components that can be integrated into websites, mobile apps, or other digital platforms. They allow organizations to display clear and concise information to users about the purposes for which their data will be used and the third parties with whom it may be shared.

User Data Consent Compliance Training

User Data Consent Compliance Training is a user interface pattern and design system that is used to educate and inform users about the collection, usage, and storage of their personal data, as well as their rights and options in regards to consent.

It is designed to ensure compliance with data protection and privacy regulations, such as the General Data Protection Regulation (GDPR) or the California Consumer Privacy Act (CCPA). The goal of this training is to increase transparency and trust between users and organizations by providing clear and accessible information about data practices.

User Data Consent Compliance Workflows

User Data Consent Compliance Workflows refer to a set of standardized and systematic procedures within a user interface (UI) pattern and design system that ensure compliance with data protection regulations and obtain user consent for collecting, storing, and processing their personal information. These workflows are designed to provide users with transparency and control over their data and to ensure that organizations are adhering to legal requirements such as the General Data Protection Regulation (GDPR) or the California Consumer Privacy Act (CCPA). They aim to establish trust between users and organizations by clearly explaining the purposes and legal basis for collecting user data and seeking their explicit consent. The first step in a User Data Consent Compliance Workflow is to clearly communicate the data collection practices to users. This can be done through informative notices or banners that highlight the purposes, scope, and consequences of data collection. These notices should be concise, easily understandable, and prominently displayed in the UI to ensure users' awareness. Once users are informed about data collection, they should be provided with options to control their consent. This involves presenting users with granular choices that allow them to grant or deny permissions for different types of data collection, processing, or sharing activities. UI patterns often include checkboxes, toggle switches, or sliders to facilitate this process, accompanied by descriptive labels or tooltips that clarify the implications of each choice. To ensure proper implementation of data consent preferences, organizations need to provide robust mechanisms for users to manage their preferences over time. This may involve allowing users to access and modify their consent settings through dedicated account or privacy settings pages. Additionally, organizations should make it easy for users to withdraw their consent at any time, providing clear instructions on how to do so and ensuring that the UI reflects these changes immediately. Overall, User Data Consent Compliance Workflows aim to strike a balance between regulatory compliance and user experience. By aligning with best practices for UI patterns and design systems, organizations can ensure that their data consent workflows are intuitive, accessible, and respectful of users' privacy rights.

User Data Consent Consultation

User Data Consent Consultation refers to the process of obtaining the explicit permission or consent from users before collecting, storing, and processing their personal data. It is an essential part of ensuring user privacy and compliance with data protection regulations. In the context of UI patterns and design systems, User Data Consent Consultation involves implementing the necessary interfaces and mechanisms to inform users about the purpose and scope of data collection, as well as seeking their consent to proceed. This typically includes displaying clear and concise explanations of the data being collected, how it will be used, and any third parties it may be shared with. A well-designed User Data Consent Consultation UI pattern should prioritize transparency, clarity, and simplicity. It should present relevant information in a concise and easily understandable manner, avoiding any unnecessary legal jargon or complex language. The goal is to empower users to make informed decisions about their personal data without feeling overwhelmed or confused. Design systems play a crucial role in ensuring consistency and coherence in User Data Consent Consultation interfaces across different platforms and devices. They provide a set of standardized components, guidelines, and best practices for designing and implementing consent interfaces. This helps maintain a cohesive user experience and ensures compliance with data protection regulations. Key considerations when designing User Data Consent Consultation UI patterns and integrating them into a design system include: 1. Accessibility: Ensuring that the consent interfaces are usable by all users, including those with disabilities. This includes providing alternative text for images, clear and logical tabbing order, and support for screen readers. 2. Flexibility: Allowing users to easily customize their consent preferences and manage their data sharing settings. This can include options for granular control over data categories and the ability to withdraw consent at any time. 3. Trustworthiness: Establishing trust with users by providing clear indications that their data will be handled securely and in accordance with applicable regulations. This can include displaying security certifications or privacy seals, prominently featuring privacy policies, and offering options for contact and support. By implementing a well-designed User Data Consent Consultation UI pattern and integrating it into a comprehensive design system, organizations can demonstrate their commitment to user privacy and build trust with their user base. This ultimately contributes to a positive user experience and compliance with data protection regulations.

User Data Consent Documentation

User Data Consent Documentation is a set of formal documents and materials provided to users to inform them about the collection, use, and processing of their personal data by a digital platform or service. It is an important component of user experience design and follows the UI patterns and design system to ensure transparency, compliance, and user consent in data handling practices. In the context of UI patterns, User Data Consent Documentation typically includes several key elements. First, it provides a clear and concise explanation of how the platform or service collects user data, including the types of data collected, the methods of collection, and the purpose for which the data is used. This ensures that users have a comprehensive understanding of the data that is being collected from them. Second, it outlines the rights and choices users have in relation to their personal data. This includes information about how users can access, delete, or modify their data, as well as options for opting out of certain types of data processing or marketing communications. The documentation also informs users about the consequences of exercising these rights, such as any limitations on the functionality or services available to them. Third, User Data Consent Documentation describes the security measures implemented to protect user data from unauthorized access, loss, or alteration. This is particularly important for building trust with users and ensuring compliance with privacy regulations. Lastly, User Data Consent Documentation includes information about the legal basis for collecting and processing user data, such as consent, legitimate interests, or legal obligations. It also clarifies whether and how user data is shared with third parties, such as partners, advertisers, or service providers. By following UI patterns and design system, User Data Consent Documentation aims to present this complex information in an accessible and user-friendly manner. This involves using clear and simple language, organizing the content in a logical structure, and employing visual elements, such as icons or illustrations, to aid comprehension. Overall, User Data Consent Documentation plays a crucial role in fostering trust, transparency, and user control in the digital ecosystem. It ensures that users are informed about how their personal data is handled and empowers them to make informed decisions about their privacy.

User Data Consent Expiry

User Data Consent Expiry refers to the duration for which a user's consent to collect and process their personal data is valid. In the context of UI patterns and design systems, it is important to inform users about the expiration date of their consent in a clear and transparent manner.

When designing the user interface, it is essential to include a prominent and easily understandable statement notifying users about the expiry of their consent. This statement should be accompanied by a clear explanation of what it means for their personal data and how they can renew or modify their consent.

User Data Consent Frameworks

A User Data Consent Framework is a set of defined patterns and guidelines for presenting consent messages and obtaining user consent in user interfaces. It is a part of the design system that organizations use to ensure consistent and compliant handling of user data privacy and consent.

The User Data Consent Framework defines the UI patterns to be used for requesting user consent for the collection, usage, and sharing of their personal data. It provides guidance on how to present clear and concise consent messages that are easy for users to understand and make informed decisions. This framework also includes guidelines for designing user-friendly controls that allow users to grant or revoke their consent easily.

User Data Consent Granularity

User Data Consent Granularity refers to the level of control and specificity that users have over the collection, use, and sharing of their personal data within a user interface (UI) or design system. It relates to the ability for users to make informed decisions and provide consent based on a clear understanding of how their data will be used.

In the context of UI patterns and design systems, User Data Consent Granularity involves providing users with transparent and customizable options for managing their data preferences. This includes allowing users to easily access and modify their consent settings, as well as providing clear explanations of the different types of data being collected and the purposes for which they will be used.

User Data Consent Guidelines

User Data Consent Guidelines in the context of UI patterns and design systems refer to a set of principles and guidelines that govern the collection, use, and disclosure of user data within a digital product or service. These guidelines ensure that users are fully informed and provided with options to consent or withhold their data, empowering them to make informed decisions and maintain control over their personal information. To comply with User Data Consent Guidelines, designers and developers are required to implement clear and transparent mechanisms that communicate to users how their data will be collected, stored, and used. This includes obtaining explicit consent for specific data processing activities and providing users with the ability to revoke or modify their consent preferences at any time. The UI patterns and design system should incorporate the following key elements to ensure compliance with User Data Consent Guidelines: 1. Notice: The interface should provide clear and concise information about the purpose of data collection, the types of data that will be collected, and any third parties with whom the data may be shared. This information should be easily understandable, avoiding technical jargon or complex terminology. 2. Consent Mechanisms: The interface should include intuitive and easily accessible consent mechanisms that allow users to provide or withhold their consent for data collection and processing. This can be done through checkboxes, toggles, or other interactive elements that clearly indicate the user's preferences. 3. Granularity: The interface should provide users with the option to provide consent for specific data processing activities rather than requiring blanket consent for all data collection and processing. This ensures that users have fine-grained control over their data and can make informed decisions based on their individual preferences. 4. Revocability: The interface should provide users with the ability to easily revoke or modify their consent preferences at any time. This may include providing a dedicated settings section where users can manage their data preferences or including clear instructions on how to withdraw consent. 5. Accessibility: The interface should be designed in a way that ensures accessibility for all users, including those with disabilities. This may involve providing alternative text for visual elements, ensuring color contrast compliance, and following other accessibility best practices. By adhering to these User Data Consent Guidelines, designers and developers can create interfaces that prioritize user privacy, transparency, and control over their personal information. This helps to foster trust between users and the digital products or services they interact with, ultimately enhancing the overall user experience.

User Data Consent Laws

User Data Consent Laws in the context of UI patterns and design system refer to the legal regulations and requirements related to obtaining informed consent from users for the collection, use, and processing of their personal data by a website, application, or digital service. These laws aim to protect user privacy and ensure that individuals have control over their own data.

The primary purpose of User Data Consent Laws is to provide individuals with transparency and control over their personal information. User consent must be obtained before any data is collected or processed, and users must be fully informed about the purposes and scope of data collection. This consent must be given freely, without any form of coercion or deception.

Designing UI patterns and systems that comply with User Data Consent Laws involves incorporating mechanisms that enable users to easily understand the data processing activities and to make informed decisions about their personal information. These mechanisms can include clear and concise language, visual cues, and user-friendly interfaces that facilitate the consent process.

It is important to provide users with accessible and easy-to-understand information about data handling practices, including how their data will be used, shared, and stored. Users should also be able to easily manage their consent preferences and revoke or modify their consent at any time.

Compliance with User Data Consent Laws helps build trust between users and digital services, enhances user experience, and mitigates legal risks. Failure to comply with these laws can result in legal penalties, reputational damage, and loss of user trust.

In conclusion, User Data Consent Laws play a crucial role in ensuring user privacy and data protection. Designing UI patterns and systems that align with these laws is essential in establishing trust and providing users with transparency and control over their personal information.>

User Data Consent Legal Compliance

User Data Consent Legal Compliance refers to the adherence to legal requirements and guidelines regarding the collection, storage, and usage of user data in an application or website. It involves obtaining explicit consent from users before collecting their personal information and ensuring that data processing practices are in line with applicable privacy and data protection laws.

UI patterns and design systems play a crucial role in facilitating User Data Consent Legal Compliance. They provide standardized templates and components that help designers and developers create user interfaces that prioritize transparency, control, and clarity when it comes to requesting and managing user data. These patterns and systems ensure that the necessary information is clearly communicated to users and that their choices regarding data sharing and privacy are respected.

User Data Consent Localization

User Data Consent Localization refers to the process of adapting or translating the user consent language and presentation to align with the local language and cultural preferences of the target users. It involves designing and implementing a user interface (UI) that clearly communicates the data privacy policies and obtains the necessary consent from users in a way that is easily understood and accepted within their specific region or country. UI patterns and design systems play a crucial role in facilitating the localization of user data consent. These patterns and systems provide a standardized set of design elements, components, and guidelines that help ensure consistency and efficiency in the localization process. They help designers and developers create UIs that can be easily adapted to different languages and cultures without sacrificing usability or compliance with local data protection regulations. To implement user data consent localization effectively, UI patterns and design systems should address the following key aspects: 1. Language: The UI should be able to switch between different languages based on the user's preferred language or the language set in their device settings. This requires the design system to provide a mechanism for storing and retrieving localized text strings, and the UI patterns to incorporate dynamic text rendering based on the selected language. 2. Cultural Adaptation: Apart from language translation, the UI should consider cultural nuances and preferences to ensure that the presentation of data privacy policies and consent options is culturally appropriate and sensitive. This may involve adapting visual elements, iconography, and color schemes to better resonate with the cultural expectations of the target users. By incorporating these aspects into UI patterns and design systems, organizations can streamline the localization of user data consent across different regions and enhance the user experience. This ensures that users can easily comprehend the data privacy policies, make informed decisions regarding their consent, and ultimately trust the organization with their personal data. In conclusion, User Data Consent Localization is a critical aspect of UI design that involves adapting the language, presentation, and visual elements of user consent to align with the local preferences and cultural context of the target users. UI patterns and design systems play a vital role in facilitating this process, enabling the creation of globally scalable and culturally sensitive UIs for obtaining user data consent.>

User Data Consent Notifications

User Data Consent Notifications refer to the messages or prompts displayed to users in a user interface, specifically in the context of requesting their consent and permission to collect, store, and process their personal data. These notifications are an essential component of user experience design and are designed to inform and educate users about how their data will be used, and to obtain their explicit consent.

The purpose of User Data Consent Notifications is to ensure transparency and compliance with data protection regulations such as the General Data Protection Regulation (GDPR). These notifications are typically displayed when users first interact with a website or application, or when there are updates to the privacy policy or terms of service that require renewed consent from users.

User Data Consent Opt-In

The User Data Consent Opt-In is a UI pattern and design system component used to inform and request the user's explicit consent for collecting and processing their personal data. It is a crucial element in ensuring user privacy and compliance with data protection regulations, such as the General Data Protection Regulation (GDPR).

When implementing a User Data Consent Opt-In, it is important to provide clear and concise information regarding the purpose and scope of the data collection, the legal basis for processing the data, and any third parties that may have access to the data. This information should be presented in a language that is easily understandable by the average user, avoiding technical jargon or complex legal terms.

User Data Consent Opt-Out

User Data Consent Opt-Out refers to a user interface pattern and design system that allows users to decline or withdraw their consent for the collection, processing, and usage of their personal data by a service or platform.

This pattern provides users with the ability to exercise control over their personal data and privacy by giving them the option to opt-out of any data collection and processing activities that are not necessary for the core functionality of the service. By offering this opt-out feature, users can choose to limit the amount of personal data that is collected and used by the platform, thereby reducing their exposure to potential privacy concerns.

User Data Consent Plugins

User Data Consent Plugins are UI patterns and design systems that are used to obtain consent from users to collect and process their personal data. These plugins are implemented in websites or applications to adhere to data protection regulations and ensure transparency and control over user data. The User Data Consent Plugins typically consist of a set of predefined UI components such as checkboxes, sliders, and buttons that can be easily integrated into the user interface of a website or application. These components are designed to provide clear and concise information to users about the data that will be collected, the purposes for which it will be used, and any third parties that will have access to it. They also allow users to make informed choices and exercise control over their data by providing options to opt-in or opt-out of specific data collection or processing activities. The design system of User Data Consent Plugins focuses on creating a user-friendly and accessible experience for obtaining consent. The UI patterns aim to present information in a concise and easily understandable manner, using plain language and avoiding jargon or technical terms. The design components are also optimized for different devices and screen sizes to ensure a consistent and seamless experience across platforms. Implementing User Data Consent Plugins is essential for website owners and application developers to comply with data protection regulations such as the General Data Protection Regulation (GDPR) in Europe. These plugins help organizations to demonstrate transparency and accountability in managing user data, which is a key requirement under these regulations. By providing clear and accessible consent mechanisms, User Data Consent Plugins empower users to make informed decisions about their data and maintain control over their personal information. In conclusion, User Data Consent Plugins are UI patterns and design systems that facilitate the collection of user consent for data processing. They are crucial for complying with data protection regulations and ensuring transparency and control over user data. These plugins provide predefined UI components, optimized for different devices, to present information and options in a clear and accessible manner. By implementing User Data Consent Plugins, organizations can demonstrate their commitment to privacy and empower users to make informed decisions about their data.

User Data Consent Preferences

User Data Consent Preferences refer to a set of options and settings provided to users in a user interface (UI) pattern or design system to manage their consent preferences regarding the collection, use, and sharing of their personal data. These preferences allow users to make informed decisions about how their data is used by the application or website they are interacting with.

The User Data Consent Preferences UI typically includes a range of options that users can select or deselect, based on their individual preferences and privacy concerns. These options may include consent for data collection, data sharing with third parties, data storage duration, and communication preferences. The design system ensures that these preferences are presented in a clear and understandable manner, allowing users to easily navigate and make choices that align with their privacy preferences.

User Data Consent Privacy Notices

User Data Consent Privacy Notices refer to a component or element in user interface (UI) patterns and design systems that are used to inform users about the collection, use, and disclosure of their personal information by a website or application. These notices are essential for ensuring transparency and obtaining user consent in compliance with privacy laws and regulations.

The purpose of User Data Consent Privacy Notices is to clearly communicate how the user's personal information will be handled by the website or application. This includes details about the types of data collected, such as name, email address, location, and browsing activity, and the purposes for which the data will be used, such as personalization, analytics, and marketing.

These notices typically provide information on how the data will be stored and secured, the rights users have regarding their data, and any third parties with whom the data may be shared. They may also outline the legal basis for processing the data, such as the user's consent or the legitimate interests of the website or application.

User Data Consent Privacy Notices should be easily accessible and understandable to users. They are often presented in a prominent location, such as a banner or pop-up, and may include a link to a more detailed privacy policy. The language used should be clear and concise, avoiding technical jargon or legal terms that may confuse users.

In UI patterns and design systems, User Data Consent Privacy Notices are an important component for ensuring a user-centered approach to privacy. By providing users with clear and transparent information about data collection and usage practices, these notices empower users to make informed decisions about their personal information. They also serve to build trust between the user and the website or application, establishing a foundation for a positive user experience.>

User Data Consent Regulations

User Data Consent Regulations refer to the legal guidelines and requirements that govern the collection, processing, storage, and sharing of personal user data. These regulations aim to protect the privacy and rights of individuals by ensuring that organizations obtain proper consent before handling their data. In the context of UI patterns and design systems, complying with User Data Consent Regulations is crucial. Designers and developers need to create interfaces that are transparent, informative, and user-friendly, enabling individuals to make informed decisions about granting permission to use their personal data. To adhere to these regulations, UI patterns and design systems should include clear and concise information about the purpose and scope of data collection. This can be achieved by providing prominent and easily understandable notices, disclaimers, and consent prompts. Designers should also prioritize simplicity and avoid complex language or jargon that may confuse or mislead users. Additionally, UI patterns should offer granular control over the types of data being collected or shared. Users should be able to understand and modify their consent settings easily without any technical knowledge or barriers. Providing options to revoke or withdraw consent is also essential to respect users' rights under the regulations. Furthermore, UI patterns and design systems should ensure that user consent is obtained through explicit actions, such as checkboxes or buttons, rather than relying on pre-ticked boxes or assumed consent. This ensures that users actively acknowledge and agree to the terms of data processing. Compliance with User Data Consent Regulations also requires designers to consider accessibility. All users, regardless of disabilities or impairments, should be able to access and understand the consent information and controls provided in the interface. Designers should follow accessibility guidelines and practices to ensure inclusivity. Overall, adhering to User Data Consent

Regulations in UI patterns and design systems involves creating interfaces that prioritize transparency, simplicity, control, and accessibility. By doing so, designers can help organizations meet legal requirements and build trust with users, fostering a more ethical and privacy-focused digital ecosystem.

User Data Consent Renewal

User Data Consent Renewal is a user interface pattern and design system that allows users to review and renew their consent for the usage of their personal data by an application or website. It is an essential component in maintaining user trust and compliance with data protection regulations.

The User Data Consent Renewal pattern typically consists of a series of screens or dialogs that guide the user through the process of reviewing and updating their consent preferences. These screens are designed to be clear, concise, and easy to understand, ensuring that users are fully informed about how their data will be used.

User Data Consent Revocation Form

The User Data Consent Revocation Form is a UI pattern and design system element used to allow users to revoke their consent for the collection and use of their personal data. It provides a clear and straightforward way for users to exercise their rights and preferences regarding their personal information.

By implementing this UI pattern, organizations can demonstrate their commitment to data privacy and give users control over their own information. The User Data Consent Revocation Form typically includes the following key elements:

1. Identification and Authentication: The form should require users to provide sufficient information to verify their identity and prevent unauthorized access to the revocation process. This may include asking users to enter their email address, account username, or other unique identifiers.

2. Consent Revocation Options: The form should clearly present users with the specific consent options that they can choose to revoke. This may include the types of data collected, specific purposes of data usage, or the sharing of data with third parties. Users should be able to select which consent they wish to revoke.

3. Confirmation and Feedback: After users submit the form, a confirmation message should be displayed to indicate that their consent revocation request has been successfully received. Additionally, organizations should provide a way for users to provide feedback or additional information if desired.

Overall, the User Data Consent Revocation Form is an essential component of any UI pattern or design system focused on privacy and data protection. It helps organizations fulfill legal requirements and empowers users to exercise their rights in a transparent and user-friendly manner.

User Data Consent Revocation Request Form

The User Data Consent Revocation Request Form is a user interface pattern and design system that is used to provide users with a formal means of revoking their consent for their personal data to be collected or processed. This form allows users to exercise their data rights under applicable laws and regulations, such as the General Data Protection Regulation (GDPR) in the European Union or the California Consumer Privacy Act (CCPA) in the United States. The purpose of the User Data Consent Revocation Request Form is to give users control over their personal data by providing a clear and transparent process for revoking consent. By presenting this form to users, organizations demonstrate their commitment to data privacy and protection, as well as their compliance with applicable data protection laws. The User Data Consent Revocation Request Form typically includes fields and elements such as: 1. User identification and contact information: This section contains fields for users to provide their name, email address, and any other relevant contact details. This information is necessary for the organization to verify the identity of the user submitting the request and to communicate with them regarding the request. 2. Data consent revocation details: This section provides users with options to specify the type of consent they wish to revoke, such as marketing emails, data sharing with third parties, or specific data processing activities. Users can select one or more options based on their preferences. 3. Additional information or comments: This section allows users to provide any additional information or comments related to their revocation request. This can include specific concerns or instructions for the organization handling the request. 4. Submit button: This is a prominent button that allows users to submit their revocation request. By clicking this button, users indicate their intention to revoke their consent and initiate the processing of their request by the organization. Overall, the User Data Consent Revocation Request Form is an essential component of a user-centric approach to data privacy and protection. It enables users to exercise their rights, promotes transparency and accountability, and establishes trust between users and organizations. By implementing this form as part of their user interface patterns and design systems, organizations can ensure compliance with data protection regulations while maintaining a positive user experience.>

User Data Consent Revocation Requests

The User Data Consent Revocation Requests UI pattern refers to the design and implementation of a user interface that allows users to revoke their previously given consent for the collection, storage, and processing of their personal data.

This UI pattern is an essential component of a broader design system that focuses on ensuring user privacy and control over their personal information. It enables users to exercise their right to revoke consent in a transparent and user-friendly manner.

User Data Consent Revocation

User Data Consent Revocation refers to the process of allowing users to withdraw their previous consent for the collection, use, and storage of their personal data. It is a crucial component of privacy and data protection, providing users with control and transparency over their information.

Within the context of UI patterns and design systems, User Data Consent Revocation involves creating a clear and intuitive interface that enables users to easily manage their consent settings. This interface should provide individuals with the ability to revoke their consent for specific data collection purposes or for the entire data processing activity.

User Data Consent Revoke Form

A User Data Consent Revoke Form in the context of UI patterns and design systems refers to a component or element that allows users to revoke their previous consent for the usage of their personal data. It is a formal and structured way for users to opt out or withdraw their consent from data collection, processing, and storage.

This form typically includes fields or options that enable users to indicate their desire to revoke consent, provide necessary personal information for identification purposes, and submit the form for processing. The design of the User Data Consent Revoke Form should prioritize usability, clarity, and transparency, ensuring that users fully understand the implications of their decision.

User Data Consent Revoke Request Form

A User Data Consent Revoke Request Form is a UI pattern and design system component that allows users to revoke their consent for the collection, use, and storage of their personal data. It provides a formal and structured way for users to exercise their data privacy rights in compliance with relevant regulations, such as the General Data Protection Regulation (GDPR).

The form typically includes several key elements:

1. Title or Heading: This clearly identifies the purpose of the form and helps users understand its context. For example, "User Data Consent Revoke Request Form."

2. Introduction or Explanation: This section provides a brief overview of why the user is being

asked to complete the form. It may include information about data protection laws, the user's rights, and the impact of revoking consent.

3. User Information: The form collects essential user details, such as their name, email address, and any relevant account or identification numbers. This information helps ensure that the request is valid and can be processed accordingly.

4. Consent Revocation Request: This section includes checkboxes or toggle switches that allow users to specify the types of consent they wish to revoke. It may provide options for revoking consent for specific purposes, such as marketing communications, data sharing with third parties, or automated decision-making.

5. Signature or Confirmation: The form may require users to provide a digital signature or confirmation of their request. This helps authenticate the request and provides a record of the user's intent.

6. Submission: The form includes a submit button that allows users to finalize and submit their consent revocation request. It may also include a secondary button for users to cancel or exit the form without submitting.

A well-designed User Data Consent Revoke Request Form follows best practices in usability and accessibility. It should have a clear and intuitive layout, with proper alignment, spacing, and typography. The language used should be concise, clear, and easily understandable by all users. Additionally, the form should adhere to any branding or style guidelines defined in the organization's design system.

User Data Consent SDK

A User Data Consent SDK refers to a software development kit (SDK) that enables developers to efficiently implement user data consent functionalities into their applications. This SDK is specifically designed to streamline the process of obtaining and managing user consent for collecting, processing, and sharing their personal information within an application or across different services.

When it comes to UI patterns and design systems, incorporating a User Data Consent SDK ensures that applications adhere to privacy regulations and best practices, providing a seamless and transparent user experience. The SDK typically offers pre-designed UI components and customizable templates that developers can easily integrate into their application's user interface.

User Data Consent Settings

User Data Consent Settings refer to a set of controls and options provided within a user interface (UI) that enable users to manage their consent preferences for how their personal data is collected, stored, and used by an application or platform. These settings allow users to exercise their rights and make informed decisions about the extent of data sharing and the purposes for which their data can be used. Consent settings are an essential component of a comprehensive privacy and data protection strategy. They serve as a mechanism to empower users and comply with relevant data protection regulations, such as the General Data Protection Regulation (GDPR) in Europe. By integrating consent settings into a UI, organizations can enhance transparency, build trust, and demonstrate accountability. In terms of UI patterns and design system, consent settings are typically presented in a structured and intuitive manner to facilitate user understanding and interaction. These settings often include a combination of checkboxes, toggles, sliders, and informative text to convey the purpose and implications of each consent option. The UI should be designed to prioritize clarity, simplicity, and accessibility, ensuring that users can easily comprehend and navigate the consent settings. A common approach is to categorize consent options into different sections or tabs, allowing users to manage preferences based on specific data processing activities or data categories. For example, users may have the option to grant or revoke consent for data sharing with third parties, targeted advertising, or data analytics purposes. By organizing consent settings into logical groupings, users can easily locate and customize their preferences based on their individual needs and concerns. When designing consent settings, it is crucial to provide users with clear and concise explanations of the implications and consequences of their decisions. This can be achieved by using plain language and avoiding technical jargon. Additionally, the UI should allow users to access detailed information about data processing practices, including the legal basis for processing, the duration of data retention, and the identity of data controllers and processors. Providing such transparency enables users to make informed choices and builds trust in the application or platform. In conclusion, User Data Consent Settings within a UI facilitate user control over their personal data by allowing them to manage and customize their consent preferences. By adopting clear and intuitive UI patterns and design principles, organizations can enhance transparency, comply with data protection regulations, and foster a user-centric approach to privacy protection.>

User Data Consent Standards

User Data Consent Standards refer to a set of guidelines and principles that define how user consent should be obtained and respected in the context of UI patterns and design systems. These standards aim to ensure transparency, control, and trust in the way user data is collected, used, and shared by digital products and services.

Consent is an essential aspect of user privacy and data protection. When designing user interfaces, it is crucial to adhere to these standards to empower users to make informed decisions regarding their personal information. UI patterns and design systems should align with the following key principles:

1. Transparency: Clearly communicate to users what data will be collected, how it will be used, and who it will be shared with. UI patterns should provide concise and easily understandable explanations of data processing activities, highlighting any potential risks or implications for the user's privacy.

2. Granularity: Offer users the ability to provide consent for different types of data processing purposes. Design systems should provide flexible UI patterns that allow users to selectively grant or withdraw consent for specific data processing activities, rather than forcing an all-or-nothing approach.

3. Opt-in and Opt-out Mechanisms: Provide clear options to opt-in or opt-out of data collection and processing. UI patterns should use unambiguous language and intuitive design elements such as checkboxes or toggles to allow users to easily control their consent preferences.

4. Clarity and Accessibility: Present consent information in a clear and understandable manner, avoiding technical jargon or complex language. Design systems should ensure that UI patterns are accessible to all users, including those with disabilities, by following best practices in inclusive design.

5. Revocability: Enable users to easily revoke their consent at any time and provide mechanisms to delete or anonymize their personal data. UI patterns should include options for users to review and modify their consent preferences and to request the erasure of their data.

Adhering to User Data Consent Standards in UI patterns and design systems fosters user trust, promotes transparency, and respects user privacy rights. By providing clear and understandable consent mechanisms, digital products and services can enhance user experiences while safeguarding the security and confidentiality of user data.

User Data Consent Support

User Data Consent Support refers to a set of UI patterns and design system components that enable users to provide their consent for the collection, use, and sharing of their personal information. These patterns and components are designed to ensure transparency, clarity, and control for users, while also helping organizations adhere to privacy regulations and best practices.

The User Data Consent Support UI patterns and design system typically include the following elements:

316

1. Consent Request: This is the initial prompt that asks users to provide their consent for the collection and processing of their personal information. It usually includes clear and concise language explaining what data will be collected, how it will be used, and any third parties it may be shared with. The design of this prompt should be unobtrusive yet noticeable enough to catch the user's attention.

2. Granular Consent Options: Users should be given the ability to provide granular consent by choosing which specific types of data they are willing to share. This could include options to opt-in or opt-out of data collection for different purposes, such as personalization, analytics, or marketing. The design of these options should be simple and easy to understand, with clear explanations of the implications of each choice.

3. Consent Management: Once users have provided their initial consent, they should have the ability to easily manage and update their preferences over time. This could include a consent management dashboard or settings page where users can review and modify their consent choices. The design of this management interface should be intuitive and easy to navigate, with clear instructions on how to make changes.

4. Privacy Policy and Terms: A link to the organization's privacy policy and terms of service should be provided in a prominent and easily accessible location. This ensures that users have access to detailed information about how their data will be handled and what rights they have in relation to their personal information. The design of these links should be visually distinct to differentiate them from other UI elements.

The User Data Consent Support UI patterns and design system should be designed with the principles of privacy by default and privacy by design in mind. It should prioritize user control, transparency, and informed decision-making, while also considering the legal and regulatory requirements related to data privacy. By implementing these patterns and components, organizations can build trust with their users and demonstrate their commitment to protecting user privacy.

User Data Consent Technology

User Data Consent Technology refers to the implementation of software or systems that allow users to provide consent for the collection, use, and processing of their personal data. It often involves the design and deployment of user interfaces (UI) that enable users to make informed decisions about their data privacy.

In the context of UI patterns and design systems, User Data Consent Technology aims to provide clear and transparent information to users about how their personal data will be used, and enables them to grant or withdraw consent for specific data processing activities. This technology helps organizations comply with data protection regulations and facilitates trust between users and service providers.

An effective UI design for User Data Consent Technology should prioritize user understanding and control. It should present concise and easily comprehensible information about the purpose, scope, and duration of data processing activities. The design should use plain language and avoid technical jargon that may confuse or mislead users.

Additionally, the UI design should provide a clear and distinguishable choice to users, allowing them to easily opt-in or opt-out of data processing activities. This can be achieved through the use of checkboxes, toggles, or sliders that clearly indicate the consent status. The design should also ensure that withdrawing consent is as straightforward as giving it.

A good UI design system for User Data Consent Technology should be adaptable and customizable to individual organizational needs and branding. It should allow for the inclusion of relevant legal information, such as privacy policies or terms of service, while maintaining a consistent and user-friendly interface. The design system should also consider accessibility guidelines to ensure that users with disabilities can easily understand and interact with the consent interface.

In summary, User Data Consent Technology encompasses the software and UI design solutions that enable users to grant or withdraw consent for the collection and processing of their personal data. It aims to provide clear and transparent information to users, prioritize user understanding and control, and ensure compliance with data protection regulations. A well-designed UI in the context of a design system can enhance user trust and confidence in sharing their personal information.>

User Data Consent Templates

User Data Consent Templates are a set of predefined UI patterns and design system components that provide a standardized format for obtaining user consent before collecting, processing, or sharing their personal data. These templates are designed to ensure compliance with privacy regulations and promote transparency in data practices.

By implementing User Data Consent Templates in a user interface, organizations can streamline the process of obtaining consent from users in a clear, concise, and user-friendly manner. These templates typically consist of various components, such as checkboxes, toggles, buttons, and informative text, that can be easily customized to fit the specific data collection or processing activities.

User Data Consent Tools

User Data Consent Tools refer to a set of UI patterns and design system components that enable users to grant or revoke their consent for the collection, use, and sharing of their personal data. These tools are designed with the aim of ensuring transparency, control, and compliance with data protection regulations. In the context of UI patterns, User Data Consent Tools typically consist of various elements such as checkboxes, switches, sliders, and buttons, which are strategically placed within the user interface to provide users with clear and accessible options for managing their data consents. These tools are used to present users with the necessary information about the types and purposes of data processing, as well as the third parties involved, and to seek their explicit permission or agreement to proceed. The design system for User Data Consent Tools adheres to principles that prioritize clarity, simplicity, and user-friendliness. The components are visually distinct, with clear labels and concise descriptions that avoid ambiguity or technical jargon. Additionally, the tools are often accompanied by contextual help texts or tooltips to further enhance user understanding and decision-making. User Data Consent Tools are essential in addressing the increasing need for user privacy and data protection. By providing users with granular control over their data consents, these tools empower them to exercise their rights and preferences in relation to their personal information. Such tools are particularly important in compliance with regulations such as the General Data Protection Regulation (GDPR) in the European Union, which emphasizes the need for informed consent and the protection of individuals' privacy rights. Overall, User Data Consent Tools in UI patterns and design systems play a crucial role in fostering a transparent and trustworthy relationship between users and organizations. By integrating these tools within the user interface, organizations can demonstrate their commitment to user privacy, build user trust, and comply with data protection regulations.

User Data Consent Tracking

User Data Consent Tracking is a UI pattern and design system that governs the process of obtaining and managing user consent for the collection, storage, and usage of their personal data. It ensures transparency, accountability, and compliance with privacy regulations by enabling users to make informed decisions and control their data. The User Data Consent Tracking pattern consists of various elements and components that facilitate the consent management process. It typically includes a consent notification banner or pop-up that informs users about the data collection practices and requests their consent. This notification prominently displays key information such as the purpose of data collection, the types of data being collected, and the entities that will have access to the data. Users can be provided with options to accept or decline the consent. To enhance user understanding and promote informed decision-making, the User Data Consent Tracking pattern also includes detailed information about privacy policies, terms of service, and data processing practices. This information can be made available through expandable sections, accordions, or links to dedicated pages. Users can

318

review these details to gain a comprehensive understanding of how their data will be handled. To ensure ongoing compliance, the User Data Consent Tracking pattern allows users to easily modify their consent preferences at any time. This can be done through a dedicated consent management user interface, where users have granular control over the specific types of data processing activities they want to allow or disallow. Furthermore, the User Data Consent Tracking pattern supports the logging and tracking of user consent choices and timestamps. This helps organizations maintain a record of consent and demonstrate compliance with privacy regulations. Additionally, it enables users to verify their consent history and understand when and how their data has been utilized. By incorporating the User Data Consent Tracking pattern into the UI design system, organizations can prioritize user privacy and respect their data preferences. It promotes transparency, trust, and user empowerment, fostering a positive user experience while ensuring compliance with privacy regulations.

User Data Consent Training

User Data Consent Training is a UI pattern and design system that encompasses the process of obtaining explicit consent from users before collecting, processing, and storing their personal data. Personal data refers to any information that can be used to identify an individual, such as their name, email address, phone number, or physical address. The purpose of User Data Consent Training is to ensure compliance with data protection laws and regulations, such as the General Data Protection Regulation (GDPR) and the California Consumer Privacy Act (CCPA), which require organizations to obtain informed consent from individuals before collecting and using their personal data. This UI pattern and design system provides a standardized and user-friendly approach to presenting and obtaining user consent. It typically involves the use of a modal or dialog box that is displayed to users when they first interact with a website or application. Within this modal or dialog box, organizations provide clear and concise information about the data they intend to collect, as well as the purposes for which it will be used. The User Data Consent Training also includes options for users to provide their consent, usually through checkboxes or buttons. Users are typically presented with a choice to either accept or decline the collection and use of their personal data. Additionally, organizations may offer users the ability to customize their consent preferences, allowing them to selectively opt-in or opt-out of specific data processing activities. To enhance transparency and user understanding, User Data Consent Training often includes links to detailed privacy policies and terms of service documents. These documents provide further information about how the organization safeguards user data, as well as the rights and options available to users regarding their personal data. Overall, User Data Consent Training serves as a crucial component of ethical and responsible data handling practices. By ensuring that users are fully informed and given control over their personal data, organizations can promote trust, privacy, and compliance with relevant data protection laws.

User Data Consent Transparency

User data consent transparency refers to the practice of clearly and explicitly informing users about the collection, use, and disclosure of their personal data, and obtaining their informed and voluntary consent before proceeding with any data processing activities. This concept is crucial in ensuring respect for user privacy and promoting transparency and trust between users and service providers. In the context of UI patterns and design systems, user data consent transparency is typically achieved through the inclusion of user-friendly interfaces and clear information provided to users. This may include the use of informative and concise privacy policies, terms of service agreements, and consent mechanisms that are easy to understand and navigate. UI patterns for user data consent transparency often involve the use of clear and easily readable text, prominent and easily accessible consent buttons or checkboxes, and visual cues such as icons or indicators to indicate the status of user consent. Additionally, design systems may incorporate standardized and consistent visual elements and language to ensure coherence and familiarity for users across different platforms and applications. By adopting user data consent transparency as a guiding principle, UI patterns and design systems aim to empower users to make informed choices about their personal data, and to understand how their data is being collected, used, and shared. This approach not only helps to comply with legal requirements and industry standards regarding data privacy, but also helps to foster a sense of trust and accountability between users and service providers. Overall, user data consent transparency is a fundamental aspect of responsible and ethical data handling practices. It involves providing clear and accessible information to users, and obtaining their voluntary and informed consent before engaging in any data processing activities. Through the use of appropriate UI patterns and design systems, service providers can ensure that users are empowered to make informed choices about their personal data and maintain control over their privacy.

User Data Consent Verification

A User Data Consent Verification is a UI pattern and design system that is implemented to obtain and verify user consent for the use and processing of their personal data. It is a crucial component of any system or platform that collects and deals with user data.

The User Data Consent Verification is typically presented to the user as a pop-up or overlay window when they first interact with a website, application, or service that requires access to their personal data. Its purpose is to inform the user about the data that will be collected, the purpose for which it will be used, and any third parties that may have access to it.

The User Data Consent Verification should provide clear and concise information, using plain language that is easy for the user to understand. It should clearly state what types of data will be collected, such as personal information, browsing history, or location data. Additionally, it should specify the purposes for which the data will be used, such as improving the user experience, personalizing content, or targeted advertising.

Within the User Data Consent Verification, the user should be given the option to either consent to the data collection and processing or to decline it. If the user chooses to decline, they should still be able to use the platform or service, though some functionalities may be limited. The option to revoke consent at any time should also be made available.

To enhance transparency, the User Data Consent Verification may include links to a Privacy Policy or Terms of Service document that provides more detailed information about how the data will be handled and protected. It should also display any relevant certifications or compliance standards that the platform adheres to, such as GDPR or CCPA.

Overall, the User Data Consent Verification is crucial in building trust and maintaining user privacy. By providing clear and easily understood information, as well as giving users control over their data, it ensures compliance with privacy regulations and fosters a positive user experience.

User Data Consent Widgets

User Data Consent Widgets refer to specific user interface (UI) patterns and design system components that are used to obtain and manage user consent for the collection, processing, and sharing of their personal data. These widgets are implemented within digital platforms, websites, and applications to ensure transparency and compliance with data protection regulations, as well as to establish trust with the users.

In the context of UI patterns, User Data Consent Widgets typically consist of interactive elements or modules that allow users to review and control permissions related to their personal data. These widgets often include clear and concise explanations of the data being collected, the purpose of collection, and the entities involved in processing or accessing the data. They also provide options for users to grant or deny consent, manage preferences, and exercise their rights, such as data deletion or modification. The design of these widgets should prioritize clarity, accessibility, and user-friendliness to facilitate informed decision-making by the users.

User Data Consent Withdraw Form

A User Data Consent Withdraw Form is a UI pattern and design system element that allows users to withdraw their previous consent for the collection and storage of their personal data. It provides a means for users to exercise their data protection rights and comply with relevant privacy regulations. The form typically includes a clear title or heading, such as "User Data Consent Withdrawal," to clearly indicate its purpose. It may also feature a brief explanation of the consequences of withdrawing consent, highlighting any potential impact on the user's experience or access to certain services. Within the form, users are presented with a series of checkboxes or toggle switches that correspond to different data collection purposes or categories. These checkboxes are typically pre-selected, reflecting the user's previous consent. To complete the withdrawal process, the user must select the relevant checkboxes or toggle switches to indicate their specific withdrawal preferences. The form may also include an optional comment field where users can provide additional context or feedback regarding their decision to withdraw consent. Once the user submits the form, the system captures their withdrawal preferences and updates their profile accordingly. Depending on the specific design system, the form may provide visual feedback, such as a success message or confirmation notification, to inform the user that their consent withdrawal has been successfully processed. From a design perspective, the User Data Consent Withdraw Form should adhere to the overall visual language and interaction patterns established in the design system. This ensures consistency and familiarity for users across different UI elements and interactions. The form should be designed to be user-friendly and accessible, with clear and concise language used for headings, instructions, and checkboxes. It should also prioritize user privacy and security by implementing appropriate data encryption and protection measures. In conclusion, the User Data Consent Withdraw Form is a vital component of a UX/UI pattern and design system. It empowers users to exercise control over their personal data and comply with privacy regulations. By providing a clear and intuitive interface, the form enables users to withdraw their consent easily and effectively.>

User Data Consent Withdraw Request Form

User Data Consent Withdrawal Form

A User Data Consent Withdrawal Form is a UI pattern and design system that allows users to easily and securely withdraw their consent for their personal data to be collected and used by a website or application. This form provides a simple and organized way for users to exercise their rights to control their personal data and comply with data protection regulations. The User Data Consent Withdrawal Form typically consists of a series of fields and options that enable users to specify which types of data they want to withdraw consent for. These fields may include checkboxes, radio buttons, dropdown menus, or text fields, depending on the specific requirements of the application or website. When a user interacts with the form, they are presented with clear instructions and prompts to guide them through the withdrawal process. The form should be designed in a way that is intuitive and easy to navigate, with clear labels and visual cues to indicate the purpose and function of each field or option. To ensure the security and privacy of the user's data, the User Data Consent Withdrawal Form should be designed to handle sensitive information with care. This may include implementing encryption and secure transmission protocols, as well as providing mechanisms for user authentication and verification, such as email confirmation or password authentication. Once the user has completed the form and submitted their withdrawal request, the application or website should process this request promptly and notify the user of the status or outcome of their withdrawal. This may include confirming the withdrawal, updating the user's data settings, or any other relevant actions that need to be taken. In summary, a User Data Consent Withdrawal Form is a crucial component of a website or application's UI pattern and design system that allows users to exercise their rights to control their personal data. It provides a user-friendly and secure way for users to withdraw their consent for the collection and use of their personal data, ensuring compliance with data protection regulations and fostering trust with the users.>

User Data Consent Withdrawal Request Form

A user data consent withdrawal request form is a UI pattern and design system used to provide a mechanism for users to withdraw their consent for the collection and processing of their personal data. This form allows users to exercise their right to revoke their consent and ensures compliance with data protection regulations, such as the General Data Protection Regulation (GDPR) in the European Union.

The user data consent withdrawal request form typically consists of a set of fields and options that enable users to identify themselves and specify the data or processing activities for which they wish to withdraw consent. These fields may include the user's name, contact details, and

321

any unique identifiers that were provided during the initial consent process.

In addition to the identification fields, the form should also include clear instructions on how to complete the withdrawal request, as well as any necessary information about the consequences of withdrawing consent. It may also provide an option for users to provide additional comments or explanations regarding their decision to withdraw consent.

To ensure a smooth and user-friendly experience, the user data consent withdrawal request form should adhere to a consistent design system that follows established UI patterns. This includes using a clean and intuitive layout, clear and concise labels and instructions, and appropriate validation to prevent errors or incomplete submissions.

Furthermore, the form should be easily accessible and prominently displayed on the website or application where the user initially provided their consent. It should be easily discoverable, preferably within a dedicated section related to data privacy or consent management.

By providing a user data consent withdrawal request form that follows best practices in UI patterns and design systems, organizations can demonstrate their commitment to respecting user privacy and complying with relevant data protection regulations. This not only helps to build trust with users but also ensures legal compliance in an increasingly privacy-conscious digital landscape.

User Data Consent Withdrawal

User Data Consent Withdrawal is a UI pattern and design system element that provides users with the ability to revoke their previously granted consent for the collection, processing, and storage of their personal data.

This feature typically exists within the user account settings or privacy preferences section of an application or website. It allows users to exercise their rights under data protection laws to control how their personal information is used by the system or organization.

User Data Correction Request Form

User Data Correction Request Form refers to a user interface (UI) pattern or design system that enables users to request corrections or updates to their personal information. This feature is commonly implemented in web or mobile applications to provide users with a convenient way to maintain the accuracy and relevance of their data.

By utilizing User Data Correction Request Form, users can easily identify and correct any inaccurate or outdated information associated with their accounts. This form typically includes fields for users to input their personal details, such as name, contact information, address, and any other relevant data. Additionally, it may also contain options or checkboxes for users to specify which information they would like corrected or updated.

User Data Deletion Request Form

A user data deletion request form is a component of a user interface pattern and design system that allows users to request the deletion of their personal data from a system or platform. This form is typically provided as a means for users to exercise their rights under data protection and privacy regulations, such as the General Data Protection Regulation (GDPR) in the European Union.

The user data deletion request form follows a formal and structured approach to ensure that users can easily and securely submit their data deletion requests. It typically includes fields for users to enter their personal information, such as their name, email address, and any additional identification or specific details relevant to their request. Users may also be requested to provide their reasons for requesting the deletion of their data, although this is not always necessary.

User Data Deletion

User Data Deletion

User Data Deletion is a UI pattern that refers to the process of permanently removing user data from a system or application. It is an important feature for maintaining user privacy and complying with data protection regulations. In the context of UI patterns and design systems, User Data Deletion involves creating a clear and intuitive interface for users to delete their data. This typically includes a dedicated settings or account page where users can manage their data and privacy preferences. The design system should ensure that User Data Deletion follows best practices for usability and accessibility. It should prioritize clarity and transparency, allowing users to easily understand the implications of deleting their data and providing any necessary warnings or confirmations. Key considerations for User Data Deletion include: 1. Clear Navigation: The design system should provide a clearly labeled and easily accessible pathway for users to initiate the deletion process. This can be achieved through a prominent "Delete My Data" or similar button within the settings or account page. 2. Informative Messaging: The interface should provide concise and straightforward messaging that explains the consequences of deleting user data. This helps users make informed decisions about whether to proceed with the deletion or explore alternative options. 3. Confirmation Dialogs: To prevent accidental deletions, the design system should incorporate confirmation dialogs that require users to confirm their intention to delete their data. This helps mitigate potential issues and allows users to reconsider their decision if necessary. 4. Granularity of Deletion: Depending on the requirements of the system or application, the design system may need to accommodate various levels of data deletion. This could include options for deleting specific data categories, such as personal information, account history, or user-generated content. Overall, the User Data Deletion pattern should prioritize user control and privacy, providing a seamless and empowering experience for users to manage their data. By integrating this pattern into the design system, it ensures a consistent and user-friendly approach to data deletion across the application or system.

User Data Disclosure Request Form

A User Data Disclosure Request Form is a UI pattern and design system component that allows users to request information about the data that a company or organization has collected from them. This form provides a structured way for users to exercise their data privacy rights and helps companies fulfill their legal obligations to disclose what personal data they have and how it is being used. The User Data Disclosure Request Form typically consists of a set of fields or inputs that users can fill out to provide their personal information and specify the details of their request. This may include their name, contact information, and any additional information that is relevant to their request. The form should also include clear instructions or guidelines on how to fill out the form correctly and what to expect after submitting it. Designing the form with a user-first approach is essential to ensure its usability and effectiveness. It should be easily accessible and prominently displayed on the company's website or any other relevant platform. The form's interface should be intuitive and straightforward, using standard input types and labels to guide users through the process. To maintain transparency and trust, it is crucial to provide users with clear information about the purpose of the form and the process of handling their requests. This can be achieved by including a concise but informative introduction or description of the form's purpose and how the data disclosure process works. Providing links to the company's privacy policy or relevant legal documents can also help users make informed decisions. Once users have submitted the form, it is essential to have a well-defined and efficient system in place to handle and process their requests. This may involve verifying the user's identity to prevent potential fraud or misuse, retrieving the requested data from relevant databases or systems, and responding to the user within a specified timeframe. Overall, a User Data Disclosure Request Form is a critical component of a design system that ensures transparency, privacy, and compliance with data protection regulations. By providing users with a structured and user-friendly interface to exercise their data privacy rights, companies can foster trust, accountability, and respect for user privacy.

User Data Download Request Form

User Data Download Request Form is a UI pattern and design system component that enables users to request and download their personal data from a platform or service. It provides users with a straightforward and efficient way to access and obtain a copy of their data for their own use or for compliance with data protection regulations.

The User Data Download Request Form typically consists of a set of fields and options that allow users to specify the type and scope of the data they want to download. This may include selecting specific data categories, date ranges, or file formats. The form may also include additional features such as the ability to choose the delivery method (e.g., email, direct download) and the frequency of data updates if applicable.

User Data Encryption

User Data Encryption is a crucial aspect of UI patterns and design systems that ensures the protection and confidentiality of user information by converting it into an unreadable format. It involves the use of encryption algorithms to transform plain text data into an encoded version known as ciphertext. This process helps to safeguard sensitive user data from unauthorized access, data breaches, and potential security threats.

UI patterns and design systems incorporate User Data Encryption as a fundamental security measure to maintain privacy and trust in digital platforms. By utilizing encryption techniques, UI designers enhance the security of user data at rest and in transit. This enables users to confidently input their personal information, such as passwords, credit card details, and personal identification, without the fear of their data being compromised.

During the encryption process, plain text data is encrypted using cryptographic keys, making it indecipherable to anyone without the corresponding decryption key. This ensures that even if an unauthorized party gains access to the encrypted data, they cannot interpret its contents.

User Data Encryption is commonly used in UI patterns and design systems to protect sensitive user information stored in databases, cloud systems, and communication channels. It plays a crucial role in secure login forms, transactional processes, and data storage mechanisms.

UI patterns and design systems consider various encryption techniques such as symmetric key encryption, asymmetric key encryption, and hashing algorithms. These techniques provide different levels of security depending on the specific use case.

In conclusion, User Data Encryption is a vital component of UI patterns and design systems that prioritizes the protection and confidentiality of user information. By encrypting sensitive user data, UI designers ensure that unauthorized parties cannot access or interpret the data, thereby enhancing the overall security of digital platforms.>

User Data Erasure Request Form

User Data Erasure Request Form is a UI pattern and design system that provides a formal and structured way for users to request the erasure of their personal data. This form ensures compliance with data privacy regulations, such as the General Data Protection Regulation (GDPR), by giving users control over their personal information. The User Data Erasure Request Form typically consists of a series of fields that the user needs to fill out to initiate the data erasure process. These fields collect essential information from the user, such as their name, email address, and a clear statement requesting the erasure of their personal data. The form may also include additional fields to help verify the user's identity and avoid unauthorized data deletion. This can include fields for the user to provide information related to their account, such as their username, account number, or any other relevant identifiers. The User Data Erasure Request Form should be designed in a way that is easy to understand and complete, enabling users to submit their request with minimal effort. The language used in the form should be concise, straightforward, and free from any ambiguity, ensuring that users understand the purpose and process of data erasure. A clear submission button should be provided at the end of the form, allowing users to finalize and send their data erasure request. Additionally, it is important to include a statement of acknowledgement or consent, informing users that by submitting the form, they understand and agree to the erasure of their personal data. Overall, the User Data Erasure Request Form is a crucial component of any user-centric design system. It empowers users to exercise their rights to control their personal information and ensures compliance with data privacy regulations. By following best practices in UI patterns and design, this form can create a seamless and secure experience for users who wish to erase their personal data.

The User Data Erasure Request Form is a UI pattern that allows users to formally request the erasure of their personal data. It employs a structured design system to ensure compliance with data privacy regulations, such as GDPR. The form includes fields for necessary information, like the user's name and email address, along with a clear statement requesting data erasure. Additional fields may be included for identity verification purposes. The form should be easy to understand and complete, with concise language and a straightforward process. A submission button is provided for users to finalize and send their request, along with a statement of acknowledgement or consent. Overall, the User Data Erasure Request Form is a vital component of user-centric design, providing users with control over their personal information while maintaining compliance with privacy regulations.

User Data Export Request Form

A User Data Export Request Form is a user interface pattern that allows users to request the export of their personal data from a system or platform. It provides a formal and structured way for users to submit a request for their data and ensures that their privacy rights are respected.

The User Data Export Request Form typically includes fields for users to enter their personal information, such as name, email address, and account ID. It may also include additional fields to specify the type and format of the data they would like to export. The form may include checkboxes or radio buttons to allow users to select specific data categories or time ranges for their export request.

The design of the User Data Export Request Form should prioritize clarity and ease of use. Clear and concise instructions should be provided to guide users through the process of filling out the form. The form should be visually consistent with the overall design system of the platform or system to maintain a coherent user experience.

When users submit the form, their request should be processed promptly and securely. The system or platform should verify the user's identity and authentication before processing the export request to ensure that only authorized users can access their personal data. Once the export request is processed, users should receive a confirmation message or email with instructions on how to download their exported data.

Overall, the User Data Export Request Form is an important component of a design system as it enables users to exercise their rights to access and control their personal data. It helps to establish trust and transparency between users and the system or platform by providing a formal channel for users to request and receive their data exports.

User Data Export

A User Data Export is a feature in a user interface (UI) pattern or design system that allows users to retrieve and download their personal data from a platform or application. It provides a way for users to have full control over their own information and facilitates data portability.

When designing a User Data Export feature, it is important to consider the following aspects:

1. User Consent: Users should explicitly give their consent before their data is exported. This can be achieved through clear and concise opt-in or confirmation prompts.

2. Data Selection: The feature should provide users with options to select which specific data they want to export. This can include personal information, activity logs, settings, or any other relevant data stored by the platform.

3. Export Format: Users should be able to choose the format in which they want their data to be exported. Common export formats include CSV, JSON, XML, or PDF. Providing multiple formats ensures compatibility with various applications and platforms.

4. Progress and Completion Indicators: During the export process, it is essential to inform users about the progress and status of the export. This can be done through visual indicators, such as a progress bar or a completion message, to ensure transparency and provide feedback.

5. Security and Privacy: Data security and privacy are paramount when implementing a User Data Export feature. The process should adhere to established security protocols and take measures to protect user data during transmission and storage.

By offering a User Data Export feature, platforms and applications demonstrate transparency, respect user rights, and comply with data protection regulations. This feature empowers users by allowing them to access and move their data freely, fostering trust and enabling data portability between different services.

User Data Objection Request Form

A User Data Objection Request Form is a UI pattern designed to allow users to request the objection or removal of their personal data from a system or platform. This form serves as a formal means for users to exercise their data protection rights and ensure their privacy. The User Data Objection Request Form typically consists of several key components. First, there is a section where users can provide their contact details, including their name, email address, and any additional identifying information that may be necessary for the request. This ensures that the system or platform can validate and respond to the request appropriately. Next, the form includes a section where users can specify the reason for their data objection. This allows users to provide a clear explanation of why they are requesting the removal of their personal data. It is important to include this section as it helps the system or platform understand the user's concerns and respond accordingly. Additionally, the User Data Objection Request Form should include a section where users can specify the specific personal data they want to be removed. This can be done through checkboxes or text fields that allow users to indicate the types of data they want to object to. It is important to provide users with the ability to be selective in their data objection, as they may only want to remove specific information rather than all of their personal data. Lastly, the form should include a section where users can provide any supporting documents or evidence to strengthen their objection. This could include screenshots, correspondence, or other relevant information that demonstrates the need for data removal. Providing this section allows users to provide additional context and enhances the validity of their objection. In conclusion, the User Data Objection Request Form is an essential UI pattern that allows users to exercise their rights to data protection and privacy. By including key sections for contact details, reason for objection, specific data to be removed, and supporting evidence, this form ensures that users can make formal and comprehensive requests for the objection of their personal data.

A User Data Objection Request Form is a UI pattern designed to allow users to request the objection or removal of their personal data from a system or platform. This form serves as a formal means for users to exercise their data protection rights and ensure their privacy.

The User Data Objection Request Form typically consists of several key components. First, there is a section where users can provide their contact details, including their name, email address, and any additional identifying information that may be necessary for the request. This ensures that the system or platform can validate and respond to the request appropriately.

Next, the form includes a section where users can specify the reason for their data objection. This allows users to provide a clear explanation of why they are requesting the removal of their personal data. It is important to include this section as it helps the system or platform understand the user's concerns and respond accordingly.

Additionally, the User Data Objection Request Form should include a section where users can specify the specific personal data they want to be removed. This can be done through checkboxes or text fields that allow users to indicate the types of data they want to object to. It is important to provide users with the ability to be selective in their data objection, as they may only want to remove specific information rather than all of their personal data.

Lastly, the form should include a section where users can provide any supporting documents or evidence to strengthen their objection. This could include screenshots, correspondence, or other relevant information that demonstrates the need for data removal. Providing this section allows users to provide additional context and enhances the validity of their objection.

User Data Portability Request Form

A User Data Portability Request Form is a user interface pattern and design system component that allows users to request the transfer or export of their personal data from one platform or service to another in a structured and standardized way.

It typically consists of a form with fields for the user to enter their personal information and select the types of data they want to export or transfer. The form may also include options for the desired format or destination of the data. Additionally, the form may provide information on the process and timeframes for the data transfer, as well as any fees or charges that may apply.

User Data Portability

User Data Portability refers to the ability of users to transfer their personal data from one application or service to another. In the context of UI patterns and design systems, it involves the implementation of a standardized method for users to export, import, or share their data seamlessly across different platforms or interfaces. The design of user interfaces plays a crucial role in ensuring a smooth and intuitive user experience when it comes to data portability. A well-designed UI should provide users with clear and easy-to-understand options for managing their data, such as exporting it in a common file format or connecting to other applications or services for data synchronization. A consistent and streamlined UI pattern for data portability can be achieved through the use of standardized icons, labels, and visual cues. This helps users quickly identify and locate the relevant actions or features related to data transfer. For example, a "Download" or "Export" button with a commonly recognized icon can be used to allow users to generate a file containing their data. Implementing a design system that promotes data portability involves adhering to established UX/UI principles and best practices. This includes ensuring accessibility, responsiveness, and consistency across different devices and platforms. By adhering to a design system, designers and developers can create a coherent and familiar user experience, regardless of the specific application or service being used for data portability. In addition to the UI patterns and design system, it is essential to consider the underlying infrastructure and protocols necessary for effective data portability. This includes supporting widely used data formats, APIs, and data transfer protocols to enable interoperability between different applications and services. By adopting standard protocols and formats, data can be efficiently transferred and interpreted, regardless of the platform or system used. Overall, user data portability in the context of UI patterns and design systems is about empowering users to seamlessly transfer their personal data between different applications or services. By implementing intuitive and standardized UI patterns, adhering to design systems, and supporting interoperable infrastructure, users can exercise control over their data and choose the platforms or services that best suit their needs.

User Data Privacy Settings

Data privacy settings refer to the options and controls available to users that allow them to manage the collection, use, and sharing of their personal data within a user interface (UI). These settings provide users with the ability to make informed choices about the privacy and security of their personal information.

In the context of a UI pattern or design system, data privacy settings should be designed and implemented in a way that is clear, easy to understand, and respects the user's preferences. This involves presenting the options and controls in a straightforward and transparent manner, without using complex or confusing language.

Data privacy settings typically include options such as:

1. Personal information: Users should have the ability to control what types of personal information are collected and stored. This may include options to enable or disable the collection of location data, browsing history, or user demographics.

2. Data sharing: Users may want to choose whether their personal information is shared with third parties or other users. This can include options to limit or restrict data sharing, as well as the ability to select specific parties or apps with which data can be shared.

3. Notification preferences: Users should have the ability to manage their notification preferences, such as opting in or out of marketing emails, push notifications, or other forms of communication.

4. Data retention: Users may want to control how long their personal data is stored. This can include options to automatically delete data after a certain period of time or to manually delete data at any time.

It is important for UI patterns and design systems to provide a consistent and intuitive experience across different platforms and devices. This includes ensuring that data privacy settings are accessible and easy to find, allowing users to easily review and update their preferences.

In summary, data privacy settings in the context of UI patterns and design systems refer to the options and controls available to users that allow them to manage the collection, use, and sharing of their personal data. These settings should be designed with clarity, transparency, and respect for the user's preferences in mind, providing a consistent and intuitive experience for users across different platforms and devices.>

User Data Rectification Request Form

A User Data Rectification Request Form is a UI pattern that allows users to request changes or updates to their personal data held by an organization. It provides a streamlined and standardized process for users to exercise their rights to rectify any inaccuracies or outdated information in their personal data.

The User Data Rectification Request Form typically consists of a simple and intuitive interface where users can input their personal details, such as name, email address, and identification number, along with a clear and concise description of the requested changes. The form may also include optional fields for additional information or supporting documents, depending on the organization's requirements.

User Data Restriction Request Form

A User Data Restriction Request Form is a UI pattern and design system component used to enable users to exercise their rights to restrict or limit the processing or use of their personal data by an organization or platform.

When implemented as a part of a user interface, the User Data Restriction Request Form typically includes a set of fields or input elements allowing users to provide their identification details, such as name, email address, and any other information required to verify their identity. Additionally, it should include dedicated fields where users can specify the data they wish to restrict, the specific processing activities they want to limit, or any other relevant details regarding their request.

User Data Retention Policies

User Data Retention Policies refer to the rules and regulations that govern the duration and management of user data within a digital interface, such as a website or application. These policies define how long user data will be stored and how it will be handled once it is no longer needed or requested by the user. The purpose of implementing user data retention policies is to ensure compliance with privacy laws and regulations, protect user privacy and security, and establish transparency and trust between the user and the organization. In the context of UI patterns and design systems, user data retention policies influence the way user data is collected, stored, and displayed within the interface. Designers and developers must take into consideration these policies to create user-friendly and privacy-conscious experiences. When designing UI patterns, it is essential to clearly communicate to users how their data will be retained and for what purposes. This can be achieved through the use of clear and concise language, accompanied by intuitive visual cues. For example, when requesting user consent for data retention, the interface should provide an easily understandable explanation of what data will be stored, how long it will be retained, and the reasons for data collection. In terms of design systems, user data retention policies should be incorporated into the guidelines and documentation provided to designers and developers. This ensures consistent implementation across different interfaces and maintains alignment with legal and regulatory requirements. The design system should outline the specific data retention periods for different types of user data and provide guidelines on how to handle data deletion requests from users. By integrating user data retention policies into UI patterns and design systems, organizations can demonstrate their commitment to protecting user privacy and complying with data protection laws. This fosters a sense of trust and confidence among users, ultimately leading to increased user satisfaction and loyalty. In summary, user data retention policies define how user data is managed within a digital interface. When designing UI patterns and developing design systems, it is crucial to incorporate these policies to ensure privacy, compliance, and trust.>

User Data Retention Request Form

A User Data Retention Request Form is a UI pattern and design system that allows users to request the retention of their personal data held by a company or service. It provides a structured and user-friendly way for individuals to exercise their data protection rights, in line with privacy regulations such as the General Data Protection Regulation (GDPR) and California Consumer Privacy Act (CCPA).

The User Data Retention Request Form typically consists of a series of fields and options that users can fill out to specify their request. This may include providing their name, contact details, and any relevant identifying information. Additionally, the form may include dropdown menus or checkboxes to indicate the specific data categories or retention periods the user wishes to request. The design of the User Data Retention Request Form should prioritize clarity and transparency, ensuring that users clearly understand their rights and the information they need to provide. The form should be intuitive, with clear labels and instructions for each field, ensuring that users can easily navigate and complete the form. To enhance transparency and user trust, it is important to provide clear information about the purpose and legal basis for requesting data retention. This can be achieved through additional text or links to relevant privacy policy or data retention policy. Users should also be informed about the potential consequences and implications of their request. The User Data Retention Request Form may also include additional features to facilitate the process, such as a submission confirmation message and an option to receive a copy of the submitted request. Additionally, it should provide a contact channel or customer support information for users to seek assistance or ask further questions. Implementing a User Data Retention Request Form as part of a design system can promote consistency and user familiarity across different interfaces and touchpoints. This helps to ensure that the form aligns with the overall user experience of the company or service, contributing to a cohesive and user-centric approach to data protection.

User Data Security

A UI pattern is a reusable solution that solves a specific design problem while maintaining consistency throughout the user interface. A design system, on the other hand, is a collection of reusable components, patterns, and guidelines that enable teams to create a consistent and cohesive experience for users. When it comes to user data security, both UI patterns and design systems play a crucial role in ensuring the protection and privacy of user information. User data security refers to the measures and practices implemented to safeguard user data from unauthorized access, misuse, or accidental disclosure. This includes personal information such as name, email address, passwords, and any other sensitive data collected or stored by an application or website. In the context of UI patterns and design systems, user data security should be a critical consideration. Designers and developers need to adhere to best practices and guidelines to ensure that the user's data is protected throughout their interactions with the interface. This can be achieved through various UI patterns and design system components, such as: 1. Secure Authentication: UI patterns for secure authentication help users establish a trusted connection with the application or website. This includes two-factor authentication, password complexity requirements, and secure password reset processes. 2. Data Encryption: Design system components should incorporate encryption methods to protect user data during transmission and storage. This includes using SSL/TLS protocols, encrypting sensitive data at rest, and securely storing user passwords using hashing algorithms. 3. Privacy Settings and Consent: UI patterns should provide users with clear options to manage their privacy settings and provide informed consent for data collection or sharing. Design system components should include privacy checkboxes, information tooltips, and user-friendly interfaces for managing personal data preferences. 4. Error Handling and Reporting: Design system components should include clear error handling messages to guide users in case of data entry mistakes or security-related issues. This ensures that users are aware of potential risks and can take appropriate action to rectify them. 5. User Education: UI patterns and design system components should incorporate educational elements to inform users about the importance of data security and provide tips for keeping their data safe. This can include tooltips, onboarding screens, and contextual help features. By implementing these UI patterns and design system components, designers and developers can create interfaces that prioritize user data security. This not only builds trust with users but also helps organizations comply with privacy regulations and avoid potential data breaches. User data security is a critical aspect of any application or website, and UI patterns and design systems provide the necessary tools and guidelines to ensure the protection and privacy of user information.>

User Data Sync Across Devices

Data Sync Across Devices refers to the functionality of a user interface (UI) pattern and design system that allows for seamless and consistent synchronization of user data across multiple devices, ensuring that the data remains up-to-date and readily accessible regardless of the device being used.

With the increasing prevalence of multiple devices (such as smartphones, tablets, and computers) in our daily lives, it has become essential for users to have their data synchronized across all these devices. This is particularly important in situations where users switch between devices frequently or use different devices for different activities.

User Data Transfer Request Form

A user data transfer request form is a user interface pattern commonly used in design systems to facilitate the transfer of user data from one system or platform to another. It is typically presented as a web form that allows users to specify the details of the data they wish to transfer and the destination where the data should be sent. The purpose of a user data transfer request form is to provide a standardized and user-friendly way for individuals to request the transfer of their personal information or other data between different systems. This form is often used in scenarios where users want to switch platforms or services, or when data portability is required by regulations such as the General Data Protection Regulation (GDPR). The user data transfer request form typically includes fields that capture relevant information such as the user's name, contact details, the type and scope of data to be transferred, and the destination system or platform. It may also include additional fields or options to clarify specific requirements or preferences related to the data transfer. The design of the user data transfer request form should prioritize simplicity and clarity to ensure a smooth and intuitive user experience. Clear labels and instructions should be provided for each field, and any technical or legal terminology should be explained in plain language. Visual cues such as icons or color coding can be used to highlight important information or guide users through the form. To enhance user privacy and security, the user data transfer request form should also incorporate appropriate measures to protect the confidentiality and integrity of the data being transferred. This may include encryption of sensitive data, secure authentication mechanisms, and adherence to data protection regulations. Overall, a well-designed user data transfer request form is an essential component of a design system, providing users with a streamlined and transparent process for requesting the transfer of their data. By following established UI patterns and principles, designers can ensure that the form is easy to use, visually appealing, and compliant with relevant regulations and standards.>

User Experience (UX) Feedback Form

The User Experience (UX) Feedback Form is a crucial component of UI patterns and design systems that allows users to provide feedback on their experience using a product or service. It serves as a medium for users to share their thoughts, suggestions, and concerns, helping the design team understand and improve the user experience. UX feedback forms typically consist of a series of questions or prompts related to various aspects of the user experience. These questions can be open-ended or multiple-choice, providing users with the flexibility to express their thoughts in their own words or select predefined options. The form may also include optional fields for users to provide additional information or contact details if they wish to be contacted for further discussion. By incorporating UX feedback forms into UI patterns and design systems, designers can establish a systematic approach to gathering user input. This ensures that feedback is consistently collected across different products or services, allowing for meaningful comparisons and analysis. Moreover, the standardized format of the feedback form streamlines the collection and analysis process, making it more efficient and manageable for the design team. The UX feedback form serves multiple purposes. First, it helps identify pain points and areas for improvement within the user experience. By encouraging users to provide specific feedback, designers can gain insights into potential issues or challenges that users may face. This information can then be used to make informed design decisions and prioritize improvements. Second, the feedback form allows designers to gather user preferences and understand their needs and expectations. By asking users about their preferences and expectations, designers can gain a better understanding of the target audience and tailor the user experience to meet their needs. This not only improves the overall satisfaction of users but also helps build a loyal user base. Finally, the UX feedback form fosters a sense of inclusivity and user-centered design. By actively seeking user feedback, designers signal that they value the opinions and experiences of their users. This helps establish a positive relationship between users and the design team, promoting a collaborative and user-focused design process. In conclusion, the UX feedback form is a critical component of UI patterns and design systems, enabling designers to collect valuable user input and improve the overall user experience. By incorporating systematic feedback mechanisms into their design processes, designers can ensure that user feedback is consistently gathered and utilized to drive meaningful improvements.>

User Flows

A user flow in the context of UI patterns and design systems refers to the defined path a user takes to complete a specific task or achieve a particular goal within a website or application. It outlines the sequence of steps and interactions that a user goes through, from the entry point to the final action, providing a visual representation of the user's journey. User flows are crucial in the design process as they help designers understand how users navigate and interact with a system, allowing them to identify potential pain points and areas for improvement. By mapping out the user flow, designers can gain insights into the user's mindset and expectations, enabling them to create a more intuitive and seamless user experience. To create a user flow, designers typically start by identifying the different user personas and their specific goals or tasks within the system. They then outline the main steps and actions that users need to take to accomplish these tasks, considering possible variations and decision points. Each step in the user flow is represented by a node, visually connected by arrows to indicate the order of progression. A user flow should be clear and easy to follow, providing a visual representation of the user's journey from start to finish. It should include all relevant interactions and decisions that the user may encounter along the way, ensuring a comprehensive understanding of the user's experience. By using user flows in the design process, designers can effectively communicate and collaborate with other team members, such as developers and stakeholders. User flows serve as a reference point for discussions and decision-making, allowing everyone involved to have a shared understanding of the intended user experience. Overall, user flows play a vital role in designing user-friendly interfaces and creating cohesive design systems. By visually mapping out the user's journey, designers can identify and address any potential issues or challenges, resulting in a more streamlined and satisfying user experience.

A user flow in the context of UI patterns and design systems refers to the defined path a user takes to complete a specific task or achieve a particular goal within a website or application. It outlines the sequence of steps and interactions that a user goes through, from the entry point to the final action, providing a visual representation of the user's journey.

User flows are crucial in the design process as they help designers understand how users navigate and interact with a system, allowing them to identify potential pain points and areas for improvement. By mapping out the user flow, designers can gain insights into the user's mindset and expectations, enabling them to create a more intuitive and seamless user experience.

User Identity Verification

User Identity Verification refers to the process of verifying the identity of a user, typically through the use of various authentication methods, in order to ensure that the user is who they claim to be. This verification process plays a crucial role in maintaining the security and integrity of a system or platform, as it helps to prevent unauthorized access and protect sensitive user data. In the context of UI patterns and design systems, User Identity Verification is implemented through the use of specific design elements and patterns that guide the user through the verification process in a clear and intuitive manner. These design patterns aim to create a user interface that is easy to understand and navigate, while also reassuring users that their personal information is being protected. One common design pattern used in User Identity Verification is the use of multi-step forms. This pattern breaks down the verification process into smaller, manageable steps, making it easier for users to complete the required steps without feeling overwhelmed. Each step typically includes clear instructions and relevant input fields, allowing users to easily provide the necessary information for verification. Another design pattern commonly used in User Identity Verification is the inclusion of visual indicators to provide feedback and reassurance to the user. Examples of such indicators include progress bars, checkmarks, and success messages, which help users track their progress and understand when they have successfully completed a verification step. Additionally, the use of clear and concise error messages is important in the design of User Identity Verification systems. When a user makes a mistake or encounters an error during the verification process, the error message should be displayed in a prominent location and provide clear instructions on how to fix the issue. This helps to prevent user frustration and allows them to easily rectify any mistakes. Overall, User Identity Verification in UI patterns and design systems aims to create a seamless and secure user experience. By implementing clear instructions, visual indicators, and concise error messages, designers can create a user interface that fosters trust and confidence in the verification process, ensuring that users can safely access and interact with a system or platform.>

User Language Preference

Language preference in the context of UI patterns and design systems refers to a user's selected or default language for interacting with a digital interface. It is the language in which the user interface elements, such as buttons, labels, messages, and notifications, are presented to the user. A design system, in the context of UI patterns, is a set of reusable components, guidelines, and standards that ensure consistency and efficiency in the user interface design. It provides a common language and a unified experience across different platforms and devices. A user's language preference is an essential factor in determining the success and usability of a user interface. It is crucial to cater to the diverse language needs of users, considering their preferences for a seamless user experience. An effective design system should support multilingual interfaces, allowing users to easily switch between languages or setting a default language based on the user's preferences or location. By incorporating language preference as a design consideration, a design system can enhance usability, accessibility, and inclusivity. Users feel more comfortable and familiar with interfaces presented in their preferred language, leading to increased engagement and satisfaction. When designing for language preference, it is important to consider the following guidelines: 1. Language Selection: Provide a clear and easily accessible option for users to select their preferred language. This can be done through a dropdown menu, language picker, or settings panel. 2. Translation and Localization: Ensure that all interface elements, including text content, button labels, error messages, and notifications, are properly translated and localized. Use language-specific files or databases to store translations and dynamically load the appropriate content based on the user's language preference. 3. Right-to-Left (RTL) Support: If the design system supports languages that are read from right to left, such as Arabic or Hebrew, ensure that the interface elements properly align and adapt to RTL reading direction. This includes the positioning of buttons, icons, and images, as well as the flow of text and layout. 4. Formatting and Date/Time Localization: Consider the specific conventions and formatting rules associated with different languages. For example, dates and times may be formatted differently in different regions. Adapting to these conventions contributes to a more natural and localized experience. 5. Consistency: Maintain consistent design principles and visual elements across different language variations. This includes typography, color usage, spacing, and iconography. Consistency ensures that users can easily navigate and interact with the interface regardless of their language preference. Taking these guidelines into account when designing a UI pattern library or a design system helps create a flexible and adaptable interface that caters to users' language preferences and provides an inclusive experience. References: - Nielsen Norman Group: https://www.nngroup.com/articles/international-ux/ - Material Design: https://material.io/design/usability/internationalization.html>

User Mentions

User Mentions in the context of UI patterns and design system refer to a feature or functionality that allows users to mention other users within a user interface. It is a way of highlighting or referencing another user within a conversation or a specific context. User mentions are commonly used in applications or platforms that involve communication, collaboration, or social interaction. The purpose of user mentions is to notify or bring attention to a particular user or group of users in a conversation or discussion. This feature can enhance communication and collaboration by facilitating direct engagement and participation from the mentioned users. It helps in addressing specific users, assigning tasks, seeking feedback, or simply acknowledging their presence in a conversation. From a design perspective, user mentions can be implemented in various ways depending on the specific UI pattern or design system being used. One common approach is to use an "@" symbol followed by the user's name or username. This convention is widely recognized and understood, making it intuitive for users to mention others. To implement user mentions effectively, it is essential to provide real-time or near-real-time notifications to the mentioned users. This ensures that they are promptly informed about their mention, enabling them to respond or take action accordingly. Additionally, it is crucial to provide clear visual cues or indicators to distinguish user mentions from regular text. This can be achieved using different colors, underlining, or highlighting the mentioned user's name. User mentions can also be accompanied by additional features, such as auto-complete or suggestions, to facilitate the process of mentioning users. This helps users find and select the desired users more easily and accurately, reducing the chances of errors or miscommunication. Overall, user mentions play a significant role in fostering effective communication, collaboration, and engagement within a user interface. By incorporating this feature into UI patterns and design systems, designers can create a more interactive and user-centered experience, ultimately improving the overall usability and functionality of the application or platform. Implementing user mentions can enhance the user experience by facilitating direct engagement and collaboration within a conversation or discussion. It provides a seamless way to address specific users, assign tasks, seek feedback, or acknowledge other users' presence. The use of recognizable symbols, real-time notifications, and clear visual cues can help ensure the effectiveness and usability of user mentions in a UI design.>

User Notification Preferences

User Notification Preferences refer to the settings that allow users to control how they receive notifications and alerts within an application or system. These preferences typically encompass a range of options that users can customize based on their preferences and needs.

The design and implementation of user notification preferences play a crucial role in providing a personalized and user-friendly experience. They aim to empower users by allowing them to tailor the types, frequency, and delivery methods of notifications they receive.

User Notifications

User notifications are an important component of user interface (UI) patterns and design systems. They are used to communicate important information, updates, or alerts to users within an application or website. These notifications are commonly displayed as banners, pop-ups, or small alert boxes that appear on the screen, usually near the top or bottom. User notifications serve several purposes. Firstly, they provide feedback to users, giving them information about the system's current state, successful actions, or any errors or issues that may have occurred. This immediate feedback helps users understand the outcome of their interactions and guides them in making informed decisions. Secondly, user notifications can be used to announce updates or new features within the application or website. These notifications can be triggered when there is a new version available, changes to the terms of service, or the introduction of new functionality. By informing users about these updates, it ensures that they are aware of any changes that may affect their experience or usage of the product. Furthermore, user notifications can be utilized to prompt users to take specific actions. These prompts can serve as reminders for unfinished tasks, time-sensitive activities, or important deadlines. By leveraging visual indicators or call-to-action buttons within the notification, users are encouraged to complete the necessary actions promptly. To ensure an effective user notification system, there are several key considerations to keep in mind. First, it is essential to strike a balance between providing relevant information and avoiding overwhelming the user with excessive notifications. Notifications should be concise, clear, and only displayed when necessary. Additionally, user notifications should be designed to align with the overall visual language and branding of the application or website. Consistent use of colors, typography, and icons helps create a cohesive and recognizable notification system. Lastly, user notifications should be designed to be easily dismissible or closable, allowing users to remove or hide them if desired. This empowers users to manage their notification flow and prioritizes their control over their experience. In conclusion, user notifications are a crucial component of UI patterns and design systems, enabling effective communication of important information, updates, and alerts to users. By providing feedback, announcing updates, and prompting actions, user notifications enhance the user experience and help users navigate and interact with applications and websites efficiently.

User Onboarding Tutorials

User onboarding tutorials, in the context of UI patterns and design systems, refer to the interactive and instructional experiences provided to new users of a digital product or platform. These tutorials aim to guide users through the initial steps of using the product, introducing them to its features and functionality, and helping them complete key tasks. User onboarding tutorials are an essential part of the user experience design process and play a crucial role in ensuring successful user adoption and engagement. They aim to reduce user friction and frustration by providing clear and concise instructions, explanations, and guidance. These tutorials can take various forms and can be presented in different ways, depending on the nature of the product and its target audience. They may include: 1. Guided Walkthroughs: These tutorials provide step-by-step instructions and guiding arrows, highlighting key elements and explaining their purpose. They often use interactive overlays or tooltips to draw attention to specific areas of the interface, ensuring that users understand how to navigate and interact with the product. 2. Video Tutorials: Video tutorials offer a visual and auditory explanation of how to use the product. They can provide a more engaging and immersive onboarding experience, allowing users to see the product in action and understand its features in a dynamic way. 3. Contextual Help: Contextual help is integrated within the product's interface, providing users with quick access to relevant information and resources. This can include inline tooltips or help icons that users can click on to get more information about a particular feature or task. 4. Gamification: Gamification techniques can be used to make the onboarding process more enjoyable and interactive. This may involve providing users with small challenges or rewards as they progress through the tutorial, keeping them motivated and engaged. By providing user onboarding tutorials, designers aim to enhance the user experience by ensuring that users understand how to use the product effectively from the start. This not only helps users feel more confident in using the product but also reduces the likelihood of abandonment and frustration. Overall, user onboarding tutorials are an essential component of UI patterns and design systems, helping new users become familiar with a product's interface and functionality through interactive and instructional experiences.

User Onboarding

User onboarding refers to the process of introducing and familiarizing new users with a product or service, ensuring a smooth and engaging experience that enables users to quickly understand and effectively use the product. It involves guiding users through the necessary steps to get started, providing clear instructions and support, and helping them become proficient users. A well-designed user onboarding experience is crucial for successful product adoption and user retention. By providing a seamless and intuitive onboarding process, users are more likely to continue using the product, reducing the likelihood of abandonment or churn. A good user onboarding experience can also contribute to positive word-of-mouth and user satisfaction, leading to increased usage and potential revenue growth. UI patterns and design systems play a significant role in shaping the user onboarding experience. UI patterns are reusable solutions to common user interface design problems, and they provide a consistent and familiar interaction framework for users. Design systems, on the other hand, are the comprehensive set of guidelines, principles, and assets that define the visual and interactive design of a product. In the context of user onboarding, UI patterns and design systems help create a cohesive and intuitive experience. They ensure consistency across different screens and interactions, allowing users to navigate through the product effortlessly. By following established UI patterns, such as walkthroughs, tooltips, and progressive disclosure, designers can effectively guide users through the onboarding process, providing clear instructions and reducing cognitive load. Furthermore, design systems provide a foundation for designing user onboarding components. By using predefined styles, components, and interactions, designers can create visually consistent and aesthetically pleasing onboarding experiences. This consistency helps users understand and recognize different elements and interactions, promoting a sense of familiarity and ease of use. In conclusion, user onboarding is a critical process in introducing and acclimating users to a product or service. UI patterns and design systems are essential tools in creating a seamless and intuitive onboarding experience. They ensure consistency, provide clear instructions, and help users become proficient in using the product. By prioritizing user onboarding and leveraging UI patterns and design systems, companies can enhance user satisfaction, increase product adoption, and drive long-term success.

User Preferences Form

User Preferences Form is a UI pattern and design system component that allows users to customize and tailor their preferences, settings, or personalization options within an application or system. It provides users with a structured and organized interface to define their choices and configurations according to their individual needs and preferences. The User Preferences Form typically consists of a series of fields or controls that enable users to modify various aspects of the application or system. These fields can include checkboxes, radio buttons, dropdown menus, text inputs, sliders, or toggle switches, among others. Through the User Preferences Form, users can specify preferences related to visual settings, language preferences, notifications, privacy settings, accessibility options, and more. It empowers users to define their experience by allowing them to personalize the application or system to align with their preferences and requirements. By offering a centralized place to manage preferences, the User Preferences Form ensures consistency and ease-of-use. It simplifies the process of modifying settings by gathering all the relevant options in one location, avoiding the need for users to navigate through multiple menus or settings pages. The User Preferences Form also enhances user control and understanding by providing clear and concise labels, descriptions, and tooltips for each preference option. These cues help users make informed decisions about the impact and implications of their choices, preventing unintended or undesired changes. Moreover, the design of the User Preferences Form should consider principles of accessibility and inclusivity. It should adhere to accessibility guidelines to guarantee that all users, regardless of their abilities, can access and modify their preferences effectively. In conclusion, the User Preferences Form is a crucial UI pattern and design system component that empowers users to tailor and customize their experience within an application or system. It provides them with a structured and user-friendly interface to define their preferences and configurations. By offering a centralized location for managing preferences, the User Preferences Form enhances usability and ensures consistency. It promotes user control, understanding, and accessibility, enabling individuals to personalize the application or system according to their unique needs and preferences.

User Preferences

User Preferences refer to the settings or choices made by individual users in a system or application to customize their experience. In the context of UI patterns and design systems, user preferences play a crucial role in allowing users to personalize their interactions and tailor the interface to their specific needs and preferences.

UI patterns and design systems provide a range of customizable elements, components, and styles that can be adjusted based on user preferences. These preferences may include various aspects such as color schemes, font sizes, layout options, language preferences, accessibility settings, and more.

User Profile Completion Form

335

A User Profile Completion Form is a UI pattern that is used to collect and organize information from users in order to create or update their user profiles within a system or application. It is an integral component of many digital products, especially those that require user registration or personalization. The purpose of a User Profile Completion Form is to gather relevant information from users in a structured and efficient manner. By providing a clear and intuitive interface, it allows users to enter their personal details, preferences, and other relevant information, ensuring that their profiles are complete and accurate. This UI pattern typically consists of a series of input fields, checkboxes, dropdown menus, and other relevant form elements. The form is usually divided into sections, each focusing on a specific category of information, such as name, contact details, address, and preferences. This segmentation helps users navigate through the form easily and understand the context of each piece of information required. To enhance usability, a User Profile Completion Form should provide clear instructions and meaningful error messages. It should include validation checks to ensure that the data entered by users is accurate and meets the specified format. Feedback mechanisms such as highlighting incorrectly filled fields or displaying error messages in a prominent and easily noticeable manner can help users address any issues and complete the form successfully. A good User Profile Completion Form is not only visually appealing but also responsive across different devices and screen sizes. It should adapt seamlessly to different layouts, maintaining consistency and legibility. Additionally, it should be accessible, adhering to accessibility guidelines and standards, so that users with disabilities can also complete their profiles effectively. By implementing a User Profile Completion Form, businesses and organizations can effectively gather relevant user information, which can be used for personalization, targeted marketing, and providing a better user experience. Successful adoption of this UI pattern can lead to increased user engagement, improved data quality, and more accurate user profiles, ultimately contributing to a more seamless and personalized digital experience.

A User Profile Completion Form is a UI pattern used to collect and organize user information for creating or updating user profiles. It consists of input fields and other elements divided into sections. The form provides clear instructions and validation checks to ensure data accuracy. It is visually appealing, responsive, and designed to be accessible. By adopting this pattern, businesses can gather relevant user information and improve their digital experience.

User Profile Dropdown

A user profile dropdown is a graphic element frequently used in user interfaces (UI) to provide quick access to a user's personal account information and settings. It is a common pattern in design systems that allows users to easily manage and customize their profiles within an application or website. The user profile dropdown typically appears as a small button or icon, often displaying the user's profile picture or initials. When clicked or hovered over, it expands to reveal a dropdown menu that presents various options related to the user's profile. Within the dropdown menu, users can expect to find options such as "My Profile," "Settings," "Sign Out," and other relevant actions. These options provide users with the ability to view and edit their personal information, change account settings, and log out of their accounts when needed. The dropdown menu itself is designed to be visually intuitive and easy to navigate. Options are usually presented in a clear, concise manner, often as a list of text links. Each option should have a clear and understandable label, enabling users to quickly identify the desired action. In some cases, icons may be used alongside the labels to enhance recognition and aid in visual comprehension. The user profile dropdown is an essential component of a design system, as it allows for consistent placement and interaction across different pages and screens. This consistency ensures that users can easily locate and access their profile information, regardless of where they are within the application or website. In terms of usability, the user profile dropdown should be easily accessible, both on desktop and mobile devices. It should be positioned in a prominent location, such as the top right corner of the interface, where users are accustomed to finding account-related features. Additionally, the dropdown menu itself should be large enough to accommodate the options and easy to interact with, even on smaller screens. Overall, the user profile dropdown provides a convenient and efficient way for users to manage their accounts and access personalized settings within an application or website. It promotes a seamless user experience by allowing users to easily navigate and customize their profiles, ultimately enhancing user satisfaction and engagement.>

User Profiles In Conversations

A user profile in the context of UI patterns and design systems refers to a visual representation or a summary of an individual user's information and preferences. It is typically used to provide a personalized experience for the users within a digital application or platform.

Within a conversation-based interface or application, a user profile is a crucial component as it helps to establish and maintain the identity of the users. It enables the system to tailor its responses and interactions based on the individual's characteristics, history, and preferences.

User Profiles

A user profile, in the context of UI patterns and design systems, refers to a visual representation of an individual or a persona within a digital platform or application. It is a structured and organized area where users can view and manage their personal information, settings, preferences, and other relevant details.

The user profile serves as a centralized hub that allows users to control their interactions and experiences within the system. It typically includes a variety of sections and features to provide a comprehensive overview of the user's identity and account information. Some common components found in a user profile include:

1. Personal Information: This section contains basic details about the user, such as their name, profile picture, contact information, and other relevant identification data.

2. Account Settings: Here, users can modify various settings related to their account, such as username, password, email preferences, notification preferences, and other privacy-related options.

3. Activity History: This section displays a summary of the user's recent activities within the platform, such as posts, comments, likes, and other relevant actions. It can serve as a quick way for users to revisit or manage their past interactions.

4. Social Connections: Users may have the option to connect their profile with external social media accounts, allowing them to share their activities or connect with friends from other platforms. This section provides options for linking and managing these connections.

5. Privacy and Security: This segment allows users to control the visibility and accessibility of their profile information. It includes options to adjust privacy settings, manage data sharing permissions, and enable two-factor authentication for added security.

6. Preferences and Customization: This section enables users to personalize their experience by customizing the interface, including themes, language settings, and other display preferences.

By providing a user profile, design systems and UI patterns ensure that users have a central location where they can efficiently manage their account-related information and interactions. It plays a crucial role in enhancing the user experience by providing a familiar and intuitive layout, facilitating easy access to relevant settings, and promoting a sense of control over one's digital presence.

User Ratings And Reviews

User Ratings and Reviews in the context of UI design patterns and design system refers to a feature or component that allows users to express their opinions, experiences, and feedback about products or services. It provides a platform for users to rate and review items, share their thoughts, and help others make informed decisions. The purpose of including User Ratings and Reviews in a UI design is to enhance the user experience by providing valuable insights and recommendations from other users. These ratings and reviews act as social proof and influence potential customers' perceptions and purchasing decisions. They serve as a source of feedback for businesses and help them improve their products or services. When designing User Ratings and Reviews, it is essential to consider the following factors: 1. Rating System: The rating system should be clear, intuitive, and easy to use. Users should be able to rate items based on a specific scale, such as a star rating system or a numerical rating out of 10. 2. Review Submission: Users should be able to submit their reviews easily. A text input field should be provided for users to write their reviews. Additionally, it is beneficial to allow users to add ratings along with their written reviews. 3. Sorting and Filtering: Users should be able to sort and filter reviews based on different criteria, such as the most recent, highest rated, or most helpful reviews. This helps users find relevant and reliable information quickly. 4. Review Display: Reviews should be displayed in a visually appealing and organized manner, allowing users to scan and read them easily. Each review should include the rating, review text, username, and date of submission. 5. Reply and Commenting: Businesses should have the option to reply to user reviews, addressing any concerns or thanking users for their feedback. Users should also be able to comment on each other's reviews, fostering a sense of community and discussion. By incorporating User Ratings and Reviews into UI design patterns and design systems, businesses can create a transparent and engaging user experience. Users are more likely to trust and be influenced by the opinions of their peers, resulting in increased user satisfaction and credibility for the brand or platform. In conclusion, User Ratings and Reviews in UI design patterns and design systems provide users with a platform to express their opinions, contribute to the community, and help inform others. It is a crucial component to enhance user experience and shape customer perceptions.>

User Ratings

User Ratings are a UI pattern and design system element used to display and collect feedback or opinions from users about a particular product, service, or experience. This pattern typically consists of a visual representation, such as stars or thumbs-up icons, accompanied by a numeric value or average rating.

These ratings provide a quick and easy way for users to evaluate the quality or satisfaction level of a product or service. They serve as a valuable source of information for other potential users to make informed decisions. User ratings can be found in various contexts, including e-commerce websites, online reviews, mobile apps, and social media platforms.

User Registration Confirmation Form

A User Registration Confirmation Form is a UI pattern and design system element that is used to confirm the successful registration of a user on a website or application. This form provides the necessary information and feedback to the user and helps establish a smooth onboarding experience. The purpose of the User Registration Confirmation Form is to acknowledge the user's successful registration and provide them with essential details, such as the confirmation message, instructions for further actions, and any additional information that may be required. It serves as a confirmation and validation of the user's identity and helps ensure a secure and trustworthy user registration process. The User Registration Confirmation Form typically includes fields or sections such as: 1. Confirmation Message: This is a prominent section of the form that displays a personalized message to the user, confirming their successful registration. It may include greetings, expressions of gratitude, and a summary of their registration details. 2. Instructions for Further Actions: This section provides clear instructions to the user on what steps they need to take next. It may include prompts to check their email for account verification, set up a password, complete their profile, or any other necessary actions. The design of the User Registration Confirmation Form should follow the overall visual style and branding of the website or application. It should be visually appealing, consistent, and easily understandable to ensure a positive user experience. Key design considerations include legible typography, appropriate use of colors and visual cues, and responsive layout to support different devices and screen sizes. By providing a User Registration Confirmation Form that is user-friendly and informative, website or application owners can improve the overall onboarding process and instill trust and confidence in their users. It serves as a crucial touchpoint in the user journey and contributes to a positive first impression, setting the stage for continued engagement and usage of the platform.

A User Registration Confirmation Form is a UI pattern and design system element used to confirm the successful registration of a user. It provides necessary details such as confirmation message and instructions for further actions.

The form must be visually appealing, consistent with the brand, and easily understandable to ensure a positive user experience and establish trust.

User Review Moderation Form

A User Review Moderation Form is a standardized user interface (UI) pattern and component of a design system that allows users to submit and moderate reviews for a product or service. It provides a structured format for collecting and managing user feedback, ensuring that all reviews are organized and easily accessible. The User Review Moderation Form typically consists of several input fields and options that users can fill out to submit their reviews. These fields may include the user's name, email address, rating, title, and comments. The form may also have additional fields such as the date of the review or location of the user. By providing a consistent and structured format, the form ensures that all necessary information is gathered from the user for a comprehensive review. Once the user submits their review, the moderation aspect of the form comes into play. The form provides functionality for moderators to review and manage the submitted reviews. This can include actions such as approving, editing, or deleting reviews based on certain criteria or guidelines. The moderation options are meant to ensure the quality and relevance of the reviews that are displayed to other users. In the context of a design system, the User Review Moderation Form is an important component that facilitates a consistent and systematic approach to collecting and managing user feedback. It follows the established design principles and guidelines of the design system to ensure a cohesive and visually pleasing user experience. Overall, the User Review Moderation Form is a crucial UI pattern and design system component that enables the collection, organization, and moderation of user reviews. It provides a standardized format for users to submit their feedback while allowing moderators to manage and curate the reviews for display. By incorporating this pattern into a design system, organizations can create a streamlined and user-friendly process for gathering and presenting user reviews.>

User Review Screen

A User Review Screen is a UI pattern commonly used in web and mobile applications to display and showcase user reviews or feedback. It is a dedicated screen or section within an application where users can provide their opinions, ratings, and comments on a particular product, service, or user experience. The User Review Screen is designed to be easy to navigate and understand, allowing users to view and contribute their own reviews effortlessly. It typically consists of a list or grid of user reviews, with each review displaying pertinent information such as the reviewer's name, rating, and comment. The design of a User Review Screen often follows a consistent layout and visual style to maintain cohesiveness within the application's overall design system. Elements such as fonts, colors, and spacing are carefully chosen to ensure readability and visual hierarchy. The use of appropriate typography and typography styles helps to differentiate between different elements of a review, such as the reviewer's name, rating, and comment. In addition to displaying user reviews, a User Review Screen may also include features that allow users to filter, sort, or search for specific reviews based on criteria such as the highest-rated reviews, most recent reviews, or reviews from specific users. These features enhance user experience by providing them with the ability to find and read relevant reviews more easily. To encourage user engagement, a User Review Screen typically includes options for users to add their own reviews. This can be done through a form where users can input their ratings, comments, and sometimes additional information such as photos or videos. The submission process may include validation to ensure that all required fields are filled and that the user review meets certain criteria. Overall, a well-designed User Review Screen plays a crucial role in providing valuable information and insights to users. It allows users to make informed decisions based on the experiences of others and fosters a sense of community and interaction within the application.

A User Review Screen is a UI pattern that showcases user reviews or feedback.

It provides a dedicated space where users can view, contribute, and interact with reviews related to a product, service, or user experience.

User Role-Based Access Control

User Role-Based Access Control (RBAC) is a UI pattern and design system that enables a hierarchical control mechanism for managing access to different functionalities and features based on user roles within an application or system.

In RBAC, users are assigned specific roles (such as administrator, manager, or user) that define their level of access and permissions. Each role is associated with a set of permissions that determine what actions and functionalities a user with that role can perform.

User Testimonial Submission Form

A UI pattern is a reusable solution to a common design problem in user interface (UI) design. It is a set of best practices and guidelines that designers can follow to create consistent and usable interfaces across different platforms and devices.

UI patterns help to streamline the design process by providing a standard set of elements and interactions that users are already familiar with. They save time and effort by eliminating the need to design every aspect of a user interface from scratch. Instead, designers can leverage existing patterns and customize them to fit their specific needs.

User Testimonials

UI patterns and design systems play a crucial role in the development of user-friendly and visually appealing interfaces for digital products. User testimonials, in the context of UI patterns and design systems, are formal definitions or statements provided by users to express their experiences and opinions about a particular interface or design element.

These testimonials serve as a valuable source of feedback for designers and developers, as they provide insight into how users perceive and interact with the interface. Testimonials often highlight the strengths and weaknesses of a UI pattern or design system, helping the design team identify areas of improvement or further development.

User Timezone Awareness

Timezone awareness refers to the ability of a user interface (UI) pattern or design system to display and handle time-related information in a way that takes into account the user's timezone. It is an essential consideration for global applications and platforms that serve users from different parts of the world.

An effective UI should be able to dynamically display time-sensitive information, such as event schedules, notifications, or timestamps, in a manner that aligns with the user's local timezone. This ensures that users see and interact with time-related data in a way that is relevant and convenient for their specific location.

User-Generated Content Upvotes/Downvotes

User-generated content upvotes/downvotes are a UI pattern and design system that allows users to express their opinion on a piece of content by either upvoting or downvoting it. This pattern is commonly used in social media platforms, forums, and content-sharing websites to enable user participation and engagement. Upvoting refers to the action of indicating approval or agreement with a particular piece of content. It is often represented by an arrow pointing upwards or a symbol that indicates positivity. Upvotes are typically used to show support, appreciation, or agreement with the content, and they are commonly displayed as a numerical value next to the content or as a visual indicator such as a count or a progress bar. On the other hand, downvoting is the action of indicating disapproval or disagreement with a piece of content. It is usually represented by an arrow pointing downwards or a symbol that indicates negativity. Downvotes are commonly used to express dislike, disagreement, or to flag inappropriate or spam content. Similar to upvotes, downvotes can be displayed as a numerical value or visual indicator next to the content. The purpose of user-generated content upvotes/downvotes is to provide a mechanism for users to influence the visibility and popularity of content within a community or platform. Content that receives a high number of upvotes is often prioritized and more prominently displayed, indicating its quality or relevance to the community. On the other hand, content that receives a high number of downvotes may be hidden, filtered, or given less prominence, signaling its potential lack of value or suitability. This UI pattern encourages user engagement, participation, and collaboration by giving users the ability to contribute to the overall reputation and visibility of content. It allows users to express their preferences, opinions, and judgments, creating a sense of ownership and community within the platform. In conclusion, user-generated content upvotes/downvotes are a fundamental UI pattern and design system that enables users to express their support or disagreement with content. By allowing users to influence visibility and reputation, this pattern fosters engagement and participation within a platform or community.>

User-Generated Content Analytics

User-generated content analytics refers to the process of gathering and analyzing data generated by users within a digital platform or website. This data includes various forms of content such as reviews, comments, ratings, and social media posts. The goal of user-generated content analytics is to extract valuable insights and patterns from this data in order to inform design decisions and improve user experience.

Within the context of UI patterns and design systems, user-generated content analytics plays a crucial role in understanding how users interact with the system and the impact of their contributions. By analyzing user-generated content, designers can identify trends, preferences, and opportunities to enhance the overall user experience.

User-Generated Content Bookmarking

User-generated Content Bookmarking is a UI pattern and design system that allows users to save and organize content created by themselves or other users within an application or platform. It involves the use of bookmarks or favorites to enable users to easily find and access content they find useful or interesting. In this UI pattern, users have the ability to bookmark or save various types of content, such as articles, images, videos, or links, for future reference. The bookmarking feature creates a personal collection or library of content that can be accessed at any time. Users can also organize their bookmarks into categories or tags to better manage and navigate their saved content. User-generated Content Bookmarking can enhance user experience by providing a convenient way for users to keep track of content that is meaningful to them. It allows users to easily revisit and engage with content that they have found valuable or want to revisit later. Additionally, it can foster community engagement by enabling users to share their bookmarks with others, creating a network of recommended content. From a design system perspective, User-generated Content Bookmarking should consider clear and intuitive bookmarking functionality. The UI should provide a prominent and easily accessible bookmark button or icon that allows users to save content with a single click. The design should also include options for organizing bookmarks, such as creating folders or tags, to enable users to efficiently manage their saved content. In terms of user interface (UI) design, User-generated Content Bookmarking should provide visual cues to indicate the bookmarked status of content, making it easy for users to identify what has been saved. This can include visual indicators such as a bookmark icon, change in color or style, or a numerical count of how many times content has been bookmarked. Overall, User-generated Content Bookmarking is a UI pattern and design system that empowers users to save and organize content within an application or platform. It improves user experience by allowing users to easily access and engage with content that they find valuable, creating a personalized library of resources.>

User-Generated Content Commenting

User-generated content commenting refers to the functionality within a user interface (UI) pattern where users are able to interact and share their thoughts, opinions, or feedback on specific pieces of content, such as articles, blog posts, images, or videos. It is a vital component of many websites and online platforms, providing users with the opportunity to engage with the content and each other.

This UI pattern typically consists of a comment section or area where users can express their thoughts and respond to others' comments. It allows for a two-way conversation between the content creator and the audience, fostering community engagement and building connections among users with shared interests.

User-Generated Content Filtering

User-generated content filtering refers to the process of managing and controlling the content generated by users within a UI pattern or design system. It involves implementing mechanisms to monitor, evaluate, and regulate the content generated by users to ensure it aligns with the desired standards, guidelines, and values of the system or platform.

This process is crucial in maintaining a safe and positive user experience, as it allows platform administrators or moderators to identify and remove inappropriate, offensive, or spammy content from the platform. By actively filtering user-generated content, platforms can create a more reliable and trustworthy environment for their users, fostering a sense of community and encouraging meaningful interactions.

User-Generated Content Flagging

User-generated Content Flagging is a UI pattern and design system feature that allows users to report inappropriate or offensive content within a platform. This mechanism relies on the active participation and vigilance of users to effectively moderate and maintain the quality of content shared within the community.

When implemented, the User-generated Content Flagging feature typically includes a small flag or report button placed alongside each user-generated post or comment. This button serves as a visual cue for users to easily notify the platform's administrators or moderators about content that violates the platform's guidelines or terms of service.

Upon clicking the flag or report button, users are often prompted to provide additional context or explanation for their concern. They may be asked to specify the reason for their report, such as spam, harassment, hate speech, or explicit content. This information helps administrators understand the nature of the reported content and prioritize their moderation efforts accordingly.

Once a piece of content is flagged, platform administrators typically review the reported material to determine its legitimacy. If the content is indeed found to be in violation of the platform's guidelines, appropriate action is taken, which may include removing the content, issuing a warning or penalty to the user responsible, or even banning the user from the platform altogether.

User-generated Content Flagging plays a crucial role in maintaining a safe and respectful online environment. By empowering users to proactively report inappropriate content, it fosters a sense of community and collective responsibility. This pattern also helps to distribute the workload of content moderation among both platform administrators and users, ensuring that potentially harmful or offensive material can be identified and addressed promptly.

User-Generated Content Follow/Unfollow

User-generated content (UGC) Follow/Unfollow is a UI pattern that allows users to choose whether or not they want to see updates from specific users or entities within a platform or social media site. This pattern is commonly used in the context of online communities, social media platforms, and content sharing websites. The Follow/Unfollow feature gives users the ability to personalize their content feeds and control the type of content they want to consume. In the context of a design system, the Follow/Unfollow pattern should be consistent across the platform to ensure a cohesive user experience. The design system should provide clear and intuitive visual cues that indicate whether a user is currently following or unfollowing a particular user or entity. This can be achieved through the use of icons, buttons, or toggle switches. The Follow/Unfollow pattern should also consider accessibility and inclusivity. Users with visual impairments should be able to easily understand and interact with this feature. Providing alternative text for icons and using descriptive labels for buttons and switches can help ensure that the pattern is accessible to all users. In terms of user experience, it is important for the Follow/Unfollow pattern to be seamless and non-disruptive. Users should be able to quickly and easily follow or unfollow users or entities without interrupting their browsing or content consumption. The pattern should also provide clear feedback to users when they successfully follow or unfollow someone to confirm their action. Additionally, the Follow/Unfollow pattern should respect the privacy and preferences of users. Users should have full control over who they follow or unfollow, and their decisions should be respected and implemented accordingly. The design system and platform should also provide clear and transparent options for managing and reviewing followed users or entities. Overall, the Follow/Unfollow UI pattern is a crucial component of user-generated content platforms as it empowers users to curate their content feeds according to their preferences, while also supporting inclusivity and user control.

User-Generated Content Highlighting

User-generated content highlighting is a UI pattern and design system that emphasizes user-generated content within an interface. This pattern is commonly used in applications, websites, and platforms where users contribute content such as reviews, ratings, comments, or posts.

The purpose of user-generated content highlighting is to acknowledge and promote the contributions of individual users, creating a sense of engagement, trust, and community. By providing visibility to user-generated content, it not only encourages users to participate and provide valuable insights but also helps others in making informed decisions.

User-Generated Content Leaderboards

User-generated content leaderboards are a UI pattern and design system that displays and ranks user-generated content based on certain criteria or metrics. These leaderboards provide a way for users to see and compare their performance or contributions to others in a visually appealing and easily understandable way.

The primary purpose of user-generated content leaderboards is to encourage user engagement, motivation, and competition within an online community or platform. They create a sense of achievement and recognition for users who generate content, motivating them to further participate and contribute. Additionally, leaderboards can foster a healthy competitive environment where users strive to improve their rankings or performance, thus driving increased activity and content creation.

User-generated content leaderboards typically consist of a list or grid-like structure with rows or cards representing individual users or contributors. Each row or card displays relevant information about the user, such as their username or display name, profile picture, and relevant metrics. These metrics can include factors like the number of posts, comments, likes, shares, or any other measurable criteria that defines the user's performance within the platform.

The leaderboard may also include visual indicators, such as progress bars or badges, to further highlight a user's achievements or progression. These visual cues can provide immediate feedback and recognition to users, further enhancing their motivation to continue participating and generating content.

Furthermore, user-generated content leaderboards often offer sorting and filtering options, allowing users to view the rankings based on different criteria or time periods. This flexibility provides users with a more personalized and tailored experience, helping them to identify patterns, trends, or areas for improvement in their performance.

In summary, user-generated content leaderboards are a UI pattern and design system that showcases and ranks user-generated content based on specific metrics. They encourage user engagement, motivation, and competition by visually displaying and recognizing users' contributions and performance, fostering a sense of achievement within an online community or platform.

User-Generated Content Mentioning

User-generated content refers to any type of content that is created by users of a particular platform or website. This can include various forms of media such as text, images, videos, and audio. User-generated content is typically generated and submitted by individuals who are not affiliated with the platform or organization hosting the content. In the context of UI patterns and design systems, user-generated content can play a crucial role in enhancing the overall user experience. One common use of user-generated content is in social media platforms where users can share their thoughts, opinions, and experiences with others. This can help create a sense of community and engagement among users. Design systems can incorporate user-generated content in a variety of ways. One way is by providing interactive elements that allow users to contribute their own content to the platform. For example, a comment section on a blog or a review section on an e-commerce website. These features not only allow users to express their thoughts but also provide valuable feedback and information for other users. Another way user-generated content can be utilized in design systems is through the integration of user-generated reviews and ratings. This can help users make informed decisions by providing them with insights and opinions from other users who have already interacted with a particular product or service. In terms of UI patterns, user-generated content can be presented in different ways depending on the platform and the type of content. For text-based user-generated content, a common UI pattern is to display the content in a structured manner, such as using cards or lists, to make it easier for users to read and navigate through. For image or video-based user-generated content, UI patterns can include thumbnail previews, lightbox overlays, or carousels to showcase the content in an engaging and visually appealing manner. Additionally, incorporating features like user profiles or social sharing buttons can encourage users to share their own content and contribute to the overall user experience. In conclusion, user-generated content is a valuable asset in UI patterns and design systems. By incorporating user feedback and allowing users to contribute their own content, platforms can create a more engaging and inclusive user experience.>

User-Generated Content Moderation

User-generated content moderation refers to the process of monitoring and managing the content submitted by users on a platform or website. It involves reviewing, filtering, and possibly removing or editing user-generated content to ensure that it is in line with the platform's guidelines and standards.

Within the context of UI patterns and design systems, user-generated content moderation plays a crucial role in maintaining the overall quality and integrity of the platform. It helps in creating a safe and positive user experience by preventing the dissemination of inappropriate or harmful content.

User-Generated Content Notifications

User-generated Content Notifications are visual indicators that notify users about new content or updates created by other users within a digital platform or application. These notifications aim to keep users informed and engaged, enhancing their overall user experience and encouraging participation in the community or social aspects of the platform.

These notifications typically appear as small, unobtrusive notifications that are strategically placed within the user interface. They may take the form of pop-ups, banners, badges, or icons, depending on the design and branding of the platform. The content notifications often display relevant information such as the type of content (e.g., comments, likes, shares), the user who generated the content, and a brief summary or preview of the content itself.

User-Generated Content Rating

User-generated content rating is a UI pattern and design system that allows users to provide feedback or rating for a particular piece of content, such as a product, service, or article. It enables users to express their opinions and experiences, contributing to a community-driven evaluation of the content's quality and relevance.

This UI pattern typically includes elements such as star ratings, thumbs up or down icons, or text-based feedback forms. These elements are designed to be user-friendly and intuitive, allowing users to easily interact and provide their ratings or feedback. The collected ratings are then aggregated and displayed to other users, helping them make informed decisions based on the overall community consensus.

User-Generated Content Reactions

User-generated Content Reactions refer to the UI patterns and design system that allow users to express their thoughts, opinions, and emotions towards a particular piece of content. These reactions can be in the form of liking, disliking, commenting, rating, or sharing. These UI patterns are essential in engaging users and creating a sense of community within a digital platform. By providing users with the ability to react to content, they feel more involved and empowered, leading to increased user satisfaction and participation. The design system for user-generated content reactions should be intuitive and visually appealing. It should allow users to easily understand and interact with the various reaction options available to them. This can be achieved by using familiar icons or symbols that represent each reaction, such as a thumbs-up for liking or a speech bubble for commenting. In terms of UI patterns, one common approach is to incorporate reaction buttons directly underneath the content. These buttons are usually represented by icons or symbols that users can click on to express their reaction. For example, a heart icon can be used to represent the "like" reaction, while a frowning face can represent the "dislike" reaction. Additionally, some design systems may include a rating system, where users can assign a numerical value or star rating to the content. This allows users to provide more nuanced feedback and helps other users identify the quality or usefulness of the content. In order to maintain a visually clean and organized interface, it is important to limit the number of reaction options available. Too many options can overwhelm users and lead to decision paralysis. It is recommended to focus on a few key reactions that are most relevant to the content being presented. Overall, user-generated content reactions are a crucial element of UI patterns and design systems. They provide users with a means to express their thoughts and emotions, fostering a sense of community and engagement within a digital platform. A well-designed system will be intuitive, visually appealing, and limited in its options to avoid overwhelming users.>

User-Generated Content Recommendations

User-generated Content Recommendations refer to a UI pattern and design system that allows users to contribute and display content within a platform. This pattern enables users to generate and share their own content, such as reviews, ratings, comments, or recommendations, with the wider community. It provides a way for users to engage and interact with the platform, as well as share their opinions and experiences.

With User-generated Content Recommendations, users have the ability to influence and guide others by providing their personal insights and perspectives. This pattern fosters a sense of community and collaboration, as users can contribute their own unique knowledge and expertise. It enables a platform to tap into the collective intelligence of its users, making it a valuable resource for others looking for recommendations or information.

User-Generated Content Reporting

User-generated content reporting is a UI pattern and design system that allows users to report objectionable or inappropriate content submitted by other users within a digital platform. This reporting feature is designed to enhance the overall user experience by promoting a safe and respectful online environment.

Within this UI pattern, users are typically provided with a clear and easily accessible option to report offensive or harmful content. The reporting process usually involves a series of steps that users can follow to express their concerns about specific content, such as uploading screenshots, describing the issue, or providing additional context.

User-Generated Content Search

User-generated content search is a UI pattern that allows users to search and retrieve content created by other users within a web or mobile application. This pattern is commonly used in social media platforms, online marketplaces, and community forums, where the content generated by users plays a significant role in driving engagement and establishing a sense of community.

The design of the user-generated content search system should prioritize ease of use and efficiency in finding relevant content. A search bar is typically placed prominently at the top of the page to enable users to input their search queries. The search interface should be visually distinct and easily noticeable to encourage users to utilize the search functionality. Additionally, a clear and concise placeholder text within the search bar helps to communicate the purpose and expected input format to the users.

User-Generated Content Sharing

User-generated content sharing refers to a UI pattern and design system that allows users to create, publish, and share their own content within a digital platform. This can include text, images, videos, and other multimedia formats. The intention is to empower users to contribute their unique perspectives, experiences, and creativity to the platform, while fostering a sense of community and collaboration.

In terms of UI patterns, user-generated content sharing typically involves providing users with intuitive and accessible tools to upload and publish their content. This can include features such as "Create" or "Upload" buttons, drag-and-drop functionality, or integrations with external services. The design system should prioritize clarity, simplicity, and consistency to ensure that users can easily understand and navigate the content sharing process.

User-Generated Content Sorting

User-generated content sorting is a UI pattern and design system that allows users to organize and arrange user-generated content based on specific criteria or preferences. This pattern provides users with the ability to sort, categorize, and filter user-created content within a digital platform or application.

With user-generated content sorting, users can personalize their experience by organizing and arranging content in a way that suits their needs and preferences. This can be achieved through various sorting options such as alphabetical order, date created, popularity, or user ratings. Sorting options can be presented to users through dropdown menus, filter panels, or toggle buttons, depending on the design and functionality of the application.

User-Generated Content Submission Form

A user-generated content submission form is a UI pattern and design system component that allows users to submit their own content, such as text, images, videos, or files, to a website or application. This form typically includes input fields and controls for users to enter and submit their content, as well as any additional information or metadata related to the submission.

The user-generated content submission form is an important feature for platforms that rely on user-generated content or community contributions. It provides a structured and standardized way for users to share their content, ensuring consistency and ease of use across different submissions.

User-Generated Content Tagging

User-generated content tagging is a UI pattern and design system that allows users to categorize and label their own content. It involves providing users with the ability to add tags or keywords to their content to make it easier to organize, search, and retrieve information.

This pattern typically includes a text input field where users can enter tags that describe the content. These tags can be words or short phrases that are relevant to the content and help to provide additional context. Users can add multiple tags by separating them with commas or pressing the enter key.

The design system for user-generated content tagging should take into account various considerations. Firstly, it should provide clear instructions or prompts to guide users on how to use the tagging feature effectively. This can be achieved through placeholder text or tooltip messages that explain the purpose and benefits of tagging.

Secondly, the design system should allow for easy editing and management of tags. Users should be able to delete or modify tags they have created. Additionally, the system can offer suggestions or autocomplete options based on commonly used tags or existing tags in the system to assist users in tagging their content accurately.

Furthermore, user-generated content tagging can provide valuable metadata that can be leveraged for search and filtering functionality. When a user searches for specific content, the system can use the associated tags to retrieve relevant results. Similarly, users can filter content by selecting tags from a list or using a tag cloud to visualize popular tags.

In conclusion, user-generated content tagging is a UI pattern and design system that empowers users to categorize and label their own content. It enhances organization, search, and retrieval capabilities by allowing users to add tags that provide additional context and metadata about the content.

User-Generated Content Trending

User-generated content (UGC) refers to any form of content, such as text, images, videos, and reviews, that is created by users or customers of a platform or website. This content is typically generated by individuals who voluntarily contribute their thoughts, experiences, opinions, or creative works. UGC has become a significant trend in UI patterns and design systems, as it allows for more authentic and engaging user experiences.

One common way UGC is implemented in UI patterns is through user reviews and ratings. Many websites and apps offer a space for users to leave feedback and reviews, which can be displayed alongside product or service information. This helps potential customers make informed decisions and builds trust in the brand or platform. Additionally, user ratings can be used to create aggregate scores, which can be displayed in various UI elements, such as star ratings or percentage bars.

Another prevalent UI pattern for UGC is the inclusion of user-generated images or videos. Platforms like social media networks often incorporate photo and video uploads, allowing users to share their experiences or creative works. These images and videos can be displayed in feeds, galleries, or interactive elements, enhancing the visual appeal and personalization of the platform.

UGC can also be utilized in UI patterns for content curation and discovery. Websites may incorporate features that allow users to create and share their own collections or playlists of content, such as articles, videos, or music. These collections can then be recommended or shared with others, creating a sense of community and encouraging user engagement.

When designing UI patterns and design systems that incorporate UGC, it is essential to consider usability and moderation. Providing clear guidelines and interfaces for users to create and manage their content helps maintain quality and relevance. Additionally, implementing moderation features, such as reporting or flagging options, allows for the management of inappropriate or harmful UGC.

User-Generated Content (UGC) Display

User-generated content (UGC) display is a UI pattern and design system that allows users to contribute their own content to a website or application. It provides a platform for users to share their thoughts, ideas, opinions, images, videos, and other forms of content with the community. UGC display is commonly seen in social media sites, forums, blogs, review platforms, and other interactive platforms that foster user engagement.

The goal of UGC display is to create an inclusive and interactive environment where users can actively participate and contribute to the content. It promotes authenticity, user engagement, and user-generated value, making the website or application more dynamic and engaging.

In terms of UI patterns and design system, UGC display involves the design and layout of elements that showcase user-generated content. This includes features such as comment sections, user profiles, rating systems, submission forms, and content feeds. The design should be intuitive and user-friendly, allowing users to easily navigate and interact with the UGC display elements.

In a design system, UGC display should be consistent and cohesive with the overall visual language and brand identity. This includes the use of appropriate color schemes, typography, and imagery that align with the website or application's style. The UGC display elements should be responsive and adaptable to different screen sizes and devices to ensure accessibility and a seamless user experience.

Furthermore, UGC display should incorporate moderation features to ensure the content shared is appropriate, respectful, and compliant with community guidelines. This may include automated filters, flagging systems, and user reporting mechanisms to prevent the spread of offensive or harmful content.

In conclusion, user-generated content display is an essential UI pattern and design system that fosters user engagement, community participation, and content diversity. It provides a platform for users to share their thoughts and experiences, creating a more interactive and dynamic website or application. By incorporating UGC display in a consistent and user-friendly manner, designers can encourage active user participation and enhance the overall user experience.

User-Generated Content (UGC)

User-Generated Content (UGC) refers to any form of content that is created, submitted, or shared by users or community members on a website, platform, or application. It is an essential component of UI patterns and design systems as it allows individuals to actively engage with and contribute to the overall user experience. UGC can include a wide range of content types such as text, images, videos, reviews, comments, ratings, and more.

In the context of UI patterns and design systems, UGC serves as a valuable asset as it provides real and authentic content that enhances the credibility and relevance of a platform. It not only enriches the overall user experience but also fosters a sense of community and collaboration among users.

User-Generated Content Voting

The user-generated content voting UI pattern is a design system that allows users to interact with and contribute to the content on a platform through voting and rating. This pattern typically consists of a user interface component where users can submit their opinions or feedback on specific pieces of content by either upvoting or downvoting. The purpose of the user-generated content voting pattern is to gauge the popularity and quality of content based on the collective opinions of the user community. It empowers users to have a voice in the platform and helps surface the most relevant and valuable content to the forefront. The design of this pattern revolves around simplicity and ease of use. Typically, the voting interface includes two buttons, one for upvoting and the other for downvoting. These buttons are often represented by icons or symbols that convey their respective actions. Clicking on the upvote button increases the vote count of the content, while clicking on the downvote button decreases it. The user-generated content voting pattern can be implemented in various ways, depending on the platform's specific requirements and constraints. For instance, it can be used in conjunction with a comment section, allowing users to vote on individual comments to determine their relevance or helpfulness. Alternatively, it can be applied to user-generated reviews, where users can rate the overall quality of a product or service. From a design system perspective, it is important to consider the visual hierarchy and placement of the voting component within the overall layout. The voting buttons should be prominent enough to capture the attention of users, but not overly dominant as to distract from the content itself. Additionally, clear visual cues should be provided to indicate the user's own vote status and the overall vote count for each piece of content. It is worth noting that the user-generated content voting pattern can be enhanced with additional features and functionality, such as sorting or filtering options based on vote count or time. These enhancements can provide users with more control over their content consumption and improve their overall experience on the platform. Overall, the user-generated content voting pattern is an effective way to engage users, encourage user participation, and surface the most valuable content within a platform. By providing users with a means to voice their opinions and contribute to the community's decision-making process, this pattern fosters a sense of ownership and collaboration among users.>

348

User-Generated Quizzes

Verification Form

A UI pattern is a recurring solution to a common user interface problem that is proven to be effective and efficient. It provides a way to standardize design elements and interactions, making them more familiar and intuitive to users. UI patterns are often used in the development of design systems, which are comprehensive collections of predefined styles, components, and guidelines that ensure consistency and coherence across an entire product or brand.

A design system, on the other hand, is a set of interconnected rules, constraints, and principles that guide the design and development of a user interface. It encompasses various aspects of design, including visual style, layout, typography, color palette, and interaction patterns. A design system acts as a single source of truth for design decisions, promoting efficiency, scalability, and collaboration among designers and developers.

Vertical Navigation

A vertical navigation is a user interface pattern and design system element that organizes and displays website or application menus in a vertical orientation. Vertical navigation is commonly used in user interfaces to provide users with easy access to different sections or pages of a website or application. It typically appears as a list or stack of links displayed vertically on the left or right side of the screen. In terms of design systems, vertical navigation is a standardized component that ensures consistency and usability across different web pages or screens. It helps users navigate through the content in an intuitive and efficient way. From a visual perspective, vertical navigation can vary in appearance. It can be designed as a simple text-based list with hyperlinks, or it can include icons or other visual cues to enhance usability and aesthetics. The choice of design depends on the overall style and branding of the website or application. When using vertical navigation in a design system, it's essential to adhere to certain guidelines to ensure consistency. The spacing, alignment, and sizing of the navigation elements should follow the design system's rules. Consistent typography and color usage also contribute to a harmonious user experience. Vertical navigation can benefit both users and designers. Users appreciate the convenience of having quick access to different sections of a website or application. Designers, on the other hand, can rely on vertical navigation as a familiar and effective pattern that helps structure and organize content. In conclusion, vertical navigation is a user interface pattern and design system element that arranges menus in a vertical orientation. It is a widely used and versatile component that improves navigation and enhances the overall user experience. Its consistent implementation in design systems ensures usability and design coherence across different screens and pages.

Video Backgrounds

A video background is a UI pattern used in web design to enhance the visual appeal and engage users by displaying a video as the background of a webpage. It is a design element integrated into a design system that provides a dynamic and immersive experience for the users. Video backgrounds can be used to showcase a product, create a certain mood or atmosphere, or simply add an element of motion and interest to a webpage. They can be found in various types of websites, including landing pages, portfolios, and promotional sites. To implement a video background in HTML, the tag is used. This tag allows the insertion of a video file that plays automatically when the webpage loads. The tag has several attributes that can be utilized to customize the video background, such as specifying the video source, controlling playback options, and setting the dimensions and position of the video. To ensure a seamless and optimized user experience, it is important to consider a few best practices when using video backgrounds. First, it is essential to optimize the video file size and format to improve page load time and reduce bandwidth usage. This can be done by compressing the video file using appropriate video codecs and reducing unnecessary details, such as resolution and frame rate. Second, it is important to ensure that the video background does not distract or overpower the webpage content. Adding a translucent overlay or reducing the volume of the video can help maintain a balance between the background and foreground elements. Finally, video backgrounds should be used judiciously and purposefully. They should align with the overall design and brand identity of the website and contribute to the overall user experience. Careful consideration should be given to the intended message and target audience to ensure the video background effectively conveys the desired information or emotion. In conclusion, video backgrounds are a captivating UI pattern that can enhance the visual appeal and engagement of a webpage. When implemented thoughtfully and optimized effectively, they can provide an immersive and dynamic experience for users, contributing to the overall aesthetic and user experience of a website.

Video Conferencing

Video Conferencing is a user interface pattern and design system that facilitates real-time audio and video communication between two or more participants located in different physical locations. It enables individuals or groups to interact and collaborate remotely, replicating the experience of face-to-face meetings through the use of cameras, microphones, and network connectivity.

Within the context of UI patterns, Video Conferencing encompasses various elements and components that work together to create a seamless and intuitive user experience. These include:

The Video Window: This is the core component of the Video Conferencing pattern, displaying the live video feeds of participants. It provides a visual representation of each participant, allowing users to see and observe the facial expressions, body language, and non-verbal cues during the conversation. The video window can be optimized for different screen sizes and orientations, ensuring a responsive design that adapts to various devices.

The Audio Controls: Effective audio communication is crucial in Video Conferencing. The UI pattern includes controls for adjusting the volume, muting and unmuting the microphone, and selecting different audio input and output devices. These controls are intuitive and easily accessible, enabling participants to manage their audio settings effortlessly.

The Chat Feature: Video Conferencing often incorporates a text-based chat feature alongside the video and audio components. This allows participants to send instant messages in real-time, facilitating additional communication and collaboration. The chat feature can include features like message history, emojis, and file sharing to enhance the overall experience.

Additionally, the UI pattern of Video Conferencing may include features such as screen sharing, recording capabilities, participant management (e.g., inviting, removing, or muting participants), and collaborative tools (e.g., whiteboard or document sharing).

Overall, the Video Conferencing UI pattern and design system aim to replicate the experience of physical meetings by combining visual and audio elements, as well as other collaboration tools to create an immersive and interactive environment for remote communication and collaboration.

Video Recording

A video recording is a UI pattern and design system element that allows users to capture, store, and playback video content. It enables users to create engaging visual content and share it with others. The video recording feature typically consists of a visual interface with controls for starting, stopping, and managing the recording process.

With the video recording UI pattern, users can initiate the recording by pressing a designated button or icon. Once the recording begins, users can preview the video in real-time, ensuring that they capture the desired content. The interface may also provide additional options such as adjusting the recording quality, choosing a specific camera or microphone, or setting a timer for automatic stoppage.

Virtual Events

Virtual Events are a type of user interface (UI) pattern and design system that enable users to engage in interactive, virtual experiences. These events replicate the aspects of in-person events by leveraging digital platforms and technologies.

Virtual events offer a wide range of features and functionalities to enhance user engagement and facilitate communication and collaboration. They can be designed for various purposes such as conferences, webinars, workshops, trade shows, and social gatherings. The design system for virtual events includes a set of guidelines, components, and UI patterns that ensure consistency and seamless interaction across different modules and screens.

Virtual Reality (VR) Interface

A Virtual Reality (VR) interface refers to the user interface design and patterns specifically tailored for interacting with digital content in a virtual reality environment. This type of interface aims to create a seamless and immersive experience for users who are engaged in a virtual world. In VR interfaces, users typically wear a head-mounted display (HMD) that provides a 360-degree view of the virtual environment. The HMD may also include sensors that track the user's head movements, allowing them to look around and interact with objects in the virtual space. Additionally, VR interfaces often incorporate other input devices such as controllers or handheld devices to enable user interaction. One key aspect of VR interface design is the concept of presence, which refers to the feeling of being physically present in the virtual environment. Designers strive to create realistic and immersive virtual worlds that simulate real-world physics and interactions. This includes details such as 3D spatial audio, haptic feedback, and accurate physics simulations. Given the immersive nature of VR, interface design patterns need to consider the limitations and challenges of the medium. For example, text-based interfaces may not be the most effective way to convey information in VR due to potential readability issues or limited field of view. Instead, designers often rely on visual cues, icons, and spatial positioning to guide users' attention and convey information. Another important consideration in VR interface design is user comfort and safety. Users can potentially experience motion sickness or discomfort if the content does not align with their physical movements. Designers must carefully consider factors such as locomotion techniques, comfort settings, and usability guidelines to mitigate these issues. A design system for VR interfaces would encompass a set of guidelines, patterns, and components that define the visual and interactive elements of the user interface. It would provide consistency in the appearance and behavior of VR applications, allowing users to quickly understand and navigate the virtual space. In conclusion, a VR interface refers to the design and patterns specific to virtual reality environments. It aims to provide users with an immersive and seamless experience by incorporating realistic physics, spatial audio, and visual cues. A design system for VR interfaces establishes guidelines and components to ensure consistency and usability across VR applications.

Virtual Tours

Virtual Tours are a UI pattern and design system that allows users to explore and experience a physical space remotely through a digital platform. These tours typically involve a collection of panoramic or 360-degree images that users can navigate and interact with using various UI components. Using Virtual Tours, users can virtually navigate through different areas of a physical space, such as a museum, a real estate property, a hotel, or even a city. The tours are created by capturing multiple images from different viewpoints and stitching them together to create a seamless panoramic experience. One of the key components of a Virtual Tour is the interface that enables users to interact with the tour. This typically includes UI elements such as navigation controls, hotspots, and information overlays. Navigation controls allow users to move between different viewpoints or areas within the tour. Hotspots are interactive markers placed within the tour that provide additional information or trigger specific actions when clicked. Information overlays display contextual information about the space or objects within the tour. Virtual Tours are designed to provide users with a realistic and immersive experience. Users can explore the space at their own pace, choosing which areas to visit and what details to focus on. This gives them a sense of control and agency, similar to physically being in the space. From a design system perspective, Virtual Tours typically follow a consistent visual style and interaction patterns. This ensures a cohesive and familiar experience for users, regardless of the specific tour they are accessing. The design system may include guidelines for the layout and placement of UI components, color schemes, typography, and overall branding. In summary, Virtual Tours are a UI pattern and design system that enable users to remotely explore and experience physical spaces through a digital platform. They provide a realistic and immersive experience, allowing users to navigate and interact with panoramic images using various UI components.>

Visitor Feedback Form

UI patterns refer to commonly used solutions or design principles that address recurring problems or challenges in user interface design. These patterns serve as a framework or guide for designers and developers to create consistent, predictable, and intuitive user experiences.

A UI pattern is a proven and tested way of organizing and presenting information, interactions, and functionality in a user interface. It helps designers and developers achieve familiarity, efficiency, and usability by providing a set of standardized elements and guidelines.

Visitor Sign-In Form

A Visitor Sign-In Form is a UI pattern that allows individuals to provide their personal information upon entering a physical space, such as a building, office, or event. This form serves multiple purposes, including verifying the identity of visitors, maintaining records for security purposes, and facilitating communication or follow-up if necessary. The Visitor Sign-In Form typically consists of a series of input fields where visitors can enter their name, contact information, reason for visit, and any additional notes or comments. These fields may include text input, dropdown menus, checkboxes, or radio buttons, depending on the specific requirements of the form. The design and layout of the Visitor Sign-In Form should prioritize ease of use and clear communication. It's important to clearly label each input field to indicate the type of information required, provide example or placeholder text when appropriate, and include any necessary validation or error messaging to ensure accurate data entry. In terms of placement within a UI or design system, the Visitor Sign-In Form should be prominently displayed at the entrance or reception area of the physical space. It should be easily accessible and visible to visitors, with clear instructions or signage to guide them through the process. When it comes to the HTML implementation of the Visitor Sign-In Form, it can be structured using a <form> element to wrap the entire form, with each input field contained within a element. The element can include a or tag to provide additional styling or formatting if desired. The input fields themselves can be implemented using various HTML input types, such as , , , , and so on. Overall, the Visitor Sign-In Form is a crucial component of a design system for physical spaces, as it enables efficient and secure visitor management. Its implementation in HTML should focus on clear communication, ease of use, and effective data entry.></form>

Visual Effects Transitions

Visual effects transitions in the context of UI patterns and design systems refer to the various types of animations and motion effects that are applied to user interfaces to enhance the user experience and provide a smooth transition between different states or screens. These transitions help to create a seamless and engaging user interface by adding subtle visual cues and feedback to guide the user's interaction with the interface. Transitions can be categorized into different types based on their purpose and behavior. Some common types of visual effects transitions include: 1. Entrance/exit transitions: These transitions are used to animate the appearance and disappearance of UI elements as the user interacts with the interface. They provide a sense of continuity and help to create a more dynamic and interactive experience. 2. State transitions: State transitions are used to animate changes in the state or appearance of UI elements. For example, when a button is clicked, it may change color or size using a transition effect to indicate that it has been activated. 3. Navigation transitions: These transitions are used to animate the movement between different screens or sections within an application or website. They help to create a sense of hierarchy and spatial awareness by visually connecting related content and providing a smooth transition between different views. 4. Feedback transitions: Feedback transitions are used to provide visual feedback to the user when performing an action or operation. For example, when a form is submitted, a loading animation or success message can be displayed to indicate that the action is being processed. Design systems often include predefined visual effects transitions as part of their component libraries. These transitions are typically designed to be reusable and consistent across different interfaces and applications. They are usually implemented using CSS or JavaScript animations, and can be customized and tweaked to fit the specific design and branding requirements. In conclusion, visual effects transitions play a crucial role in enhancing the user experience by adding motion and animation to user interfaces. They provide subtle cues and feedback that improve usability and engagement, and are an important component of a well-designed UI pattern and design system.

Visual Storytelling

Visual storytelling in the context of UI patterns and design system refers to the practice of using visual elements and techniques to convey a narrative or message within a user interface. It involves the strategic use of imagery, color, typography, and other visual elements to guide users and communicate information effectively.

In UI design, visual storytelling helps to create a cohesive and engaging user experience by providing users with a clear understanding of the interface's purpose, layout, and functionality. It goes beyond simply arranging elements on a screen; it aims to guide users through a specific sequence of actions or provide them with a story-like experience.

Voice Assistants For Accessibility

A voice assistant for accessibility is a user interface pattern and design system that utilizes voice recognition technology to provide assistance and support to individuals with disabilities. It is designed to be accessible and inclusive, allowing users to interact with digital devices and applications using their voice instead of traditional input methods such as keyboards or touchscreens.

By enabling users to control and navigate through digital interfaces using spoken commands, voice assistants for accessibility aim to remove barriers and provide equal access to information and services for individuals with disabilities. These voice assistants can be integrated into various devices and platforms, including smartphones, computers, and smart home devices, making them widely accessible and versatile.

Voice Command Navigation

Voice Command Navigation is a user interface (UI) pattern that allows users to navigate through a system or application using spoken commands. It leverages voice recognition technology to interpret and understand the user's verbal instructions, enabling them to interact with the UI without the need for traditional input methods such as typing or clicking.

With Voice Command Navigation, users can perform various actions, access different features, and navigate between screens or sections by simply speaking their commands. This feature is particularly useful for individuals with disabilities or those who prefer a hands-free approach to interacting with technology.

Voice Commands

Voice commands refer to a user interface (UI) pattern that allows users to interact with a system or device using spoken language. This pattern is particularly prevalent in design systems that incorporate voice recognition technology. Voice commands enable users to perform various actions or tasks by speaking specific phrases or commands. The system then processes the spoken input and translates it into actionable commands. This UI pattern is often used in smart speakers, virtual assistants, and other voice-activated devices. When designing voice command interfaces, it is essential to consider various factors to ensure usability and effectiveness. First and foremost, the system must accurately recognize and interpret the user's spoken input. Natural language processing (NLP) algorithms and machine learning techniques are typically employed to achieve this. Additionally, voice command UIs should provide clear and intuitive feedback to the user. This can be achieved through audio and visual cues to indicate that the system is actively listening or processing the command. Feedback should also be given to inform the user of the command's execution or any errors that may have occurred. Furthermore, voice command UIs should support a range of user interactions. This includes the ability to navigate through different sections or functionalities, perform specific actions, and retrieve information from the system. Providing a comprehensive set of voice commands and ensuring they are easy to remember and use is crucial for an effective voice command UI. Designers must also consider the context in which the voice command interface will be used. Factors such as ambient noise, user location, and language preferences should be taken into account when designing the system's speech recognition capabilities. In summary, voice commands are a UI pattern that allows users to interact with a system or device using spoken language. They rely on speech recognition technology to translate spoken input into actionable commands. Designing effective voice command UIs involves accurately interpreting user input, providing clear feedback, and supporting a wide range of user interactions. Considering the context in which the system will be used is also essential for a successful voice command interface.>

Voice Feedback For Accessibility

Voice feedback for accessibility refers to the use of spoken responses or audio cues provided by a user interface (UI) system or design pattern to assist individuals with disabilities in navigating and interacting with digital content. This feature is designed to accommodate users who are blind or visually impaired, as well as those with certain motor or cognitive limitations that make it difficult to rely solely on visual cues.

When it comes to creating UI patterns and design systems that are inclusive and accessible, voice feedback plays a crucial role. By integrating spoken responses and audio cues into the user experience, designers can ensure that individuals with different abilities are able to understand and interact with the interface effectively.

Voice Feedback For Confirmation

UI patterns refer to reusable design solutions that address common user interface challenges and provide a consistent and intuitive experience for users. They are a set of best practices and guidelines that help designers and developers create interfaces that are visually appealing, functional, and user-friendly. UI patterns are crucial in the development of a design system, which is a collection of reusable components, guidelines, and resources that ensure consistency and efficiency in creating user interfaces. A design system provides a set of rules and guidelines that govern how different components should be used, how they should look and behave, and how they should be implemented. Design systems are essential for large-scale projects or organizations with multiple products, as they help maintain brand consistency and improve overall user experience. They streamline the design and development process by providing a library of pre-designed components that can be easily integrated into different interfaces. UI patterns and design systems work hand in hand to create a cohesive and standardized user experience. UI patterns provide the individual design solutions for specific UI challenges, while the design system ensures that these patterns are implemented consistently across different interfaces. By following UI patterns and using a design system, designers and developers can save time and effort in the design and development process. They don't have to reinvent the wheel for every interface element, as they can rely on established patterns and components from the design system. This results in a more efficient workflow and a more consistent user experience. In conclusion, UI patterns are reusable design solutions that address common user interface challenges, while design systems provide a set of guidelines and resources for creating consistent and efficient interfaces. By incorporating UI patterns and design systems into the design and development process, designers and developers can save time, maintain brand consistency, and enhance the overall user experience.

Voice Feedback For Errors

UI patterns refer to established design solutions for common user interface challenges. These patterns provide a standardized approach to user interface design, allowing designers and developers to create consistent and intuitive user experiences across different applications and platforms. A design system, on the other hand, is a comprehensive set of guidelines, components, and assets that define the visual and interactive design of a product. A design system ensures consistency and efficiency in design and development by providing a centralized source of truth for all design-related decisions and assets. Voice feedback for errors is a UI pattern and design system component that provides users with spoken feedback when they make errors or encounter issues while interacting with a user interface. Instead of relying solely on visual cues, voice feedback helps improve accessibility and user experience by providing additional auditory information. Voice feedback for errors can be implemented in various ways, depending on the specific needs of the user interface and the target audience. Some common approaches include: 1. Error message narration: When a user encounters an error, a voice component would narrate the error message or provide auditory cues to help the user understand the issue. This can be especially useful for users with visual impairments or those who prefer auditory feedback. 2. Audio confirmation: When a user successfully completes an action or submits a form, voice feedback can provide an audio confirmation message. This helps to reinforce the user's actions and assures them that their input or request has been successfully processed. By incorporating voice feedback for errors, designers and developers can create more inclusive and accessible user interfaces. However, it is essential to consider the following best practices when implementing this UI pattern: 1. Clear and concise messages: Voice feedback should provide clear and concise instructions or error messages to guide users in resolving the issue. Avoid lengthy or confusing statements that may overwhelm or confuse the user. 2. Volume control: Provide users with the option to control the volume or mute the voice feedback. This allows users to customize their experience based on their preferences and environment. Voice feedback for errors enhances the user experience by providing users with an additional modality for interacting with the interface. Whether it is narrating error messages or confirming successful actions, voice feedback helps to improve accessibility and usability. By integrating this UI pattern and design system component, designers and developers can create more inclusive and user-friendly interfaces that meet the needs of a diverse user base.

Voice Feedback For Feedback

A UI pattern refers to a recurring design solution that is widely used and helps in addressing common design problems in user interfaces. It is a set of best practices that have been proven to be effective in creating user-friendly and intuitive interfaces. UI patterns are commonly used in design systems, which are a collection of reusable components, rules, and guidelines that define the overall look and feel of a product's user interface. These design systems ensure consistency and coherence in the user experience across different platforms and devices. In the context of UI patterns, each pattern has a specific purpose and solves a particular problem in the user interface. Examples of common UI patterns include navigation menus, search bars, and notification alerts. These patterns have been extensively tested and found to enhance user engagement and satisfaction. Design systems are essential for larger projects with multiple designers and developers working together. They provide a shared language and a common understanding of how the interface should look and behave. By using a design system, teams can save time and effort, as they can easily create and reuse components that have already been designed and tested. One of the key benefits of using UI patterns and design systems is that they enhance usability and make the user interface more intuitive. By following established patterns, designers can leverage users' existing mental models and expectations, making it easier for them to interact with the interface. This results in a more enjoyable and efficient user experience. In conclusion, UI patterns are recurring design solutions that address common problems in user interface design, while design systems are collections of reusable components and guidelines that ensure consistency and coherence in the overall user experience. By utilizing these patterns and systems, designers can create more user-friendly and intuitive interfaces, leading to increased user satisfaction and engagement. >

Voice Feedback For Navigation

A navigation system refers to the user interface patterns and design system that are utilized for organizing and providing easy access to the various pages, sections, and features within a website or application. It serves as a roadmap for users to navigate and explore the content and functionality of the system.

In the context of UI patterns, navigation commonly consists of a set of menus, links, or buttons that are strategically placed and labeled to guide users through the system. It helps users comprehend the structure and hierarchy of the overall system while allowing them to easily switch between different sections or pages. The design of the navigation system should be intuitive, visually consistent, and seamlessly integrated into the overall user interface.

Voice Feedback

A UI pattern refers to a recurring solution or approach used in user interface design to address common design problems. It is a reusable solution that helps in creating a consistent and visually appealing user experience across different parts of a website or application. UI patterns are based on research and established best practices in the field of user experience design. They serve as a guide for designers and developers to create intuitive and user-friendly interfaces. By following these patterns, designers can ensure that their designs are familiar and easy to use for the users. A design system, on the other hand, is a collection of reusable components, guidelines, and assets that are used to build and maintain a consistent visual and interactive experience across various platforms and devices. It encompasses a set of design principles, rules, and standards that define how different components and elements should be used in the user interface. A design system helps in promoting consistency, efficiency, and scalability in design and development processes. It provides a common language and framework for designers and developers to collaborate effectively. By using a design system, teams can ensure that their products have a cohesive and unified look and feel, regardless of who is working on them. In summary, UI patterns and design systems are crucial elements in the field of user interface design. UI patterns provide reusable solutions to common design problems, while design systems facilitate consistency and efficiency in design and development processes. By leveraging these concepts, designers and developers can create well-crafted and user-friendly interfaces that enhance the overall user experience.

Voice Notes

Voice Notes is a UI pattern commonly used in design systems to allow users to record and store audio messages. This pattern provides a convenient and efficient way for users to create and save voice recordings within an interface. Voice Notes typically consist of a button or icon that triggers the recording functionality. When the user clicks or taps on this button, the device's microphone is activated, and the user can begin speaking to record their message. Once the recording is complete, the Voice Notes pattern often includes playback controls that allow the user to listen to the recorded message. This may include a play button to start and pause playback, as well as a slider or progress bar to navigate through the recording. In addition to playback controls, Voice Notes may also include options for editing or deleting the recorded message. These options allow the user to trim or enhance the recording and manage their stored voice notes. Voice Notes are particularly useful in scenarios where textual input may be cumbersome or time-consuming. For example, in messaging applications, users can quickly record and send voice messages instead of typing out long texts. In note-taking or productivity apps, users can easily dictate ideas or reminders instead of typing them out manually. From a design system perspective, incorporating the Voice Notes pattern allows for consistency and familiarity across different interfaces and platforms. The design system provides a set of guidelines and components that ensure the Voice Notes pattern is implemented consistently, making it easier for users to understand and interact with voice recording functionality regardless of the application or device they are using. Overall, Voice Notes enhance the user experience by providing a convenient and efficient method for recording and storing audio messages within an interface. The pattern allows users to easily create, listen to, and manage voice recordings, making it a valuable addition to any design system.

Voice Search

Voice search, in the context of UI patterns and design systems, refers to the ability for users to search for information or perform actions on a digital platform using voice commands instead of typing or clicking. It is a user interface (UI) pattern that leverages voice recognition technology to enable hands-free interaction with a system. With voice search, users can simply speak their queries or commands, and the system will interpret their voice input to generate relevant results or trigger specific actions. This form of interaction can be especially convenient in situations where users have limited mobility or when they are occupied with other tasks and cannot use their hands to interact with a device. From a design system perspective, incorporating voice search requires careful consideration of the following elements: 1. Voice Recognition: The system should utilize advanced algorithms and technologies to accurately recognize and interpret users' voice commands or queries. This involves analyzing the input for relevant keywords, context, and intent to generate the desired output. 2. Natural Language Processing (NLP): The design system should incorporate NLP techniques to understand the meaning and context behind users' voice inputs. This enables the system to provide more accurate and context-aware responses or actions. 3. Error Handling: Since voice recognition systems are not perfect, there should be a mechanism in place to handle errors or misunderstandings. The system should be able to provide suggestions or clarifications to users in case their voice input cannot be correctly interpreted. 4. Feedback and Confirmation: It is essential to provide users with feedback on their voice inputs, ensuring that the system recognized their commands correctly. Visual or auditory cues can be used to confirm the action or query initiated by the user, providing reassurance and preventing potential errors or misunderstandings. Overall, voice search is a UI pattern that enhances the accessibility and ease of use of a digital platform. By enabling users to interact with the system using their voices, it offers a more convenient and intuitive way to search for information, perform tasks, and navigate through the interface.

Voice search is a hands-free interaction method that enables users to search for information using their voice commands.

It utilizes voice recognition and natural language processing technologies to interpret users' queries and generate relevant results or trigger actions.

Voice User Interface (VUI)

A Voice User Interface (VUI) is a design pattern and system that allows users to interact with a computer or device using voice commands and natural language instead of traditional graphical user interfaces (GUIs). It enables users to perform tasks, retrieve information, and control various functionalities through spoken language. VUI design focuses on creating a seamless and intuitive experience for users, leveraging advancements in speech recognition, natural language processing, and machine learning technologies. It aims to understand and interpret user commands accurately, responding with appropriate and meaningful feedback. VUIs can be found in various applications, including virtual assistants, voice-controlled devices, and speech-based navigation systems. The primary goal of VUI design is to provide users with a more efficient and hands-free means of interacting with technology. It eliminates the need for physical input devices such as keyboards or touchscreens, allowing for a more natural and accessible user experience. By employing conversational interfaces, VUIs aim to mimic human-like interactions and provide a more personalized and engaging experience. One key aspect of VUI design is the concept of dialogue management, which involves handling user requests and providing appropriate responses. Designers must carefully consider the system's capabilities and limitations to ensure an optimal user experience. Clear and concise prompts, as well as context-aware responses, are essential to guide users effectively through the conversation flow. Another important consideration in VUI design is error handling and recovery. Since voice-based interactions are prone to errors, designers must anticipate and handle situations where the system misinterprets or fails to recognize the user's intent. Providing clear error messages and offering alternatives or suggestions can help mitigate frustration and enhance usability. Overall, VUIs present a unique set of challenges and opportunities in UI design. They require a deep understanding of user behavior, language patterns, and system capabilities. By leveraging the power of speech recognition and natural language processing technologies, VUIs provide users with a more convenient, accessible, and intuitive way of interacting with technology. In conclusion, a Voice User Interface (VUI) is a design pattern and system that enables users to interact with computers and devices using voice commands and natural language. Through efficient dialogue management and error handling, VUIs provide a seamless and intuitive conversational experience for users.

Voice And Video Calls

Voice and video calls are user interface patterns that allow two or more individuals to communicate with each other in real-time. These patterns are commonly used in various communication platforms and are essential for maintaining effective and efficient remote communication.

In a UI design system, voice and video calls are typically represented by icons or buttons that users can click on to initiate a call. These icons are usually placed in the chat or messaging interface, allowing users to seamlessly transition from text-based conversations to audio or video conversations.

Voice-Controlled Assistant

Voice-Activated Home Automation

Voice-activated Home Automation is a UI pattern and design system that enables users to control and interact with various devices and systems in their homes using voice commands.

This technology utilizes speech recognition and natural language processing to understand and interpret user inputs, allowing for seamless and convenient control of connected devices. The primary goal of Voice-activated Home Automation is to simplify the user experience by eliminating the need for physical interaction with devices. Instead of manually pressing buttons or navigating through menus, users can simply speak commands or questions to control their smart home appliances, entertainment systems, lighting, security systems, and more. Voice-activated Home Automation typically includes a voice assistant or virtual assistant, such as Amazon Alexa, Google Assistant, or Apple Siri, which acts as the intermediary between the user and the connected devices. These assistants are equipped with voice recognition capabilities and are trained to understand natural language commands, making the experience more conversational and intuitive. Designing for Voice-activated Home Automation involves creating a user-friendly interface that guides users through the process of setting up and controlling their smart home devices using voice commands. The design system should consider factors such as voice feedback, confirmation prompts, error handling, and contextual suggestions to ensure a seamless and responsive user experience. In terms of UI patterns, Voice-activated Home Automation may include features such as voice-enabled buttons, voice commands displayed on the screen, dialogue boxes for confirmation or error messages, and voice-controlled navigation menus. The design system should prioritize simplicity, clarity, and accessibility, as users may have varying levels of familiarity with voice-activated technology. Overall, Voice-activated Home Automation aims to enhance the convenience and accessibility of controlling smart home devices by leveraging the power of voice commands and natural language processing. By eliminating the need for physical interaction, this technology offers users an intuitive and effortless way to manage their homes and simplify their daily routines.

Voice-Controlled Accessibility Features

Voice-controlled accessibility features refer to user interface (UI) patterns and design systems that enable individuals with disabilities to interact with digital devices, applications, and websites using their voice commands. These features allow users to perform various tasks, navigate through different user interfaces, and access content on digital platforms by simply speaking.

Implementing voice-controlled accessibility features involves integrating speech recognition technology into the UI design. The system recognizes and interprets the user's spoken words or commands, converting them into actionable tasks or interactions within the digital environment. This technology enables individuals with motor disabilities, visual impairments, or other accessibility needs to overcome barriers in traditional input methods, such as keyboards or touchscreens.

Voice-Controlled Entertainment

Voice-controlled entertainment is a UI pattern and design system that allows users to interact with entertainment devices or applications using voice commands. This technology enables users to control various aspects of their entertainment experience, such as playing music or videos, adjusting volume, navigating menus, and even searching for specific content, all through natural spoken language.

By integrating voice control into entertainment interfaces, users can enjoy a hands-free and more seamless experience. This is particularly beneficial in scenarios where manual control is inconvenient or impossible, such as when cooking, exercising, or operating devices from a distance. Voice-controlled entertainment utilizes speech recognition technology to identify and interpret user commands, converting them into actions that the system can perform.

Voice-Controlled Gaming

Voice-controlled gaming is a user interface (UI) pattern and design system that allows users to interact with a video game using voice commands. Instead of using traditional input methods such as a keyboard, mouse, or controller, players can use their voice to control and interact with the game. Voice-controlled gaming relies on voice recognition technology to interpret and understand the spoken commands of the player. The design system includes various commands and responses that are programmed into the game, allowing the player to perform actions, navigate menus, and interact with characters or objects within the game world. One of the key benefits of voice-controlled gaming is the potential for a more immersive and intuitive gaming experience. By using natural language and vocal expressions, players can engage with the game in a more fluid and expressive manner. This can enhance the realism and emotional engagement in storytelling games, and also provide more precise control in action-oriented games. However, voice-controlled gaming also presents challenges for designers and developers. Voice recognition technology is not perfect and can be prone to errors, especially in noisy environments or with accents and dialects that differ from the training data. Designers must account for these limitations and provide alternative input methods or fallback options to ensure a smooth and accessible gameplay experience for all players. In terms of UI patterns, voice-controlled gaming often includes audio and visual feedback to guide the player and provide confirmation of their commands. This can include text or visual prompts on the screen, as well as voice responses from characters or narrators within the game. These feedback mechanisms help players understand how their commands are being interpreted by the game and provide a sense of control and agency. In conclusion, voice-controlled gaming is a UI pattern and design system that allows players to interact with video games using voice commands. It offers the potential for a more immersive and intuitive gameplay experience, but also presents challenges related to voice recognition technology and accessibility. The inclusion of audio and visual feedback helps guide players and confirm the interpretation of their commands.

Voice-Controlled Home Security

Voice-controlled home security refers to a system that allows users to control and monitor their home security features using voice commands. This technology integrates voice recognition capabilities with the home security system, enabling users to interact with their security devices hands-free.

The user interface (UI) patterns and design system for voice-controlled home security aim to create a seamless and intuitive experience for users. The design focuses on enabling users to easily navigate and interact with the system using their voice, reducing the reliance on physical interfaces such as buttons or touch screens.

Voice-Controlled Smart Appliances

Voice-controlled smart appliances refer to household devices that can be operated and controlled through voice commands. These appliances utilize voice recognition technology to interpret and execute user instructions, offering a more convenient and user-friendly experience. UI patterns and design systems for voice-controlled smart appliances prioritize simplicity and ease of use. The goal is to create an intuitive and efficient interface that allows users to interact with their appliances using natural language. The design should minimize cognitive load and provide clear feedback to the user, ensuring a seamless and enjoyable interaction. In terms of UI patterns, voice-controlled smart appliances typically feature a "wake word" or "hotword" that activates the device when spoken. This pattern allows users to initiate commands without the need for physically pressing buttons or navigating through menus. Once the device is activated, the user can simply speak their instructions, which are then processed and executed by the appliance. Another common UI pattern is the use of voice prompts or cues to guide the user through the interaction. These prompts can help the user understand the available options, provide context, and confirm successful execution of their commands. Voice-controlled smart appliances should also provide clear and concise auditory feedback to indicate device status, such as completion of a task or an error. Design systems for voice-controlled smart appliances should aim for consistency across devices and platforms. Colors, typography, and icons should be chosen carefully to ensure readability and accessibility. Additionally, a cohesive visual language can help establish brand identity and familiarity for users. When implementing voice-controlled features, it is crucial to consider usability and accessibility. The interface should be designed to accommodate different accents, speech patterns, and languages, while also taking into account potential background noise or other environmental factors. Providing clear instructions for optimal voice input and feedback when voice commands are not recognized can help prevent frustration and improve user experience. In conclusion, voice-controlled smart appliances offer a convenient and hands-free way to interact with household devices. UI patterns and design systems for these appliances should prioritize simplicity, intuitiveness, and consistent branding. By focusing on usability and accessibility, developers can create a seamless and enjoyable user experience.

Voice-Controlled Smart Lighting

Voice-controlled Smart Lighting refers to a user interface pattern and design system that enables users to control their lighting fixtures using voice commands. It is a technology that combines the use of voice recognition with smart lighting systems to provide a hands-free and intuitive way of controlling lights.

The primary purpose of Voice-controlled Smart Lighting is to enhance user experience and convenience by eliminating the need for physical switches or manual control. Users can simply speak commands to adjust the brightness, color, or on/off state of their lights without having to interact with any physical controls. This technology is designed to simplify the process of controlling lighting fixtures, making it more accessible and user-friendly.

Voice-Controlled Thermostats

Voice-controlled thermostats are a type of user interface (UI) pattern and design system that allows users to control the temperature in their homes or buildings through voice commands instead of traditional manual controls. This technology uses speech recognition and natural language processing to interpret vocal instructions and adjust the thermostat accordingly.

As part of a larger smart home ecosystem, voice-controlled thermostats enable users to have hands-free control over their heating and cooling systems. By simply speaking commands like "increase the temperature to 75 degrees" or "set the thermostat to eco mode," users can easily adjust the climate settings without needing to physically interact with the device.

Voice-Controlled Vehicle Features

Voice-controlled vehicle features refer to the functionalities and capabilities of a vehicle that can be controlled and accessed through voice commands. These features are designed to enhance the user experience and provide a seamless and convenient way for users to interact with the vehicle's systems and controls. Voice control has become increasingly popular in the automotive industry, as it allows drivers to keep their hands on the wheel and their eyes on the road while still being able to perform various tasks and access different features. This technology uses speech recognition to interpret and understand the user's voice commands, enabling them to control various aspects of the vehicle's operations without having to manually interact with physical buttons or touchscreens. Some common voice-controlled vehicle features include: 1. Navigation: Users can simply provide voice commands to set destinations, search for points of interest, or receive turn-by-turn directions. This feature greatly enhances the driver's safety and convenience, as they can access navigation functions without taking their hands off the steering wheel. 2. Entertainment: Users can control the vehicle's audio systems, such as adjusting the volume, changing radio stations, or playing specific songs or playlists, all by using voice commands. This allows for a more enjoyable and personalized music experience while driving. 3. Phone and Messaging: Voice control enables users to make hands-free phone calls, answer or reject incoming calls, and dictate and send text messages without manually interacting with their mobile devices. By integrating with the vehicle's infotainment system, these features ensure safer communication while driving. 4. Climate Control: Voice commands can be used to adjust the temperature, fan speed, or airflow of the vehicle's climate control system. This enables users to maintain their desired comfort levels without taking their attention away from the road. 5. Vehicle Information: Users can obtain real-time vehicle information, such as current fuel levels, tire pressure, or maintenance alerts, by simply asking the vehicle through voice commands. This feature provides drivers with important updates and allows them to better monitor and manage their vehicle's status. Overall, voice-controlled vehicle features offer an intuitive and hands-free way for users to interact with their vehicles' systems and controls. They provide increased safety, convenience, and ease of use, creating a more enjoyable and user-friendly driving experience. Voice-controlled vehicle features are an essential element of modern user interface (UI) patterns and design systems. They significantly contribute to enhancing the accessibility and usability of automotive interfaces, enabling users to interact with the vehicle's functionalities using natural language commands. By seamlessly integrating voice recognition technology with the vehicle's user interface, designers create a cohesive and intuitive experience for the users.

In conclusion, voice-controlled vehicle features refer to the functionalities that can be accessed and controlled through voice commands. These features provide users with a convenient and hands-free way to interact with their vehicles, allowing for safer and more enjoyable driving experiences.

Voice-Driven Survey Analytics

Voice-driven Survey Analytics refers to the use of voice commands and natural language processing technology to collect and analyze data from surveys and feedback forms. This technology allows users to engage with survey questions and provide their responses simply by speaking, rather than typing or clicking on buttons.

As a UI pattern in the context of design systems, Voice-driven Survey Analytics involves designing the interface and interactions that facilitate the voice-driven survey experience. This includes the design of voice prompts, response options, error handling, and overall user flow.

When implementing Voice-driven Survey Analytics, it is important to consider the following design principles:

- Clear and concise voice prompts: The system should provide prompts that are easy to understand and guide the user through the survey process. The prompts should be concise and avoid ambiguity to ensure accurate responses.

- Dynamic response options: The system should dynamically adjust the available response options based on the context of the survey question. For example, if the question asks for a yes or no response, the system should only accept those specific answers and provide appropriate feedback for other inputs.

- Error recovery: Since voice recognition technology may not always accurately capture user responses, the system should be designed to handle errors and provide options for users to correct or clarify their answers.

- Privacy and data security: It is crucial to maintain the privacy and security of user data gathered through voice-driven surveys. Design should ensure that personal information is collected and stored securely, and that proper consent is obtained from users.

In summary, Voice-driven Survey Analytics leverages voice recognition technology to enhance the survey experience by allowing users to provide their responses through spoken commands. The UI patterns and design system associated with this technology focus on creating intuitive and user-friendly interfaces that guide users through the survey process, handle errors, and prioritize data privacy and security.

Voice-Enabled Settings

Voice-enabled settings are a type of user interface (UI) pattern and design system that allows users to interact with and adjust settings using voice commands instead of manual inputs. This technology can be integrated into various devices and platforms, such as smartphones, smart home assistants, or even web applications. Voice-enabled settings provide a hands-free and convenient way for users to control and modify various system preferences and options. By leveraging natural language processing and voice recognition technologies, these settings allow users to manage and customize their user experience simply by speaking commands or requests. In terms of UI patterns, voice-enabled settings often incorporate a microphone icon or a specific voice command trigger to indicate that voice inputs are accepted. When users activate the voice-enabled settings, they can speak their desired commands, which are then processed and interpreted by the system. These commands can include instructions to change display settings, adjust sound levels, enable or disable certain features, or even provide system feedback. Design systems for voice-enabled settings should consider factors such as voice command recognition accuracy, user feedback, and error handling. To ensure user satisfaction, the system should provide clear and concise feedback to acknowledge successful commands or indicate any errors encountered during voice recognition. Additionally, the design system should provide options for users to confirm or cancel certain commands to prevent unintended changes. Voice-enabled settings can significantly enhance accessibility for users with physical impairments or those who prefer a hands-free interaction. This technology allows for a more intuitive and efficient method of interacting with settings and preferences, eliminating the need for manual navigation through complex menus or options. Overall, voice-enabled settings offer users a more seamless and personalized user experience by allowing them to interact and modify system preferences using natural language commands. This UI pattern and design system leverage voice recognition technology to provide a hands-free and convenient alternative to traditional manual inputs.

Voice-Guided Cooking

Voice-guided cooking is a user interface pattern and design system that incorporates voice technology to guide users through cooking processes. It provides step-by-step instructions and assistance to users in real-time, using audio prompts and voice commands. The main aim of voice-guided cooking is to simplify and enhance the cooking experience by allowing users to follow recipes and instructions hands-free. By relying on voice commands, users can keep their hands and eyes focused on preparing the food, reducing the need for manual interactions with kitchen devices or smartphones. This UI pattern leverages natural language processing capabilities to understand and interpret user commands and queries. It can recognize and respond to voice inputs such as "What's the next step?" or "How much salt should I add?" in a conversational manner. The system provides immediate feedback or guidance, ensuring that users can proceed smoothly through the cooking process. To implement voice-guided cooking, a design system is employed to create a consistent and intuitive user experience. This system includes a set of pre-defined voice commands and responses, ensuring that users can easily navigate and interact with the cooking assistant. The design system also takes into account the context of cooking, providing tailored prompts and clarifications based on the specific recipe or task at hand. Voice-guided cooking can be integrated into various devices, such as smart speakers, kitchen appliances, or mobile applications. It has the potential to revolutionize the kitchen experience, particularly for individuals with limited mobility, visual impairments, or busy lifestyles. In conclusion, voice-guided cooking is a UI pattern and design system that leverages voice technology to provide step-by-step instructions and assistance to users while they cook. By allowing hands-free interactions and incorporating natural language processing, it simplifies the cooking process and enhances the overall user experience.

Voice-Guided Tours

Voice-guided tours refer to a user interface pattern and design system that provides audio instructions and guidance to users as they navigate through a digital platform or physical environment. These tours are designed to offer a seamless and intuitive user experience by leveraging voice commands to assist users in real-time. Voice-guided tours can be implemented in various contexts, such as mobile applications, websites, smart home devices, or even physical spaces like museums or tourist attractions. The primary purpose is to enhance user engagement and provide step-by-step guidance through complex processes or locations. In the realm of user interface patterns, voice-guided tours offer an alternative to visual cues and text-based instructions traditionally used in user interfaces. By leveraging human-like voices or synthesized speech, these tours provide a more immersive and interactive experience for users. From a design system perspective, voice-guided tours require careful consideration of the audio content's structure, tone, and clarity. The audio instructions should be concise, straightforward, and easy to understand, ensuring that users can follow them effortlessly. In addition, the design system should include mechanisms to handle different languages, accents, and speech speeds to accommodate a diverse range of users. In terms of UI design, voice-guided tours are typically triggered by specific user actions, such as a voice command, a button press, or even a proximity sensor. Once initiated, the system guides users through a series of predefined steps or prompts, offering clear and concise instructions to accomplish a particular task or explore a space. The audio content can be supplemented with visual elements like on-screen indicators or animations to create a more cohesive and multimodal experience. Overall, voice-guided tours are an innovative approach to user interface design, leveraging voice interaction to facilitate user understanding and navigation. By providing audio instructions and guidance, these tours offer an inclusive and accessible experience that can benefit both visually impaired users and those seeking a hands-free and intuitive interaction with a digital or physical environment. Voice-guided tours pave the way for more immersive and engaging interfaces, where users can rely on audio cues and voice commands to navigate, learn, or explore.

Voice-Guided Workouts

Voice-guided workouts are a type of interactive fitness experience that provides audio instructions and guidance to users during their exercise routines. This UI pattern and design system is designed to enhance the user's workout experience by giving real-time feedback and instructions, eliminating the need for visual prompts or constant monitoring of a screen.

By leveraging voice technology, voice-guided workouts offer a hands-free and eyes-free approach to fitness training. Users can follow along with their workouts while listening to audio prompts that provide step-by-step instructions, motivational cues, and additional details about each exercise. This allows users to focus on their form, pace, and breathing without the distractions of constantly looking at a device or a screen.

Voice-Powered Surveys

Voice-powered surveys are a user interface pattern that leverages voice recognition technology to collect feedback and gather user data through spoken responses. This pattern is designed to replace traditional text-based survey methods and offers a more intuitive and efficient way for users to provide their input.

By implementing voice-powered surveys, users can simply speak their answers instead of typing them out, making the survey-taking process faster and more accessible. This pattern is particularly beneficial for users who may have difficulty with traditional input methods, such as those with limited mobility or visual impairments. Additionally, it can help reduce user fatigue and improve engagement by providing a more interactive and conversational experience.

Voice-Powered Virtual Shopping Assistants

Voice-powered virtual shopping assistants are a type of user interface pattern and design system that utilize voice recognition technology to assist users in their online shopping experiences. These assistants are designed to provide a more streamlined and intuitive way for users to interact with online shopping platforms. By utilizing voice commands, users can navigate through product catalogs, search for specific items, add products to their shopping carts, and complete the purchasing process without the need for traditional keyboard and mouse inputs. The design principles behind voice-powered virtual shopping assistants focus on creating an accessible and efficient user experience. The use of voice commands allows for a hands-free shopping experience, which can be particularly useful for users who have limited mobility or who prefer a more natural means of interaction. To facilitate a smooth user experience, these assistants are built with robust voice recognition technology that can accurately interpret and respond to user commands. This involves implementing advanced algorithms that can accurately identify spoken words, phrases, and context, and quickly provide relevant and helpful responses. The design system for voice-powered virtual shopping assistants also encompasses the creation of a conversational user interface. These interfaces aim to simulate natural human conversation, with assistants using language that is clear, concise, and easy to understand. By mimicking human conversation, these interfaces can help users feel more engaged and comfortable throughout the shopping process. Furthermore, the design system takes into account the importance of personalization and tailored recommendations. Voice-powered virtual shopping assistants can utilize data analytics and machine learning algorithms to understand user preferences, browsing habits, and purchase history. This allows assistants to provide personalized product recommendations and suggestions, ultimately enhancing the overall shopping experience for users. In conclusion, voice-powered virtual shopping assistants are a user interface pattern and design system that leverage voice recognition technology to enable a hands-free and intuitive online shopping experience. By incorporating natural language interfaces and personalized recommendations, these assistants aim to streamline the shopping process and enhance user satisfaction.

Voiceprint Authentication

Voiceprint authentication is a UI pattern and design system that uses a person's unique vocal characteristics to verify their identity and grant access to a system or application. It is based on the fact that each individual has distinct vocal features, such as pitch, tone, and rhythm, that can be captured and analyzed.

When implementing voiceprint authentication, the system typically prompts the user to provide a spoken passphrase or series of predetermined words. These spoken words are then recorded and converted into a digital representation of the user's voiceprint. This digital voiceprint is compared to a stored template that was previously created during the user's enrollment process.

Volume Control

Volume control is a user interface (UI) pattern used in design systems to provide users with the ability to adjust the audio levels of a device or application. It allows users to increase or decrease the volume of audio playback or output as per their preference. In UI design, volume control is commonly represented by a horizontal slider that can be dragged or clicked on to adjust the audio volume. This slider is often accompanied by icons or labels indicating the current volume level, such as speaker icons or numerical values. The design of the volume control should be visually distinct and easily recognizable to ensure its purpose is clear to the user. The volume control UI pattern is crucial in providing a seamless and intuitive user experience. By offering users control over audio levels, it allows them to personalize their audio experience based on their environment or personal preferences. For example, users might want to lower the volume in a quiet setting or increase it when listening to music in a noisy environment. When implementing volume control in a design system, it is important to consider accessibility guidelines. Providing alternative methods for adjusting volume, such as keyboard shortcuts or voice commands, can enhance the accessibility of the feature. Additionally, incorporating visual feedback, such as highlighting the slider when it is being interacted with, can improve usability for users with motor or visual impairments. A well-designed volume control should be responsive and adapt to different screen sizes and orientations. It should seamlessly integrate with the overall user interface design, maintaining consistency with the design system's visual language and styling. In conclusion, volume control is a UI pattern that allows users to adjust the audio levels of a device or application. It is represented by a horizontal slider and plays a crucial role in providing users with personalized audio experiences. When designing volume controls, accessibility and responsiveness should be considered to ensure an inclusive and seamless user experience.

Volunteer Opportunities

Volunteer Opportunities in the context of UI patterns and design systems refer to the various ways in which individuals can contribute their time and skills towards the development and enhancement of user interfaces and design systems.

These opportunities are typically provided by organizations or communities that focus on creating and maintaining design systems, UI patterns, and related resources. By volunteering, individuals can actively participate in the continuous improvement and evolution of these systems, while also gaining valuable experience and knowledge in the field of UI design.

Volunteer Signup Form

A volunteer signup form is a UI pattern used in a design system to allow users to sign up to volunteer for a certain cause, event, or organization. It typically consists of fields where users can input their personal information such as name, email address, phone number, and any other relevant details. The form may also include additional fields to gather specific information related to the volunteering opportunity, such as preferred volunteer roles, availability, and any relevant experience or skills. The purpose of the volunteer signup form is to streamline the process of recruiting volunteers and collect necessary information to match volunteers with suitable opportunities. It provides a structured approach for users to express their interest in volunteering and ensures that important details are captured for later reference. The design of the volunteer signup form should be intuitive and user-friendly, making it easy for users to fill out the necessary information. Clear labels and placeholders should guide users on what information should be entered in each field. Validation can be implemented to ensure that the information provided is accurate and complete, reducing errors and inaccuracies. In terms of layout and visual design, the form should follow the established design system to maintain consistency with other components and elements across the website or application. This includes consistent typography, colors, and spacing to create a cohesive and polished user experience. By utilizing a design system for the volunteer signup form, organizations can ensure that the form adheres to best practices and usability guidelines. This helps to create a cohesive and seamless experience for users, improving the overall success of volunteer recruitment efforts. In conclusion, a volunteer signup form is a UI pattern that allows users to sign up for volunteer opportunities. It collects essential information from users to match them with suitable volunteer roles. The form should follow the design system and be visually consistent with other elements. It should also be user-friendly and intuitive for ease of use.>

Walkthrough Tours

Walkthrough Tours are a UI pattern and design system used to guide users step-by-step through a series of screens or pages in order to familiarize them with a new interface, feature, or product. This pattern is commonly employed in onboarding processes or to assist users in understanding the functionality and navigation of a website or application. - A Walkthrough Tour typically begins with an introduction screen that provides context and explains the purpose of the tour. This screen may include a brief description or a series of images or videos to engage the user. - After the introduction, users are presented with a series of sequential steps or tasks. Each step is usually accompanied by a short description, instructions, or examples of how to interact with the interface. Visual cues such as arrows or highlights may also be used to draw attention to specific elements or actions. - Walkthrough Tours often include interactive elements that allow users to control the pace of the tour. This can be done through buttons or gestures that allow users to navigate forward and backward, pause or replay steps, or skip the tour altogether. - Along with the sequential steps, Walkthrough Tours may also provide additional information or tips in the form of tooltips, pop-ups, or overlays. These can help clarify complex concepts or provide further guidance on specific features. - Walkthrough Tours can be designed to be dismissible or persistent. Dismissible tours allow users to exit or skip the tour at any point, while persistent tours require users to complete all the steps before accessing the main content or functionality. - To enhance the user experience, Walkthrough Tours should be visually appealing, consistent with the overall design system, and accessible for all users. Clear typography, legible colors, and intuitive navigation are important elements to consider in the design of these tours. - It is also essential to test and iterate the Walkthrough Tour design to ensure that it effectively guides users without overwhelming or frustrating them. Usability testing, user feedback, and data analysis can help identify areas for improvement and refinement. In conclusion, Walkthrough Tours are a valuable UI pattern and design system used to guide users through a series of steps and familiarize them with an interface or product. They help improve user onboarding, reduce learning curves, and enhance overall user experience.

Weather Forecast

A weather forecast in the context of UI patterns and design system refers to a user interface element that provides information about the expected weather conditions for a specific location or time period. It is designed to present this information in a clear and visually appealing manner, allowing users to easily understand and plan for the weather ahead. The weather forecast typically includes key data such as the temperature, precipitation chances, wind speed, and humidity. It may also include additional information such as sunrise and sunset times, UV index, and air quality. The forecast is usually presented for a specific time period, ranging from hourly to daily or even weekly predictions. This UI pattern often uses visuals, such as icons or illustrations, to represent different weather conditions. For example, a sun icon may be used to represent a sunny day, while a cloud with raindrops can represent rainy weather. These visuals provide users with a quick and intuitive way to grasp the expected weather conditions at a glance. In addition to visuals, the weather forecast UI pattern also commonly utilizes textual information to provide more detailed descriptions of the weather conditions. This may include statements such as "Partly cloudy with a high of 25°C" or "70% chance of rain in the afternoon." Textual information helps users understand the forecast in more depth and make informed decisions based on the weather conditions. Design systems play a crucial role in ensuring a consistent and cohesive weather forecast across different platforms and devices. They provide guidelines for the visual design of the forecast, ensuring that it aligns with the overall design language and branding of the application or website. The design system also helps maintain consistency in the way weather information is presented, making it easier for users to understand and navigate the forecast. In conclusion, a weather forecast in the context of UI patterns and design systems is an interface element that presents information about expected weather conditions. It utilizes visuals and textual information to communicate the forecast in a visually appealing and easily understandable manner. Design systems ensure consistency and cohesiveness in the design of the forecast across different platforms and devices.>

Webinar Viewer

A webinar viewer is a user interface (UI) pattern and a component of a design system that allows users to attend and participate in webinars, which are live online events where a speaker or a panel of experts present information, conduct discussions, and answer questions. The webinar viewer is designed to provide users with a seamless and engaging experience during the webinar. It typically consists of multiple sections that serve different purposes. The main section is the video player, where users can watch the webinar in real-time. The video player is usually accompanied by controls that allow users to play, pause, rewind, and fast forward the webinar. In addition to the video player, the webinar viewer also includes features that enhance the user experience and facilitate interaction. One common feature is a chat box, where users can exchange messages with other attendees and ask questions to the speaker or panelists. The chat box is often located next to the video player, allowing users to follow the conversation while watching the webinar. Another important component of the webinar viewer is the presentation view. This section displays the slides or visual content that accompanies the webinar. It allows users to view the slides in full-screen mode or side-by-side with the video player. The presentation view may also include navigation controls that allow users to jump to specific slides or sections of the webinar. To ensure a consistent and cohesive user experience, the webinar viewer follows the design principles and guidelines defined in the design system. It adopts a visually appealing layout with clear typography, colors, and icons that are aligned with the brand identity. The UI elements are organized in a logical and intuitive manner, making it easy for users to navigate and interact with the webinar viewer. Overall, a webinar viewer is an essential component of a design system that enables users to attend and actively participate in webinars. It provides users with a user-friendly interface that combines video playback, chat functionality, and presentation view, creating an immersive and interactive experience for webinar attendees.>

Wishlist And Favorites

Wishlist and Favorites are two UI patterns commonly used in web and app design systems to allow users to save and organize items or content they are interested in for future reference.

A Wishlist is a UI pattern that enables users to create a list or collection of desired items or products. It serves as a personalized shopping guide for users to keep track of the things they want to purchase. In the context of e-commerce platforms, a Wishlist usually includes a product image, title, price, and a "Add to Cart" button. Users can add or remove items from their Wishlist, as well as view and manage the existing items in their list. This pattern helps users to easily manage and prioritize their shopping preferences, providing a convenient and efficient way to browse and track desired items.

Favorites, on the other hand, is a UI pattern that allows users to bookmark or save their preferred or frequently accessed content, such as articles, images, or videos. It provides a quick way for users to revisit their favorite content without having to search or navigate through the entire website or app. The Favorites UI pattern typically uses a heart or star icon to indicate the saved status of the content. Users can easily add or remove items from their Favorites list, as well as view and organize the saved items. This pattern enhances user experience by enabling users to easily access and revisit the content they enjoy or find useful.

Wishlist

A wishlist is a user interface (UI) pattern commonly used in design systems to allow users to create and manage lists of desired items or future tasks. It serves as a tool for users to keep track of items they wish to purchase or events they wish to attend at a later time. In the context of UI patterns and design systems, a wishlist typically consists of a container where users can add, view, and modify their desired items. It often includes features such as adding items to the wishlist, removing items from the wishlist, and managing the quantity or priority of each item.

The wishlist UI pattern is designed to provide a convenient and organized way for users to save items of interest without committing to immediate action. It enables users to browse through products or events, select the ones they find appealing, and save them for future consideration or purchase. A typical wishlist UI pattern starts with a clear indication that a wishlist functionality is available, such as a dedicated button or icon. When clicked or activated, it opens a modal or overlay that displays the user's saved items. Within the wishlist UI, users can add new items by clicking an "Add to Wishlist" button or similar action linked to the desired item. Users may also have the ability to remove items from the wishlist, usually achieved through a "Remove" or "Delete" action associated with each item on the list. To enhance usability, a wishlist UI pattern often incorporates features such as drag-and-drop functionality to reorder items within the list, or options to adjust item quantities or priorities. Design systems typically provide guidelines and components to implement the wishlist UI pattern consistently across different interfaces and platforms. These guidelines ensure a consistent visual and interactive experience for users, regardless of the specific application they are using. In summary, a wishlist is a UI pattern used in design systems that allows users to create and manage lists of desired items or future tasks. It provides a convenient way for users to keep track of items they wish to purchase or events they wish to attend at a later time. The pattern often includes features such as adding and removing items, and may incorporate additional functionality like reordering or adjusting item quantities. Design systems provide guidelines and components to implement a consistent wishlist experience across different interfaces and platforms.>

Withdrawal Request Form

A Withdrawal Request Form in the context of UI patterns and design systems is a user interface element that allows users to submit a request for withdrawing funds or other resources from a system or account. The Withdrawal Request Form typically consists of a set of input fields and submit button that the user can interact with to provide necessary information regarding their withdrawal request. This information may include details such as the amount to be withdrawn, the destination account or recipient, and any additional instructions or comments. The form is designed to be easily understood and navigated by the user, with clear labels and placeholders in the input fields to indicate the type of information required. The design of the form usually follows established design patterns and guidelines to ensure consistency and familiarity for users. To ensure a seamless and user-friendly experience, validations may be implemented to verify the accuracy and completeness of the information entered by the user. This can include checking for the proper format of account numbers or verifying that the withdrawal amount does not exceed the available balance. Once the user has filled out all the required fields, they can submit the form by clicking on the submit button. After submission, the system may display a confirmation message or perform additional processing based on the nature of the withdrawal request. In summary, a Withdrawal Request Form in the context of UI patterns and design systems is a user interface element that allows users to formally submit a request to withdraw funds or resources from a system or account. It is designed to be intuitive and user-friendly, guiding users through the required fields and providing necessary validation for accurate and secure information submission.

A Withdrawal Request Form in the context of UI patterns and design systems is a user interface element that allows users to submit a request for withdrawing funds or other resources from a system or account.

The form typically consists of input fields for relevant information like the withdrawal amount, destination account, and additional instructions. It is designed following established patterns and guidelines to ensure consistency and familiarity for users. Validations may be implemented to verify the accuracy of entered information, and upon submission, the system may display a confirmation message or perform further processing.

Wizard Form

A wizard form is a UI pattern used in design systems that guides users through a step-by-step process to accomplish a specific task or goal. It provides a structured flow by breaking down complex tasks into smaller, more manageable steps. Wizards are commonly used for processes that involve multiple inputs or decisions, such as creating an account, making a purchase, or configuring settings. In terms of HTML structure, a wizard form typically consists of a series of screens or steps that are displayed one at a time. Each step is logically connected and has a clear purpose in the overall process. Additionally, wizards often include indicators or progress bars to help users understand their current position in the workflow and how many steps are remaining. From a usability perspective, the wizard form pattern has several benefits. Firstly, it reduces cognitive load by dividing a complex task into smaller, more approachable parts. Users can focus on one step at a time, which can improve their understanding and reduce errors. Secondly, it provides a sense of control and transparency as users have a clear sense of progress and know what to expect at each step. Lastly, wizards can increase user engagement by making the process feel interactive and dynamic. To implement a basic wizard form in HTML, two key elements are necessary. Firstly, each step should be contained within a separate `

` tag. This helps maintain a clean structure and ensures that each step is distinct. Secondly, a progress indicator can be added using another `

` tag. This can be a simple text-based representation of the user's progress, such as "Step X of Y" or a percentage indicator. For example: ```html

Step 1: Choose a username and password

Step 2: Provide your personal information

Step 3: Select your preferences

Progress: Step 1 of 3

``` In conclusion, the wizard form is a valuable UI pattern that helps users navigate complex processes in a user-friendly and manageable manner. By breaking down tasks into smaller steps and providing clear indicators of progress, wizard forms enhance usability and engagement in web applications.

## Wizard Progress Bar

A Wizard Progress Bar is a user interface (UI) pattern and design element that is commonly used in the context of multi-step processes or workflows. It provides a visual representation of the progress made by the user through the different steps of the process. The Wizard Progress Bar is typically positioned at the top or bottom of the screen and consists of a horizontal bar divided into sections or steps. Each step represents a distinct stage or task that the user needs to complete in order to progress to the next step. The purpose of the Wizard Progress Bar is to enhance the user experience by clearly indicating the user's current position within the overall process and the remaining steps. It helps in providing a sense of orientation and context, enabling users to easily understand where they are in the process and how much more is left to be completed. One common way to represent the progress is by using visual indicators, such as filled or highlighted sections, to denote completed steps, and empty or inactive sections to indicate the remaining steps. This visual representation allows users to quickly assess their progress and motivates them to complete the remaining steps. The Wizard Progress Bar can also be interactive, allowing users to navigate directly to any completed or upcoming steps. This navigation functionality enables users to go back and forth between steps, which can be particularly useful when editing or reviewing information in a multi-step form or process. In terms of design system, the Wizard Progress Bar should adhere to the overall visual language and style guidelines of the UI system. It should maintain consistency in terms of colors, typography, spacing, and alignment to ensure a cohesive and intuitive user experience across different applications or screens. To implement a simple Wizard Progress Bar in pure HTML format, you can use two paragraph tags to represent the completed and remaining steps. For example:

Step 1

Step 2

In this example, "Step 1" represents a completed step and "Step 2" represents a remaining step. By visually differentiating the styles of the two paragraphs, you can create a basic representation of a Wizard Progress Bar.
```

Wizards

A UI pattern is a commonly used solution for a specific user interface design problem, which aims to provide consistency and familiarity to users. It is a proven approach that defines the structure, behavior, and appearance of elements within a user interface. A design system, on the other hand, is a comprehensive set of guidelines, principles, and assets that are used to create consistent and cohesive user experiences across different platforms and applications. It includes a collection of reusable components, patterns, color palettes, typography, and other design elements that ensure visual and functional consistency. UI patterns within a design system are like building blocks that can be combined and customized to create different user interfaces. They provide a predefined and tested solution for common design challenges, making it easier for designers and developers to create interfaces with a consistent and familiar look and feel. By using UI patterns within a design system, designers can save time and effort by not having to start from scratch for every design element. They can leverage existing patterns, modify them to suit specific needs, and ensure a consistent experience across different screens and devices. Additionally, by following a design system with defined UI patterns, companies can establish a unified brand identity and create trust and recognition among users. Consistency in design helps users learn and understand interfaces more easily, leading to improved usability and overall user satisfaction. In conclusion, UI patterns are a set of predefined and proven solutions for common design problems, while a design system provides a complete set of guidelines, components, and assets for creating consistent and cohesive user interfaces. By integrating UI patterns within a design system, companies can ensure consistency, efficiency, and a positive user experience across different applications and platforms.

Workout Plans

A workout plan, in the context of UI patterns and design systems, is a structured and organized approach to designing and implementing the visual and interactive components of a user interface. It serves as a guide or blueprint for designers and developers to create consistent and cohesive user experiences across multiple screens, devices, and platforms.

The purpose of a workout plan is to establish a set of guidelines, principles, and standards that ensure consistency, efficiency, and usability in the design and development process. It helps to streamline the workflow, increase productivity, and improve the overall quality of the user interface by providing a systematic approach to UI design.

www.ingramcontent.com/pod-product-compliance
Lightning Source LLC
LaVergne TN
LVHW041203050326
832903LV00020B/424